## See what others have said about Peter A Hubbard's 'Tears' trilogy

**The US Review of Books** *"The result is a masterclass of investigative acumen, psychological insight, and global coordination."*

**HOLLYWOOD Book Reviews** *"The writing style has a literary structure that crafts poignant visuals drawing you into the intensity of the moment, such as a mushroom cloud described with sooty grey contrails against the blue sky and compared to a canvas from Dante's Inferno."*

**Pacific Book Review** *"The action and intensity of the plot balanced out the depth of relationship building that occurred with this cast of characters, from the protagonist's own traumatic past that brought her into the field and into a life of government and military service, to the tragedies which befell the children who would become the faces behind the movement which these terrorists fuel their campaign with."*

**Christina Avina-Professional Book Reviewer** *"As a fan of this genre, I was enthralled with the author's writing and was even more moved by the rich themes developed in this book, including the heavy look at the morality behind those who are radicalized or brainwashed into committing such heinous actions after having witnessed or experiencing their own brand of injustice early on in life. The cycle of violence and destruction plays a major role in this thriller."*

http://peterahubbardbooks.com/

# the tears of joy

THE TEARS OF HOPE TRILOGY – **BOOK 3**

PETER A. HUBBARD

ISBN: 979-8-88945-254-6 (paperback)
ISBN: 979-8-88945-256-0 (hardback)
eISBN: 979-8-88945-255-3

Brilliant Books Literary
137 Forest Park Lane Thomasville
North Carolina 27360 USA

ADVERTISING I DESIGN I DIGITAL I PRINT

Look for the psychological thrillers by Peter A Hubbard

The Tears of Hope
The Tears of Wonder
The Tears of Joy
The Island of Tears

https://peterahubbardbooks.com/

Due to the apocalyptic events wrought on the world by terrorists corrupting the genius of refugee women, there are over 30 million deaths, very little infrastructure, and all carbon-based fuels have been destroyed.

Among the chaos, however, nanotechnology has been adapted to provide a form of solar power and a sliver of hope for humanity exists. That is, until, a series of devices appear. Devices that can be weaponized with atomic material to cause worldwide annihilation...

*The Tears of Joy* is the final book in Hubbard's monumental *Tears of Blood* trilogy. There are several considerable character shifts and some subtle differences. Captain Jessica Riley is now Commander of Interpol Section 5, taking the helm from Colonel PJ Anthony.

Colonel Indigo Kashasini and Arie Rosenberg are still central. Both men carry their trajectories convincingly, and there are some new faces, all of whom are written with nicely individual quirks combined with concrete observation.

As before, the chapters involving Riley are written in first-person from her perspective, and all others are written in close third-person. Therefore, in this outing, the reader is fully engaged in every thought, decision, and action process that Riley takes as Commander rather than her observations and reactions as a subordinate.

It takes a while for Riley's voice to settle as Commander. She can be jarring with some unnecessary asides, such as the continuing reference to the physical appearance and mannerisms of the other Section 5 women, especially Sandra Thomas.

Regardless, she is an undoubted *tour de force*. This novel makes it apparent that an axis of strong, principled, albeit opposing, women is at the heart of the trilogy. The interrogation scenes between these female factions are fascinating, fraught with tension and ideological complications.

Notwithstanding, Hubbard's writing is strongest when he switches perspective and takes the reader into the terrorists' arena. Malik Badawi is especially well-depicted and, although briefly present, Gerhart von Speer and his surroundings were perfectly realized.

The viewpoint change also allows Hubbard to be less subjective and unfold events from a detached aspect, benefiting what is essentially a fictional terrorist thriller, parts of which are reminiscent of early Ken Follett.

Although, as with the previous novels, Hubbard has an uncanny awareness of the *zeitgeist*, addressing the issues of refugee children, female empowerment, and the rise of artificial intelligence with a single-minded focus that provokes thought outside the remit of the novel.

Hubbard's geographical use, insight, and descriptive imagery of people and places are sharply observed with effortless segues into different cultural mores and customs. The scenes set in Ireland are nicely atmospheric and Brother Francis's deceptively rustic portrayal is beautifully nuanced.

He excels with military details and political power play. Correspondingly, the action scenes are brilliantly choreographed. They never lose continuity or purpose, guaranteeing that vast swathes of the story are truly riveting as Hubbard piles on twist after twist in Section 5's desperate search for the devices.

The science behind the plot is mind-boggling. However, although the technicalities of what the terrorists and their nuclear scientists are attempting is cloaked with scientific jargon, the concept remains largely accessible and intriguing to read.

*The Tears of Joy* is a sprawling, complex, yet compelling, novel that provides the equivalent of a literary thrill ride. Hubbard stratospherically ratchets up all elements in the previous two books to produce the trilogy's most action-packed and fantastic installment.

This book is dedicated to Lyla Brooks, Agent extraordinaire, without whom this would not have been possible.

# Chapter One

We had chased terrorists together from continent to continent.

We had escaped certain death together more than once.

And then we had personally executed unarmed, confined prisoners together, shot them in the head and in the heart, and left their bodies to rot in a three-hundred-year-old subterranean prison underneath a beautiful island in Venice, where thousands of tourists once walked in the effervescent sunshine.

But the world had changed, thanks to a cadre of women terrorists who had started their lives as abandoned, parentless refugees on the world's scrapheap. No oil, no gas, no coal, but unlimited power from the sun, had literally changed the face of the Earth in less than six months.

No internet, few computers, or anything electronic that worked, changed the way we communicated, reminiscent of what we did as a species back in the 1950s and '60s.

Local, very much not global, except for certain military and private networks that had been protected at the time of the worldwide hack.

And millions upon millions of innocent people were killed by panic, chaos, and home-grown militia that forced migration around the world on a scale never before seen.

But thanks to the invention of a nanomachine by a brilliant young Israeli genius, herself a refugee, the world was slowly regaining hope as devices able to convert the sun's power more efficiently than ever thought possible popped up around the country.

That was the good news.

The better news was that Sandra *'just call me Sally'*, my partner in crime and the bubbliest person I had ever had the privilege to be around, and I were now enjoying the tropical sun together, sipping cold drinks in long glasses with little umbrellas in them, the images of the executions and what followed now just a dim memory.

"Did you get the banks to release the funds from the terrorists' accounts?"

The boss, lying flat on his stomach, his lounge chair buckling from his weight, squeaked as he moved his head to look at me. Behind him, Pete, recovering from three bad bullet wounds, was asleep on his back, snoring slightly, while his inamorata, a world-class cellist, slept beside him. If you didn't know, you would only see a group of friends relaxing around the pool without a care in the world.

If you tried to come over and be our friends, large well-dressed people would politely stop you, throw a million words at you in Italian so fast your head would ring, then turn you around to where you had started. If there was one thing other than his monstrous expresso machine that Indigo guarded with his life was us, which was stupendous because it allowed us to act like normal people when we were anything but.

"Yes. We had to threaten them with Red Notices, but Sandra got the last of the funds early this morning, and the monks now have several billion to play with. I have given them a list of what we need funds for and requested another fifty minicomputers. Stefarino was very happy, a lot of his private funding dried up because of the terrorist attacks, and he is linking our Italian headquarters to his cavern. He sends his regards and wants to have a conversation with you at some time." I received a grunt for my trouble and decided to drink more of the wonderful green thing that sloshed around in my glass. It tasted like a tropical fruit bomb but had a sensitive kick on the palate that was unmistakably a high-quality rum base of some sort.

I looked up as Indigo returned, accompanied by a beautiful woman, who I recognized as Fay Remer, our latest recruit from the FBI. Like Sandra, she was positively glowing, having just completed the Interpol boot camp, which had the driest international legal subject matter in the known universe. She had then completed the physical training for attachment to Section Five, and that was obviously what had put the color in her cheeks. The fact that she was dressed in the skimpiest bikini with a flowing silk thing over her shoulders didn't fool me for a second.

"Commander, great to see you at last. Thanks for the invite."

A guard hastily set up another sun lounge, and she plopped a handbag big enough to hold a child, a towel, a smaller bag which I assumed held her weapon and credentials, then a huge floppy straw hat.

"Intend on staying long?" Sandra asked, mumbling over her drink as she shielded her face from the sun with one delicate hand as she looked up at Fay.

Fay just laughed, plonked down on the lounge, and pointed to my drink. "I'll have one of those, thanks, Indigo."

He beamed at her. I promise you, his whole face lit up. *"Sarà un piacere per me, e scusa questo maleducato qui, la farò rimuovere se lo desideri!"*

"Yeah, you can try!" Sandra didn't exactly mumble, but the humor came through, and obviously, Indigo's invitation to throw her out of the pool area hadn't concerned her in the least.

Indigo took the coward's way out when faced with determined women and left to organize Fay's drink.

"How was the training?"

"Excellent. The HALO (High Altitude, Low Opening) jumps were the best, and the one we did in daylight was over Sardinia, and that's a sight I won't forget in a hurry."

"What about the weapons training? Learn anything new?"

Sandra was getting into the swing of it now, sitting up next to Fay, looking like a supermodel in her multi-colored top, baseball cap, and aviator glasses. Between her and Fay, I would forever look like the ugly sister.

"Yes. How much the modern squad weapons weigh, and how loud a flashbang is without ear protection!"

They both laughed. In my day, the big event was surviving the gas chamber without a mask, but that test now seemed old school.

I let them bubble on and turned back to the boss. "Have you spoken to Roger lately?"

Roger was the head of the FBI and a lifelong friend of the Boss's and had been one of the instigators in involving Interpol in solving the terrorist attacks. He looked at me with one eye open, the other shut, and it squeezed his face into an even more distorted look than his usual scarred appearance.

"Earlier today. All good on his end, they have three plants up and running, and they are happy to maintain the status quo for the time being." I gave him my hardest look over the top of my sunglasses, but half-naked, with a silly drink in my hand, it was difficult to pull off bad arse. He just closed his open eye and shrugged, causing the lounge to squeak again.

"What do you mean 'for the time being'?"

"You don't goad the bear in his own cave and expect to come out unscratched." I settled back. To a certain extent, I had anticipated what the Americans might do by placing the UN in charge of the international distribution and installation of the ecological plants that had been designed and built by the terrorists. And left the nanomachines firmly in the hands of Israel and Amira, who was now one of our agents attached to the Israeli Security Service. Or, in truth, was an Israeli agent attached to Interpol.

"I had hoped that they would at least play the gracious savior for a while longer." He turned to face me, both eyes open this time, his serious look anchored between his scars.

"They took a huge hit-the Catholic and Jewish, and for that matter, Muslim communities in the States are quite large, West Point was an attack on their very militaristic soul, and the smart way the terrorists pushed the immigration of thousands of refugees on them still rankles." I nodded, put my drink aside, and considered my next move. I pulled my towel off my lap and dived into the pool.

The water was crystal clear, comfortably cool, and invigorating. I lazily swam a few laps, letting my muscles warm up, testing my recovering shoulder a little, wishing this quiet time could last a little longer. But the boss had been pulling in information from all over the world, and all his nefarious contacts in the deepest and darkest places on the planet said the same thing.

In the vacuum created by the terrorist attacks, the lack of fuel, water, and food, and an almost complete lack of international will, was driving the creation of a whole new subset of bad behaviors.

And there was a new actor on the block with the resources and the skills to cause several of our supporting member countries to become very nervous.

I smelt a hard stop to our little vacation down the road.

And in countries where camels, horses, and donkeys were viewed as state-of-the-art transportation, and hard men and women made their living off the land, the balance of power had once again shifted away from technology and civilization to campfires and word of mouth. And no intelligence agency in the world had ever been particularly good at intercepting the spoken word, often in dialects unknown outside of tribal boundaries, without their agents literally losing their heads in the process.

Afghanistan was the center of it all. In the half-decade since the American withdrawal, it seemed that an endless series of new versions of ISIS had erupted, spewed their venom and hatred on anyone in their sights, mostly unarmed and innocent civilians, then self-destructed like one of their suicide bombers. But there were rumors emerging of a newly formed group, disciplined, as yet unnamed, and unidentified, working with some sophisticated weaponry. Didn't know what that was all about and didn't want to until it was on our radar.

We had just spent shy of two months fighting to save the planet, literally, and we needed to decompress, heal our wounds, find our centers as people, not puppets, and regain our balance. When you killed a person one-on-one, no matter the circumstances or how righteous that kill was, it affected you deeply, and you couldn't just shrug it off and pretend nothing had changed.

Unless you were a narcist and a sociopath. And if you were, you would not be working for the world's preeminent anticriminal and antiterrorist organization, Interpol.

I let the water flow over me like a liquid blanket, upped my tempo, pleased with the lack of any twinges or discomfort in my shoulder. The doctors had done a good job, and the physiotherapist that had been assigned to me, straight out of an East German gulag, I swear, had worked me to the bone, cheerfully destroying any excuse I came up with to evade her massive hands. The only good thing I had to hang onto was Pete telling me his recovery from his wounds had been worse than mine. But he didn't have that haunted look he had just a month ago, so he must be close to fully recovered.

The next thing I knew, I was sinking to the bottom of the pool; the sound of crashing water filled my ears, and the rolled-up body of Pete was sitting on my back. We both bobbed back up to the surface, spluttering and laughing like loons, most unladylike and certainly not the done thing in a prestigious military organization. I funneled water into my hands and pushed it into his face, having the time of my life. His laughter lifted my spirits. I had been worried about him, he had been shot three times while protecting me, and while I was not the cause, I always felt I was the root. Being around me could be a very hazardous occupation. "Children, children, play fair. No hurting each other unless you mean it!" Pete ignored the Boss, and reached over and dunked me again. Now I had options. I could punch him in his manhood, pull him under and drown him, or just let him have his way with me.

Seeing his live-in partner of some fifteen years looking at us over her blue-tinted glasses, with a smirk on her face, lying back and talking it seemed the best option. He let me up, still laughing like a loon but starting to look like the shooter I had entrusted my life to on more than one occasion. The new scars were only obvious from the old ones because they still looked like painted-on pale, puckered healing holes on his otherwise suntanned skin, and his ropy chest muscles flexed and rippled in a very nice manner.

It was hard to believe that it was less than a month ago that I had helped load him onto an Israeli C-17 with blood running freely down his chest from three bullet holes that clustered just below his collarbone. And I had been shot as well, but that seemed trivial at the time. And for the life of me, I couldn't remember why.

I drifted to the side of the pool, completely relaxed for the first time in days. "You look relaxed."

"I am. How're the wounds?"

"Getting me plenty of sympathy, Jenny and I are off back home tomorrow. The Boss has made it clear I'm off call for at least the next six weeks."

"You'll go stark raving mad," I said, climbing out of the pool. He grabbed the side of the pool and levered himself up and out with a nimble twist of his lean body that had more scars than I remembered. But then, I hadn't seen him naked for quite a while.

"Has Jenny got any concerts planned?" He looked over at his life partner, smiled when she grinned at him and turned back to look at me.

"Yes, one in New Zealand, a benefit for their recovery program. They have resettled nearly two thousand children in the site they built on the Wairoa River at Dargaville. The New Zealand government has approved the construction of ten more townships spread across the country, and that means that another twenty thousand girls will be taken in. There are families putting their hands up from as far away as Samoa."

"Chalk one up to Mohammad bin Azaria and 'Helen'." I didn't let the bitterness creep into my voice, but it took all my effort not to. He gave me a hard look, but I suspect he saw what was under my less-than-warm response. He just nodded and walked back to Jenny. I reached for a towel and sat back on my couch. The boss had one eye open again, a sure sign I was going to get blitzed.

Not quite.

"One thing I picked up from Arie this morning, you might find interesting. Just as the French promised the world that they would remove the radioactivity from the Arabian oil fields, persons unknown clagged up the wellheads all the way across the desert and shut it down permanently." I sat up, this was news, and it might mean that we had missed one of the mercenary terrorist groups.

"Do we know who did it?"

"No. And the French, as you can imagine, are seriously pissed about it."

"Why? Surely the radioactivity was enough. Those fields were out of action for thousands of years."

"Seems like the tech heads got it wrong. They changed their forecast to less than thirty years, and within a week of that being made public, the well heads and pipelines were attacked with the nanomachines, and that ended that."

"Who had that capacity? That would have taken five or six simultaneous attacks across different countries, those fields were the biggest in the world."

"Maybe, but out of play since yesterday. Think about who had the nano technology—the canisters from Canada, the ones we collected. Amira estimates that it only needed around four to do the job. And no, before you ask, she hasn't been cooking up nano bugs out the back of Mossad, and she assures me that the nano-machines in use in the plants would have a different effect on raw oil. No, this was someone left over from the original attacks, someone we missed, being very selective and very, very fast." I thought about it and couldn't see how it could have been done without state-level resources and, most of all, a supply of nanomachines. Who? How? Did it matter? There weren't any oil or gas pipes or coal fields anywhere as far as I knew that hadn't already been attacked, so was this a once-off?

"Arie's view is that the 'shut it down' message that Trotsky had us broadcast was incomplete. No way to prove it, one way or the other, and Arabia and the French are pursuing it themselves, don't want anyone else involved."

"Do you think there are mercenary terrorists connected to 'Helen' still out there?"

"Don't know. There is no movement in the bank accounts that we tracked, according to the geeks. We have one hundred percent of them locked away, matched by the data from the accountant and from Trotsky's own files. It is possible that there are some stragglers out there, but unless we get asked by one of our member nations, we're out of it for the time being." I thought about that, let it roll around my mind for a bit, then just nodded. Yes, we were out of it, but Interpol, in the main, would remain connected to the data and keep us informed of anything that looked like we should get on our bikes again.

Interpol was a huge international coordinating intelligence and data gathering agency, with one hundred and ninety-four member nations, and the agents neither had the power of arrest nor carried guns. That's why Section Five was created, providing a military-trained and well-equipped group, who working with a sponsor country and backed by the Intelligence from Interpol, could arrest and carry weapons and use them with deadly force on those occasions that demanded it.

A shadow fell over me, and I looked up to see Indigo standing at ease, smiling, but with two of his burly guards flanking him.

"Commander, you have a call in the conference room, if you please?" I stood, causing Sandra to stir on her couch, then she was up like a cat. Her energy really was incredible.

"Hi, Indigo, where are we going?" she asked in her bubbly voice as she wrapped a lightweight gown over her bikini.

"*Tenente, il Comandante ha una chiamata sicura nella sala conferenze. Possiamo accompagnarla se preferisci stare al sole?*"

"*Grazie, Indigo non vale l'ira del boss per lasciarla andare a giocare da sola!*" I just laughed. Arguing about who would escort me was a battle I would never win, so I walked with Indigo and was shadowed by Sandra. She had also been promoted within the tight ranks of Section Five the moment she had qualified some two weeks ago. Fay still had the nominal rank of Senior Special Agent (SSA-FBI), but that would change as her training caught up to her. The ranks were equivalents, simply so other military forces could see where we fit. In our system, a colonel was the equivalent of a two-star general and a commander a one-star.

Indigo was the odd man out, still holding his rank in the Italian Carabinieri Special Intervention Group (CSIG), as well as being our head of operations in Italy. But what mattered the most in Section Five was how well you could think under pressure and how well you could shoot. Yes, we were the police force, but one structured to work on any continent or in any jurisdiction, cross any border, and deal with anything that our member nations needed help with.

We went into the smallish conference room and found Malcolm's cheery face center screen, with Luigi and Shami in little boxes underneath.

"Sorry to spoil your holiday, Commander, but what would you interpret this as meaning?" A line of Irish floated into the center of the screen, with Malcolm a faded shadow behind.

*"Éiríonn fir na bhFíniní arís"* I looked at it very hard, racking my brain. The Finnians had been the center of the Irish rebellion for tens of years, an organized terrorist group that had been very hard to put down, but in my mind, there hadn't been any mention of them for some time. The IRA had well and truly taken over their bailiwick and then, in turn, been beaten down to just the occasional flicker of annoyance.

"The Fenian men rise again," I translated, looked at the screen, dialed up some data on my minicomputer, and read it with interest.

*In 1858 the Fenian League of Irish was formed in the United States, dedicated to promoting revolution and the overthrow of the English government in Ireland. They raised money and even a small army of expatriates, who were to sail to the SireLand around 1862-3 and wage war. This rag-tag army was also called `The Fianna'. They were not successful.*

"The Fianna Fail party of Eanmon de Valera was elected to the Dail Eiream in 1927. They are still a predominant Party in the Irish Parliament. Fianna Fail means `The Armed Men of Ireland.'*

I flicked the data up onto the big screen and gave everyone on the call enough time to read it and absorb it.

"Why do you bring it to our attention?"

"We found this posted on an old bulletin board that survived the internet hack, and on it was a picture of a training camp. We'd been tracking training camps in Afghanistan for some time, just a satellite flyover every now and then, no schedule they could prepare for, then a year ago, it just disappeared. Exactly the same as your 'black holes' we solved recently. So we applied the same technology, and guess what?"

"You found the camp again.

"Yes. That's not the real concern here."

"What is then?"

"Who's in that camp."

"Malcolm, don't play games, please; I was enjoying the sun and a lovely tall drink with an umbrella in it." The words disappeared from the screen, replaced by three facial recognition photos with their distinctive yellow grid lines. My heart skipped a beat, and I felt Indigo stiffen.

"Al Bar al Shirak. They blew up the shopping centers in Israel, linked to our mercenary terrorists, but used the remote-control devices developed by the women to drive the vehicles. That's Amir Abbas, one of Hamas's top leaders, and Malik Badawi, he's a Bedouin thought to be one of the leaders of this group. Who's the woman? And has Arie seen these?"

Shami's head grew in size until he filled half the screen. He looked stressed, tired, and in need of some comfort.

"Commander, yes, Arie has seen these pictures. He's the one who told us to contact you. The woman is Irish, or so her passport says. She is suspected of being one of the very heavy hitters in the Republican movement. She was on every watchlist but slipped through with this identification which somehow managed to be inserted in every system across Europe. Sound familiar? And she fits the profile we built for you three months ago when we were chasing the original women terrorists."

"So she could be a refugee pulled out of the camps and placed with an Irish family?"

"Yes."

"Didn't we arrest two Irish women in Helena?"

"Yes, both very young, but they came from Ireland — Elizabeth Kane, Moya O'Halloran — one, a writer, the other a painter, supposedly to write the history of the Westhall property, and there's no proof of their families, which again, fits the profile of the women terrorists."

"Where's the money?" Sandra had remained quiet until now, but I could feel her vibrating beside me.

"Good question. No data on it, not from Mohammad bin Azaria's files or the accountant, Shetani's files, or Trotsky's."

"It could be in Ireland, Afghanistan, or any damn where, and based on our experience so far, it will be a lot of money they have to play with."

"Wait! Ireland was one of the countries that were designated for an environmental plant and migration of children. Where was their funding lodged?" Shami's face reduced in size again, to be replaced by Luigi's.

"A trust account set up six years ago in the family name of Charles Stewart Parnell the Third, and if that isn't a clue, I don't know what is."

"Parnell. That name rings a bell all the way back to the eighteen hundreds and the 'Home Rule' movement. And the Fenians tried to usurp British rule in Ireland with a serious uprising during the first World War."

"Okay, enough already. Who has control of the trust?"

Silence was the answer for around three minutes. Then Luigi held his hand up as if to stop traffic.

"A firm of accountants, name of Reganit and Sons, Belfast. Who the beneficiaries are is under seal."

"Break it." Then I thought how rude that sounded. "Please." My holiday in the tropics had not really improved my humor, and I could tell I was anything but centered and in balance. I started to wonder what might change that.

Then I had a brilliant idea. The boss and I had made a plan, maybe this was time to use it. "Sandra, get the G4 ready. We're going to Chicago."

She looked at me with surprise all over her face but nodded and reached for her minicomputer.

"Thanks, everyone. Follow up and keep me posted. I'll be available via my mini for the next three days." And I walked out of the room, leaving a few startled faces on the screen and one or two in the room.

I mentally composed a text to the boss — *'running away for three days, taking the jet, let me know where to come back to.'*

Packed in record time, met Sandra at the portico where a black-windowed limo waited, handed my bag to the Italian guard, who practically fell over trying to bow and collect my luggage in the same movement and climbed into the cool of the limo.

"Chicago's your home base?" I looked at Sandra, dressed as usual, like a runway model, all flowing curves and exotic colors. How anyone could ever mistake her for an Interpol agent was beyond me, but she cheered me up, and right now that was the most important thing on my mind.

"No, not really. It's where I was posted early last year. I was in Ukraine chasing some of the stragglers from your people smuggling op. Just as a matter of interest, how many of us are there in Section Five?"

"Not as many as we would like. We have pairs here, and there — Japan, the UK, and a few spots in the EU backed up by single agents who are ostensibly Interpol but trained by us; we call on them as needed. The original concept was a hard-core team of five or so; that could collect assets as needed, but that didn't last very long due to the caseload. So the answer is today, including Fay, our most recent recruit, probably twelve full-time, and another six on the fringe." Sandra's reaction was not what I expected. She smiled and bounced around on her seat.

"Fantastic! So I got a guernsey because of my cross-training with the FBI counter-terrorist group and SWAT in Chicago."

I couldn't help but smile back. Her energy was infectious.

"That's the direct result of the boss being able to negotiate with military and law enforcement seemingly everywhere. I don't know how he made all his contacts, but his system works. And we steal the best of the best from everyone, but only a little at a time, so no one gets pissed at us."

"Like Fay." We both paused our conversation and swapped the limo for our jet, settled in, then picked up where we had left off as the roar of the engines took us to another world.

"Exactly like Fay. She managed her team exquisitely well in Point Roberts, then again in Seattle, and Helena, took on everything thrown at her, and in case you didn't know, she is only twenty-eight, and was already a senior special agent with the FBI. That takes some balls." Sandra nodded, thinking to herself.

"And for full disclosure, she is a refugee just like the women we chased down, so she and Amira have a lot in common." When she turned to look at me, it was with her deep blue eyes wide open as if I had zapped her with a Taser.

"So where does Pete come into it? I get Tom and his crew, even Bob and his, but as I understand it Pete joined you and the boss right at the very start. How does a retired Master Chief get called up by Section Five?"

"Easy. Pete worked with the boss in a former life in the Teams. When Section Five was formed, the boss recruited Pete to devise the training program, and run it for the first year, which he did, then retired back to his home in northern Australia. The boss calls him in from time to time when we need a hard-core shooter, which on this operation, we thought we would." She nodded to herself again, fitting the pieces of the Section Five puzzle together.

"Indigo runs Interpol Italy?"

"Yes, and more besides, he manages Interpol resources across six or seven countries as well as Italy."

"And he's a member of Section Five?"

"One of the very first the boss recruited. He also makes the best expresso in the known world, and I'd have him on my team just for that alone."

"So the Section Five 'outliers' as I'll call them, work for Interpol in the usual manner, until we call them up, yes?"

"Yes. An example is our Interpol agent in Islamabad-Drishya Singh. She moved there from New Delhi, runs the office out of the barracks of the Pakistani SSG (Special Forces), nothing unusual until we knock on her door, she guns up, changes her credentials, and goes to war for us. Exactly the same as Nokomoto Senji and Aikido Namoki in our Tokyo office, although they spend most of their time working for us because of the large volume of criminal activity in that region."

"They are the ones that broke up the Innomatchi operation."

"Yes. Took some of Tokyo's finest in with them, killed around twenty heavily armed Yakuza and a few private guards, and took the head of that organization into custody, located the ship sets, then shut the company down. The way they tell it, they didn't even get a bruise in the gunfight." Again, Sandra smiled, her face lighting up.

"I'd like to meet them." I looked at her and tilted my head to one side. "Be careful what you wish for."

I closed my eyes, parked my head on the side wall, and let myself go.

# Connection

It had been a meeting waiting to happen for over a month since Amira had first been able to talk to Michele, her first true love, but one that abandoned her in a treacherous move when she stole most of Amira's work in nanotechnology, and special coding that allowed the user to create 'black holes' over locations on the Earth that made them invisible to satellites or any type of photographic surveillance. Amira was in a heavily secured small room at the rear of Arie's office, her computer was air-gapped and heavily filtered. Where Michele was located remained a secret, but the geeks had calculated somewhere in China. Her face showed no stress or strain and the background was completely neutral. "Hello, Amira."

"Michele." She smiled fleetingly, then looked Michele straight in the eyes. "How are you?"

"Fine as can be expected, you look good." Amira nodded. She felt good, she had managed to put the past away in a little box, and her current work ensured she had little time to consider it.

"Do you think it will be possible for us to work together again?" Michele looked curious and tilted her pretty face to one side, causing her long black hair to ripple around her shoulders.

"I don't see how that could be possible. Your masters will want to throw me in a very deep, dark hole and keep me there for a very long time." Amira dropped her shoulders, and her head followed, and for a split second, she looked defeated. Then she straightened herself up and pulled herself together.

"You know what the terrorists did. You would have seen for yourself how they have all but killed the hope of the ordinary person, even in China, if that's where you're hiding, has been affected. Millions dead or dying, people starving, no power, fresh water, how can you walk away from all that chaos?" At the mention of 'China,' Michele had visibly blanched, then regained her composure.

"Yes, I have seen it for myself. But as we spoke of many times in the past, the world will be a better place without oil, gas, and coal."

"But when we spoke of it, we talked about a gentle progressive transition, not an assassination on a global scale." Michele raised her eyebrows at this, seemed to consider it, then shook her head.

"Too late now. Why would you want to work with me?" Amira looked stung, obviously hurt at the sharp tone Michele used.

"Oh! Perhaps I'm really stupid, I don't know, maybe to finish off our work on the nano bugs? Remember all the great ideas we had? Biofuel, panels, living buildings?" She shrugged her shoulders in dismay, remembering how Michele's creamy brown skin had felt under her hands. She realized that was the real problem. She was still in love with what Michele had been when they had been at Harvey Mudd College together, now almost six years ago. It had been the most exciting time of her young life, and Michele had been a considerate and experienced lover. And you didn't forget your first love easily.

"Again, too late. My information is that the plants created by the women are producing biofuel, panels, and power supplies. I haven't been able to see one, but the people I'm working with have been inside one, and we got photos." Amira just nodded, accepting that she was wasting her time. She looked up into the camera, did her best to smile, then just shut the connection down. She silently mouthed the words, 'goodbye Michele', as a single tear worked its way down her face.

"That was very hard on you," a gruff but warm voice said, making Amira smile for real.

"Yes, it was, Arie, but now it is behind me, and I can move on. It's interesting that someone is spying on the plants, but I suppose it's to be expected." Arie, being one of the most experienced spy masters still alive, merely nodded.

Of course, they were. While the UN had control over the distribution of the ship sets, the Japanese, in partnership with the UN control over the manufacture of everything that went into a ship set, and Israel had control over the nanomachines needed to make plans viable, there wasn't a spy agency on the planet that wasn't trying to circumvent the process to their own countries' advantage. He patted Amira on the shoulder, just like a kindly grandfather would.

"Come, let's get some tea, we have a new puzzle to solve, and I'd like your opinion."

# Chapter Two

Sandra and I deplaned at the military end of Midway International Airport, straight into a small black SUV, windows blacked out and manned by what looked like FBI agents but weren't. I ignored them. Sandra giggled a little, then followed my lead. She didn't have to wait long for an explanation.

"The moment the G4 crew filed their flight plan, we had high cover from the US Navy, and once we were feet dry, the Airforce. These good people will be someone's special forces, and don't be surprised if Tom's face turns up unexpectedly." Sandra took all this in, wondering why such a high level of security was necessary for what should have been just two agents, off duty no less, making a short visit to Chicago. There was a lot she had yet to learn about geopolitics, she thought to herself. The experience she was getting working with what amounted to the head office of Section Five was a huge step up from being a single agent manning a desk in someone else's front yard.

"You knew this would happen?"

"I suspected as much. The boss has not let me out of his, Pete's, or your sight since the second week of the terrorist operation, so either something spooked him, or there is a fatwa on my head. Who could be bothered with such a thing now? I can only imagine." Sandra looked at me, a hard look in her eyes. I was dressed in jeans and a bland tee, a loose jacket thrown over my shoulders, a style I had adopted since I had temporarily lost the use of my left arm. I was sitting as calmly as I could, casually discussing my death sentenced by persons unknown but persons undoubtedly very serious about their cause.

What was I supposed to do? Throw up my hands and scream? In direct contrast, she still looked like a supermodel and was outrageously happy. At least one of us was.

Sandra had initially been surprised at Pete's attachment to Jessica and then her own when Pete had been shot. No one had given her an explanation other than the boss's gruff *'don't let her out of your sight, not for one second'*. She had assumed, incorrectly as it turned out, that she had been allocated as an assistant to a very busy person trying to bring to heel the worst terrorist attack in living memory.

"Where are we going?" Sandra looked around the inside of the SUV, then looked back at her principal, for that was now how she regarded Jessica. She now understood the stakes, and she would be doubly prepared.

"We have a choice. We can pretend that nothing is going to happen, you go your way, and I'll go mine, then we can meet up back at the plane."

"Or? And there's no way in heaven you're going off by yourself. I like my new job and my promotion, and I don't want to end up managing an office in Bumfuck Alaska." The sour look on Sandra's face was such a change I smirked.

"Bumfuck Alaska? No way, we send all our rejects to the Antarctic. Much better, there's a little office the Argentineans keep open for us just for the purpose." This time she laughed, and the tension dissolved, and I gave some thought to her question. I didn't want my mother in anyone's crosshairs, and this was the real reason I had come to Chicago. She had kept her maiden name, so there was no way anyone could track her through me. And I knew my professional file had been redacted some years ago as a precaution.

"I am going to see my mother, but not in this vehicle, and probably not with you. I'm thinking about how to manage all that." She gave me another hard look, and an edge crept into her voice.

Outside the speeding vehicle, the evidence of the chaos that followed the terrorist attacks was all too plain to see. Buildings were burnt and gutted, piles and piles of rubbish on the roadside, and the very few people who were out on the streets had that scared and haunted look about them. For that alone, I hated the terrorists with a vengeance.

"No solo performances, period. Work something out."

In a sense, I expected nothing less and realized I would have to come up with a plan that allowed her to fulfill her duty as my shadow. My mum still worked at the truck stop. She no longer had to. She got five-eighths of my salary every month and had since the day I had been press-ganged into the Navy. But she kept her job, loved it, in fact, and flirted with every driver from every state to the point where she was probably one of the best-known waitresses in the business. That gave me an idea. I tapped the agent in the shotgun seat on the shoulder.

"We need to swap vehicles, one to draw anyone away, one to take us to the Navy pier."

"Yes, ma'am, give us five. But you do know the pier has been destroyed?"

He pulled a little handset out of his pocket, spoke quietly into it, snapped it shut, then just relaxed as if he had played the shell game all his life. Our driver left the freeway, headed into a massive parking garage, drove up several floors, stopped, and the shotgun agent jumped out and opened the door for us. Silently, a small SUV slid up, the door swung up, and we both climbed in. Just one agent this time, but the same blacked-out windows, albeit in a different color. Our original ride drove off and down the exit ramp. Our new driver waited a few minutes, then engaged the drive, looked over his shoulder at me, and grinned.

"Navy pier?"

"Yes, please."

"You know it's been destroyed?"

"Yes."

We lapsed into a comfortable silence, with Sandra's head on a swivel, obviously watching for anyone attempting to follow us. I put my hand on her knee. "Relax, if we're going to be hit, it will happen when we least expect it and when we are stationary."

"That's so comforting. I can't thank you enough."

Luckily, I recognized sarcasm when it dripped over my jeans, so I just smiled and sat back. I had recognized some of my younger self in Sandra when I had first met her, fresh from the Chicago office. Young, extremely intelligent, and highly trained in all the arcane arts we needed to survive in Section Five. And she was pretty, had amazing energy, and literally lit up every room she entered.

"So, your plan is to draw whoever is targeting you to a location we can control, get rid of them, then go see your mum somewhere?"

"It sounds simple when you say it quickly."

She gave me another hard look, reached into her shoulder bag, and pulled out a dull black H&K MP47, which she pulled the magazine out of, checked the load, slipped it back in, then cocked the weapon. It disappeared back into her bag, and I suddenly had a whole new respect for her. I had been with her for weeks, on planes, on foot, in and out of gun fights, and I never had for one second suspected she carried such a potent weapon.

"Something the Chicago SWAT taught me." I just smiled, thinking my own defense would have to rely on my old handgun, a weapon I had carried over from my NCIS days, a mimic of the boss's Sig Saur P226, which he loved so passionately. At least I had another thirty rounds in two magazines hitched to my belt in the middle of my back. I stopped thinking about such morbid things, even as I unconsciously reached behind and pulled the mag pouch to my left-hand side and paid more attention to the destruction of the once beautiful Chicago landscape.

It was like a series of big bombs had gone off downtown, tall buildings with shattered glass, black holes where whole floors had been destroyed, bent frames, still smoking rubbish choking the streets, and literally thousands of cars smashed together as if some giant hand had collected them and thrown them carelessly away. I wondered why the city fathers hadn't cleaned up the streets, then felt the patter of small arms fire peppering the car. Several shots smacked into our side windows with a 'thwack!' Sandra didn't do so much as flinch. She just let her hand slide into her bag, which was now resting on her lap.

"Not to worry, we always get shot down here," the cool voice of the driver rolled over the bullet strikes, which stopped as suddenly as they had started. Outside, the scene got even more depressing as the guttered and burnt-out buildings that had paralleled the Pier swam past our windows. The Pier itself was broken towards the end, bent down with one end just sticking up, still attached to the warped and buckled Ferris wheel. A hot dog stand lay on its side, reminiscent of a toy carelessly disposed of by a spiteful child. The skin crawled up my back, and the hairs on my arms stood to attention like the good little soldiers they were. We were being observed, and I could feel the eyes outside somewhere on us.

"Stop here, please." We drifted to a silent stop. "Go back around a mile past the start of the Pier, and wait for our call."

He just nodded, flicked a switch on the dash, and the doors swung up and opened like a pair of gull wings.

Nifty.

We climbed out, Sandra trying to project calm, but I could feel her vibrating. "The plan is simple. If there is someone trying to kill me, they'll come out here and have a go. They won't succeed, I've taken precautions, and I have you."

The look she gave me would have frozen a normal person in place, but at least she had the look of a hunter in her clear blue eyes and not the hunted. She still looked like a fashion model, but I was learning that there was a very strong steel core under all that color and polish. I just hoped it didn't get chipped along the way.

We waited, sitting on either side of a concrete bollard that was lying on its butt. I looked up, couldn't see anything in the dark blue sky, and turned to look out to sea. Nothing there either, as far as I could tell. The attack, if it were coming, would come from the land side. I was counting on it.

Then they appeared like ants, swarming out of the broken concrete and shattered buildings, dressed in all manner of urban dress, from rippled concrete-colored camos to jeans and leather jackets. And all carried long guns, wore sunglasses, and bright red bandanas, obviously gang colors. I sighed; this would be easier than I thought.

"Sandra, kill as many as you like, but I want at least one left alive."

She just smiled and settled down over her sights. If I had set this encounter up correctly, she probably wouldn't even get to fire her weapon. A ghost that looked like a moving part of the roadway slid alongside me, and I saw Sandra jump with surprise before a huge grin split her face. She really was a bubbly personality!

"Hi Tom, fancy seeing you here." He grunted, whispered into his fist, then turned to look up at me. "Jessica, what's a nice girl like you doing in a wreck of a place like this?"

"Contact front!" Sandra's cry was controlled and soft and filled me with pride. "Hold fire."

She did, and my pride grew stronger. Tom was looking over his sights, then fired just the one suppressed shot. The nearest attacker went down, and the entire ant hill opened up, spraying bullets everywhere. You could hear them singing as they flew over our heads. One of the things I loved about urban gangs-and for that matter, most terrorists-was their propensity to spray and pray, the concept of a single aimed shot as an insult to their manhood, and the number of rounds in their magazines. Behind the swarming ant hill, a series of single shots rang out, and suddenly there we only three or four gang members left. A stray round smashed into the concrete bollard, causing chips of concrete to fly around like lethal projectiles. And, of course, one ripped my face, and now I had warm blood running all over me. I slapped my hand on the cut, figured it to be relatively small, then dropped my shoulders in a sigh. I sighted the nearest gangster and shot him or her twice in the head. She-he fell, leaving only two that I could see.

"Sandra, go get me one of them, please. I don't care what you do with the other."

She rose up, her eyeline over her sight, her Kevlar vest over her rainbow-colored shirt, the tail of which was fluttering out from under it, creating a weird sight in combat terms. Tom flew up beside her, and they both took off firing shots around the gangster. Then one of them hit his leg, and he threw up his hands, and his gun fell down, supported only by the sling he had around his neck.

While Tom held him at gunpoint, Sandra cuffed him, frisked him, then cracked him behind his knees with the butt of her machine pistol, forcing him to the ground. I stood up and walked to the gangster, now bleeding more than my face was, and that made me happy for a minute. I kicked him lightly in the chest, got a full-face scowl for my effort, and sworn at in Russian and Spanish, as blocks of concrete came to life all over the battlefield, moving towards us.

"Tom, search them all, take everything they have on them, leave the bodies, ditch then weapons."

"Yes, Commander."

Now he was formal, and as I saw some of his troop now in range of us, I understood why. They looked half asleep, their weapons held at the port-arms position, but with their barrels pointing down and their heads continually turning as if on swivels. Only eight of them, and I wondered if they were the same team we had with us earlier in the month. I called our driver, grabbed our gangster by his hair, and pulled him to his feet, then forced him along in front of me. Then I kicked him behind the knees, and he collapsed again.

"Buggar this, I really don't have time to play nice. Who wants me dead, and who's paying for it? Sandra, if he doesn't answer in the next thirty seconds, shoot him in his other leg, then work your way up."

He looked at me, a full-face sneer and bloodshot eyes, and before he could say anything, the soft 'pop' of Sandra's suppressed MP47 hissed through the air, and his knee erupted like a volcano of blood and bone fragments. He grabbed at it, rolled around in the filth of the roadway, and was about to scream when Sandra reached forward and pushed the barrel into his crotch. He held up one bloody hand, then fired a string of Russian at us, and I watched impassionedly as tears streaked down his face, making little muggy tracks. He was pathetic. And I had what I needed. I waved Sandra down, looked at Tom, nodded my thanks, then walked towards our SUV.

We had been driving for five minutes before Sandra spoke. Her vest was folded next to her on the seat, and her leather bag was piled on top. She was drinking a Coke, I was sticking to water, and she was casually reloading her magazine one-handed.

"Why didn't you brief me on what we were going to do?" I looked over at her, still bubbling, probably the adrenalin rush working its way through her system. She had stood up extremely well, and she deserved a full explanation.

"The boss and I decided to keep this on the down low. We wanted to see if they could track us, if they knew our movements and if they would actually make a move on us. Now we know who they are, and hopefully, Malcolm or our own geeks will have some idea how they tracked us and timed their assault so well."

"You think they are still inside our electronic systems?"

"Yes, without a doubt. When you look at all the money they had, all the time they took to set up the first round of attacks, their 'Plan B' with the refugees and the environmental plants, the fact that they tried to kill all the prisoners we had in Israel twice, it suggested that we had only seen Act One. Shetani and his goons are out of the picture, 'Helen' and Mohammad bin Azaria are accounted for, so we need to find the new kids on the block." Sandra took that in, thinking of her own role in 'accounting' for the terrorists. One in the head, one in the heart, and a World Court judgement supporting the execution thrown onto the jail floor.

"Did you understand what that creep was saying?"

"Who? The lovely tourist you shot the kneecaps off?" She laughed, reminding me that she was a well-balanced and very strong woman.

"Yes, that one, and I shot him in his other leg as well."

"Did you just. I'll remember never to take you out for a lazy walk in the park again."

"You do that. But did you understand him?"

"Yes. Russian is one of my languages, thanks to the NCIS. How many languages do you speak?"

"Spanish, Italian, and a little Chinese." I nodded my approval. In our business, an ear for languages was a huge asset.

"Basically, what he told us was that his gang was contracted by an Arab, whose name was unintelligible, offered five million USD for proof of death, and was briefed continuously on our movements for the last three hours, including our flight arrival, all the way from our tropical paradise. I'd really like to know how they managed that and who they are." Sandra went silent, in deep thought, probably running through all the communication options she could think of.

"So this was just to expose their network a little, not a serious attempt to put terrorists in the ground?"

"Yes. And I didn't brief you because I wanted to see how you would react unprepared. I have big plans for you."

Her eyes widened as she took all this in, but I could see the insult slithering just under her smile. No professional liked to be set up, it tended to lead to trust issues, and I hoped that our little jaunt wouldn't have that effect on her. We sat in silence as our SUV drove through the devastation that had once been the proud city of Chicago, each lost in our own thoughts.

The terrorists hadn't done the damage. The population had — ordinary people breaking out and acting out in the worst possible way. Fueled by marauding gangs and an almost complete breakdown in policing, a desperate lack of food and clean water, and literally no power, thousands had taken to the streets and then destroyed everything and anything they thought was responsible for the terrible conditions they found themselves in. And as social media had died at the same time as the world wide web hack, people's ability to shout electronically and abuse the systems with bytes and passion and remain anonymous had turned into physical violence not seen since the civil war, when both North and South routinely sacked towns and villages to deny the enemy comfort and access.

"Okay, I can forgive you for not briefing me, but if they are able to track us that accurately, what's to stop a second or third gang from having a go at us?"

"Nothing. I came here hoping to see my mother and take a little personal time to wind down, but's that probably out the window now, so we have a choice."

"Set another trap or go home?"

"Yes. And let me guess, you want to set another trap."

The smile on Sandra's face told the story, but I had a few things to work out first. Like the cost-benefit of taking out another gang versus getting us safely to our next destination, which the boss had not yet let me have. I needed intelligence and information, and I thought about the safest way to get it.

"Tom, where can you and your team set up so we can get a quiet half-hour to talk things over?" The little communicator I was using was so small it just looked like a gray blob in my palm, but the reception was first-class and clear as a whistle.

"We're front and rear tailing you now, so you choose." I brought up the map of Chicago in my mind, mentally marked an 'X' where we were now, where the airport was, then looked out the window. Lots of wrecked buildings, vehicles upended and scattered all over, not really very appealing to the visiting tourist.

"Sandra, you worked the Chicago office. Where can we go that will be relatively safe and we can have a chat?"

She looked out her window, saw the same carnage and wanton destruction I did, shrugged her shoulders, then looked at me with a sparkle in her eyes I could only envy.

"Given what's outside our windows, I'd say a hangar at the airport if you want to be invisible to satellites, and if you really want to see your mum, why don't you arrange for a truck convoy?" My time to smile was simple, elegant, and very doable. Why hadn't I been able to think of that?

"Tom, we're going to use hangar three, and there will be a lot of trucks coming and going. We're going to play a little shell game." I got three clicks as my response, so my next call was to a wily trucker named Harry, one of mum's frequent suitors. I had been using him for months to get messages to and from her again, so no one could tie her to me.

"Harry, mount up, shell game, hangar three, Chicago International, bring mum, we will have troops on the ground, and your guys need to be on the lookout for any gangs and send your vehicle IDs to this code." Three clicks, he was eighty-six if he was a day, always had a three-day scruff on his wrinkled face, now a warming snowy color, and professed to have been in love with my mum for as long as I had known him, so in a very nice way, he was family. He didn't know what I did, only that I worked for Interpol somewhere overseas and that I needed his help to keep mum safe.

"So, tell me, while we have this quiet time together, why were you so keen to get out of the office?" She shrugged, and kept looking out the window.

"That big child smuggling operation you worked two years ago made my head buzz. I read and reread the report twenty times, looking for all the bits you left out. Then I ran across a soldier who was doing some refresher training with the Chicago SWAT team, and he told me he had been with you for two months while you hunted the bastards across Europe and Asia. He didn't share any secrets other than the fact that he had never seen such precision and purpose in the way you and the boss went about the operation. He was amazed at the way you meshed with the local militia or police seamlessly, was always in control no matter how much the local help outranked you, and he thought you were cute."

"He thought what?" I was shocked. Cute? Me? You've got to be kidding. "He definitely said cute. And that you were a hell of a shot, and he was very glad to be on your side of the argument."

"Huh." I didn't know what to say. But then, soldiers in the field often fantasized and created images in their heads to keep sane in the most insane conditions imaginable.

"So you wanted to go off and hunt bad guys?" I looked at her out of the corner of my eye, waiting for a reaction. She turned from the window, all smiles, and to look at her, you would be very hard-pressed to see someone who had just survived another vicious firefight and shot a gangster in the leg, then blown his kneecap off at close range.

"No, not really. A year ago, when I was scheduled for training with the FBI hostage team and then the Chicago SWAT, I asked my supervisor in Washington what was up and if we were going to be allowed to carry firearms at last. She said no, there had been an instruction from HQ to train up certain single-person offices and to ensure we had the best training available. That was when I started to get my first tingle. Then I read the report of your operation, with all that it didn't say, and I got another buzz. I was very happy when I was called out to work with Fay. She had an excellent team and really knew what to do and how to do it." I thought about that. The reason she had been called out was that she had been cross-trained with the FBI and SWAT; if she hadn't, I would have pulled a more experienced and qualified agent in from somewhere else.

The world worked in mysterious ways. "Okay, here we go."

And our SUV drove into the hangar, where six Pantechs were lined up side by side. Their drivers were busily disconnecting the cabs from the trailers, and as we slid to a stop, I saw my mum sitting in the shotgun seat of Harry's cab. I put my hand out to Sandra.

"Give me a few with her alone, maybe thirty yards. I'll walk her over to that little office." I got out, and the moment I did, my mum jumped down from the cab and ran to me.

"How did you cut your face? And are you hurt anywhere else?" She reached to my cheek, rubbing the dried blood away.

I just hugged her and let myself go for the first time in about a year. She hadn't changed in the slightest, still thin as a rail, still pretty as a picture, dressed in her truck stop uniform with a red cardigan over the blue dress with white trim, her alligator handbag carelessly thrown over one shoulder, her hair now more gray that I remembered, but still shiny and well cared for. Bright red nail polish! No wonder every truckle from both coasts was in love with her!

I had given her the handbag as a Christmas present because it was beautiful Cajun workmanship, all soft and warm, with the pattern of the scales just a subtle change in color. She had loved it from the get-go, and it warmed my heart to see it on her.

I wasn't alone. Six really big beefy, and roughly dressed drivers, some spitting tobacco on the gray epoxy floor of the hangar, formed a loose circle around us. It was quite warming to see how much they cared for her. Sandra, her hand in her bag, which was casually thrown over her shoulder, walked with them, but in spite of the procession, I sensed no fear, no trouble, just a strong love for my mother, who had done everything in her power to raise me, protect me, and love me, no matter what the circumstances might be, including being at my bedside when I came to after a horrific crash where five of my friends had been killed. We were all very young, stupid, and probably drunk. That had led me to be brought before a judge, and as the police couldn't prove that I had been driving the car, and I couldn't prove that I hadn't, he had given me the choice of joining the military or going to jail.

Hello Navy, and hello, NCIS. Hello Boss, who I had shot six times in the chest as he crawled into our base chasing terrorists, and then a short time, later he had recruited me into Section Five. I had aimed for his center of mass; he had worn body armor. After that experience, I had always aimed for the head of anyone I shot.

We walked out of the protective circle and into a little utility room where we had a modicum of privacy.

"Hi, mom. You look as lovely as always." Tears were falling from her eyes like little jeweled waterfalls, and I pulled a stained bandana out of my pocket and wiped them away. "Don't cry. I'm not hurt. My face is just scratched from being careless. What have you been doing with yourself these last few months?"

She gave me that look that only a mother can as if seeking the truth deep in my soul, but I was good at hiding my feelings by now, so she only saw the love I had for her. She sniffed, then sat on a little metal chair, pulled a tissue out of her handbag, wiped her face, sniffed again, then gave me that 'don't lie to me' look.

"When the fighting broke out, our drivers built a ring around the truck stop with their trailers, they moved all their families into the rooms out the back, and they protected us from whatever came at us for over a month. Then we got word that the fighting had been brought under control by a lone trooper in a beat-up police van, and things went back to sort of normal. The boys started getting orders to move freight, so they teamed up, and we managed to open the truck stop again to anyone passing. That's pretty much it until I got your message this morning. You can believe that created a ruckus!" I smiled at that. My call to Harry would have been the first outside communication they would have received in months.

"Harry didn't have any trouble organizing the convoy?"

"Darling, we had every driver and their crew volunteer! They couldn't wait to get going." Her eyes started to leak again, and it was my turn to sigh.

"I'm sorry to put you through all this, but I really wanted to see you, make sure you were okay. Do you need anything?" She looked at me out of her hazel eyes, now sparkling with happiness, and rubbed my shoulders, giving comfort.

"No, thank you. I have everything I need, and Harry looks after me as if he were mine, and I don't mind that one bit." I smiled. The idea of the giant man who looked like he crushed cars with his fists for sport looking after my mum was lovely because he was the original 'gentle giant', and you only had to look at him to see that he had eyes only for my mum. I leaned in, hugged her, and held on as long as possible. Then I sighed, nodded, smiled at her, gave her a kiss on each cheek, then fell forward and gave her another hug.

"Got to go, mom. Thanks for taking the time to see me. I love you." And I walked back out to the marauding group of drivers, joined up with Sandra, waved to Harry, and got back into the SUV. We drove the short distance to the G4 and climbed back into the lush and overly expensive interior that only a government department could afford.

"We've got some thinking to do, my young apprentice. Let's see what happens on the way back."

"Way back to where?"

"No idea. But I expect we'll find out soon enough. And I want you to work through how the bad guys tracked us so efficiently." I flicked open my mini, and dialed my favorite FBI agent.

"Anna, how goes it?" She looked rested and relaxed, her silky haircut shape revealing the chiseled edges of her pretty face, one that would seduce you into confessing once you saw the hard look in her green eyes with their faintly gold surrounds. From the background, she was in her office, the crossed flags of the USA and the FBI framing her perfectly.

"Hi, Jessica. Who did you piss off this time?" I reached for the cut on my face and was surprised to feel it leaking a little.

"A concrete block. It went off pretty much as you anticipated, but we really need to find out how they tracked us. Have you got an update from Helena?"

"Vernon moved in last week, and he gets his refugees next week. He has opted to take two, and his wife is totally on board, so we are waiting for the next step. His partner, now that you have stolen Fay, is working the local area out of the office, acting as the senior special agent, and we've posted another pair of agents in from Los Angeles. The agents shadowing the barges report nothing unusual. Our background checks on the people handling the distribution are coming up normal, as in families, IDs, references, and qualifications all seem genuine, but we intend to dig as deep as we can to make sure. But if you want my first glance summary, no one in the distribution chain was a part of the attacks."

"Okay, that's good to know. How to go the engineers at Point Roberts?"

"They have three new structures up, the first one commissioned last week."

"How long did it take Amira to jump-start the process?"

"Three days. And the third day was simply her being anal. I have to say, even with everything we know and applying our brightest people, we still don't have anyone even half as good as her. It will take time, I think, and another Amira before we can duplicate the process."

I smiled at that; it meant the Americans probably couldn't take over the world as fast as they hoped!

"Did anyone try for Amira?"

"No. The Israelis masked her movements expertly. My feeling is that the terrorists always wanted the plants to succeed, so attacking the one person that can make that possible would go against the grain."

"Then why are they tracking and attacking us?" She looked confused and tilted her head to one side.

"Jessica, you stopped them in their tracks. You took out their leadership and made a huge dent in their program. You can't really be all that surprised?" I shook my head, no, I wasn't, but I didn't appreciate the focus being kept on my people or me.

"Next, Tom's left some rubbish that needs to be collected at the Navy Pier. Can you take care of that, please?" Then the look she gave me was one of amusement. "Already done, and we shadowed you to your-or should I say, our-plane. That was an interesting convoy you arranged."

"Okay, thanks. Next, are we officially off the hook with you and the general, so we can go back to doing what we love?" This time she just smiled, the real humor of my question showing in her eyes.

"Yes and no. Officially, the FBI, NSA, and CIA have taken over your role, but the general has made it very clear to Roger, Julius, and Frank that she wants to keep you in the loop."

"Well, that makes sense, someone in your camp is leaking like a sieve, and you want us to share with them? I don't think so." Dripping sarcasm wasn't my usual style, and Anna knew it.

"Jessica, we all have a long way to go before this is resolved. All I ask for is a little patience. You are using our resources as part of your private army; we want very little in return other than pertinent information as and when it is applicable." The stern school teacher had returned, reminding me that while she came across as soft and girly, she was the senior FBI agent next to the director and had all the experience to support her position.

"Yes, ma'am, at once, ma'am. Happy now?" She just smiled at my response.

"What's got your cranky pants on?" I heaved a huge sigh and let my shoulders slump, dropping my head into my hands.

"All I wanted was a few hours with my mum, not a bloody circus." I felt her warmth through the tiny screen, and she leaned into the camera to make her contact more personal.

"Jessica, the fact that you were able to see her at all is a minor miracle, given the current circumstances. None of us will have a smooth personal road for some time to come." I lifted my head, looked into those challenging eyes of hers, and saw the truth in them.

"Yes, I know. Sorry. Back to the main story. The geeks and our special electronics squad are working out the how's and why's of our little trip, so it will have served its purpose. Have you had any pressure put on you regarding the special electronics squad?"

"Yes, I did initially, until Frank accepted that it was an Interpol thing, and he didn't really have to worry about it, just use the minis and then the pipeline they provided. The details stay with me, and I know Malcolm will go to his grave before he tells anyone, is that what you wanted to hear?"

"Yes, thank you. Protecting Indigo's brother is of primary importance. I'll have more to tell you about that when I get back to wherever the boss is sending me now. Thanks for everything." I shut the lid on the mini, thought for a second, then lifted it again.

"*Moshi moshi*, Commander?" The earnest young face of our agent in Toyoko swam into focus with the docks behind him. It was either night or very early in the morning, as the harsh light of an overhead halogen carved his face in two, one side in deep black shadow, the other almost burnt out. I decided to deescalate the implied importance of the call, the better to make my agent feel at ease.

"Nokomoto-san, good to see you. Are you supervising the loading of the shipsets?"

"*Hai*, just these last two, one for Estonia and one for Finland."

"Have you established the owners of the trust accounts in those countries?"

"*Hai*. My partner, Namoki-san, worked with Colonel Kashasini and found the companies managing the trusts and the contacts for unlocking the funds. We have put a Red Notice on each and informed the local authorities in each case."

"Excellent. Have you got Innomatchi back up and running?" He grinned, his eyes turned feral, and I swore I could feel the tension or passion rippling off him in waves.

"Commander, Innomatchi sent more soldiers to our homes and then to the office. I have to report that we made quite a mess cleaning them up." I sat stunned; this information had not reached me.

"Were you or your partner hurt? Your families? Casualties? Media?" Now he just smiled, and I felt the tension go out of my shoulders.

"No, Commander, we were not hurt in any way. Our families are safe, the Yakuza not so much. They came in waves. We killed about thirty; the Nihonkoku Shoukan Wiki, who was working with us, took some minor casualties and many prisoners. The police special assault teams here are quite fierce, as I'm sure you know." I just nodded, adding this attack to the one we had experienced back in Chicago and the two attacks on the prison cells and hospital in Israel. There was a pattern there, and I suspected it went all the way back to us broadcasting the so-called 'cease fire' message from 'Helen'. That gave me another idea, so I put my best smile on and bowed to the camera.

"Thank you, Nokomoto-san. Keep us in the loop. I will have more for you in an hour."

"*Sayōnara, arigatō* Commander."

I shut my screen, then opened it and dialed again. "Indigo, hello from Interpol Atlantic Ocean. How goes it all?"

He looked cheerful, happy, and relaxed and his background was in our operations room under the old church in Venice. "*Ciao, Comandante, è bello vederti ancora tutto intero!*"

"Tom and a few beefy truck drivers looked after us. I have a question for you. Have you and the geeks mapped all the black holes yet?"

"*Si*, we have. What do you need to know?"

"Send me a world map with the black holes highlighted. Please, in fact, send it to the plane's data center."

"At once, Commander, are you heading home?"

"Ask the boss."

I snapped the lid shut to stop any further dialogue from running into my thinking, I was nibbling at an idea, and I didn't want it to run away. I looked over at Sandra, relaxing in the wide, plush seat next to me. She was all but sleeping, the mini on her lap. We still had five hours to go before reaching Venice, and I toyed for a second to let her continue sleeping. Then I just reached over and gave her a gentle shake. If we ever wanted to get on top of this, time was of the essence.

"Wakey, wakey, time to go back to work."

She rolled over in her seat and gave me a warm and very soft smile, obviously still in the throes of her dream, then her eyes suddenly focused on me in the real, and she snapped back to her normal, happy, alert self.

"Must have been an excellent dream," I said, with a wicked grin on my face.

"It certainly was. No need to describe the tall, tanned, well-built naked man that was running me down?"

"No. Absolutely not. Keep your prurient fantasies to yourself!"

She laughed, and so did I, the idea of sex such a remote idea I had forgotten it had ever existed. "Have you found out how they tracked us?"

"Yes and no."

"Give me the yes."

"The geeks and Malcolm have managed to follow us in the G4. That was, according to them, the easy bit. Few aircraft are flying. We used the G4 in the US, we took it to Israel, etc., etc. They did okay until we switched vehicles but were still able to follow us again because of the lack of traffic. They watched the firefight go down in real-time, followed us to the airport, lost us in the hangar, and picked us up again at the G4. Now that's the good news, and they were using a combination of what the US has got back up and our own technology."

"You mean the monks."

"I mean the monks."

"What's the no?"

"The no is a very big scary piece of data that Malcolm provided. If you remember, about a month or so ago, the US said they had shut down all the backdoors in their airways system and in the government and corporate databases."

"I remember."

"Good. It was bullshit. They may have thought they got all the back doors, but according to Malcolm, during our flight and road transport, several sites lit up, he says, like the proverbial Christmas tree, and when he pulled the data, it showed our movements in detail, in real-time, and the data was being transmitted via the type of hardware we recovered from Helena, Point Roberts, Innomatchi, and New Zealand."

"So they can track us where ever we go?"

"It may seem like it, but Malcolm believes that they are totally unaware of the technology the monks are using, what our minis are using, and that our exposure is only when we go public, as it were."

"So, if we changed aircraft, went to ground, then completely changed the way we move around, we might manage to escape their surveillance."

"Something like that. The real issue is that, as we believed, the French weather satellites are being used by the terrorists to receive and transmit, and we now have access to that data, but perhaps we should consider shutting them down?"

"What does Malcolm say about a secure satellite network we could use?"

"Well, as you know, the Internet hack only took out computers, routers, modems, and data stores that were active at the time. Took out their individual chipsets, via their Mac addresses. So anything in orbit is useless until it can be repaired. However, there is a company that had just launched twelve hundred satellites into LEO (Low Earth Orbit) just before the terrorists attacked, and the satellites have not been turned on yet. So with a little bit of persuasion, maybe we could invoke some law or other and get them for ourselves?"

"Some law or other? Just what exactly did they teach you in International Law school." She just smiled, and started to bounce around in her seat again, making me feel tired just by looking at her.

"Is Malcolm in contact with this company?"

"He is, but they have been the target of multiple attacks, their Spaceport in Texas was raised to the ground, and several of their car and battery plants have been destroyed, not to mention the six thousand constellation of LEO satellites they lost in the hack. The point I'm making is that they may be leery of doing business with us."

"No. We have the perfect bargaining tool. We trade them chipsets for satellites. They're already in that business. We need to talk to their main decision maker."

"There's two to choose from: the founder, owner, and chief scientist/engineer, the other is their Chief Operations Officer, and of the two, I'd suggest her for the first round."

"Then find him or her, get them to a secure location where we can talk to them."

"Yes, boss." And she dived into her mini, and I switched my attention back to the idea that had been forming at the back of my mind. When your enemy could track your every move, you needed to find a way to work without having to move. A distributed network approach that half the world had learned the value of during the recent pandemic might work. Now, how could I pull that off with so few resources? And another thing, were we on a clean-up detail or preparing to fend off another attack? The waters were murky, and I needed to sift through the muck to see way clearer.

# Chapter Three

Malik Badawi had dirt under his fingernails and blood on his hands and had never been happier. Nearly fifteen years ago, he had met the Iman who called himself 'Al Hemish al-bin Mohammad Karesish' in the desert, and the physical scale of his whole world had changed. He had been promised money, so vast the size of it beggared belief. He had only to make two promises, and he would become the most successful terrorist in known history.

The first was to limit his preference for little boys and girls and stay out of the limelight of the sex and people trade. He had managed that, mostly, right up to the time his major network had been taken down by Interpol just over two years ago. He had been safe, of course, sitting in a luxurious apartment in Dublin, entertaining people who were the opposite of everything he believed in and as far away from the carnage and misery of the people trade as it was possible to get.

Still, he had lost a huge part of his investment, and his anger fizzled just under the surface at the thought of all those delicious little children being taken from him. At a little over six foot in height, with a strong-boned face and long black hair that curled over his shoulders, whether he dressed in the traditional garb of the Bedouin desert warrior or a high-end Italian suit, he looked handsome, sophisticated even, and carried himself with style and a certain panache. People of money did that, he had seen it all his life, and the irony was he had dedicated himself and his terrorist band, Al Bar al Shirak, to bring down as many of the monied heathens as he possibly could, by any means possible, while silently drinking champagne and the world's finest wines in their very midst.

Did he believe in God? Only when it suited him, and mostly when he had his hands or other body parts wrapped in the creamy skin of a young girl or boy, as they pleaded for their lives. As in, 'thank you, God, for what you allow me to do.' How did he maintain leadership and control over his terrorist band, with his duplicitous nature? Easy. He simply killed anyone who resisted after torturing them. And he was very, very good at it, and during the centerpiece of the Iman's grand plan, he had been sequestered within the Hezbollah neighboring Israel, from where he had been able to mount two excellent attacks on shopping malls, killing thousands of innocent targets using remotely controlled vehicles.

Now he was playing the part of the Bedouin terrorist, supposedly working with Hamas's top man, Amir Abbas, in a well-designed training camp on the fringes of Afghanistan. What interested him the most were Hamas's ability to move things around the terrorist world without detection, and as far as he could see, that was their only real value from his narrow point of view. Of course, his main interest on this visit was the stunningly beautiful Irish woman he had brought with him, Siobhan O'Cleary, who dressed in the traditional Arab abaya, a rich dark blue swath of silk with silver trimmings that sparkled and shone in the sun, was also one of the world's foremost experts in nuclear science and nanotechnology.

Right now, with a group of heavily armed onlookers standing a respectable ten meters away from her, she was examining a dull gray beautiful machined series of interlocking cylinders, resting in a 3D printed casing, shaped like a small torpedo. She ran a small electronic instrument over the cylinders looking for flaws, but found nothing. She looked up into the dark eyes of her lover and nodded. She packed her tools away and stood by his side.

"Here is a list of destinations where we want each complete set delivered, and on proof of receipt, we will transfer one million euros for each to your offshore account. We will give you one million now, allowing one hundred thousand euros for transportation and expenses for each delivery. And we need all ten delivered within eight weeks, no exceptions." Amir Abbs, one of the very top leaders of Hamas, all but rubbed his hands in glee. This money from the tall man of the desert would fund untold terror attacks on his hated enemy, Israel, and would give him more power than he had ever held over his contemporaries in Hamas.

Maybe it was time for him to make his move.

Malik and his lover moved over to a camouflaged Black Hawk helicopter, abandoned after the withdrawal by the USA and its surrogates at the end of the so-called war back in 2021. They watched as the huge desert-colored net was removed and climbed inside, leaving the gunner's door open to allow air to circulate. Within minutes the huge blades were turning, creating their own slipstream, which started to whirl the desert sand up into circles as the power was applied. Just as it seemed the artificial sandstorm would engulf them, the aircraft pitched up, tilted its nose down, and flew out of the maelstrom. Unknown to anyone on the ground, or in the helicopter for that matter, the whole event had been faithfully recorded by a satellite, and as the aircraft winged its way back out to Pakistan, the digital film was being retrieved and sent to Arie Rosenberg, previously retired director of Sin Bet (Shabak).

"Well, what do you see" Amira, still smarting from her abortive call with her former lover, tried to relax as the images flowed over the huge screen.

"Stop. Zoom in, please. Center in on that metallic object." The frame froze, then slowly moved into a close shot of the torpedo-like object. The face of the woman was so clear Amira could see the blue eye lines she had used when she tilted her head up to the tall man who stood at her shoulder. She heard Arie mutter something off-camera, and the telltale yellow triangular ID dashes suddenly appeared on the woman's face.

"Female identified, Irish citizen, age twenty-nine, current passport issued last year, in the name of Siobhan O'Cleary. File note, leading expert in Nuclear Science, studied at MIT and the INSTN —- *Institut national des sciences et techniques nucléaires* — the National Institute for Nuclear Science and Technology in France."

"Quite the pedigree."

"Yes."

"I'm sorry. What did you say?" Amira looked up from where she had been peering at the screen, having captured the metallic object, and pulled it onto her personal laptop for a closer examination. Arie waved her away and smiled as if apologizing for distracting her attention away.

"What do you think it is?"

"Are they making these in Afghanistan?" she asked, her mind-boggling at the technology exhibited by the metallic object. It was obviously finely engineered and had both additive and 3D components, something you usually only saw in the lab.

"Possibly. Probably. The Americans and the British left a lot of hardware when they vacated four years ago. It's not a long stretch to assume that the hardware to make things like this were left behind." Amira looked at Arie, and the way she looked suggested he take another tack as fast as he could.

"Give us the room, please?" And the four technicians, short-barreled automatic weapons strapped to their backs, filed out, leaving Arie and Amira alone.

"Even if the machinery was first class and the engineers of a similar quality, it would take maybe two years to perfect something like this, and that would be in a climate-controlled lab with plenty of money."

"So, for the sake of the exercise, assume both. What is it?"

"It's the outer shell casing and transport system for a nuclear missile." Arie's face registered shock, and he tilted his head to one side.

"Are you sure?"

"Without physically inspecting it, that's my best guess."

"A missile, as in shot out of a cannon or dropped from an aircraft?" She looked up into space, focusing on a small spot of mold on the ancient roof, then shook her head.

"No, this is a torpedo meant to be fired out of a rifled barrel."

"A mortar?"

"Maybe. Perhaps a shoulder launcher, like the antitank ones we have here." Arie searched through his mind, tapped a keyboard, and a series of photos came up of MANPADS (Man-portable air-defense systems).

"Which one of these would be the best suited?" She peered at the choices and looked at the RBS 70 NG, the FIM-92 Stinger, Mistral MANPADS, and the 9K333 Verba. She shook her head in frustration.

"How could I know? The diameter of the torpedo is seventy millimeters. Which of those would it fit into?"

"The Russian RBS 70 MG. A lot of them were left lying around when the Russians vacated Afghanistan, so that might be it. Or they might have just designed and built something else we don't know about. Either way, please keep this to yourself for the time being, even from your friends at Interpol." She nodded, realizing she owed a huge debt of gratitude to this wonderful old man, even though she had come to love Jessica and Anna like sisters.

"Do me a personal favor. Sketch me what you would design and build to fire this at someone so I have something to show my masters."

"Yes, sir, do you want me to secure the footage?" He looked at her like a kindly old grandfather would smile and nod. And left her to it. She worried the skin on her nail with her forefinger, a new worry creeping into her subconscious. She had invented and developed the nano bug that had been turned against humanity, with disastrous results — no useable oil, gas, or coal left on the planet, chaos across the world due to ordinary people breaking out and showing their displeasure with lethal results, and now a world on the very edge of a minor extinction event.

The death toll had passed thirty million worldwide, and there were probably twice that many again that no one had the energy to count. But there was hope. The very nano bug that had been used to destroy all carbon-based fuels had again been mutated to provide, in combination with modern technology and common sand and seawater, environmentally sound solar collectors and power supplies, which were now being distributed around the world, based on some strange formula established by the terrorists.

The nano bug she had invented had eaten up oil spills with relish; the bug the terrorists had refined ate up oil, gas, and raw coal deposits with as much gusto, but rather than turn the elements into harmless sludge that sank to the bottom of the ocean, the terrorist's version had clagged up the pipelines, refractories, terminals, and mines destroying the precious materials for eternity.

And now there was evidence of her work having been hijacked yet again, work that Arie and his team had no knowledge of. She thought back to her work at Harvey Mudd university and the three labs she had under her control. One for nano work, one for deep fake coding, and the other for additive and 3D printing from new metallic materials. The photo she had seen looked exactly like a model that had been produced in her lab just before she had gone on the run.

Arie had asked her to keep this discovery to herself, and she felt conflicted. She had to let Jessica and the Interpol team know she was a sworn agent of Interpol, and it was not just a cursory membership. But she was also a sworn member of Sin Bet, a condition of her release from custody.

She walked into Arie's office, where he was in deep conversation with Colonel Shami Borowitz, his chief geek. Arie looked up from his notes, pulled his reading glasses off his nose where they had slipped to, and sat back in his worn leather seat.

"You need to tell Jessica or colonel Anthony about your work at Harvey Mudd?" She looked at him with amazement, then smiled to herself. One of the world's preeminent spies, why should she be surprised.

"Yes, sir, if it is what we believe it to be, Jessica should know about it as soon as possible."

"We agree. Give her a call." And he pointed to a keyboard sitting on a small table with an air-gapped computer sitting under it on little feet.

"Hi Jessica, where are you?" The background was plush leather, with just the hint of a royal blue curtain to one side.

"At forty thousand feet somewhere over the Atlantic. Hello Arie, Shami, what gives?"

"I'll let Amira fill you in." He turned to Amira, gave her a huge smile to encourage her, then sat back with his folded arms across his chest.

"Ah, Jessica, I don't know how to tell you this, so forgive me if I get it out of order. You know that I went to Harvey Mudd?" If I looked puzzled, it was because I was. No secret about Harvey

Mudd, that's where the destruction of the world had started, quite innocently, but nevertheless that's where the carbon-eating nano bugs were first perfected.

By Amira.

"Well, the second lab was developing the digital code that was eventually misused to create the black holes in the satellite coverage, and I guess you know all about that."

"Yes, we do. What's the real problem now?" I asked, a hint of sharpness creeping into my voice, I hated mysteries, and even more hated video calls where I wasn't setting the agenda. Actually, in truth, I just hated video calls, full stop. My mood was moderated by the lost look on Amira's face, so I took a deep breath, and calmed down.

"I had a third lab, purely experimental. We were developing additive and 3D printing using new metal-based materials. Small scale, we were going for the gold in terms of accuracy and precision. We had some great success, but as it wasn't my core work, I only kept a casual eye on the development. But just before I left, the team showed me a series of cylinders that fit together with amazing precision, something that had not been achieved previously, and I thanked them and let them play with it to their heart's content."

"And?" My skin was crawling with irrational fear. I had no notion of what she was really talking about, but having witnessed the chaos her previous efforts in the lab had gestated, and the fact that she was calling me from Arie's office worried me to the bone.

"And it looks like the terrorists managed to steal that work as well. We've just received these pictures from Afghanistan." And a close-up of the metallic cylinders in their torpedo-shaped housing swam up, and my fear turned to dread.

"How old is the data, and what is it?"

"Five weeks old and a projectile of some type, Arie believes that could be fired from a Russian MANPAD." I calmed down a little. A new projectile fired from a MANPAD didn't seem to be that much of a new threat. I was missing something.

"What am I missing, Arie"

"Think fissionable material."

"What?" I practically yelled across the Atlantic. Sandra heard me, filed whatever she was doing, and turned to look at me with a worried look in her eyes.

"Think dirty bomb, or even real bomb, we don't know at this stage, but the shape and nature of those cylinders can be found anywhere you look on the Internet — if we still had one-under the heading of 'using fissionable material to make an atomic bomb.' I trust you can still access a database on the subject?" I was in shock, but under the gaze of Sandra, miss happy and bubbly, I pulled myself together.

"I'll call you back."

"Sandra, use the big screen. Get the boss." She stepped forward to the controls, and within a minute, the boss's ugly face swam into focus on the aircraft bulkhead. Before he could talk, I cut right across him.

"Data on fissionable materials, containers, methodology of bomb-making, everything we've got." His stare showed the same degree of dread as I had, so I was calmed by that. If he was worried, it wouldn't matter so much that I had been. Within seconds he dialed up our registry, pulled the requisite section open, scrolled down to the nitty gritty, and right there in the photo file of 'preferred containers for maximizing the explosive effect of nuclear materials' was a miniature version of Amira's photo.

"*Merde*. I'll call you back."

"Arie confirmed. Where did this come from?"

"Afghanistan. The images are at least a month old, possibly older. There's no real way to time/date stamp them. But I believe this image is from the week after we had the first terrorist bombing of our Tikvah shopping center."

"How the hell did they do that?" If he was offended by my language, his face didn't show it.

"American leftovers, two years development. I'm told by Amira and lots and lots of money."

"But that's world-class engineering. Where on Earth could that be manufactured in Afghanistan?"

"We're looking, but for now, you have two known terrorists, one linked to Hamas, the other to Al Bar al Shirak, and an unknown Irish woman with no history, family, and a fake passport."

"And a container that can be used to deliver a nuclear weapon."

"And that."

"Okay, thanks, Arie. We'll take a good look at it." I sat back in my seat. It might be plush, beautiful leather, and stylish, but it now felt like a jail, holding me back from moving forward. Sandra gave me one of her happy looks, eyes sparkling from the sun as it moved across the window, and it made my day.

"At least we won't have time to get bored," and I had to smile, no truer word I could think of. But the key was the money, so I turned to her with a raised eyebrow. "The Irish trust fund has been frozen, and the Army Ranger Wing (ARW) is on the ground at the accountant's office, Reganit and Sons, Belfast, waiting for your instructions. But I think there's a stash somewhere that is outside our data. I think we have a new player on the block, utilizing the technology the women terrorists created." I gave her a hard look.

"Why?"

"Because for the last three or four months, we have been chasing persons of interest from the intelligence we received from multiple sources, collecting them up from all over the world, or just eliminating them, without a single sniff of these new guys."

"Not true. Arie confirmed that Al Bar al Shirak was behind the bombing of the shopping centers, and they used the automated AI technology designed by the women to drive their vehicles to their targets. Arie even identified their leader, Malik Badawi, so they have been playing with us previously."

"Okay, I'll give you that, but those attacks were in the context of the overall terrorism we were experiencing at the time."

"Or it was a dry run to prove the technology." Sandra's face lit up, her eyes shot wide open, and she sat back in her seat, looking a little deflated.

"Oh! I didn't think of that. In fact, I doubt if I would have ever made that connection." I smiled. She was very hard on herself. At the time of the attacks, she had just left manning a desk in Chicago to chase down the principals of the terrorist organization and lock them away, so you might say she was distracted by current events.

"So we have a puzzle. Terrorists in Afghanistan a month ago looked at a device that could be weaponized with atomic matériel, and we all know how easy it is to get some of that. A cryptic message at least a year old on an Irish bulletin board. A possible link through the funds deposited five years ago in Dublin, supposedly to support the building of an ecological manufacturing plant, the migration of refugee children, part of a worldwide project initiated by the terrorists. We know from Point Roberts how the plants work and what they can produce. We know from New Zealand and Helena how the migration of the refugees works."

"And we know the terrorists can track and attack us anywhere they like." Sandra wasn't even bitter, more excited; what was it with this young woman that she thrived on the prospect of being shot at?

"We have that. And we suspect that there is a large sum of money hidden away somewhere else funding whatever it is the terrorists are planning now. Money that was hidden long before the deposits into the nineteen countries destined for the refugees."

"Okay, question, let's suppose there are homemade nukes being assembled somewhere. Let's assume the Irish separatists are involved. What would be their natural targets?" Sandra started bouncing in her seat again. If she didn't stop it, I would tie her down!

"Not the right question, not the right suppose!" She squirted across the aisle, tapped on the keyboard, and brought up the photo of the two terrorists and the female nuclear scientist on the big screen, with the picture of the machined cylinders in a small box at the bottom. She turned to face me, her eyes lit up like touches, her smile so broad it filled her entire face. Her energy was infectious, and I started to feel myself lift.

"Suppose different interests or targets for each person in the photo. Where does that take you?" I looked at her, she was bubbly but bright, and the speed at which she was unpicking things made me feel old and slow.

"Maybe Israel, maybe the UK, who knows? Using a weapon of mass destruction (WMD) is a whole new ball game. And given the state of the world at present, what would you gain by blowing somewhere up?" She looked at me as if I had two heads, then she smiled again.

"Jessica, my friend, and mentor, you're missing the point. The one thing the terrorists have always wanted is recognition for their cause and, in a sense, respectability for their point of view. What better way to resolve an outstanding issue than to blow somewhere right off the map? Then threaten other places with the same fate unless the terrorists' demands are met? Think about it. A WMD is the perfect bargaining chip."

"Prove you can do it somewhere that might not matter in the grand scheme of things, then hold the world hostage."

"Yes. And given the chaos and instability of most countries at the moment and the dangerous positions most governments find themselves in, it's the perfect time to launch such an attack."

"The demonstration target has to be close enough so that people feel the threat viscerally, but far enough away not to pollute somewhere important."

"Yes. You've got it. We did a lot of this type of scenario planning at Quantico, mostly looking for weak spots in the major cities on the US continent. But the principles were the same for any large population area, and that's why the US created the NEST (Nuclear Energy Support Team) program." I thought about NEST and the huge effort the US had put into setting up radiation detectors at every port around the country post-9/11.

"Commander, this is your captain. Buckle up. We are under attack!" The sharp command from the pointy end got the required result, Sandra flew back to her seat, and we both tightened our seat belts and peered out our respective windows.

'Can't see a thing."

"Neither can I." I picked up the handset built into the arm of my seat, was immediately squeezed into the corner, then flung across to the other side like so much refuse. Then the bottom dropped out of my stomach, and bits and pieces hit the roof and sidewalls with a crash and thud.

"What's the attack profile?"

"Missiles, heat seekers, I'll come back to you!" And we rose up precipitously, then, like a roller coaster, started down the other side, the cabin at such an acute angle that now had whatever was not tied down smashing into the forward bulk-head. I watched in amazement as a single plate seemed to hover in mid-air, then smash itself to bits on the cockpit door. A huge fireball scorched Sandra's side of the fuselage, the bright orange, and yellow flame causing a strobing effect as the light flickered through the oval windows. To my amazement, she was watching all this with a huge grin from ear to ear.

The whole airframe shuddered, then the cabin exploded outwards, and all the loose stuff flew out the gaping hole that had opened next to the galley. Oxygen masks dropped down, swinging in the torrid air as if they didn't have a care in the world. I reached up and grabbed one about the same time Sandra did, and we turned to look at each other, looking like Martians with our yellow snouts and inflatable oxygen bags. The plane steadied, still, nose down, and the shuddering and vibration had dropped to just a constant buzz.

We were still flying over the ocean somewhere, losing altitude rapidly, either because the engines had been damaged or because the pilot had to get us below ten thousand feet because we had lost our pressurization. I looked towards the cockpit door figured my best move was to stay seated, at least until it became obvious the pilot had been injured as well, but as we started to slowly level out, and I could clearly hear the roar of the starboard engine somewhere behind my seat, I mentally crossed my fingers.

"Okay, that was close, but no cigar, down to one burning and turning, all good otherwise. How y'all back there?" I picked the handset back up from where it had lodged in the back of the seat in front of me, looked around the cabin, and made my assessment.

"Big hole behind the cockpit door starboard side, a bit of a mess on the floor, otherwise okay." The hiss of highspeed air came back at me through the handset, and I suspected that the hole in our side may have also impacted the cockpit. "Are you okay?"

"Ah, not really. If one of you could come forward with the first aid kit, it would be appreciated." Sandra started to get up. I motioned her down, took off my oxygen mask, then crawled forward over the mess that was now our floor, dug the first aid kit out of its wall mount, then broached the cockpit door.

Big hole on the co-pilot's side, lots of smashed windscreens, instrument glass, and wall panels, and the pilot was down to one arm, his entire right-hand side streaked with blood, his uniform hanging in tatters. We hit a small bump, and we both juddered up and down, and I made a snap decision. I turned back and yelled for Sandra. Checked to see that the autopilot was still engaged and that we were in straight and level flight, with good airspeed.

Sandra arrived, took one look, and nodded to herself.

"Help me pull him out into the co-pilot's seat." She leaned forward, undid his five-point harness, used the electric runner to move his seat backwards, then, getting his injured shoulder under her own, twisted and shimmied until pilot, still conscious but only barely, was in the seat. The instrument panel in front of him was trashed, a piece of fuselage sticking out of it like a flag. I handed her the first aid box, swung down into the pilot's seat, and ran it forward and up to align my eye level with the little red balls on the windshield.

I strapped in, tightened the harness, and ran my eyes over the instruments. One of the first things the boss taught me when I was learning to fly was *'do nothing quickly'*. Pilots under pressure had a tendency to make things worse, but the need to be focused and quick in determining our location and state was its own motivation. I pulled my mini out, slid it into the slot in the control column, and dialed the boss. Before he could speak, I summarized our condition.

"Took a missile hit starboard side, down to one engine, pilot injured but not totally out of it, level at nine thousand six hundred feet, heading zero eight four, indicating three bars off course. Holes in the fuselage, fuel state showing as two thousand pounds, and dropping. Looking for options."

"Wait, one." His head bent and bobbed up and down a little, then his blue eyes focused on mine, and I felt confident for the first time in minutes.

"Dial-up Alpha Charlie Lima on your FMC (Flight Management Computer), select alternate, select 'go to direct', tell me what you see." I punched the designation into the FMC, selected the alternatives the boss had instructed and watched the indicators and needles on the instruments move themselves as the aircraft banked to the right, then settled down with the needles centered in the head-up display. I told the boss. He asked about the pilot. I looked at Sandra. She shook her head, and I shrugged my shoulders.

"Airspeed?"

"One forty indicated, one sixty-five ground speed."

"Fuel state?"

"Showing seventeen hundred pounds."

"Okay, you're good for the Azores. They will be ready for you. Just keep it smooth. Remember, on your approach, you will have a lot of asymmetric swing going on, the pilot will have trimmed most of it out, but as you descend and slow down, it will become much more noticeable. How much time do you have in the G4?" I looked at my analogue watch with its pretty pink band, a present last Christmas from my mum. I had only put it on because I was going to meet her, and my tactical watch was still in my carryall.

"I think about ten minutes in total, so far." His smile was only outshone by Sandra's, who by now had the pilot well and truly bandaged up. He was looking a little less pale, so maybe I wouldn't have to land this thing by myself. I had considerable jet time, but mostly in trainers and smaller executive jets and a little bit in the C-17s, we kept finding ourselves in.

"No matter how we land, you get him out and to safety. That is your priority, understand?" She gave me a very hard look, seemed to think twice about arguing, then just nodded. The airport symbol was moving up in the HUD, and the GPS was showing forty-two nautical miles to run. I started a very, very slow descent, using the autopilot, one hundred feet a minute descent rate initially, waiting for the airframe to tell me what it objected to.

"Active?"

"Straight in approach runway one fife, you are cleared to land, emergency vehicles standing by. And you will be met by the local militia, who are Portuguese, so play nice with them."

"You're just loving this, aren't you?" I dripped my words with as much sarcasm as I could, and he just smiled all the harder. I looked at Sandra.

"Get our carryalls, take the pilot, sit down somewhere, belt your-selves in. The moment we land, pop the door, inflate the slide, then get the pilot out." She nodded and went back to do my bidding, taking the now very shocked pilot with her. He reached over and squeezed my shoulder, mouthed *'good luck'*. I would need it. I checked the bars on the airspeed indicator; the orange one was set at one hundred and twenty knots; the green one at one hundred and ten. I was already using just a single engine, so I only had to keep us flying long enough to hit the ground reasonably safely.

I tested the hydraulics by selecting five degrees of flaps. They ran out, I felt the resulting lift, and the nose rose slightly. Went for twenty degrees. The airspeed dropped ten knots, the airframe shim-mied from side to side, then settled down. It would have to be a high-speed approach. I hoped the brakes worked. But the higher speed would eliminate some of the asymmetric swings I had to anticipate as one wing tried to climb over to its less-working brethren. I increased the descent rate and pegged the marker on the altitude bar at five hundred feet.

My plan was simple. Long, flattish approach, hold one thirty knots, no flare, just pull the good engine to idle over the threshold and bang it on. I dialed up one twenty-one point five, gave a standard mayday call, warned of my approach and condition, then just shut up. Another lesson from the boss filtered through my mind. When the s-h-one-t hits the fan, aviate, navigate, and communicate in that order.

The runway appeared where it was supposed to. Looked like a nice evening, the island was well-lit, almost festive, and I could make out the winking red and blue of the emergency lights on the fire trucks. I snapped the mini closed, took manual control as gently as I could, got a real shimmy for my efforts, watched the airspeed fluctu-ate wildly, then settle down, which helped my nerves and my attitude, and as close to my airspeed as I could hold, and in less time that it takes to tell it here had the G4 on the ground, in one piece, slewing from side to side, standing on the brakes for all I was worth, my good port engine in full reverse.

We started to spin, and I realized the starboard side undercar-riage had collapsed, and we were busy burying the wing in the weeds.

I cut the fuel, and the power, pulled the fire bottles, and unconsciously put my hand up to protect my face, then with a series of rips, yaws, and bangs, we stopped. I heard the door open and the slide inflating with its characteristic '*pop, hiss*', and just sat and caught my breath. Clicked my harness open, grabbed my mini, climbed out of the cockpit, found the open door and chute, and jumped into it. Sandra grabbed me at the bottom, then gave me a little hug.

"Make a note, when I get home, to update my flight log, Gulf-stream G4, thirty-one minutes flight time, IFR, one landing, PIC."

"Do you want me to take a picture for your log?" she asked imp-ishly, turning to look at the wreckage. Our beautiful G4 was lean-ing on one side, one wing was broken, smoke billowing out from the undercarriage, and small flames licking at the rear, where the fire-fighters were pouring on foam with gusto. The slide had buckled, and the cockpit looked like someone had taken a very big hammer to it.

"You can do that, but then I would have to kill you, and it would be such a pity to have to train someone new." I watched as the pilot was loaded into the ambulance, took my hold all from Sandra, slung it over my shoulder, and started to walk to the terminal building. We didn't get there, as we were intercepted by a police jeep, lights flashing and carrying two very determined-looking gentlemen.

"Commander Riley?"

"Yes, sir, that is me."

"Commander, please come with us. We have somewhere you can stay while we sort all this out." Sort all that out? We had our bent, broken, and still smoldering G4 just off the main runway, the pilot on the way to the hospital, and Sandra and I on our feet and uninjured, unless you count my pride. I just rolled my shoulders and climbed into the back seat with Sandra, who had gone all paranoid on me and now had her hand in her bag, giving our driver and his companion the fish eye. My weapon was in my bag, so I would be a slow start to any gunfight. I wondered what had set Sandra off? She was normally the calm, happy, bouncing battery bunny. Just as I was forming that thought, a pair of F-35s roared overhead, broke formation with a fast hard turn, and streaked parallel to the runway. The two police, if that is what they were, looked at each other, then the jeep stopped suddenly. They both turned, drawing their guns and found themselves looking down the barrel of Sandra's H&K MP47.

"*Joguem suas armas!*" she shouted in Portuguese. They both froze, giving me time to reach into my bag and grab my Sig. Sandra motioned both of them to get out of the jeep, which they did, and now we had an uncomfortable situation of being on foreign soil, holding guns on supposed police, with a crashed and burning plane at our backs. The F-35's landed in formation with a roar, and a minute or two later, they were parked in sight of us, canopies raised, green helmeted monsters staring out at us from their cockpits.

The thump thump of a helicopter cut through the air, and out of the clear starlit sky, a sleek navy MH-60s Nighthawk floated down, its pressure wave flattening everything under it for a hundred feet in every direction. It had barely sunk down on its undercarriage before six heavily armed black-suited sailors ran out. Four swarmed around the jeep, and the other two headed to the ambulance.

"Thank you, sirs. We will take it from here." Polite, and effective, as the two policemen lowered their hands, standing embarrassed at what they had tried to do, and for reasons we might never know. And for about the millionth time, I marveled at the boss's connections, his intelligence-gathering skills, and his ability to get me out of the really smelly stuff with such ease.

We marched to the helicopter, Sandra pushing the neat H&K back into her bag. The two sailors ran past us with the pilot between them and pushed him into the cabin. We climbed in after him and, as we did, saw the two F35s drop their canopies and start taxing. No one spoke, we were not offered coffee, tea, or biscuits, and the entire crew kept their flash shields down and looked anywhere but at us. If it worried Sandra, it didn't show. She just looked out the open door and grinned like a twelve-year-old as we flew across the Atlantic Ocean. I had a fair idea of where we were headed. I had seen the code on the tail of the Nightwalk CSG-11 (Carrier Strike Group 11). The F-35's had stopped too far away for me to see their tail feathers.

It only took about thirty minutes, and the carrier group came into view as we crossed one of the picket Destroyers, then flared to land on the massive, dark carrier deck. The pilot was unloaded and rushed away, and we were hustled out to the base of the island, where we were met by a lieutenant commander in at-sea camos. He saluted, I returned the courtesy, and we followed him up to the flight control deck, where we were ushered into the captain's space. He was a big man with broad shoulders, graying hair in a brush cut, a warm craggy face, and twinkling green eyes that stared at you until you blinked. Knowing no more than this, I decided never to play poker with him.

"Commander Riley and Inspector Thomas, Interpol, Section Five. Permission to come aboard, sir." He saluted back and smiled.

"Granted. I understand you've had quite a day."

"Yes, sir." I paused for a second. "Sir, how is my pilot?" He looked me square in the eyes, then turned and nodded to the officer who had accompanied us.

"Sir, your pilot is recovering in sick bay. He is ambulatory at this time." The captain smiled; he was probably as relieved as I was to hear that. He nodded and motioned to our escort.

"Take these two ladies to our guest quarters. Perhaps you would like a shower, a hot meal. We can debrief in an hour if that suits you?"

"Yes sir, thank you, that would be excellent. I need to contact my boss. May I use my own secure comms unit?" He gave me a hard look, probably wondering what sort of device I thought I had that was more secure than his navy communications center. But I knew the terrorists were somewhere in the backend of the US electronic systems, and if they heard me my talking to the boss, it could paint a huge target on the battle group. People kept getting shot and blown out of the air around me. I didn't need a carrier group on my conscience.

We reached our temporary quarters and thanked our escort.

"Ma'am, there will be a sailor outside your door. Anything you need, just ask. Place your clothes outside when you are ready, and we'll have them processed for you." I closed the door behind him, threw my bag on the bunk, rubbed my hands through my hair, and looked at Sandra, who still managed to look bubbly and happy.

"Take the shower first. I want to bring the boss up to speed. I don't know what we will do about clothes until we get ours back." She silently opened the door of the large closet, which hung various sizes of navy camo overalls. I smiled, at least they would be clean, and for once, we would be equal in the dress stakes! After bringing him up to date, I asked the questions that were thumping me behind my eyes, creating a headache I really didn't need.

"How did they attack us in the middle of the Atlantic Ocean? And how did they get to the police so fast?" He looked at me for a few seconds, then dropped his head slightly as if in apology.

"The geeks are working on it. We just got the pilot's statement via Milnet. your ship facilitated a conversation between him and Frank. Frank was seriously pissed off. He considered G4 as his personal jet. The pilot said that there were four missiles, he thinks heat seekers, he avoided or deflected three, the fourth got you in the starboard engine, the rest you know. The G4 had the usual military specification defense systems as as it belonged to the NSA, but as you suspect, you must have been attacked by a jet of some sort, and we're looking into that now."

"The bigger question to me is why are they so invested in attacking me? I'm just one person. Interpol has hundreds of agents. It doesn't make sense." He gave me that hard look again as if to say, 'get over yourself', but I held his stare. Whoever it was had tried to kill me twice in one day, and the second time had used resources that still required nation-level support.

"We're working on it. In the meantime, enjoy your stay aboard the Gerald Ford. We'll get you back home soonest." And he went to black, his eyes told me he knew something I didn't, and that started a slow boil, completely spoiled by Sandra popping out of the shower like a human laughter bubble, all joy and happiness, wrapping her luxurious hair in a towel.

"That shower was mag, great pressure, and hot, hot, hot!" She bounced around the small stateroom, finally sitting on the edge of the bunk. She looked at me as if to ask why I wasn't following her lead, shrugged her tanned shoulders, then bent to the drying of her hair, vigorously rubbing long shiny bundles of it up and down. As well as clothes envy, I now had hair envy, my cap of light brown hair just a tangled mop of unruliness. Which was usual, as my personal grooming style lacked a certain sophistication, according to Anna, my favorite FBI agent, another clotheshorse. Just because I felt running my hands through my hair once or twice a day was all I needed to do, didn't make me any less of a woman.

"For someone who has just been unceremoniously shot out of the air, then nearly kidnapped at gunpoint, you sure have a bright and breezy attitude." I stripped off my jacket, dumped my weapon and mags on the bed, stripped off my shirt and body armor, which had its own sour smell at this point, turned my naked butt to the princess in waiting and her long fabulous hair, and hit the head.

She was right about the shower, great pressure, great heat, and I luxuriated in it far longer than I normally would. By the time I got out looking for my set of overalls, Sandra had bundled all our clothes up and disappeared them out the door, got dressed, and was now wearing a shoulder holster. Her bag was still on the bed, and I wondered if it would stay there with her lethal H&K. Why she was gunned up on our aircraft carrier, I didn't bother to wonder about. I would leave my Sig in the stateroom, I didn't have a shoulder rig, and I didn't have a belt.

We opened the door, and the sailor stood smartly to attention. Sandra acknowledged him and pointed back to our bags on the bed.

"These bags are to be kept secure, please." He nodded, closed the door, then placed his back against it and assumed the at-ease position. The officer who had escorted us earlier magically appeared, confirming that they had the stateroom under video surveillance. He glanced at Sandra's weapon, his face remained neutral, and his voice remained calm.

"This way, please." We followed his lead down a green-painted flight of steel stairs, his combat boots clanking, our slippers making no sound, and Sandra's head rotating like a radar tower. I almost told her to relax, but before I could, we turned into a well-lit cabin, set up for meal service, with two burly soldiers dressed in soft clothes, but carrying arms in a relaxed pose, one in each corner of the squat room. They suddenly braced.

"Captain on deck!" And the man referred to walked in, barked an order to 'stand at ease', gestured to the three of us to sit, and was immediately followed by two orderlies, one with a steaming silver jug of coffee, the smell so strong it took over the room, the other with a huge platter of burgers and fires.

"Your General tells me you need coffee to function, and I picked the meal to make you both comfortable. Your pilot is sleeping, but I have his recorded statement available for you when you want it." I just accepted the coffee, smelt the richness of it, then dived in. Boy, was I missing the magic of Indigo and his massive expresso machine. This was almost as good.

"Captain, thank you, the coffee would have been sufficient all by itself. My boss relayed the pertinent data on our shoot down, but perhaps there is a question of two you might care to answer during this debrief?" He laughed, helped himself to a burger from the plate, grabbed a handful of chips.

"I'm not usually allowed to eat comfort food. Got to keep the weight down. But yes, I will answer your questions. I have been ordered to give you the run of the ship and any assistance you request. You have powerful friends in high places." It was our turn to laugh. We knew the friends he was referring to, but high places were really a step too far! We helped ourselves to the burgers, and the mess orderlies left. The two soldiers moved out behind them and closed the door.

"The lieutenant commander here is my Intelligence officer. I asked permission from your general to include him in this debriefing. He approved it on the proviso that we seal the recording and send the video with you when you leave. He nominated the president's military chief-of-staff as the only recipient of a copy."

"General Bridges has worked with us from day one of the attacks, and the United States has provided massive resources and support throughout. And we spent most of the first month on US soil hunting the terrorists. In fact, we still have ongoing operations there, now under the direct control of the FBI."

"That would be in Point Roberts, Helena, and Roanoke." I looked at him with respect, he was well-briefed, and I mentally kicked myself again for being so closed-minded. Of course, he would be, while the military had only been involved in cleaning out the mercenary terrorists, in their collective mind, the threat still existed, and today's events proved that beyond doubt.

"Yes, sir, as well as some other minor locations the FBI have under surveillance on the west coast.

"Those would be the delivery sites for the power packs?" He really was well briefed.

"Yes, sir." He smiled, finishing off his burger between sentences.

"Let's get to the nitty gritty. Who shot you down? I hear on the grapevine the director of the NSA is really pissed at you; it was his G4, wasn't it?" He took a small handful of chips and seemed to inhale them, suggesting his need for fat and salt was as bad as mine for caffeine.

"Sir, were you advised we would be flying through your airspace?" He put a remaining chip down and wiped his fingers on a monogrammed serviette. He looked at me with a twinkle in his eyes.

"Yes."

"And you would have positioned your Electronic Warfare destroyers along that corridor?"

"Yes, again. You seem to know your navy order of battle."

"Sir, I was NCIS before Interpol. Did either of your destroyers record the attack?" He looked at me, his gray eyes looking almost blue in the light, but you could not escape the intensity. Being ordered to share intelligence and resources didn't always translate into sharing intelligence and resources. I could see him weighing what to tell us in his facial expression. Maybe I would play poker with him after all. "We have the full attack on laser video and data file. Would you like to see it?" I looked at Sandra, who had gone a little tense while the captain was contemplating whether or not to share with us, and gave her a little smile to let her know it was okay. The captain was just being a captain. He didn't know us, he might have got a solid briefing on us, but that was just data. You really had to see, feel, smell, and touch someone to get the whole story. What sat before him was one slightly ragged woman looking a little worse the wear, and a bright, bubbly, effervescent younger woman, who even in navy overalls, looked like a runway model and openly wearing a sidearm in his mess.

"Yes, sir, thank you. You were obviously monitoring most frequencies before and after the attack. Would it be possible to have a spectrum analysis as well please?" He looked at me with a quizzical gaze, turned his head towards his intelligence officer, and nodded. The officer stood and walked out of the room. As the door opened, I could see the two soldiers standing on either side. Were they keeping people out or us in? I smiled at the thought. Not much we could do on a ship with over five thousand crew, who would defend their captain and their ship like rabid dogs in heat, and to the death.

Warrior culture.

Interpol had it, but dressed it down, because so much of our work was out in the civilian world where normal people went about their normal lives, or at least did until the terrorist attack had literally turned the planet on its collective head. The worst riots worldwide ever. No oil, gas, or petrol. Water contaminated, food scarce, roaming gangs of militia and hardened criminals, taking advantage of the chaos the terrorist had created. Civilization, as we knew it, was brought to a shuddering halt as we searched for the new normal.

Just five years before, we had all been doing the same thing, but this time in the wake of a pandemic that grew from an epidemic and changed the concept of personal security on its ear. This time the solution was anything but clear, and in the majority, the smaller the group of people, the better the success of riding out the vast changes forced on everyone. And that had me thinking again; air traffic was down to less than five percent of pre-terrorist levels due to a lack of aviation gas. Bio-fuel was now available, thanks to the terrorist-in-spired ecological plants, but aircraft had to be adapted to the new fuel, and that took time and resources.

The intelligence officer returned, a small metal can in his hand. He put it on the table in front of my half-finished burger.

"The big screen will have the flight data for you. This is a complete summary, as well as the spectrum analysis you asked for." I looked at the captain. Time to show a few of my cards.

"Sir, were you aware that we tracked the terrorists via their use of burst transmissions carried by French weather satellites?" He gave a little grin, which made his tanned, handsome face all that more attractive. For a fleeting second, I wondered if there was a Mrs. captain waiting for him in some exotic port.

"Commander, we have been thoroughly briefed on all aspects of your hunt, the tactics, the timing, and the various outcomes you achieved. It was, in my opinion, one of the most brilliant and efficient uses of resources I have ever seen under such circumstances."

"Thank you, sir. I'll pass that on to my boss, who was responsible for both the success and the efficiency." With a huge grin, Sandra turned to me and embarrassed me to my nonexistent boots.

"And you, Commander, were responsible for the brilliance." The captain and the intelligence officer smiled politely as I cringed and probably flushed bright red from the neck up. The big screen lit up, and a series of graphs and charts swam into sharp focus, saving me from further embarrassment, and the intelligence officer pushed a small controller across the table to me. I flicked the laser pointer on and circled the frequencies we picked up way back at the Ranger Station, where we first came under attack by a swarm of terrorists or militia. It was only weeks ago, but it felt like months.

"These are the uplink and downlink frequencies, so the same pattern we have seen previously. Captain, may I have your permission to make a call?"

"Go ahead." And his grin turned into a study of concentration when I pulled my mini out of my leg pocket and dialed up our geeks. He probably wondered how we were making a call deep in the bowels of an aircraft carrier, in the middle of the Atlantic Ocean, given the Internet had crashed and satellite coverage as well. The truth was, I didn't know, and I didn't particularly want to know. That's why we had geeks!

"*Luigi, ciao*, some help, please. Analyze this data," and I held the mini up to record and send the graphs on the screen, "Then call me back with the coordinates. *Pronto!*"

"At once, Commander. I take it you are recovered from your latest adventure?" he asked with a cheeky grin. I just shut the mini on him and slipped it back into my pocket. Looked at the intelligence officer and shook my head.

"Sorry, you won't pick that up on any frequency scanner, can't help you there. When it comes to geekdom, I'm a complete putz."

"Yes, I'm sure." I recognized sarcasm when I heard it, so I just ignored the officer and asked for what I really wanted to see. The shoot down. The screen cleared, then devolved into two images, side by side. On one, a ghostly image of an aircraft being followed at a distance by a small blob, the other a much darker image that shimmied and shook, blurring the images a little. The blob emitted a sharp flare that evolved into a streak, closely followed by another, then another, and finally a fourth one. The aircraft turned suddenly, dropped, ejected chaff and flares, and the first missile took the bait. The second chased the fireball and added to it. The third exploded alongside the aircraft but I couldn't judge the distance that separated the aircraft and the exploding missile, and the fourth rammed into the rear and exploded.

Having lived through all that for real, it made sense and explained the damage to the aircraft we had both observed onboard and later on the ground.

In my humble opinion, we owed the pilot and the designers of the G4 our lives. We should be dead.

"Can you backtrack the blob?" The intelligence officer signaled for the controller. I slid it to him, and he fiddled with the controls, then hit the screen with the laser pointer and circled the blob. The aircraft and missiles froze in mid-impact, then disappeared. The blob increased in size and moved into the center of the screen. It didn't move, but the position indicator did until it obviously moved out of range of the laser camera. I didn't have paper or a pen, so I had to roughly estimate the distance from the attack point the blob had started from. I guessed at sixty nautical miles. Still in the middle of the Atlantic Ocean, well off the normal airways, as we were, usually a civilian airliner flying US to Europe would take the great circle route north-we had taken our own great circle route south. More ocean and fewer places to land, but we were on a military flight and didn't expect to be shot down.

The image ran forward, and less than a minute in, our aircraft symbol moved over the blob, moved away, only to be followed, but at a far slower rate. Then the missile launches could plainly be seen. I needed the data on that, distance, airspeed, and how far in the trail the blob had been when it had fired. They hadn't found us; we had found them.

I might be a little slow and more than a little tired, but my brain was wide awake and driving me insane with questions. Did the terrorists cover all possible routes? Or only this one. How did they know which route we would take? And what did they have that could match the speed and range of the G4? But the blob had been less than half the size of the image of the G4-so what the hell was it? And in the tail chase, the blob and the aircraft had been moving away from each other, so it wasn't as fast as the G4.

"Sir, I need the latitude and longitude of the start point and the attack point, and can we match the transmission data to the real-time imaging, please?" The captain looked to his intelligence officer, who once again stood and left the room.

"You know, this would all be easier in our C-in-C (Command and Control) center." The captain looked serious, so I headed off the inevitable.

"Sir, we need to keep this to ourselves. This might give us valuable intelligence on how this new group is resourced and working." He nodded, obviously having considered that conclusion himself.

"You said, new group. Were you being superfluous or literal?" I looked at him, my best poker face on, having just realized that I had inadvertently let something only three of four of us in Interpol knew. Buggar. I hoped this didn't come back to bite us on the arse.

"Sir, I apologize. I may not have been quite as literal as I should have been. These attacks on us today are new. We don't know who or why as yet. That's the new part-it may be the same actors, or it may be just someone working in their shadow. We know the crazies in Afghanistan have formed several breakaway terror groups, some you would know of." He looked at me with his big gray eyes, but I wasn't fooled by his placid look for a second. Then he just smiled as if accepting we would not share any more intelligence than we absolutely had to with him, and that was okay because, under similar circumstances, he would have done the same.

"Okay, let it go at that. Finish up here, and grab some rack time. You fly out at 0600 tomorrow." He stood, looked at both of us, smiled, and left. Right on his heels, the officer returned, this time with a file and a data store.

"Here you go, ma'am. Are you ready to return to your quarters?" I looked at Sandra as she shoveled the last of her fries in.

"Yes, thank you, could we go by way of the sick bay?" He nodded and stood back to let us pass. We both waited for him to shut the door to the mess, then followed him down the myriad of corridors and stairways that made up the innards of the modern battleship, remembering to duck at every watertight door, and lift my feet, so I didn't crack my shins on the buffer edge. If I had to remember how to get back to our quarters, I fervently hoped that Sandra was paying attention!

We reached the sick bay, there was only one customer, and in the low light, he looked in reasonable shape. I would see to it that he got a commendation in his jacket, he had flown us out of the death zone of the missiles, and if it hadn't been for the proximity explosion, we probably would have landed normally, with him still at the controls.

"Thanks, happy to go to our Stateroom."

We followed the leader up and across hallways, down the stairs, through the ubiquitous watertight doors, until we reached our room where the sailor stood at ease, with his back against the door.

He straightened up into attention at the sight of his officer, then relaxed slightly at my hand signal.

"Thank you, seaman, that will be all for tonight. Will you call us at zero four thirty, please?" The officer nodded, opened the door for us, then shut it behind us. Before I could say a word, Sandra pulled her shoulder rig off and threw it on the first bunk, pointing to the second against the far wall.

"You there, me here, I'm going to shower again, then sleep in my underwear that someone had generously washed and ironed!" She literally bubbled over with happiness as she held up a pair of frilly black knickers. I shook my head. Only Sandra would dress for an ambush with terrorists or gang members in black lace underwear!

Zero four-thirty came too fast, so we showered and dressed, making sure our body amour, which had not only been cleaned but now smelt like a forest, went on under our shirts. We gunned up, checked the room for anything we had left, then walked out to find our seaman at the door waiting for us.

'This way, please." We followed him to a different mess, this one three levels below, and with some naval aviators sitting down to steak and eggs, toast and jam, and most wonderful of all, hot coffee! I didn't wait for an invitation, just marched to the massive steel urn and filled a mug to the top. Sandra all but shoved me out of the way. I just hip-bumped her back, then turned and sat.

"You're our crew?" If the sight of two women dressed in varying degrees of civilian fashion, openly carrying weapons partially covered by lightweight jackets, caused any angst, it was well hidden.

"Yes, ma'am, lieutenant colonel Tawdry at your service." The pilot looked barely old enough to be able to order a beer, let alone command an expensive naval aircraft, and I wondered what type it would be and where we were headed.

"Excellent, Tawdry, and what might your call sign be?" The crew broke into laughter, and another pilot, I guessed the co-pilot by his age and the wings on his flight suit, punched Tawdry in the arm.

"Miss-U!" he shouted, and the crew broke into even more noisy laughter. Tawdry just dropped his head in mock shame, letting the ribbing run its course.

"I supposed you got that when you missed the deck a few times?" Sandra asked, hoeing into the steak and eggs that had been handed to her by the mess steward.

"A few times? Are you kidding? He parked an Osprey on the corner of a ramp, fifty feet in the air!" The laughter was infectious and, in truth, a great way to start the day.

"Is that what we are flying?" The laughter tricked down, and the pilot looked a little serious for a moment.

"A version of it, yes, ma'am, the CMV 22-B, a specialized naval version. It's been upgraded in the last three years, and now it's a genuine beast!" The pride in his voice was telling me you didn't get to be a lieutenant commander in the marines if you were a dummy, and you didn't get to play with millions of dollars worth of aircraft if you couldn't fly, so I suspected, like so many other callsigns, his was a badge of honor.

"Why do you call it a beast?"

"Well, ma'am, since the last upgrade, we have ourselves a twenty-mike-mike Gatling gun forward, a sling mount for the smaller seven-point-sixty-two in the rear, and sling mounts on both sides. Plus, the digital controls are awesome, and we have a picture-on-screen heads-up display. It's a prince!" The co-pilot also had pride in his voice, and I was starting to feel comfortable risking another aircrew. I knew of the aircraft, and of its genesis, a cross between a helicopter and a plane, with two massive propellers stuck out the ends of small narrow wings. The engines rotated up for takeoff, then rolled forward for normal flight.

And with the armaments, the co-pilot described, from a ground pounders point of view, a beast it would be, for sure.

"Destination?"

"Sorry, ma'am, classified until we clear the deck." I looked at him, gave him the full force of my very best unladylike glare, and to his credit, he met my hostility without blinking. "Apologies, ma'am, orders from the top." I nodded, if it was from the captain, it was operational and tactical, and we were, after all, just guests. I decided to eat my steak and eggs, grab another coffee, and maybe have some toast and jam. Sandra was giving me the fish eye, I don't know what her problem was, but I didn't like my future in someone else's hands. Never had, never would.

We ate in relative silence, then were surprised by the captain appearing at the door. "Commander, can I have you, please, for five minutes?" I stood, wiped my lips, and turned to meet him in the corridor, Sandra on my shoulder. He was momentarily surprised by her presence but masked his feelings professionally. He led the way back up to the C-in-C, where he stopped in front of a wall of radar scopes, laser cameras, and big screens. It only took me a second or two to work out what was happening. In the center screen, the blob that had shot us out of the sky the day before was being approached by two markers from different directions. The laser camera jerked, and the image increased in size by a factor of twenty. The blob resolved itself to be a small aircraft-sized drone, with two missiles still visible under its wings.

"What you are looking at is twelve hours old. We dispatched two F-35s just after you arrived on board. The drone is the NVX-7, so that gives you a start on identifying it, and the missiles are advanced ARM-12 heat seekers. Only three countries have those, as far as we are aware. I had to get clearance to show you this, and we have a copy for you to take."

"Clearance from whom?" He didn't look fazed at my question, handed me a slim electronic storage device, and then led us back down to the ready room. The aircrew we had breakfast with were all sitting in their high-backed theatre seats, and a briefer ran through the weather outlook, a large map of western Europe behind her on yet another massive screen.

We were both handed life vests, helmets, and waterproof carry bags, which filled quickly with our electronic booty and our carryalls. If anyone was surprised when Sandra pulled her H&K out of her bag and slung it across her chest, no one commented on it. We stood until the weather briefing was completed, fitted ourselves out, put on the helmets, the comms cord dangling like the tail on a monkey, and followed the crew out to the deck. The captain leaned forward, shook my hand, then Sandra's, and with a big grin, wished us luck.

The flight, for once, was uneventful. We sat in the center cabin, relatively insulated from the noise of the massive engines by our helmets. We had company all the way; first F-35's from the carrier, then Eurofighters with Spanish markings, then finally Italian F-22 Raptors. When they peeled away, I knew we were close to home, and sure enough, we rotated the engines, and then with an unholy roar, did a helicopter landing in a far corner of Marco Polo airport. As we were swarmed by a fuel truck, Italian police, and a small UAV, the rear ramp dropped down. We thanked the pilots and walked out into the bright sunlight. A crew member took our flight gear, and Indigo took us physically in a series of hugs that would have been embarrassing if we didn't know him.

Forty minutes later, the insane driver and his cigarette boat were disappearing in the distance along the grand canal, and Sandra, Indigo, and I were being politely ushered into the tunnel that led to our headquarters.

We were home, at least for a while, and who knew what lay ahead?

# Chapter Four

The penthouse apartment in the Capital Dock development took over the entire top floor and had been savagely remodeled the moment it had been handed over to its new owner. Walls had been smashed down, floors pulled up, and windows enlarged until only the outer shell remained, primarily to meet the City's requirements for conformity of the exterior of the building. Because it was planned to be thirty-two stories high, the tallest residential block in the whole of Dublin, there had been protests against its very nature for two years prior to the Council permits being issued.

Like any modern city, money spoke volumes, and with the permits obtained and well paid for, construction started and was completed in just fourteen months. Then the owners of the building took another eight months to complete the penthouse. There were some three hundred other apartments in the building, but as the penthouse was served by its own twin elevators and a six-car secured garage, the other residents never saw anyone enter or leave, no matter how hard or how often they looked.

Standing in front of the blue mirrored double-glazed tinted glass, watching the dark of the ocean occasionally break with the white caps of an angry sea, Malik Badawi slowly nipped the exposed neck of his companion, her long, silky red dress slightly askew on one shoulder. Malik was tall for a Bedouin, at six feet three inches of chiseled, ripped and toned muscle, his long silky black hair reaching below his shoulders. His face was that of desert god, chiseled and shaped perfectly so that the aquiline face perfectly suited the intensity of his blue eyes.

And he was the epitome of the modern-day terrorist. Rich, aloof, remote from the action, and able to dress appropriately for any audience or any occasion, be it the board room or the desert. The perfect camouflage for the urban dissident whose only agenda was to profit from his actions and the weaknesses of others. And he rated most of the scheming, ideological terrorist fraternity as his bounty because they were so easy to part from their money and resources and always provided a lovely clear, physical and emotional target to distract the authorities and the media.

Chaos was his friend, the terrorists who had turned the world on its head, his brothers and sisters, and from them, he would gain wealth beyond reason. Had gained wealth, he thought to himself as he nibbled a little lower, his full generous lips now just cresting the rich, silky-smooth rise of a breast. He already had over ten billion dollars tucked away, his large hands around the pretty waist of one who controlled another five billion, and a way to siphon off another twenty billion in the next few months.

Who said terrorism couldn't be profitable?

"Fair enough, I think, my love, or would you be going to eat me all up before we leave?" Siobhan O'Cleary looked up at Malik, noted the desire and sparkle in his deep blue eyes, and hitched her shoulder just a fraction, then reached up and replaced her strap.

"I would love to, but as you remind me, we have to be relatively on time tonight. It's important."

"Yes, it is. Can we go now?" She looked at him, all polished and suave, and not for the first time, she wondered how she, a girl from the small, rural, and muddy village of Castleshane, just two miles from the border with Northern Ireland, could have been attracted to such a powerful person. A man she now knew travelled in interesting circles in many countries.

They moved to one of the elevators that stood ready and silently and effortlessly dropped the four hundred feet to the garage level. The matte black town car waited; the driver, unmistakably an Arab, resplendent in a black suit and a black and white keffiyeh, which flowed down his back. He bowed to Malik and opened the rear door, softly closing it as the last of the red skirt was pulled into the seat.

Inwardly, he smiled, marveling at the skill with which his sayyid had wound the beautiful nuclear scientist around his little finger.

He drove them quietly and quickly to the little Irish pub on the waterfront, which had been closed for the evening, and shepherded them in through the low brick entrance. Inside waited for seven hard men, sitting around a large table in the center of the bar area, the rest of the floor clear but not necessarily clean. Four very large men dressed in black pants, combat boots, and loose, flowing, dirty green combat jackets stood at the rear, hands folded across their stomachs, the obvious giveaway that they were personal protection. There was no beer or other drink on the table, no misty smoke from a peat fire stroking the roof, and in fact, a slight chill in the air. And no music, other than the occasional scuffle from someone shifting their feet on the old concrete floor.

*"Marhaba,"* Malik offered one hand over his heart, bowing slightly to the man at the end of the table.

"Hello yourself, Mister Badawi. Please sit yourself and your lady down here." He pointed to two clean seats on one side of the table. Malik and Siobhan sat as requested, and their driver filled the doorway, mimicking the stance of the four personal guards. Malik smiled to himself. These Irish peasants playing at being revolutionaries really didn't know what they were facing.

"Mister Badawi, call me Tom, and can we get to the business as quickly as you like, as none of us here really appreciate being so far in the lion's den? As it were, we'll all be a far happier back up and across the border."

"I appreciate your courtesy, Tom, but this is the safest place we could think of to have this conversation." They eyed each other across the table, neither letting the other see any weakness. Siobhan rested her long fingers flat on the table and leaned slightly forward.

"Tom, have you received the delivery you were promised?" Every head turned to look at her, most with suspicion. When something as important as this was under discussion, none were sure that a woman had any place in it, but none could ignore her beauty and the lilt in her voice.

"Oh, aye, we have three boxes as you described, and we've received word from our friends across the pond that they have received theirs as well." Malik looked surprised, his eyebrows furrowing together.

"How did they communicate with you?" he asked, suddenly fearful that his whole plan might have been compromised. Tom looked amused, his old craggy face a mix of furrows and creases, and his short-peaked hat only just covered a few wisps of silver-gray hair. His baggy shirt was stained, and his jacket not much better, with a red patch on one elbow. He was dying for a pint, and his pipe, which he considered necessary for life, but the brothers who had set up this meeting had been firm on what could and could not be done before and during the meeting.

"Well now, lad, we used one of the oldest methods or talking between friends ever devised, so as you can be sure that only the nine of us will know the message if you don't count the men at either end of the room." Malik thought as hard as he could. The only reliable method of secure long-distance communication was the burst transmitters the woman, 'Helen' had given him over a year ago during his visit to Syria. One had been careful not to use it yet, as he really didn't trust the woman or her cohort. Yes, he had personally met Al Hemish al-bin Mohammad Karesish. It had been he who had started him on the path to riches. But he had always been leery of the woman; she seemed-and in thinking about it, he marveled at the contradiction-too hardline for his tastes.

"I get the image of two paper cups joined by string, but I'm having difficulty seeing how you would get the string all the way across the Irish Sea to England." Malik's smile took the sting out of the implied insult and recognizing it for what it was, the men around the table laughed. Tom reached into his pocket and pulled out a dead pigeon with a little silver and blue canister strapped to its leg. He pushed it across the table to Malik.

"Nothing more secure, hasn't been for hundreds of years, we used them to beat the bloody British off several times, and I've no doubt we'll do it again." Malik looked at the dead bird and smiled. Old school, very old school, and brilliant, and he had to acknowledge this to move the meeting into the space where he wanted it to be.

"Tom, this is excellent, I would never have imagined it, and once again, you have demonstrated why we want to work with you for your cause." Tom preened at the compliment, nodded, and instinctively reached for his pipe, which ended up as a pat to his pocket. He looked around the table at his men, all as old as him, and all as committed to the cause, and all hopeful that this time they would be successful. It was one thing to entertain a bargain with the devil, for surely that was what this immaculately dressed foreigner was. It was another to lose sight of the dream of generations.

"What is it then you would have us do now," he asked, a firm and thoughtful look on his face. Siobhan leaned across the table again and, in a soft but firm voice, answered his question.

"Tell your friends across the pond to sit tight until we get to them, have your men deliver one box to Ennis, one box to Dublin, and the last box to Belfast, Mister Badawi with giving you the addresses once they are delivered your part is completed until it's time to strike."

"And when will that be, missus, if you don't mind me asking?" She gave him a long look, then a gentle smile.

"Tom, we strike before the next Easter, on the Thursday night before, and finish what our forefathers weren't able to a hundred and five years ago." A thumping sound broke out as the seven men around the table struck their fists on the tabletop. Malik looked amused, handed a small piece of paper to Tom, and put a hard look on his face.

"Burn this the moment you have memorized the addresses. You understand?" He held the old man's eyes, looking for any sign of weakness or duplicity, saw none, then nodded and stood.

"Thank you, gentlemen, *ma'aasalaama*." Malik and Siobhan walked out, paused to take in the brisk air, the strong salty flavor not unwelcome after the sterile atmosphere of the pub, then climbed into the town car. They drove away in silence, then malik reached over and put one hand on Siobhan's warm thigh.

"Well, we have our beard. Next, stop the backup, then we need to put the rest into play." She looked into his rich blue eyes, saw the intensity sparkle in them, and felt his hand stroke her, arousing heat and a strong emotional feeling that flowed from her stomach all the way to her toes. Here was a man of strength, of plans, of the new world, and right now, she felt as powerful as he looked.

# Chapter Five

Of all the low and high technology that ranged around the walls of our headquarters, the one thing that drew my attention was Indigo's massive copper and steel espresso machine. It puffed and chuffed, little spurts of steam shooting out of spigots, the pleasurable plops and drips of rich coffee slipping into cups and mugs like lovers kissing in the dark. Before I could reach it and embarrass myself, someone handed me a monogrammed mug full to the brim, and I lost myself to the rich flavor of the smell. Sandra deserted me for a moment, shrugged off her jacket, parked her holdall, then grabbed her own mug with both hands.

"Indigo, we have to work out a way to take you and your excellent machine with us when we go somewhere!" A bright burst of laughter rang through the room, and technicians, agents, and geeks joined in the mirth. Rumors of our day away had preceded us, and there was more than one worried face staring at us, looking for signs of damage. I held my hand up to get everyone's attention.

"All good, no holes or scrapes, I won't say we enjoyed ourselves, but it is nice to be home!" A round of hand-clapping burst out, then settled as people went back to work. Throughout all this, the boss just stood leaning against one wall, feet crossed at the ankles, a stoic look on his face.

"Frank Reynolds wants to charge you for his G4," he said, in a laconic style that suggested spaghetti western. I smiled, I could imagine Frank on his high horse, but with what I got each month working for Interpol, it would take me about a thousand years just to pay off the interest! "Jessica, saddle up. You and I have a short trip to make." Sandra looked around her mug, about to find somewhere to put it down, when the boss signaled her to stay where she was. Indigo walked over with four of his elite Col Moschin-the 9th Assault Parachute Regiment-all dressed in smart black cargo pants and matching parachute jackets, royal blue caps with their red stripes on at a jaunty angle, and their Baretta AR-70s strung across their chests.

"These gentlemen will go with us Sandra, take a break. Enjoy it. You're back on guard dog duty the moment we get back." She gave a thin smile, not sure if she liked the 'guard dog' quip, but concentrated on her coffee. We exited the headquarters and jumped into a small military boat, which sped away almost before the last person had boarded. It raced around the pier, cut across the canal, then idled to a stop against a blackened rock façade that was hauntingly familiar.

It was where the boss, Indigo, Pete, and I had been attacked by the mercenary terrorists, and in the process, had given us our first real lead on who they were and who they were affiliated with. The boss and I entered the long corridor with Indigo leading, the boat sped off, and Col Moschin melted into the walls. We reached the detection arch and shed everything metal or electronic except for our mini, which Indigo indicated we could take with us.

*"Fratello, benvenuto, Colonnello, Comandante, benvenuto anche, come sono state le tue avventure di recente?"* Indigo's brother, the head monk of this centuries-old secret organization dedicated to preserving religious artifices and icons irrespective of their religious bias, hugged his brother as if he hadn't seen him in years.

"Brother Stefarino, we had some fun and a little trouble, but otherwise, I hope you managed to learn things for us about the terrorists and how they trace us," it may have been rude of me, but I cut to the chase, the whole exercise of me leaving the tropical paradise and long drinks with umbrellas in them was designed to expose the terrorist's methodology and abilities. We had set it up with the help of the American military, as in Tom's SEAL team, the Secret Service Personal Protection Unit, who had provided the vehicles and drivers, and the president's military chief of staff, general Bridget Saunders, who had approved the operation on American soil, and arranged for military coverage along the route by the navy. For which I was very thankful.

The Americans had a vested interest. They wanted to know how deeply the terrorists had penetrated their electronic systems. They had already closed multiple 'backdoors' that had been detected earlier, but the realization had come that there were more bugs in the system than they had detected.

So the boss had volunteered me as the bait, the NSA G4 had been called into service, and away we had gone. And we had told no one in our team except Indigo who told his brother, so they could use their incredible technology to assist the NSA track the terrorists tracking us. It sounded convoluted when you said it slowly, but we had been ambushed, then blown out of the air, so from the aspect of getting their attention and a reaction, it had worked.

"Commander Riley, yes, we have had some success. Do you have the data from the US Navy, please?" I gave him that look that said, 'how did you know about that?' but he just smiled at me the way he did and held out his hand. The boss filled it with the data stores and the tape from the aircraft carrier. He bobbed his head in thanks and fired off a stream of Italian to his geeks, but it was so fast and so much geek I really couldn't tell you what he said. The boss motioned me over to a long soft couch, and we both hit it simultaneously, setting up a rippling wave that looked like the wind against the tide at the beach.

"You mentioned Stefarino wanted to see us before I took off?"

"Yes. He does. Let him get his geeks in a row, and we'll ask him." I closed my eyes and leaned back. I was tired, right down to my socks. We sat in the quiet buzz of geeks working keyboards, swiping at screens, muttering under their breath in Italian, Spanish, Portuguese, French, and Chinese, a real United nation of geekdom. Finally, Stefarino came back, pulled a small chair up, and sat facing us.

"Thank you for that, Colonel. We will have everything you need in a few minutes. It is obvious the terrorists thought deeply about how they wanted to compromise your systems, it took years of patient work, and I suspect it will take even more years to eradicate the results. I want to offer you an alternative solution." The boss sat up, leaned forward, and reached his hands out to the monk.

"Anything you can do to help us will be appreciated. We're between a rock and a hard place, but we need to address this as soon as we can. There's a storm brewing. I can feel it in my bones. The terrorists are not done with us, but we have no real view of what their next move might be." The monk nodded, pushed his linked hands further into the folds of his brown robe, gave them a quick shake, then stood.

"You have provided us the financial resources and security we have always lacked, and we thank you for that, but the larger issue is what these terrorists have done to the psyche of the ordinary person. It is hard enough to have faith when you are starving, homeless, cold, and dispossessed, but add to that the untenable conditions of no work and no power, and you quickly see the human spirit diminished. We have here in our vaults the history of mankind, as far back as materials and icons were created for the purpose of recording what life was at that time. We intend to preserve it, add to it, and use it to help people regain their hope and faith. We need you to stamp out these terrorists once and for all. Can you do that?" The boss and I looked at the monk and sensed a pain that went beyond the physical.

"Stefarino, we can only promise to do our best and keep at it for as long as we can."

"I'll take both promises, thank you, please come with me." He stood and walked towards a dark doorway, in front of which sat a single monk at an old wooden desk transcribing some sort of parchment. He didn't even look up at our approach, as focused on his work as he was. Stefarino walked through the doorway and turned on a red lighting system. The dark cavern had long, deep shadows that not only looked creepy but also made my skin run cold. Little rivulets of water ran down the walls to be collected in some sort of gutter. The sound was relaxing, but it didn't offset the spookiness of the dark shadows. In the middle of the room, a modern stand-up table had been erected, and on it sat a maze of wires and small boxes, and small flashing LEDs covered the boxes like a lice infection. A mini-computer like the ones the monks had provided us sat open next to the rats-nest of cables.

"You already have these, and we have got the additional ones you requested earlier in the week." The monk picked up the mini, turned it over in his hands, seemed to contemplate something, then shut the lid and replaced it on the table. "We know that you have used them for large-audience conferences and thrown the images up on big screens. We suspect that just doing this may have compromised your data." The boss looked shocked, and I had trouble remembering all the times we had used the minis to connect to bigger systems, mostly in the US but a few times in Israel.

"You can't be serious?" I asked, my voice horse. What had we spoken about? Everything. Particularly in the US, when we have been working with the president and her cabinet, this was a serious breach of security, and I was not sure how we could recover from it. We had taken the minis to the US and freely distributed them to the NSA, CIA, and FBI, and by my count, there were probably ten units in total spread across the country. Plus, we had sent units to our agents in Pakistan, and Tokyo, Arie, and Shami had one each, Tom had one, Bob had one, and who else?

Before I could think further, he folded his hands in his wide sleeves, dropped his head onto his chest, and looked at us from under his bushy eyebrows.

"Not to worry. We have a solution for you. It's here in this little box. All you need to do is provide one to every person you have given a mini to, get them to attach it to the base like this," and he pulled his hands out, picked up one of the little silver boxes, the mini, and with a fluid movement snapped the two together, and handed it to me. It didn't weigh all that much more than my mini did now, so that was a comfort. Then I had a thought, and I tilted my head to one side to let it get out in a coherent manner.

"This will do two things-firstly, you can throw the data up to any screen or system, and it cannot be hacked, and secondly, it will send us back data on who might try to hack you and leave them with a nasty virus." That last part didn't sound very monk-like, but I guess as a geek, you got your fun wherever you could find it.

"Stefarino, the boss and I did not talk about my little adventure on our minis. It was face-to-face, and no one else knew about my trip. Oh!" and I put my hand across my mouth, what about the calls to the general, Frank, Julius, Roger, and Anna to set the trap up? But then I remembered that it had been mini to mini, with no big screens involved. "Are you saying mini to mini can be hacked?"

"No. Only when you send the signal to another system, like a big screen." I relaxed, and a wash of relief rippled through me from head to toe. I hadn't been leaking data all over the planet. But the question remained.

"Then how did they learn of my movements and intentions?" The look he gave me was one of concern, and I wondered what his answer was going to be.

"I know Malcolm and his team at the NSA traced back all the backdoors that had been inserted into the enterprise-level systems going back to 1999. I know that they also discovered other hacks right across Europe in shipping, transportation, health, and education, and specifically in distribution. And that is where your current problem still sits. Who did it is unknown, and now, nearly thirty years later, possibly even unknowable. But there is tracking software in the European and US systems connected to shipping, aircraft, and mass transit."

"What do you mean by tracking software?"

"Once you identify a person, using entry codes, biometrics, personal data, government records, all the way down to vehicle data, the operator puts a little flag on you, and the system from that time on basically follows you wherever you go. All this data is pulled off and stored in the cloud, not on any of the systems from which the data is accumulated, and there is no trace of the data being pulled off in the first place. Before the Internet crash, every CCTV camera on the planet sent data somewhere, and this system swept that up as well. Post the net hack, the systems have been severely compromised because everything that had a computer chip with a MAC (Media Access Control) address, which effectively was every chip on the planet-that was engaged at the time of the hack-was fried."

"This must have limited the amount of data that the trackers have access to?" We knew that computers or systems that had not been connected at the time of the attack still worked. This was what we were using to get some balance back. And we also knew that selected people and countries, if we were to be truthful about it all, had been forewarned, so they had everything they needed turned off and unplugged before the attack. The French weather satellites were one such example we knew of, as they were still carrying the coded transmissions from the terrorist's burst transmitters. Whether or not the French knew of this was a moot point.

"Yes, you are correct, Colonel. But consider this. At this time, with the world in chaos, and given that we have precious few electric ships and planes, even with the possibility of biofuel conversions such as your G4, who do you think would be travelling the most?" I thought for a minute, and suddenly it became apparent how they had done it.

"Stefarino, you're saying that before the hack, the tracers could follow anyone they designated and follow them anywhere in the world, in real-time, continuously?" He gave me his little grin, like a school teacher rewarding a student for getting five plus five right.

"Yes. I can show you a tape we made one day tracing the trackers, and you can see for yourself how detailed the data is." I didn't want to see it. Being in the military had taught me that personal privacy was a state of mind, not a real practical thing; I knew it was an illusion, but this was a step too far, but once I got over myself, it all made sense. That's what the unintended consequences of the computer age had beget-total, immersive and continuous invasion of individual privacy on a worldwide scale.

"That's what the terrorists used against us with their black holes." He shook his head.

"Only in part. You got back a lot of the data they hid, but you never got back specific data on the terrorists-just the peripheral data that had nothing to do with the terrorists." I nodded. That was exactly what we had uncovered. The more useful information was the location of the burst transmitters, which led us to the terrorists in spite of their famous black holes.

"You're saying that they deleted the data on specific individuals so they would be invisible to the system?"

"Yes."

"What about now?"

"Same rules apply. We don't know who they have hidden. There is no record in the files from Trotsky or Mohammad bin Azaria, nothing in the data you recovered from Shetani." I nodded. It made sense, if I was launching a thirty-year pogrom against humanity, I would very much want to protect the identity of my key players, and in retrospect, we had not tracked down any of the participants we currently had in concrete cells via their personal information. It had been by their manner of communication with each other.

The burst transmitters.

"But the whole attack makes some kind of warped sense if you look at the outcome in narrow terms-prompting attention be paid to the refugee camps and causing the migration of young, intelligent female refugees. What else could be on their agenda that meant so much to the planners?" His smile got a little warmer, but his eyes were still dark and dead, showing no emotion.

"That is something unfortunately you will have to uncover. We will do everything in our power to help you, but you will have to come up with the questions." I nodded, I expected nothing less. These amazing monks had basically set aside their life's work to help us in the first place, had been attacked by a boatload of terrorists, forced to move their entire establishment as a result, and were even now helping us with their advanced technology and wisdom in a way that was fast becoming comfortable. I would have to watch that. They deserved to be able to choose their own future without the pain, suffering, and death that usually went along with helping anyone from Section Five!

Specifically, working with me.

"Stefarino, can you take the data from the Afghanistan terrorist camp, please, and upload the data for the three principals we saw there, and give us a history of their movements before and after the web hack?"

"Yes, we already have that on the way. It raises one question in my mind. If the terrorists were busy hiding specific people from us, why would they allow these three to be seen and identified?" That threw me back a step. I ran the three faces through my mind; Amir Abbas, a top leader of Hamas and potentially the co-leader of the terrorist group Al Bar al Shirak; Malik Badawi, a Bedouin, also thought to be a leader of this terrorist organization; and Siobhan O'Cleary, a nuclear physicist, with impeccable credentials, who may or may not be linked to a Republican movement in Ireland. Why would the terrorists allow these three to be visible? I asked the boss the same question, he just smiled, his face creasing and underlying his tiredness. We might have had a short tropical break, but none of us had really rested.

"I suspect the answer to that is an easy one. Firstly, in the case of Abbas and Badawi, they have to have local credibility with their troops on the ground, or they wouldn't be able to operate. They both have run terror campaigns out of the Gaza strip. You may remember the two truck bomb attacks on the supermarkets that Arie reported? Both were traced back to Al Bar al Shirak, and both used the remote AI devices designed by the terrorists. As for the woman, if you were building a threat, such as a nuclear attack, what better way to establish your credentials than to have a nuclear expert on hand, and visible, at least at some point of your workup?"

"So you think this whole Afghanistan thing is simply a 'show and tell' by the terrorists? And the data is, what, at least a month old?"

"Makes the most sense to me. They hid everyone else they wanted to. We still don't know the extent of their network, and look at the trouble we just went to so we could flush out how they were tracking us." That gave me pause for thought, so I switched tracks, opened my mini, and dialed my very best friend in Japan.

"Senji-san is not available for the moment; how may I help you?" The diminutive but resilient Aikido Namoki, dressed in her traditional goth outfit, ears resplendent with silver rings and a golden one piercing her eyebrow, eyes blackened top and bottom, making her gray pupils pop out like searchlights swam into focus.

"Aikido-san, hello. I hope there is no trouble?"

"Nothing we can't manage. A small group of yakuza, we understand, employed by Innomatchi launched an attack on our office. As you would be aware, we share the office with the 16th. Special Assault Team, so it really wasn't a fair fight. Senji-san is working with the prefecture to identify some of the bodies." I paused, not sure how to proceed, but from all accounts, the pair were two of our best operatives in the South East Asian area, so I asked what I had called for.

"Aikido, I need you to check the shipping files from Innomatchi— we need to track anything sent to Pakistan, Afghanistan, or Iran, going back three years. I'm looking for additive and 3D manufacturing machinery, rotational molding, and anything that could produce the item in this photo. I also need you to keep it totally secure and share this with no one. Can you expedite that, please?" She blinked, her eyebrows furrowed in concentration, and she slowly nodded.

"Commander, that might take a day or two. The situation around Innomatchi is a little fluid. Can you give us that time?" I thought for a moment. Trusting the local man on the ground was Rule #1 in our business, but did we have two days? No choice.

"Yes, but be as quick as you can, please. Our best to Nokomoto." I closed the mini. The boss looked at me with a question in his eyes.

"Why only back three years?"

"The ecological plants established by the terrorists go back three years, so the manufacturing for the hardware had to be ready around that time. I'm guessing that if the hardware was shipped to Afghanistan, it would have been around that time frame."

"Three years ago was just two years after the US left. Right on the cusp of the pandemic turning into a world-wide problem for real. Millions dead worldwide; more were killed in the US than at any other time, and millions were out of work, a lot like now-except this time, the economies collapsed by the removal of all oil, gas, and coal. Interesting comparison."

"This is where the terrorists have been really smart. All their migration destinations are small towns, all largely self-sufficient in terms of power, water, food, and all the locations of thousands of displaced people from the larger cities and towns due to the chaos. We need to get back." He nodded, took Stefarino by the hands, and thanked him for his hospitality. One of the geeks handed me a bag, heavy and loaded with the little silver bottoms for the minis. We left, climbed back on the police boat, and sat in silence until we arrived back at our headquarters.

"What do we do now?" He looked at me and tilted his head to one side.

"We have the bones of something. We don't know what it is. It may or may not involve Irish Republicans, Arab terrorists, and nuclear weapons, but it does involve our previous enemy in that these new guys are using their technology, their systems, and to an extent, their playbook. But until someone asks us to do something, all we can do is collect data, intelligence, and put a case together we can present to one of our member countries who can then invite us to the party."

"If that's all you're worried about, I can get Arie to invite us almost immediately."

"Just hold off for a day. Let's get the data from Stefarino and his geeks. Let's see where these three have been and what they have been doing, and then we might have a better handle on it." The boss was correct. We didn't have enough to know a target, or even if there was one. We just had some scribble on a data wall, a year old, some forty-day-old satellite images of three people, two of whom were known terrorists, and a grainy photo of what might be the shell for a nuclear weapon.

As we walked back into the main room, Indigo greeted us with large steaming mugs of coffee, and I just stopped thinking for a minute and concentrated on the intoxicating smell of the coffee. It worked; I suddenly had an idea. I walked over to a small couch, plopped down, put my booted feet up on a chair, and one-handed opened my mini and dialed my favorite agent in Pakistan.

"Drishya, are you secure?" The background looked like a concrete block with wires running all over it. Drishya, with her head covered with a beautiful pink hijab, reminded me of both her cultural heritage and the sensitivity of her position in our office. What I was going to ask her to do might push those boundaries a little harder for her.

"I am now commander; how can I help." Her earnest but beautiful copper-colored face was framed by her hijab, her lips bright red, her eye shadow a misty blue. All in all, I fleetingly thought she could give my two supermodels, Fay and Sandra, a run for their money in the great looks department.

"Who do you know in Afghanistan?" She would be a great poker player, her eyes never dilated, flickered, or her facial expressions change a whit.

"What do you need?" Intelligent as well, always get all the data before making any commitment. It was what could keep you alive in this business of international terrorism.

"We believe someone is making-or has already made parts for portable nuclear weapons somewhere in Afghanistan. We can send you the data, and we can guess at the type of equipment they would need to achieve this in the country. I need you to find where, when, who, how many, and what they did with them. And I need you to do it yesterday." Not a flicker, just the hard stare of someone paying close attention to what was being said.

"Here is a photo of the metallic parts of the casing. We estimate seventy millimeters in diameter, around eight hundred centimeters long, and probably made out of brass or a copper/brass composite. It could weigh as much as one hundred kilos."

"How do you think they were made?"

"Our intelligence, based on what we have seen of these terrorists previously, is additive and 3D manufacturing, specialized machinery, robotics, AI, and possibly nanotechnology. Can't be sure about the nanotechnology at this point, but don't be surprised if you come across it." Still, no flicker in her eyes or her face. What a poker player she would be!

"Physically, it might be hard for me personally to enter Afghanistan, given the current view they have of women. Can I recruit for this job?"

"Only from Interpol ranks, but they don't have to be Section Five qualified. And then, only people you know personally. Two years ago, when you helped us clean up the people smugglers, you had two agents from your local area working with you, both of whom I met. Where are they now?" Still nothing. This girl was a rock!

"Sandista Yang is working out of our Indian office, and Phon Yarmuth is in Singapore. The last contact I had with them was a month ago when we were checking into the offices of Innomatchi."

"They don't have minis, do they?"

"No, Commander, we sent them home after that operation ended and have only used inter-office communications with them since then."

"So you could have been hacked, and the terrorists might know their names and data?"

"Probably not, ma'am. We used one-time code pads and personal couriers with diplomatic bags."

"Of course you did. Apologies, I completely forgot that. Okay, here's what I want you to do. I'll send you the briefing package to your mini at the conclusion of this call. Get them to whatever location you can absolutely control for at least a month, brief them, then call me. Got that?"

"Yes, Commander, it will take three days to arrange that, plus two days for them to get to me. It is nice to be working with you again." Now I had two additional elements in play, a search for the manufacturing equipment and a search for the location where it may have been utilized. Five days was nothing unless it all blew up in our faces somehow. We'd just have to wait and see.

# Chapter Six

The town of Helena, Montana, once boasted a population of 324,555. In the last three months since the terrorist attacks, that had swollen by an additional 105,450. And added to that, just in the last week, another 1,233 migrants had arrived, most to be placed in homes only finished the week before. Looking from the outside, it was a constant stream of humanity moving one way and then the other. But at its heart was the most significant migration of refugees in history. John Vernon, the latest Senior Special Agent, FBI, to run the Helena office, looked at his new house with pride. Made from a sparkling-colored material that acted as solar panels, providing one hundred and fifty percent of all the power the house required to provide every electric service imaginable, including heating a spa, it looked modern, elegant, and bright.

He had purchased the house three weeks prior, and because he and his wife had agreed to take two refugee girls, the price of the house had been discounted by fifty percent. They would also be compensated annually for the refugee children, as well as have full education and support for any of their own children they decided to have. At the end of the day, they had obtained a four-bedroom, two-bathroom, fully furnished, free-standing house with a yard for fifty thousand dollars. It was not only amazing, but it was also a sheer, upfront, and unmitigated bribe worked out by the terrorists that had turned the country on its ear. And there were over twelve hundred houses being completed at present, with room for another five thousand in months to come.

As he and his wife waited expectantly, having submitted their personal details at the time of purchase, he wondered what it would be like adopting two young girls, at this point, origin unknown, other than they spoke basic English and were orphaned. The adoption process wasn't shrouded in secrecy, as much as it was extremely confusing, with over a thousand children arriving on buses within hours of each other. This meant that hundreds of pairs of parents-to-be waited in the same football park, waiting for their chosen children to appear from the mass of confusion. It was not a good look, and not, John thought to himself, a good start.

However, with the pressure of his wife's hand increasing by the second, he stood tall, dressed in a western-style flannel shirt, jeans, and low-heeled boots, searching the mass of people and children for any sign of the Aid worker to whom they had identified themselves.

Her name was Roslin Albreck. She was just twenty-three, a nurse at the Helena hospital, drafted by the city council to help with the transfer of the children to their parents. What had seemed to be a well-planned process had now turned into a milling mass of people, all looking for the same thing but not having a single clue how to find it. What was missing, she felt, was discipline and system. She lifted the small bull horn to her lightly colored lips and, raising it slightly towards the sky, which, thankfully, was blue and not gray or black, called for quiet.

"Thank you. This would go much faster and smoother if you could please organize yourselves into rows and if you held your identity cards up at chest height." There was a low rumble from the crowd, then a small movement towards one end of the field, and then a slow if not a reluctant movement of the mass of people, until a crooked line faced the center of the field, curving around the ends in the shape of the low fence. The children had been held behind a rope barrier, all looking pretty but mostly frightened and scared. They had been prepared for the transition from refugee camp to a private home, but as in all things where the quantum of change was huge, the intellect took a while to catch up with the practical.

"Again, thank you. Once you have your child or children, please move to the far side of the ground to get the health and education records and register your family. You will find a full set of instructions in your care pack, as well as your first year's stipend. Owing to the lack of electronic systems, the registration process will be manual, as will the records that you receive. Thank you all for your patience." As she spoke, the first of the children were being led to the far end of the line of parents, and before long, the line of children and careers were moving ever so slowly as they looked for the specific families with whom to place the children. As the children flowed past him, Andrew saw the tension in their eyes, the flash of curiosity, the occasional smile, but the underlying emotion he felt in everyone was hope laced with fear.

It took nearly an hour before a small woman, who looked a little fragile, stopped in front of them with a child in each hand. "Mister and Missus Vernon?" she asked in a quiet voice. John nodded, amazed at how beautiful the two children who now stood in front of him were. Soft, almost elegant, in new jeans, tee shirts, and pullovers, their hair pulled back into tails, held by pretty ribbons. His wife moved forward, went down on her knees, reached forward, and hugged the two girls, tears or happiness slipping down her face like little sparkling drops of champagne.

"Hello, I'm Elizabeth. This is John. What are your names?" Her face said it all-happiness, worry, fear, and happiness again, as she tried to hug the girls while letting them speak.

"My name is Kona," the little brunette said, holding a delicate hand out. "I'm eight years old, and I am happy to be here." The tears turned into a flood, and John bent down to be at the same eye level as the girls, took Kona's hand, and gave it a gentle squeeze.

"Hi, I'm John. Welcome to our family." Tears were running down his face, not as many as his wife's, but noticeable. Nothing tugged Elizabeth's heart more than seeing her tough, seasoned, broad-shouldered, strong FBI agent husband cry, and she reached into one of her jumper sleeves and pulled out a silk handkerchief. She wiped her eyes, handed it to John, then looked at the second little girl. She was a little taller than Kona, a little thinner, and she had a small scar running up her neck from out of her collar. Bright yellow hair cut in a short style framed her face, and she looked anything by happy.

"My name is Aya, I'm ten, and I don't want to leave my friends." As she spoke, she looked around as if lost, looking for someone she recognized. On one hand, she had a stained Rubik's cube that had seen a lot of action. John spotted it and pointed to it.

"Aya, what is that you're holding?" She stared at him, her eyes narrowing and just the faintest smile creeping over her coffee-colored face.

"It's a Rubik's cube. Want to try to beat me?" John laughed, a genuine sound that drew other heads towards him.

"Yes, please." Aya quickly mixed the sides up until there was a complete jumble of colors on every side. John took a deep breath, he hadn't played with a cube in twenty years, and he hoped he didn't make a fool of himself. He started the matching process, moving row after row, and at around the three-minute mark, recognized that he had, if it were possible, made it worse. Aya smiled at him, held her little hand out, and took the cube back. And in a blur of movement, she turned the six colored sides into a perfect cube in less than twenty seconds.

"Wow! You've been practicing." John stood up, simply amazed at her skill. And without realizing it, he immediately thought of Amira, the super smart refugee whose inventions had turned the world on its head once they had been bastardized by the terrorists. Now he had a real feel for what the terrorists had been able to accomplish. Before he could develop his thinking, Aya held the cube out to him.

"You can try again; I haven't mixed it up so much." He took the cube and, shaking his head, tried again. This time he managed to marginally improve on his first attempt, but somewhat frustrated handed the incomplete cube back. Aya had it perfect in seconds and looked very pleased with herself.

"No one could beat me on the boat, so maybe you could practice a bit, or I could show you how to do it." John nodded, standing and then taking her little hand in his.

"Let's all go and get the paperwork done. Then would anyone like ice cream?" Both little girls looked up at him, curiosity in their eyes.

"What's an ice cream?' Aya asked, curiosity overcoming her fear of asking an adult a question. Just weeks ago, that would have earned her a beating with a cane and no food for the rest of the day. She wondered if she would get beaten by these two white people, even though they seemed nice.

She shrugged her shoulders. She had learnt in her short life she had no control over anything, so she decided on the spot to hold herself, ready to run if she needed to, patting her pockets where she had hidden scraps of food just in case. And she worried about Kona, who seemed to be far too friendly and trusting. She would have to watch her carefully and wait to see what happened next and started to do the fifteen times tables in her head.

# Chapter Seven

"Commander, we are all here." The pretty face of Drishya Singh popped into the frame, and she panned the mini around to reveal her other two agents, Sandista Yang, a mild-looking short agent with thinning hair, and Phon Yarmuth, in contrast, a huge man with black hair, and the darkest skin I had ever seen on a person. I knew them both. They had worked with Section Five during the roundup of the people smugglers two years ago. And if memory served me correctly, agent Yarmuth had been shot during a fierce fight with a group of very angry terrorists.

"Phon, how are you? Have your wounds healed?" His smile told me all, but it was nice to see him in action again.

"Commander, thank you, all good. Why did you interrupt my holiday in Singapore?"

"Holiday?"

"Well, it might as well have been. The people we were tracking did exactly nothing for five full weeks. It was driving me crazy." I laughed, as did the other two agents.

"Let me offer you a new adventure. You have been briefed by Drishya, so all I want to do is fill in the gaps." He smiled, reassuring me that he had been briefed and he was on his game again. Good. We needed every advantage we could muster at this point of the investigation. Nothing concrete, just supposition, web traffic, photos, and a tickling in the back of my neck. As an investigator, I placed a great store in the back of my neck and its tingles.

"Are you both authorized to carry weapons?" They both looked a little sheepish. Of course, they were carrying weapons, but not necessarily with Interpol's authorization. I fixed that in a heartbeat.

"You are both TDY (Temporary Duty Transferred) to Drishya as your immediate commandeering officer, Section Five, and all that this entails. Copy?"

"Just like the last time."

"Yes, exactly, except Drishya is your immediate supervisor, not me. You report to her and follow her instructions to the letter." The chat went quiet as both agents absorbed the ramifications of that order. Sandista was the first to nod; being Indian and working out of our Indian office, reporting to a woman was culturally easier for him. Phon had reported directly to me during the people smuggling operation, so this should not be an issue for him.

"I need you to go in as openly as you can, preferably legitimate, so pick your cover well, and Drishya has a device you will take with you to report back to her. It's a minicomputer, secured, and can't be hacked, tracked, or jammed. The reason you report back to her and not directly to us is we want to keep this investigation local and under the radar as best we can. Questions?" They both looked a little serious, probably thinking through how to mount a legitimate, visible, and, therefore, challengeable foray into the enemy-held territory. Since the Americans had left Afghanistan four years previously, the Taliban, ISIS, and around twenty bastardizations of those terrorist organizations had made living and working in the country an absolute hell.

But countries, even ones controlled by terrorists, relied on a basic economy to survive, and that required trade across borders. And that was what I was counting on. The one thing we knew from looking at the plants the terrorists had set up in Point Roberts and New Zealand was the machinery used to produce the power cells and power packs, and even the biofuel, required heaps of power-huge big continuous gigawatts of power-and the cleverest design of all, the buildings, with their in-built solar panels providing that power.

So we were looking for either the sparkling giveaway of the terrorists' solar panels or a factory in a civilized area with access to commercial quantities of power, and I had my money at Kandahar

International Airport. Throughout the Russian occupation and then the American invasion, the airport had remained essentially intact and, in fact, during the American stay, had been improved considerably. New runways, new buildings, and improved infrastructure at every level.

I ran through my thinking with them and then clicked off to let the team decide for themselves what approach might work best.

"Sandra, what are you doing, and why are you doing it," I demanded in as harsh a tone as I could manage. She never flinched, just smiled and lay back in her chair, her screen a myriad of images. I turned in mine to better see her and realized she hadn't moved from her workstation in hours.

"Looking at all the possibilities for making a nuke. And boy, oh boy, are there a lot of them!"

"What does Luigi say about the material?" She turned in her chair, tilting her head from side to side, probably suffering the same neck stress I was.

"Well, how scared do you want to be?" I shrugged my shoulders, I was already scared of the possibilities, and to a certain extent, that fear would only be reduced by hard facts. During our earlier investigation into how the terrorists had stolen a quantity of atomic material with which they poisoned the Arabian oil fields with disastrous consequences, Luigi had, at the boss's request, duplicated the theft in less than thirty minutes and had demonstrated just how unsafe the whole process of moving nuclear materials around was.

"Luigi says there is no way to backtrack to find out what has been stolen, even with the new protocols Interpol introduced after the last attack. He says that Strontium wouldn't be the material of choice for a nuclear weapon. He prefers Plutonium, more traditional, used in atomic bombs for years, lots and lots of data on how to maximize its yield, you know, the drill."

"And?" There was always another level to anything Luigi, one of the smartest geeks I had ever come across, came up with. Teamed up with Indigo, Shami, the Israeli colonel, and Malcolm, the head of the geek squad at the NSA, then throw in Stefarino and his geeks, and you could literally control the geek world.

"And he has successfully taken three hundred kilos of Plutonium out of the system and shipped it to a warehouse in the United States. It took him longer than before because he claims he had to wait for the optimal conditions."

"How much longer?"

"Three hours."

"You're kidding. Three hours to steal three hundred kilos of one of the most heavily guarded and protected materials in the known universe!" I shook my head in wonder. I had trouble grasping the enormity of what we were so casually discussing.

"What could that do in the article we have the photo of?"

"Firstly, they probably have stolen much more than three hundred kilos. That was just the optimal position Luigi described. As in at that point in time, that was the most susceptible shipment. But to answer your question, the bomb dropped on Hiroshima contained sixty-four kilos of atomic material and produced a blast the equivalent of sixteen thousand tons of TNT. Very big bomb, even by today's standards, so our bomb, by comparison, is a baby. We estimate it might hold around six kilos of Plutonium for an explosive force of one thousand five hundred tons of TNT. That's around three times the size of the explosion that leveled parts of Beirut back in 2020."

"And not counting the radioactive fallout."

"And not counting the radioactive fallout."

"Shit!"

"Yes. Very much so. And we don't know how many devices they made, where they were shipped to, and what they intend to do with them."

"Then you've been slacking off!" It was the best insult I could think of. The mere idea of a Beirut-sized explosion on steroids plus radioactivity that would last for twenty thousand years or longer sent chills up my spine so hard my back was going cold. We had to find them before they could be put into play.

But how? I flicked my mini-open. Its buzzing irritated me. In fact, everything was starting to irritate me.

"Yes, Senji-san, how may I help you?" He smiled and bowed to the camera, resulting in his magnificent head of hair falling all over the screen.

"Commander, I hope to be able to help you. Namoki-san passed your request to me, and I have the information. How would you like me to dispatch it?" I thought quickly and asked a question. He nodded, and I made up my mind.

"Mini to mini, encoded, one-time code. Use the one that fits you best." He gave me a long look, then bowed again, more hair all over the screen, then data started to flow so fast I couldn't read it. I waited, and when the screen finally went black, I pulled the data up and flicked it up to the big screen in the middle of the room.

"Sandra, use one-time code #63. Decrypt this, please." All conversation in the room stopped, and every head turned towards the big screen, where line by line, data and photos appeared as if being pulled off a pasta machine. I flicked the mini-open, and dialed Nokomoto.

"Excellent, make sure no one has access to this data, and also thank Namoki-san for me. Good job!" And I snapped the mini closed, then opened it again. Now, at least, we knew what we were looking for, so I dialed Drishya, checked she had the little silver base on her mini and started to forward the decrypted data.

"This is what you are looking for. Hardware-wise, you will see from the schematics how it was laid out, and you can see the specifications for the support machinery required. Go find it!" She just smiled that lovely demure smile she had, and the screen wet to black again.

"Sandra, get this to the geeks, Arie, Malcolm, and where the hell is Fay?" Indigo came over, a huge mug of espresso in his hand, patted me on the shoulder like you would an out-of-sorts five-year-old, handed me the coffee, and smiled.

"*Comandante, Jessica, l'hai mandata in America, proprio ieri, dovrebbe essere lì ormai?*" I had? Why didn't I remember? Then it all came flooding back. I had sent her back to Helena and Seattle to distribute the silver bottoms for the minis, which involved stopping in Washington, then to the mid-west. She had taken a smallish mid-sized jet the Italian Airforce had lying around, already converted for biofuel. Indigo had arranged the whole thing because I had forgotten it the moment I had pointed to the door and shouted, "USA!"

"Does she have a backup?" I remembered only too well being shot out of the sky earlier in the week.

"*Sì, comandante, due dei miei migliori sono con lei, e abbiamo organizzato scorte attraverso l'oceano e nel paese.*"

Good. Two of Indigo's best with her, and covered all the way across the Atlantic by firstly the Italians, then the Americans.

"Thanks, Indigo, it slipped my mind." He just smiled a bigger smile, if that was possible, and moved back to his beloved espresso machine. The data had finally unscrambled itself on the big screen, and I started to get a feel for what we were facing. A floor area of around eleven hundred square meters, with a feeding area twenty meters long. And my intuition about the power was spot on. They would have needed a lot. And I wondered if we could trace the raw material? Before I could ask, my mini buzzed again, so I gave in to the inevitable and opened it.

"Commander, we agree with your assumption. The only facility with this sort of continuous power supply will be the airport."

"Good. Go for it." I dialed Fay. "Where are you?"

"Nice to see you too, Commander, sitting with general Saunders, who is, as we speak, fitting her security bottom to her mini. Would you like to talk to her?" I shook my head.

"No. Thanks. Call me when you are secure." Telling the Americans anything about what we were running down would be premature and only cause more grief for the president and her cabinet. With the migration of the refugees in full swing in both Helena and Roanoke, she had her hands full. I needed more information but hesitated to call up Stefarino. He had been really good at getting data to us as he processed it. I wanted to know where the three people in the satellite shot had been, were going, how they travelled, what their alias was, and most of all, what they were planning.

"Amira, hi, how are you?" she looked worn down around the edges, and I wondered what had gotten to her this time. I could see her steeling herself to talk to me. Not good. It was hard to remember she was still very young in her age years, even though her intellectual level was off the scale.

"I'm fine, Commander. How can I help you?" I fired the data that we had shared with our team in Pakistan. She had marginally run the lab where the first prototype of the device had been made at Harvey Mudd university.

"What do you make of this? And would it use any nanotechnology?" She peered at the screen, then obviously flicked it up to a bigger one because she swam in and out of focus as she changed cameras.

"This big machine here," and she pointed to a green and black monster that had three clear sides, a huge bucket-like shape at the base, and silver bars running across the top, "is the 3D printer. These smaller machines are additive printing machines. I suggest sizing for a specific component. If, as you suspect, copper or brass was used for the origin material, then perhaps nanomachines may have been used to meld the two materials at the atomic level, but I would have to see a physical sample to be sure."

"Is this how you did it at Harvey Mudd?"

"No. We only had one printer. And it was much smaller than this one." She panned around the schematics. "We changed the platen several times, that's why it took almost two years to make something."

"Can you tell, just by looking, if the object in the satellite images could have come from this machinery?" As I said the words, another box opened up, and the satellite images ran through, freezing and then zooming in on the torpedo-shaped object the three terrorists were looking at.

"It's possible. Can you give me some time to do a proper analysis?"

"Yes. Sorry, 1 didn't mean to push. You look unhappy. What's wrong?" She hung her head, the background graphics morphing in and out of different shapes, reminding me of an early-style cartoon.

"I spoke to Michele."

"Oh." No way to fix a conversation between lovers who have been torn apart by greed, treachery, and world events.

"It's okay, we parted as friends, but we won't get any help from her."

"We can survive without that. Call me when you're ready." The images faded. I closed my mini and looked for somewhere to throw it.

Having a digital phone was one thing. Having a digital video phone was quite another, especially with all the people who kept calling me for one reason or another. And just as I was ready to 'accidentally' leave it on a chair, it buzzed again. Fay swam into view.

"Hello again from the battlements of Washington."

"You sound cheery?"

"Well, Frank is pissed at you, so they barely notice me. The general is a general. I've passed out the security attachments and explained what we think is happening in the back end, I got a lot of grief from Malcolm, as you would expect, but he called me just now to apologize. Seems he had a long chat with Luigi and Shami, and they talked to him long enough in geek to convince him that it wasn't his fault."

"Okay, I want you to make a diversion. Roanoke. See what's really going on there. Summary only, don't get involved, ask Anna for cover, maybe you can slip back into an FBI suit for the occasion." She smiled at my sarcasm, a good sign, she had only officially been with us for three weeks, and I had cast her out of the nest and into the wild with the barest of briefs, straight back where she had come from. I wanted her personal update, as she had been heavily involved with myself and Sandra in Point Roberts, collecting their senior management and taking them into custody, had survived an ambush in Helena by the terrorists, and managed the agent who was now running the Helena FBI office and had first-hand knowledge of the Seattle office and the distribution chain for the power packs. Her insights would be invaluable.

"On it. I'm sure Anna has a suit she can lend me." And with that little shot across my metaphorical bows, I hung up.

Between her and Sandra, I had my hands full. Effervescent, vivacious, highly intelligent, and dressed in a way that made them look like supermodels. Against them, I came off boring, dull, and old-fashioned.

Too bad. I was just adjusting my attitude to being the third best-looking female agent in Interpol when my accursed mini buzzed. Again. I snapped it open. Arie's face filled the screen, and the look on it made my skin crawl.

"Jessica, I called the colonel, but he was engaged. We have uncovered a second message on another old social media board, this was written in Gaelic — *'rachaidh mic chlann na bhFianna ar stailc arís ag meán oíche, an lá roimh an lá is naofa ar an Domhan'* — and they list Ennis, Belfast, London, Dublin, Manchester, New York, Rome, Glasgow, and Paris. Translated, it simply says the sons of the sons of the Fenians will strike again at midnight, the day before the holiest day on Earth."

"The Thursday before Easter. How long does that give us?" I felt panic in my bones, but I held it down, the attack on the world wide web was having a catastrophic effect on our intelligence-gathering abilities. Arie looked surprised at my question, but he gave me that grandfatherly smile again, suggesting he forgave me for my ignorance.

"Nine weeks if they are true to their word." I thought furiously. Not much time to locate an unknown number of nuclear bombs, if they existed, and if we could find a way to detect them. Think logically, like the great investigator I was supposed to be.

Locate the factory where the bombs had been made. Track the bombs to where they had been delivered. Find the bombs, and take them out of commission.

But there was one thing we could do right now, locate the three terrorists in the satellite images from Afghanistan, and sweat the details out of them. And the bloody Irish might not even be involved in the nuclear bombs. It could be a totally different attack profile, although, in my bones, I felt that this was a bridge too far.

I hung up on Arie, and dialed Stefarino.

"The tracking system. Can you please tell me where those three people in the satellite images are?"

"Yes, and no. We have Badawi and O'Cleary making a brief appearance in Dublin, then disappearing. Abbas simply disappeared once he left — if he did, in fact, leave Afghanistan. It's perplexing. The system is working perfectly, as we are tracking other individuals in real-time as we speak, but these three seem to be able to hide at will.

"Thank you, Stefarino. Your help is appreciated." I cancelled the call, then just sat and let the energy in the room flow around me and, hopefully, into me.

Geeks were buzzing around like busy bees, and the normal complement of analysts was beavering away at their consoles without a care in the world. I had to get a handle on something tangible, something I could give the team to work with. Then I had a real, genuine new thought.

Motive.

Why place bombs anywhere? You wanted something, all the usual reasons — power, control, retribution, political gain, financial gain, economic gain, sheer terror, pick your poison. If it wasn't just terror, then someone wanted something, and that something would be, by the very nature of the attack, very large.

We could rule out financial and economic gain. We knew the Irish had over five billion euros at their disposal, kindly given to them by Mohammad bin Azaria when he had control of the Sovereign Wealth Fund. It was supposed to support the building and running of an environmental plant, producing panels and batteries and biofuel, then support the immigration of refugee girls, but the evidence suggested it may have been hijacked by the terrorists-or perhaps another group of terrorists-for a purpose that was not yet transparent. And one of the terrorists was an Irish nuclear scientist.

If it were the Irish, they would want a free state from both Ireland and the United Kingdom. Since Brexit, Northern Island has followed the EU in the common trade agreement. Britain still included it in the four countries of the United Kingdom. The Republicans wanted a united Ireland and had for decades. But the bad blood still lingered between the north and the south. Was this strong enough to provoke the threat of a nuclear attack?

I really didn't think so.

The original terrorists — if I could call them that — had a definite agenda — destroy the world and our way of life and force the migration of thousands of young refugees into selected countries. What was left for these 'new' terrorists to achieve? Terror, pure and simple, and if I looked at the world like the skeptic I was, the biggest issues were getting rid of the State of Israel, the oligarchs getting total control over Russia, and a whole range of smaller nation-states who wanted to rid themselves of their neighbors, and take over their resources.

What had kept the world mostly sane during the decades-long 'cold war' was 'MAD'-Mutually Assured Destruction'-where the threat of nuclear retaliation threatened the attacker and protected the target. There hadn't really been any shift in that emotional balance except for the threat of portable 'suitcase' nuclear weapons and the so-called 'dirty bombs'. Throw together some nuclear waste material, wrap it in an explosive, blow it up, irradiate the target and make it unoccupiable for thousands of years. Hadn't been one to date, plenty of threats, most nipped in the bud or flushed out before their perpetrators could pull the trigger.

Now we might have a new credible threat involving an unknown quantity of torpedo-shaped bombs capable of holding a mere six kilos of nuclear material, creating a yield of approximately fifteen hundred tons of TNT. Sadly, while that sounded small, if you remembered the devastation in the Beirut harbor back in 2020, a six-kilo warhead would be approximately three times that size-a blast radius of twenty to thirty miles-plus the radioactive fallout which would pollute another thirty to forty miles, depending on the wind strength. But the real question was why when the terrorists had access to the 'black hole' technology, which had effectively hidden the terrorists from our view almost for the entire time we were chasing them down, why hadn't these new terrorists used it to cover what they were doing?

Simple answer — they wanted the world to know what they were doing at certain points of their attack. So, the old message board is revealed, the satellite images from Afghanistan, then the brief appearance of two of the terrorists in Dublin. Create the scenario for a credible threat.

We needed more data. We needed intelligence. We needed to find things out and quickly.

# Chapter Eight

The boat was three hundred and fifty feet long, had four decks, and was originally designed and built for the sum of seven hundred million dollars for an Internet billionaire, who had many, many parties, then gone bust. The ship had been sold for one hundred and fifty million, then sat in a San Francisco shipyard for three years until it was purchased by Loni Traveler, a young man who had made his millions off conning people by selling land that didn't exist. He also had a lot of shipboard parties but subsequently went to jail. The boat went back to its berth, where it sat unloved for another two years until it was purchased by a trust managed by Reganit and Sons of Belfast.

They had put a prized crew onboard and sailed the ship back to Ireland, where for the relatively low cost of one hundred and three million dollars, the ship had been returned to its former glory.

On the outside.

The crew consisted of four stewards, two chefs, a captain and a first mate, an engineer and her assistant, two physicists, one plasma scientist, and a mechanical engineer. The entire lower deck, slightly below the waterline, had been gutted and fitted out as a modern, state-of-the-art laboratory with laminar flow rooms, a controlled environment, and the ability to handle nuclear materials with complete anonymity and safety.

The very top deck, once the prized location for orgies and drunken drug-fueled non-stop parties, was now configured with a custom-made one-hundred-millimeter tube with a rifled barrel and three support expansion rings running the twenty-meter length. It fired a rocket-assisted sabot round that had been developed specifically for the tube. A rail gun mechanism fired the round the first five nautical miles, then using technology perfected by the Russians for their submarine-launched missiles, the rocket at the base of the sabot lit and propelled the round for another one hundred and twenty nautical miles. It was cleverly hidden against the side as a decorative feature in what was now a collapsible theatre, with a full sliding rooftop and a screen that ran the full width of the beam of the ship. As the room was always dim or just dark, the unique features of the tube and its loading mechanism and support rail gun mechanism were never noticed.

Long before the crew had been allowed to board, a special weapons team had practiced using the tube in the dead of night, firing a bean bag into the ocean, and were happy to report to the owner, a tall good looking Arab, that the tube could be ready to fire manually in just three minutes, the roof opening and the walls falling into specially made recesses, and that the test of the automatic firing run by the AI could open, fire, and close the room in less than half a minute, and that the fired shot was undetectable from more than a hundred meters away. But a new round would have to be loaded into the breech manually. That suited Malik Badawi's plan perfectly, as he intended to spread his attack out to maximize the damage he intended to create. And he intended to create a lot!

The technology was not all that far removed from that used by the terrorists to bomb the sports stadia from the trucks the month before, just on a much larger scale and using the sabot design rather than a drone. There were ten sabot shells laid out side by side in the laboratory, the nose painted a dull black, the middle cradle a mild blue, and the rocket tail bright red. When you looked down at them, it looked like the nose and the tail were held together by thin straps until you saw the cover that wrapped around the completed weapon. And the nose had a mix of laser, GPS, and ground-mapping navigational software, giving an accuracy of just one meter.

On a long rubberized bench, behind each sabot, sat a brass/copper composite torpedo, each seventy millimeters wide and eight hundred centimeters long, with fine microscopic lines demarking the machined sections of the torpedo, which now lay open and in sections. The torpedoes looked like a puzzle, with two separate chambers linked in a figure of eight and the other pieces showing locking blocks and sleeves which seemed destined for each other. One completed torpedo sat in a specially constructed cradle, looking exactly like the photo Interpol had pulled off the satellite pictures.

Malik Badawi stood tall and proud, looking over his arsenal, his arm around the waist of Siobhan O'Cleary, hugging her in a rare exhibition of emotion.

"This will be your finest work," and he bent down and sought the lush lips of the nuclear scientist, which were warm and moist.

They shared the kiss, let it go a little deeper than usual, and Siobhan found herself panting slightly when Malik released her.

"Wow! Where did that come from?" Wearing jeans, sturdy boots, and a thick woolen pullover, she didn't look particularly attractive until you saw her face, which was radiant, and glowed with health and vitality. She looked up at Malik, smiled, and brushed her long silky hair back from her face.

"*Leannán*, what the world has suffered so far will pale into insignificance when we let these beauties fly! No one will be able to resist us, and we will have everything we want."

"Your Irish is getting better, but I'm still not sure what it is you want?" He looked at her and smiled a deep smile, his eyes sparkling in the muted overhead light. "You will get your free Ireland, and we won't have to fire a shot. Fear will rule the day for us, and we won't even be in the same part of the world. As for what I want, it's simple. I want justice for my brothers and to make the point for once and all that you cannot let cancer grow and disrupt the world without consequences." She looked at him with sadness in her eyes, perhaps realizing for the first time just how hard this man of hers was. She grasped his hand a little firmer, trying to provide comfort while mentally preparing herself for arming the torpedoes she saw spread out before her. But first, she had to get the material that would bring the little fabricated torpedoes to life.

"When will we get the core for the bombs?"

"It's being arranged now; we should have it within a week. Let's go and watch the stars."

And he took her by the hand, walked out onto the command deck, and watched the ocean swim by, rich, frothy white crested waves being forced back on either side of the sharp bow in a beautiful ballet, underscored by the swish and crash as each wave crested and collapsed against the side of the hull. From the cockpit, the two looked like merged shadows in the wan moonlight. The first mate took the call on the satellite phone, looked a little serious for a moment, then walked the handset out to the foredeck.

"Sir, a call for you."

The first mate retreated back into the cockpit as Malik turned from Siobhan and held the handset to his ear. He listened, then threw the handset into the ocean. Someone had locked up his funds, and the excuses offered by his accountants in Dublin seemed hollow and insincere. He would remedy that; in the meantime, he had to find sufficient additional funds to secure the most important purchase he would ever make.

# Window Shopping

Sandista Yang and Phon Yarmuth moved to the hangar as if they owned it. Dressed in smart suits, starched shirts, and club ties, while culturally different at their roots for this mission, they were brothers, posing as Pakistani Military researching possible locations for setting up a maintenance facility. The manager of Kabul International Airport, while being a staunch member of the Taliban, was also a realist, and the 'access fee' he was charging the two officers would feed his family for months. Besides, the Taliban council wanted desperately to develop the business side of the airport in an attempt to lure back the outside world.

One by one, they were escorted through the hangars until they reached a large double-ended one in which sat three old Russian jets, all sitting on flat perished tires, looking very much the worse for wear, and a clean area with machinery sitting mute, exactly like the photos they had memorized. Amazingly, refuse bins stuffed to the gills sat in a row, flowing over with dull metallic leftovers. Sandista made a point of fingering some of the waste and looked at their guard with a quizzical look, eyebrows hitching up in a silent question.

*"Hadhih baed alnufayat almutabaqiyat min mihnat sabiqat, yumkinuna 'iizalatuha ealaa alfawr 'iidha kunt targhab fi aistikhdam hadha alhazirati."* The guard almost bowed as he offered to have the hangar cleaned out. Sandista gave a noncommittal nod, carefully pocketing a handful of the shiny material. He decided to try for additional information but was beaten to it by his partner. The guard seemed to think for a moment, then held up seven fingers.

117

*"Kanuu yaemalun huna limudat sabeat 'ashhuru?"* The guard nodded quickly, confirming that the previous users had been here for seven months. Both agents assumed a politely bored expression and started to move onto the next hangar, and as they turned to leave, Phon also pocketed a handful of the shiny material. Now they had an additional problem, how to get the samples to Venice.

He had an idea about that and increased the pace to the next hangar.

# Chapter Nine

Amir Abbas had led the Hamas group for nearly ten years, and as luck would have it, his partner in chaos Malik Badawi had found the holy grail of terrorism through an old man he had met in the desert fifteen years ago. Now Malik had needed a secure place to manufacture some exotic materials from which a real, undetectable dirty nuclear bomb could be constructed. Five had already been spirited away in a Russian helicopter, a destination unknown to Abbas. More, Malik had paid for the manufacture of an additional twenty bomb sets and then had promised an extra million dollars each for the delivery of ten of them.

They had been dispatched as specified, three to Ireland, four to England, and one each to France, Germany, and Italy. But the ten million dollars had not been transferred to his accounts and would not be until proof of delivery had been provided. It had taken the best part of three months to set up the delivery of all the bombs, as they would be moved from dowl to small boats, to bigger ships, then back to horse-drawn carts. Primitive but effective. Slow but secure, using a network of child and weapons smugglers he had been using for over twenty years.

His ambition was simple. To remove the state of Israel from the map. Completely and forever. And these interesting little bombs would make that possible, as Malik had assured him that three of the ten bombs Malik had moved himself would be dedicated to that task. But Abbas had a backup plan, having made more than the twenty bombs he had been paid for, and he looked at the two he had kept to himself as the light slowly ebbed from the day. The incredible golden reflection and sparkles the sun made as it sunk below the western horizon on the shattered glass of the broken buildings were lost on him.

He was sitting on a small hill, his bombed-out headquarters behind him, on one side of the Gaza strip. He had a mathematical problem. From the conversations he had held with Malik's whore of a scientist, he knew each little bomb, if delivered properly, would create a blast that would decimate around thirty square kilometers and eradicate a further twenty. And that meant that no matter where he exploded the bombs, the Gaza strip would be affected. Not necessarily from the blast, but surely from the fallout. As he looked around the rubble and the ruins of what had once been a proud little city of the faithful, all he saw now were misery and pain. Hamas may well fire rockets into Israel, but Israel returned that fire one hundred times over with bombs and cannon fire that indiscriminately killed all before it.

He considered his options.

Did he really care about the people still trying to eke out a living in the Gaza strip?

No, not really. If they became martyrs to the cause, all the better and all the more international condemnation. That was an aspect he had paid attention to in seeking out radioactive material that had the unique signature the Israelis used to distinguish their radioactive waste from all others. Consequently, he needed the ten million dollars Malik owed him to pay for the delivery he expected within the week. Or at least six of it, to secure twelve kilos of plutonium and one of Uranium-235. Rare as hens' teeth, he thought to himself, he had to go all the way to the United States to secure some, and even now, it was still two weeks away from being delivered.

But then he would have something much more potent than just a dirty bomb — he would have a real atomic bomb with which to shake his world. Make that two.

He stood, pulled his dirty robes around him against the evening chill, and slowly walked back to his guards, who had been standing in the shadows.

He had to get his money from Malik.

He reached for his satellite phone, checked the time, and noted that the single satellite that he could use would not be in range for another three and a half hours. Bloody female terrorists! They had killed the Internet, satellite phone calls, computers, and a whole host of other useful communication tools, with no regard for the people who depended on them!

# Chapter Ten

**"I**'ve got samples of the copper/brass substrate on their way here from Pakistan, I got the geeks tracking the three terrorists in the satellite photo, I've got Fay running around the US getting eyes on the various activities running there, I've frozen the bank account the terrorists set up in Ireland, and I have a full accounting of where the money has gone on its way here by courier. What have you done?" I fired the question at Sandra, she looked too relaxed and pretty to have been doing anything more than trimming her nails, but the fluid eye roll and her face full of laughter almost put me off my game.

"And who got out of the wrong side of the bed this morning?" she asked, not bothering to hide her mirth. She walked over with a small portfolio and signaled to Indigo for life-giving coffee. He arrived first, a steaming mug in his hand. I just inhaled it, then sipped strongly, and I could feel the rest of me wake up.

"Okay, Indigo, you can live another day. This is wonderful. You," and I pointed to Sandra, "had better have something interesting, or I'm sending you to South America."

"What's in South America?" she asked guilelessly.

"Nothing good. Now, what have you got?" And I held out my spare hand, almost imperiously. I was cranky, I had slept badly, and I had kept seeing little atomic explosions going off in a whole bunch of different cities while we beavered away uselessly in our Venice headquarters. The skin peeled off the faces of babies, mothers torn apart by the blast, and the rotten skin of someone dying from radiation poisoning.

"Well, I have a video of our attacker being shot down, ID on the drone and the missiles and a track of its movements from start to finish. I also have the tapes from the carrier C-n-C and the data from the flight recorder on the G4. The pilot, by the way, is recovering nicely and should be back in the air in another week." And just like that, she turned my head. I had completely forgotten about our pilot, so consumed was I with atomic explosions.

"Excellent. Now get yourself with a couple of Indigo's best to the airport and make sure the sample from Pakistan gets onto the Israel helicopter without any fuss. And bring the data stores back with you so we can review them together." I turned away, not wanting her to see I was a little upset at having forgotten about the pilot. I snapped my mini-open, dialed Fay, and waited until she finished her conversation, with whom I couldn't see and really didn't care at this point.

"Commander, you called?"

"Get back here quickest, please." I waited for a reaction. She merely looked a little quizzical, then she nodded.

"Yes, ma'am." Now, who else would I need? I looked over at the boss, still camped in a huge leather armchair without a care in the world, pretending to sleep. I walked over and kicked him in the shins.

"Wake up. You're needed." I got one eye pointed at me, he didn't look all that happy with me disturbing him, but it was time for him to get his head in the game as well.

"You seem to be stirring things up quite well all on your own. What could I possibly do?" The sarcasm was dripping. I moved my boot to avoid it getting scarred and sat on the wide arm of his chair. I let my shoulders sag, circular breathed, and tried to center myself, bring the 'now' into focus, and differentiate between the facts and the maybe's. The boss would not respond to emotional bullshit, not even from me.

"We're going to need grunts on the ground, multiple locations, possibly all over Europe, UK, Ireland. I'd like to have a quiet hour to think things through, then I'd like a bull session involving Arie and his geeks. They are the ones who have found most of the data, I need Amira to analyze the material from Pakistan, and I need the information from the accountants from Ireland." He opened his other eye and shifted slightly so he could see all of me perched over him.

"You think this threat of dirty or nuclear bombs has merit?" I paused. What I said now would set the tone of the conversation going forward.

"I suspect that our nuclear scientist, Siobhan O'Cleary, is one of our women terrorists, although I don't know that for a fact. We are checking her family as we speak. I suspect that linking up with the Bedouin and Amir Abbas is just another version of the women using Shetani and his mercenary terrorists. If the photos from the satellite are true, then we have sophisticated genius-level engineering, which Amira was dabbling in when she was at Harvey Mudd. Everything else is supposition, or at best old data that can't be confirmed without boots on the ground. Our current communication limitations limit what we can do and how fast we can do it. And if the Irish message is not just a load of pompous crap, we have around seven weeks to solve the puzzle."

"But no country yet inviting us to the table?"

"No. As you know, Interpol's main function is to gather intelligence across the world relating to terrorism, major crime, and anything that threatens peace and stability. We need to use our resources as fast as we can to get as much intelligence as we need to form an accurate threat assessment."

"If you look at the baseline as Amira's work at Harvey Mudd and how the terrorists took that work and bastardized it, then bought the world to its collective knees, you have to take seriously any other technology she was working on at that time. Do you think these torpedo things are real? And if I had told you no oil, gas, or coal two months ago, would you have believed me?"

"No. No one would have; it was impossible to imagine. And as for the torpedoes, yes, I do. Why they have been designed that way, all the interlocking spheres and barrels and their relatively small size makes no sense, yet, but once we understand the technology, maybe the application will become more apparent."

"The real question is, why this type of attack? Every country in Europe is fighting to survive, millions of people have been disposed of, borders are flooded with migrants, there are real food shortages, a lack of clean water, and we're heading into spring, which might help alleviate some of the distress. But attacking anyone under these conditions makes no sense — what could you possibly ask for with any guarantee that you would get it?"

"The motive worries me. With the funding the terrorists have had access to, thanks to Mohammad bin Azaria, money would seem to be out of the question. The Irish threats are largely hollow; with the Northern Ireland take-up of the European Union back in 2020, the whole independence movement went quiet; they virtually have it now, so why all the fuss? But there are some larger questions here — how you deliver these bombs, if that is what they are, and where do you get the nuclear material? We now have every disposal of nuclear waste under physical monitoring, end to end, following our last little experience and under Interpol control."

"That doesn't mean they won't get their material."

"No, it doesn't."

"So, back to the boots on the ground. I'll do a little investigating and see what we can put together. You go off and have your hour down. For what it's worth, I believe there is a credible threat, but to whom, how, and why, we have a lot more work to do." I looked at the boss. Having him agree with me based on the little intelligence we had was major, and I started to feel a little better about it. I started to move away when Sandra burst back into the room, all smiles and bubbly energy, and I immediately felt tired and dull next to her brightness.

"Samples on their way, Amira is ready at her end, and I have two guests for you." And as she waved her hand in the classic 'come in' gesture, Sandista Yang and Phon Yarmuth walked in, escorted by Indigo's uniformed officers.

"Commander, nice to see you in person. Agent Singh believed we should debrief you personally, and we have photos and video for you as well." Indigo flashed over with two mugs of steaming coffee, the agents, surprised as they were, bowed graciously, but both took the time to smell before drinking, suggesting they had not eaten in a while, so I looked at Indigo and mimed spooning food into my mouth.

"*Subito, comandante, dammi cinque minuti.*" And with that, he disappeared into the bowels of the office.

"Colonel Kashasini will organize a meal for you. Please take a seat. I'll be with you in a minute." They both nodded, looked over to the seating area we had in front of a giant screen, then walked over and sat. A geek took their data stores and started to upload the material they had brought with them. I opened my mini and dialed up Drishya Sing.

"I have your agents here in Venice."

"Yes, Commander, thank you for confirming their arrival. After talking to them, I realized you needed to hear from them personally. I don't understand a lot of what they observed, but I'm sure you or your people will." I nodded at the camera, this was a wrinkle I hadn't anticipated, but I had learned the hard way you always trusted your man or woman on the ground. Particularly when they were as experienced and smart as Drishya Singh.

"Thanks, I'll get them back to you as soon as I can, but that may take a while." My planned hour had succinctly evaporated, so I moved over to the two agents, who were now eating a meal off their laps.

"While you eat, please run through for me what you think I need to hear." Sandista put his spoon down and rested the curry bowl on his lap. He looked a little tired, and his suit was creased in the crutch and armpits, suggesting he had not had it off in some time.

"Commander, using the diagrams you supplied, we tracked down the equipment to a hangar, which was being used as a dump for old soviet air frames. A third of the hangar had been resurfaced, and the equipment was laid out as per the blueprints. There was a twenty-meter area that acted as a feed-run and evidence of a sinter bath that led to one of the bigger machines, and according to our escort, who was one of the airport management, the machines were in use for two months, after a five-month build. There were nine workers involved, three of who were women, authorized by the local Iman and protected by Taliban militia, and they flew in and out every week. The five males bunked in the hangar and were fed by local caters attached to the airport.

"It was clear that the women were in control, even though they spoke through one of the males and one of the women was identified by the satellite photo you sent to us. He also confirmed the identity of the two males and mentioned that the Bedouin, Malik, had visited the site frequently in the last few weeks. He arrived by helicopter, an American SR-60, which was in very good condition, according to the airport staff. No one had been at the site in the last month, and the locals had no idea what to do with the equipment.

"He confirmed that several hundred million euros had been paid for the use of the area and the security. He also confirmed that they had direct access to the base power station, and we saw evidence that several substations had been linked together at some point. We were not able to get any readings from the area, but we were able to get samples of the waste, which your agent took off us and loaded into a helicopter at the airport where we had just arrived. The helicopter had Israeli markings if that is important."

"What have you got on the video?" The agent looked up at the big screen and offered a commentary.

"Here is the main area, here are the machines, and here is the run-in. This shot shows the substations hooked together, and here is the long view of the entire working area."

I thought for a moment, then realized that there was only one person who could properly interpret this data. I dialed Amira.

"Sending you some video and recently recorded audio. Can you look at this, please and let me know your thoughts? And have you got the samples yet?"

"They have just arrived, Commander. Give me an hour, please, and I'll get back to you." I hung up and looked back at the two agents.

"You both could have relayed this via video. Why did Agent Singh really send you here?" Phon Yarmuth stood up, folded his hands together, and looked me straight in the eye.

"Commander, we both had a strong feeling that the equipment was not left unattended accidentally and the refuse container not emptied also was no accident. We can't prove anything, so Agent Singh decided to let us tell you in person what our feelings were about the site."

"What specifically leads you to this conclusion?" Phon Yarmuth looked at his fellow agent, seemed to get his support, then dropped his head slightly as if in apology.

"Commander, we both live and work in environments where the cost of business is often in cash or portable assets and sometimes a little more than the sticker price. The people who used this hangar paid hundreds of millions of euros for the seven-month lease, plus the security of the women and the security of the site. Getting rid of the evidence would have been second nature to the airport management if only to protect themselves from questions being asked by the more rabid Taliban. The fact that the site was left, literally, in pristine condition, power still connected, both ends of the hangar open to anyone who wanted to look, waste bins left full to overflowing, suggests that this action was deliberate."

"I see." I thought about what he had said. It made sense to me, just like the amazing shots obtained by the satellite during a time when the terrorists had cloaking technology that hid the terrorists' movements from us quite effectively. And the clues left on the Irish chat board. We were being played, set up for something, and I hoped we could get ahead of whatever it was before it went "bang!" in the middle of the night.

I was saved from further musings by Indigo moving into my line of vision with a data pack.

The serious nature of his package was highlighted by his use of perfect English, so I flexed my toes and mentally readied myself for the more bad news. I motioned to the data center setup, and he moved to it and inserted the device. A whole row of figures scrolled across the big screen so fast it was incomprehensible. Then a list appeared, with photos, and the screen went still.

"I take it this is the report from the accountants in Ireland?"

"Yes, Commander, I have someone summarizing the numbers, but at the end, here you can see how they spent some of their money."

"They brought a boat."

"Yes, Commander, and a very big one at that. They also spent considerable time and money refurbishing it, and according to the data here, it went back into the water in Dublin almost six months ago. And to answer your next question, no, we don't know where it is now or who might be on it."

"What are these expenditures for here? The one million euros times twenty-four?"

"No idea, but they all went to the one account in Pakistan, so we may be able to trace them." I looked at our two agents, saw the interest in their eyes, and nodded. "Okay, Indigo, get these agents back home and collate all that data. I'd like to brief you in an hour, and when you're ready, can we have a private chat, please?"

"*Certamente comandante, cinque me dieci minuti per favore.*" I turned to the two agents.

"Thank you both. Your insights are invaluable, make sure agent Singh is aware of your report and ask her to let me know the outcome of your financial hunt." Both agents stood and followed Indigo out of the room, leaving it strangely empty in spite of the twenty or so people working at consoles and desks. I walked to the espresso machine, looked hopelessly at all the dials and controls, shrugged my shoulders, then saw the boss in a corner on his mini. I decided to walk outside and get some fresh air.

The sun was fighting a band of low gray clouds, the air was crisp, and the concrete wet, so we had some rain over the past few hours and as I smelled the scent of the ocean, I was reminded that I was spending far too much time inside. The light wind was causing small ripples on the water, so probably the tide was turning one way or the other, and in the distance, I could see the rare sight of a gondola with, I presumed, tourists waggling along the canal. There had been very few tourists since the terrorist attacks, so I wondered who it might be.

The boss emerged from our cave-like entrance, ranged himself against the cobblestone wall, crossed his ankles, and looked magnificent with his rugged untidy hair in the dying light, and for a split second, my unrequited love for him blossomed into full bloom before I tamped it down like I would an exploding grenade. He gave no sign he had registered my emotional turmoil, but then he was a master of disguising his own emotions, so who knew?

"Do you have any grunts for me?" I asked to break the silence and help myself get back on an even foot.

"Anticipating we will need trained operators who can hunt down radioactive signals, I've put the word out to a few friends, and we should have answers shortly. Understandably, with all the chaos in most countries, no one is rushing in to volunteer their best people."

"They might if we can show them a credible threat." He looked at me, his deep blue eyes slightly darkened by the fading light, but you could not mistake the intensity in them.

"Yes, that always makes a difference. In ten words or less, what do you think the threat is?" He looked at me with those intense eyes, still slouching, and I knew that he had formed his own opinion and wanted to see if mine was the same. I brushed my hands through my hair, not stalling so much as filtering what I knew from what I suspected. I looked out over the canal, letting the peace and quiet fill me. If we were on song, we would have a potentially bigger problem than the last terrorist attacks that had leveled the planet. Who could have envisaged, just three months ago, that within weeks the world would have no oil, gas, or coal to fuel our power, transport, and manufacturing demands? And quite frankly, I didn't know that anyone could cope with more disaster, doom, gloom, and despair.

I knew I couldn't, and maybe that was the whole point of the exercise. I hunched my shoulders and looked back at the boss.

"There may be as many as twenty devices in play, maybe more, may or may not be radioactive, they have been built using the technology the terrorists have used previously for their power panels and packs, there are three women involved, and two identified male terrorists, one of whom we know is a seriously bad arse."

"And how these new players are connected to our previous group is not obvious — other than their use of the same technology — and neither is their motive."

"Agreed. The first group-if I can call them that-had a clear objective; make the world aware of the appalling conditions in the refugee camps, and bring that realization home in practical form by destroying the world's supply of oil, gas, and coal, attacking the major religions, and forcing the acceptance of the migration of thousands of children from the camps with their environmentally orientated panels and power packs."

"Yes. And at this point, it seems to have worked. Reports from Helena, New Zealand, and Roanoke suggests the migration is going as well as can be expected, and fifteen of the nineteen countries that the terrorists set trust funds up in for similar migration have accepted their ship sets and will build their plants progressively, knowing that they have been targeted for specific numbers of children. And there's still something in the background that niggles at me. Can you guess what it is?" I looked at him, saw a faint smile crease on his craggy face, and realized he was teasing me. I course, I knew of his niggle; I had worked with him for nearly six years now, and I knew every crease and wrinkle.

"How the Red Crescent has managed and still manages all the migration of the girls."

"Exactly. They claim they have been paid for it, paid well, and have no connection to the terrorists except for the possibility of funding, but we have never been able to prove that. The bastards set it up too well and hid the details. We have seen their overall plan, it's excellent, and the money is buried too deep for us to prove anything."

"But why would we now? Why deny all those little girls the possibility of a future? The terrorists have used them. They have had nothing to do with the chaos caused by the terrorists, other than a few of the early girls were helped in developing their natural talents and then had the results of their work bastardized."

"Spoken like a woman." I looked at him. That was a comment I had not expected from him.

"Like a woman?"

"Yes. From day one, I have watched you wrestle with your conscience as their plan unfolded, struggle with your internal battle to prosecute the women versus your natural nurturing instinct of protecting them." Seeing that I had personally ended the life of one of the female terrorists and had orchestrated the permanent incarceration of many more, some as young as twenty, I wondered about his 'nurturing' comment, but he was right, sometimes it had been a battle for me to keep everything lined up in the correct columns.

"I say again-why now?" He stood up, waved his hands at me, then folded his long arms across his chest.

"I'm not saying anything to the contrary. Just pointing out how difficult it has been for you to do the job. A job, by the way, you have done exceptionally well."

"That's why you promoted me." I let a little chill slip into my voice. I did not like the way this conversation was going.

"That's one of the reasons. We needed you to have a higher equivalent rank so you could boss around more of the rank and file. Look at how you handled that carrier captain." His mild laughter underscored his comments, and I suddenly realized he was having a very serious conversation with me, so I calmed down and really tuned into what he was saying.

"What's your point?"

"Simple. You're really good at the digging, the investigating, the people management, and when the time comes, you can pull the trigger better than anyone else I know except Pete." I had a mental image of Pete the day I had left him back on the island, his shoulder still healing from the three bullets he had taken capturing the terrorist known as 'Helen'. Yes, he was a shooter and had the scars to prove it, but I had never put myself in the same category. He was ex-SEAL teams, and I was ex-NCIS, as far apart as you could get in terms of rules of engagement. On the one hand, you had muscle and a killer instinct. On the other, a Law book and Rules that only worked if you followed them to the letter.

"I'll take all that as a compliment. What are you leading up to?" He looked at me, a serious look on his face, and he unlocked his arms and took both my hands in his.

"Our general is retiring, and I have been asked to take over from him. You will take over from me. The only advantage I have over you operationally at this time is my military and intelligence contacts, all of which I will have transferred to you later today. As of now, you run Section Five."

"I run Section Five?" The astonishment in my voice betrayed my nerves. This was not the transfer of the management of the local pizza parlor. This was a fundamental shift in the power structure of the entire policing network worldwide.

"As a commander, you have the equivalent rank of a one star and as the head of Section Five, you have the added authority of the World Court and UN behind you. I know you can and will do the job. I'll still be contactable if you need anything. You have only to ask."

"Does anyone else know?"

"No. I'll make an announcement at a town hall meeting via our minis later today. It won't become public knowledge, but it will eventually leak, and that means the bad guys will hunt you as a matter of course. But you're used to that." I thought about it, the boss had let me run every investigation for the last three years and had only inserted himself when a strong military presence was required, but even then, he had left most of the running up to me. He took a small notebook out of his pocket, its corners were bent from use, its leather cover faded in places from a deep burgundy to a faint pink and handed it to me.

"Here's every contact I have, legal and illegal. They will only know of the change when you tell them. You might lose some, but none of those who really count. Keep it safe." He held my hand with the book sandwiched between his and mine, looked me straight in the eyes, and smiled.

"Relax, Jessica, you were born for this. Just remember to have fun." His smile was infectious, and I found myself smiling as well.

"You are a bastard, but you know that, don't you?"

"Takes one to know one." He let my hand go and walked back inside.

# Baby Steps

Special Agent John Vernon was out of his depth. As an FBI agent chasing bad guys, he knew what to do and when to do it. As a newly minted father of two refugee girls, one ten and the other just eight, he hadn't the faintest idea how to manage them. Luckily for him, his wife Elizabeth had all the instincts needed to manage a family and manage it well. Both children had a rudimentary understanding of English, and the speed with which they were picking up more and more of the language every day suggested an intelligence above the average. Both were innately curious, both were very quick studies, and both were well-behaved, if not a little introspective. But they had been transplanted into a totally different environment in a matter of months and given precious little information about what to expect. Taken from a miserable experience in an overrun refugee camp to a modern, twenty-first-century living experience with all the bells and whistles.

Green grass to run and play on; other children with similar backgrounds to play with. And books, and videos, and a school, and an electric car, and a supermarket with so many things on the shelves both children had been too shocked to be able to select anything the first time they had been there. But they were learning and learning fast. They discovered that they liked ice cream. And pizza. And hot dogs-although Aya wasn't exactly sure she liked the BBQ sauce all that much. Her battered Rubik's cube had been enhanced with a board game that used the cube as a die and a video on the mathematics involved in solving all the different puzzles a cube could generate.

Neither girl had given a thought to running away, and both real-ized they had been given the chance of their short lifetimes. Living in the house was like emerging from living in a wet and soggy cardboard box to living in a palace. And the food! Neither of them had ever seen as much or as varied a selection of food that had been put in front of them every day. Their first week had been spent learning the names of all the vegetables and watching how Elizabeth cooked them. And slowly, ever so slowly, they both began to feel a warmth for both of their new parents, something they had not ever experienced before.

So when the tall lady in the bright red dress came to visit, her long blond hair flowing in the wind, they sat next to Elizabeth and listened intently to what was being said.

School will start next week. No one would be graded initially. That wouldn't happen for a month or two. The focus would be on helping the children with their English, learning to read, how to use the massive physical library and what the various roles in the commu-nity were — doctor, dentist, pharmacist, how the city council worked, and where they could go to play the different sports that were being set up. Demonstrations with the local children were being set up, and coaches and support staff were being recruited from the families who had migrated to Helena.

And then, the local zoo set up a temporary animal farm on the school grounds, and their whole world changed.

Kona, the beautiful brunette, all eight years old (she thought), fell in love with a cat.

Aya, the equally beautiful blond with the scar running down one cheek, fell in love with a dog.

John and Elizabeth agonized over their choices for a full week, carefully trying to manage the expectations of the children before finally caving on the weekend and taking them to the animal shelter up the highway.

The girls would have to take care of their new pets. Feed them, clean up after them, wash them, and take responsibility for them. Both girls agreed, not really understanding what all those words meant. But they learned, and in no time at all, the family had grown to six, and the pet door in the kitchen snapped open and shut on demand as the cat and the dog claimed either the outside or the inside. The cat watched the antics of the little dog with royal disdain and suspicion in her green eyes. The dog watched the antics of the cat with humor in his brown eyes, his tongue rolling out the corner of his mouth.

And at night, when they slept on their pet beds in the laundry, the girls would silently slip down the stairs to rub their bellies and stroke their fur, innately afraid that someone would come and take them away in the dead of night.

# Chapter Eleven

"Indigo, I have a favor to ask you. It concerns your brother." He looked at me with smiling eyes, and not for the first time, I felt that nothing was beyond his reach. It was a comfort I enjoyed, and buoyed by his calm told him what we needed. His face turned serious for a second. He nodded, then walked away to speak to Stefarino.

One down, plenty to go. I signaled to Sandra, and she waltzed over to where I had set up my little desk. As usual, happiness and joy bubbled out of her like a fountain.

"Tell me the story about the drone that shot us down."

"Visuals, or just the summary."

"Summary."

"Okay, it was an NVX-7, long-range, designed to sit in a battlespace for two or more days, just loitering until a target turns up. It was prepositioned where it shot us down just an hour after we flew into the States. Where it launched from is not clear, they used the same black hole technology that has been dogging us from day one. The missiles were ARM-12 heat seekers, again long range, and the fact that our pilot avoided three of them speaks to his incredible skill."

"Who owns the drone, and who owns the missiles?"

"The drone is, or was, on the US Airforce register; the missiles came from Israel, and Shami has confirmed they went missing two months ago, around the time we started looking for how the weapons were stolen from the US."

"Have the Israelis checked their current stock of weapons?"

"Full physical search currently underway, same with the Americans. The drone went missing three months ago, before the first terrorist attack on the Vatican."

"Okay. What does the video from the carrier show?"

"The drone flying a slow racetrack pattern, aligning itself with our flight path as we flew under it, the missiles firing, then a bit later, the drone being shot down by the Agis Destroyer."

"Was our flight path so predictable?" She broke out into a full-face grin, obviously enjoying me peppering her with questions. Not once had she looked down at her notes. Her eyes had never left mine.

"Really good question. Prior to the terrorist attacks, most aircraft from the US flying to Europe took the northern great circle route have been doing it for years, with more land area for them to make an emergency landing on. Since the attacks and the loss of access to aviation fuel, most transport flights now use the southern great circle route, it's an hour shorter. We used it because of military flight, and we didn't expect to get shot down."

"But military flight, so the carrier group just happened to be almost underneath us?" She smiled again; at this rate, I would have to put a bag over her head.

"Well, the short answer is the nature of the cargo in this case; apparently, the boss called the general, and the general called an admiral, and so it goes. But lucky for us, in any case." I thought that over and nodded. If the navy hadn't turned up when they did, the police might well have managed to take us prisoner, although, to be honest, I couldn't visualize how they would have survived the nasty little H&K MP-47 Sandra had tucked away in her shoulder bag. I had seen her shoot up close and personal, and I had every confidence she would have shot our way out of trouble in a heartbeat, and it would all be on her because at the time the police turned their guns on us, my weapon was still in my shoulder bag!

"Next, I have a new role for you. You've just been promoted to my intelligence officer, unpaid, immediate, on top of anything else you need to do. I want you to gather all the data from the Pakistanis on the money flow from Ireland and onwards; I want everything Amira has, as she has it; I've already organized boots on the ground in Ireland, speak to Indigo and get the details, then keep me posted. And I want a conference with all the geeks in geekdom within the hour, including Indigo and his tribe, and I'll give you an agenda shortly. Questions?"

"Only one. What's the boss on about with his Town Hall meeting at fourteen hundred hours?" My time to smile. It felt good to actually know something 'just call me Sally' didn't.

"Guess you'll have to wait to find out." I shooed her away with a hand wave and started to get my head around how to package all the disparate data we had and turn it into a cohesive picture. Indigo won my heart again, handing me yet another mug of his excellent espresso. I waved him to the seat next to me, and he sat, turning his chair so we could see each other.

"I spoke to my brother, and he will work out how to do as you asked. He feels that it is taking their movement in a new direction, but because it's you asking, he is prepared to make that move." I gave that some thought, the monk and his ministry were very much concerned with recording everything they could about the history of all religions and all the artifacts that had been gathered in the various churches, monasteries, and dungeons over the centuries. And suddenly, a question occurred to me. "How did the bombing of the Vatican affect your brother's business?" He looked a little puzzled by the question, then seemed to get the intent of it.

"He had two monks in the Vatican at the time of the attack, and he suffered for that, as you would expect. But his Order had a good relationship with the Vatican for many years, so they had recorded and documented much of what was stored in the Tombs. He expects to be able to present much of what was lost in the physical form back to them virtually at some point, perhaps when they have elected their new Pope."

"I feel for your brother's loss, and I apologize for not thinking of it earlier."

"Commander, you have had many things on your mind, it is good you ask now, and I will pass your sympathy onto my brother when next we speak." I nodded my acceptance, wondering how all the people in the world who had lost family and friends in the chaos of the last three months were coping, as just the thought of two dedicated monks being vaporized brought an ache to my heart and tears to my eyes. I nodded again, not trusting myself to speak for a moment. As if sensing my emotional state, Indigo reached out and patted me on the shoulder, smiled, stood, and marched back off into the fray, the noise from the geek squad suddenly filling my ears again.

"Commander, you called for me?"

I looked up and was surprised to see Fay standing in front of my desk, wearing a very creased green suit, her usual luster and shine missing. Flying for thirty or forty hours would do that to you.

"Hi Fay, thanks for getting back as quickly as you did. Go have a shower, freshen up, grab a meal, and see you back here at fourteen hundred hours." She picked up her overnight bag and disappeared into the bowels of the office. Before I could catch my breath, Sandra was back, open mini in her hands and a look on her face that spelled trouble.

"Over here," and I pointed to a little private set up in a dark corner with a large screen and a thick black curtain that could be pulled around us to give privacy. She flicked the image from her mini to the screen, and once it settled, the lovely young face of my favorite genius swam into view.

"Amira, hi! How are you?" She beamed at me, then her face tilted slightly and she seemed a little less happy.

"You might not like me all that much when I tell you what I have found?" I smiled. This poor girl had the roughest of times during this whole chaotic disaster, first being thrown in jail as a hacker/terrorist, then being questioned by three security services, each of whom wanted to throw her into a deep dark hole, then released with a tracking bracelet on her ankle, until she was finally released in my care to help solve the identity and location of the terrorists. Terrorists had stolen her work and turned it into the deadliest attack on the planet ever experienced since the extinction of the dinosaurs.

"Amira, without you, we would not have put the terrorists behind bars. What have you found?"

"The techniques they used were identical to the ones I developed back at Harvey Mudd. However, they used the nanomachines to meld the copper and brass substrate at the molecular level to produce a composite with a very fine stratum. If you look at the torpedo shape we saw in the satellite images, you can see that the various sections meld together in such a way as to form a contiguous metallic substrate."

"In English?" She smiled, as did Sandra, who undoubtedly understood the ramifications of what Amira was describing.

"Well, if, for example, you had a radioactive substance inside the torpedo, the radiation would not be able to be detected."

"How?"

"The brass/copper substrate has a different atomic composition, and the radioactive molecules can't get through it."

"If it were a bomb, it would be undetectable by normal means?"

"Yes. You could fill this up with uranium, plutonium, strontium, anything you like, stand next to a radiation detector, and you would get a negative reading."

"And you estimate this vessel could hold six kilos of atomic matériel?"

"Yes." So now we potentially had a dirty bomb that couldn't be detected by the infrastructure most countries had installed post-9/11.

"What was the main thrust of your work with this at Harvey Mudd?"

"It was very much a sideline. It was being worked by some of my students, almost as a spare time activity. I was looking for the effects of using the nanomachines on different substrates and any long-term effects they might have. I didn't even take my notes with me when I ran. It was that low on my priority list." I thought very hard for a moment, then noticed Sandra bouncing up and down on her seat.

"Yes?"

"Amira, does the new substrate have an atomic number?"

"Yes, of course, a brand new one, but it does have one."

'And could you detect it from a distance?" She bounced even more, almost to the point where I wanted to tie her to her seat. On the other end of the call, Amira had gone very quiet, then she suddenly looked at the camera and grinned.

"Give me an hour." And she closed the circuit. I looked at Sandra with a critical eye.

"What do you know that I don't?" The sly grin she gave me suggested she thought the list was long, so I just ignored her, sat back, and folded my arms. And waited her out. An investigator's greatest tool-silence. She folded in less than a minute, laughing as she poked me in the arms.

"You know my background, I studied with Chicago SWAT, and they had a division dedicated to tracking and disarming dirty bombs. One of the things I learned is that every metal gives an atomic signature at the molecular level when it gets excited."

"Excited? How?"

"Well, different metals, different wavelengths. And most of the detection was at close quarters, like inside a factory or building. I don't know if it will work in this case, but Amira will figure it out if anyone can."

"Humm. You might be useful to keep around a little longer."

All I got for my sarcasm was a bigger smile and bigger bounces on the chair. I thought about what to do next, as the idea of an undetectable dirty bomb sent chills up my spine. But given the chaotic state of most nations due to the aftermath of the terrorist attacks, I couldn't see for the life of me what the motive could be. What could you ransom? What could you demand? I saw the boss walking back into the room and stood to meet him.

"Boss, I've got civilian boots on the ground in Ireland, England, France and Germany. How have you gone otherwise?" He looked at me with that speculative gaze he used so effectively to distract people, then shook his head. I got the message. Not now, not here. He nodded towards the big screen, took me by the shoulder, looked deep into my eyes, and smiled.

"It's time."

I mentally flinched for the first time in a long time, not sure of what would happen next. We walked over to the central workstation in front of the huge wall screen. The boss nodded to Indigo. He barked a string of instructions in Italian, and the screen started to fill with little boxes, then people.

"Good afternoon, ladies and gentlemen. You are all using our secured mini-computers?"

Every head nodded, including that of General Bridges and the heads of the FBI, NSA, and CIA. Arie, our recent exports back in Pakistan. Tom, where ever he was, Bob, same deal, John Vernon and his partner in Helena, Senji-san and Namoki-san in Toyoko, even Pete in faraway Daintree Forrest, and a few agents I hadn't met or worked with yet, but obviously had been issued minis.

"As of this time, control of Section Five will pass to Commander Riley. She will lead Section Five as I am moving into the chair in Geneva." Silence, total and absolute silence, and from the look on the faces on the screen, not a little surprise. "That is all. Thank you for your good work. It has been my privilege to work with you all." And the big screen went blank, and for the first time that I could remember, the entire office was silent, almost as if we were frozen at the moment. Then one of the geeks started on his keyboard, and bit by bit, normal life returned to the office. The boss took my arm, and led me to his little hideaway in the corner, shut the door behind me, and pushed me gently into a chair.

"Okay, good, that's over. Pete looked good, didn't he?" I shook my head to clear my thinking, this was the last thing I had on my mind, but when I pulled the image of Pete in, I nodded.

"Yes, he did. Recovering quickly. How long do I keep him off the role?"

"If it were me, at least another month or two. He was badly wounded, lost a lot of blood, and yes, he heals well, but he needs to be one hundred percent before we abuse him again." I nodded, I had only been shot once, just seconds after Pete had taken his hits, and my shoulder still wasn't at full capacity.

"When do you leave?"

"Now. Questions?"

I looked at him and tried to remember the first time I had seen his camouflaged face in the night scope, just before I pumped six shots into him, center mass, and then taken him in handcuffs to the base hospital. It seemed like yesterday, but it was now six years ago, probably the best six years of my career, if truth be told. We had taken down the very worst of the worst together, and I had trusted him implicitly and looked to him for leadership, inspiration, and answers. I had grown accustomed to his presence, his unswerving support, and the intangible stimulus he always provided for my thinking.

And at times, he had irritated the hell out of me, just on principle! I stood up and gave him a full-body hug, squeezed as hard as I could, and let my chin rest on his broad shoulder.

"You're a pure bastard, but you've been my pure bastard, and I'll miss you." I pulled back so I could see into his deep blue eyes. "Thank you, I'll do my best not to let you down." He just hugged me back, then pushed me away at arm's length, and rolled his shoulders.

"Don't let yourself down, and I'm always there if you need a chat." I nodded, walked out of his little cubbyhole, you could hardly call it an office, and straight into Indigo.

"*Mi scusi, comandante, ha una chiamata urgente da Amira.*" I pulled my mini out as I went back to my little desk and opened it to find Amira's face full screen. "Commander, we can track the copper/brass substrate. We are still working out the exact details, but in simple terms, when we excite the metal with a laser, we get a reaction that we can pick up on a specific frequency. We need to determine the best frequency for both the laser and the detector. We will have that by closing of business today. I just thought you should know the good news as soon as possible."

I smiled, a genuine full-face monster. I almost yelled out to her, then realizing what had transpired just minutes before, pulled myself back into control and lowered the volume of my happiness.

"Amira, thank you, that is the best news possible." I sat there, seeing a way forward, even without the fine detail. I had a new and different role to play now. I had to provide both the leadership and inspiration that was needed to drive multi-cultural teams of investigators, soldiers, and scientists to their best possible performance. Half of me was still bewildered by the newness of the role, the other half petrified I would stuff it up.

"Commander, I have the information from Pakistan. And there is no family in Ireland that can be traced to our nuclear scientist." Sandra was still her usual bouncy self, but I noticed she was a fraction more contained, like she had wound down the happiness meter to eighty percent, and I hoped the transition in our organization would not affect her bubbly personality too much.

"Yes, please, let's see where the money went." I looked at the figures and blanched. This was not good news. Not good at all. "Call Arie immediately. Pass him this data, please. And check all the universities she supposedly went to, see if they have records."

She walked off to make the calls, and I looked at the data again. The funds-all twenty million euros had been first deposited into a local bank in Islamabad, then had been immediately transferred to a local Hawala, one we knew had its main head in Gaza and was controlled by Hamas. And Amir Abbas, the head of this terror group, had personally launched the two attacks on the Israeli supermarkets, using automated technology to drive the trucks into the venues and explode them.

And now he had twenty-two million euros to play with and nuclear-capable shells.

Heaven help Israel.

# Brotherhood

F rancis Alistair was named for his grandfather, a rotund barrel of a man, given to huge belly laughs and massive generosity. A father of five, he and his wife Morea had adopted another five 'to even the odds', as she was wont to say to any who commented on her massive brood. As luck would have it, the family ended up with five boys and five girls, all crammed into a little wooden hut that had more juts than doorways, built by Francis senior and added to as and when the demand came along. Peat fires warmed every room. There was a chicken shed and yard, not that the chickens were ever inside them, three sheep, a cow, and a vegetable patch that, with a lot of love from Morea and a little magic, produced a good supply for the table year around.

When he was not adding to their ramshackle house, Francis worked at anything that needed doing, from plumbing, woodwork, roofing, digging foundations, or just generally helping out. And while most jobs paid a little, most did not, but provided a table for bartering services and goods, again, as needed.

The village of Ballybay, in County Monaghan, had never boasted a population bigger than twelve hundred souls, so it was as it should be in the emerald island that everyone knew everyone else, and over the centuries, the families had mingled and matched, and as Francis Senior loved to say in the local pub at the top of his bawdy voice, "My sister's granny is your cousin's mother and I can prove it!" to the mirth of all in earshot.

Over the years, the town had modernized, and its strategic position between five major roads leading north, south, west and east had allowed it to stretch its roots and combine modern thinking with old-world values. It had been home to the Alistair's for over three hundred years, and while the wooden house had expanded, been modernized, and even made to look like it belonged in the current century, its original makeshift charm remained, and Francis, the younger, retired to it as often as he could. As a religious scholar and now lecturer at Belfast University, he enjoyed all the privileges the university had to offer while enjoying the freedom to roam the entire length and breadth of Ireland on the little stipends he was able to scrape together from interested parties, searching for stories and artifacts of the fabulous and mystical history of the country.

The fact that an overly large proportion of his work involved understanding magic, fairies, and tall tales was made all the more easier when he found the forgotten stone dances (DoChara) across the country, mostly off the beaten track, and where little or no tourist traffic ventured; some of the stone dances had been dated at over three thousand years old, as proven by the university science lab. What drew him were the stories told about the dances by the locals, stories passed down from generation to generation, stories that had at their heart the very soul of the Irish people. So he faithfully recorded all these stories in pubs and homes, some that would rival his own for their unique style and manner of leaning into the wind, and passed all that he learned back to the university and to his brother in faraway Venice.

And he had kept a handwritten diary in an old leather journal, now forty years old, in the hope that one day he could put together a story to take to his parish and make them proud of their ancestors.

He was trusted as much in the north as he was in the south, had wandered the countryside in his dusty and sometimes sodden robes for thirty years, and in that time, had learned the names of every man or woman who ran a pub or little boarding house. As he was currently on a short sabbatical, hoping to visit his ailing aunt in faraway Ashborne, being asked to make a small detour to Dublin was no effort at all. Plus, his brother had offered to pay for his whole trip, plus a healthy bonus for the local parish if Francis thought it necessary.

So he packed his meager belongings into a shoulder bag, bid his mother, sisters, and brothers goodbye, and amongst the hugging and well-wishers, set out on foot for the south.

He had not travelled ten minutes when the first lorry stopped, piled to its limits with wood and hay.

"Can I offer you a ride, father?" The face was weathered, wrinkled, and bore a scar or two but warm and friendly, with an old battered pipe leaning out one side of her mouth. "I'm Molly, and I'd be off to Ardee if that's of any help to ya."

Francis smiled at the kind woman, climbed in the rusted door, made the sign of the cross, and settled in amongst the bridles and leather gear that struggled for a room in the cab.

"Molly, I thank you, I would be Brother Francis, and I think I know your father."

She burst out laughing, pulled the truck back onto the bitumen, and sucked on her empty pipe. "Francis, me boy, if that be so, you know he hasn't moved from his seat at the pub in these ten years or so!"

Francis joined in her laughter and relaxed. "It's your truck, Molly. My own Da has worked on it a time or two. Even had it at our house one time, waiting for parts. Sean McGuire is no stranger to us, and I'm pleased to finally meet his brilliant and beautiful daughter."

She looked at him out of the corner of one eye, keeping the other fixed on the big rig that headed towards them on the wrong side of the road. Being part of the European Union was a fine thing for Northern Ireland, but the uncertainty of the European drivers as to which side of the bloody road they would occupy at any one time made for some interesting passing maneuvers!

"And who said I was brilliant, as I surely am?"

"Your Da kept mentioning it every time we saw him. The way you run the mill and the family now that your mother's past, God bless her, the pride in you was naked on his face." She looked at him with a thoughtful look, having survived the passing of the b-double, which had moved to the right side of the road just in time to avoid a head-on crash.

"Well, he's been a good father to me and mine, so perhaps I can forgive him for babbling. Where might ya be headed, young Francis?"

The pale blue sky had little wisps of clouds playing hide and seek in the misty morning air, and the early sun hung low on the horizon. Apart from the racking and coughing sound of the old truck's motor, all was still and quiet.

"I'd be making my way to Ashbourne initially to see an aunt who's feeling a bit poorly, then to Dublin when I can." She just nodded, thinking of the health of her own family, now that the chaos from the terror attacks had quieted down a little. Being staunch Catholics, the attack on the Vatican had devastated her and her family, and the stupid youths that took up bricks and stones to smash at things in the aftermath had been put down without ceremony by the local Garda.

So the chaos had only lasted a few days, with the small towns and villages all over Ireland closing up around their long-suffering citizens in an attempt to help them heal. While religion had been at the foundation of the Irish Troubles for a century or more, every denomination rallied around the Catholics as if they were their own. It had been mentioned more than once in more than one pub that this healing had brought the country together more so than anything in the history of the Emerald Island.

Her family was particularly long-lived, and while it had been some time since she had celebrated her seventieth birthday, she had a sister and a brother a decade older than her, and wasn't that a worry? She turned to look at the young priest, for that is what she thought of him as, noticing that his cassock had been mended in several places and the collar of his shirt was frayed around the edges. "If you're not in a hurry, it might be I can get you to Ashbourne later today, and I know a good friend who drives to Dublin every other day if you'd be interested in a lift."

He looked over at her, not in the least amazed at her kind offer, he had experienced the generosity of the heart of hundreds of locals over the years, and he was, and always would be, humbled by it.

"Would you allow me to contribute to the cost of your fuel, perhaps?" he asked, reaching into his bag to grab a pound note. She laughed and shook her head.

"No, brother Francis, not at all. But you can buy me a pint when we get to Ardee."

He smiled in return, put his only pound away, and nodded his acceptance. A bargain well done.

They drove in comfortable silence, the kilometers rolling by at a steady rate until they hit the outskirts of Ardee.

"We'll just drop off the timber at the golf club, then the hay at the riding club, grab a sandwich and a pint at the local, then I'll take you to your aunt's."

"And I thank you, Molly McGuire, for your kindness."

It only took half an hour to unload the timber, with the help of the groundskeeper, another half an hour at the riding club, where three young women in smart riding jodhpurs and polished boots helped move the hay, and then in another two hours, they were in one of the oldest pubs in Ireland, the Pig 'n Whistle, where the walls exuded the smoke and smell centuries old, the floor stained with both beer and blood and the locals giving the gimlet eye to anyone they didn't recognize.

"Molly, my love, come sit on my lap, and who's that strapping lad you've brought with ya?" The voice was crusted with laughter, and the face was as old as sin. The baggy pants, hanging on a shrunken frame, were only outdone by a patched and tattered woolen shirt partially hidden by a leather motorcycle jacket also patched.

"Don't be fussing with me, Michael O'Connor, or I'll sit on yer lap and cause you a heart attack!" The pub erupted with laughter, and pints were poured with generosity as the monk and his friend was welcomed. An hour later, they parted, and an hour after that, the monk said his goodbyes, with the address of the truck driver he would call on in the next two days for a ride down to Dublin.

# Chapter Twelve

The geeks had split up a huge task between themselves and squeezed it in around everything else they were doing. But after only three days, Indigo had a list of refugee women whose families did not exist, an element that had been determined would help pinpoint who was playing the terrorist game and who wasn't.

As he had been requested by Jessica, the results of the world-wide search were sent to every country, forty-seven all told, which was quite a surprise to everyone concerned. Mohammad bin Azaria had been much busier than Interpol had expected. All told, six hundred and fifty refugees had been placed over a twenty-year period, and the search had discovered that twenty-two had disappeared from their families, over and above those already in custody. There were a few exceptions-the Anaisha family, Reve, and Nazreen had been in plain sight due to their adopted mother's need to be seen to be running her Asia-wide technology giant, Innomatchi, which had manufactured all the terrorists' hardware for the environmental plants, the production of the nanites, and the artificial intelligence games that had created the attack plan the terrorists had used so successfully.

So as Jessica read the summary, deducting the names she already knew from having locked them up just a month ago, she calculated that they now had potentially twenty new faces to uncover, having already seen the photos of Siobhan O'Cleary. And she would put her next paycheck on the fact that nineteen of the women would be located in the nineteen countries scheduled to receive one of the boxed environmental plants.

Which left just one more.

And who and where she was a mystery for another time, as she had a far bigger problem on her mind.

Did they, or did they not, have a large number of dirty bombs in play, and if they did, where in hell were they? She had to push Amira to speed up her research. It had become her priority mission since she had first woken to the silence of the canal outside her bulletproof window. It was one of those weird days in Venice where the air was crisp and clear, a little warm, but the promise of a very humid day was lurking on the horizon in the form of rolling black thunderheads, which while very beautiful as a spectacle, in practical terms would trap the warm air over the canals underneath them and create a steam bath for the locals.

She showered, noticed her bullet scar had faded just a little, rolled her shoulders to prove it, then dressed in office casual, in this case, cargo pants, a tucked-in silk shirt, and her well-worn dull brown combat boots. Not very lady-like, she could count on Fay and Sandra to get the men's blood flowing, but immensely practical, given what she would do today. She opened her door and almost walked into Sandra, resplendent in a light gray pants suit, with matching low-heeled boots, her longish flaxen hair tied up in a bob.

"What are you doing up so early?"

"You're up, I'm up." She simply turned on her heel and headed for the communal kitchen, where Indigo was grilling bacon and eggs in a huge black cast iron pan. "You know, the 'where you go, I go' thing is over and done with, don't you?" She turned back, looked at me, and smiled.

"No, it isn't. If anything, it's even more important now than before. The bounty on your head went up overnight to ten million euros, so you can count on all the crazies coming out of the wood-work." I shook my head, completely unhinged by the stupidity of whoever was posting the bounty.

It wasn't the women. I had a strong feeling about that. No one had been directly hurt by any of them, though I had to admit millions and millions had been indirectly killed or hurt by their terrorist attacks.

"The geeks have cleaned all of us off the data files. No one can track us now as they did before." She looked a little serious, which stopped me in my tracks. Miss battery bunny was saving some of her normal sunshine to make her point with me, so I took notice.

"That may be so, boss, but having seen up close and personal just how far the crazies will go to take you out, I'm not going to let you take any more chances than you have to." I smiled, patted her on the shoulder, and walked towards the table that had been set for breakfast.

"What, so a little ambush in Chicago and getting shot out of the sky gets your knickers in a twist?" I said, letting the amusement in my voice soften my words. Her face didn't lose its seriousness. She just sat opposite me, reached for a coffee mug just as Indigo reached over to pour, looked me straight in the eyes, and said nothing.

Powerful, very powerful. I decided to play it straight. 'What would you have me do?"

"Limit your outside exposure for the next week, give the geeks time to back-track the bounty, then we can take it from there." I thought for a minute exposure wasn't my problem. Not enough time was if we really did have a pile of nukes out there just waiting to go off. And besides, I was dressed for a trip I intended to make today. A platter of bacon, eggs, toast, and jam took my attention off my immediate problem 'call me Sally', who had resumed her bouncy, smiling, overly happy persona as she had been served her breakfast.

"I'm making a short trip today, you can select the transport arrangements, but I want to be in Amira's office ASAP." I dug into my breakfast, warmed by the spices Indigo had woven into the eggs. Sandra chose to ignore me, so I worked on cleaning up my plate and grabbing another cup of coffee. By the time I had finished, Fay had arrived, and now I had two competitors for the best dressed of the day. She wore a fitted suit of dark blue over a crystal white blouse, the collar of which had little silver piping things running around the edge. I shook my head, wouldn't last a minute in a firefight, and with this thought, I had an epiphany.

Neither Sandra nor Fay had long-term exposure to constant threats. Fay had come out of the FBI, where she had only drawn her weapon twice in six years and fired it in heat only once. Sandra had great training with SWAT, but again, had hardly used her weapon under combat conditions. The boss and Pete, on the other hand, had constantly lived in the theatre of kill or be killed, had deep, dark military backgrounds, and the use of weapons was innate. Maybe the passing of command had also passed a lessening of the military mindset? I would have to watch that, Section Five was the pointy end of Interpol, and we had been created specifically to manage the worst of the worst and terminate threats to the countries who were our members.

Just as I rounded off my introspection, Indigo tapped me on the shoulder.

*"Mi scusi comandante, la sua barca è fuori e un elicottero sarà pronto per lei all'aeroporto."*

"Thanks, Indigo. I'll be ready in five." I wiped my mouth and stood up just as Sandra and Fay rose, mirroring my movements. We moved into the conference area. I checked the status board, checked to see where everything was at, noticed the night shift was changing over, relaxed in the cool, calm atmosphere that floated around the room like a warm blanket on a cold night, then walked out to the jetty, where a police boat bobbed in the early morning swell. Two of Indigo's uniformed guards held the boat still. I climbed on, then got a gentle push from Sandra as she followed me.

The helicopter was waiting, and inside a few hours, I was inside Amira's secret lab, watching her work behind a glassed-in Level Four isolation area. In a full pressure suit, helmet, face shield, and wearing glasses and an oxygen mask, she could have been anyone, except for her sharp look when I arrived. That's all I got because she bent to whatever she was doing and ignored us.

I turned at a tap on my shoulder to see Colonel Shami Borowitz, surprisingly in uniform, smiling and holding a submachine gun across his chest.

"Shami, I hope you haven't been using that?" I said, pointing to the weapon. "No, Commander, just training. After those two attacks, while you were here, the brass wanted to tighten things up, so even we geeks have to play soldier three days a week." I smiled at him. The idea of any Israeli playing a soldier, given the number of attacks they suffered every day, was so far from possible as to be fiction.

"Good to see you. How is Arie?" As I asked this question, Arie walked into the lab, looking just a little more worn than the last time I had seen him on the big screen.

"Hello, Jessica and Inspector Thomas. Good to see you both again."

"Hi, Arie. I was just asking after you. Could I get five minutes with you, please?" He smiled and waved us over to a glassed-in office, a huge microscope filling one corner. We squeezed in and sat on the metal chairs, forming a loose square.

"What's on your mind, Jessica? I can see the wheels turning from over here!" My turn to smile again. He had this grandfatherly way of speaking, with just the hint of a twinkle in his eyes. As the so-called retired head of one of Israeli's prime spy and intelligence agencies, he had been roped into working again by the terrorist attacks, one of which had taken out a giant chunk of the Dome of the Rock, as well as the Western Wailing Wall, virtually at the same time as the Vatican was bombed out of existence. Arie had worked closely with us to shut the terrorists down permanently.

"We need to form a rapid response team, probably six to eight people, shooters and scientists, capable of defusing a dirty bomb or at least containing it. They will need to be highly mobile, attached to Section Five, and multi-lingual."

"Languages?"

"Arabic, French, Italian, German, English, Russian, Chinese, and all the dialects — in my mind, this is one of the eight, a professional linguist, not necessarily a shooter, but able to shoot if needed to defend." He went very quiet and very still. Shami mirrored him, then dropped his eyes to his toes. Then he looked up and smiled at me.

"Commander, we have one such person already on our team, he works with my section, but I fear he may not be available to you."

"Shami, I know who you mean, and you are correct. However, there is a woman who we know from her time here in Israel studying some years ago, who is reputed to be able to speak and read in almost any language, currently working for the UN. She is Lebanese by birth, now a naturalized citizen of Israel. We know of her because she has helped us out from time to time." Shami looked at Arie, a sour look on his face.

"You mean Bazif Akili?" Arie looked at Shami and nodded.

"Do you have an objection to that?" he asked softly, letting us know that there was something between Shami and Bazif. He looked down again, then slowly nodded his head.

"She will do what she will do. It's nothing to do with me." He stood, nodded to us, then left the room, closing the door quietly behind him.

"They were an item?" Sandra asked.

"Yes. For some time, until Bazif moved to Geneva. She felt contained here, like so many of our young people do, but I'm sure if you ask her, she will stand for your team. Do you want all eight from Israel?" I shook my head.

"No, Aire. I've already asked Indigo, and he'll give me four. And I haven't approached the Americans yet. I think they might give us a whole team if it looks like they may be involved."

"Good. I'll work on who to send to you. Do you want me to contact Bazif?"

"Thank you, that would be excellent. As far as rapid response goes, can you help out there? Indigo can give us a helicopter, a fast boat, and a mid-sized fast jet. What I'd like from you is a very big drone, maybe two, long-range. We can control them from Venice once you release them to us."

"Weapons, cameras, sensors?"

"Yes, please, all three. Hellfire's or their equivalents, something that can take out a large boat, a b-double, that scale of a target. You might care to deidentify them, and we'll need to move them around Europe, starting with Ireland." He thought about that. It had been an Israeli drone that terrorists had stolen and used in the attack on the Dome of the Rock, so undoubtedly, some sensitivity still remained around that choice of weapon.

"I can give you one of our C-17s, the same aircraft you used to fly to Libya in. We can posit it as an exercise and get preapprovals from the EU and UK Air Traffic Control. The biggest issue we will have is fuel." He thought for a moment, then held up his hand. "And I think we can give you a transportable control cockpit for the drones on board the aircraft."

"That would be excellent. And if you give me a list of key airports, I'll set the fuel up with the UN." He gave me a look I hadn't seen previously from under his thick eyebrows.

"The UN? They have aviation fuel sequestered away?" I just grinned.

"No names, no pack drill, we'll have what you require wherever you need it." I thought for a moment, collecting all the little bits and pieces that seemed to fly around in my mind more and more these days. I really needed breathing space to collect them all into little organized bubbles. "Aire, as yet, we see no direct threat to you, but could you formally commission us to act on behalf of Israel?"

"Absolutely. This has been our intention since we uncovered the web material from Ireland. And to be frank, a dirty bomb is one of the things we fear the most."

"Why?"

"Because they are so hard to detect. Amira tells us that the design of these torpedoes is such that it would not allow radioactivity to escape, so you would not be able to detect it by normal defensive means."

"We might have a solution for that. That's where the drones come in." He gave me one of his hopeful looks, and my heart went pitty-pat just once. He should have met my mother; they would have been a perfect pair!

"Amira is experimenting with a way to make the bombs visible. I don't know the details. She's still working on it, but she was excited, so I expect a good result."

"When was the last time Amira wasn't excited?" Sandra smiled, pointing to the figure of Amira in her Level 4 bio-suit jumping up and down in the containment area, waving at us through the glass. Arie pressed a little button on the desk, and her shouts became clearer.

"Jessica, Jessica, we can track them!" I stood, turned to Amira and gave her the thumbs up, tapped my wrist, and opened my arms, miming, 'how long'?

"I'll be out of deco in ten minutes."

"Can you wait with us, Arie? What she tells us might change our equipment requirements." We all stood and walked out into the holding area in front of the laboratory.

"Is that what you want the drones for?" I nodded.

"Based on what Amira told us initially, it suggested we might need an illuminating source and a detection source, so two drones." His turn to nod, and we settled into a comfortable silence, only broken by Amira's enthusiastic emergence from the decontamination chamber.

"Jessica, we can track the bombs!" I smiled and patted her on the shoulder. Even with the top half of her bio-suit folded down over the bottom half, she still radiated energy and natural beauty that had taken my breath away from the very first time I had met her, with her hands and feet in chains. I had three strong and vibrant women in my life that dressed better than I did; they looked fantastic at the worst moments of their lives and constantly buzzed with excitement. I was getting old.

"Okay, tell us how to do it." Waving her hands, she painted a picture in the sky, which, even as a non-geek, I understood.

"We iridate a wide area with a laser. I have the exact frequency for that, then using a detector I have rigged up but will be productionized for you, you can paint the brass/copper substrate to within half a meter. If we use a combination of light detection and ranging (LIDAR), a ground penetration style radar, and this little gadget I just invented, you can look at a broad beam scope overlayed with mapping data and pinpoint where they are."

"Can you tell if it is carrying radioactive material?"

"No. But we can measure the density of the bomb and tell you if it is carrying more than just the shell."

"How do you do that?" It sounded like science fiction to me, but then, as I have said a million times, not a geek! She looked at me as if I was testing her, so I held my hands out in a vulnerable position.

"Not a geek, remember?" She laughed, wriggling out of her bio-suit, which pooled at her ankles. Sandra bent to help her, and in seconds Amira appeared as if from a chrysalis, jeans and tee shirt untucked and very worn and faded. And even then, she looked like a beautiful young, full of energy, and happy woman. I envied her but was thankful she had been able to put all the betrayals behind her and move on from what the terrorists had done with her brilliant work. She walked to a whiteboard hanging on the wall and, using a marker, drew a lot of indescribable diagrams and equations. I looked on in amusement while Sandra walked closer, ran her fingers across the data, nodded, turned to me, and filled me in.

"Working on the density of the substrate, the size, and estimating the volume of the cavity, we can get a baseline density and weight of the torpedo. Using the scanners, we can then set a mark, and if it is above that, the bomb has something inside it. She paused, then continued.

"Very clever, Amira, Chicago SWAT was working on something like this last year, but they had to give it up due to a lack of skill." I looked at the board and had an idea.

"We estimated a six-kilo mass for the prime explosive, plus the trigger, so using your calculations, what does an empty bomb probably weigh?" She moved to the board, scribbled again, and long lines of equations streamed out beneath her fingers. I was almost sorry I had asked.

"Using the data we first accumulated back at Harvey Mudd on minimum wall thicknesses, etc., this bomb is seventy millimeters in diameter and eight hundred centimeters long. Or for you, Jessica, think six inches by two feet eight."

"That's not very big."

"It is if you put a six kilo-fifteen pound-nuclear material inside it, you'll get the explosive force of approximately one thousand five hundred tons of TNT. In layman's terms, that's a Zone 1 blast radius of ten to fifteen miles, Zone 2 of thirty to fifty, with the radioactivity spreading out another twenty to thirty miles, depending on the prevailing wind and the material used."

"What would make the worst type of nuclear bomb?"

"Plutonium and uranium, the usual suspects."

"And every nuclear power station produces plutonium all day long."

"Yes. But we have our eyes and ears on every known power station since the first attacks on the oil wells, but nothing's perfect." No, I thought to myself, it wasn't. But I learned another vital piece of information. My very own 'call me Sally', Sandra, was able to read high math and understood what went into a nuclear bomb. She never ceased to amaze me.

"Okay, thank you all, but answer my question. Loaded, what will they likely weigh?"

"We estimate twenty kilos or fifty pounds." I nodded. That lined up with what our geeks had guessed from the satellite photos.

"How far will your laser scan?" Amira looked at me with question marks in her brilliant eyes. It was nice to know I could momentarily befuddle a genius! Sandra saved me from further embarrassment.

"What Jessica is asking is if we mount the laser in a drone, for example, what would be the surface area we could cover?" My turn to smile because I knew part of this answer.

"Assume we cruise at twenty thousand feet-say six thousand meters. What would the width of the scanned surface be?" Amira went into her deep-thinking look, head down, eyes partially closed. One hand absently wiped the hair back from her ears.

"With enough power, I can give you a ten kilometer-sixteen-mile-scan. The detector will match that, and if you're thinking of one drone for each, they are small and light enough to fit in one airframe. The power source will supply them for thirty hours between charging, so if you take two drones, you could have continuous coverage 24/7."

"How long does it take to build your equipment and fit it to our drones?" Amira looked at Arie, who, in turn, looked at me. He shrugged his shoulders.

"I can have the drones for you in two days, the C-17 at the same time. Amira, how about your build time?"

"Two days will be great. And if I can come with, I can make any repairs or alterations as we go." Arie smiled as if he had been anticipating his agent's move to be included. But she was already attached to Interpol, so it shouldn't be an issue. He just nodded in his grandfatherly way and smiled.

"Okay, Arie, send me the list of airports where you will want fuel, and we'll expect the C-17 and its cargo three days from now. That gives you a day to fit everything and test it?" He nodded again, and Amira swooped up her bio-suit and literally ran out of the lab.

"Amira, make a second set or two for the Americans, please."

"I haven't seen her this happy in weeks."

"We'll do our very best to keep it that way."

# Making Friends

Brother Francis had seen his aunt, reassured himself that her family had her in hand, arranged for his brother to send his stipend for the trip to them, then walked off to find Molly's driver friend to hitch a lift to Dublin. Where he would stay, he didn't know. How he could afford anything, he also didn't know, having spent his sole punt on Molly's pint. But none of this uncertainty worried him. He had often set out on a search for a new Stone Dance or Faerie Hill with nothing but the cassock on his back, and a sturdy pair of old boots.

He believed, utterly, that what was meant to be would be and that if his need was great, some kind soul would provide for him and his quest. He pulled his cassock around his shoulders, the chill of the early morning cutting into him like a small knife made of ice. He sang himself an old Irish ditty about a 'rover boy', smiling the smile of the contented. His oft-repaired cassock flowed around his solid frame like a rich brown cape, and the hood at the back bounced up and down to his internal beat.

He found Molly's friend and, in two hours, was dropped off at a church that had survived over four hundred years, several invasions, and a fire or two yet still retained its original heft stone magic. He entered, bowed, used the holy water in the baptism font, then worked his way to the front pews, where he sat, admiring the filtered colored light that streamed in through the stained-glass window in the shape of a cross. Angles and cherubs danced and flew across the glass in perpetual happiness, lit by the bright streams of heavenly beams.

Here was peace and solitude, peace and harmony, peace and faith, where a travelling soul like himself could find balance. He was joined in the pew by a robed priest, who knelt in prayer before sitting back and patting the brother on the arm.

"Peace be unto you, and may the good Lord smile upon your quest."

"Thank you, father. On this quest, I will need all the help I can get."

"What do you need, my son?"

"Some time ago, two people met with some northern folk to negotiate a business deal. My brotherhood needs to know where this meeting occured and what was said. The safety of the world might depend on it."

"I see. Do you have a description of the two people?" The monk reached into his shoulder bag and pulled out three photos that had been laminated in plastic. These were blow-ups from the satellite picture taken in Afghanistan.

"It may well be only two of these three, but anything you can find out for us regarding any of them, such as where they live, what work they do, if any, what they might be doing now, will be gratefully received."

"Do you believe these people to be evil? Will they bring more pain and sorrow to our community?" The monk turned to face the priest, seeking his eyes, the better to see that he had the truth of it.

"My brothers believe that these three, or others associated with them, are planning an attack timed with the Easter festivities that could have a devastating impact on our community. I can't give you more details than this, it is all we have, but I believe with all that I am that we must take this seriously." The priest nodded, seemingly looking into himself as he spoke.

"The terror attacks of the past months have been a tragedy of unimaginable proportions, but thankfully the full effect of them has not been felt here in Ireland, apart from the thugs and stupid youths that acted out in the aftermath. Of course, we are all suffering from the lack of oil and gas, but we've been a peat economy in terms of small-scale heating for hundreds of years, and the move to electric vehicles two years ago has given us a head start."

"Aye, I agree. I see signs all over the country of life going on, with not all that much hardship. Except in the cities, where unemployment is rising by the day." The priest lowed his head and nodded to himself.

"Yes, here in Dublin, we've many a family out of work and in need of food, and again, being used to providing for ourselves, we're managing to help them as needed." They sat in comfortable silence for a minute, then the priest turned to the monk.

"I'll get these around for you. Where will you be staying, then?"

"I'm not staying anywhere in particular at this time; I can come back in a day or two to see what you have found." The priest looked at the monk, surprise in his gray eyes.

"You've not got anywhere to overnight? Then, of course, you can stay here at the rectory with me and Father Brian. Do you, by any chance, play cards?"

"Well enough to pay for my keep!" The monk laughed from deep in his belly, once again having been provided for by faith alone. Deep in his bones, he hoped against hope that he got answers on his quest that would prevent the unimaginable from happening, for he had been well briefed by his brother in faraway Venice, and it was all he could do to not fall to his knees and pray for all he was worth.

The next day, several punts richer, he walked into the boat yard that had been identified from the data provided by the accountants.

What he learned from the workers and staff meant nothing to him, so he passed it on to his brother with the schematics and pictures they had taken during the rebuild of the biggest boat they had ever worked on. The photos included the three strangers in the satellite blow-ups.

That night in the rectory, he lost all that he had won and enjoyed himself more. He was deep into his second pint when the blue minicomputer he carried in his satchel buzzed, so he excused himself from the game and opened the lid.

"Brother Francis, God be with you. The information you have found is excellent. We need one more favor from you. Can you take the photos of the people and try to establish where they might have lived?" The monk gave the question some thought. There was always a way to find people, and in this case, two were clearly Arabs or, at the very least, from that part of the world, and the woman was beautiful and had a known history — even though that may well be false. He nodded at the small camera.

"Brother, I will do my best."

"Blessed be, brother, your work is in God's hands, and we thank you for your efforts." The screen went blank, and the monk retired the mini to his pocket and re-entered the game, where his last chip sat proudly on top of his cards.

"Would ya be making a bet, Brother Francis, or would ya be begging to be let out of this hand?" The monk looked at his antagonist, a weedy man of just five feet, his black suit hanging on his skinny frame, his clerical collar flopping down his creased neck. He gave the priest a huge smile, then pushed his single chip into the pot.

"I'll call ya. There's no taking advantage of me justly because I had to answer a call!" The laughter rolled around the table, and the priest and monk turned over their cards to see that they both had exactly the same hand-two twos, two fours, and a king. And in the way of all those that had come before them, without an argument over which suit trumped which, a third of the pot went into the orphans' fund, the rest split between the winners. As the monk swept his chips towards him, he noticed that the cuff on one arm was frayed again and shook his head. He'll have to patch it some more. There was no sense in letting such a good robe go to waste!

# Chapter Thirteen

I looked at the boss in his uniform, a sight I would remember, as I couldn't remember seeing someone so uncomfortable in my entire service life.

"You look manly." He didn't smile. He just looked uncomfortable.

"I'm paying my respects to the UN. There's a formal change-over in Lyon later today. Right now, I'm in the Hague."

"Well, you look pretty. I'll be sure to tell the troops."

"What do you want, Jessica? I'm on the clock here." I smiled my very best girl smile; it was the first time I had really seen the boss uncomfortable.

"Your little black book didn't have anyone nominated as an expert on advanced weapons." He looked blank for a second or two, then dropped his eyes towards the ground.

"What type of weapons?"

"Nuclear." His head shot up at a rapid rate, his eyes opened wide, and he moved from where I had no idea, but his background blurred with the motion.

"Those little torpedoes in Afghanistan are nuclear bombs?"

"Don't know yet, haven't put all the puzzle pieces together. I need an expert on weapons delivery, someone who can look at blue-prints and drawings and divine what the hell is going on. I don't know if I'm looking at a delivery system, a bomb manufacturing factory, or a sexy new way of building a spa." He smiled at my attempt at humor, and right there, I saw the real boss, thank God.

"Send them to me, and I'll give them a look over. It will be a couple of hours until all this ceremonious stuff is over. Talk to you later." The screen went dark, so I just dialed the next person on my list.

"Stefarino, good morning. Thank you for taking my call. As usual, I need your help." He just smiled. I had only ever seen two expressions on his face, outright happiness, and thoughtfulness, he was perhaps the most centered, calm, and balanced individual I had ever had the pleasure to meet.

"Jessica, or should I call you Commander?"

"Jessica's just fine, Stefarino. They only gave me more rank so I could boss more people around." He laughed, enjoying the joke.

"Stefarino, I need you and your geeks to find a ship for me. Your monk has the latest and best information. Please thank him for us. Left Dublin three or four months ago, and I have no idea where it went. I'm sending you all the details we have, so can you look for 'black holes' over the oceans, see what you can find, and let us know the outcome, please?"

"Certainly. And I have a view of the ship data if you're interested?"

I felt myself goggled. What on earth would a band of monks dedicated to recording the religious history of the world know about high-tech armaments? He saw my confusion and widened his smile.

"Don't panic, Jessica, one of my geeks came to us very late in life, and he worked for the General Atomics Company for many years before he found the light. From his observation of the schematics, you have a high-powered rail gun, able to be elevated twenty degrees, firing a round that might weigh up to forty-five kilos. When he looked at the satellite images, then compared them to the mechanics of the rail gun, he drew this for us." And the head monk held up a beautiful pencil drawing that looked like a three-dimensional model of a long rocket with a pinched middle and little fins on the tail end. In the middle of the model, he sketched the outline of the torpedo.

I knew this weapon shape — it was called a sabot round, mostly used to kill tanks. In that use, it was a depleted uranium core encased in a body that gave it aerodynamic shape and mass, fired at high intensity to the point where on impact, it literally pulverized its target. In this iteration, according to the drawing, this round separated into propulsion, warhead, and guidance sections once fired, and on reaching the proximity of its target, dropped off the propulsion and guidance bits just leaving the torpedo to smash into its target, at supersonic speeds, that could well trigger a nuclear explosion.

"Where did the rail gun fit in?" I asked Stefarino.

"Our weapons expert suggests that the rail gun could be used to propel the round ten to twelve kilometers when the rocket in the tail ignites and flies the round to its target."

"What would be the extended range of the weapon?"

"We can only guess without seeing an actual round, but possibly another ten to fifteen kilometers."

"Outside the initial blast area of a nuclear weapon that size."

"Hypothetically. Remember, we are extrapolating here from drawings, schematics, and third and fourth-hand verbal reports."

"How was this rail gun fitted to the ship?"

"The reports suggest facing the stern, from the very topmost deck. Further, it would appear that the roofline can be tilted up, providing an unencumbered firing aperture."

"Someone is very serious about delivering these bombs."

"Yes, it would appear so."

"Stefarino, as always, thank you, I think we have to find this ship as soon as possible." He nodded, smiled, and hung up. I thought about my next call, mindful of the fact that crying wolf would damage our reputation irrevocably, but not giving the earliest possible warning could have disastrous consequences of monumental proportions. Then I thought about my team here in Venice and the agents we had scattered around the world and decided on a course of action we could not come back from.

"Sandra, get Fay a private room. Bring Indigo." She looked at me, had been sitting quietly across the desk, her face expressionless throughout my calls. I had decisions to make, but I welcomed her silence during the calls and her lack of questions. One of the biggest decisions was how to use my key people.

"Indigo, I want a summary of what we have here and what I am about to tell the US, in short form, sent to everyone who has a mini. At this time, eyes only. No action is required unless something triggers a response, but be on the alert. But first, we have to have a quick chat with Nokomoto-san."

"Nokomoto, full briefing in a minute, sending you some schematics. Need you to check Innomatchi and see if they are involved in any way, please." I hung up and group dialed, getting Malcolm, the directors of the NSA, CIA, and FBI, the general, Tom, Bob, agent RuPaul, and every agent with a mini right across the world. My mini was filled with little boxes with faces in them, and I flicked the screen up to the big one so I could as least see their facial expressions.

"Gentle people, this is a warning-out at this time. If anyone has information they think is relevant, contact me at the conclusion of this call, please."

No one said anything, even the general in faraway Washington held her peace. "Interpol believes there may be as many as ten small nuclear devices in play, there may be more, but let's stick with ten, and the timing may or may not be linked to an Irish Nationalist site. It may be that they are being carried in a ship. This information is speculative at present, but we felt it necessary to inform you of the possibility at this point."

"How sure are you that this is a credible threat?" The general had asked the question that was on everyone's lips, but she seemed calm on the screen, something for which I was thankful.

"General, we only have bits and pieces of the puzzle, but I would not have called if our confidence level was not greater than fifty percent."

"What size blast do you anticipate?"

"One thousand five hundred tons of TNT equivalent, plus fall out."

"Huh!" The general seemed to be reading from another portable computer as she looked off to one side momentarily.

"That's a Zone 1 blast radius of ten to twenty miles, Zone 2 of thirty to fifty miles, with the radioactivity spreading out another twenty to thirty miles, depending on the prevailing wind and the material used."

"That's the same information that we have."

"Well, we have good antiradiation detection and protection at every port and entry point on the continental United States, so we'll start looking."

"Won't do you any good. The bombs, in this case, are manufactured from a substrate composite of copper and brass, melded by nanites that have the same derivation as the ones used in the oil, gas, and coal attacks. I'm told no radioactivity will escape the cavity."

"Is this that Israeli woman's work?"

"No, not directly, just something that was taken from her lab while she was at Harvey Mudd. It was a third-level experiment. She hardly paid any attention to it."

"What are you doing about it" Now, there was a sharp edge to the general's voice, and her tonality left me in no doubt as to whom she was pointing her anger. Goes with the job, I thought to myself and mentally gave myself a big hug for having thought to ask Amira for a set of lasers and detectors for the Americans.

"We will have a detector device available in two days, we will cover Europe and Asia Minor, and I'll have a set of the devices sent to you for you to duplicate. There is a strong suggestion that any attack is planned for the Thursday before Easter, but there is a very large ship involved somewhere. What role it will play is not clear, but you might think in terms of setting up a picket line."

"So, let me get this clear. We may have ten nuclear devices with a kill range of twenty miles, plus another twenty or thirty for radiation, undetectable, may or may not be on their way here by ship, and we may have six weeks to find them?" I smiled when you said it succinctly and quickly. As the general had, it really didn't sound so bad.

"Yes, general, that just about sums it up." No one on the screens moved or added to the conversation. So I signed off, closed my mini, and looked at the three people now crowding my space. Indigo was the first to move, predictably off to his espresso machine. He returned with four steaming mugs, set them down, then stood behind Fay.

"Commander, what would you have me do at this time?" I looked at Fay and Sandra, seeking any reaction to my general broadcast, but got none. I rolled my shoulders.

"We have to put a team in the air, Arie's giving us a C-17 and two drones fitted out with detectors. Amira will be on board as the technical adviser. I want to scan all of Ireland and then move progressively across Europe. There's no reason why we can't scan on the way across to Ireland. That will give us a sense of how things work. Arie is going to scan his immediate area as a test of the system, and he'll let us know the outcome. Then we have an eight-man rapid response team being put together, four from Israel, four from Italy, plus one of you in command. The team will have a language expert to help with any translation required. There are a lot of holes in this plan initially. I hope to address them before they get us into the s-h-one-t up to our eyeballs. Comments, suggestions, speak up now or forever hold your peace!" Everyone laughed. Quoting Shakespeare was just quirky enough to ease the tension. Indigo stood tall, puffed his chest out, and almost saluted but managed to reign himself in at the last moment.

*"Comandante, sarà un piacere prendere la squadra di pronto intervento sotto la mia ala protettrice!"* I looked at Indigo, both Sandra and Fay turned their heads, and all three of us smiled at his offer to take the rapid response team 'under his wing'.

"All yours, Indigo. Work out how to get anywhere very quickly, from Ireland to Israel." I looked at Fay, and she must have sensed what was coming because she smiled and, in perfect Italian, took on the role of commander of the drones. I smiled again, this was the perfect solution, and one I would have proscribed if it had been necessary. They both walked away, and Sandra turned to look at me.

"What's your plan for me?" I looked at her, dressed today in a slinky pale lemon pants suit, with a bright red jacket, cuffs rolled up to below the elbow, her weapon just managing to peek out from under whenever she moved. And, of course, her hair was shining, flowing around her pretty face with little wisps here and there. Against her, I was dull and dressed from the op shop, but life gave you what it gave you, and you either worked with it or went mad.

"Well, you have to keep me alive and decipher all the technical stuff for me. Is that enough for you?" She picked up her shoulder bag, no doubt hiding her precious H&K MP-47 machine carbine. I had no illusions about being targeted, having just survived two attempts on my life just this week. The first was by a motley crew of militia and thugs in Chicago, the second by being shot out of the sky with prejudice midway across the Atlantic Ocean, and that was when the bounty on my head was only five million euros!

Now it was supposedly ten million, and every crazy in the world would crawl out of their holes at every chance they could get. I put it away in my 'too hard to worry about' basket and considered my next action.

"We need to set up a fast reaction communications capability. It has to be mobile, it will need command and control capabilities, and whatever shape it takes, we need clearance from all one hundred and ninety-four countries and any that aren't members. Dress it up any way you like, but get us approvals ASAP. I'll work Indigo for our transport." She gave me a very hard look, screwing her eyes up in concentration.

"You want cart blanche to cross borders wherever and whenever you like, land, sea, and I suppose air, armed to the teeth, for how long?" I held up eight fingers.

"It will either be over then, or it won't matter. Get us two months and a list of every special forces' commander in every country. And find me that translator Aire talked about." She continued to stare at me with her hard-arsed narrow-eyed look, so I just waved her off and dialed my good friend, the general.

"Hello, General Saunders. Fancy seeing you again." She had the good grace to smile, probably wondering what I was up to now.

"I need Bob and his team, and Tom and his team, for at least two months, they need their own transport, air, sea, and land, one team to Dublin ASAP, one team to Greece, make that Araxos International Airport. And it would be a fine idea if you could drop one of your carrier groups into the Mediterranean Sea, on maneuvers, as it were, and forewarn your excellent captain of the battle group that collected us from our little incident, we may well drop in on him again." She seemed to be thinking, went very quiet, then looked into the camera, her eyes sparkling.

"You're assuming the nukes are in Europe, and the attack may be seaborne?"

"Mostly. The numbers don't add up, neither do the players. On the one hand, we have two well-established terrorists with long reputations for bastardry and chaos, mixing with an Irish scientist, who may or may not be on a crusade based on the famous 'Troubles'. Then you have money being spent on making the substrate casings for the bombs, money that went via Pakistan straight back to Gaza. And then…."

"You have the data from the year-old bulletin board claiming attacks on London, Dublin, Manchester, New York, Rome, Glasgow, and Paris, and God knows where else." I nodded. She might have cut me off at the pass but had added a critical piece of information to my summary.

"Why do you want Tom and Bob's teams specifically?" I smiled. That was an easy one to answer.

"I've shed blood with both of them, they know me, my style, and I know them. If only ten percent of this data is accurate, we will need to kick some very sensitive arse and take no prisoners, and I can't think of anyone better to do that with under the circumstances."

"There's one thing you haven't mentioned."

"The women?"

"Yes."

"Your president made them redundant. I didn't think you would want to go there again." She seemed to think again, then, with a sigh, rolled her shoulders.

"You can tell the boys or me. We'll keep it to ourselves. How many this time?" The boys, in this case, were the directors of the CIA, NSA, and FBI.

"More than twenty, including the scientist. We have no idea where they are, who they are now, or even if they are involved in the new scenario. The scientist, yes, she has been identified, but as you would expect, no provable history anywhere other than her university qualifications, which are first class."

"You don't see us as a target?"

"No, not at this time. The list included New York, but with the present logistical problems, this seems to be a hit in Europe, and we suspect more political than the last attacks. If it is Amir Abbas and Al Bar al Shirak, then anyone who has pissed them off in the last hundred years needs to duck for cover. Personally, you were the prime target for the refugee girls, so I don't see the need to punish you further."

"It's a pity that Mohammad bi Azaria and Natasha Trotsky aren't around so we can ask them what's up." My turn to generate a steely look. How did she know? Their summary executions were held in close secret, and to my knowledge, only four people on the planet knew. And two of those were in the same room, and the third was out getting ready to deploy, and the boss was kowtowing to the mucky-mucks in Lyon or the Hague somewhere.

"Yes, it is, but you know the one about love and war?" She had the good grace to smile, so I put her barb behind me. But I'd still like to know how she knew we had removed the two from further temptation.

"Do you want technical staff with your teams?" She was referring to nuclear specialists, of that I had no doubt.

"No, our rapid reaction squad has that covered. I want the teams to be very sharp and pointy bulldozers. I've run hundreds of scenarios, but I can't yet see what we are really up against. If that changes, you'll be the second to know." She smiled.

"How is General Anthony?" she asked with a laugh in her voice. I smiled, imagining him in his shiny uniform, bowing and scraping to the hierarchy in the UN and Interpol.

"Well, everyone gets promoted to their ultimate level of inefficiency, so I guess he will rise to the occasion!" She laughed with me, and I suddenly realized that I had become trusted, a huge step from my side.

"Don't undersell Anthony or yourself, Jessica. What you have between you is special, and before this is over, I think you'll both need everything you've got." She waved and closed the link. I dialed Arie, having thought of something I had forgotten. And buried the general's pithy comment as deeply as I could.

"Arie, hi, sorry to interrupt, but I need Amira to make at least two sets of portable scanners, handheld or on a trolly of some sort, if the powerpack is too heavy." He nodded, a grim look on his face.

"Jessica, I was just about to call you. You need to get here as fast as you can with your reaction team. Anything else you will need, I'll provide." I looked at the face of a tired old man, aged in the last day beyond his years, and wondered what could have possibly caused such a change in him? Then my skin went cold, and a shiver ran up my back that literally froze me in place.

"You've found the nukes?" I almost whispered. Such was the shock I felt. He nodded and held up two fingers.

"Where?"

"Gaza, right on the edge of the ocean, both in small vehicles, and according to Amira, they may not be loaded with any explosives at this time, but she can't be sure. The equipment was a test article we mounted in a helicopter. It all worked better than expected." I looked at him in horror. It was Israel's worst nightmare, the possibility of a nuclear attack.

"Have you got Commando Troupe 104 on call?"

"Yes, New Commander, waiting on your orders." The import of what he had just said reverberated through me like a snowball down the back of my neck. Me, responsible for the future of Israel? Preposterous. Then I mentally shook myself back into shape, the boss had given me this job because he thought I was up to it, and by God, I would be.

"Hold everything, keep the helicopter wherever it is, monitor the sites, and add whoever you think we might need to the 104. We'll be there as fast as we can." I slipped the mini into my pants pocket and took a mental inventory of all the other things I had in play.

"Sandra, Indigo, front and center!" They both magically appeared from where ever they had been hiding, both with quizzical looks on their faces.

"Combat gear, including vests, Indigo. We need the fastest transport to Israel you can get, and we need it now, and I need your share of the rapid deployment team with us."

"Immediately, Commander!" and he scurried off to places unknown. Sandra turned to walk back to her room, froze on the spot, and gave me the hurry-up signal. I sighed and, not wanting to waste energy on a useless fight, stood up and followed her out.

Ten minutes later, we were geared up and following Indigo and four of his special forces team to a helipad that had been hastily erected on a tennis court at the back of our headquarters. A very sleek Augusta 139 sat on its squat legs, rotors spinning, while overhead, two deadly Cobra gunships buzzed around like busy bees at a honey pot. We boarded, and before we could strap in, the helicopter lifted into the air, and with one gunship on either side, we flew off to deal with the atom.

Or maybe not. Arie had said Amira thought the torpedoes were not loaded, so I had my fingers crossed. It would take one hundred and fifty minutes to get to Israel, so I shut my eyes and pretended to sleep.

I was woken by an elbow in my ribs, attached to Sandra, who jumped up and ran out of the helicopter as if it were on fire, only to come to a screeching halt two yards away as she waited for me. As befitted my rank and status (ha-ha!) I slid decorously or as smoothly as one could, carrying a forty-pound pack, battle helmet, and assorted weapons, and joined her. Aire was there to greet us, as was Amira. We followed Arie into a hut, presently guarded by the ugliest and toughest-looking group of soldiers I had seen since the last time we worked with Commando Troupe 104.

"This is 104's new commander, Josephine, she is a lieutenant colonel, like her predecessor, and I have instructed her to take her orders from you and anyone you delegate." A rough, calloused hand reached out for mine. The handshake was strong and firm but not bone-crushing, which told me she was aware of her strength, and in control of it. Her shoulders would have put a professional weightlifter to shame, and in her tight combat pants, you could see the outline of massive thighs and the ripple of very strong legs. If I wasn't being put to shame by my own people dressing like fashion models, it seemed I would be shamed by this beautifully crafted soldier!

"Josephine, call me Jessica. This is Sandra, my number one, and Colonel Kashasini, who will command the rapid response team. I'll brief you in a minute. I need to catch up with your scientist and General Rosenberg. Indigo, collect your team while I get briefed."

"*Subito, comandante!*"

I motioned Sandra in front of me, and Arie disappeared into a little alcove, followed by Amira. I tapped her on the shoulder, and she turned to face me.

"Hi, Jessica. Sorry, we had to get you here so fast."

"Not a problem. Wasn't doing very much in any case," She smiled, then fired up her mini and flicked the image up to a larger screen mounted on the wall.

"He's what we found. We were only doing an air test to check the scanning range and calibrate the system. We flew the helicopter along the shoreline. Here you see the visual images we shot for reference. We decided to combine the detector into a map reading program, and just before we turned to get back into our airspace, the alarm went off, so we flew away to avoid letting anyone know what we were doing, flew a couple of circles, then ran back up the border just here, and got the targets locked in."

"How far are they across the border?"

"As of now, around one and a half kilometers. They are contained in two small vehicles parked next to each other in front of this shed. There have never been any attacks from this part of Gaza previously, so this is probably why they are there." I looked at the map and the two blobs the detector had picked up and tried to decipher the gobbly gook on the screen. 'Call me Sally' came to the rescue.

"Boss, the data lists the calculated mass at the bottom of the baseline. This means there are no explosives in them yet?" she asked Amira, who shook her head. "No, it seems that they have not been armed yet." I turned to Arie and asked the question that I bet was on everybody's lips but unspoken until now.

"Arie, what happens if you invade this section of Gaza? World war three?" He looked at me and smiled. Shook his head. Turned to a map he had on his desk and pined it up on the wall next to the screen.

"This area of Gaza is sort of neutral territory. Hezbollah, ISIS, the Sons of Islam, Palestinian Islamic Jihad, and Hamas all prefer to shell us to the south. It happens that one of the very few Iman we talk to works in this area, and I suspect he is unaware that Al Bar al Shirak is using his front yard to store nuclear weapons. Remember the two attacks they launched on our shopping centers? He and I met during that, and he helped push the terrorists back into their holes."

"Good to know. But Hamas rule the Gaze strip, don't they?"

"Yes."

"And Al Bar al Shirak is a sanctioned group in Gaza?"

"Yes, again. But they are not represented on the council. It seems their methods are too extreme even for Hamas."

"Then how do we take those bombs from under their noses without massive retaliation?"

"Do you think Hamas wants to attack us with nuclear weapons?"

"Do you?" The room went deadly quiet. We all knew that while there was no real answer to that question, it was known that some of the more militant members of Hamas wanted the end of Israel by any means, and weapons of mass destruction were not beyond their imagination.

"Then let me ask another question. Can you get into that area, take the weapons, get out again, and not cause World War Three?" Arie really looked old and tired, and I felt sorry for him, having to manage this potentially country-scarring issue. But he had not got to the top of the intelligence pile with Shabak (Sin Bet) because he lacked clarity of vision and couldn't solve a puzzle, so he laid out a plan that would give us the best chance of success without setting the region on fire.

I liked it, so I took Sandra back out with me, linked up with the 104, called Indigo, and formed a briefing circle on the stony pathway outside the little hut in the shadow of the helicopter. I asked the three helicopter pilots to join us and laid out my plan. Timing would be everything, and like all good battle plans, the chance of it surviving the first shot was very low. I liked the odds!

# Friendly Fire

The shed was fifty meters long and twenty wide and originally stored grain and machinery imported from Europe. Now it was dusty, dirty, and occupied by nine people whose last bath had been some time ago. Preferring the black and white checked head scarf of the terrorists they had seen depicted in magazines and newspapers, they now only had one purpose in life. To guard the two small electric carts parked outside the open doors, currently chained to the ground.

They had mounted two heavy caliber machineguns to the sides of the doors and had an excellent field of view, but all they had seen in the last two weeks were common people going about their business, foraging for food, or moving from one side of the small compound to the other. None of the locals had dared to come closer, as the word had gone out that this was a refuge for some very nasty people, a reputation the men enjoyed, even though it had yet to be earned.

Incessant rain showers had made the floor of the shed and the compound muddy, and while they rotated the guard in teams of four, with one on kitchen duty, boredom had set to the point where only three turned up for each outside shift, and instead of walking the perimeter, they sat and smoked sitting on piles of well-worn tractor tires. A rough lean-to kept the majority of the rain out of their eyes, but there was no mistaking the lack of enthusiasm they showed for their task.

It was just on dusk when the trouble started, the three outside guards falling from their perches with a messy thud! In seconds, black shadows moved into the shed, and the remainder of the guards died where they stood without a single shot being fired in response. The second group of shadows moved stealthy to the vehicles, dismantled the rear sections, removed the two shiny torpedoes, looped them into canvas carry-alls, and disappeared back into the night. The bodies were stacked inside the shed. Petrol was poured over them, then lit. Explosive charges were placed around the walls and on the vehicles. Rude signs were spray painted on the walls in Arabic, claiming that ISIS ruled the Muslim world and that Hamas was just a pretender and should leave Gaza as soon as possible.

Nothing blew up for six and a half hours, and when it did, it looked like one of the terrorist groups that freely roamed the Gaza strip had attacked the shed and blown up everything in their anger. Thanks to the odd items left behind adding salt to the wound, when a replacement crew arrived two days later, they had no doubt that a terrorist group had attacked their comrades. The thermite bombs that destroyed the vehicles had reached such a high temperature that each entire vehicle was melted, and only a messy slag heap and puddle of burnt rubber survived to sizzle and spit in the rain.

The locals supported the contention that it had been terrorists that had attacked, provided excellent eyewitness accounts, and even agreed on the color of their uniforms and the weapons they had used. So when word finally reached Amir Abbas, who was hard at work in France trying to arrange for the theft of twelve kilos of plutonium from the Mont LeClair atomic power station, there was little he could do but scream and rage in his little hotel room, just prior to shooting his two bodyguards after knifing them several times.

Now he had to either leave or clean up the blood that had pooled all over the carpet and floor tiles of the bathroom.

He decided on a better exit strategy, called for his car, and left a homemade bomb ticking in the small kitchen, which, when it exploded, removed all evidence of any wrongdoing if you were stupid enough to accept that the massive fire that threatened the whole top floor of the hotel was an accident.

# Chapter Fourteen

I climbed out of the helicopter and followed the four specialists who carried the torpedoes. It was a relief to be back and absolute relief to know we had zero casualties, zero people wounded, and as far as the world knew, one of the Gaza terrorist groups had attacked another and burnt down their shed. And there was a little joy in my heart because Sandra, in her black jeans, shirt, vest, and weapons harnesses with black camouflage all over her pretty face and a black watch cap pulled down over her beautiful hair, looked no better than I did! It was small of me, I know, but a girl has to get her jollies wherever she can!

And with that thought, I suddenly recognized the main difference between the boss's management style and my own. He had preferred to set things up, help with the strategy and tactics planning, then move into the background letting everyone else do what they did best. I liked to strategize and plan like everyone else, but I also liked to lead from the front. It was a significant difference, so I mentally cautioned myself not to cramp anyone's style with my natural bent to get involved.

I needn't have worried on this occasion because the two teams had performed brilliantly as if they had worked together for days, not hours. The Commando 104 had slipped into the compound and, using silenced weapons, killed the guards, killed the remainder in the shed, then taken care of the signage and set things up to go "boom!" in the night. Indigo's blended reaction team had scooted up the bombs in record time and reduced the vehicles to puddles of rubber and slag. I had tailed Indigo's team with Sandra, but we had been superfluous, hadn't needed to fire a shot, issue, and order, and in fact, we could have stayed with the trucks that had crossed the border.

Lesson learned.

Amira met us at the door to the laboratory, took the bombs, then shut us out by climbing into her level 4 bio-suit and snapping the airlock shut behind her. The girl had moves, but no manners! Sandra and I decided to go see Arie and listen to the debrief, which was underway when we arrived. Indigo performed his magic by producing two steaming mugs of coffee, so we sat and listened.

Josephine, in her black uniform, war paint, and lethal account-ments hanging off her, looked soft and cuddly until you saw the deter-mination on her face and listened to her voice.

All business. A short, sharp, and detailed report, no frills, then she turned to me and pointed.

"We did not see the Commander until we were exiting the shed, the small vehicles were burning, and the reaction team was well in front of us on the way back to the trucks."

"We stayed with Indigo's team. You seemed to have it in hand." She looked at me, smiled, nodded, then stood.

"Thank you, if we are no longer needed, I would like to retire my team for a meal and rest." I nodded, understanding the unspoken hierarchy. Arie was the senior person in the room, but I had been in operational control of the mission. Arie held his hand up as if seeking permission to speak.

"I spoke to the Iman and explained what you were doing, and his early reports are that the locals are saying with some force that a ter-rorist group attacked the shed, killed everyone, then blew it up. There were messages left in the ruins of a shed in Arabic claiming ISIS was the perpetrator, and broken AK-47s. There is no mention of us and, apparently, no evidence of us having ever been involved."

"That's good. Your people are first class. They got in and out in less than four minutes. Indigo's team had just started their run out when they exited. I hope we can keep them for the next adventure." He smiled and nodded but didn't say anything. I looked at him for a minute, then decided to move the agenda forward.

"Will we still have the C-17 and drones tomorrow?" He nodded.

"Yes. That is well in hand. But I'd like you to stay while Amira and her team examine the torpedoes if you can." I looked at Sandra, and she looked back at me with a wan smile, we were not really dressed for a social event, and I suspect Arie's long experience tipped him off about our silent chat. "We'll get you something to wear. Use my facilities to shower and clean up."

So we did.

And enjoyed a lovely hot meal dressed in black overalls, with our combat gear snug in little carry-alls at our feet. Amira joined us, took a coffee from Indigo, and with a huge sigh, filled us in on the science.

"The good news is that they have used almost an identical formula to the one we developed at Harvey Mudd. The bad news is that they have tweaked it a fraction, so you will need some nanites with you to neutralize any further finds."

"Can you explain that for me, please? Remember, not a nerd!" The mild laughter settled everyone down, and I noticed Sandra had her mini out and was entering data into it.

"To split the substrate open, say, for loading an isotope into the center chamber, you need to use a nanite spread over it like sunscreen. Easy to apply, but tricky in the open air, as it turns into a chalky paste in seconds. Whoever developed this from my original work knows their nanotechnology, but I haven't found any signature as yet."

"Signature?"

"Yes. Arie will tell you that every bomb maker has a 'signature', a certain way, they do something in the construction of the bomb. Nanotechnology is the same — you can usually tell who did the molecular bonding in the nanite; after all, when I left the university, there were only four people who knew what I did. If you take away Michael, that leaves just two people to find. The university records might help, but I suggest we look in my files because I have everyone who worked with me in all three laboratories, their photos, histories, and their skill evaluations. You took all that material some weeks ago if you remember. After all, I had to submit a progress report every quarter to maintain our funding, or so I thought."

"Who can find that data for you?"

"I gave Luigi all the access information he needed before I left Venice. I can call him now for you if that suits you?" I held my hand up to stop her from moving away.

"No, not just yet. My non-geek mind still needs a little help. How do we disarm one of these bombs if it is loaded with nuclear material?" The room went very quiet. Talking about disarming a nuclear bomb did that. Amira looked like she was thinking deeply, then she nodded to herself.

"You don't. I'll make you a ballistic sleeve out of nanomaterial that you can slide over the weapon, and that will keep it inert. The trigger has been built into the nose cone and requires an impact force of eighteen hundred meters per second to engage. So as long as you don't drop it or throw it onto a concrete floor, you should be okay."

"Or hit it with a hammer." We all laughed as Sandra's dry comment lightened the mood again. She had a sweet touch when it came to making people feel comfortable. But I wasn't feeling very comfortable at all. Put it together — rail gun, rocket propulsion, planned high-speed impact — the bad guys were going for the gold as far as delivery was concerned, using a very simple method-explosion by impact, no complicated fuses, detonators, or much possibly of an accident.

At the back of my mind, our task just got a little easier, but first, we had to find the bastards and neutralize everyone involved.

"Okay, Arie, we need to get the detection system airborne as soon as possible. Amira, make thirty of those nano things, just in case, and make sure they are easily transportable. The slings we use today worked well. No need to change that, but Aire, I really think we will need more manpower." He gave me that grandfatherly look again. It was a hard one to negotiate around.

"Have you asked for any other support from anyone?"

"Yes. Tom and Bob's team from the States, and Indigo is lending me four more for my personal collection." Everyone laughed again, making me feel warm.

"What's your order of battle?"

"The C-17 with Inspector Fay Remer commanding, Amira as science guru, will scan the European coastline all the way to Ireland, where we'll do a whole-of-island search. Then we'll move from country to country until we get back here. Indigo's team will follow the C-17, ready to deploy if we find anything. I'll be following in a specially equipped jet with C and C capability, with a small backup team of shooters. I'll have Bob in position in a day in Ireland and Tom's team in Greece."

"Then I'll keep the 104 here with me until you really need them, just in case your little episode this morning creates any blowback." I nodded. He was right. I was overcomplicating the problem, a habit I would kill in the bud, as in right now. If I was going to be an effective commander, I would have to trust my judgement, and that of my troops.

The C-17 acting as a drone scanner detected nothing all the way along the coastline of Europe to Ireland. Word was received via our minis that both Bob and Tom's teams were in position, there had been no word from Israel that Hamas or others were arcing up more than usual over our dawn attack, and as it had been said in a war movie decades ago, it was 'all quiet on the Western front'. Our little pocket rocket had made it to Dublin long before the C-17, as it had bobbed and weaved along the northern coast of Africa, creating a three-hundred-kilometer corridor that would have been scanned at least once.

We were billeted in an old army barracks on one corner of the airport, provided with two big SUVs and a close protection unit from the Army Ranger Wing, most of whom Sandra fell in love with the moment they opened their mouths.

"It's the accents, boss, all the 'aye' this and 'ahhh' that. How could you not love it?"

I held my comments, not wishing to spoil her prudent fantasies. I was too busy studying the scans from the C-17 that was now crossing the water from Africa to Spain. I was beginning to realize that it was going to be a timing thing, as in how long would it take the terrorists to preposition the bombs once they left Afghanistan. We had to assume slow manned transport and small boats. Otherwise, there was too much chance of them getting caught up in the continual chaos initiated by the earlier terrorist attacks and the massive migration of millions still underway.

And there was, literally, no oil-based fuel in Europe other than that stashed away by the military. The satellite images were over a month old, and we had found two of the nano substrate bombs in the Gaza Strip, but that was just a hop, step, and a jump from Afghanistan, around eleven hundred miles as the crow flies, and even allowing for a modern electric vehicle and traversing all the Muslim-held areas would only take a few weeks. The major cities mentioned on the Irish website were considerably further away.

And we could assume that they would be dropped off in a logical fashion, as in Rome, Paris, London, Manchester, Glasgow, then Dublin. I had no idea how they intended to get one to New York under the current restricted transatlantic travel arrangements. Why carry a heavy object further than you need to?

As much as I mulled it all over, I lacked intelligence, information, and data, and the clock was ticking.

Six weeks to go.

So I did what any reasonable person would do. I called Fay in the C-17 and handed her temporary operational control. Then I packed Sandra and Indigo's four guards into one of the SUVs and headed off to church. If we were being tracked, this would be the perfect opportunity to attack us again, so I had insisted on full combat gear, covered by lightweight waterproof, great coats, with long guns slung from the shoulder and hidden beneath the folds. We told no one of our destinations. I was driving, and everyone in the back, seasoned veterans of bloody wars and deadly skirmishes all over the globe, cowered in fear as I took off on the wrong side of the road!

Sandra, to her credit, just swore a most unladylike oath and clutched the panic stick over her shoulder like a newborn holding onto her mother's finger.

"Boss, the speed limit is sixty kilometers. This is a well built-up area, we can expect some counter traffic, and you're on the wrong side of the road." She didn't exactly screech, but the panic in her voice was palpable. I swerved over to the left-hand side of the road, saw a large farm truck coming at us, and relaxed. It was the first time I had driven in a long, long time, and it felt good to be in control of even something as simple as a vehicle.

"Relax, I'll slow down in a minute. I just need to get the dust out of the engine." The muttering from the back seats, strong Italian invectives, and expletives reminded me we were an international team, and I was supposedly the one in charge. I was having fun, couldn't help but smile, waved at the troops in the back, and reassured them as best as I could.

*"Ehi, ho una patente di guida internazionale, valida per altri sette anni!"*

"If it were up to me, Commander, I'd take it off you for life!" And they all laughed, releasing the tension. Sandra just shook her head, reached in, adjusted her H&K, which had swung across her chest, and glared at me.

"Not funny, Jessica, not funny at all." The first time I had ever heard her pissed, so I slowed down to seventy, and seeing the little church a few blocks away, its white painted spire shining in the flickering sunlight, I started to work out how to pull over and stop. Which I did, without further cursing from the self-loading cargo, and we dismounted progressively and walked into the annex. The church was made of huge stained blocks, possibly Byzantine in origin, certainly in design, at least three or four hundred years old, with the most magnificent stained-glass windows behind the pulpit I had ever seen. The sunlight streamed through, creating a series of colored rainbows that reached all the way down to the old and well-worn stained floor, illuminating the pews, obviously hewed from very old wood as they had blackened with both age and use.

I felt a sense of calm and peace that flowed through the place like an invisible mist, and I felt very out of place wearing combat gear and carrying weapons. Sandra shared my feelings, her face told the story, amazement and wonder all over it, her eyes sparkling in the reflected light. I motioned the four troopers to wait and moved down to the front pew, where I sat, a little uncomfortably given the circumstances. Sandra stood behind me in the next row but kept her hands clasped in front, right hand over left, the typical pose for a close protection operative.

A very old priest, his black cassock hanging a little from his gaunt frame, walked in from what I supposed was the rectory, genuflected as he crossed the alter, then stood, arms folded in his cassock, and smiled.

"How would I be assisting you, my child?" His voice was soft but heavily accented, but his face was radiant, as only a true believer can manage. I stood out of respect and felt Sandra move to one side.

"Father, I come in peace, seeking an associate I believe has sought sanctuary with you these last few days." His gaze didn't flinch, his body language was impossible to read because of the cassock, and his face remained impassioned. I definitely would not be playing poker with this guy!

"And who would be your associate, I'd be asking, for we've not granted sanctuary to anyone these last few years. Sure you are. You have the right parish?" I looked at him, forming a small grin, wondering what I could say without compromising our contact. Using Interpol credentials was out of the question. Bullying him would do no good. I could sense a steel backbone of considerable strength, then I had it.

"His brother sent me to give him a message and to speak with him about his quest." And I left it at that, it would either get me to our contact, or it wouldn't, and we'd have to come up with a better plan.

"And what would be his quest, might I ask, as curious I am about why his brother would send you and not let him know of your visit?" Now his face registered curiosity, but I saw no guile or prevacation, so I took another chance.

"Brother Francis is well known to me and mine, and I'm as sure as you are that his brother did reach out on one of these," I said, pulling my mini from the folds of my coat, "and warn him of my visit. It would be wrong of me to claim that the time was given, but I'm sure there was a message." He just stared at me, a neutral look, obviously one he practiced on errant children.

"Well, let me see if we have anyone here that is interested in meeting with you, and by what name would I be introducing you?" The trap question was answered the wrong way, and we would be out on our collective ears. I furiously though what Stefarino might have called me. The last time we met, he had known of my upgraded rank, so I went for the formal and hoped for the best.

"Commander Riley." He nodded, turned on his heel, and walked back into the rectory. I literally held my breath, and Sandra had her H&K across her chest but hidden under her coat. She was as tense as a wolf about to strike, and I must admit she was making me nervous. Then the monk walked out, beaming a one-hundred-watt smile, his patched brown robe bouncing as he walked, the priest behind him, arms still folded in his cassock.

"Jessica, hello, I was wondering when you would get here, and who's this pretty girl with you?" I smiled, waved Sandra down, walked around the end of the pew, and reached forward with my hand, which was enveloped by a meaty one in response. Sandra was forced to let her H&K go as he held his hand out to her. He continued to smile, turned to look at the priest, then, in Gaelic, reassured him we were who he had been expecting. I pointed to the pew, and we sat side by side, with Sandra now sitting behind us.

"Sorry to burst in on you this way, but we are on the clock." He nodded. His brother had briefed him well and thoroughly. "And you may need to move on. Our coming here might put a target on your back." He nodded again, still smiling, as if all was right in his world.

"I'll be leaving now that we've met, and the local boys will look after the church, as they've done for all these years past, of that you can be sure."

"Did Brother Stefarino make provision for your return to your home?"

"All taken care of, my friend. The truck driver will get me back to Moly's place, and from there I'll get home quick enough. I had hoped to see a Stone Dance. I've got this interest in me way back, but that's not to be now." I looked at him, saw the disappointment of the scholar denied his pleasure, and felt sorry for him. But I could give him hope.

"All I can promise you is we are here to prevent a tragedy of huge proportions, and once we have succeeded, you will be free to roam the country as you were before. The information you have is critical to our success."

"Aye, my brother did say you've important things to do when he asked me to take my sabbatical. So, do you want what I have found now?"

"Yes, please." He reached into his patched robe and pulled out a battered and well-worn leather journal.

"I've a habit of writing things down, as my memory isn't what it used to be, not that it was ever great by any means. The folks in the pictures you sent me were only known by two, the tall, dark man and the pretty young woman. The man with the keffiyeh was known to none that I spoke with." So Malik Badawi, the Bedouin, and Siobhan O'Cleary, the scientist, were in play here, but Amir Abbas, the leader of Hamas, had not been seen.

"Where were the two that were seen?" He turned a grubby page, ran his finger down the edge, scrunched up his eyebrows in concentration, then turned to look at us. Out of the corner of my eye, I could see Sandra writing everything down on her mini. One day I would have to tell her about my photographic memory.

"The first time was at the shipyards here in Dublin, then over a period of time for some four months, on and off, never more than a few hours at a time. Then I have a report of them being seen at this club here," and he pointed to a scrawled almost illegible name, "and once in a private elevator in this building. But I've spoken to no none who had sighted them in the last month or two. Would you be interested in their names, then?"

"Yes, please."

"He calls himself Thana Praxidike and herself Adriana Nichols."

"What?" I turned to look at Sandra, who had all but shouted.

"That's a Bedouin retribution name-Thana is from the Greek meaning 'death', and Praxidike is the name of the Greek Goddess Exacting Justice." I looked at her, amazed at what she knew, and a chill ran down my spine thinking about a seasoned terrorist who had managed to remain in play for at least two decades and now sought justice. For what? Or whom? And from whom? And in a multi-billion-dollar ship nearly three hundred feet long, with, maybe, ten or fifteen nuclear bombs on board!

"Do you have anything else?" I asked the monk, wondering how I could show my appreciation. He had been invisible to all the people he talked to, with no perceivable threat, and now we had some real intelligence to analyze.

"Well, I did manage to visit their building during one of my long walks, and it seems that the apartment on the top floor where it is said they stayed the most is vacant, locked up, and not expected to be in use again this year. I learned that from the cleaners they used, a lovely couple got paid up to the end of the month." I processed that, not sure what it meant. Dublin was one of the specified targets, so they might just be getting clear of any possibility of being killed in any attack.

Or it could be a deliberate move to convince us that an attack was brewing. There were so many intangibles in this puzzle — the fact that the Irish website had magically stayed up; that a satellite had managed to photograph the three main players and a torpedo when satellites that worked could be counted on one hand, and their orbits were well known and documented. And that the academic history of their nuclear scientist remained visible for anyone to find if they looked. It smelt bad, as if we were being set up, but for the life of me, set up for what?

"Brother Francis, is there something practical we can do for you to thank you for your excellent efforts?" He laughed and put his journal away in the folds of his robe, the cuffs of which had been recently sewn up with little leather strips. I marveled at his faith and his humility, and his God-given strength and sense of humor.

"Well, now, a donation of sorts for this little parish wouldn't go astray." I smiled and motioned to Sandra, who pulled out a wallet, unzipped it, pulled out a stack of Euros, folded them in half, and handed them to the monk.

"It's all we have on us, but we can send more if it's not sufficient." He laughed again, took the notes which disappeared into his robe, then took Sandra's hand for a soft and gentle shake.

"It'd be plenty, I should think, and will more than compensate the good priest and his friends for putting up with the likes of me. God be with you both, blessed be." And he walked out back to the rectory, not aware that he had given us the first piece of reliable information since this madness had started with the call from Arie.

"Let's go." We walked out of the church and, with the guards, fed back into the SUV. I motioned to Sandra and climbed into the passenger seat. She looked at me for a split second, then raced to the driver's side before I could change my mind.

"Do you have an international driver's license?" One of the guards asked, and it sounded like the one who had sworn at me in Italian for my driving skills on the way in.

"Of course not. But I'm a fast learner."

# Chapter Fifteen

The bronzed couple on the foredeck of the ship looked nothing like the most wanted terrorists in the world and possibly the most wanted scientist in the world. In fact, their worldwide infamy meant nothing to them, so secure were they in their skins, and in their new personas. As far as the world knew, Thana Praxidike and Adriana Nichols were a young Greek couple enjoying the fruits of their parents' hard labor, taking the time to relax between visits to the exotic bars that had returned to the riviera after the terrorist attacks and civil unrest had settled down, or the casinos that remained standing.

The jet set of the Mediterranean coastline had not really been inconvenienced by the chaos that spread across the world like cancer, being insulated by both their wealth and their resources. Yes, there had been casualties, and over the latest cocktail, those that had the misfortune to get mixed up in the death and destruction were lamented for their foolishness. And the police boats and warships were keeping the floating migrants at bay, sinking one or two each day to discourage the others.

Calm and warmed by the sun as he was, Malik Badawi had a problem of monumental proportions.

The money he was counting on to purchase the nuclear components for his bombs had been cut off, his supplier was not a patient woman, and he now had only three days left to raise funds — a half billion dollars, or four hundred and thirty thousand euros. Cryptocurrency would not be accepted, and the supplier was quick to point out that having skillfully removed the base material from a French nuclear power station undetected and had the initial machining done to turn the plutonium into precise slugs and the Uranium 235 into equally precise little balls, it had already cost her twenty million dollars a set.

Yes, it was expensive, so if he could find someone else to do the work, he was welcome to do so, but after he paid her the five hundred million he already owed. The threat had not been made but was always just under the surface of every conversation — Interpol, or perhaps even the Gendarmerie National would be very interested in an international terrorist with the making of nuclear bombs sitting around on a boat on the French Riviera.

He had his feelers out, but unfortunately, his lack of funds had also created a problem with his friend and co-conspirator Amir Abbas, to whom he also owed considerable money, so he couldn't count on anyone in the Gaza Strip or the usual clutch of terror groups for help. But he had one very strong source of funds, who had committed to the project way back over a year ago when it had first been raised in casual conversation. The family had a long history of supporting Middle Eastern conflicts, traced their personal fortunes all the way back to the seamy side of the Second World War, were wealthy beyond reason, and all he had to do now was make contact.

And it was just this simple element that he was giving his deepest thoughts to. How and when.

He had deliberately timed his exposure in Afghanistan to provide the satellite with his face and that of his two companions, as well as the brilliant substrate torpedo. He counted on it being retrieved by a Security Force smart enough to work out what it was. He wanted the level of uncertainty and fear to underpin his strategy. He wanted the security forces around the world to be looking in the wrong direction. And he was counting on his friend, Amir Abbas, to stuff his side of it up so badly that the security forces would be chasing their tails for years. He knew Abbas had taken two extra shells; he had counted on it.

It had to be in person, and it had to be in character, and it had to be today. His plane was at the Côte d'Azur airport in Nice, a twenty-minute speedboat ride. His benefactor was at his chalet in Buchenbuhl, just near Nuremberg Airport. It was less than three hours of flying time. If he left now, he would be back by the start of the cocktail hour, something his Irish companion enjoyed immensely. And given that when he was successful in straightening out his little financial problem, she would be in a level Five Biohazard suit, locked in an airtight room, for hours at a time building all his bombs, it would be smart to keep her happy. Probably on her knees a lot of the time, and that image made him happy with anticipation.

"Adriana, my love, I need to make a quick trip to Germany. Would you care to come or stay here on the boat?" She rolled over on her stomach to look at him, a gorgeous man from head to toe, his long black hair flowing over his broad shoulders, the smile on his face highlighted by his orange-colored sunglasses. As she rolled, her bikini, which had been undone, slipped off, revealing her perfect, creamy breasts as she leaned up on her hands, supporting her beautiful face.

"I think I'll stay here, if you don't mind, it might be the last time I can spend time outdoors for a while, and it's the perfect day for just lying around catching the sun." He smiled. It was the reaction he had anticipated and the one he wanted. It didn't do to take strangers to meetings, even when he knew both parties and trusted them with his life. He leaned down, drew her in for a warm, soft kiss, then, stroking her red hair, stood.

"*Ciao*, my darling, I'll be back in time for cocktail hour." He walked down the companionway, dressed in his stateroom, then climbed into the beautiful wooden replica of a sixty-year-old Riva Aquarama. Her topsides shined to perfection, making her ribbed planked hull look gorgeous in the sunlight. The boat sped off and, within minutes, pulled into the little port that served the Côte d'Azur airport. Within another few minutes, he was deposited at the stairs to his plane, the engines sending out a hazy hum, the air from the exhausts ripping up the sky in waves.

Three hours later, he walked down the airstairs into a fog, heavy rain, and strong wind. Half an hour later, he was sitting on the wide portico of his benefactor's castle, marveling at what real money could buy. All his life he had lived mostly hand-to-mouth, and this crusade, his last, would give him riches beyond imagination. He smiled to himself; he'd had his hands on five billion euros just weeks ago, only to see them slip from his grasp due to a Red Notice from Interpol.

He blamed the weak-kneed accountants in Dublin for that, and he had a special reward for their perfidy that he would deliver personally when the time came. He looked over to his host, Gerhart von Speer, and marveled at his stature. For an eighty-eight-year-old man, his back was straight, his head was covered with a silver mane of flowing hair, and his face looked like that of a much younger man. The blue and red robe smoking jacket he wore sat over a starched pure white shirt and conservative club tie. The glass of Christal champagne he held was in a cut, long, stemmed flute with golden trim, and the whole effect, he thought to himself was one of being in the presence of royalty.

"Sir, I am humbled by your generosity. Is there anywhere, in particular, I could send a message for you, one that would be irrevocably final and the consequences of monumental proportions?" The old man looked at his guest, noting the Armani suit, highly polished brogues, and light blue silk shirt covered with a pale blue silk tie. The Bedouin knew how to dress like a gentleman, and his manners were impeccable, something he was thankful for, as his experience of terrorists in the past had always been an uncomfortable one.

"When we spoke early last year, you mentioned you may be in a position to hit multiple targets in a way that would send a message as unmistakable as it would be powerful. Is that still the case?"

"Yes, but the cost of each strike will be quite high, given the risk we will take in prolonging the attacks." The old man sipped his champagne, looking through the fog and rain as if seeking divine intervention. He put the magnificent flute down on an antique table, so old the wood had turned deep black with age.

"If I could get you, let's say, upwards of thirty billion euros, or the equivalent in USD, or gold, your choice, could you consider a target list of as many as six or seven? And could you eliminate them within the remainder of this year?" Malik thought to himself, did a mental inventory of his original list of targets, and rapidly worked out what he could compromise on his list in the interest of thirty billion worth of gold, something that would only appreciate in value given the current chaos around the world, and what he planned to do.

"Sir, if I could be assured of two billion euros in cash in two days, delivered to a location, I will confirm, and the thirty billion in gold at the current euro exchange rate delivered to an address I will provide, I can give you your choice of seven targets." The old man nodded. He had expected at least a small back and forth with the Bedouin, just for form, but realized that the capriciousness of the terrorist had got the better of his negotiation skills.

So be it.

"Do you have the ability to deliver by air?" Malik looked at the old man, surprised by the question. As it currently stood, he didn't, but if he had the money in two days, he would make that a certainty.

"Yes, I do."

"And it will be completed this year?" Malik nodded, picked his flute up, and saluted the old man.

"With certainty and to your health, Sir."

The flight back was seemingly faster than the trip out, and Malik took the time to work through how he could air deliver a weapon that had been designed specifically to be fired out of a rail gun. But then, the principle of the sabot was to hit a target with such kinetic force that the core penetrated through the wall of the target, even if it were a six-inch steel armor plate.

Unfortunately, he had personally killed his armorer back in Afghanistan as a precaution against a leak, thinking that the dim-witted man had done all that was necessary. He had slit his throat from side to side, reveled in the blood that had oozed out all over his shirt and the wicked grin the man had formed in his death throws. It wasn't often Malik got to see the results of his work up close and personal, and he realized at the time that this new way of dealing with death, while many times more powerful, lacked the personal touch.

He worried about this all the way back to his ship, and even as he went to collect his prize for the night, he tried to visualize how to make the system work with an airdrop.

Luckily, Adriana — or Siobhan as she had been christened by her parents, now long dead — had been extremely anxious to see him back, and as the cocktail hour stretched into the night, and he finally stretched into Adriana, he let the question fade from his mind.

Plenty of time to come up with a solution. He had better than eight months to deliver on his promise, all the time in the world, if he stopped to think about it!

# Chapter Sixteen

"**F**ay, Tom, Bob, Indigo, listen up. We have the names the terrorists used as recently as a month ago. We have photos and schematics of the ship they fitted out in Dublin. It sailed over fifteen weeks ago. No idea where it is now. Nothing is located at this time, we may be early as far as deliveries of the shells go, or we might be looking in the wrong place. And there's a technical aspect to this that is causing us some grief. The good news is that we have taken out of circulation two weapons from the Gaza strip, and we will have details on that for you later today. Any questions?" No one on the screen moved. No hands went up, so I just nodded and closed the meeting.

"Thank you all. Stay on your toes." I sat back in my seat; the big screen that had been rigged opposite me looked completely out of place in the executive layout of the fast jet. More used to silky suits and champagne cocktails, the interior now smelled of sweat, coffee, and more coffee. We had purloined a small but efficient espresso machine back at the airport, and I had made it a condition of entry that anyone who boarded, including the aircrew, had to know how to work the machine on demand. And Army marched on its stomach, or so it was said, but this Army marched on caffeine and plenty of it!

"What's the technical hitch you mentioned in the conversation?" Sandra sat sprawled across two lush seats, now in casual black jeans and a matching tee shirt, her weapon slung casually over one shoulder. Her combat boots, a little the worse for wear, perched on one chair, crossed at the ankles, the rest of her on the other. Her mini was open on her lap, but the glazed look in her eyes told me she was in thinking mode, not reading mode, so I paid her more attention than I otherwise would.

She was relatively new to Section Five, had proven herself several times in a very short time, and I was growing to really like her as a person, not just as an asset. She bounced around like a battery bunny and had a very sunny disposition, but she could pull the trigger in cold blood equally as well as the best of us.

Or the worst of us, depending on your point of view.

"Here, read this," and I threw a rare printed copy of the data Amira had sent me privately, which Sandra caught without apparent effort with one hand. Good reflexes. I'd have to note that down somewhere.

"Amira estimated that a speed of eighteen hundred meters per second would be reached with the profile we have from the boat. That's faster than a rifle bullet by a factor of two and a half times. She estimated that at least half this velocity would be needed to crush the firing stud in the nose, which forces the plutonium into the uranium, and poof! Lovely mushroom cloud." She studied the data a little longer, then turned to look at me, jumping up to a sitting position at the same time, creating the impression that she was on springs.

"Wait a minute, what if they wanted to deliver one by air?"

"And that's the technical problem." She nodded, her eyes glazing over slightly as she settled back into her seat.

"You've got the issue of the radius of the blast, then the radius of the radiation, so any airburst or air delivery would need to be a stand-off, maybe as far as twenty kilometers away. It couldn't be a glide bomb because even at terminal velocity, it wouldn't be fast enough to crush the plug. Now, this torpedo thing is eighty centimeters long, eighty millimeters in diameter, and weighs in at around forty-five kilos, so what air-launched missiles would that fit in?" She closed her eyes, then sprung up again. "Got it. There are two, the French Rafael Anti Air Missile, model 90, has a beyond-the-horizon range of one hundred kilometers plus, and the American equivalent, the AAM 104."

"You forget one other. What took out the space station?" She looked at me as if I had asked her the hardest question on earth, then grinned and fell back into her seat.

"That was a beast. Anna told me that only two of those babies had even been made, and then over ten years ago. And no, I don't know the designation."

"Find out." I turned my head to the window. I hated chipping at her happy gloss, but to be truly effective in this job, you had to know your enemy and what they could bring to bear against you. It didn't take her very long.

"A heavily modified Rafael 160 munition with an after-booster attached, from most of a weather rocket that was common at the time, grafted on. The weather rocket was nineteen feet high — that's approximately six meters. And yes, the diameter of the instrument package was one hundred centimeters by one meter. But to make that work for this substrate shell, you would have to modify it significantly."

"Draw it up for me, most plausible arrangement, make sure you work out attachments and firing mechanisms, consult with Indigo and anyone he suggests, run the theory by Tom and Bob, talk to anyone they suggest, pretend you want to send me to hell with it, so make it real, and make it fast!"

"I'll do that," she replied, her voice so soft it almost didn't carry over the hum of the jet engines. I turned to look at her and saw a look in her eyes I hadn't seen before. Thoughtful horror. Plenty of that going around on this case, and anyone who wasn't affected shouldn't be working the possibilities. Nuclear Weapons of Mass Destruction (WMD) were the creepy figure hiding under the stairs in the darkest of the dark, the stuff that genuine nightmares were made of, and in our history thus far, there had only been four really serious nuclear accidents, but in every case, the fear, uncertainty, and paranoia created in the ordinary population by each failure went far beyond the physical reach of the actual disaster and lasted years after the event.

If you didn't count the multiple atomic and hydrogen bomb tests carried out so openly by the Russians, Americans, Chinese, North Koreans, French, English, Indians, and Pakistanis between 1945 and 2017, you were left with the SL-1 accident in 1961, Three Mile Island 1979, Chernobyl disaster 1986, and the Fukushima Daiichi power plant meltdown in 2011. And the radioactive fallout from that one had been detected as far away as the west coast of America over a year later and still detectable in the fish supply two years after that.

And every country on the planet was hypertensive about the possibility of portable nukes carried by terrorists in suitcases and the so-called 'dirty bomb', which used a normal explosive to spread radio-active material.

And now, it seemed, we had a well-heeled, well-funded terrorist group with ten or more nuclear-capable weapons, all based on tech-nology invented by our very own Amira, a genius-level scientist whose research had been bastardized to kill the world as we knew it. The question was the 'or more' part of that thought. Just how many were we really chasing? And where was this bloody ship, as big as a foot-ball field, not something that could hide in a shallow cove? And that thought gave me an idea.

"General, hi. Sorry to bother you, but have you got anything in the Mediterranean at the moment?" The look she gave me was pure 'fuck off, how dare you ask', but I didn't flinch. I respected both her and her position as the president's liaison with her military, and having worked with her these last three tension-filled months, I had developed a healthy respect for her decision-making powers and her smarts.

"If I had, why the hell would I tell you?" the sneer didn't come out exactly as she had planned. The humor that hid just under it spoiled the effect. I smiled, aware that we were negotiating, and this time I had some worthy chips.

"If I told you I'd have to kill you, so 'fess up, general."

"Huh! The ever-secretive Section Five. I won't confirm or deny any naval presence anywhere, but I will say if you got shot down again — an event I pray for every hour of every day — you just might be lucky and get plucked out of the sea." I thought about that. It inferred a spread of warships right along the Mediterranean Sea, something we could possibly use. I made an instant decision and knew it would give part of our strategy away. She had the smarts, after all, and had demonstrated them on many occasions.

"Warn them I might drop in unexpectedly and have the coffee strong and black!" And I shut the mini, turned to look at Sandra beavering away on her mini, and wondered how the boss had always seemed so calm when we started out on a serious case. I was a bundle of nerves, my brain was trying to drive me crazy with all the different strings we were tugging, and in spite of sitting in a warm and plush seat, in my commandeered fast jet, with four burly Italian special forces and Sandra sitting next to me, I felt very lonely. I dialed Amira.

"How many portable sets of detectors have we got?" She bent her head as if working, and I guessed she was at her makeshift bench in the hold of the C-17.

"If you give me another hour, we'll have four more, and I've modified the laser so it will run off any sufficiently large power supply."

"How about a frigate, or one of the American's Arleigh Burke-class destroyers, or an America-class amphibious battleship?"

"Perfect. I can attach the laser to their broad scan radar mast and cover hundreds of square kilometers with each sweep, but the detector will still have to be airborne.

"Smallest possible drone to carry it?" She looked up, gave a really cold look, shrugged her shoulders, and shook her head, sending her shiny hair flying.

"How would I know? Use the drones we have already fitted out as a reference." Buggar, the boss, would have figured this out in a heartbeat. Weapons were his specialty or one of them, I thought. He actually had a few.

"Sandra, all the details on the drones we have and match them to American equivalents. Soonest." She looked over at me, mildly aggravated at having her concentration broken. She would have to multi-task, and we didn't have time to pull one string at a time. With a grunt, she bent to her mini, and suddenly the big screen on the seat in front of me came to life.

"General, happy to disturb you this time. Do you have one of your factory ships in the vicinity, possibly able to work with high-end technology? I'll supply the genius, you the grunts, and the spare parts." The look she gave me this time was more considered. "And I'll need a few of your drones, nothing smaller than the ARD 34, and you'll have to provide a twenty-four-hour monitoring crew."

"Is that all?"

"For now." And I shut the mini, hopefully making my point. Then opened it again.

"Indigo, can you please arrange for helicopter transport for Amira, say, three hours from now? Get them to collect me first, and we'll be flying into the med, so range might be a factor."

"With pleasure, Commander, expect it within the hour." His use of Oxford English said it all. Serious times. So, we had the makings of a seaborne detection system that covered one aspect of the problem. But there were many others. When we found the two bombs in Gaza, they had been stored inside the guts of small electric vehicles. And they had not been fitted into a sabot shell. Did that mean that not all of the torpedoes were designed to fire the same way?

Sandra leaned over towards me, gave me one of her million-watt smiles, and pointed to the big screen.

"Boss, the Americans have a number of autonomous helicopters based on the old Bell 212 design. They use them for remote resupply, communications, and sub-hunting. It might be smarter to use them rather than drones."

"Buggar it, you're right. And don't call me 'boss'." I tried to look irritated, but the smirky look she gave me in return indicated I had only managed sulky, so I gave in, leaned back, let my shoulders relax, and released a big sigh.

"Sally, keep it up, and I'll promote you out to the farthest reaches of the known world, further even than bumfuck Alaska or even the tin shed we have down at Tierra del Fuego. Follow me through. Correct me if you dare, but this is what I'm trying to establish." I pointed to the screen, where a map of the Mediterranean from Spain to Turkey floated, with little range circles that looked like right-angle ticks over-layed. A tick was the approximate range of the sabot, given the data we had so far. But the screen did not show any possibility of an aerial attack, and I was very much aware of our limitations in that area.

"I want to use the Navy to cover the Mediterranean Sea, so we can concentrate on the landside of the target areas. Frankly, I doubt that the terrorists have gone to all this trouble and expense just to get caught out in the ocean, but maybe we can force their hand with a more visible presence. Ideas?" She looked serious for a second, then that agile mind of hers sparked. I actually saw it reflected in her eyes.

"Jessica, sir, ma'am, commander, whatever, if you want a deterrent, you don't actually need hardware on platforms — or at least on all of them. All you need is a lot of coordinated noise and a wide channel communications strategy to make sure everyone who can get the message." She looked like the cat who had just eaten the mouse, who had just eaten the cheese. She was bouncing on her seat again, something I was starting to admire.

"Explain."

"Well, for starters, no one but our friends and us will know how many detectors we really have, or for that matter, how they work. Correct?" I focused on her with my most serious, thin-lipped look, challenging her to continue.

"Well, say we establish an electronic picket line in and out of the Med, maybe one spotter in the middle, but set up a broadcast regime that creates the impression that we have hundreds of spotters swarming all over the Mediterranean Sea. For that matter, anywhere the Navy has deep water boats. Maybe a less broadcast frequency strategy there with the messaging, but we'll gain the same effect."

"What if we drive them underground with all that noise?"

"I don't think they want that. Why all the clues, the seemingly mistaken synchronization with the satellite flyover, giving us their faces, see their handiwork with the substrate, then let us take two bombs with little or no fuss from them in the Gaza?"

"I hate it when you're right. So, how many detectors do we give the Navy?"

"Give them four, and tell them they can make as many as they like so long as they coordinate their search zones with us."

"And the small matter of only the one rapid reaction team?"

"Emphasize that point, highlight the technical aspects of recovery without making a bang, work in partnership, etc., etc., you're good at all that huggy kissy stuff." And she smiled again, and it was all I could do to not lean over and cuff her ears. She was bright, very fast on her feet, and she managed tension and terror equally well. I had seen her in action, mano-a-mano. The general and I needed to have another chat. I needed to rethink my management strategy. The boss had pretty much left me alone to run the operational side of most cases, but I was more hands-on and needed that to keep my focus on pulling the strings. I had to find the balance between my needs and a style that kept everyone engaged and owning the outcomes.

"General, third time lucky. Thanks to my able padawan, we have a revised strategy for you to consider." And I laid it out for her to get her reaction. She sat back and folded her arms.

"Tell me why we can't stand up a rapid reaction team?"

"Easy. There's nano technology involved and a protective sleeve, and until we can train someone, we only have the one expert who can manage it without setting the bomb off."

"Amira."

"Yes."

"Is she with your team in Ireland?"

"For the moment. I'm planning on shipping her to your floating factory, wherever it is." Still, with her arms folded and a crease running between her eye-brows, she signaled to someone off-camera.

"We need to read in the president. Wait one." The screen froze, then two boxes popped up, one with the general, one with the president, obviously sitting in the Oval Office, and obviously with others in the room.

"Yes, Bridget?"

"Madam President, we have an issue we need to brief you on. It is immediate. I apologize for breaking into your conference." The president waved away the general's apology, asked for the room, waited until it was empty, then looked back at the camera. "Madam President, Commander Riley is also on this call, and I'd ask her to brief you."

Nothing like being dropped into the deep end of the ocean, sharks circling, wearing a weight belt that was too heavy, and bleeding like a pig!

"Madam President, good to see you again. I'm calling you airborne inbound to Ireland. We have a situation I was just getting the general's advice on." I had learned this trick from the boss, who always believed in taking down as many others with him as he could, should circumstances dictate, "I'm up to date on the purported threat of the nuclear bombs as of my last briefing on the subject. What's up now? And I understand you have taken over Colonel Anthony's role. Is that correct?"

"Yes, ma'am, he has moved up to take over from our general. As you know, we believe our science team has developed a method of detecting the new substrate these bombs are made from. It involves a two-part process, one a very high-tech modified laser, the other a detector that can pick up the reflected signals from the substrate. We also have a methodology for encapsulating any bombs we find that contain nuclear material and neuter them."

"You can kill a nuke?"

"Yes, we can. If there's one thing I have learned about our women geniuses is that they are never wrong when it comes to making statements about cause and effect."

"Women geniuses? The women are back in play?" She sat forward in her seat so quickly that the camera momentarily lost its focus.

"New players, at least one in this specific operation, might be more behind the curtain, but we have the old style, identifiable terrorists leading the charge, so we can focus on them and not mention the women."

"So, these will be nuclear bomb attacks by known terrorists?" Her government had decided to blame the entire terrorist activity that had shaken the world and nearly brought it to its economic knees while killing more than thirty million people, displacing another fifty million, and creating havoc and chaos the likes of which had never been experienced before, on identifiable terror organizations. They had never mentioned the role the refugee women had played in the development and delivery of the weapons, and she preferred to keep it that way. As the first tranche of refugee women was either in deep dark holes or dead, it didn't bother me a bit to concentrate on known bad guys. Section Five wasn't in it for the headlines or the reflected glory. We were a sharp, pointy stick and worked best behind the skirts of our client states.

"The front runner is Hamas, courtesy of Amir Abbas. We took two bombs off him in the Gaza Strip just recently. Now we are chasing at least ten or more across Europe, possibly one headed your way, which is why I asked the general's help." She seemed to be thinking, so I gave her a little more of what we had.

"The next target is a Bedouin, Malik Badawi, aka Thana Praxidike, and his girlfriend, Siobhan O'Cleary aka Adriana Nichols. He's attached to Al Bar al Shirak, and she's an Irish refugee nuclear scientist, seriously talented. It's her work you see in the photos of the bomb, she is part of the initial group placed around the world, and we have her academic records, her photo, but precious little else."

"I see. Just how many of these women are there likely to be still out there?"

No one had asked that question, and it was the one thing that bothered me day and night. Would these women come at us in waves, as they were now, and would we have to live in fear of the next genius-level WMD? And if the refugee children were their true cause, what more could they ask of the world under the present circumstances?

"Madam President, from the evidence we have collected, there would appear to be at least twenty very smart women out there some-where until they declare themselves they're invisible." She nodded and looked anything but happy, but what could I do except tell her the truth?

"Thank you, Jessica, Please keep me in the loop." And she clicked off, leaving me and the general to share the screen. The use of my given name suggested she was not angry with me so much as the circumstances, which bolstered my spirits a little.

"Jessica."

"General."

"I'll send you the location of our factory ship, I'll warn the cap-tain you'll want to take over, and I'll clear you for access to all sensitive areas. Who will you have with you?"

"Amira, as science adviser, Sandra as my deputy, maybe one or two Italian special forces, it depends on who Indigo will let me go with."

"You're still a target of opportunity?"

"Want to collect ten million euros? I'm your girl." Her face turned serious, as she considered my banter. To me, it was just an annoyance, but to those around me, a target had been painted on their backs as surely as it had been on mine.

"Have Indigo send me your flight details, and we'll arrange for an escort."

"Thank you. Appreciated."

"Don't thank me, I don't want you crashing down on any of my ships! Go get those bastards!" And I was left looking at my own image, shrunken down to a little square on the bottom of the screen. I didn't recognize the face. It looked too tired and fatigued, worry lines all over the place. It couldn't be me, could it?

# Chapter Seventeen

M alik had a headache, his mood was foul, and his whisky was slopping over the rim of his cut crystal glass, and his companion, while not fearing she would be physically attacked, had shrunk back into a corner of the stateroom from the verbal lashing he had just delivered. Siobhan had simply told him the truth, nothing more, nothing less. She changed her mind about physical abuse when the whisky glass shattered next to her head.

"Stop it! You contracted me to create a sophisticated device that could act as a nuclear bomb, be undetectable, with a range of thirty kilometers, using rail gun technology. The case had to be easy to assemble, load nuclear material, and only be detonated if certain criteria were met. Namely, a velocity of eighteen hundred meters per second, with a plunger system that forces the prime material into the secondary material. This I have given you, and now you shout at me and rage about it not being able to be dropped from the air? What stupidity are you going on with?" She stopped to wipe some whisky off her face, one delicate hand clenched, ready to fight if she had to.

She had no illusions. She had been by Malik's side when he had shot two workers, gutted a third, then smashed his chief weapons designer to death with a hammer after stabbing him several times. While she managed not to register any physical reaction at the time to these wanton acts of terror, the only thing keeping her on the boat was the promise of the second half of her funds, fifty million euros, which would enable her to do the things she had promised her mentor. How had she ever got mixed up with this crazy Arab?

Pride. She had been too wrapped up in her own story to notice that subtle seduction taking place, week after week, as she was courted, romanced, and finally wooed to his side. Yes, he was attractive, and he was pleasant to be around most of the time, but his temper was like a volcano going off, and he did not usually focus on just the implied guilty party.

"All right, I'll give you that you have built me exactly what I said I wanted. But why did you make them so limited in how they can be used?" She looked at him, his face red, his long black silky hair disheveled, his usually immaculate suit creased from his flights to and from Germany during the day. She held up her hands as if to keep him away from her.

"You specifically said eighteen hundred meters a second, and the firing mechanism to be via the rod in the nose penetrating the first chamber, causing it to collapse and crush the second chamber, to create the explosion. You were pedantic about this. You went on and on until my ears started to bleed." He seemed to calm down, dropped his head, let his shoulders sink, then looked back up at her with the full force of his anger.

"I want you to pack seven of the casings, secure them in their cradles, box them, have them stacked, and leave the sabots behind. We're moving to another location, so I can work this clusterfuck out." She looked astonished. He had told her he was going to Germany to get the funds they needed for the nuclear material. She didn't know what had changed so much that he was now at the point of uncontrollable rage.

"And take everything you need to load the material, don't mark the boxes, don't tell any of the crew what you are doing. You will be loading them in a different facility, you'll have everything you need, and if you don't, you'll just have to make do." He turned on his heel and stomped out of the cabin.

Make do? Not likely, she thought to herself. Loading the casing with the two nuclear materials was the hardest single part of the entire operation. One mistake, and you were potentially killed instantly by intense radiation, and that was only if you didn't blow yourself and everyone around you up with a nuclear explosion first.

She walked down the corridor and took the staircase down to her laboratory, which had been specifically fitted out as a Level Five radiation hazard zone, with negative pressure, nuclear dampers, sealed cribs with their long rubber and lead-lined arms and gloves, and the multitude of instruments she needed to measure and manage the installation of the nuclear material in the casings. She had ordered the material to be provided in two forms, the larger component, the plutonium, in preformed slugs to her exact measurements, weight, and physical properties, and the secondary material, Uranium 235, in precisely sculptured balls. She had designed the casings so that an impenetrable substrate membrane would separate the two until punctured by the nose plug.

And yes, the plug would not be able to penetrate the first chamber, breach the membrane, and provide the pathway for the two atomic elements to combine in a beautiful nuclear explosion equivalent to around one thousand five hundred tons of TNT, a blast radius of twenty to thirty kilometers, and with a radiation radius of another twenty to thirty kilometers, unless the projectile impacted at eighteen hundred meters a second. A deadly blast, an equally deadly secondary level of fallout, but not big enough to really do irreparable damage to a city with heavily built-up areas.

The term 'tactical nuke' came to mind, and she smiled. She knew people who had been dreaming of being able to make something like this for tens of years, and now she had done it. The proof lay at her feet, ten beautiful, perfectly machined torpedoes, made from copper and brass, bonded at the atomic level using nanotechnology, which, when loaded to the gills with nuclear material could not be detected if you placed a radiation counter literally on top of the weapon. She smiled, her sisters would be proud of her, and the money she would have once this was over would establish their little conclave in Ireland, where they could adopt a significant number of child refugees who even now were being collected by the International Red Cross and the Red Crescent.

That, plus the environmental plant she would help build on the edge of the Atlantic Ocean. What Malik did not know is that she and her sisters had moved some three billion Euros out of the trust account well before Malik had become involved, thanks to a very sympathetic accountant who just happened to be a refugee herself. And the fund set up in Ireland was twice the size of the funds set up in other countries.

Plans within plans, as her mentor had said, would be needed to navigate the chaos and destruction the terrorists had forced on the world, and while she was sorry for the heartache and emotional storm the attacks had created, she firmly believed that the world needed to suffer as the refugees had before any real change could be counted on.

And there was something else Malik, for all his brutality and pride, did not know or understand, and that was the power of hope. She and her sisters would give hope to new generations of refugees for years and years to come.

She packed the first projectile, located the sealed tube that contained the nano-machines that would both open and close it during the arming process, lay it next to the weapon, then placed a small parcel of metal-wrapped material next to them both. The box was customed designed, and its outside was a bland dark green color with a huge red cross stenciled on top. The words 'DANGER-Toxic Medical Waste' was stenciled on one side, and a yellow band ran around the whole box.

When she had packed all seven, she placed the little wrapped metal packages in a shoulder bag, swung it over her arm, and left the laboratory. *Plans within plans*, she thought to herself and smiled. Not only had she guaranteed her own safety, but she had also made it impossible for anyone to replace her.

She smiled all the way to the shore, noticing that it was turning out to be a beautiful evening, with the moon just cresting the horizon and stars starting to fill the crisp sky. She wondered where they were moving to, but in the end, it didn't really matter.

She and her sisters would prevail, in spite of the aggravation and chest-thumping of the terrorist!

# Chapter Eighteen

The captain of the USS Resplendent, an aging floating factory ship whose genesis was in the first Gulf War, stood on his helicopter deck, hands on his hips, his pristine blue and white at-sea camouflage uniform looking entirely smart, his hair loose and flying in the aftereffects of the rotor wash. A general he had only known of by reputation had warned him to expect visitors and give them the run of the ship. A call to his immediate admiral had confirmed the instruction, with an override, and that the entire operation was to be kept Top Secret, all shipboard cameras and CCTVs were to be turned off for the duration, and anything a Commander Riley asked for, she got. That instruction, alone, put his back up, he was a twenty-five-year veteran with an impeccable service record, and he did not take kindly to being told to take orders from someone he had never met, let alone ever heard of. And a woman.

His back went even further up when the so-called commander deplaned, surrounded by four heavily armed guards, who were dressed identically in black jeans, black military top vests, body armor, dark glasses, and caps. One of the guards had blonde hair creeping out from under her cap and a modern automatic carbine in hand but slung across her chest. A soldier was fussing over the cockpit door to the pilot, but the angle prevented him from seeing why. The group stood rock still, two of the guards facing the rear, making it clear that they were ready for any attack, and just as his vision started to go red from the implied insult, two gunships roared overhead, swung around, so their multi-barreled Gatling guns faced the captain and the helicopter, only to see the blond raise one hand in the air with her thumb up.

The helicopters swung around and disappeared the way they had come. A second group deplaned from the helicopter, which he recognized as belonging to the Irish Special Forces by its markings, and this time it was a stunning young woman, carrying a large metal box with the help of yet another stunning woman, armed to the teeth. Two others soldiers stood by her side at the ready.

*Ready for what?* He thought to himself, why would they be ready for a shootout on the deck of his ship? Then he noticed what looked like bullet holes just under the nose of the helicopter, moved slightly to the side, and saw the holes had peppered the side of the aircraft all the way along the tail boom. The two gunships appeared again, this time one at the bow and one hovering over the stern, and as he recognized them as US Marine Corps by their tail feathers, he relaxed slightly. Something was up, and it was big, so he fell into his training, motioned to the two groups still poised under the helicopter rotors, which were now slowly spinning down, turned on his heel, and led them down a sheltered staircase to a large platform, where his own contingent of marines stood relaxed. Before he could take control of the situation, the commander, or whoever she was, pointed to the cockpit and shouted out for medical help. He didn't look back but continued down to the first level of the ship.

"Incoming, friendly, armed, anxious, and suspicious, so weapons locked, physical escort only at this point."

"Sir, yes, sir!" The squad master chief shouted, motioning to his troops to lower and secure weapons. Just as the last marine secured her weapon, the visitors started to emerge from the stairwell.

"Captain, permission to come aboard. I'm Commander Riley, this is Colonel Kashasini, in command of our mobile forces, and this is Inspector Thomas, my second in command." I pointed to each person as I introduced them, waited until Amira's team arrived, then pointed to her and her precious box. "I need medical assistance immediately for our pilot." I hope my stare got through to him. Having him ignore me the first time started little balls of fire rolling in my gut.

"This is Agent Abramowitz, our scientific adviser, and Agent Remer, her assistant. The colonel and the three agents are with me, and Interpol, Section Five, the troops are special forces lent to us by both the Italian and Irish Governments." I noticed Indigo saluted when he was introduced, but the captain did not return it. That got my hackles up because I knew the level of support the captain had been instructed to give us.

"Permission granted, but I must ask you to disarm and allow my marines to provide any security you may require." Now my hackles were up around my neck, and Sandra must have sensed it because she stepped in front of me, halted three feet from the captain, and gave him one of her 'you'll still love me in the morning' smiles.

"Captain, not only is that not going to happen, but if you have not received clear and unambiguous instructions from your higher command, we can solve that for you very quickly." He felt intimated, unsure of his position, and had never been challenged by a woman ever before in his life, civilian or military. I could see it in his eyes, and in his posture. He was old school, still locked into very old ways, but he was the captain, and while we wouldn't play by his rules, the stakes were far too high for that. We would let him keep his face. I opened my mini, dialed the general, and handed the mini to Sandra, who handed it to the captain.

The marines were getting nervous with the standoff, and shuffling feet and moving bodies signaled something I did not want to evolve.

"Stand down, Amira, Fay, front and center. Everybody relax." While the captain enjoyed his conversation with the general, Amira shuffled forward with her box and Fay, who held one end and stood immediately behind me. Indigo had also moved up, so Amira, Fay, and I were succinctly flanked by Sandra and our troops. The master chief recognized the formation and, caught between a rock and a hard place, visibly rolled his shoulders and his posture. Indigo nodded to him and mirrored his stance. It took one to know one, and I had learned that military respect, warrior to warrior, was the strongest bond next to love. The tension visibly went out of every military person on the deck, except the captain, whose face told the story of his little chat with the general.

He handed the mini back to Sandra and, with a little nod, looked straight at me for the first time, his face tight with frustration.

"Commander, my ship is yours. What do you need?"

"One of my pilots is injured, he's being tended to by our copilot, but I'd like him to be professionally treated; you can have my helicopter assessed as to its flyability, and if necessary, we will call up a replacement. However, the most urgent need we have is for Agents Abramowitz, Remer, and Colonel Kashasini to be taken to your workshop and laboratory, so they can commence their work. While that is going on, I'd like to brief you on what happens next." His look was not quite stoic, and there was no warmth in it at all, so I would have to be very careful with what I said and how I said it.

Two medics ran up the stairs, so my pilot would be looked after at last, but I had made a mental note that would not please the captain. The pilot had been wounded quite badly, in the chest and in the legs, and his side window had exploded in his face, but you would not have known it by the way he continued to fly the aircraft all the way down to the deck. Sitting in the back as we were behind the transmission hub, we had only heard and felt the impact of the rounds from the drone, and as the pilot had been in the right-hand seat, we had not been able to see either the extent of the damage or the injury to the pilot.

But we had seen the explosion of the drone as it was shot down by one of the gunships. The flare and glare from it had filled the cockpit and nearly blinded us. How had they tracked me? Stefarino had told me we had all been removed from the automatic tracking software worldwide. How were they doing it? And who were the 'they'? This was the third time I had been attacked in five days and the second time my crew had been injured. It really was becoming hazardous to be around me. Which brought me to my biggest fear, that by our very presence, this ship would become a target for some sort of attack.

Amira and Fay, with two of our people, were ushered down another set of stairs, and we were led into an anteroom on the main floor of the ship, outside of which we could see amphibious vehicles, rigid inflatables, and even three helicopters in various states of repairs. I gave in to my need to be transparent. We were, after all, Interpol, so I moved to the Captain and skillfully moved him out of the group.

'Captain, we need an urgent conversation with whoever is your commander of this fleet." The look he gave me would have frozen a normal person on the spot, possibly causing them to void their bowels or at least piss themselves. I was far from a normal person, thank God, and I only had one change of clothes for this trip.

"That would be Admiral Rogers, Commander in Chief, Mediterranean Fleet Thirty-Eight (CinCMFTE). Why do you need to talk to him?" Suspicion hung on every word, and I'd have to get around that if we were to succeed.

"Sir, our escorts will have reported to your command that we were attacked en route, and the likelihood of you now being in the cross-hairs is very strong." He looked horrified, then his face snapped back into a more skeptical look as his brain caught up with his emotions.

"Why would anyone want to attack a factory ship of the US Navy sailing in international waters?" I looked at him, trying to work out what to say and how to say it. Sandra, who had attached herself to my shoulder like a leech, solved the problem for me but possibly created another. Time would tell because as she leaned forward, the barrel of her H&K swung towards the Captain, an innocent but noticeable move that had the master chief sucking his teeth.

"Because the fucked-up bastards that are trying to kill the commander are the same terrorists that tried to kill the world just three months ago. You remember that, don't you?" And her smile had been replaced by a polite look I had never seen before, and I could literally feel her vibrating inside her combat uniform. Whether it was the situation or the after-effects of the attack, I couldn't tell, or it just could have been the obvious male chauvinistic attitude of the Captain. My money was on that, as I had never seen her metaphorically get off her bike over something as simple as being shot at.

"And in case you don't read the papers, this is the same commander who led the attacks that took the terrorists out of commission."

He looked horrified.

"We rely on our destroyer and submarine escort, and when we have it, carrier air cover. Our ship is not really equipped to fight off an air attack. We can manage small boat incursions, and our marine detachment is first class, but we're part of a team." He almost whined the last statement, and I pitied the sailors under him. I gave up and dialed the general again.

"General, I'm here with the Captain. He is attending to our needs, thank you for that, but the bigger problem is we might just have turned your lovely little factory ship into a target of opportunity."

"I worked that one out when your escort reported back. I've arranged for a permanent air cover for you. How bad is your helicopter?"

"Don't know at this point. It's being examined as we speak. But I'll need a crew replacement, even if it can fly again."

"We can manage that. Do you remember the captain of the carrier group that picked you up out of the Atlantic?" I smiled. How could I ever forget him? Apart from his looks which were first class, he had helped us without question, looked after my injured crew, and then got Sandra and me safely back home without incident.

"Yes, I remember him well."

"He's now running MFTE, and he'll be on your ship by fifteen hundred hours today with his 2IC. They will make everything happen for you from that point on and get your sorry arse back in one piece."

"I want to know how they tracked us. Malcolm is in that loop. Have you spoken to him?"

"I had a quick chat with Frank just now. He is as perplexed as your own people back in Venice. The real question is where did they get the drone from, who was flying it, and how many more do they have?"

"Yes, that occurred to me as well. Thanks for your help. It's invaluable."

"Just don't let the bastards get one aimed at us." And as usual, she clicked off without saying goodbye. I pocketed the mini and looked at my watch, we had just over an hour to go before the Admiral got here, so I took the cowards way out.

"Sir, any chance of getting a meal for my team, please? We haven't eaten in quite a while" He looked shocked, as if I had asked for the life of his firstborn, waved furiously at his chief, turned on his heel, and stalked off. The chief moved over to Indigo, saluted him, turned to me, saluted me, and in the deepest voice I had ever heard, asked us to follow him.

We did.

The mess was well fitted out, all stainless steel and gray topped tables, and only had a few sailors eating at this time. I motioned to the chief.

"Master Chief, could you take my 2IC here to the laboratory, please?" He nodded, stood up, and waited for Sandra. I whispered in her ear. She nodded, tapped Indigo on the shoulder, and followed the master chief out. I didn't want the torpedo we had brought with us to be unpacked until after the Admiral and I had our next chat. I went about eating the steak, eggs, bacon, and toast that had been put in front of me by one of Indigo's team and tried to forget the hostility of the captain.

Sandra walked back in and sat down beside me, and Indigo slipped her a tray of food passed to him by the master chief.

"Thanks, master chief, appreciated." He just nodded and got his own tray. I noticed that some of his team had arranged themselves next to ours and were earnestly trying to pry information out of them.

"*Mi scusi, dispiace, non parlo inglese,*" rang around the table, and I smiled to myself. There were more multilinguists in our team than they probably had at the UN, but it was fun to watch the marines try to pry information out of our boys and girls, and it made me very proud of them. The master chief suddenly sprang to his feet.

"Sir!"

"Master Chief, kindly escort the commander to the bridge." The Captain disappeared as fast as he had arrived, so I stood with Sandra and followed the master chief out, signaling to Indigo to take over. A gracious nod was all I got back, but the hardened look in his eyes told me he was not losing his focus.

"Sir, yes, sir."

After the usual torturous climb up and down narrow metal stairs, ducking through watertight bulkheads fitted with the usual shin cutters and headbangers, we arrived on the bridge to see the captain standing rigidly at attention next to the tall, weathered admiral who had only been a captain the last time we had met. His silver-gray hair was cut very short, his shoulders those of a linebacker, and his ramrod-straight posture told me he was pissed. Maybe that's why the Captain had been sent on messenger duty.

"Commander, welcome. Good to see you again." I came to attention and saluted, which he returned. Sandra was still on my shoulder, and she was looking anything but happy. The Admiral looked around, noted the master chief and the bridge crew, and then with a shoulder turn, started to step out.

"Come with me, please." We did, the master chief did, but everyone else on the bridge remained where they were. I noticed that two destroyers had formed up in a close protection detail and that the two gunships were still hovering over our fantail and our bow. An officer, I assumed, was the Admiral's 2IC, met us in front of a large open space that looked like a recreation area. As we entered, the master chief shut the door and stood in front of us in the at-east position, arms behind his broad back. The officer leaned forward to shake my hand.

"Jordan Summers, 2IC to Admiral Rogers, and it's a pleasure to meet you both." Sandra shook hands and almost went back to her guard dog stance, then sensing the dynamics had changed, relaxed and stuck her hands in her pockets. I made a snap decision, something I was known for, and signaled to the master chief. "Sir," I said, looking at the admiral, "I need the master chief to take Inspector Thomas back to the science laboratory and ask both my team to come here with their package." The Admiral nodded to the Master Chief, who left the room, trailed by Sandra, who gave me a dirty look over her shoulder. "It would be of help if colonel Kashasini could also attend." He looked at his 2IC, who also left the room. "Jessica, for the next little while, why don't you call me Paul, and why don't you relax a little. Your pilot is in an induced coma, his wounds are treated, and he is expected to make a full recovery. You seem to be making a habit of getting your pilots shot," and his face lit up with a smile, taking all the tension out of the room and some of the pain I felt. He was right-two pilots in seven days. Getting another crew might prove problematic! I kept my anger about how long it had taken us to get medical assistance to myself.

"Paul, thank you, it really is good to see you, and congratulations on your promotion." He smiled, as I expected he would. He was an utter professional. It had shone out of him the last time we had met on the bridge of his carrier.

"It's only 'acting' at this point. There's no Congress to ratify it!" and he laughed as if he couldn't care less. "However, the speed with which I was promoted, then moved to MFTE was probably your doing, and I'm told from those that know, the president is very firm on us helping you in any way we can. Can you tell me why?" I looked at him, and just then, the door opened, and Amira and Fay walked in, the huge metal box between them, closely followed by Indigo, who halted at the door and saluted the Admiral.

"Sit down, make yourselves comfortable, Master Chief. Take the door, please." We all sat, Sandra back on my shoulder, Indigo on my other side, with Amira and Fay looking very uncomfortable with the box between them on the deck.

"Sir, can you confirm that this room is not under surveillance of any type?" The return to formal address caused him to narrow his eyes, but he looked at the master chief, who nodded, then nodded to me.

"Sir, what I am about to tell you is classified beyond top secret, president's eyes only, and must remain that way until she says otherwise. Agreed?" He looked very serious, his face revealing nothing but intense interest.

"I can agree to that and see that it is enforced." My turn to nod. I pointed to the box, then looked Amira in the eyes. She read what was in them, opened the box and took the torpedo in its black Kevlar bag out, and laid it on the floor. Fay reached down, and pulled the sheath off, laid it to one side.

"Sir, what you have here is a purpose-designed bimetal substrate shell that can contain nuclear material, and when it does, it cannot be detected by any radioactive detection means we know of and has been designed to be fired from a ship fitted with a rail gun, and then accelerated by a rocket motor, all fitted into a sabot shell. Once again, nanotechnology developed some five or six years ago has been used to manufacture this device." I paused to let it all settle in their minds and watched as amazement turned to fear as the ramifications sunk in. There were highly trained military minds at the very top of their profession, and there wouldn't be very much that they didn't know about the nuclear attack and its aftermath.

"The range is estimated to be between twenty-five to thirty-five kilometers, the initial blast radius some ten to twenty kilometers, the secondary twenty to forty, and the radiation radius out beyond fifty kilometers." I paused again to let them absorb the data.

"There are at least ten of these in play and may be as many as twenty-five. We have a possible target list left on an old website by an Irish splinter group, and amongst the list, New York was mentioned." He reacted to this, I hadn't run him, but he possibly had family in or around the five boroughs.

"Our scientist, agent Abramowitz, and her team have developed a means of detecting these shells, it is a two-part strategy, and we are onboard this ship in the hope that we can manufacture multiple devices and have you install them and operate them throughout the Mediterranean Sea. Many of the parts you will need are available from our laboratory in Israel and can be flown in once we know what you will need." I paused again, I was carefully watching the master chief, whose eyes had gone deep black, and his stance had tightened as if we were preparing to jump. I understood his emotions. I had a similar reaction the first time I learned about the torpedoes.

Arthur C. Clark, a prolific writer of science fiction and one who predicted satellites and worldwide communication in the nineteen sixties, once said, 'Any sufficiently advanced technology is indistinguishable from magic'. And that's what we had here, in effect. Nanotechnology enabled two metals to be bonded at the atomic level, creating a nonporous substrate that could contain two of the most potent radioactive elements known to man and not be able to be detected by Giger counters.

"Sir, I know this is a lot to take in, but we have been working this case for a couple of weeks now, and we know some of the who, maybe the when not the why, or even what happens next. But we are working on it. Questions?" The master chief looked like he was going to jump out of his skin, and I was pleased to hear his question.

"How much do these things of yours weigh loaded?" I smiled at him. "Come on over and pick it up." He left the door and hefted the torpedo with little effort.

"Add six kilos fully loaded, and there you have it. If it is fitted into a sabot shell, then you can expect to add another twenty or thirty kilos." The look on his face said it all. Horror mixed with surprise as he lifted the shell up and down as if weighing it.

"This little bastard is very bad news. You could hide it anywhere, carry it in anything. It must be a terrorist's delight." I smiled at the master chief; his appreciation of its damaging potential was similar to my own.

"What are your priorities?" the Admiral asked. He took the shell from his master chief, and repeated the same lifting up and down gesture, then shook his head.

"We have been worried about suitcase bombs for decades, but this takes the conversation to a whole new level. I assume that this nano process can generate any shape?" I hadn't thought of that, points to the Admiral, so I looked to Amira.

"Yes, sir, theoretically, you could manufacture any shape or size you wanted."

"Back to my question, Jessica, what are your priorities?" His use of my given name reassured me that he was going to listen to me and, hopefully, see the logic in what I proposed.

"Sir, step one is to fit one of the two systems we have brought with us to one of your destroyers, then deploy it to the coast and start the search for the bombs that we believe are salted somewhere between Spain and Turkey." I paused to let him assimilate what I had just said, and I could see his thinking reflected in his eyes.

"Step two is to manufacture additional lasers and detectors, then get them on ships in the Atlantic and the Pacific." He turned to look at me. I had caught him momentarily off guard.

"Why the Atlantic and Pacific?"

"Sir, our intelligence is that the terrorists may have fitted out a ship, some three hundred and fifty feet in length, that has the capability of firing these bombs fitted in sabots. In fact, at this point, and not to be taken literally, it may be the only way to deliver these bombs and have them explode."

"Explain."

"Amira?"

"Sir, the design of this shell is that it has a bulbous nose in the shape of a rod, and," she said while performing her magician's trick of opening the shell up into two halves, laying them side by side, "you can see here this metallic membrane between the two chambers?" He nodded.

"Our research indicates that the rod at the front is designed to break away from the casing, penetrate the first chamber, then continue through the membrane into the second chamber, with the resultant mixing of the two nuclear materials leading to a nuclear explosion." He leaned forward, ran his hands across one half, bumped his fingers up and over the membrane, and looked straight at Amira.

"One of these chambers is designed to take a plug of what?"

"We think plutonium."

"And this ball cavity?"

"Uranium 235."

"Tried, tested, and proven. Well, well, you do find interesting work, Jessica. Have you estimated the force needed to push the plug all the way into the second chamber?"

"Our calculations show a force of around fifty-four thousand newtons or around one thousand pounds per square inch. Velocity wise, that is eighteen hundred meters per second, with an assumed full weight of thirty kilos or more."

"Master Chief, what is the standard velocity of a sabot round we fire?"

"Sir, the standard one-hundred-millimeter sabot has a velocity of eighteen hundred meters a second." The Admiral nodded to himself; the data was lining up in a way that was becoming inescapable.

"Okay, Jessica, we interrupted your flow. You were saying we cover both major oceans. Consider that acknowledged. What's next?"

"We use my C&C to coordinate the detection possibilities in all areas, and we have a rapid reaction team that colonel Kashasini commands on standby, and they can neutralize the bombs on the spot. We have a support aircraft in Ireland with two drones, already fitted for transmission and detection. They are already airborne as we speak. We have a command-and-control aircraft in Dublin and a support team of shooters sitting in Greece. We know the bombs were moved from Afghanistan ten or twelve weeks ago. We just don't know where or by what means.

"We are assuming road and sea, low tech, and we took the first two bombs into custody in the Gaza Strip, so we are using that as a baseline reference in terms of time and distance. The targets mentioned in the Irish bulletin board were London, Dublin, Manchester, New York, Rome, Glasgow, and Paris, and we have already scanned the inland corridor to some extent, but we think we may have been a little early, and that if anything we may have been in front of the transport, whatever they are using. Or simply on the wrong side of the Mediterranean."

"The mast height of this ship is twice that of a destroyer. Is that an advantage?" I looked at Amira again.

"Yes, sir, and if you could move fifty kilometres off the coast, that would be perfect." He nodded and looked at his 2IC.

"Rob, make that happen, get whatever manufacturing support you need, and inform Fleet HQ we are maneuvering, but no details." He turned to look at me again.

"You want your people off this ship?"

"Yes, sir, as soon as you have a team that can produce the lasers and the detectors. However, I'm not sure my helicopter is going anywhere soon, and I'll need a pilot."

"I can call in a chopper for you, and that will solve the pilot problem, and Rob and I will stay with this ship for the foreseeable future. Do you have a secure means of communication? I've heard rumours." I bet he had. I looked at Indigo, who reached into his backpack and produced a mini.

"This will connect you directly to me, and there is a very short list of others. Do you want to know who they are?" He looked directly at me, a thin smile, his only noteworthy facial feature.

"I can guess, but for now, you will do. I take it that this is also not to be mentioned in general discussion?" My turn for a thin smile.

"This is the most closely guarded secret in Interpol, and we'd appreciate you keeping it that way." He stood, reached out his hand, shook, then took his 2IC by the shoulder and walked towards the door. The master chief opened it for them, then just stood there as if waiting for his next order.

"Amira, Fay, Indigo, back to the salt mine. Let me know when you have an estimate for bugging out. Sandra, with me. Thanks, Master Chief. We appreciate all your help." As we walked through the door, I got the feeling that the master chief was itching to say something, so I stopped and turned to him, raising one eyebrow.

"Master Chief?"

"Ma'am, should you need more boots on the ground, my team is trained in counterinsurgency and hazardous materials recovery that covers nuclear, biological, and chemical. Love to help!" And the light in his eyes was as strong as a searchlight, so I smiled, then thought of something I needed to know.

"Master Chief, how do you dress the ship for a nuclear attack?"

"We have topside water guns that produce a deluge down the sides of our hull, and across the decks and topsides, we have bio suits for the standing watch and airtight and radiation-proof cabins for the rest. We can last fifty hours before we run out of clean air, and we can treat low dosages of radiation poisoning in our sick bay." I nodded, taking all that in and hoping against hope that none of it would ever be necessary.

It took three hours, three hours I had used to chat with my team in Venice, Malcolm, and Luigi, with regards to how we had been tracked, and a quick call to Arie for an update. All good there, no retaliation so far for our little incursion into Gaza, and a call to Anna to test the temperature in Washington, then check-in with both Bob and Tom, and the whole time Sandra snored little delicate grunts as she slept alongside me. I must admit, I nearly nodded off a couple of times, but finally, Amira and Fay appeared, carrying their silver box, with Indigo in trail.

"Jessica, we have made two more sets. The technicians are making another twenty to distribute to the fleets, which will take them a day or two due to them needing parts, and the ship is ready for a test when you are." I sat up, dug my elbow into Sandra's midriff, was surprised by the hard muscle it hit, then stood myself, rolled my shoulders, then stopped in my tracks. How to do this without engaging the Captain? I reached for my mini.

"Admiral, I understand you are ready to test the equipment?" His face looked off-center, then I realized he was holding the mini while trying to balance a coffee.

Coffee! My nose twitched, and then I realized I was on board a navy ship, and coffee only had to be requested as a matter of policy!

"The master chief will escort you." He clicked off. I wondered what was so all-consuming that he had been short with me. I didn't have time to develop that thought as the master chief arrived and led us to the bridge. We left the box outside the door and entered. The Admiral met us, waved us over to a very large radar screen, waved everyone else away, signaled to his 2IC, who called 'battle stations, one cee, this is not a drill' into the inter ship tannoy and watched as the bridge crew fitted flash protectors over their heads, then slipped goggles and a battle helmet on before standing up at their stations. The 2IC handed us the same equipment, and we fitted ourselves out as quickly as we could.

"The system we are using for the test has your detector mounted on the hull of one of the gunships, Bravo Two; the laser is mounted on our topmast antiaircraft radar dish, we've slowed the rotations down to the slowest speed we can, and any signal the chopper picks up with being bounced to this screen."

"Sir, where are we in relationship to the coast?"

"Twenty-two nautical miles off the French Rivera, heading east, approximately abeam Saint Tropez, passing Cannes in five minutes. Scanning now." I suddenly thought of something.

"Admiral, keep the chopper above one thousand feet, three hundred and twenty meters, don't let them stop if they detect anything. Just record and report." He handed me a microphone, so I spoke to the gunship pilot and laid out what I wanted.

"Thank you, sir," I said to the Admiral as I passed the microphone back. He just smiled. Then the most amazing thing happened, and alarm went off, and every head turned to the radar screen.

"Contact, three objects, continuing flight plan." And there, as clear as day, three bright blobs sat in a row, on what I couldn't tell yet, but we had found some more of the torpedoes. I opened my mini, then snapped it shut. We might not have that much time. I held my hand out, and the admiral gave me back the microphone.

"Bravo two, I need pictures of that location."

"Transmitting now." And on a large computer screen, the top-down images of six very large boats swam into focus, and there, bright and shiny, was our three hundred and fifty footer, in all its glory, and the overlay from the detector showed the three bombs to be on board, just aft of the centerline. And it was well over three hundred feet long, surprise, surprise.

"Bravo two, remaining fuel?"

"We have two hours loiter time, sir."

"Nearest airport?"

"That would be Cote d'Azur on this heading, or if we backtrack, Cannes Mandelieu. Advise?"

"Admiral, can you get them refueled and hold them on the ground for my orders?"

"We can do that. What are you thinking?"

"Wait for one," I said to him, opening the channel to the pilot, "Cote d'Azur, fuel will be arranged. Sit down, and wait for instructions. Can you go weapons hot?"

"Yes sir, we have an anti-air plus ground attack, full load."

"Stand by Bravo Two." I handed the microphone to the 2IC, who had watched this little interplay with fascination in his eyes. He had probably never seen someone take over a ship or gunship in the admirals' presence before, but then neither of them had worked in the trenches with me before, either.

"Admiral, I have two problems. I need to neutralize that ship immediately, and I need to take possession of those three bombs. My rapid reaction team is three hours away. Can I use your marines to achieve objective one while they travel?"

"Our technical staff are trained in handling nuclear materials if that's any help?"

"Under normal circumstances, it would be, but our team has the ability to neuter those bombs if they are hot. So basically, I want to storm the ship with your marines, use the gunship to shove its missiles and guns right up their guts to intimidate them, then stabilize the situation until my team can get here. Indigo, have you arranged that?"

"*Sì, comandante, sono in volo.*"

"*Allora atterra a Cannes, faremo prendere un rame e farli atterrare sul ponte del nostro obiettivo.*"

"*Sì, comandante.*" I looked at the admiral, his 2IC patiently standing by, the bridge crew looking on but trying not to look if you know what I mean, and I realized I really had taken over the ship.

"Apologies, Admiral. I should have asked your permission before acting."

"Forget it. What did you just discuss with your colonel?

"Apologies again, Admiral. Colonel Kashasini is the head of our rapid reaction team. I asked him if they were airborne, then told him to get them to Cannes, where we would chopper them to the boat. If that is okay with you, sir?"

"Rob, make it so call our closest sheepdog in behind us to lend support, have everyone else reduce speed, and hold the position."

"Jessica, do we dress the ship for a nuclear attack?" Every head turned towards me, and I had to weigh what we would do next with what could go wrong.

"Sir, at this time, I suggest we don't. Can you get us to the harbor asap?"

"Yes. How many?" I looked at Indigo. He held up four fingers, I would need Amira and Fay at some point, but I needed Fay now as well.

"Eight for trip one. When we are secured, I'll need the remainder of my crew. Can I take your master chief with me, and can he have secure comms back to you" He nodded, and the master chief ran off to get his equipment, so I took the opportunity to brief the bridge crew, and the Admiral, without appearing to do so.

"Listen up, this will be an Interpol police action sanctioned by both the UN and our client states of Israel, Italy, the UK, Ireland, and the US, we are hunting terrorists, and all weapons will be hot. Do you understand what I have just said?" I looked around the crew, only saw confusion in their eyes, and wondered what I had said that didn't resonate. Then I got it. Military minds, military speak.

"There are verified weapons of mass destruction on shore. We are tasked with retrieving them and consider this to be an action where we will shoot first if necessary and apologize never. Now, are there any questions?" The smile on the Admiral's face told the crew that they were in it up to their flame-protected necks, and before any further conversation could take place, the master chief ran in, dressed for war.

"The fast boat is waiting for portside, ma'am. Ready when you are." I turned to look at the Admiral, he just saluted me, then stood in the at-ease position, so I saluted him back and followed the master chief out.

The rubber inflatable boat was a favorite of special forces. They were really fast, easy to maneuver, came in various sizes, and had a relatively low profile. Their nickname was 'ribbie". I bent until I was adjacent to the master chief's ear.

"Get us alongside the smaller boat, two down from the target. Follow us until you have a clear view of our attack, call the chopper in at your discretion, and anticipate a reaction. I don't know how many, but over the last seven days, they have come at us three times, from a squad of twenty doped-up louts to a drone shooting us out of the sky mid-Atlantic, and today another drone tried to kill our helicopter and us with it. Weapon's free, Master Chief. This is a kill mission, not capture, and keep your head down." I turned back to my team.

"Indigo, Fay, you and two flank them to starboard. Sandra and I, with four, will go to the port. I want the ship neutralized. A prisoner or two would be nice, but you already know my feelings on that, safety first, and no one gets away, understood?" Just nodding heads, and Indigo and his team jumped out, split off, ran around some infrastructure. This being a very socially orientated location, there were bars, shops, and civilians everywhere. They would get a great show for their money, and with luck, none of them would ever know what went down.

I led my team to the port side, and noticed that as the ship was stern in, a large plank joined it to the shore, with a silver rail on each side. We had limited options with respect to boarding. Sometimes you get the doughnut, sometimes the hole.

I ran forward, crouching over my sights, and felt Sandra against my shoulder. We hit the deck and rolled behind a large enclosure, then bounced up and ran into a saloon of some type, brightly lit, with four tough-looking males sitting around a large bar, all of whom now looked startled, and started reaching for what I presumed were weapons.

"Halt!" I shouted, then Sandra repeated it in Italian, French, Arabic, and just to show off in Gaelic! I saw our four running down the outside deck and Indigo's team running down the starboard side, then a fifth person burst into the saloon from behind a cutesy curtain firing a sub-machine gun. His shots stitched the floor around our feet. My three-round burst hit him in the center of his face, Sandra's in the middle of his chest, and of course, being heroes, the other four musclemen tried to use the distraction to get their own guns out, so we had no choice, I took the two on the left, Sandra the two on the right, and as the silence settled on the room, our ears ringing from the gunshots, we heard more fire from up forward, and over our heads.

We ignored it and climbed the stairs to the upper deck, which in the plans we had seen, should lead us to the weapons area. It didn't work at first. We ran straight into a laboratory of some sort, just as two grubby people, one a man and one a woman, dressed in dirty overalls covered in grease and dirt, raced around the corner holding long knives, so we both knelt and shot them multiple times in their center of mass until they stopped running. We raced through the laboratory and straight into what looked like a store room, and sure enough, three mylar baskets were mounted in little cradles that sat in indentations on the floor, with little silver metal packages sitting next to them. There were seven other indentations, all empty. We had the three bombs that had shown up in Amira's magic locator system.

Were they hot? I didn't know, and I wasn't going to touch them or let anyone else touch them until I had Amira. Now I had to secure the ship, hold it until our larger team arrived, and keep everyone calm.

"Go get the Master Chief."

"No. Send someone else." I looked at Sandra, her H&K giving off little trickles of smoke from the barrel, her head swiveling like a radar, shrugged my shoulders, opened my mini, called Indigo, and settled the issue. The master chief ran up to us, his weapon held in the port arms position, looking pissed.

"You had all the fun. Ma'am." His disappointment notwithstanding, I pointed to the three cradles.

"Sorry we didn't have time to call you earlier. We need to secure this ship. What I would really like to do is sail it away from here. Do you think that's possible?" He looked at me with a fierce grin, reminding me of my childhood when I had seen a small boy's face when given a toy, and then someone had tried to take it away from him. Indigo and his team trotted in and formed up a live barrier between us and the shore.

"Commander, there is much movement on shore. It is possible we could be attacked." That decided me on the spot.

"Master Chief, take anyone you need except the crew here. Get us out to sea soonest."

"Yes, ma'am." He grabbed two soldiers just as the gunship arrived over our stern, making an incredible racket, then lowered itself onto our roof. If that didn't give the bad guys pause, I didn't know what would. Deep below my feet, I heard the rumble of engines, two soldiers threw mooring lines off onto the dock, and as we started to move, the plank that had joined us on the dock fell into the water. In a matter of minutes, we were hiding behind a destroyer, in sight of the factory ship, and wondering what to do next. The problem was solved when another rubber duckie pulled alongside, and a bunch of marines and sailors climbed aboard.

One of them worked their way to us, saluted, then, in the deepest southern drawl I had ever heard, asked me what we wanted to do with the bodies, of which there were plenty.

"Strip them, search them, take ID and anything else we can use forensically, then bury them at sea."

"Yes sir." He saluted again, then left. I needed a coffee, so I leaned forward and tapped Indigo on the shoulder.

"Indigo, can you hustle coffee from the galley, please?"

"*Certamente, comandante, piacere mio!*" Sandra smiled again. Good, she was regaining her sense of humor. I walked over to the cabin wall, slipped down with my back against it, my weapon across my lap, and tried to relax. Not unexpectedly, she slumped down beside me, but between the stern and our position. She was taking this guard dog's duty seriously. Post-action adrenaline was racing through my system, and the calm that had followed the storm felt very uncomfortable.

Killing people was not my forte, but in this business, you tended to get into kill-or-be-killed situations all too often. It seemed like none of the bad guys wanted to have a conversation with a pair of lonely women.

Chauvinist pigs!

And before I could develop that particular thought, another ribbie pulled up, and the admiral and his 2IC climbed aboard with that innate grace that came from having spent years and years at sea. We both stood up and almost made it to the attention position when he waved us back down and scrunched next to me. His 2IC stood loosely in the middle of the room, watching the body bags get filled.

"Jessica. I let you go off on your own, and you make a mess. What am I going to do with you?" His smile underscored his sarcasm, then he got serious.

"My master chief tells me you stormed the ship and, in less than two minutes, took on over thirty armed terrorists, not to mention three potentially armed nuclear bombs, then stole the ship from under the noses of a bunch of guys with guns on the shore who from all accounts, were seriously pissed with you." He turned to look at me, a grin telling me he was okay with my actions and those of my team, so I took the opportunity to let out a significant sigh, releasing some of the built-up tension.

"Your master chief stole the boat; we just came along for the ride." That got me a gut laugh, and I noticed the master chief had joined the 2IC standing in the middle of the room. Just then, Indigo and one of his team walked in with a tray of steaming coffee, handed one to each of the men standing guard, then worked their way over to us.

"*Comandante, il tuo espresso, posso fare qualcos'altro per te in questo momento?*" I took my mug and just gave him a foolish grin. The adrenalin was washing through my system, and I was almost back to normal and would be in five glorious slurps!

"*Grazie Indigo, se volessi una moglie, saresti la mia prima scelta!*" He laughed at my invitation to be my wife and moved back to his team, who were now sipping their espresso like they were possessed.

"Jessica, what do you want us to do next?" I looked at the admiral, slurping a mug of espresso, slumped against the bulkhead, looking relaxed and comfortable in his skin, and hoped I could demonstrate such strong and inspiring leadership to my own team when the occasion demanded.

"Sir, my rapid reaction team is half an hour away. They will need to be collected and flown here. They will defuse the bombs if necessary, secure them, and then we will need to transport the shells back to our laboratory in Israel. My team and I will have to get back to Ireland and start the search for the other bombs. It occurs to me that if you allowed us to train up a response team from your sailors and marines, it would give us an advantage when we locate other bombs. However, if you do that, they will have to transfer to my command for the duration." That got me a tight look, the idea that he would lose direct control over some of his men and women not immediately sitting comfortably with him.

"Sir, this is my fault. We reacted too fast initially, our resources were not sufficient for what we needed to do, and I have been making our tactics up on the fly. The cradles in the storeroom indicate that there are at least another seven devices out there, and Europe is a very large hunting ground."

"Jessica, from what I have seen, you did exactly the right thing at the right time. But maybe we can help going forward with more than just resources and manpower." I looked at him with a question or two in my eyes, wondering what this large, seemingly gentle man who had recently commanded a carrier group in the Atlantic and had been moved specifically into my area of operations by the president's general, was thinking.

"What do you have in mind, sir?" He stood, handed his empty mug to his 2IC, who had moved towards us at the movement of his boss, looked at Indigo's team barricading the deck, looked up at the continuous thump of the gunship's rotors, then back at the cradles.

"Why don't you get these bombs dealt with, then meet me back on the bridge, and we can talk it out." I nodded. I could do that and felt the gunship lift off the roof, the pitch of its rotors increasing to a vibrating roar, only to be replaced by an even louder roar as another helicopter landed on the roof.

Bomb defusing time.

I had asked for Amira to be sent over, and she arrived just before the Rapid Response Team (RRT). They formed a huddle around the first torpedo, and we could hear the odd mutter in Hebrew and Italian, with the odd English curse thrown in for good measure.

Amira waved me over, holding a small instrument in her hands. The three sheaths had been stripped of the bombs, and they gleamed and shone like evil messengers from Hell.

"Jessica, these shells are not hot. However, each bomb has a proximity explosion linked to it, and they need to deal with it first. We will bag them, but they are exactly the same as the two we took in Gaza." I thought about that. In a way, that was good news. The terrorists hadn't had the time to get the nuclear materials. The bad news was that they had left their launching system behind on the boat, so what were they planning now. And where were they?

"Bag them. Give me a minute." I walked over to Indigo, whose team was still guarding our rear.

"Indigo, you need to train the locals in rapid response, fit them out with sleeves and nanomaterial, and make sure they are comfortable and properly equipped.

"Once they are up to standard, get your team back to Ireland. We're going to have to split our attention between here and Ireland for the short term. I need you with me when I meet the admiral. Link up when you see us start to move out." He nodded and patted me on the shoulder. It made me feel good, and not quite as much behind the eight ball.

"Sally, my girl, you and I have a lot of thinking to do."

"How do we manage two teams half a continent away, maintain control, find the nukes when or preferably before they become nukes, that sort of thing?" I nodded, mindful that while she wore black lace underwear under her combat clothes, she was not only a great shooter but had a very active mind and was as smart as anyone I had even met-except maybe Amira, but we can't all be geniuses!

"Got it in one. Few other things, but that covers the main points." Indigo emerged from the group, crouched over the bombs, waited until I saw him, then pulled me aside.

"Commander, where do you want these bombs to be sent to?" I looked at Sandra, then at Indigo, and saw the answer in their eyes.

"Call Arie, get him to collect them. Let's go talk to the admiral."

We were not exactly piped aboard, but this time we were actually welcomed, with lots of grinning faces, high fives, and even a little finger clicking. A navy ship's crew was the most incestuous of social gatherings, and word of our little adventure would have spread like wildfire. We were escorted straight to the bridge, and I immediately noticed the absence of the captain. I let it ride. Politics was not my strong point.

"Sir, permission to come aboard?" And I saluted him, received one in return, and then we were led to a small stateroom that had a large planning table against one wall.

"Commander, we have your two prisoners ready for interrogation when you are ready. In the meantime, let me show you where we are up to." He used a small laser pointer to highlight parts of the map. "We now have three destroyers deployed with the laser devices you designed, and the gunship we used the first time has been joined by its partner, and we now have two detectors that can fly the coast. Our radar can reach one hundred and fifty nautical miles, the destroyers one hundred and twenty, and our geeks calculate that if the choppers fly at seventeen hundred meters, around five thousand feet, we can scan that wide a corridor in four sweeps. At the moment, both are holding on board, waiting for your instructions." My head was ringing from the after-action effects, and I desperately needed to think.

"Sir, may Inspector Thomas and I afford ourselves of your facilities, have a shower, and change into something more suitable? Could we then pick this up in, say, thirty minutes?" Indigo gave me the tiniest of nods, Amira and Fay remained neutral, but I knew Fay had worked out what I was doing. The admiral nodded and pointed to a sailor on the door, who started out, and we followed.

We hit the head, were given privacy, our carryalls were delivered, we stripped off our combat clothes, and sure enough, Sandra was wearing a frilly black lace bra and panties, and I shook my head in wonder. In contrast, my dull khaki sports bra and matching shorts put me to shame in the glamour stakes.

"Sir, Commander, Ma'am, Jessica, whoever you are at this moment, why do you need a break, and what is it you are so concerned about?" I looked at her soaping herself up, all tanned, muscular, sharply framed, supporting long blond hair that even wet looked sleek and like the pelt of seal, and a face so commanding and naturally beautiful it could sink ships. How had someone so elegant and good-looking gotten into the business of hunting and killing terrorists? I washed the soap out of my eyes, rolled my head back to let the hot water run over my face, and soaked in the heat. In direct contrast, my choppy hair sat like a wet floor mat, waiting for someone to scrape their boots across.

"Padawan, little cricket, Sally, think on this. You are a bad-arsed terrorist with a bunch of bombs that can be turned into tactical nukes with a bit of work, yet you abandon the launching platform that you spent months and hundreds of millions of euros building and fitting out, and then for no apparent reason you suddenly up and run away with an armful of your bombs, to go where? How?" She stopped her rinsing motion, tilted her head slightly to one side, and the water ran over her face and breasts like a miniature waterfall.

"I run away because the big bad Interpol is about to attack my boat?" I shook my own head, letting the water splash over the walls, thinking that this was why dogs loved getting wet. So they could share the joy with everyone around them!

"They didn't know we were coming. Did you sense any awareness when we boarded?"

"No."

"Any sign they were expecting a visit?"

"No."

"So, why move seven casings off the boat? I need Amira's confirmation, but that laboratory looked like it could handle the nuclear materials. This ship was purpose-built, don't forget, why leave it? And, I might throw in just to tease you, why leave the launching system?"

"At the risk of being sent to bumfuck Alaska, let me speculate on that. Last point first. They are going to launch them using some other method." I smiled. She was not only bright but very fast. That was my number one concern. If they were changing their launch strategy, we had a whole different ball of wax to melt and pull apart. The rail gun gave us a range limit. If they changed the delivery system, with the small size of the bombs, they could go anywhere and hit anywhere.

"Exactly. And?" We both started to dry ourselves, the faded blue navy towels living up to their reputation for thinness, so I used three without any compunction. Sandra used that many just on her hair. She was such a girl!

"Well, seeing I've survived so far and using the evidence we have collected to date, I speculate they have had trouble getting the core materials for some reason. So maybe the move was to get closer to a source, or maybe their battle plan had changed for reasons unknown, and they intend to launch the bombs from other devices, maybe even from the air." I nodded, climbing into my favorite pair of black jeans, which I noted were getting a little light on in the material department on the knees, so a shopping spree was in my future, and wouldn't that be fun? Ten million euros on my head and no online shopping anymore meant a physical visit somewhere. I returned my attention to Sandra, who was now slipping back into her sexy underwear, this time in flamingo pink!

"Yes to both. You do remember we put a Red Notice on the funds in Ireland, the Sovereign Wealth Fund is still frozen, and we have taken over all the trust funds around the world that supposedly were to support the building and running of the environmental plants. Look at the timing."

"The ship was rebuilt months ago, the bombs were made months ago, and we shut off the Irish funds the week before last."

"Yes, and we know-or suspect-the funds were used for the bombs, at least the manufacturer of them in Afghanistan, and that six or seven weeks ago, one of them was photographed on the ground with our terrorists. So we were late to the party, but our arrival has caused them some pain."

"I feel good about that, but there is another question in there you haven't asked."

"I haven't?"

"No. And I don't want to be sent to Terra del Frago, so I volunteer this observation in the spirit of us being partners, even if you are older than I am. You haven't asked how they moved seven bombs so quickly." Again, I was amazed at her smart thinking. The transportation question had been on my mind from the moment we boarded and saw seven of the bombs had been removed. I had delegated the task to Indigo, and he had one of his team chasing it down. Sandra had not been in that quick conversation, it had been mini to mini, and she had been doing her guard dog thing and not watching my hands. And I chose not to be pissed at the old comment.

Yet.

I finished dressing, bundled my combat fatigues, vest, hat, and boots up into a laundry bag we had been given and started for the door.

"Yes. We should have that answer by the time we rejoin the admiral. But the outtake of all this supposition and speculation is that our battle plan is shot to shit, and I need something to convince the admiral we still know what we're doing so we can stay in control. The last thing we need is various military forces running around the place looking for nuclear bombs and creating panic. We have enough panic and chaos in the world to last a lifetime as it is."

"And, how, my excellent guide, mentor, leader, and all-around good guy, do you intend to manage that? Fear of tactical nukes has driven some people to the madhouse, even though we have yet to experience one."

"Sucking up will get you nowhere. Listen and learn, my padawan. Your turn at the wheel is not so far away as you think." Our laundry bags were taken from us by a sailor with a huge smile and a cheery wave; formality was seemingly done and dusted, and now we were dressed in civilian attire. However, we were still gunned up, a habit neither of us was able to shake.

Ten million euros is a hell of an incentive for anyone to change sides.

We met the 2IC coming down the corridor, and he stopped, making getting past him impossible.

"The admiral requests you join him in his briefing station. I'll take you there, but first, is there anyone else you need at the briefing?"

"Yes, thank you. Agent Remer, colonel Kashasini, and I'd like my two special forces' commanders on the screen. Inspector Thomas will give you a device that will connect to them." Sandra handed him her mini, already dialed into Tom and Bob. "And your master chief, if possible, please, he may have some insights on what went down." He nodded, spoke into a small communicator on his wrist, and we entered the room. Nothing fancy as you would expect on a ship attached to a battle group, but it was set up extremely well, with my favorite person in the whole world standing in front of a large industrial coffee maker.

"*Indaco, tu adorabile uomo, sposami e fai i miei bambini!*"

"*Comandante, mia moglie sarebbe molto gelosa della tua bellezza, meglio se rimaniamo amici!*" We both laughed, happy that he was already happily married, and I just loved him for his coffee! But again, that would have to change in the not-too-distant future because having survived the second contact with the enemy had made me realize we were not structured properly, and that needed to change. I saluted the admiral, who just nodded, smiled, and continued to drink his coffee. Fay came in, and it was obvious that she and Indigo had also used the ablutions, and when the master chief arrived, that made it five for five in the clean stakes.

"Commander, perhaps you would like to take the floor. We are at your disposal."

"Admiral, thank you, I'd like to give you a report on where I believe we are at, the next steps, where you and your beautiful ships may play a role, and then I have a little begging to do." He smiled. The master chief took a mug of coffee and retired to stand against the wall, managing to keep everyone in the room in his eyesight. Indigo and Fay were also armed, so in his mind, he had four outsiders standing next to his admiral, all openly wearing weapons, and I know how uncomfortable that would make me feel were I in his position. I decided to defuse any anxiety first before starting the after-action report.

"Sir, I apologize for my team wearing weapons. It is a habit we have adopted because of the nature of our work. I am happy for us to remove and store weapons at your call." He looked at his chief, who shook his head minutely, so he just waved it away, and that was that.

"Thank you, sir. Sir, we have secure resources that at this time exceed yours due to the internet being taken down and the hack attack on our technology." Interestingly, both Tom and Bob's faces were up on the big screen, patiently waiting for whatever was in their future. I motioned to Sandra, who held up a mini from her knapsack, which at least was on her shoulder, and not by her side, where she could get her H&K out in a heartbeat.

"This is a secure way to communicate with us and all those listed on the comms screen — you'll notice that as well as our key agents, the general, who is the president's liaison with the military, is top of the list, as are the directors of the NSA, FBI, and CIA. There are also a few select FBI agents, the head of the Israeli Intelligence forces, and odd military persons, all of whom are in key locations. Sir, please consider this the only secure way to communicate with my team or me, and use it accordingly." He pulled his mini out, looked at the one his 2IC had placed on the console and looked back at me. He was no dummy. The implications of what I had just said resonated in his quick mind.

"You're implying that our military communications net has been hacked."

"Yes, sir." I let my answer hang.

"So everything we did back in the Atlantic, all the footage we got of the drone, the shoot down, every transmission we made was intercepted by the terrorists?"

"Yes." Again, I let that hang. Then I decided to remind him of the stakes. "They have been tracking us for months, using something embedded in our systems, which we only just managed to locate and defuse in the last two weeks. However, they are after my team and me, the bounty is ten million Euros, so after today we can expect that to be increased, and your whole flotilla will become a target of opportunity the longer we stay here." He just smiled and flexed his shoulders.

"Let them come. Back to business. What are you planning to do next?" I gave him a hard look, his hubris did not make me feel any better, but I had a job to do, just as he did.

"Sir, I need a report from my colonel, if I may?" He nodded, and Indigo stepped forward, braced his shoulders, and put his hands behind his back in the parade rest position.

"Commander, I initiated a track and trace as you requested, and it led to Cote de Azur airport. I contacted our head office and had them initiate a scan two days ago, and we found what we believe to be the terrorist's jet. However, there were two trips taken, one yesterday to Germany, returned the same day, then today to Aleppo, in Syria. Interestingly, a freight plane left the same airport in Germany early today and, landed in Aleppo. More amazingly, a plane we backtracked to Chaumont, France, also landed at Aleppo airport in the last hour. There have only been these three movements into Aleppo in the last three days." I immediately thought of Stefarino, but then an urgent impulse had me reaching for my own mini.

"Arie, sorry to bother you and others on this call, but we need HUMINT (human intelligence) on Aleppo airport, the last two days, all aircraft movements, ground transport, and any data on personnel. Possibility of hot material in this vicinity, get 104 booted up. Luigi has the data. Can you expedite, please?" He just nodded and disconnected. The admiral looked at me from under his eyebrows, a solid query on his tongue, which he swallowed with some effort. I had one. One thing to do first, and I just hoped the admiral's patience wasn't wearing thin. I used my mini again.

"Amira, Indigo will get you to Greece. Connect with Tom, and wait for my instructions." I looked up at the big screen and saw Tom acknowledge that he had heard me, then I closed the mini and bent my head in thought. No one moved, no one spoke, perhaps the sheer speed with which I had acted had dazzled them, but from the vibrations I felt beside me, Sandra had worked out what the intelligence meant and was bouncing up and down on her toes.

"Do we run a double bluff on them?" I asked her quietly, every head turned to us. Indigo looked at his usual calm self, the master chief looked puzzled, the 2IC looked out of his depth, and Fay was also humming. I think she had picked up on the theme, but the admiral was just looking on with a slightly bemused look on his face.

"They told me to expect this, but I must admit it's a real pleasure to see it for real. What are you thinking?" I turned to look squarely at him. For my new plan to work, I would need all his resources, intelligence and will.

"I want to run a double bluff on them. I want fast jets over their head, breaching sovereign airspace. Arie will take care of that. I want to flood Aleppo with ground troops, again, breaching sovereignty, Arie again, and I want you to flood the north side of the Mediterranean with ships and helicopters as if you are looking for bomb casings. Then I want you to position this ship as close to Syria as you can get and not draw too much attention to yourself, and have the master chief ready with your Rapid Response Team and shooters to attack with very little notice. My team in Ireland will continue to look for bombs, but I think that any we find will not be hot, were never intended to be hot, so I see that as a clean-up mission, no longer the primary." He stood perfectly still, considering all that I had said. Fay was looking at me, waiting for me to tell her what her next mission would be, she was with the C-17 before I brought her here, and she had just heard me tell everyone that, in all probability, the Irish side of the terrorist plan was no more than a distraction.

"Admiral, I know you might be a little confused with such a rapid change in plans, but we have a very narrow window to work with."

"You figuring one of the planes into Aleppo carried the nuclear matériel?"

"Yes."

"And the other two?"

"Bombshells and the crew from the ship, the other one no idea, but we will find out."

"How? And who is this 'Arie' you called?" I wondered if I was breaking any confidence answering him, then opted for safety first.

"A contact we have in the Israeli military." And left it at that. And reached for my mini again.

"Boss, need you to get Syria to agree to overflights and boots on the ground. Coordinate with Arie soonest." And I cancelled the call.

"Sir, I apologize for my lack of manners, but if we can get the bomb shells before they are loaded, we will have saved ourselves and everyone else a whole lot of grief. I hope you understand." He nodded, poured himself another cup of coffee, perched on the arm of the long, empty couch, and just smiled.

"Commander, Jessica, I feel your pain, and I am instructed to provide anything you need, short of giving you an actual ship, although I expect you could handle that just as well. I've seen planning on the fly before, even been guilty of it myself, but never so competently and quickly. Can I assume you just arranged for the invasion of Syria?"

"Actually, the invasion would have started with my call to Israel. Now we have covered it with a UN-sanctioned police force action, world court authorized, and their government will allow it or be pushed out of power. There are terror groups, thugs, and any number of vested interests who want the government out, and we'd be happy to trigger a régime change. However, not our mandate."

"Where will you set up your operational HQ?" I looked at him with renewed respect, no questions, no second guessing. He was not presented as the typical Navy senior officer. I liked him, something that didn't happen all that often in our line of business.

"With your permission, while Syria is the focus here." He nodded, having arrived at that conclusion on his own. Then my mini buzzed.

"Jessica, boots on the ground, two aircraft held and immobilized, several casualties, the third aircraft, the one from Côte d'Azur airport, got airborne, and surprise, surprise, it is no longer trackable. They have a new 'black hole' mechanism of some type. Shami is on it, with help from the other geeks. Interested to know what was in the two aircraft we did catch on the ground?" I hesitated, then made a snap decision and gestured to the technician standing by the console, he nodded, so I flicked the image up to the big screen. If you wanted to be trusted, you had to trust first.

"Arie, meet Admiral Rogers. He's CMFTE. We're aboard one of his supply ships in the Med. Admiral, this is Arie Rosenberg, Israeli Intelligence, formally head of Shabak. He has been assisting Interpol from the very first days of the initial terrorist attack on the Dome of the Rock. Aire, what was in the two aircraft you took?"

"A lot of cash, euros, we're still counting it, bit over a six hundred million so far, and the second aircraft is stacked with tubes like this," and the picture cut to a line of metal tubes around a meter long, with radiation symbols on each end, and a series of small square boxes, "and the rad count is off the chart."

"How many of each?" He smiled, warming his creased face up a little. "Thought you'd ask. Ten sets."

"Can you tell if the nuclear material is still in the containers?"

"We have only opened three so far, and the answer is yes. We'll have the rest opened in the next hour."

"Do you need backup?" He looked surprised at the question, then smiled. "Thank you for asking Jessica, but the 104 have three teams with them, we have fast jets and gunships overhead, and so far, the government, officially at least, is denying any knowledge of the terrorists, protesting everything other than our presence, which they describe as responding to a crisis they identified, but no one has any idea of what we have found, why we are here, and we will keep it that way."

"Good. Anyone hurt on our side?"

"No, thank you for asking."

"Question; once you have examined the material, can you fly it to this ship?" He gave me a very long look and seemed to be considering all his options, handling nuclear material to anyone was always a gamble, and Israel was hyper-sensitive about it, but he finally nodded slowly.

"How about we keep two sets of tubes and containers for our geeks to play with, and we send you the rest?" The admiral was watching the screen closely, probably amused by the casual manner in which Arie and I conducted our conversation. But then, I had been in the trenches and under fire with Arie and the commando 104 more than once in the last three months, and we trusted each other implicitly. And he was my stand-in grandfather, for the one I never had.

"Thanks, that will be fine. Can you stand by for a group chat with the geeks?"

"Give me fifteen to watch the clean-up, then I'll dial you in. Do you want everyone in Venice on the call?" Yes, but I couldn't take the risk of the monk's secret being shared, so I shook my head.

"Just Shami, Luigi, Malcolm, maybe Frank, and Julius. I'll have Amira, Fay, Indigo, Sandra, and maybe one geek from the ship." The big screen went black. I pocketed my mini and looked longingly at the coffee urn. Indigo saw my look and took my mug from me, and refilled it. I smiled my thanks. The admiral looked just a little dazed at the casual way I had referenced the directors of the NSA and CIA.

"Admiral, you can expect radioactive material in quantity, and once here, we will want to examine every tube and box, analyze the material, then bury it somewhere safe for the duration. Can you manage that, please?"

"Yes. We have a working nuclear laboratory on our hangar deck, with level Five containment facilities. Let me set that up for you." He motioned to his master chief, the technician at the console, and they all marched out, shutting the door behind them. I made a hurried call to Amira, asked her to meet us here, hung up. I gave them three minutes, during which time my team filled their mugs and settled into the couches and chairs to wait for Arie to dial us back in. Then I laid back, closed my eyes, and let out the sigh I had been holding in since Indigo's report about the aircraft.

Sandra settled in beside me, handed me a fresh mug of coffee, flipped her shiny blond hair out of her eyes with a 'come-hither' look, then nailed me with a full-on stare.

"You work well under pressure. We changed tactics three times in as many minutes as I was counting, so what miracle are you going to pull out of your arse now?" I looked at her out of the corner of my eye, saw no malice, sensed none, just friendly amusement, so I relaxed.

"If the containers all hold nuclear matériel, then I think we might have dodged a bullet. If they don't, we will at least know how many shells they can load up. This 'black hole' thing worries me. I want to get Stefarino on it. I'm hoping Arie or Shami will have done that. I want those bastards in chains."

"But you don't want the Americans to know about the monks?"

"I don't want anyone to know about the monks." She looked at me and nodded her agreement.

"The longer this plays out, the harder it will be to keep them to ourselves."

"I know. We are now three months in, we have a new crop of super-intelligent refugee women, we can only identify one of them, we don't know what they want, and we have been reacting from the get-go."

"Have you given any thought to interrogating the two prisoners the Navy brought back for us?" I stretched out, releasing the tension that had been building in my back and buttocks.

"Yes. But they won't know anything. They were just hired muscle, and not very good ones at that. This scientist of theirs, Siobhan O'Cleary, if she's anything like Amira, she'll work alone. The way those torpedoes were designed, and the way the nuclear material was ordered, tells me that the fitting of the material is a relatively simple step, albeit potentially a very dangerous one. And they went to extraordinary lengths to make the shells foolproof; only one way to explode them, the massive velocity required and locked in a sabot round. That tells me Malik Badawi, our roving Bedouin, wanted simple, simple, and fool proof."

"You live in the desert, you work with terrorists, you limit the possibility of a friend taking your bombs and using them themselves, maybe even against you?"

"That's what this whole setup says to me. The rail gun was built into the ship. The design of the ammunition. The simplicity of loading the material. When you think about it, apart from your scientist, no other technical help is required once they left the factory."

"So, the fact that they left three of the shells, and all ten of the sabot outers behind, suggest a change in plans — maybe a change in the delivery method?"

"Yes. From what Amira says, eighteen hundred meters a second velocity is hard to generate unless you use rocket propulsion and a lot of it. The sabots worked because the rail gun fired the missile five kilometers away at speed, then the sabot round fired its rocket motor, and bang! You hit what you aim at, and nuclear explosion. I asked her what the alternative might be, and she said to drill through the nose of the torpedo and retrofit a slug that could penetrate the membrane at a much lower velocity. She suggests the missile you researched would be adequate, not only for its range but its speed."

"So they need a machine shop with a powerful drill, need to make the slugs, fit them, arm the bombs, then fit them into an air-to-air missile, and deliver them?"

"Yes, all that, plus the delivery system, and since we have been attacked twice this week by drones, that's what my money's on. A drone firing the missile. The advantage of the missile is that they can load the front end up with all sorts of navigation equipment, optical, laser, not GPS, because, no satellites, so inertial or ground mapping. And I have a theory on what that money was all about."

"You do? Of course, you do. What is it, spill!" She was excited again, bouncing up and down in her seat.

"We seized the remaining funds in the Irish trust account. We froze all the other trust accounts worldwide. We know what they spent the missing amount from the Irish trust on-the ship and building and transporting the shells all over Europe. What if stopping that account prevented them from paying for the supply of their nuclear material?"

"That's what the euros were for?"

"Some of them. But think about it. Our terrorists flew into Germany — specifically Nuremberg Airport — where they stayed for around three hours, then flew back to Côte d'Azur. Then the next day, they load up seven shells and fly to Syria and are shortly joined by an aircraft from Nuremberg and one from Chaumont, France. Sally, my padawan, what is that region of France famous for, other than some fermented grapes?" She looked at me as if I was mad. Maybe she was right, time would tell, but that region of France was world-famous for something that fitted right into my scenario. She finally got it.

"Nuclear power plants."

"Yes. Seven of them within two hundred kilometers of Chaumont. Wouldn't you think terrorists going shopping on a Saturday morning might drop into their local nuclear plant and purloin something they need?"

"So the second aircraft was carrying the payment for the material?"

"A reasonable assumption, as is the one about the providers of all that lovely material being supremely pissed when they don't get paid."

"How much?" I looked at her and frowned.

"You should know the going rate for material on the black market. It's part of our mandate to monitor any potential threat." She dived into her mini and, after a few mutters under her breath, snapped the lid shut and pulled her hands up as if signaling a touchdown.

"Latest offer on the dark web is half a billion euros for one hundred kilos, but that's a straw horse. No one buys that much, so figuring these guys only needed sixty kilos of plutonium plus the U-235, machining, packing, shipping, probably around six or seven hundred million euros."

"Yes, that's what I figured. So the spare cash would have been used for other purposes. Now, let's play another guessing game. If you go to Germany for one point five bills, might you consider taking more money for a target of opportunity that your money man might like taken out, permanently?" She considered my question, went very quiet, very still, closed her eyes partially, and put herself in the shoes of the terrorists.

"Targets of opportunity, you take them out, I pay you handsomely. But cash is clumsy, bulky, that 1.5 bill filled that jet, and I'd have to think changing the strike package this late in the game would be a very expensive exercise."

"Good point. So, given the world has gone to Hell in a handbasket, millions dead, millions more migrating from somewhere to nowhere, the banking and financial systems wrecked for the foreseeable future, no internet, no ATMs, what would you ask for that could enable you to survive long term under these conditions?"

"And maintain its value?"

"Yes."

"Gold, diamonds, exotic minerals, a good bottle of rum." I smiled, her bubbly nature made what we faced a little easier, but she had a brain, knew how to use it, and I was starting to rely on her for more than just keeping me alive.

"I think gold, the universal standard in every war, in every century, in every millennium for that matter. And what is the one thing that is true about gold?"

"It weighs a shit load! We need to be scanning for very large transport trucks, ships, and anything that move tons and tons, and if Nuremberg is the locus, we need to dig into who lives near there and who is a billionaire, and we need to do it now."

"Go on then, but make it fast. I want you back here when Arie tunes in." She raced off to Fay, who immediately huddled with Indigo, and all three jumped on their minis and, with heads bent, tried to lever out some suspects. I knew how I would go about it, but I wanted to see what Sandra produced. New ways of thinking, not yet polluted by hardcore action that all too often turned to stress-inducing disaster. My mini buzzed, and the admiral's face swam into focus.

"Nice toy, Commander. Just to let you know, we have moved your helicopter into our main hangar. It's not fit to fly at this time. We'll be one hundred fifty nautical miles off Syria in another two hours, and I have five of our destroyers racing up the northern coastline, all in international waters, and our Helios are scanning as requested. And guess what we just found?" I looked at his face, all serious and formal, he was enjoying something, but I didn't know what.

"You found another torpedo." He smiled and nodded.

"Not just one, but what is reading as three images."

"Where?"

"On a wooden work boat, around fifty feet long, off the coast of Greece, the crew on deck, dirty sails, under an auxiliary motor at present, we have overflown it but are keeping it in sight awaiting your orders." An admiral waiting on little old me for orders? That just highlighted the incredibly difficult and strange position we found ourselves in.

"Sir, our approach would be to storm the boat, taking only those prisoners we thought had sufficient intelligence to make it worthwhile risking our lives for theirs, recover the target, and sink the vessel. We can do that under our mandate from the UN and World Court. Some paperwork is involved, but doable. You can't do any of that as a US Naval flotilla. Your rules of engagement do not allow for an approach like ours. How far away is this boat?"

"Eighty nautical miles from us, five off the coast of Greece."

"Sir, I have a strike team in southern Greece. Can you please arrange a fast helicopter for my team and collect them, then allow us to engage this vessel and secure the shells?" He looked at me with astonishment, then his face creased with a frown, and he tilted his head to one side.

"Two provisos-one, you take my master chief, and this time keeps him at your side, and two-you come back in one piece."

"Affirmative to the first, and I'll promise my hardest to meet the second. And we'll need at least four ribbies for the attack." I hung up on him, dialed Arie, brought him up to date, then looked at my team.

"Gear up, same rig as for this morning. We'll allocate teams and tasks when we get Tom. Questions?"

"I was just getting comfortable in these jeans," Sandra moaned dramatically. "Suck it up, Sally, you girl you!" And as the room filled with laughter, I moved quickly out to where we had left our combat gear. It was dirty and still smelled, and it fit my mood perfectly.

It was going to be a long day, and for some unlucky terrorists, not a particularly good one!

# Intermission

The flight attendant lay in a bundle of bleeding limbs, and hacked torso parts, his usually pristine uniform now shredded by the vicious knife strikes Malik had inflicted on him. Broken glasses, crockery, carrying trays, and various things from the galley lay scattered and in pieces all over the floor of the aircraft. Malik himself, now somewhat calmer, slumped in the one leather seat that he had not yet attacked in his fury at having both his nuclear material and his money denied him by whoever the masked attackers had been. Dressed head to toe in neutral black, they had swarmed out of the sky and land vehicles like wasps, firing at the cockpits of the aircraft, killing both pilots in the two other jets and his co-pilot, shattering the windscreen which had forced his surviving pilot to fly below ten thousand feet as he had no pressurization, and didn't as yet know what would still work, and what would not.

Additional rounds had penetrated the fuselage, and streams of sunlight now filtered across the interior and flittered across the ceiling like fairy lights. He was royally pissed, his temper beyond the edge of immediate recovery, and only the sight of the boxes containing his precious torpedoes kept him from dispensing equal measure on his scientist, who even now was still cowering in the toilet. She had screamed and cried and waved her delicate hands in the air from the moment of the first attack, typical female, he thought to himself, as his badly holed jet raced across the floor of the desert in Iran.

He didn't know about the 'black hole'. All he knew was he had to get somewhere safe where he could reassess his options. He thought about going back to his ship, but that was in the opposite direction. News of its demise had not yet reached him.

The factory he had constructed in the hangar in Afghanistan was off-limits. His highly-paid airport staff had gotten a message to him about the visit by strangers who turned out to be Interpol agents. Besides, he still didn't trust those sand jockeys. They changed sides too often. And the factory was of no use to him if he were to change the weapons so they could be launched from the air.

His gold was on the way, he had confirmed that before he had left his ship, it would take some days before it was in his hands, but he could afford to wait now that his immediate plans had effectively been killed at the starting gun.

Thinking through all this, he calmed somewhat, lurched his way forward, recovered the only surviving bottle of scotch, weaved back to his seat, and drank from the neck once he had removed the cap with his bloody knife.

Life was a bitch, and then you died! But until then, he would find a way to deliver retribution and collect his gold. Heaven help any who stand in his way.

# Chapter Nineteen

I had broken our team up into four groups-Indigo commanding one, Tom the second, Fay the third, and the master chief the fourth, and we approached the vessel from the four points of the compass at around fifty knots. The rigid rubber hulls flew through the choppy water, bouncing every now and then on a wave; the admiral had arranged for one of his destroyers to approach directly towards the target, and fire a series of warning shots that landed all around the wooden boat.

It had not responded except to slightly increase its speed, and head more out to sea and away from the coastline. We each had a fifty-caliber machine gun on our bows, which we engaged at one hundred meters. We chopped the topsides and anyone hiding behind them to pieces, and I saw the main mast shred, then collapse on itself. Our gunner moved his stream to the stern and chopped the engine and rudder to bits, and the dowl then slowly drifted to an uneven, sloppy stop. Several automatic weapons poked over the sides, firing wildly at us, but were soon silenced by the gunners.

We slid to a stop, and our teams boarded as fast as they could, the odd shot being fired to suppress any resistance. The rapid reaction team went below in a hurry. The dowl was already listing badly to starboard, sinking into the Mediterranean Sea. One by one, the green boxes were lifted into the ribbie, and once secured, its coxswain swung the inflatable around and headed out to sea, its companion following and protecting its rear.

Sandra and I boarded, found a survivor, had a quick conversation, as the water was now very obvious by its presence lapping at our boots, and extracted what little they knew about the situation. They were just simple terrorists who had been paid a small fortune to move the shells from a team they had met on the beach in Syria. Turns out that there were three dowls involved that had the remaining seven bombs. Where were they?

Didn't know, but now we had transport method and a timeline, so we left them to their own devices, and as our ribbie motored away, I gave the order to sink the boat, so we spun around, and our gunner did just that.

We saw no survivors, didn't expect any, but waited five minutes just in case, then reversed course for the Navy ship.

"Do you always shoot first?" the master chief asked, hunkered down next to Sally and me. At fifty knots, the spray came in over the bows, from the sides, and I swear, from over the stern, we would not only be bloodied but seriously soaked when we got back.

"Pretty much," Sandra said, hugging her H&K to her chest to prevent the seawater from spraying all over it. The barrel was tucked under her armpit!

There was a love affair I had to respect and put in mind the boss's relationship with his precious Sig, which I had never seen him without, even in the shower, in the six years I had worked with him. I wondered how he was going all dressed up and nowhere to go? I felt a need to soften Sandra's cryptic and somewhat dry response.

"Master Chief, the people we chase down, are usually killing wantonly, indiscriminately, men, women, children, without conscience or regard for any rules or social norms. It's why Section Five was created by Interpol. Usually, Interpol collects precious data and intelligence on the world's worst criminals, terrorists, child traffickers, people, and drug smugglers, and shares this information with police forces all around the world. But with the increase in terrorism, and since the pandemic four years ago, we have, frankly, had our hands full trying to stop the flood of attacks."

"But I've watched you work twice now, and none of you ever hesitate to kill. It's hard to accept that." I looked at him, a true warrior who still felt the weight of fighting by the rules of war, which, unfortunately, our terrorist enemies never did. I shrugged my shoulders.

"Horses for courses, chief, nothing more, nothing less." He just looked at me with a lost look on his face. Beside me, Sandra all but scowled at him, her reaction hidden by a huge wave that chose to try and flood us.

Back to reality.

We reached the ship and noticed that the three boxes had already been unloaded and moved inboard, so Sandra, the master chief, and I moved on up to the bridge. Fay, Tom, and Indigo followed us. We were all soaked to the skin, had blood on various parts of our bodies, and looked like we had been working in a dirty cesspit, which I suppose described the interior of the terrorist's boat to a tee.

The admiral saluted us, and we returned the acknowledgement, he motioned to one side of the bridge where the on-deck crew had cleared some space, and I brought him up to speed.

"Two other boats?"

"Yes, sir, and I suggest we create a picket, say fifty nautical miles further out than our intercept point, and scan for them." He looked at me, working the puzzle through in his head, and I added to his mental picture. "I can get our team in Ireland to work towards the picket line. They can cover the area in less than a day. These bombs are headed somewhere, and I am starting to feel as if they might be the base of the Irish website threat. We obviously have two different agendas, one by the Boudin, Malik Badawi, and one by an as yet unknown operator."

"So you see these shells, bombs, call them what you will, as heading for Ireland, the UK, France, Germany, and Italy? On what do you base your supposition that there are two agendas, two operators?" He looked quite critically at me, he had almost the same information I had, but he hadn't joined the dots.

"Sir, the fact that the ship we took this morning was outfitted with a railgun, and there were ten sabots and three shells left on the boat, suggests that at least ten of the missiles were destined to be fired by that mechanism. Badawi only took off with seven shells. Then we have three more shells turning up on a terrorist boat out of Syria and a report of two other boars carrying seven more. It very much smells to me as if we have two teams with very different agendas. Otherwise, why were the shells we captured just now not on the ship? Why wasn't Badawi interested in them? And then we have the two shells we collected in Gaza. We have Amir Abbas, who leads Hamas, one of the worst terrorist groups in Gaza, on camera, with Badawi, the scientist, and a shell. That, in my opinion, was deliberate." He looked at me as if I had two heads.

"How do you make all those assumptions?"

"Sir, it's a pattern. An old magician's trick of sleight of hand. I believe that the shells we found on the boat just now are part of that sleight of hand, but your discovery of the shells on the ship destroyed the illusion. Badawi had already left for Syria, so as we reasoned, his agenda has changed, we still don't know what it is, but we do know now he has less money to work with than before and no nuclear material — or at the very least, a major supply has been interdicted. Sir, please excuse me. I have to take this call." I walked out onto the docking stage, where engine telegraphs rested in big white boxes, and took my mini out. The buzzing had been an annoying interruption in trying to get the admiral to understand my reasoning. "Jessica, very bad news. Some of the containers were stuffed with dummy material and salted with some radioactive waste to throw us off. Can't tell if the cylinders were interfered with before they arrived on the plane, but someone somewhere may have three sets of nuclear material machined to fit into the torpedoes." Arie's face was a pasty gray, Israel's biggest fear was an enemy with nuclear capability or just a suitcase bomb. They lived on a small plot of dirt the locals had been fighting over for thousands of years. Had the supplier run out of source material and dummied up the three containers to collect all the money? Had someone else siphoned off the material somewhere in transit? I just shook my head, worrying that it would not solve my immediate issue.

I had to convince the admiral that there were two strategies in play, and we had to attend to both of them.

"Sir, three of the canisters were dummies." He looked at me, shook his head, then leaned back on the bulkhead and folded his arms, a posture that usually meant someone was tightening up their attitude, didn't want to listen, or was bored with the conversation. Trouble for me.

"Did the people you interrogated on the boat tell you when the other two vessels took to sea?"

"No, sir, only that they were some days ahead of them due to the trucks with the shells arriving before theirs did."

"Navigator, what was the average speed of the boat we just sunk?" The small woman moved very quickly, punched some data into a handheld, and looked back at us. "Sir, it was sprinting at fifteen knots every hour, down to ten knots every other, allowing for average sea state and tidal data for this time of the year, twelve to thirteen knots."

"So at thirteen knots, worst case, say four days, they could be some twelve hundred and fifty nautical miles away, or anywhere in between, or another three hundred nautical miles further away."

"Somewhere adjacent to Spain, assuming they didn't stop any-where. Your destroyers and gunships had been scanning the coast and have only picked up the ship we took today. Our drones will scan all the way from the English Channel down to the start of the Mediterranean Sea, then inbound until they either hit or reach us. Does that seem feasible to you, sir?" He looked unhappy, but I really couldn't do anything about that at the moment. I needed to get with my people and get their input. I needed to talk to Arie out of earshot of any of the crew, and I needed coffee.

"Sir, may we retire to consider our options, get the drones in the air, get the RRT repositioned, we have a second team on standby close to Spain, and reformat our teams for what's to come?"

"Dismissed, Commander. I'll call for you in an hour for an update."

"Thank you, sir," and I followed Sandra off the bridge. She was obviously in a hurry to get somewhere; it would be interesting to see if the master chief joined us. I turned to Sandra, with Fay and Indigo behind Tom and me just behind them. "Do you think we fired too fast or too early just now?" I had kept my voice low; I wasn't interested in the ship's crew overhearing.

"Commander, one question. How many casualties have we taken in the attacks on the ship and the boat?" I looked at Indigo, a little confused. He had been on both boarding parties. He should know that answer.

"None," I said, a little crossly. He waved his hands in the air as if scaring away mosquitoes.

"And how many of the terrorists did we encounter during both attacks?"

"Thirty or more on the ship, and I guess twenty to twenty-five on the boat."

"Exactly. If my memory serves me right, we had eight people on our team that took the ship and the shells. A few more for the boat, but that was strategic. Would you agree?"

"Yes. But what in the name of hell are you getting at?"

"It's simple, Commander, fifty plus terrorists, on their own home turf, so to speak, all happy to shoot first, and a smaller number of us, having to board and rush into unknown territory, and not one of us sustained so much as a torn fingernail." Only Sandra would use a metaphor that related to glamor!

"Commander, I would say, on behalf of all our team, we shot at exactly the right time and in the correct manner, and frankly, I thank you for that." Indigo gave me a little bow as we entered the wardroom that we had taken over as our working area. I shook my head, I knew our tactics were good, even sensible, considering the type of terrorists we were facing and the extraordinarily high stakes we were playing for, and my team had just thanked me for not getting them shot! I just shook my head in wonder and put it all behind me.

"Jessica, the admiral, and his master chief are used to fighting an enemy that declares itself and fights by observable rules. We don't have that luxury." Tom walked past and headed to the coffee machine. I joined him, punched him on the shoulder, and nodded.

"That's exactly what I told the admiral before we set off." And I felt the tension building in my shoulders again, and as I did, a memory flashed into my mind of the boss sitting at the controls of a Hercules L-100, reproducing the route a similar aircraft had taken days before when it had dropped two massive bombs on the Vatican, destroying thousands of years of religious history and icons, killing essentially the entire head of the Catholic church, as well as thousands of innocent people who were doing no more than waiting for the new Pope to be proclaimed. He had casually put the aircraft on autopilot, his feet up on the cockpit coaming, and without visible effort in the midst of the carnage and chaos the attack had unleashed, come to the conclusion that had tipped the balance in us finding the terrorists responsible.

Somehow, he had managed to relax under that intense pressure and let his mind sift through all the evidence to find that single kernel of truth that eventually led us to the terrorists.

At my comment, Tom shrugged his shoulders, took his coffee, slid down the bulkhead, and crossed his feet at the ankles. He was soon joined by everyone else, and the only sound was the slurping of coffee and the burbling of the coffee machine. I gave myself a few minutes to decompress, trying to emulate my mental image of the boss, but I still had to brief Arie, the boss, Fay had to get the drones in the air, and then we had to get the admiral back onside to set up the picket line. And find the missing radioactive material if it was, in fact, missing, find the Bedouin and his shells, and find the other two boats and their shells.

And find and confiscate an unknown quantity of gold from an unknown location.

It was all very easy if you said it quickly!

# Chapter Twenty

There was a dangerous flaw in Malik Badawi's plan for the distribution of the substrate shells around Europe. Malik had negotiated with Amir Abbas, the leader of the terror organization that was known as Hamas. At the time, he had been in a leadership position with the group and had financed a number of their attacks and provided technology for some of them, most notably the remote-controlled vehicle attacks on the Israeli shopping centers. At that time, Al Bar al Shirak and Hamas had worked together, almost in harmony.

Abbas had already purloined two shells from the end of the production line in Afghanistan and replaced them with dummies, which had been shipped as negotiated.

Unfortunately, two of the stolen shells had been detected as they sat inside small electric vehicles in the northern end of the Gaza strip and had subsequently been seized by Israeli Special Forces.

What no one knew other than Abbas was that he had also stolen two additional shells from the ten he was responsible for delivering all over Europe and also replaced them with dummies, making the total of real bombs actually shipped just six. Ten boxes were all marked appropriately, but only six shells could be used as designed-tactical nukes.

And as fate always turned up a surprise or two when no one was looking, purely by accident, three of the dummies had been shipped together. The other dummy included three real shells that still survived. Three of the remaining real bombs had been seized by the

Interpol attack on the wooden boat that had been detected by the Navy on its way past Greece.

And due to the funds having been cut off by Interpol, Abbas had not been paid the one million euros per bomb for delivery; he had lost two of his bombs, as he thought of them to the accursed Israelis, he still had two left, but as yet no nuclear material to load them with.

But he hadn't become and held the top position in a feared terrorist organization without support from other powerful people, and once he regained his composure from the loss of his bombs, he had plotted and planned, and with the right contacts at Aleppo, the first person to board the aircraft from France had been a bogus customs officer, who swapped out three sets of canisters and replaced them with mildly radioactive dummies, right under the nose of Malik, who had been sleeping in a semi-drunken stupor in his aircraft with his scientist.

One of his men had also managed to retrieve several bricks of euros from the destroyed aircraft from Germany, an added bonus, and when it had been counted, Abbas found to his delight that the amount owed to him by Badawi had been paid in full, with interest!

So he now had two shells hidden away, the ability to turn them into nukes, and three loads of deadly nuclear material, which he held in reserve. The ten boxes that contained the mix of real and dummy bombs had reached the beach in Syria and been loaded onto the three boats over four days he had organized for the purpose, and as far as he knew, were now on their way to their ultimate destinations in Europe, England, and Ireland.

He only had one problem.

He needed someone to load the nuclear material into the shells, a process he had been warned by Badawi was potentially dangerous and life-threatening unless the proper facilities were provided and could easily result in a nuclear explosion.

But he knew people who knew people. That was how he had learned of the three aircraft flying into Aleppo. And as he was still in France, where he had been negotiating what he needed to turn the shells into nuclear bombs, he was perfectly positioned to take advantage of his windfall in Aleppo and at last have what he had always wanted — a way to strike fear into the hearts of the Israelis, and bring them to their knees once and for all.

His two remaining shells were hidden away in Quetta, Pakistan, his nuclear material and his money in Syria, and his laboratory-to-be in France. He thought hard, and though long, to bring this together, he would need a cover of some sort that would keep the authorities off his back and looking elsewhere. He had plenty of money and, chuckling to himself at his cleverness, picked up his satellite phone, a gift courtesy of Badawi, and checked the time. Having his calls limited by satellite overflight time was an irritant, but the security of the system more than made up for the inconvenience.

After speaking for almost twenty minutes, he had what he needed. On his payroll, an accredited member of the Atomic Energy Commission (AEC) a beautiful new French executive jet with a crew, just waiting for him in Toulouse. He figured a maximum of three days for the round trip. He pondered going himself, then dismissed the idea something could go wrong, and he liked his freedom. He made contact with another of his supporters and negotiated a personal courier deal, fully securitized, and smiled. He liked the way the new world worked. Money had always talked, but in the chaos and disaster of the new world, money shouted at the top of its voice. Get your freedom here. No waiting!

However, now he had to wait, so he'd use the time to obtain laboratory facilities so that he could load his bombs, And wouldn't that be fun!

# Chapter Twenty-One

S andra and I stood on the bridge, dressed back in casual clothes, fresh from another wonderful shower, a good snack, and great coffee. The admiral and his 2IC lounged back against the navigation platform, seemingly relaxed, but I sensed a tension in the air, only heightened by the deck crew keeping their eyes on the front, pretending to ignore our presence. The master chief entered, dressed in ship day, camouflaged with cover, saluted the admiral, then stood at ease.

"Report."

"Sir, we interrogated the two prisoners, and basically, they said the same thing. They had been recruited, along with two other boat crews by representatives of Hamas, to move ten boxes to different ports in Europe, where they would be collected by others. Due to their injuries, we couldn't question them as hard as we would have liked and got little else from them."

"Thank you, Master Chief. Stand by." The admiral turned to me and very pointedly asked me why we hadn't interrogated the prisoners on our return to the ship. I thought about just flicking him off, but we still needed his support, and at some point, he would have to recognize our tactics would never be as clean and neat as his.

"Sir, we already had that data. We saw no point in an interrogation due to what else was happening at the time." He went into thinking mode, a frown creasing his broad face, his eyebrows shooting up into a classic inverted 'w' shape.

"I spoke to general Saunders again, told her I was uncomfortable with your tactics, and she supported my opinion and then told me to leave you alone with the planning and strategies you wish to employ. So, we don't condone your methodology, but we will support you. I think in future operations, should there be any, you may need to use your own people." I nodded. In essence, this is what we did anyway, and I now had Tom and his team if we needed to do any more dirty work. I wish I had my own ship; it would make it easier on all of us, and then I had a brilliant idea.

"Admiral, could you please arrange for us to be transferred back to the ship we took this morning and lend us a helicopter and crew for the duration and perhaps a couple of your excellent ribbies?" His frown deepened, then his face softened. He tilted his head to one side and nodded.

"We can do that. You have a crew who can manage that ship and helicopter pilots?"

"Yes, sir, some of our people are cross-trained land/sea/air, and our current contingent of specialists on loan from your good selves, thanks to the president and the general, include pilots and sailors as well. Mostly ex-teams, so you would know their level of training." He nodded, turned to his 2IC, gave the necessary orders, and within an hour, we were ferrying the first of our motley crew to the ship. It took seven loads. The ribbies would arrive under their own power from the destroyers in the area and would be housed in the internal storage the ship had in its stern. While we were refueled from a tanker, I gathered my team on the uppermost deck, the one with the sun lounge, spar, and wide couches, and grinned as many of the hard bodies, shirts off, lay around as if playing on the Rivera. Interestingly, of all the women on our teams, only one had lacy underwear.

Guess who?

"Okay, listen up please, Tom's crew over there, Indigo's over here, everybody else over here. Now, who wants to be captain of the good ship. I don't know. We have to give her a name yet. Who wants to play navigator? Amira, the laboratory is all yours. Fay, the comms center will be reconfigured so you can use our private net and talk to the C-17 and drone managers. We'll limit comms with the navy to minis. I want four-hour shifts, we could be at this for a long time, and we need a shopping expedition. Also, who wants to be the helicopter pilot, co-pilot, or loader? You need to be able to fly on five minutes warning." Tom and Indigo had gotten together, and seemed to be working out who did what, Fay was looking at me with a hopeful look, so I addressed her one-on-one.

"Fay, what is it?" she looked around for a spare empty space, saw one, and motioned me over to it. Sandra stuck to my shoulder as if she had been glued there.

I'd have to do something about that soon. I couldn't spare someone as talented as her for bodyguard duty.

"Commander, our drones have picked up the signature of more shells, three in all, similar boat to the one we sank, anchored off the coast of Mallorca. There is no other activity in the area. At this point, I've instructed the drones to keep flying, and I've instructed the C-17 to land at Palma de Mallorca Airport."

"Tom, distance to Mallorca?"

"Approximately ninety nautical miles, three hours at maximum speed."

"Too slow. Tom, pick four, Indigo, three plus you, whoever won the pilot job we leave in five, Tom, stay here, take who is left when you get close enough in the ribbies, but only launch if we call you. Sandra, get everyone selected and geared up. Move!" And everyone did. The Rivera look soon replaced with that of the warrior, long guns slung across chests, hands gloved with naked fingers protruding through the tips, lightweight armor loaded with spare magazines, comms gear, emergency med packs, and in one instance a small blackened teddy bear hanging off a carabiner.

No comment.

We scarpered to the helicopter pad, where the massive blades were already turning, climbed in, and fitted ourselves to thick rappelling ropes anchored to the floor, or at least I hoped they were. I didn't remember seeing them when we flew in.

"Indigo, port side, weapons hot. I'll lead out the starboard; pilot, fast and low, pull up as you cross their stern. We will rappel out very low, so make sure you come to a hover as fast as you can. There are no door gunners unless we really lose the plot. Clear?" Every helmeted and goggled head nodded, a brisk "Sir, yes sir!" from the cockpit, and so we lay across the floor, crushed almost one on top of the other. I risked losing my mini in the slipstream called Fay.

"Status?"

"Still no traffic, no movement other than a few gunned-up guards roaming the top deck." I hung up and dialed the boss.

"Sorry to bother you, but I need official cover for Mallorca, immediate, WMD, yadayadayada. How's your day?" He just hung up on me, and I'd punish him for that the very first chance I got. I kept the mini out, the slipstream was now spitting at us as we flew through some low-hanging clouds, but I could still see the white caps of the waves under us, so the visibility wasn't that bad.

Forty minutes later, the pilot turned on the red jump light, we bunched up the backside to the front side in a long stick, gripped the rope as if our lives depended on it, and I felt Sandra's hand on my shoulder, where it shouldn't be, and then the chopper reared up pressing us to the floor, then rolled upwards and flat, the red turned to green, and we were out, falling down the rope like so many ants on a sticky flower stem. I shot two terrorists on the way down. I felt the bullets from Sandra's H&K snap past my ear. We hit the deck and immediately had a wall of terrorists shooting and shouting at us. Sandra took a hit. I felt my legs go out from under me, then sustained fire from our side as Indigo's team hit the deck and leveled the playing field until the only sense of movement came from the rocking of the boat, having been insulted by our rapid and noisy arrival. Tom's team was moving forward. I tried to join them but found it hard to stand, then realized Sandra, covered with blood from shoulder to crutch, was pulling me down to the deck. Just as she did, a rocket whizzed over my head, smashing into the coaming, turning the front part of the boat into matchwood.

I turned as one with Sandra and shot the five figures who stood off from our stern in a small metal tender and kept firing until there were enough holes in their boat to qualify as a colander. I stood, blood leaking out of my thigh on one side and my calf on the other, Sandra stood shakily, and we both hobbled forward, but we could see that Tom's team, as well as the front of the boat, had gone, leaving just a waterlogged cabin without a roof, and four green boxes slowly sinking into the bay. Four boxes. Fay's team had only detected three. Something to sort out later. My mini was smashed, and I could feel pieces of plastic in my thigh, but with luck, it might have just mitigated some of the force a bullet usually arrived at, and I would be able to say, with a straight face, "just a flesh wound, boys, just a flesh wound." I looked at Sandra, being tended to by one of Indigo's team, which was looping pressure bandages around her chest and lower extremities. She didn't look like her normal happy self, and again I reflected that being around me was a constant hazard.

"*Comandante, ti raggiungo tra un minuto, sei gravemente ferito?*" Was I badly hurt? I didn't know. I looked down to see my boots swimming in blood, gore, and seawater and idly wondered how long before we sank. Then the trooper was sitting me down unceremoniously, snapping at me in Italian, which I chose to ignore as he bandaged my thigh, pulling pieces of the blue computer out before he applied the pressure bandage, then attacked my calf, and for the first time, I felt some real pain. I ignored it and looked at Sandra.

"Thank you. I never saw them." She just shook her head, obviously in some pain, but managed to pull herself up so she could balance on the steering pedestal.

"I did, but too late. I think I got hit about the same time as I saw the reflection off the side of the tinny."

"I'll hold Fay down while you beat her up. She said no traffic." She just smiled and shook her head as if trying to clear it.

"Not her fault. You didn't talk to her for the last ten minutes, plenty of time for the tinny to slip in behind us. Anyway, that's not the issue. How do we tell Tom half of his team were taken out by lousy terrorists?"

"Indigo!" I turned to see him crawling out of the mess that used to be the bow of the boat. He just shook his head and moved back to us.

"Tell this sadist to leave me alone, is anyone else hurt?" He shook his head, reached down, and gave Sandra's shoulder a squeeze.

"We need to recover the bodies of our team and those four boxes. Do you think the ribbies can get here before we sink?"

"Jessica, the bottom of the hull is quite sound, we have taken on water, but we are in balance, as it were. We should be okay for an hour

271

or two, and Tom is heading here as fast as he can." I nodded, pulled Sandra to her feet, and moved her back to the stern, then sat her down against the small box that probably held lifejackets and other boat detritus.

Had we been careless, not seeing the tinny in time? And why hadn't the chopper gunned them down? My fault. I had told them no door gunners.

Overhead, the helicopter buzzed around like a moth looking for a flame. The pilot was obviously upset that the terrorists had been able to fire a missile at us while he had been flying around and obeying my instructions. Indigo and his team squatted opposite us in the hope that our combined weight would counterbalance the amount of seawater we had taken aboard.

"How many tangos?" Indigo looked over at me, looked back at the shattered bow, then handed me a water bottle.

"Commander, we estimate around thirty, plus the boat load you took down. Hard to tell now, owing to the damage the RPG (Rocket-Propelled Grenade) did. But we counted four boxes, and Fay mentioned only three?"

"Yes, we'll clear that up when we get them back to our ship." I sat and played back every step we had taken, and even though we had good visibility just before we had roped down, I had not seen the tinny. Where had it been hiding? I would have to look at a map, something I had not done before we took off. I was attacking a boat on the water, but I now realized again that my propensity to lead from the front was causing me to experience tunnel vision, and I made a mental note to not make the same mistake again.

On reflection, we were extremely lucky that we had only lost four members of Tom's team, something I would have to account for if only to me.

# Chapter Twenty-Two

Malik Badawi's jet was seriously damaged, and the fuselage was starting to exhibit some of the stress caused by the rush across the desert. The pilot, knowing that he risked his life and that of his passengers, had flown as smoothly as possible, at a reduced airspeed, in an attempt to get somewhere he could land without crashing or being shot out of the sky.

Outside, the late afternoon sun was creating a golden hue on the skyline, and the ridges in the sand dunes were turning black, creating a contrast that, at any other time, he would have enjoyed. Another massive shudder rippled through the airframe, and his airspeed suddenly decreased to just above where the airframe would stall, so he gently increased the power to compensate. Then once the airspeed rose again to a safer level, he pulled the power back down. It reminded him of riding a roller coaster.

It would be a balance between thrust and drag, with the damaged fuselage creating more drag than it had been designed for. This is where a pilot earned his money, he thought to himself, one of those moments of terror that spoilt the usual calm and gentleness flying usually entailed. He knew where he was, but he didn't know how much further he could go. His mapping software showed him his options, and Ramadi in Iraq looked like the best bet.

A city with a checkered history, one that had seen all-out war, insurgency, and terrorism, sacking by religious zealots, occupation by foreign invaders, and was still a hotbed of religious fervor. But it had a dirt strip just graded in the last few months, the nearest real airport being Baghdad, fifty kilometers away, where he definitely did not want to go. He doubted if there were any aircraft flyable in the area that could shoot him down, and he was flying so low that the possibility of being detected by radar was slight. If he could land, what happened next would be his passenger's responsibility.

He tentatively started a gentle descent, opted to keep his flaps up, and lowered his landing gear, only to have at least one hang-up. His nose wheel light remained stubbornly red, so he changed his mind about his flaps, lowered them fifteen degrees, and felt the whole airframe shudder. The airspeed decreased rapidly, so he added a little more power judiciously, then lined up on the long dirt strip that had been carved out of the desert. The airframe tried to roll over to the left. He fought it with both opposite rudder and ailerons and managed to get back to marginally straight and level, then the jet just fell out of the sky from fifteen meters. He rammed the power levers full forward, and managed to get his airspeed back up, reduced the velocity of the fall marginally, just as the main wheels hit the desert floor, and with a shudder, started to slew off to the right.

He could feel the aircraft trying to fight the dynamics of slowing down, the main undercarriage digging into the sand, swinging them left then right.

He held the nose up as long as he could, then it thumped down with a huge mound of dirt exploding as the wings ran out of lift, with sand being thrown up over the cockpit like a huge wave at the beach. He could only imagine the dust storm he was creating.

He corrected as best as he could, pulled the fire bottles for the engines, turned the fuel off, and mentally crossed his fingers, a time-honored tradition for pilots in trouble since the first flight of the Wright brothers one hundred and twenty-two years before. With a huge audible sigh, the aircraft slid to a stop, immediately immersed in a heavy red and yellow sand storm, which started to leak into the airframe through the bullet holes. The clicking of the turbine blades winding down was the only sound.

Until Malik Badawi burst into the cockpit, gun drawn, screaming and shouting so loudly the pilot was initially deafened. He turned to meet the wild-eyed terrorist, only to be shot three times in the face, then as many times in the chest, his five-point seat belt the only thing stopping him from flopping all over the control console. His blood seeped across his seat, sinking down between the power levers, into the radio control panel, then dripped courageously onto the cockpit floor and over Malik's feet. He was so mad he simply turned and stormed out of the cockpit, yelling for his scientist to get out of the toilet.

She did, but wouldn't move past the first body, the unfortunate steward who had now turned a little ripe, not only staining the carpet but also the air having voided his bowels and bladder when he had been killed.

Badawi suddenly realized his mistake. He didn't know where the pilot had landed them! He pushed the lever that dropped the main door and found it jammed. He fired his gun at it, only managing to put dents in the fabric that covered the back of the hatch. He threw his gun at the obstinate door, swearing in both Russian and Arabic, his face red with emotion. The scientist, seeing her opportunity, stepped over the unfortunate steward, hit the little handle over the emergency escape window, and like a rabbit being hunted by a rabid dog, squeezed herself out the window, then slid off the back of the wing into the roiling sand and dust.

Before she could catch her breath, Badawi flew after her, his very large knife flashing in the fading light. He swore at the scientist in Russian, and Arabic, then suddenly calmed down, realizing he was making the situation worse, and in her current state of fear, she would be useless to him.

"I apologize. I'm sorry. The whole being shot at and then crash landing rattled me. I let it get out of control. Please accept my apology." And to underlie his sincerity, he slipped his knife back into its sheath and back under his coat.

She looked at him with fear still in her eyes, her body language indicating she was ready to run, so he let his hands fall by his side and stood perfectly still.

"Siobhan, I am really very sorry for losing control. Can you forgive me?" He saw that she hadn't fully relaxed, but was starting to stand up slightly, a good sign.

"You killed everyone. Why?" Her face looked strained, her hair muddy, covered with the dust and sand that the jet had stirred up. Her eyes had white rings around them, making her face look like a mask. Here was his opportunity to calm her down. He had lived with and slept with her for over a year, and he thought he knew all her moods and soft points. He had never had as long a relationship with a woman like this before, so he softened his body stance, looked her straight in the eyes, put a gentle smile on his face, and he tried to look contrite.

It came off as a badly managed sneer, but he held the pose until she straightened up a little more and relaxed fractionally.

"Siobhan, I lost control. You know what this project means to me, to us, and for a moment back at the airport, I saw it all crushed to dust. I apologize. I did not mean to scare you." She looked like a sulky teenager, the bottom half of her slim dress covered in blood and mud. She had left her shoes back on the plane, as well as her hand-bag, so as well as feeling scared, she was feeling somewhat naked. Her introspection was rudely interrupted by the arrival of a jeep with five very dark, robed, masked, and seemingly angry soldiers waving guns.

Badawi moved over to them, waited until the dust settled, then fired off a string of Arabic so fast Siobhan couldn't follow. One of the soldiers climbed out of the jeep, strutted to Badawi, and leaned into him as if he were seeking a fight. And Badawi pulled his knife out and cut his throat, not bothering to step away so that the blood gush from the open neck wound would miss him. Initially, the other four soldiers were stunned, then as one, they levelled their guns on him, shouting at the top of their voices. One soldier stepped down and, raising his hand for silence, walked to the terrorist.

A short conversation followed in Farsi, which Siobhan did follow, and her amazement at the content both shocked her and amazed her. Before she could process it, Badawi walked to her and, in a soft voice, asked her to cover her head. He handed her his red and white keffiyeh, which she quickly wrapped around her hair, pulling it down to the crown of her head.

"It's all right now. They are friends of friends, they will take care of us, and in a day or two, we will be able to continue our journey and complete our mission." She looked into his eyes, deep black orbs flecked with gold around the iris, and felt herself calm down. She had survived over two years with this man, followed him all over the world, and had been with him when he had met with a number of very strange people. She would take her time and watch carefully for any opportunity to get away. In her mind, at least, while her life was worth the cause she fought for, she no longer thought Malik Badawi was even remotely interested in it.

And he scared her right down to the bone. Her only ace in the hole was she was the only one who could turn the substrate torpedoes into nuclear bombs, and without the railgun, she was the only one who knew what modifications needed to be made to enable them to be detonated.

She hoped that would be enough to keep her alive until she could flee.

# Chapter Twenty-Three

Our ship took two and a half hours to reach us, the ribbies just one. We were rebandaged and warm when we transferred the boxes and the remains of Tom's team but anchored around one hundred meters from the terrorist boat due to the ship's draft. Sandra was receiving professional medical care, and I was next, but first, I had to make my bones with Tom.

I found him on the stern, alongside the four body bags of his compatriots, holding their identity tags in one hand, the other shading his eyes, hiding his tears. I squeezed his shoulder and remained still.

"It's okay, Jessica. Indigo told me what went down, there was nothing you could do, and the chopper gunner caught it all on his camera. They were lurking behind the small headland and popped out as you rappelled down, you were all looking the wrong way, and I doubt even the noise of their motor could be heard over the gunfire. We're very lucky we didn't lose more of us."

"Never saw them, Tom, totally focused on the swarm from the bow, maybe twenty or so. We had to shut them down. We had no choice." He turned his head upwards, looked over his shoulder at me, then stood, the dog tags swinging in his hand. "The way I heard it, you and Sandra went out first, suppressed fire from the tangos all the way down, got shot for your trouble, then the rest of the team got down and cleaned up after you. Then the Tangos in the tender fired the RPG, you and Sandra killed them all, and that was that."

"Accurate, but that doesn't stop me from taking responsibility for your team. I'm sorry, Tom, they were an excellent group of soldiers. We will miss them." He looked at me with his tear-stained eyes, his hair all over the place, stood tall, then saluted me. I saluted him back, wondering what this formality was all about.

"Commander, in my humble opinion, you did more than your best under heavy fire, led from the front, as you always do, and going in, we always knew we might take casualties. Permission to dress my team for burial." I stood stock still, this was a SEAL Team leader telling me I 'done good', standing over the dead bodies of four of his team, who had been killed on my watch. I just nodded, not trusting myself to speak. He marched away towards the main saloon. I looked down at the body bags one last time, then walked a little unsteadily to where the medic was treating Sandra.

"How're you going?" My voice was a little squeaky, so I just plonked down next to her. Her long blond hair, which she had tied up before the mission, was now hanging long and straggly down her shoulders. With her body armor, shirt, and battle pants either cut off or pooled around her ankles, she no longer presented as the fashionista model of a few hours ago. Her lacy bra was hanging down from her shoulder, held up by a full chest pressure bandage. Two other bandages crisscrossed her lower torso and her thighs. She looked a mess, but I detected her bubbly personality lurking just under the surface, which was smeared with blood, dirt, grime, and something indistinguishable.

"Hope you're had your tetanus shots," I moved a little to ease the pressure on my thigh. She just looked fatigued. The medic finished up, I looked at him, asked the question silently with my eyes, and he gave me the thumbs up and smiled.

"She'll be fine in a day. All three rounds went through and through, and nothing vital hit. I've prescribed meds for her, which are on the way from the nearest destroyer. I'll add to that list when I look at you." Sandra was helped up to her feet by Indigo, then the medic turned his evil intention to me. He pulled, probed, cut, and sliced my uniform, ripped the pressure bandages off with no regard for how I might feel, then painted me with some smelly ointment, rebandaged me, and laughed.

"Two of the luckiest soldiers I have had this month. Both flesh wounds, both through-and-throughs, I'll double up on the antibiotics, and you'll be fine." I heaved a sigh of relief; it was always good to have your own diagnoses backed up by a professional. I heard the sound of a helicopter. It rattled the ship from stem to stern with its rotor wash, then landed right over our heads on the top deck, the compression washing over us like a storm. Everything was not tied down, and that included the old bloody bandages the medic had just removed from Sandra, and I went flying over the deck and into the ocean. I had bent my head behind my arms to protect my face, and when I looked up, the admiral was standing in front of me, with a big canvas bag with red crosses on its side.

"You called?" he asked, his voice only mildly sarcastic. I stood, saluted him, and he just grinned. "Leave you alone for half a day, and look what you get yourself into." He handed the bag to the medic, who hurriedly left the stern.

"Wasn't looking for trouble, but it found us, and we have recovered another four of the shells. I do not know their condition; we've been a little busy, as you can see." He turned to look at the body bags, came to attention, and saluted. He held the pose for a full minute, then turned back to face me.

"How and who?"

"Four of Tom's team, RPG direct hit just as we took control of the boat." He nodded, thinking through what damage an RPG round could do to the human body, then his face went to neutral.

"Any other injuries?" He looked at my bandages and torn uniform, and I mentally shrugged.

"Just one other. Inspector Thomas sustained three flesh wounds. She's been treated and cleared." The look he gave me was as hard as I had ever experienced from a superior officer, and that included the boss, whose frosty look could freeze you to the spot.

"So the two of you get shot, we lose four valuable SEALs, and you go about it as if it's business as usual?"

"Sir, it is. Every encounter we have with terrorists is out of any normal playbook. And these particular gentlemen, if I can call them that, had four potentially armed nuclear devices under their control, and it was my judgement to take them by surprise and hit as hard as we could and as fast as we could." He still gave me his frostiest look, but his body language softened slightly. Again, you didn't get to be an admiral in one of the world's biggest navies if you were a dummy.

"Do you have footage of the attack?"

"Yes, sir."

"I'll look at it before I make any further judgement." I nodded to one of our Italian Special Forces who had taken over from Sandra as my personal shadow. He turned to his counterpart, snapped out an order, and in a minute, returned with one of our minis.

"So, you and Agent Thomas rappelled out first, star formation, shooting all the way to the ground, both got shot for your efforts, then ten seconds later the rest of your team get into it with suppression fire, then this smoke trail comes from the RPG?"

"Yes, sir."

"No one saw it?"

"Not until they fired, then Inspector Thomas and I were able to deal with the terrorists and their boat and prevent any more damage." He looked at me curiously.

'Why were you worried about damage? And to what?"

"Four potentially live nuclear weapons and the superstructure of the boat, which had its topsides ripped off by the RPG." He watched the video again, then snapped the lid shut and handed it back to our guard.

"Why didn't the helicopter see the other boat?"

"They were facing towards the bow and focused as we were on the terrorists. And I had instructed the door gunners to not fire unless I gave the order. It was one of the gunners who got that video."

"Commander, who do you report to?" My turn to give a frosty stare, which given my sloppy and damaged physical appearance, probably came off a little less like a hard look and more like confusion.

"Sir, I am responsible for Section Five, its strategic and tactical decisions, and execution of same. As a matter of courtesy, I submit after-action summaries to my general and sometimes seek his input and advice when our actions cross his areas of expertise."

"Who did you include in the planning of this raid?"

"My senior team; Team Leader of our SEALs; Colonel Kashasini, representing the Italian Special Forces; my 2IC, Inspector Thomas; Agent Remer, whose team spotted the boat, and our pilots, both Italian Special Forces." He looked at me, probably considering all the talent I had at my back, trying to understand how we could have gotten into the trouble we did. I decided to remind him of the rules the other side didn't play by.

"Sir, do you recall pulling us out of the Atlantic a week ago after we had been shot down?" His eyes sparkled; it was obviously a happy thought.

"Sir, did you hear us receive a warning or did anyone instruct us not to fly that route before we were shot down?" He shook his head.

"Asymmetric warfare is a bitch. No rules, no declarations, and no borders, and to match that, we have to respond in kind. Section Five stood up to address that issue, and we trained to fight the same way. We are small in comparison to most of the terrorist units we come up against, but again, we train for that. And a big part is having the attitude necessary to hit very hard and very fast, with not a lot of information going in." I let that sit for a moment, then fired my last shot.

"In less than seven days, we have identified two internationally wanted terrorists, uncovered a plan to create weapons of mass destruction that were thought to be undetectable; worked out how to detect them; and located, identified, and taken down four well-armed and equipped terrorist cells and recovered potentially twelve of the WMD's. Sadly, it has cost us a few flesh wounds and the lives of four of our team. On balance, I don't suspect any of our dead would see themselves having wasted their lives doing what we have done."

He just looked at me, working through what I had just said. The navy fought by rules, declared themselves before any action, had the luxury of massive intelligence resources, and they never ever got into a fight they didn't think they could win. Somehow, our team seemed to do the exact opposite nearly every day! He continued to give me a very hard look, but I could see in his eyes that he was considering what I had just told him.

"What do you intend to do now?" Here we go again, I haven't fully processed the last op, and I need to have a plan for the next, with no intelligence! I didn't grimace, or at least I hope I didn't. I was bone weary, my wounds were hurting like a bitch, and I needed coffee. Coffee! I looked at my Italian stud of a guard, motioned drinking with my hand, he smiled and fired a rapid string at his compatriot, the one who had got the mini for the admiral, and he rushed off like a man of a mission, probably knowing I might completely fade away if I didn't get a caffeine fix pronto! And to no one's surprise, Indigo appeared as if by magic with a tray and mugs of steaming coffee bouncing on top. I had the wherewithal to let the admiral select a mug first, then motioned to the guards, then, with a very deep breath, and a huge sigh of relief, got my own. Indigo gave me that look that asked, 'this guy giving you trouble?' so I just shook my head, hoping it would be misconstrued as me reacting to the strong black liquid to which I currently owed my life. I turned to face the admiral.

"Sir, debrief this mission, rest and recover for a spell, continue the search for the rest of the shells, find the missing nuclear material, try to track where the Bedouin fled to, find his shells, and a few other things I can't think of now."

"Can't or won't?" Here comes that steely glare again, and I had to remind myself that while I needed him and his flotilla onside, he was not in my chain of command. Tricky.

"Sir, with all due respect, I have been out of the information loop for over an hour, and as you have seen for yourself, our world moves fast, very fast when you think about it. I need time to catch up." He just hunched his shoulders, turned on his heel, and started to walk up the stairs to the rooftop helipad.

"See you on my bridge in eight hours, Commander, don't be late." I stared at his boots as they disappeared up the stairs, wondering what my punishment might be if I were. I retreated into the command center we had set up between the top and mezzanine decks, found a shiny leather chair, and fell into it.

"Indigo, get everyone together, please, keep the coffee coming, but I want you here."

"*Certamente, comandante, come desidera!*" And one by one, my team entered and took their seats where they found them. Sandra was helped to a chair next to mine by one of the Italians, Tom was the last to arrive, looking a little worse for wear, so I decided to address his issues first.

"Tom, we've lost four good soldiers. I know you can't go back to the Teams for replacements at this point. Can you handle a suggestion or two?" He looked at me, his face neutral, his hair a messy testament to his mood.

"What are you thinking?"

"We have at least three sources for replacements, and I know your men and women cannot simply be replaced. That's not what I am suggesting. But we have Bob and his team on standby; I can ask Arie for some of the Commando 104, or Indigo can get us more of his team from Venice. Which avenue would you prefer?"

"We only want four shooters?" I nodded, looking at Indigo for confirmation.

One of our unique strengths, I believed, was our small size compared to most other militarized groups, and I really wanted to maintain every advantage I could as far as hunting terrorists with WMDs was concerned.

"What have you got in mind for Bob's team?"

"Either to back you up or form a second Rapid Response Team, depending on our needs at the time." He thought for a minute, then nodded.

"Then let's leave them alone. We still have shells to find and bombs to defuse." He seemed to be thinking about the Israeli commandoes he had worked with previously, then he turned to look at Indigo.

"Colonel, can you lend me four of your best must-have English, one a long gun shooter, one a medic?"

"Master Chief, Tom, it would be our pleasure to serve with you. You can have all of my team here now. I will arrange for a new team to join us as soon as they can." He positively beamed at Tom, then his face creased for a moment as he thought of something. "Tom, if it doesn't inconvenience you, I need one of my team to remain with the commander until Agent Thomas has recovered fully. I apologize for this. I can send for another soldier if this is a problem." Tom smiled, looked at me, then over where Sandra lay slumped almost asleep, her bandages quite prominent under her coveralls, which had not been closed up the front.

"Colonel, I humbly accept your offer. The way the commander has taken a liking to be shot up and shot down, she definitely needs a minder. I'm just glad it's not me!" And the laughter that rippled around the room broke the tension that had been building since the admiral dropped in, so I moved us along to where we needed to be.

"Fay, any sign of the other boat?" She turned the big screen on and flicked live images from her mini to it.

"Yes, it's one hundred kilometers further west, almost abeam Algiers, but there are no shells painting." That didn't make sense. The terrorists back in Syria said three identical sixty-foot boats, the same paint scheme, all carrying twenty to thirty armed terrorists, and all carrying some of the shells. We had so far intercepted three back in Syria and now four here in Mallorca, and they had counted ten boxes loaded. I had a strange thought and called Amira.

"Hi, sorry to break your concentration. How are you going with our latest collection?" She looked like someone on the moon. Her orange level 5 bio-suit expanded out of all proportion to the usual human frame. She sat on her haunches in from of three shiny brass/copper torpedoes, one of which lay with its guts laid bare.

"Jessica, only three shells. The fourth box had a concrete slug in it. These are not active; I've closed two up and was about to close the third when you called." A concrete slug? My mind froze. There was a nagging fear building which I would have to tamper with very quickly if I was to lead my team appropriately. First stolen radioactive material from the aircraft in Aleppo, or maybe even before that, way back in France somewhere. Now a missing shell. I tried to sort it all out in my head, got nowhere, call the room to attention.

"Take notes. Questions will be asked. I need all your help working this out. Hypothesis one; the terrorists build twenty-plus substrate shells in Afghanistan with the help of a scientist, Siobhan O'Cleary, with two main terrorists involved, Malik Badawi and Amir Abbas, both known to associate with Hamas and Al Bar al Shirak. Got that?" Every head but Sandra's nodded. She just rolled her eyes at me and closed them.

"Assume they split the shells between them, ten each, with maybe Abbas getting another two somehow. We take those off him in Gaza with Arie's help." Still nodding heads, I used my fingers to work out the next part.

"Let's assume Badawi sets up the ship with the scientist and moves his ten shells to the boat. We find the boat thanks to Amira and the Navy and take back three shells, with seven missing. Badawi takes them in his aircraft, which we discover, the Israelis attack. He flies off, leaving his money and nuclear material behind in two other disabled aircraft. We recover ten sealed capsules of supposedly radioactive matériel, only to find three of them are empty. Following me so far?" Now there were some serious faces in the room and a lot of scribbling on notepads and mini-screens.

"So, assumption two, Badawi has seven shells, no nuclear material yet, and he and his jet are in the wind. What happens next? We find the first small terrorist boat in Syria, and we take three shells from it and learn there are two more boats a few days ahead in the med somewhere."

"One of which we find down in Mallorca, and we take four boxes but only three shells. Now, we locate boat three, but no shells are detected. What does this suggest?"

"If it has boxes, they will be dummies as well." Sandra's voice was so low I almost didn't hear her, but I smiled. I might as well have known she would be paying attention, no matter how much she hurt.

"And that gives us four missing shells, and we'll assume Abbas is the culprit, and I also see him for the theft of the radioactive material."

"That's not the real issue." Amira was still squatting on her haunches in the laboratory, her orange suits still inflated, and her voice sounded a little metallic.

"What is?"

"I opened two of the canisters Arie sent us, and in my judgment, if they have the skills and the equipment, they can easily make up four nukes, smaller yield, say around thousand tons of TNT, but still plenty big enough to give someone a real headache." That gave me pause. I was still thinking literally and not allowing my mind to wander into the 'what ifs', but I could see what Amira was saying, and frankly, it scared the hell out of me.

"Alright, let's assume they have the skills. If we plot this all out, we have a very large shipment of gold coming from the middle of Germany to the Mediterranean coast — I don't know the quantity or the destination. We have three sets of nuclear material either stolen in Aleppo or back in France, and we have four shells stolen somewhere between the factory in Afghanistan and Syria, where the boats loaded the boxes. And we have Badawi with his aircraft and seven shells somewhere in the middle east."

"My brother and our geeks are looking for the aircraft as we speak, but I suggest we need to prove the other three shells are dummies, and then find this Abbas as quickly as we can. He has shells, possibly nuclear material, not sure about the skills, but all things can be obtained for cash in this day and age."

"Fay, are we positive the third boat has no shells?"

"If you believe our technology, which I do, then yes, they probably have empty boxes, and the boxes show up clearly on our scans." I smiled, suddenly, I had a job for the admiral, but I had to think carefully about what I needed. I opened my mini.

"Sir, apologies for interrupting you, but we have found the third boat, carrying at least three boxes, but we don't believe they have shells in them. Could you arrange for one of your destroyers to attack the boat and capture the boxes for us, please?" He looked astonished as if I had asked him to get me to the moon or something, then he smiled, shook his head, and called his 2IC over.

"Send the coordinates of this target, and we'll see what we can do."

"Thank you, sir. We need to know if the boxes are empty as soon as possible." He just grimaced and cancelled the call. He had his own rapid response team; we had just trained them before we left his factory ship. I had an ace up my sleeve, and I used it. A quick call to Washington.

"General, hope this finds you fit and well. I need your backup, please. I've just requested your admiral to locate and sink a ship we have identified as carrying the boxes that may contain some of the shells. In this case, we believe the boxes are empty, but we need to confirm it as soon as possible." She was wearing a bright-colored shirt with the collar up and had a beautiful string of pearls around her collar, her short-cropped copper-colored hair was shining in the light, and she was obviously either entertaining or planning on going out. Some people had lives, something I constantly forgot.

"Are you sure there are no live nukes on that boat?" I held her gaze, eyeball to eyeball. It was a fair question and one I could only answer one way.

"We believe so. Our detection system has located twelve of these shells in the last forty hours. We know it works, and it works well. If I could, I would mount the attack myself." She nodded, I had told the absolute truth, and she sensed that we had now been working together for three months, and the trust had built steadily but strongly on both sides based on what we had said and what we had done.

"Would it help if you were aboard the destroyer when it mounts its attack?" I thought long and hard about that, and the possible reaction of the admiral and mentally shook my head.

"No, general, much as it pains me to say no, the attack has to be mounted hard and fast. On past experience, these terrorists are well-armed and have large contingents of nasty people. Your rules of engagement need to be as direct as ours are-shoot on sight, we don't need prisoners, but we do need those boxes."

"Can you get us a UN or Interpol cover?"

"Yes, general, you will be covered under the Terrorist Laws as modified in 2022. I will have a Red Notice issued immediately."

"No publicity, no reports, and the ship's video remain classified."

"Agreed." My screen went black, her usual way of completing a conversation. I dialed the boss, told him what we needed and where to send it, then hung up and looked around at my team.

"Everyone gets a hot meal, take four hours down, and meet back here at fifteen hundred hours. Questions?" No one spoke, Indigo moved over to assist Sandra in getting up, and the team moved out.

# Big Brother

The destroyer was one of the very new littoral cruisers, all sharp angles and low superstructure, designed for close in-shore dirty work, and carried a contingent of highly trained marines and a fleet of rubber duckies (ribbies) as well as multiple barreled fifty caliber automated machine guns on both sides of the superstructure. In a sense, the perfect solution to an anchored fifty-footer in shallow water, holding thirty-plus heavily armed terrorists, and green boxes that may or may not be carrying WMDs.

The Captain, a commodore in rank, was itching to see his crew in action. They had yet to be bloodied in battle, had no colors, but plenty of very young cannon fodder, all anxious to shoot at something other than a training target. On orders from the admiral, the USS Repentance swung broadside onto the target boat after steaming in at thirty-five knots, four ribbies full of marines hidden behind their starboard flank.

At fifty meters, the automated machine guns open fire, raking the deck, and reducing the cabin to matchwood. Three RPGs fired almost simultaneously, all three hitting the bridge and radar stack, and in seconds the ship was electronically blind. The automated machine guns ran down, deprived of target information. Automatic fire from the boat raked the sides and command deck, leaving little white stars in the armor plate and bulletproof windows.

The ribbies attacked, two from the stern and two from the bow, their bow guns firing, another RPG fired, hit the first ribbie and killed everyone onboard. Its mate immediately turned its guns on the shooter, shredding him to pieces, taking return fire from hidden shooters firing through small potholes. The two ribbies coming in from the stern pulled alongside the now burning boat. Marines leaped aboard, met withering fire from the bow, returned it with intent, and in two short minutes, only the fires all around the boat moved, black fumes and smoke reaching up into the sky like signals to the gods that a battle had been fought and won.

The boxes were secured, the marines collected their dead, charges placed on the boat detonated, the boat sunk, and the commodore prepared his after-action report for his admiral.

Damage to the hull of the ship and bridge deck via inbound rocket rounds, seven sailors killed in action, five wounded; thirteen marines killed in action, eight wounded; two ribbies destroyed/out of action; four boxes retrieved, awaiting the report from Rapid Response Team.

When the admiral read the report, he winched, shook his head, and mentally made a note to never challenge Commander Riley's tactics again.

The Rapid Response Team confirmed the boxes were empty.

# Chapter Twenty-Four

"Jessica, I have news from my brother." Indigo looked a little sheepish at having wakened me before I had my full four hours, but next to me, Sandra still slept with a little snoring effect, not unlike that of a cat purr.

Tom was one bunk down, and Fay and the Italians filled out the rest of the row. I sat up, crawled out of the bunk, and reached for my jacket. It was a little cold, and I followed Indigo out into a small salon that the previous owners had used as a library.

A guard posing as a steward held mugs of coffee, and Fay, Tom, and I all took them like people possessed. We sat at a round bench/table affair reminiscent of an old-style diner back in Texas. Indigo remained on his feet, holding his mini.

"Commander, my brother, using technology shared with him by Amira and the geeks, has adapted one of the satellites they use to act as a point source and scanner, so they followed the jet that took off from Aleppo all the way to where it crashed landed in Ramadi, in Iraq. A small vehicle went to the crash site, and a second one arrived a little later and took two people away. One was a dark-skinned man and a white-skinned woman, wearing a keffiyeh. The man has been identified as Malik Badawi, the woman as Siobhan O'Cleary." Next to me, Tom huffed.

"We've already invaded Iraq twice, and look how that turned out. How the hell do we get in there without creating an international situation?" I held my hand up to halt further comment. I reached for

Indigo's mini and dialed my favorite Israeli. "Arie, hi, don't know the time there, hope I haven't woken you up. I need your help."

"Jessica, you look tired and a little worn down. Are you okay?" His tired gray eyes looked into mine, and the affinity I felt for this wonderful man filled me with an emotion I almost couldn't control.

"I'm fine, just a little sleep-deprived," I said, looking straight at Indigo, who held his hands up over his face in mock shame. "Arie, we have tracked the Bedouin to Iraq. He had seven shells. They are inert, as far as we are aware. If I get you accurate coordinates, could you dispose of them, please?"

He tightened his face, and his whole body went rigid. I could feel his intensity all the way through the transmission. "You're serious?"

"Deadly."

"Can you get UN and Interpol cover for us? I don't want to start a war."

This much I knew, so I tilted my head and thought. Remembered the boss's little black book. Held my hand up again to stop anyone from talking. Opened the torn leather cover and found an entry for Iraq, it was a colonel in the Imperial Guard, one I had read about some years ago, and I knew he also served as a minister for international affairs with direct access to the current dictator who runs the country. Now, how did I contact him? Then I had a rare flash of inspiration.

"Arie, exact coordinates to you in one minute. Appreciate it if you would deal with this soonest. You will have all the cover you need. Thank you." I turned to Indigo.

"You heard that? Get Arie the coordinates as fast as you can." I dialed up the boss again. It was becoming a habit.

"Boss, I need you to contact your friend in Iraq and inform him we are about to destroy an aircraft on a dirt strip in Ramadi. It contains seven shells, potential WMDs, and get a UN and Interpol cover for Arie. And I know I'm a pain in your arse, but you're the one who swanned off to play with the guys in suits." And I took a leaf from the playbook used by the general who looked after the president of the United States and hung up without saying goodbye.

"Indigo, get your brother to mount an overwatch, Tom. Best guess, cruise missile flight time to target?"

"Twenty-five to thirty minutes." I thought about that and then had another of my brilliant ideas. It might work, or it might not. That's what made it brilliant. I dialed the Admiral and the General in Washington.

"General, Admiral, the UN, and Interpol will provide cover. Can you order an immediate cruise missile strike to kill a downed aircraft on a dirt strip in Iraq and make your communications clear, acting on behalf of Interpol and a Red Notice we will have issued?" The admiral started to point out all sorts of things, and the general cut him off.

"Jessica, how many bombs, and what is their state?"

"Severn shells, not loaded as far as we know, and we have additional support being provided by another country, but we need you to keep that very much to yourselves." She looked like a well-dressed mother, but her stern face suggested an intensity beyond the normal household traumas of wild children and cheating husbands.

"Admiral, execute immediately on my authority." For a change, the general didn't hang up, the admiral did, and the background moved behind the general as she moved to a quieter area.

"Jessica, you move very quickly, and I appreciate that, but as a nation-state, we have to observe protocols and procedures, as I'm sure you know. Leave it with us, and let me know the outcome as soon as you have one." And she clicked off. I looked at my team and only saw the surprise on Tom's face. Sandra waddled in, still looking weary, but at least she had her coveralls buttoned this time. She also had her weapons harness over her shoulder, but she looked anything but battle ready. She snagged a mug of coffee from the table, drank greedily, then screwed her nose up.

"It's cold, buggar it," and she slammed the mug back on the table. Indigo turned and took off, no doubt to get her a hot mug. I hoped he had transmitted the coordinates of the Bedouin's jet.

"There's a good chance of collateral damage." Tom's face was as sober as I had ever seen it, then I remembered that he had served in the middle east, Afghanistan two tours and likely had an affinity for the indigenous people of the region. "Yes. My responsibility, my call. I don't want those shells in play. I hope you can accept that." He nodded, looking very thoughtful.

"Who are you blowing up this time?" Sandra asked, slurping at her coffee. Fay smiled at her and pushed a tin of biscuits over to her.

"Here, have a cookie. You look like shit." Sandra looked at Fay across the table from under her eyelashes, which were quite long.

"If you weren't sitting half a continent away, I'd have you for that." But she smiled, and the color was coming back into her face. Indigo was looking down at his mini.

"Missiles away, it looks like two from the west and three from the east. Should be quite a show." So the general and her admiral had come through. I always knew Arie would. He wanted those shells removed from the game board as much as I did. If Israel had a phobia, it was about suitcase nukes.

It seemed like forever, but it was, in fact, exactly thirty-three minutes before Indigo announced "hit one", followed by "hit two", "hit three", and then we waited on the next salvo, which took another twenty minutes. I looked at Indigo. He spun the mini around to we could all see the small screen, and as the desert sand, dust, and smoke from the burning debris cleared thanks to a strong wind, the long shape of a graded runway came into focus, with the bottom third completely obliterated, with no sign of the downed aircraft. And as there was no mushroom cloud, our guess that the shells had not been loaded with nuclear material had proven correct. I let out a sigh I had been holding in since my call to Arie, realizing that I had now instigated attacks on sovereign soil for the third time in as many days, and I really hoped it didn't come back to bite me in the arse.

Now, what was left on my to-do list?

Find the missing nuclear material; find the missing shells; find the gold; find the terrorists'; find the scientist; find out what this latest attack was really all about. As I ran all these little chores through my tired mind, I formed a picture of the terrorists learning that their shells had been destroyed or captured and smiled. I would love to be a fly on the proverbial wall if that happened.

# Fake News

Amir Abbas was just a day away from having the money he stole off the aircraft in Aleppo, and the nuclear material which he had also stolen, joined with the two shells had acquired by sleight of hand during the manufacturing of the substrate torpedoes in Afghanistan. The French registered private jet and private courier he had hired had left Toulouse two days ago and had successfully landed in Aleppo and recovered his money and his canisters of nuclear material. It had cost him more in 'fees,' and outright bribes than he thought was reasonable, but he had stolen the money in the first place, so easy come, easy go.

And now his private courier had called him on his secure satellite phone, using the short window the satellite was visible to him and confirmed that the two shells were being loaded in Quetta, Pakistan, they were refueling, and planned to be airborne in an hour. Flying time was around six and a half hours to Blagnac International Airport, just outside Toulouse, subject, of course, to weather.

What he didn't know was that Interpol had swept up all the shells he had sent on the three boats, as well as those in Gaza. In that, his former bedmate and co-captain of Team Al Bar al Shirak, Malik Abbas, was equally ignorant of the fact that his precious seven shells that he had left in the crashed jet in Ramadi had been totally destroyed by an Israeli and American cruise missile attack. And he had yet to learn that his boat had been seized, and the three shells on it also taken.

Of the original twenty-five shells that had been manufactured, only two remained, and of the ten sets of machined nuclear slugs, only three sets had survived. Neither terrorist knew of the other's plight, and neither had any safe communication means to bring each other up to date. Badawi had his satellite phone, but Abbas had given his to the private courier, who was calling an unsecured landline in France.

But when the two terrorists learned of their misfortune, they had two completely different reactions.

Abbas had sulked for a minute or two, then brightened when he realized he now held all the power; he had two shells and the nuclear material which he could turn the incredible substrate shells into small atomic bombs. He hadn't worked out yet that he couldn't use them due to their inherent design.

Badawi had a meltdown, killed everyone within his sight, was shot by his hosts for his efforts, and his precious scientist used the fray to cover her escape. To where? She had no idea, but she was more free now than in the last two years, so she thought only of getting to civilization and getting home.

# Chapter Twenty-Five

I had a decision to make. Did I accept that we had removed the threat to the cities originally listed on the Irish website? Namely, London, Dublin, Manchester, New York, Rome, Glasgow, and Paris? And had we taken the Bedouin off the board, now that we had all ten of his shells, as well as his launching system on his boat? And if twenty or more shells were originally manufactured, were we correct in assuming only two were left? And if so, where were they? And where were the three missing cylinders of nuclear material? Had they been stolen at the point of origin, France, or lifted in Aleppo?

My tingles told me that Abbas had the answers, but we did not know where he was. So, do I pull the C-17 and drones off the search focused on Ireland, the UK, and Europe, or do I keep them there, hoping to catch Abbas before he can do real damage somewhere? And what about the gold we believed was in transit from Germany to an unknown destination? We had out an all-points bulletin and Red Notice on it, and we now had the police forces of fifty nations monitoring their traffic, looking specifically for it. But all fifty countries had major issues with armed rioting, looting, and mass migration either to their borders or through their borders. There was virtually no fuel, oil, or gas, food was scarce, and the average community's mood was fearful and angry.

I did not have confidence that they would pay attention to a simple movement of a huge mass of gold.

And where was the Bedouin? Our sources told us that he had gone to ground after the missile strike on his aircraft, possibly killed, or had crossed the border into Iran or Syria. Lots of options to choose from, maybe wounded, maybe not.

But our geeks, with a little help from their friends, the monks, had traced a satellite call to a landline in France, and voice recognition had identified Amir Abbas. So now I knew where he was, and I knew the shells had been picked up in Quetta, Pakistan, and that a flight that we were now tracking in real time was on its way back to France. My instinct was to pull everything back and concentrate on that area; if Abbas was planning on fitting the shells out in a laboratory in France, that cut our search down to possibly twenty facilities that could handle Level Five biohazards. Then there were all the nuclear power stations, lots and lots of power stations, so our target was more like forty.

But France did not like Interpol very much at the moment, we were seen to have influenced the Israelis in the overthrow of the Arabian Government, and they blamed us for the killing of the Arabian oil supply in that we had not acted quickly enough in capturing the terrorists responsible!

France had played a double game and been caught out by circumstances, and a terrorist by the name of Shetani, and now they wanted control over everything that was happening with the terrorist hunt and nothing to do with us.

But they did not control space, and our geeks and the Americans had regained use of an unknown constellation of communications satellites, and we had realtime tracking ability of any identified target, and right now, the aircraft that had originally left from Blagnac International Airport, had flown to Aleppo, then to Quetta, where the phone call had been intercepted between an unknown male and Abbas and was now headed for France, or so we thought.

And the possibility that this plane had the two remaining shells onboard was high, given that the phone call had referenced 'two boxes as requested'. Time will tell.

I had the choice of having the aircraft shot down over the Mediterranean Sea, impounded wherever it landed or tracked and traced. I knew my friendly admiral would not shoot down a civilian aircraft without absolute proof, and I couldn't blame him for that, and I could always call on Arie if a shoot-down was an option. Personally, I preferred a force-down on the territory I controlled, and I had to think carefully about that because we could be wrong in our intelligence assessment. I decided to get some help in thinking this through. But before I could act on that thought, my mini yelled at me. I opened the screen and saw the shocked face of Luigi. "*Comandante, perdonami, abbiamo perso l'aereo, è diventato invisibile per noi!*" The geeks had lost the aircraft!

"Same black holes as we saw before?"

"No, Commander, not the black holes." Then what? New technology? Developed by whom? We knew the scientist was one of the refugee children taken from the camps and educated in Ireland. Were there more of them out there?

"Is Stefarino aware of the problem?"

"*Si, comandante.*"

"Can you call him into this conversation, please?"

"*Si, comandante.*" And the old monk's smiling face filled half the screen, and seeing me, he bobbed his head.

"Hello, Commander. I hope you are well."

"Stefarino, how big a wrinkle is this new black hole?" He smiled, reminding me I had never seen him less than amused at all the antics we had gone on with during this terrorist hunt. I wished I had his inner calm.

"It caught us by surprise. One minute we had a perfect lock on the aircraft, the next, it had vanished. We tried everything we had learned from the last experience with the black holes, but nothing worked." I rocked back on my heels. This was not good news, we had potentially all the makings for two nuclear devices in play, and they had disappeared from under our very eyes.

"Keep on it. We'll see what we can do at this end." I thought for a moment, then remembered a conversation I had had with the admiral back when he was running a carrier battle group. Just two weeks ago!

"Admiral, good to see you, how did your interlude with the terrorist boat go?" His face took on a scowl, and I saw worry and fury in his eyes.

299

"Sorry for your losses, but I need you at your very best in a matter of hours." He looked at me with such a hard look I nearly looked away, but I held on, and he relaxed fractionally.

"What do you want?"

"You have air defense radar that can see how far?" His face turned into a puzzled look, and a sparkle came into his eyes, a much better look than his scowl.

"Classified. Why don't you tell me what you want, and I'll see if we can provide it?"

I nodded, I understood his wariness, and I needed an outcome, not the specifications.

"I'll send you data on an aircraft we were tracking out of Quetta, Pakistan, when it disappeared from our sensors. I need you to set up a picket off the coast of France and on the direct route from Quetta to Blagnac International Airport. We need to find that aircraft, it potentially has the two missing shells, plus it may have the nuclear matériel needed to turn them into nuclear weapons."

"And I suppose if we find it, you want us to shoot it down?"

"Would you?" I asked in surprise. I was sure his rules of engagement explicitly prohibited him from doing that without probable cause.

"No, so get that out of your head once and for all. Our little excursion with your terrorist boat cost me the lives of good sailors and marines and damage to my ship. You need to pull the trigger on anyone. You do it yourself." I heard the bitterness in his voice, and I could understand his pain. The boxes had been empty, so in a sense, it must feel like taking all that pain over empty boxes just wasn't worth it, but in this game, you always had to eliminate potential threats, the nature of terrorism left you no choice.

"Sir, I'm sorry for your loss, but the risk was too great not to prove those boxes were empty." He just looked down at the camera lens, his face a mix of pain and sorrow. I knew what it was like to lose men and women under your command. It was the hardest thing on earth to experience and stay balanced.

"Anything you can do to help on this occasion would be gratefully appreciated." I arranged for the geeks to send him the data. I was just about to dig into my earlier thoughts to see where I had left off when the mini yelled at me.

"Commander, where in the hell did you get this satellite data from?" The admiral's face this time was angry, and it surprised me. Then I suddenly realized we had kept our use of satellites completely secret, except for Arie, who had been around when the monks had first included us in their little technological miracle. What did I tell him? I settled on the part of the truth, just not the part that involved the monks.

"Admiral, the French managed to maintain some weather satellites during the technology hack, we don't know how, but we have managed to use them for our own purposes."

"Interpol has those technological skills?"

"Yes, sir, we do. Our geeks are very, very good." His face registered some surprise as he absorbed this information, then a question occurred to him, and his eyes opened significantly.

"Do our people know about this?"

"Yes, sir, NSA, CIA, FBI, and the president's general."

"I see. Thank you, I'll let you know what we can do to help." Blank screen again, I'd try to recall where I was up to before I was so rudely interrupted about a hundred times, then through the fog, my original plan emerged, somewhat a little tarnished by current events. I walked into our bunk room and found Sandra sitting on the edge of her bed, still looking a little the worst for wear, with Fay sitting at a small desk pounding away on the miniature keyboard of her mini.

"Fay, Sandra, I need to bounce some stuff off you both. First, Fay, what's the status of your scanning?"

"Nothing in Ireland, nothing in Spain, we're holding just outside France's airspace. We have permission to land the C-17 in France. Arie arranged for fuel at four airports. We're waiting on you for direction."

"Hold time for the drones?"

"Seven hours."

"The C-17?"

"Will need to land and refuel in four hours, tops."

"Okay, put it on the ground now, refuel, and wait for my go before relaunching. Keep the drones where they are."

"WILCO" (Will comply). She bent to her mini again. I looked at Sandra, the color had come back into her cheeks, there was light in her eyes, and I could feel the vibes starting to come off her, albeit at a much-reduced frequency. She must still hurt like a bitch. I know I did, and my wounds were far less severe than hers.

"I need your input on our next moves."

"Current sitrep?" (Situation report).

"Navy has taken out the third boat, confirmed three empty boxes. Geeks were tracking an aircraft we believe is carrying two shells and nuclear material out of Quetta by way of Aleppo. They lost them just now. Tracking went blank, similar to the black holes we had to deal with last time." Sandra looked at me, a question in her eyes. Her long blond hair was really messy and needed a wash, and why was I thinking of that right now?

"You've got the Americans looking with their antiair search radars?"

"Yes." She nodded, making no move to stand. I wondered just how to hurt she really was.

"You know, back in the second world war, during the battle of Brittan, and before radar had been perfected, the English erected huge listening towers that could detect German aircraft crossing the French coast. Not suggesting that for a second, but eyeballs can't be fooled by technology trickery, the airways are down to less than ten percent traffic, it shouldn't be too hard to find then knowing they are landing in France, somewhere."

"What if they divert?" Her shoulders slumped, almost as if the conversation was wearing her down.

"Take a few hours more down. Fay and I will take it upstairs." And signaling to Fay, I walked back out to the open deck. It was a windy, choppy day, and the overcast was threatening to rain. It made me feel even more miserable than usual, and I needed something solid under me, so I called for Indigo.

"Can you get us a warehouse or hangar, France preferably, if not Spain or Italy but very close to the border, and get our geeks set up, full command center, room for Tom and Bob's teams, plus us, and maybe you get a few extra of your special people? And at least one expresso machine, giant size, and I'd like to be in and settled by tomorrow." He smiled at me, nodded enthusiastically, and raced back inside. Tom approached so stealthily that I felt my skin start to crawl, and I shivered. Lived with silent people all my working life but never got used to them creeping around.

"Commander, I overheard your instructions to the colonel. What can I do to help?" I smiled, letting him know I wasn't put out by his eavesdropping and pointed to the bow of the ship.

"Find somewhere to park this until we need it again, help Indigo with the accommodations, and get everyone packed up and ready to move." He threw me a mock salute and marched away.

I started to think about finding an invisible aircraft, a mountain of gold, a level five biohazard capable laboratory, and two terrorists.

I turned to Fay, who had been watching me like a hawk.

"I need all your FBI-trained instincts on this." I stared at the water, churned up by the wind pushing against the tidal flow.

The wind had risen in the last few minutes, and I could smell a storm building, and the horizon was showing signs that the gods were angry.

"We seem to be in a technology battle. Every time we make a breakthrough, they come back at us with a new, improved version of something. I can't believe that the two terrorists from Al Bar al Shirak have the skills we keep seeing. We know they had help from one of the refugee women, but somehow, we need to find any others who are playing with us this time around. I'm an investigator first, but I just can't see the trees for the woods."

"We lack motive. I remember when I first learned of the women's motive when this whole situation started, and thinking to myself, 'I was a refugee child. I was taken out and placed with a loving family. Why wasn't I asked to contribute to their plan?' And then I met the CEO of the plant in Point Roberts, and later Amira, and I understood why no one had tried to coerce me."

"Your choice of career made you unattractive to them?"

"Maybe. But I think it also had to do with placement. Every person we arrested had reached superstar status in their field at a very young age. By my mid-twenties, I had risen to SSA (supervisory special agent) and had my own team, but I was still very low on the FBI power ladder. I never reached the heights so that I became a real asset to them."

"But you are a most valuable asset to us. Your work in Helena, Point Roberts, and New Zealand gave us most of their team. I look at you, and I see their Achilles' heel." Fay gave me a strained look as if she hadn't connected the dots.

"They had their strategy and money guy, Mohammad bin Azaria; the operations manager in 'Helen', then their implementers, the pilot, the scientist, the engineer, the CEOs of their plants, their gamers, their corporate supporters like Innomatchi, but they didn't have anyone who could look at all the levels of the puzzle and cross those boundaries. They went for compartmentalizing all their players, centralized control, and countered on us never being able to link it all together." She nodded, seeing the logic of what I was saying.

"This feels different. I think we have two main players, working almost against each other, certainly not in concert, supported by the women at some technological level, but not intimately involved as they were last time. Just as an aside, do you know how the geeks are going in Israel getting the nano bug to eat the one that is clogging up the oil and gas pipelines?" She looked surprised. None of us had talked about that little project started by Amira some weeks ago.

"Yes, and no. At this point, it seems unlikely they will find a solution. If anything, from the data I have seen, every attempt makes it worse. I suspect that they need Amira back, or even the mythical Michele, before and if they can get a solution. But I thought that was very low on your priority list?"

"It is. The question just popped into my head because I was talking to you, and I suddenly remembered dropping that little project on you back in Venice." She nodded, accepting the situation and no doubt putting it behind her as she chewed on what I was really asking of her.

"If you weren't running the drone program but sitting back in your FBI office in Seattle, what questions would you be asking, and who would you be asking them of?"

"Like you, I don't know the 'who', other than our two terrorists and certainly the scientist. But the motive bugs me. I can't see a win for the refugee argument by using a nuclear weapon anywhere on the globe. Unless you deliberately want to make new refugees. And when you look at the timeline, it seems a really long stretch to link this attack with the ones we just managed to eradicate."

"Why?"

"The Irish bulletin board, set up over a year ago, predates the first terrorist attacks by the women or Shetani by nine months. The ship we're sitting on was being rebuilt nine months before the first attack and finished around the time of the first attacks. The pictures from Afghanistan are six weeks old, right in the middle of the first and second wave attack timelines. Want me to go on?" I closed my eyes for a second, nodded, then raised a question I thought she had missed.

"If you look at 'Helen', Natasha Trotsky, she had a thirty-five-year timeline on her activities, so lead and lag in the terrorist's attack profile doesn't really seem to be an issue?" She looked at me and smiled as if sensing I was challenging her logic. "We got all her data from her computers, a list of all her recruits, full information on the families, distribution of funds, terror groups involved, and a detailed timeline of all the attacks, but in the thousands of pages of data, there was not a single mention of Amir Abbas, Malik Badawi, or Hamas or Al Bar al Shirak. From that, we deduce that what we have now is a separate group, no doubt financed by some of the funds deposited in those nineteen countries where the plants were destined for, but running a different attack profile."

"Who is the 'we'?"

"Sandra, Indigo, and I had a chat about it after you and Arie and the 104 took the shells out of Gaza."

This is what I had been missing. We had been reacting from the very first, running around chasing our tails, fighting the good fight, but without the benefit of being able to stand back and look at the threat overall. This is where the boss and I had meshed so well-he had orchestrated and led the running around, and I had managed the investigative overview and provided the warm body with a gun when he needed it, mostly to throw in some bad guy's face. But he was always sitting in the background, looking at the big picture, or trying to put one together.

And now I had my direction. All I had to do was work out who to put where. I sat quietly beside her, reflecting on my choices. Can't duplicate what we had before the boss moved on, different personalities and different times, but I did have a deep well of talent to call on.

On the far horizon, the sun, which had turned a brilliant orange due to all the smoke in the air, fought its way through the dark threatening clouds, seemed to hang in the sky, then silently crawl into the sea, forming a glaring figure of eight, as if it was being split in two, or the sea was eating it. The top slowly merged with the bottom until only the afterglow of the magnificent sunset rippled on the horizon, slowly sending out little flashes on top of the waves.

Life. I had to get one, and I promised myself to attend to this matter the moment the little issue of terrorists playing with nuclear weapons of mass destruction was settled.

During the morning, we moved everything and everybody into a sturdy empty hangar in Turin, mostly used by Alpine Mountain Rescue, which had a bevy of Turbo Porters and Bell-212 helicopters, painted bright red over white with orange strips on the wings and fuselage, all the better to see them after they had crashed into the snow-covered mountains, which they did a couple of times a year. All this proved was that the area was exceedingly dangerous for the unwary, both on the ground and in the air. There was a mixture of eight planes parked out the front, next to our C-17, which had been quickly rebadged as Italian Airforce, and the two drones were kept in the hangar when they weren't flying.

Indigo and I had briefed the Colonel who ran the rescue unit, and she had been absolutely thrilled to act as a front for us, even giving us the high-visibility outerwear, so we looked the part. That had given me an idea, and Amira, Tom, and Fay were presently busy fitting detectors and laser broadcast units to the Turbo Porters and 212s, who would start flying scanning corridors for us tomorrow.

I had politely asked the admiral to maintain a blockage of the Mediterranean Sea, and to park a destroyer off the coast of Europe every one hundred nautical miles, all the way to the edge of Cyprus, and fly noisy and visible helicopter patrols along the coast and inland, three times a day. He hadn't grumbled. He had even sent over four

Marines to man our ship, which we had arranged to return to its original mooring. Before they left the ship via the ubiquitous navy helicopter, the marines had enabled the video and motion detector system the geeks had installed right throughout the boat. This system was monitored twenty-four hours and right now filled the main display area.

As a piece of bait went, the multimillion-dollar price tag was probably excessive, but let's see what it caught before we wrote it off. The marines had reported a lot of interest land-side as they flew off, and I could hardly wait to see who turned up.

Now it was rubber-hitting the road time, and I pulled my teams in for a briefing. Tom and Bob had posted their teams around the perimeter of the hangar, and the two massive doors had been pulled closed. As we had moved in the very early hours of the morning, in one coordinated shift, it was unlikely that we had been tracked. But just in case, the aircrew of the C-17 sat in their cockpit, keeping a watch on the approaches, which were very tight and very narrow.

Hard to penetrate, easy to defend.

"Settle down. If you haven't got a coffee, get one now. You all know the situation and our priorities. We are looking for two terrorists, two shells, and potentially two nukes, and we have a focus on what they need to make them a real threat. I'm going to break us up into teams — Bob, you have eight in your team. You'll work with Indigo, he will match your eight, and each team will have a French/ Italian/ German speaker. I want every nuclear power station in France, then Germany visited and their level Five biosecurity labs inspected. And I want every level Five independent lab inspected, and I want that done as fast as humanly possible. You will have an Italian helicopter at your disposal, UN/Interpol credentials, Red Notices, and warrants, and you will not be expected. You arrive, you inspect, and you do not take prisoners, and if you hit, you sit and call everyone to you. Clear?" Bob looked a little perplexed and looked at Indigo, who gave him a high-five and a huge grin.

"Tom, you've got four at this point. Indigo will lend you four more. Again, you will have multilinguists. I want that gold found, and I want it secured. The same goes for your own helicopter, full documentation, and when you find it, sit and call home. Your bailiwick is Germany. Start where that aircraft with the money originated before it was shot to pieces on the ground at Aleppo. Questions?" He shook his head, happy to have a defined target.

"Fay, I want you to team up with Indigo. He will lend you four of his best. I want you to find Amir Abbas. He is somewhere in France. Think it through and pin him down. Be mindful that we lost his aircraft, and we don't know where it is now. You have a more open brief, if you find him, end him and any with him, and if you need backup, you know where to find it. Indigo, make sure the four you give Fay are Section Five qualified, please. We will not want any hesitation." He nodded to me. He understood what I wasn't saying. This was a 'kill' mission.

No are prisoners required. We couldn't take the risk.

"Indigo, you will work with Luigi, Amira, and the geeks, find Abbas's plane, and find anyone who is playing in the shadows. Does anyone have any questions?"

"No? Good. Move it, people, keep your heads down, and make it fast." I looked around the room, confident that if anyone could nip this potential nuclear attack in the bud, they were in this hangar. Sandra hadn't said a word during the briefing, just sat sipping her coffee, occasionally looking up to see who I was targeting next.

"Are you treating me like the walking wounded, or have you a role for me?" There was no sarcasm in her voice, something that worried me a little, but then she had been out of it most of the last two days, so she was probably feeling a little left behind.

"You and I have the hardest task. We have to find Amir Abbas, he is the central character in this disaster, and I want to nail his arse to the wall. We need to work out his motive. Who does he really hate?" She looked up, mildly interested, so I asked her the one question she couldn't duck.

"Are you up for this?" I got a face full of frown. She shook her head, rotated her shoulders, and stood so suddenly her hair, now washed and shiny again, flew up and down as if it had been in a cyclone.

"Yes. Just haven't been shot before, don't like the experience, and you continually piss me off the way you just march around with bullet holes all over you as if it doesn't matter!" I thought about my reply and decided there was no benefit in pulling any punches.

"Well, to tell the truth, it does get a little boring after a while. You'll get used to it." And that made her laugh, and she was back. Thank God, I had missed her bubbling, cheerful self. She stood still, looking dead into my eyes.

"Do you really believe we can stop them before they let one off?" I stared back at her, not blinking.

"Yes. I absolutely do. Look what we've done so far and how fast we have done it. And on buggar all information." I held her gaze. She smiled, then punched me lightly on the arm.

"Then let's go get the bastards."

# Chapter Twenty-Six

The airfield just outside Cour-l'Évêque, in the Haute-Marne department of northeastern France, had been built by the Germans in the early years of the occupation during the second world war. Hitler had seen it as a strategic location from which his freedom bombers could take off and bomb England into submission. Originally a grass strip of some one thousand meters, the German engineers had extended it to three thousand meters and laid concrete blocks down over the grass, which, stubbornly, if you listened to the locals, continued to grow between the cracks as if it hadn't a care in the world.

Several abandoned hangars lay in various stages of ruin, the fight against rot, rust, and poorly made concrete having been given up decades ago. The locals had tried to have a gliding club established in the mid-sixties, but that had failed miserably, and a local farmer continued to run his industrial-sized mower over the entire paddock once a year, simply to keep it from looking like what it was—an abandoned and forgotten memory from difficult times.

Amir Abbas had heard of the site from one of his acolytes, who had run away from home to join in the fight against everything, having washed out of his entrance exams for the Foreign Legion. Abbas had taken little notice at first. After all, why would a terrorist work to crush Israel with an abandoned airfield in the middle of France? But on his recent trip, he had decided to drive by and take a look for himself. And what we saw got his juices going. Using his forged papers, declaring him to be an Inspector with an obscure branch of French Intelligence, the DPSD, formerly *Securite Militaire-SM*-Military

Security, he hunted up to farmer and his mower and paid him ten thousand euros to mow the grass immediately and lower the blades to their finest level for the strip. He had located the owner living some kilometers away and hired the field for three months in the name of the government for just five thousand euros. Cash. Because this was French Intelligence, both the farmer and the local council member were sworn to keep the information a secret on pain of imprisonment.

He had organized six of his followers from the south of France to drive up and dressed as military policemen. They took up positions around the paddock and camped in their vehicles, which for the turbulent times, was not an unnatural thing to do. Then he found a spot in one of the deserted hangars where he could set up camp and make himself comfortable. With him was his purloined official from the Atomic Energy Commission, who had been effectively duped by Abbas's fake credentials, and the one hundred thousand euros he had been promised for essentially seven days' work. While they both spoke French, Abbas had insisted they speak only English, as the three guards he had brought with him did not. He huddled out of the drizzle in one corner of the hangar, feeling invincible.

"Henri, if I show you some diagrams, can you help me to understand them, please?" The inspector, a long, sad willowy man of some forty-eight years, his hair shredded to just wisps across a bald, stone-white skull, offset by a miserable mustache that dropped at each end as if trying to find somewhere to hide on his shrunken face, shuffled over, wrapped in a patched dark gray greatcoat that was two sizes too big for him.

"*Oui, monsieur.*"

"Henri, English please."

"Yes, sir, my apologies. I forget these days very easily." Abbas nodded as if he agreed with him, and in fact, he did. Only Henri's credentials in manipulating nuclear materials had brought him to Abbas's notice. The man was ugly, to say the least, had the manners of a pig and snored in his sleep. Abbas held out the blueprints for the torpedoes and let the inspector paw through them. He muttered to himself under his breath, flipped them over once or twice, and actually held one up to the fading light as if he could see through the dark blue ink of the blueprint.

"If it were possible to make these, they would be magnificent and very hard to work with." His eyes shone with pleasure in his humdrum, mundane life back in Paris. All he ever saw was the dreary refuse handed to him by a supervisor who hated his guts. Never had he seen such clever technology, and sadly, he could not envisage how such beautiful shells could be made to such exacting tolerances.

"Why hard to work with?" Henri pointed to the third page, where an expanded section showed the tolerances and the precise fitting of the membrane and nose plug.

"Sir, opening and closing these shells would entail a technology I am not familiar with. And this plug here, you see?" he said, pointing to the dolphin-like nose on the shell, "is designed to push through the entire body of the shell, penetrating the first chamber, then the membrane, then into the second chamber. Yet there are no seams on the plug, you see?" No, Abbas, in spite of having been present when Badawi and his witch had produced the shells, did not see anything special in the nose, just a horrible barrier to his plan. But he had a persona to protect, so he played out his role as best as he could, keeping his temper under control as much as he could, but in truth, he needed the smell and touch of blood on his hands, and he needed it now.

Killing the AEC Inspector was not an option. Unfortunately, he needed him and his miserable skills to solve the loading of the nuclear matériel's into the shells, which were due soon, and looking down at his watch to prevent the dumb inspector from seeing his own death in Abbas's eyes, noted that they would arrive in the next hour. He started to mentally prepare for their arrival, thinking through all he had to do. He stood, looked out over the bleak featureless paddock, pulled out a stolen satellite phone, and, as he started to walk away, barked out an order to the unfortunate inspector.

"Take your time, but I want to know how to make those shells work before the end of the day. Use your imagination. Pretend money is no object. Your government is depending on you! And your life, Abbas thought to himself, although that was forfeit in any case, dead man walking, as they say, the only variable was the time. He looked at the display on the phone, which indicated no satellite in range. He swore to himself, not having remembered the schedule. He kept walking, the need for the smell and touch of blood pushing his self-control to its very borders.

He stood on the edge of the closely mown strip, which disappeared off in both directions, straight sides, flat surface, in contrast to the higher cut on the surrounding grass. He kicked at the edge of one concrete block, stubbed his toe, cursed, then, in a fit of temper, almost threw his phone on the ground, pulling back at the last moment as his brain caught up with his temper. He sucked in deep breaths, letting his chest expand and his shoulders rise, and slowly, ever so slowly, regained his calm.

He missed his home back in Gaza, he missed his cohort with whom he had proudly raised terror to new heights for the past decades, and he missed the ability to kill anytime he wanted to and anyone he wanted to. These bloody bombs of Badawi had better work, and they had better work as promised, or he would go on a hunt and track him down and kill him in the worst way possible.

Slowly and with great care and attention to detail!

# Chapter Twenty-Seven

Tom, an ex-SEAL, now working for an off-book government agency, and seconded to Interpol, specifically Section Five, had seen a lot of Europe in the last three months. Initially, he and his team had become involved in the first terrorist attacks when his life-long friend, one Colonel Anthony, PJ to his friends, had coopted him to manage a small investigation concerning the Hog attack on West Point. That had only taken a matter of hours before his friend had shot off back to Italy in a dead black SR-71, one of only two still flying. That in itself should have been a clue. Why would the American government give a member of Interpol such an asset? But at the time, he had just been very happy to reacquaint himself with his ex-partner and follow the bouncing ball.

All the way to Milan, and then over the next few weeks, when the hunt for the terrorists really heated up, he had been shot at in the desert, attacked by wild militia in the mid-west, nearly crushed by a tank back in the Arabian desert, only to have the opportunity to meet and serve with the most incredible group of people he had ever experienced.

Not the least of which had been the then Captain-now Commander, Jessica Riley, at the time PJ's 2IC. A woman who literally broke the mold of feminity. Dressed in her Armani power suit, her weapon securely covered by her well-cut jacket, capped off with polished rubber-soled low-heeled boots, she looked like someone who haunted the boardrooms of the biggest and best of corporate empires. When she changed into what for her was classed as combat fatigues, hip-hugging jeans, tight tank tops, slinky body armor, a Sig carelessly hung on her narrow hips, all covered with a lightweight but the stylish bush jacket, with her short auburn hair freely flowing every which way in the wind, she managed to cut a swath through everything and everyone in her way with a flick of one dainty, but calloused hand. She had been seriously wounded during the capture of the terrorist known as 'Helen'-Natasha Trotsky-who was an ex-Stasi German operative responsible for setting up families all over the world for the refugee children, having been trained by the Russians at a place called 'USAville' in the nineteen sixties and seventies. She had also controlled some of the terrorist attacks out of her headquarters in Libya. 'Helen' had worked with Mohammad bin Azaria for over thirty-five years, setting up the framework, the systems and processes, the technology and communications, and the accounting for all his success, as well as managing the terrorist group she had hired in on his behalf run by the devil-Shetani-a six-foot six Afrikaans mercenary, who had effectively closed down every oil and gas well, and coal mine, worldwide. Shetani had also overthrown the King of Arabia and had survived a coup attempt by the French, only to be blown to bits a day or two later by an Israeli commando troop which Tom and his men were proud to have been attached to.

It was rumored among the Section Five troops that Riley had personally shot Mohammad bin Azaria to death, one in the head, one in the heart, in a subterranean jail cell back in Venice, which was silently lauded given the magnitude of his crimes against humanity. The same rumor had also mentioned the demise of the German, Natasha Trotsky, but the details of who had pulled the trigger on her were vague. But it was hinted that Riley's 2IC, the long-legged blonde, had been with her at the time.

And now, just a few weeks later, he again found himself thrown into the fray, but this time he had lost half his men due to a rocket explosion while they had been attacking a terrorist boat carrying nuclear-capable shells along the Mediterranean Sea. Commander Riley had again been shot, he remembered, leading the charge onto the terrorist boat via a helicopter rappelling line. She was a bullet magnet, no doubt about that, and her courage was unequalled. And now, having been given command of Section Five, she had tasked him and his men with finding the gold bullion that was somewhere in Germany, supposedly making its way to the Mediterranean coast. He looked at the four new members of his team, on loan from the Italian Special Forces. Not one of them over five feet ten, not one of them over thirty years of age, and not one of them in the least bit fazed with their new team leader.

"Gentlemen and women, or I suppose that's what you are," he said, pointing to two women with masses of black curly hair bubbling out from their caps, "and if you're not, I don't want to know about it!" The laughter was genuine, and one of the troopers blew him a messy kiss. The other made the heart sign with her dainty hands and pulsed it over her chest with a huge smile.

"Buggar me, what did I do to deserve you?" He settled down, pulled the one-in-five-hundred-kilometer scale map over, laid it on the floor, and invited them all to look at it critically. "Now, if you were going to ship tons of gold bullion from here in Germany to here on the Mediterranean coast, how would you do it?" One very young face looked up at him, a cheeky grin from ear to ear, his automatic rifle poking up over his shoulder caught his attention.

"Master Chief, or can wea call you 'boss'?"

"'Boss' will do."

"*Grazie*. You knowa howa much gold?"

"The Commander thought ten to twenty billion euros. Let's settle for the sake of the argument on fifteen."

"Youa knowa howa mucha that weights?"

"We're going to get ourselves caught up in imperial versus metric. Let me work it out for you the way I know, then we can convert it at the end. Agreed?" Everybody nodded, immediately taking the weight off Tom's board shoulders. He loved the Italians. He had served alongside Indigo and his troopers a number of times, and their courage was never lacking, or their sense of humor, he remembered, so he relaxed fractionally. He might be an older person. Good grief, he was just shy of forty! He wasn't ready for a box by any means, but the seriously young faces of the four specialists he had been 'lent' by Indigo had marginally scared him.

"Okay, here we go. A long ton is 1.12 of a short ton. Keep that in mind. A ton is valued at approximately forty-seven million dollars. So fifteen billion would weigh approximately 320 tons. Convert that to short tons, and you have, again, approximately 358 tons. Got that?" Lots of nods again, then the young face broke into a smile.

"Boss, that'sa lots of trucks!" And everyone laughed. The safe load for a truck was twenty-two to twenty-five tons, so even at maximum capacity, you'd need fifteen trucks, which in convoy, would be very hard to hide, especially at the truck measuring stations that were placed at regular intervals along the freeways, autobahns, and major roads. And to move any real volume of bullion, you would need paperwork-point of origin, destination, authorizing persons, everything to prove the providence of the bullion. And security.

"Boss, where do you think the bullion came from?" This from one of Tom's team, a smart boy from the wilds of California, blond hair and all. He spoke with a twang, he claimed he had picked up like a disease from a woman he had dated when he was at college.

"We figure around here where the aircraft with the money took off from." Tom pointed to Nuremberg airport. He traced his finger all the way down to the Mediterranean coast and nodded to himself.

"We don't know the destination, but we can work out the mechanics. Where do you store that much gold for long periods of time? How do you load it onto transport? How do you move it freely along the road system? How do you cross borders with it? That's a big one. How do you cross borders with it? Then unload at the end of your journey into what? Any ideas? We are talking the equivalent of fifteen freighters loaded to the gills or more trucks carrying less. Not easy to hide."

"There can't be that many places that store bullion. They would need government approval, ease of access for transport, and most of all, very good security." Our blond-headed beach boy was no slouch, drawl, and all.

"Correct. Let's start there, find the source, find the transport." And the biggest treasure hunt of the twenty-first century, in fact, in living memory, got off to a whimper, nine people all dressed for war sitting on the floor looking at an old-style paper map, pointing with their gloved fingers, taking notes by hand in little notebooks!

# Chapter Twenty-Eight

I nterpol France has a unique setup in that its National Central Bureau (NCB) in Paris is part of the National Criminal Police (DCPJ), whose director is also the head of the NCB. One man, many roles, but in this case, it expedited the connection between multiple arms of the police force in their incessant fight against professional gangs who smuggled people, weapons, children, drugs, and all manner of other criminal activities, that usually involved the police, gendarmerie, and customs services. Having one single point of coordination not only sped up the operation to stop the criminals in their tracks, but it also allowed several departmental budgets to be pooled, enabling the most modern technology to be utilized in the fight against crime. Unfortunately, like the rest of the world, their technological advantage was made moot by the attack on the web and worldwide hack on routers, computers, and anything else that had a MAC address chip in it. But they still had the boots on the ground and a typical superior French attitude that drove them to the edge of perfection, albeit with an insolence that frustrated practically every other country in the world.

When Alphonse Joubert received notification that his entire unit, across all sectors of policing, was required for a specific task on behalf of Section Five, his bushy eyebrows rose in tandem as he studied the telex. Signed by a Commander Riley, someone he didn't know personally, but he had worked previously with Colonel Anthony, whom he called on his old landline immediately. It took almost ten minutes for his exchange to run the good colonel down but was finally connected with crackles and snaps indicative of the age of the ancient equipment.

"Alphonse, how can I help you?" Anthony inquired, having been warned by his PA that it was the head of Interpol France calling. He remembered a bear of a man with wide shoulders, a pugnacious face, bushy eyebrows, and lots of unkempt hair, with a temper that sat just barely under the surface. But a good investigator, he had helped on a case nearly two years ago that involved child smuggling on a massive scale. And he knew that the man had no patience for anyone not in a uniform.

"Colonel, I have just received a message from Interpol Italy, signed by a Commander Riley, requesting I shift my attention to the matter of a missing terrorist believed to be here in France." PJ listened carefully for the subtext, not bothering to correct him on his rank. He was now a general, remembering that Alphonse had previously dismissed the women in the Interpol team almost out of hand. Old school. And probably a little set in his ways.

"Alphonse, you may remember my 2IC, Captain Jessica Riley, two years ago when you helped us shatter that kiddy smuggling ring?" He could actually hear the Frenchman stroking his mustache.

"Ah, yes, I seem to remember her." The lack of conviction in his voice left PJ in no doubt that he most probably didn't, so he smiled inwardly, relaxing into the call.

"Alphonse, she has been promoted to commander, our equivalent of a one-star general, and took Section Five over from me recently when I was moved to head office. What has she asked you to do?" Alphonse paused. This was no trivial matter. If this woman had been promoted to run Section Five, she was no slouch, and theoretically, she outranked him by at least three or possibly even four ranks. He respected Anthony and had worked well with him and his team, so he was left with little choice but to pay attention to this new person. Whomever she was.

"She has asked me for a nationwide physical search for a terrorist known as Amir Abbas. She has given me a last known location, and had asked that we drop everything else for the next forty-eight hours." As he listed the requirements, his voice got tighter and tighter. How could he possibly stop every investigation currently running in all the adjoined police forces in every department across the whole of France?

"Did she give you a reason?"

"Yes, she mentioned a Red Notice on this person, on suspicion of having a portable nuclear weapon and nuclear materials that can be used in the construction of same." PJ mentally shrugged. If that hadn't gotten through to his French counterpart, he wasn't sure what would.

"Alphonse, if you remember the recent terror attacks that have tipped the world on its collective backside, Commander Riley personally led the raids that netted the mastermind, and then the organizer, and then all the senior cadre as well as managed the entire operation around the world from start to finish. In the last ten days, she has personally managed to sweep up some eighteen potential tactical nuclear bombs, three of which were parked on your doorstep. We are working in five jurisdictions at present, so if she is coming to you directly, you can count on it being at the highest level of threat." PJ paused to let all that sink in, then dropped the hammer. "And, just as an aside, Paris was one of six cities on the terrorist's attack list."

"*Bon dieu! Paris!*"

"Yes, Paris. The Commander moves very quickly and very deliberately, so I suggest you help her as much as you can."

Phone calls were made, telexes sent, and police on bicycles spread the word, and in less than four hours, over two hundred thousand members of the various police and military forces in every department in France were out and about, looking for Amir Abbas.

In the next hour, details filtered back to Paris concerning a secret government operation at an airfield just outside Cour-l'Évêque in the Haute-Marne department of northeastern France. No such operation was admitted to, and upon a deeper investigation, the so-called agent in change's face fit the photo that had been circulated from Interpol's files. One of two of the most wanted terrorists on the planet, Amir Abbas, was working freely and openly out in the French countryside, building nuclear bombs!

Just thirty-five minutes later, a blue van with a flashing blue light loaded with some of France's best rural police stormed the hangar unannounced and was cut down to a man by concentrated fire from the guards who had initially let them through the fence. As the guards were dressed in police uniforms, the trap was simple and easy to execute. Amir Abbas shouted, screamed, kicked the lifeless bodies of the dead policemen and women, fired his weapon at the roof, which did nothing to improve its ability to keep out the light drizzle that fell relentlessly, then finally realized where he was, and what had just happened.

In rapid Arabic, which the AEC inspector did not understand, as he was busy hiding under a table, Abbas instructed his men to move to the aircraft and physically turn it around, as the concrete was not wide enough for it to manage this without sinking into the soft grass. This took the better part of thirty minutes when Abbas dragged the hapless inspector by the collar and finally boarded, then shouted at his men to guard the gate, as he would be back in three hours. Whether they lived or died was no longer his concern. Like most things in his life, they were, having failed him as he saw it, disposable.

They scattered, the pilot, who until the gunfire had erupted had not thought anything was particularly wrong with the charter flight, as rich people always changed their minds about destinations, and this grass strip was no stranger than some of the other ones he had landed on in past months. But now he was concerned, but before he could climb out of his seat where Abbas had told him to stay, Abbas was at his shoulder, a very large handgun now pointing directly at him.

"Change of plan, now you fly to here, direct route, no deviations. Understood?" One look at the crazed eyes of his customer told him all he needed to know about his options, so he started the engines and mentally prepared his flight plan. Gush Katif Airport, approximately 2 nautical miles to the north of Kahn Yunis, in the Gaza strip. Now he really did worry. He had no way of gaining permission to land in the Gaza and would probably be shot down for his trouble in any case. Taking his life in his hands, he turned to the terrorist who now stood jammed in the cockpit doorway.

"Sir, we will need permission to land at that airport."

"Leave that to me. You just fly the plane." And Abbas thrust the gun forward until it hovered just an inch from the pilot's eye. He turned to stare blindly out the cockpit window, the rain now so heavy he switched on the windshield wipers. He did the only thing he could think of. He turned his transponder to the international distress frequency and crossed his fingers. Pushing the throttles forwards, he called out his velocity speeds to himself, 'V1, V2, rotate' and pulled the jet off the concrete and into the heavy overcast, which immediately swallowed him in a threatening collage of black and gray mist, with streaks from the rain running up the windshield. He turned the wipers off and focused on his instruments, this was the most dangerous point of any takeoff, losing all outside visual reference and flying immediately into instrument meteorological conditions (IMC), and he let out the breath he had been holding since first being shirtfronted by his customer.

"Good. Don't stop." And Abbas deserted the cockpit, moving back down into the cabin. From a navigational point of view, now that worldwide GPS was no longer functioning, he had to rely on his inertial systems, so he plotted a great circle route and turned onto a heading that would capture the mythical blue line on his way out of France. He had to be careful because Italy and Germany both had fast jets that would intercept him if he strayed into their airspace, so his plan was to cross the Mediterranean, then parallel the African coast, but in a manner that would not bring any attention. As he thought this through, he suddenly realized that his passenger would kill him on landing. He had clearly seen that in his eyes, so perhaps a good strategy would be to get noticed and allow someone to force them down.

He adjusted his flight path, now planning on deliberately crossing into Italy, then Greece, then possibly Turkey, on his way down to Gaza if he could disguise his intentions. As he passed through ten thousand meters, he started humming to himself, happy for the deep clouds that surrounded them, hoping against hope that they would stay with him all the way.

Back in Paris, the director of Interpol read the report of the initial gunfight, where all his men had been killed, then of the jet taking off, then of a second gunfight where a prisoner had been taken alive, and only seven of his eight men were killed. He summarized the report and passed it on to Lyon with a heavy heart, who immediately passed it on to Venice, where a bright-eyed Italian agent dialed her commander and passed the message on, only to be instructed to contact Colonel Kashasini on his mini.

Which she did, and Indigo, in the darkened belly of the C-17 crossing the French border, took the call in all its gory details. Fay, sitting next to him, slapped her hands together, snapped an order out to their pilot to change course, clapped Indigo on the back, jumped up, and rolled her shoulders.

"Indigo, tell them to have him available in Paris post haste." Indigo, in a similar mood to Fay, just smiled and started the relay back to the director. He could see the same sense of purpose and energy in Fay as he often saw in his commander, and he smiled, enjoying the experience. He only had one regret, and that was the bubbly, effervescent Inspector Thomas had lost a little of her sparkle since being shot, and he sincerely hoped she got it back soon because, with these three women at the top of their game, the terrorists had no chance of succeeding!

As luck would have it, the C-17 beat the police van by an hour, which enabled Fay and Indigo to get a really impressive cup of coffee and a fresh croissant in the director's waiting room and decompress a little. The director, faced with yet another unknown woman of power, decided that valor and French pride required him to stay through the entire ordeal and sulked in his office.

When the prisoner was finally brought in, the long chains linking his hand-cuffed wrists and ankles causing him to shuffle, a large bloody bandage over his shoulder and collar bone, the director held his peace, letting the Section Five agents have first use of the terrorist, now wearing the more traditional white and blue striped overalls of the French prison system.

Indigo asked him his name in Arabic, Urdu, French, Italian, Spanish, Farsi, Hebrew, and Persian but was ignored in all of them, except for the dilation of his eyes when he had spoken in Hebrew. He smiled, then addressed the terrorist in English. Another Jew-hater, he would break easily.

"Sir, in actual fact, your name is unimportant. When Amir Abbas discovers you have survived and spoken to Interpol, your life will be forfeit in any jail or prison we send you to. You know this to be true. We only want to know one thing." As he finished speaking, Fay pulled her weapon out of its holster on her back hip, pulled the slide back, checked the load, stood, and pointed it at his head, holding the barrel just centimeters from his nose.

"*Directeur, mes excuses, nous pourrions salir votre sol.*"

"*Vous* êtes *excusée madame, le personnel de nettoyage s'occupera de tout gâchis.*" Good, Fay thought to herself. The director was on the same page, understood the real threat, and would have his cleaners look after any mess she made. Something she had learned firsthand working with Jessica was never postured, never draw your gun if you didn't intend to use it, and she did, and the terrorist saw it in her eyes. He put his manacled hands up in surrender, bent his head to the side as if to duck a bullet, and started to whimper.

A really rapid conversation then ensued between the terrorist and Indigo, in what Fay interpreted as Farsi, a language she had yet to master. She could see by the change in the director's demeanor that he understood the conversation, and he was not enjoying it. In fact, his face was turning redder and redder, and he was clenching and unclenching his fists.

"Indigo, we take him with us." He looked at Fay, nodded, and the director realized that the woman was giving instructions to an Italian colonel. But he had heard the conversation about the nuclear material, and the shells, and his blood had run cold while his emotions had run riot. They wanted the prisoner? All theirs, with a handshake, to seal the deal. He couldn't get rid of this dangerous prisoner fast enough. His view of women hadn't necessarily changed, but perhaps he was a little more ready to acknowledge their skills, and certainly, he thought to himself never to get on the wrong side of them! He had noted that the woman's hand had not shaken even a millimeter while holding her gun on the terrorist.

Fay and Indigo followed the guards who had the prisoner between them all the way to the ubiquitous blue van.

"Aéroport d'Orly." The ride was rapid and bumpy, and they were thrown from side to side at each corner, as the police driver exploited his god given right to barrel through every intersection and round-a-bout on two wheels. The four dour policemen seemed to enjoy the ride, but refused to smile. Fay didn't care less, and minutes after the van pulled up at the ramp of the C-17, she had the prisoner chained to a cargo bolt on the cabin floor, and was drinking a cup of hot steaming coffee with both hands, her Italian contingent hustling Indigo for information.

"Where to next?" Indigo asked, sitting down in one of the red webbing seats, stretching out his legs, and crossing his combat boots at the ankles, something the boss was wont to do, and it hit her that he was no longer part of their daily fabric. Indigo looked tired, but that was no more than the adrenalin let down after the charge of getting to the terrorist and hearing his pitiful story.

"Tell me all." Indigo sighed, aligning his thoughts as Fay joined him on the row of seats. Fay looked at him, at the anxious troops, and at the prisoner, now lying prone, looking miserable and extremely uncomfortable. She waved her hands at him in the 'come on' gesture, her eyes holding a glint.

"Fay, in response to your superior interrogation technique, the prisoner described Abbas to a tee, has been with him this last week as Abbas visited a number of nuclear power plants. and some private laboratories, none of whom would take his money for the use of their facilities. He had himself a person from the Atomic Energy Commission, who he had hoped could negotiate a successful outcome and then do the work to load up the shells and turn them into bombs. The shells and the nuclear material are on the aircraft. It is a French jet with three engines, one mounted over the tail, single pilot, but it has or had a bonded courier dressed in a fine black suit, white shirt, and navy tie. His shoes had been highly polished, and he had winced at walking on the wet grass in them, which had all the guards laughing. All his men were recruits from Hamas, from three cells in the Paris region. They stole the police uniforms a week ago. Abbas paid them all fifty percent of what he promised them from the money on the aircraft, and according to the courier, before he was hacked to death, he told one of the men that the money and the nuclear material were picked up in Aleppo, and the shells in Quetta, Pakistan.

The reason he had been butchered was that he had told the guards this story, thinking he was a valuable asset. Abbas had overheard him, then diced and sliced him to death, and then shot him several times for good measure.

Most importantly, he did not know where Abbas was going now. However, they had all been promised a flight to Gaza to join the main terrorist force and fight the Jews. As she was processing all this, Indigo's and her mini started to howl, so they both flipped them open.

# Chapter Twenty-Nine

"Hello, Team. Sorry to interrupt your busy days, but I have an update for you all." I waited until I saw all their faces register the call, noted their backgrounds and their tired looks in the case of Indigo and Fay, and crossed my fingers that I wasn't pushing them too hard.

"Firstly, thanks to the great work by Indigo and Fay and their team, we've found Abbas. He's fled France for points unknown, so Bob, you are your team no longer need to check on the labs. How was that going, by the way?"

"Seven down, all negative. What do you want to do with us now?"

"Meet up with Tom, work with him on finding the gold. I'm particularly interested in a destination because, at some time, Badawi will want to claim his bullion." His face showed nothing, and he nodded silently, so I moved on to the next thing on my agenda.

"Sandra and I, with four of Indigo's best boys and girls and an Israeli interpreter, are at the crash site where Badawi was put down, and the Americans and Israelis subsequently hit with cruise missiles outside Ramadi. We have two locals helping us, thanks to Arie. If we can't find him, when you find the gold, we will set a trap. How is that going, Tom?" He had a big smile, low scrub running past his image, and I could just hear Italian chatter in the background. I rounded off the conversation.

"We have first-hand accounts that suggest nothing was offloaded from the aircraft, and Badawi took off in a four-wheel drive heading towards Fallujah. The missiles only missed him by a matter of minutes. But he was wounded, not seriously, according to the men on the ground."

"So any shells he may have had or containers of nuclear matériel are destroyed?"

"Yes."

"But can we prove it?"

"No." The line went quiet as everyone thought through the import of what had just been saying. I had another piece of news, and I had tossed up whether or not to share, but my team deserved to know what the stakes were. They risked their lives every minute of every day. I took a deep breath.

"Do you all remember when our Pakistani agents went into Afghanistan?" Heads nodded, so I continued. "Well, based on what we found originally, our resident director, agent Drishya Singh, with agents Sandista Yang and Phon Yarmuth, decided to go back in, this time armed with a lot of spending money. They took a different approach, tracked down the materials providers, truck drivers, support personal, and had another go at the airport manager, and we now think that a total of thirty shells were manufactured, one was destroyed in testing, but all other twenty-nine were shipped out.

"Five went first, by helicopter, days before the next shipment. One lot of ten was taken directly by Badawi personally and was flown out somewhere in an ex-Russian helicopter, but we now assume these were the shells we located holders for on the ship. Abbas was responsible for ten, which he transported by truck to the boats in Syria, and somewhere along the line stole at least four of them that we know of."

"The two in Gaza, they were also his?"

"Yes, but he has four more shells. We know he has two shells on the plane with him now, which leaves us missing two others. The good news is, well, maybe not so good in reality. He only has material for three bombs. Although Amira did say they could shave down the ingots and slugs, reduce the yield by twenty percent, and get four good bombs out of it if they have the skills."

"So, if I've followed you correctly," Fay interjected, "we know two are on that aircraft, where ever it is, and now we have another two to track?"

"Plus, the first five shipped out. Absolutely have no idea where they are or who has them. One other thing. Right at the beginning, we thought the shells would be fired from shoulder-launched Man Pads (man-portable air defense weapon), 80 millimeters. The electro-magnetic rail gun on the ship distracted us into thinking that we knew how they were going to launch them. But we didn't count on Abbas going native, and in all probability, he was always going to use a Man Pad of some description. And that means he had to prepare for this six weeks ago, at the very least."

"Effective range?" I pointed to Sandra; this had been one of her first tasks on this operation.

"The Russian SRV-70 would be the easiest to get, and if they build the sabot to encompass the shell, stick any available rocket on the back end, don't get fussy with electronic targeting, you might have five thousand meters range."

"Predicted radius of both blast effect and radiation fallout?" I snapped this out, not meaning to, but suddenly this was all getting a little low-tech, and it scared me to the bone.

Sandra snapped back at me. The first sign I had was that she was recovering from her sulk at being shot.

"The original figures were based on six kilos-eighteen pounds-of nuclear material inside the shell. You'll get the explosive force of approximately fifteen hundred tons of TNT. That's a Zone 1 blast radius of five to ten miles, Zone 2 of twenty to thirty miles, with the radioactivity spreading out another twenty to thirty miles, depending on the prevailing wind and the material used."

"Do you shave that by twenty percent if you stretch the nuclear material out over four shells?"

"I can work that out for you, but for now, just think that the damage zones will be approximately the same."

"That's still a very effective weapon, not to mention the scare factor."

"Yes."

"Then firing the bomb from five thousand meters away would still be very dangerous."

"Yes."

"But then, if you didn't care about the welfare of your men, it wouldn't matter."

"No."

"And we know Abbas is a psychopath, sociopath, and flat-out murderer, so to him, the sacrifice would be a good thing."

"Same goes for a jihadist. Instead of a bomb vest, they can go out with a bang and a mushroom cloud."

"Ouch!" and at that, everyone laughed a little, breaking the tension.

"Okay, people, listen up. Find that gold, or at least the destination. We have a trap set on the ship. I'll get the navy to start sweeping as far as they can inland down this end of the Med. Fay, get your drone fleet mobile. We need to scan from the coast of Syria all the way to Russia. Bring the C-17 back as well, but keep it ready to fly. Maybe park it at Sde Dov. I'll talk to Arie about that. Good work, everyone. Think outside the box, and stay safe." And now I had the hardest call to make, to my friend the admiral, because I needed him to move his ships again.

"Admiral, I hope this finds you in good spirits." He looked anything but his starched whites a sharp contrast to the overcast sky and boiling thunderheads.

"We've just buried our dead from the raid on the boat. Very hard on all the crew, specifically the marines. How is your search going?" The image behind him panned as he moved, probably to seek a measure of privacy.

"Well, we've managed to chase one of the terrorists down in France. He got away and headed for the Middle East. We can't track his flight path. It is invisible to us. And we have just learned that Abbas, whose boat you took out, has four shells, not just the two we thought were left. So now we are concentrating all our efforts on smoking him out." He looked serious for a moment, then nodded to himself.

"You will want me to move my ships towards Gaza?"

"Yes, sir, but please don't remove any ship you have blockading the Mediterranean. We know they are mobile, but we don't know their plan."

"I've seen your work up close, Commander. What are you mentally preparing for?" I looked at him, all stiff and formal, his whites glaring in the fleeting sunlight that managed to penetrate the overcast and grieving for his lost sailors and marines. I would give him my best guess and not hold it against him if it came back on me. I looked at Sandra, now standing a few feet away from me, out of camera range, hands on her hips, her long blond hair swept back from her face. She nodded her agreement.

"Full-out attack on Israel. Abbas has always been after Israel and has made no secret about it. I think he was in France to get the nuclear material he needed for the shells. I suspect he and Badawi had different targeting preferences, broke up after the manufacturing process was completed, and Abbas delivered the shells to the boats as part of his arrangement with Badawi. I think he was always going to attack Israel, and Badawi changed his target list after he visited someone in Germany. I also suspect that Badawi was never going to arm the shells he sent West. I think that was part of some plot or other cooked up in Ireland and was meant to throw us off his main agenda and chase our tails. I also suspect he was offered the gold bullion for his troubles, which we are also tracking."

"What draws you to these conclusions?"

"A lot of guessing, speculating, some hard facts, and the way it has all unfolded. Badawi definitely had help from the refugee women. We don't know how much or for that matter, how many. But it is very hard to see where nuclear bombs fit in with the women's larger agenda with the refugee children. It could just be as simple as Badawi seeing an opportunity for himself with the women and using them for his own purposes."

"Which might be?" I laughed. This was a question that haunted me day and night.

"Sir, not a single clue at this stage. And there's one other small matter." His smile was a grimace that barely split his lips.

"And what would that be?" It was all I could do to not smile at his formality. It wasn't funny, it was tragic, but the sight of him in his crisp whites was such a contrast with the grubby unkempt appearance of our team in the warehouse.

"We now suspect there are five shells hidden somewhere we haven't looked yet, they we placed in position nearly two months ago." I saw his frown, his eyes scrunched up as he took this new information in, then he just shrugged his shoulders.

"Commander, we're all putting a lot of trust in you and your team, don't let us down". And he disconnected. Sandra sat back down on the bed, looking more herself now we were back on the hunt. While she and I worked from the room of a hotel in Bagdad, our team, comprising two of Indigo's special forces, two of Arie's commando 104 troops, and the very good friend of Shami, Bazif Akili, a renowned linguist, who could speak, read and write, every dialect in the Arab world, including many of the 'forgotten' languages. They were out in a traditional dress, following the scent of Thana Praxidike, the name Badawi was using as he moved from place to place.

He didn't know we had gotten his alias from our monk in Ireland, and I was hoping against hope he didn't know we had taken his ship. But that wasn't important now because he and a small band of terrorists he had picked up on his way through Iraq were now headed for Syria in a big expensive four-wheel drive, and three well-fortified trucks, which my team confirmed were well-armed and armored. They were on their way back, waiting for our next move.

Something Sandra and I were currently debating.

"I don't think he is going to Syria to improve his tan. He knows we bombed his shells and anything that was in that crashed aircraft. He knows we destroyed his nuclear material and money back in Aleppo, but does he know what Abbas has done?" I shook my head.

"No. We have the frequency of his satellite phone, we know his schedule, and we know that Abbas is on the run from France not having received or made a call for at least a day. My guess is that Badawi doesn't know Abbas has the shells or the material."

"But according to the prisoner Indigo and Fay interrogated, Abbas has the AEC inspector, and I wonder what his purpose might be?"

"When Abbas was hunting the Level Five containment facilities, and possibly the material, my guess would be the inspector was to get him into a facility legitimately, initially, at least. Now, without knowing what this inspector's specific skills are, I have no idea what his worth is."

"Do you believe he could assemble the bomb?"

"I checked with Amira on that, and she says no, the handling of the slugs and the shells is a delicate matter; the front slug has to be fitted first, then the section up to the membrane sealed using the nanites; then the ball has to be fitted, and sealed. The scientist with Badawi had the skills. No doubt she designed the shells. But she has disappeared and is no longer travelling with Badawi. So to me, it looks like they still need a scientist or two brave enough to tackle nuclear loading materiel into the shells and comfortable working with nanites. Screw either process up, and bang!"

"And the ship, which we have under surveillance, has the rail gun launcher."

"Yes. But don't discount using a Man Pad. We know that is possible, shortens their reach in terms of target, but can still be very effective."

"What's our next move?"

"We wait for the team to get back, then move into Syria some-where. You might like to look at that before they get back." Sandra gave me one of her long looks, shrugged her shoulders, then opened her mini. Being shot had pissed her off, but being kept out of the field was pissing her off even more!

# Flash In The Pan

"**A**dmiral to the bridge!"

Usually, it was the captain who was called this way, but since the captain had been transferred to another ship, the admiral was the effective captain, and the tannoy caller, being only just twenty and still wet behind the ears, didn't know what else to call him. Thankfully, the admiral appeared, dressed in slacks and a sea jumper, his hair a little mussed from the short nap he had tried to get in the previous captain's day room.

"Sir, contact bearing zero three four degrees, height thirty-five thousand feet, tracking zero eighty-eight, speed five hundred and twenty knots. Radar paint is not available. We are tracking a transponder broadcast on the international distress frequency." The radar operator, his headphones bulging large over his smallish head, his eyes reflecting the eerie green of the fluorescent wash from the radar scope, pointed to a red flashing symbol that had been tagged 'UT 001' on the digital map. It showed the POI to be over one hundred nautical miles inland from the Italian coast, heading for Turkey if it held its present course.

The admiral thought for a moment, then dialed Jessica.

"Commander, we think we have a contact with your aircraft out of France."

"Where is it?"

"One hundred nautical miles inland Italy, heading for the Turkish border, but if you draw a course line in somewhere, then the Middle East is its destination."

"Have you got a radar paint?"

"No. Transponder only."

"Will you shoot it down, please?"

"No."

"What if I told you one of the world's most wanted terrorist is on board, with shells and enough nuclear material to make four atomic bombs?"

"Still no. Can you prove that?"

"Yes, I can, but you would not accept all the evidence at this point. Please, can you continue tracking it until the destination, and can you be ready to attack on my command if necessary?"

"Yes to the tracking, no to the attack. This is the US Navy; we have very defined rules of engagement. Prove it, and we will act."

"Thank you, Admiral. Keep in touch. Appreciate the heads up."

I closed the mini and looked at Sandra, who had popped up off the bed at the call like a battery bunny. She looked at me with a snarly face that did not suit her runway model aspirations.

"Pussy."

"Yes, but our pussy. And acting within his limitations. Let's get the proof."

# Chapter Thirty

Amira was deep in conversation with Luigi, Shami, Malcolm, Indigo, and a brace of geeks from the Israeli Intelligence Service and the NSA. The subject was how to disguise an ordinary civilian aircraft from radar. And it had become a very heated argument. The baseline was the 'black holes' the women terrorists had developed and deployed for the first month of the attacks, which had subsequently been defeated by Amira and the geek team being able to create an algorithm that could 'see' through the computer code that had created the black holes.

Now they had something different. Electronic transmissions could escape the invisibility cloak. They had proof of this because the US navy was tracking an aircraft that they couldn't see on the radar but could detect by its transmissions via its transponder, a device fitted to aircraft to enable them to have a discrete signal to make their identification easier by air traffic control.

The French Security Services had found the charter company, confirmed the aircraft type, found the company that had supplied the bonded courier, and knew the name of the pilot. The aircraft had to be near the end of its range, as it had only refueled once since it had left France, and it had flown all the way to the western edges of Pakistan, then back to France, and was now headed for places unknown.

It was flying down the tip of Turkey, still invisible to radar, apparently heading for the Middle Eastern coast somewhere.

"Amira, how can they be nullifying radar waves?' Luigi asked, almost at a loss as to what to do, which for a serious geek, was a humiliating state of affairs.

"Modern fighter aircraft use radar deadening materials and triangular shaped fuselages to bounce the waves off, but this is a civilian three-engine jet, modified for biofuel, so it has to be something the terrorists have on board."

"It would have to be plugged into the jet's electrical and electronic systems?"

"Electrical, yes, not sure about the electronics."

What principal would it be using?" This question came from the American NSA analyst, a super geek himself, who, when he wasn't surfing, was playing with his computers. Amira shook her head, her long hair flying uncontrolled around her pretty face. Sitting next to her, Luigi rubbed her shoulder, mindful that they had loaded up this young woman with issue after issue since the first time they had detected her hacking into Israel's most secure military system. Amira responded to the friendly touch with a smile.

"My guess, and this is a guess, is that they have built an artificial intelligence, possibly using quantum decryption, and the AI is capturing the radar waves, analyzing them, then broadcasting an interference signal using its quantum application to mask the physical aircraft. At least, that's how I would do it."

"Good enough for me. How do we defeat it?" Amira thought for a moment, reached for a marker, and started scribbling on a whiteboard with a vengeance.

"Amira, share your screen with me. We have done some work on that." Malcolm looked to his screen, saw Amira's scribble, and immediately added lines of code to hers, then created a moving diagram that combined both lines of thinking. "I see what you are doing," chipped in one of the Israeli geeks, who posted his electronic board onto the screen, and now three lines of code appeared, each eating up each other whenever they intersected. After a furious few minutes, the coding stopped, the diagram rearranged itself several times, obviously testing different solutions, then steadied and sent a blinking cursor to the far corner of the screen.

"Got it. In theory, in any case."

"No, this will work. Shami, can you get your lab to fabricate this?"

"I can and I will. What do we do with it when we get it?"

"Get it into an aircraft with a strong antiair radar, and look for the plane using its transponder signal as a base."

"Can you get the Americans to keep monitoring that transponder?"

"Yes." And listening in from the sidelines, I answered the question for Amira because I was sure the admiral would do that to the best of the ability of his fleet.

But I needed to speak to Arie, so I dropped out of the conversation and dialed his direct line.

"Jessica, it seems you have my entire geek squad working for you now," he said, smiling to remove any inference of offense in what he said.

"Arie, they are the best, and they may have given us a way to find the missing aircraft. Are you up to date with that?" He nodded, still looking like I hoped my grandfather would have if I had one.

"Question. Are you hampered by the same rules of engagement as the Americans?" His face tightened considerably, giving nothing away. You would expect that from a seasoned spymaster.

"We obey the intent and the letter of international Law, right up until it might compromise our borders and lay us open to attack."

"Would you shoot this aircraft down if we find it, based on the case we are building against the terrorists? But short of taking the aircraft physically out of play, we can't yet prove beyond a doubt."

"Jessica, if you tell me that aircraft has shells and nuclear material on board and is headed in our direction, that would be enough for me to invoke 'Pikuach nefesh', which is a Jew's obligation to attack to defend another life. I would prefer to do this privately and in international airspace. But the short answer is yes because you have our complete and utter trust in this." I nodded, mindful that I now carried the entire fate of Israel on my shoulders, and I mentally sagged with the virtual weight. Well, I wouldn't let it bother me unduly. I looked at Sandra, who was chatting on her mini with our boys in the field, thanked Arie, and hung up.

She looked at me, snapped her lid shut, and raised her eyebrows as if to ask me what's what.

"You heard my conversation with Arie?" She nodded. "Comments?"

"Our team is moving further inland, heading towards the western border of Jordan. They are six hours behind Badawi and his men, they have one big SUV and seven trucks now, all full of armed people, and our clever interpreter, Bazif, managed a conversation with a trader they stopped for, and he gave her a lot of detail on their caravan. Badawi is dressed for the desert, is wounded, but not life-threatening, there are no women in the trucks, and they are well supplied."

"We should move. Where do you suggest?" She pulled out an old army ordinance map, Circa 1990 and spread it on the bed.

"On the basis that they are running for the Gaza strip, I think Be 'Er Sheva would be a great place to sit and wait to see what eventuates."

'We won't get the aircraft in the air."

"No. The geeks will build something, but even if it only took a couple of hours, by then, they will have landed somewhere. I think our best bet is the long-range search radar on the destroyers, and our drones, which Fay said will be with the C-17 in eight hours."

"That might be too late. We've been chasing our tails from the get-go on this. The Irish blind was a good move, although the way it has panned out, I do not see any other way to have done what we have done so far, based on what we actually know."

"If it's any help, I agree. Half the time, I can't see what you're thinking tactically, but then you do something, and it makes total sense. I have to learn how to do that."

"Yes, you do, but give yourself some time. I worked with the boss for six years, and I got to understand his thinking patterns and the way he could leap between one set of facts and another, build a case out of thin air, then have everyone else prove it for him."

"You were a good apprentice." I smiled, I had never seen myself in that role, to be honest, but it was amazing what you could pick up watching someone work at the very top of their game.

"You'll be a better one, and you have Fay to help you."

"I do?"

"Yes. She's FBI-trained. They think a totally different way to us, build a case differently and pursue the facts and the evidence. She will learn from you how to be a prime shooter, move quickly, move decisively, rely on small teams, and work across borders; you'll learn how to slow down, think it through, and dig deeper than you are used to. And I think you'll enjoy it." She looked at me out of the corner of one eye, not necessarily suspiciously, but perhaps a little wearily.

"Do you know how Indigo and Fay got all that information out of the prisoner the French police took at the airfield?" I smiled. I had enjoyed Indigo's telling of it and Fay's almost competition for the opposite report, where she had left out a lot of the dramatic bits.

"The way I heard it, the French director agreed to clean up any mess, Indigo asked politely, and Fay held a gun to his head."

"And you're not worried about that?"

"No. The stakes are too high. We have an upside-down world, fractured and in chaos because of the terrorist attacks, the loss of most of the oil, gas, and coal we all took for granted, the massive uncontrolled migration across borders, and the almost complete economic collapse of nearly every country you can name. To have a nuclear disaster on top of that would be the final straw, and one we might not be able to recover from for decades."

"Well, when you put it that way." I gave her a hard look, then realized she was stringing me along, so I just laughed and fluffed my unruly hair. She flicked her head with a shoulder roll, sending her long blonde hair flying, and also laughed. "Okay, pack us up, organize us a move, let's see what the next few hours brings us."

# Chapter Thirty-One

Tom, a twenty-year veteran of the Teams, faced off with his counterpart, Bob, who had worked with the presidential guard for two decades, so between them, they had a boot full of experience. Initially, Tom had been charged with finding the gold and Bob with finding the laboratories, which with Abbas fleeing France, was now moot. Jessica had put both teams together to find the gold bullion and locate where it was being delivered to. But like all great commanders, instead of flying off around the country, they plotted and planned before they allocated tasks. They had two helicopters between them and four trucks, so transport wouldn't be an issue.

And they had a starting point. Nuremberg. So they broke out their minis, and located the state-controlled bullion stores, plotted them on a map, then found the Minister for State Taxes and EU compliance, and planned a call on the Minister of Finance in his offices in the Detlev Rohwedder Building in Berlin. Tom and Bob tossed a coin to see who would pose as the Interpol inspector, a role that usually would be fulfilled by the senior Interpol Section Five staff, who were currently off chasing terrorists in the desert. After all, they were hired muscle, shooters, not usually strategic, but they had the bit between their teeth and played it out.

"Heads!"

"It's tails, bad luck, and no two out of three." Bob laughed. Maybe he would see how this Interpol thing really worked. He looked around the gathered troops, mentally checked the qualifications of each, then picked out three.

"Ryan, Joy, Antonio, find suits and ties. You need to look like executives. We will take one of the choppers, in the meantime, call every bullion store, get the name of their comptroller, inform them an Interpol Red Notice has been issued related to terrorist activities, and that we will expect their fullest cooperation. Tom, I'll leave you to organize that. In the meantime, I need to call the Commander." Tom nodded his agreement and moved his team and their maps off to a corner of the room.

"Commander, my apologies for interrupting your busy day. We need a series of Red Notices issued and Interpol credentials for a team we have put together." I listened to Bob, then passed the mini to Sandra, who was in the middle of the truck, bouncing up and down and looking like she was on a joy ride.

"Sandra, organize this for Bob." I handed over the mini, heard Bob reiterate everything he had told me, watched my plucky padawan work through it all and noticed that the sparkle was back in her eyes.

Good. No one enjoyed being shot, and it was the second time, and I think she felt personally aggrieved by the whole incident. She'd get used to it.

I watched as she hung up on Bob, then called Lyon, spoke rapidly in French, then Italian, nodding at various points, then disconnecting and recalling Bob.

"All organized, Bob. Good luck!" And before he could respond, she hung up. "What do you think their plan is?" She gave me a hard look, squinting her eyes, trying to see behind my question. She slowly turned her head to one side, obviously thinking hard. "When I realized I had to use everyone more and lead from the front a little less, moments like these were inevitable. In days gone by, you and I would be paying a visit to the Minister of Finance and scaring him shitless. Now we have to let others do it for us." She nodded, then turned to look outside at the desert as it swept by.

"But Bob is a great choice. He has long executive experience working with the presidential guard. He's not just a soldier but possibly a little bit of a diplomat. Tom is Tom, I love him to death, but I've never seen much subtly in him." She nodded.

"I see what you are doing now, and maybe at some point in the future, you can outline your plan for me." I laughed. Good question, one I would willingly answer the very second I had worked it out!

The Italian helicopter landed in the car park of the Detlev Rohwedder Building, located in the Wilhelmstraße in Berlin's historical government quarter, to an overt ceremony of sirens and armed police. There were literally thousands of protesters being held back by the Army and the police, all unhappy with the rampant inflation and economic chaos precipitated by the terrorist attacks.

The team dismounted and, after their credentials were examined, were escorted into the long, dark, but beautifully decorated corridors of the building. It had been designed with style, panache, and a little bit of cheek, as it was the largest office building in Germany when completed in 1936 and taken over by the Nazi party soon after. It had sixteen kilometers of corridors, and as expected, the office of the Minister was almost at the very end. The walls were lined with frescos and art worth millions, and the building had the air of a well-preserved museum.

The team noticed that their rubber-soled boots made no noise on the polished marble floor, but the click-clacking of the police escorting them made for an interesting rhythm. They reached an antechamber and were met by a tall, statuesque blond with amazing deep blue eyes, wearing the tightest-fitting red dress Bob had ever seen. Every curve was highlighted, and the shimmering low cut 'V' was adorned with a double string of pearls, so perfect they were almost translucent.

"You are the Interpol, yes?" Her voice was husky, reminding Tom that they were on enemy territory, and he felt his team bracing for something he couldn't quite define. Then he realized that in the last three months, none of them had seen a beautifully dressed woman, a clean corridor that ran as far as the eye could see, and a wonderfully restored old building that shouted style, grace, and calm.

"Yes, I'm Inspector Robertson, and these are my staff." She gave him a shrewd look as if to challenge him on something, but with a flick of her head, she motioned them through a door. On either side, busy people sat working computers, all taking in hushed tones, no doubt doing what needed to be done to prevent Germany from sliding into a deep, dark depression. He wondered where all the working computers had come from, then noticed the black channels on the floor covering cables running between desks. They entered a large pair of double doors made from a rich old timber that looked black with age, then found themselves facing a fat, balding man in an impeccable suit sitting behind an expansive desk.

*"Herr Direktor, die Leute von Interpol."*

"Thank you, Freida, that will be all."

He rose, tucking his bright blue tie in between the lapels of his jacket, allowing his crisp pink shirt to create a point of focus. As well as fat and bald, he was short, no more than five feet two, and Bob wondered who they were really speaking to.

"Sir, thank you for seeing us. We come at the request of the Inspector-General of Interpol and with the authority of the World Court." The little man still stood behind his desk, nodded at Bob's introduction, smoothed his tie again, then sat down, waving them to visitor's chairs that had been carefully arranged in a semicircle. As soon as Bob sat, he realized the little man was sitting on a platform, as they were eyeball to eyeball. Inwardly, he smiled at this, having experienced the wiles and ways of short bureaucrats back in Washington.

"We are trying to track a large shipment of gold bullion that is being used to promote terrorism, and under the Terrorist Laws as modified in 2022, your ministry may well be embroiled in the case as an accessory to the acts of terror as specified in the Red Notice that has been issued." The director pumped himself up as if being filled with compressed air, his face turned red, and for a moment, Bob thought he might explode. Then in a flash, the little man decompressed, returning to his original size, as he took a very deep breath staring at Bob as if he were demented. He hit a button under his desk, the two massive old doors flung open, and two guards dressed in German police uniforms strode in, looking very uncertain as to their role.

"Sir, you need to hear us out and stand down your guard if you are to survive this encounter." The little man stared at Bob as if he had spoken in Chinese, started to bubble over in protest, then caught his breath again, pulled a pure white handkerchief out of a pocket, and wiped his brow very hard several times.

"What do you mean, 'survive this encounter?'" he wheezed. His face was starting to go red again, and Bob was afraid he would have a stroke if he didn't calm down.

"Sir, we are empowered to take you into custody if we do not get the answers we seek and the help the World Court has requested of you. It is that simple." The guards rocked back and forth on their feet, still unsure of the situation. Ryan, Joy, and Antonio, dressed impeccably in dark suits, starched shirts, and ties, with their briefcases on their laps, had all swiveled their chairs around, so they had the German guards in view but had not yet reached for their weapons. If fact, they looked so loose and uninspiring. The guards had taken them for flunkies, who in their experience swarmed around people of power like moths around a flame.

Little did they know that each briefcase which had sailed through the electronic screening on entry without fuss, contained enough firepower to hold off a small army and that the three supposedly unimportant people sitting next to the inspector from Interpol were some of the most highly trained and combat experienced troops in the world. Bob held his breath, hoping the director would calm down and provide them with the answers they needed. As he was thinking through his next move, the luscious female who had escorted them in ran in on her three-inch-high heels, waving her arms.

"*Herr Direktor, diese Leute sind von Interpol, mit Erlaubnis des Ministerpräsidenten!*" The little man took this shouted statement at face value, stood up again, and bowed.

"Please excuse me. I misunderstood who you were. Accept my apologies, these are difficult times, and I was confused. If the Chief Minister has cleared you, I will answer any questions you have." The tension went out of the room. The assistant shooed the guards out, gave the director a last, filthy look, then pulled the heavy doors shut behind her. Tom wondered what the dynamic was between them, then decided it didn't matter.

"Sir, who is moving an estimated fifteen billion euros of gold bullion from German storage at this time?" The director looked nonplussed as if he hadn't heard the question.

"Fifteen billion euros? Of bullion? Impossible!" He pressed another button on his desk, and the assistant pranced back in, this time more composed but still obviously angry.

"Sir, you called?"

Her English was Oxford-perfect, whereas the little man's was heavily accented, creating a contrast that was not lost on the team. He waved his stubby arms at her and almost spluttered.

*"Diese Leute beschuldigen mich, fünfzehn Milliarden Euro Goldbarren transportiert zu haben! Sagen Sie ihnen, dass das unmöglich ist!"* She looked at him, then at Bob, shrugged her shoulders slightly, then addressed herself directly to him.

"Inspector, my apologies. It seems my director has become confused as to what you are saying. Would you mind repeating what you said, please?" Bob smiled, held his mini out to her, showed her the Red Notice, the permission slip from the Ministry, then held up his credentials.

"Madam, I asked the director who is moving an estimated fifteen billion euros of gold bullion from German storage at this time." Her face froze over, but she caught herself very quickly, something Bob appreciated.

"Inspector, under the current conditions in the country, as in many others, trying to move that amount of bullion would amount to suicide. The mobs would tear to pieces anyone involved before they could get the bullion on a train." Bob nodded. He had the same thought on the helicopter when he looked down at the massive civil unrest surrounding Berlin.

"I agree, it would be difficult, but our information is someone in Germany is trying to move that amount of bullion. We have inspectors on their way to every bullion store as we speak. I was hoping that you, as the ministry responsible for taxes and EU monetary compliance, might help us discover who is moving the gold." She gave Bob a very hard look and thought about his request, which she knew that thanks to the Red Notice, was not really a request, but a demand backed by the full weight of the World Court and the UN. She doubted the imbecile behind the desk would be any help, so she chose her battleground and issued her challenge.

"Come with me, please, gentlemen. Thank you, Director, that will be all," and she turned on her amazing heels and marched out, leaving the director spluttering behind his desk.

Ryan, Joy, and Antonio took up positions, so Bob was covered from the rear and sides, and the maneuver was not lost on the assistant as she led them into her office, which was sparsely furnished compared to the luxury fit out of the director's.

"Now, there is too much military in your bearing for you to be just an inspector with Interpol. Who are you really, and what do you want?" She sat gracefully in a chair in front of her desk and crossed her legs delicately, revealing a good tan and thin ankles. Around one rode a small silver bracelet. She folded her hands together and looped them over her knees.

"I'm major Thomas Reynold, the head of the presidential guard, White House, Washington, on secondment to Interpol since the original terrorist attacks three months ago, and I hold the acting rank of full inspector within Interpol, Section Five. My team is also Section Five, handpicked for this mission. Does that clear it up for you?" If she was shocked about any of the details, it didn't show on her face, and Bob gave her credit for that.

"Section Five, I've not heard anything about this section. What is it?" Bob gave her a long, long look, thinking through what he could say and what he should say.

"Section Fire was created by Interpol with the backing of the World Court and the UN to prosecute on behalf of both terrorists of all callings and anyone else who threatens a nation-state who is a member. We took the lead in hunting down the terrorists that attacked us all just three months ago, then came into play just a month ago when a second level attack was mounted and is now the lead agency with this third attack."

"How successful have you been?" Bob decided to get to the heart of the matter, this conversation was taking too much time, and he resented the role he was being forced to play.

"One week ago, we became aware of terrorists manufacturing shells that could be converted into nuclear bombs. They made thirty odd, lost one during testing, and since then, we have recovered all but four of the other shells. I need the details on the movement of the bullion, and madam, forgive me, but I need it now. We believe the bullion will pay for attacks on unspecified targets, and if they are successful, you and your director, and any who work with you, will spend the rest of your days rotting in the deepest hole I can throw you into. Do you understand me?" Her face had turned a puce color during Bob's dissertation, and she visibly shook. She rolled her fingers over each other as if washing them, then obviously reached a decision.

"Give me five minutes, please. Let me use my computer." She stood unsteadily and moved behind her glass-topped desk. She tapped keys with a purpose, muttered under her breath, but her eyes were alive, and the color had come back into her cheeks. Bob decided to make it a little easier for her.

"How did that clown get to be a director?" She stopped what she was doing and actually smiled at him.

"The director was killed last week on his way to work, his assistant was also killed in a car accident, and the current director was promoted only because his father is in the ministry and quite highly placed." Bob nodded, having suspected something like that had happened. It was a recurring nightmare, with good people all over the world being killed by roaming crowds of vigilantes or just angry people out for vengeance. The civil unrest was on an unprecedented scale, and those that tried to maintain a normal working relationship with their environments were having great difficulty getting to and from their offices. Government service was the hardest hit, as they were the most obvious.

And with the internet down and most computers out of use, working from home, as had become the norm during the pandemic crisis three years ago, was not an option. She looked up from her computer, almost smiled, then remembered the subject under discussion and kept her face neutral.

"There are three companies registered who have over five billion in gold bullion that is currently scheduled for movement, and all capital gains tax has been paid by one individual."

"Who is the individual?"

"Herr Gerhart von Speer."

"His address?"

"One sixty-one Bundren Strasse, Buchenbuhl, which is near Nuremberg Airport."

"How much bullion does Herr von Speer have registered?" She ran one delicate finger down her screen, then looked up again.

"He has nine storage sites listed, they are well spread over Germany, and he has paid taxes on all deposits for many years."

"Can you tell us when the movement from those depositories is planned?" The finger did its work again. This time she looked curious.

"The three of them are currently reporting the withdrawals, have booked security and government oversight, and trains are being prepared as we speak."

"Can you please print out the address and senior contact at each location, and issue them with a 'HOLD' notice, give them a real reason. I suggest that you use a security issue and make the hold only three days. That will give us time to get to each depository. I will mention your excellent assistance to our director general, and I sincerely wish you luck with your director." A printer on the edge of her desk hummed, and three sheets of lilaccolored paper rolled out gracefully, a sight that startled the four Interpol agents.

"Thank you, miss-I'm sorry, I didn't get your name?"

"Fräulein Seidensticker."

"Thank you, your help is gratefully appreciated." Bob stood, bobbed his head at the assistant, then led his team out of the room and back into the long corridor.

No one spoke, and Bob noticed his three companions swiveling their heads like radar towers searching for aircraft and smiled to himself. It was good to have a team you could trust, and the Italians had mixed in so seamlessly with his own troops to the point he had forgotten that Antonio was one of Indigo's men. They reached the doors and were collected by both an army and police escort, and just as they reached their helicopter, firebombs rained out of the crowd, being held back behind massive red and black barricades, spreading dense smoke and flame across the car park.

"Get in, strap in. We don't react to this. Go!"

Small arms fire followed, and within a minute, there was a full-scale attack on the barricades. The helicopter rose rapidly into the air, and they heard rather than felt rounds pinging off the fuselage.

"Bloody hell, that's the last time I'll voluntarily go to a Tax Office!" The team shared the joke, the pilot hunched his backside as a round ripped through his cockpit door, and the helicopter gradually gained both speed and altitude.

"The one good thing about this is it wasn't personal."

"So you say," replied Joy, reaching into her field pack for a pressure bandage. Blood suddenly ran down her arm, smearing and pooling around her boots on the floor. Ryan had reached over and clamped one meaty hand on the wound, which he removed as the pressure bandage was applied.

"I want danger money, boss. This shit has completely ruined my suit!" The laughter overcame nerves, and the flight settled down into a normal one between destinations. Then Bob remembered he hadn't told the pilot where to go. And now he had a wounded soldier to consider. Then he thought of Jessica and Sandra and how they had both been shot boarding a terrorist boat, then still managed to kill a bunch of terrorists who had fired a rocket into their boat, killing four of Tom's team. "Clean yourself up as best as you can. Use our water to clean your sleeve. Nothing changes, okay?" Three heads nodded vigorously, understanding that their task came first and personal comfort a distant last. This was what they had all signed on for, and they would see it through to the finish.

Bob opened his mini and dialed Jessica.

"Commander, you look like you're having fun?" The background behind us jumped all over the place as our truck hit every pothole for kilometers around, and it was all I could do to hold the small computer still on my lap.

"Bob, what news do you have?" He broke into a huge smile as if enjoying a joke. "We have a name and three depositories which are setting up to move bullion. We have requested a hold on the movement, invoked a Red Notice, and have three days to get around and sort things out. We have one wounded, high-arm wound treated on site, but it will require professional attention at some point; my plan is to visit the name, visit each depository, and shut them down. We're sending an advance team to each location as we speak. Tom is organizing that."

"Remember, we want the destination the bullion was to be shipped to and confirm the means."

"Yes, ma'am, top of the list." Problem. The 'name' might be an issue, and I didn't want Bob to get engaged in any heavy stuff with the locals.

"Hold off on the name for a moment. Bob, where were you based?"

"We were in a hotel room in Frankfurt. Tom and his team and the remainder of mine are there waiting for our instructions."

"Okay, I'll talk to Tom. Get yourself back there, but get two-man surveillance teams to each location, well disguised and hidden if necessary, as fast as you can. I want data on the location and force projection for the 'name,' and issue each team a mini. Tom will need his original four troops; come to think about that, get Tom plus one on the 'name'; you can take the rest. I need to think about this. Give me five." I turned to look at Sandra, who was enjoying the bouncing and swaying of the truck as if she was riding a carnival ride at an amusement park.

"Closest Israeli airport to us?" She buried her head in her mini. "Where we are going-Be 'Er Sheva."

"Thanks," I called Arie.

"Welcome from the Negev desert. I need your help again." His bushy eye-brows simply rose in a question mark, and a wan smile crossed his face fleetingly "You can be up to no good there. What are you doing?"

"Driving. Arie, I need a very fast transport for two, Be 'Er Sheva to Nuremburg, collecting one, possibly two or more hostile passengers, returning to Be 'Er Sheva, prisoners to your location or Venice, and it would be nice if one or two of your commandoes 104 were along for the ride, and I'd really like Josephine of the big thighs if she isn't busy." He gave me a long look, nodded slowly to himself, then waved politely and cancelled the call. I dialed again.

"Fay, where ever you are, in the next hour, I want you to be in Be 'Er Sheva, the airport, and bring Indigo with you." My turn to be rude, as I snapped the lid shut before she could respond. I looked Sandra straight in the eyes and let her feel the intensity I was working up.

"Who would you trust my life to?" She looked at me with a puzzled look and shook her head from the side in a very positive manner.

"No way, the boss personally put me on you, and that's that." I just smiled. "The boss has moved on, and I need you to head up the team that takes the 'name' into custody, and I suspect there will be a serious fight along the way somewhere. I'm sending elements of the commando 104 as a backup for you, and you'll have Tom plus one, but only an officer of Section Five can carry out a sanctioned retirement. I'm also sending Fay along with you to see first-hand how we manage the tough shitheads."

"And you need to stay here in case Abbas breaks ground."

"Yes. Don't want to, but sometimes you have to split the team to create the most effective battle plan. Seeing as how you have already been bloodied in the retirement stakes, you will know what to do when and if the time comes. Are you up for it?" I looked at her critically just as the back axle of the truck rose three feet in the air, throwing us all around into an untidy heap. Sand flew everywhere, and somewhere underneath me, I could hear someone swearing in Italian. We sorted ourselves out and brushed off the sand as best as we could, but I could feel the grit of it in my hair, and I was really looking forward to my next shower.

"Okay, contact Lyon, present our case against the 'name', aiding and abetting acts of terror, financing WMDs, make it as complete a list as you can, get a trial in absentia with the World Court, a judgement under the Terrorist Laws, we already have a Red Notice out, all you need is the 'name'."

"Who is it?"

"A German industrialist called Herr von Speer, eighty-nine years of age, goes all the way back to Bavaria and the second world war. He lives at one-sixty-one Bundren Strasse, Buchenbuhl, which is near Nuremberg Airport, so that's handy for you."

"Bob is covering the depositories?"

"Yes, and he is securing each site as we speak but will be invisible unless you really need him. Remember, Bob is American, military, and they don't have the same latitude we do in wrangling these terrorist bastards."

"Got it. To answer your first question, if I didn't have your back, Tom, Indigo, or Fay would be my preference, in that order. Tom has a hard edge to him, has worked with you and the boss before, and understands the rules of engagement. Indigo goes without saying, and I suspect Fay is a lot harder than either of us expect, from what I heard about the interrogation of the prisoner in France."

"I want Fay with you, on your shoulder. It should be a great learning experience for her. Tom is busy sorting out the bullion issue, which leaves Indigo. I'll leave it to you to brief him." And I switched my mind to our other problem. Where in the hell was Abbas? I called the admiral.

"Commander, I won't lie and tell you how good you look. I just hope the other guy looks worse."

"Try speeding through the Negev desert at breakneck speed and see what you'll look like. Where is Abbas?"

"No idea. We lost his transponder twenty minutes ago, and we have the last heading. It still looks like Gaza or Palestine, I've got a destroyer fifty nautical miles away, but he is still invisible to our radar."

"Buggar. Can you estimate a time of arrival from his track speed?"

"Fourteen twenty your time, but that is a big guess. He could be going anywhere, may even have landed already in Turkey." I thought about that and shook my head, Abbas's other two shells had been found in Gaza. He was going home.

"Thanks, admiral, keep looking." And I hung up, an abrupt habit I was perfecting by frequency of use! I was just settling into some serious introspection when my mini yelled at me.

"Jessica, you have a fast jet inbound. Colonel Aria and four of her best are onboard. Please return them to me in the condition you receive them." I smiled at that request. I was an acknowledged bullet magnet, I had a ten-million-euro bounty on my head, although that could have increased recently, and everyone that worked with me got shot one time or another. Pete back at the headquarters of Natasha

Trotsky, the ex-Stasi officer Mohammad bin Azaria had recruited thirty-five years ago to set up his terror organization; Sandra, the second time during the attack on the terrorist boat that held capable nuclear shells, where we had also lost four of Tom's team of SEALS; and now 'Joy', one of Bob's team in an ambush on their helicopter. And that didn't count the pilots and co-pilots I had run through in the past month!

"Arie, I'll do my best, but my record speaks for itself."

"That's what I'm afraid of!" And he disconnected, beating me to it by a hair's breadth.

"Okay, we've got some reinforcements. You'll have five from commando 104 with you, colonel Aria has fought with us before, and she has taken over from the Sgen Aluf, who was killed on one of our missions." As I said that, the image of the beautiful man with the angry face who had fought side with Pete, the boss, and I came to mind, and I mentally wished him well in the afterlife, if there was one for people like us.

"Here's what I want you to do. Get the 'name', get the destination for the bullion, secure the 'name', and anyone else you need to, by any means you need to keep our people as safe as possible; get Bob's teams to shut down the repositories, firmly but surely, leave people at each site, if necessary, we'll get the German police to backfill once we know the lay of the land. Then get back here. Clear?" When you said it quickly, it sounded easy. But it was a sure bet the German industrialist had armed guards on his property, something I was waiting on Tom's team to confirm. That could take up to an hour, so I settled back to let the truck destroy what was left of my kidneys with what I hoped was a stoic look on my face!

# Chapter Thirty-Two

Amir Abbas had landed at Çukurova Regional Airport (Çukurova Bölgesel Havaliman), which served the cities of Adana, Mersin, and Osmaniye in Turkey, and had only been finished the year before. He had a large armoured truck waiting and twenty heavily armed followers from the local branch of the ISIL. The two boxes containing the shells were unloaded, as were the sealed tubes holding the nuclear material. When it came time to unload the millions of dollars of euros, he allowed each terrorist to pocket fifty thousand each and had arranged for small canvas rucksacks to hold the currency.

Then he played his trump card. He motioned to his temporary second in command, speaking in English because he knew no one else understood it and laid out his requirements.

"I will pay you two hundred and fifty thousand euros and your men an additional one hundred thousand each for providing me with a chemistry laboratory, secured, and a chemist able to handle sensitive materials. I also will need four Russian MM-57 Man Pads, six rounds for each, delivered to the laboratory. I need all this done today, ready for work first thing in the morning."

"*Ra'is*, it will be done. We already have the facility. However, we cannot get the MM-57s, but we can get the model 68."

"Specifications?"

"Eighty-eight millimeters, two meters twenty in length, weight thirty kilos, range ten kilometers. They will cost us three hundred and fifty thousand lira, cash, or ninety thousand euros."

"Can the rounds be disassembled?"

"Yes, *Ra'īs*, they can be broken down into three sections."

"Can you get me an armourer familiar with that weapon?" The young man who had yet to shave, his hair long and matted, his dishdasha mottled and filthy, the boots on his feet well-worn and scruffy, nodded, excitement bubbling just beneath the surface of his weather-beaten face. This could be the most important operation of his life, one that would propel his people onto the front pages of every paper that could still get an issue out, and if nothing else, he would know he had died doing his best to free his people.

"We captured a Russian last month and kept him alive. He was taken with the Man Pads and a lot of other Russian hardware that was being smuggled into the country for another group-one we are not aligned with. We can convince him to help you."

"Excellent. Have my aircraft fuelled, and I will need a replacement pilot two days from now." He looked hard at the young man, saw the eagerness and a little fear in his black eyes, nodded to himself, and moved off to the jeep that was waiting for him.

He could make the shells work in the Man Pad rounds. He would then fly to a location from which he could attack his target. But first, he had to retrieve his other two shells, and he put his mind to this problem for the next hour, sitting on a rock, watching the seagulls fight for supper in the late afternoon sun.

He idly wondered how Malik was fearing and suddenly realized he didn't really care. He would check in with him when he felt like it. He picked up a small rock and spun it into the water, a broad smile breaking over his face when it skipped six times before finally splashing into the ocean. He visualized his shells skipping over the ocean of air on their way to their destinations and smiled so hard he broke out laughing.

He knew he personally couldn't fire the shells. Even eleven kilometres away, the blast or the fallout would kill him, but he had a cadre of young, eager jihadists ready and willing to sacrifice themselves to do his bidding.

Not that he would tell them anything other than the target. And he would kill everyone used in the loading of the shells to preserve his security. He was happy he had loyal followers who would die for him, but they didn't have to know all the details!

He got back into the jeep, drove to the address his recruit had given him, and immediately approved his choice. A large building, brick, two stories, secure fencing around it, and nothing else close enough to be a bother. The big double doors were open, so he drove in and parked behind the armoured truck. Four guards were posted around the truck, so he stopped and asked where his boxes and tubes were and was pointed to a set of stairs that led down. The heavy metal roller door slammed shut behind him, creating a sense of security, if not isolation. The only noise he could hear came from some sort of ventilation system.

He found his man standing outside a heavily glassed enclosure, behind which he could see huge yellow suits hanging in an airlock.

"What was this place?"

"A chemical company used to make medicines and pills here, but the war last year sent them broke. Everything still works, and Amar here is the caretaker who is renting the property to us. He will show us how everything works. He only speaks Farsi." Abbas thought for a minute, then decided to keep his language skills to himself.

"Ask him how he is. Does he need anything?" The recruit fired off a string Farsi, the caretaker looking like a shrunken caricature of a man, stoop shoulders, blue overalls stained and patched in several places, what little hair he had was stringy and sat on his mostly bald head in splotches, bowed several times, gabbled his answer, then looked at Abbas out of the corner of one bloodshot eye.

"He says he is happy the factory will be used again, prays for our success, and asks if he could be spared a hot meal or two during our stay." Abbas smiled, bowed to the little man, and walked over to his two boxes and their guards.

"He can eat with us at every meal. Where are we sleeping?" The recruit pointed up, so Abbas followed him up the stairs, across the floor past the jeep and the truck, then up another flight of stairs, which led to a massive office area with glassed-in cubicles.

"There is an industrial kitchen in the far corner, and I suggest we use the offices for our camp, *Ra'is*, as they will enable us to see everything that is going on." Abbas nodded and waved in the general direction of the kitchen.

"Prepare a meal, vegetables and rice, and tea. I will sleep in the laboratory."

"At once, *Ra'īs.*" Abbas pulled his satellite phone out of his stained suit coat pocket, checked the time on his old analogue watch, then dialed the number Badawi had given him. He noticed that three of his new recruits had gathered on the floor, so he moved away for privacy.

"English, I am not on my own." Abbas smiled at Badawi's immediate reply, he didn't sound comfortable, and that suited Abbas's purpose perfectly.

"You still owe me for the transport of the shells, my friend. Do I have to hunt you down to get what is mine?" The laugh from the other end of the phone was strained, so he held his silence, forcing Badawi to continue the conversation.

"Why would I pay you for losing all my shells to rogue terrorists who sunk all your boats? And do you think I don't know you stole other shells from me? And took my money and material from my planes in Aleppo with the help of the accursed Jews? And thanks to this call, I now know where you are, so if you want to stay alive, remain where you are because I will have your location surrounded in less time than it will take you to hang up." Abbas suddenly realized he had played his cards the wrong way. Turkey was one of Badawi's strongholds, from where he had recruited hundreds of dissatisfied terrorists from all the different bands and groups that had been a problem for the Turkish Government for years. Abbas controlled the major terror groups in Gaza and Badawi the same in Turkey, which is why he had linked up with him in the first place.

He decided to negotiate.

"My friend, I did not steal from you so much as see that some of your precious materials we saved from the Jews. And for your information, according to my sources, it is not terrorists who sunk my boats, but the US Navy." The silence on the satellite phone was so pronounced Abbas's ear clicked in an attempt to hear something.

"And just so you know, they also took your ship and everything on it." The cursing that came down the line was violent. Abbas could hear gunfire, screaming, thuds, and the sound of someone choking. He hoped against hope it was Badawi at the end of the pain and anger, but he suspected, correctly, that he was the source and not the recipient. He wondered who Badawi had killed in his wrath but then just as quickly decided he didn't care. So long as he could keep Badawi at arm's length, he would be safe.

"Are you absolutely sure of that?"

"Yes."

"Then what you have is useless to you." Abbas felt threatened, as he always did around Badawi, by his superior presence and knowledge, but he kept his mouth shut and played the underling, a role had perfected these last six months.

"If we were to work together again, could you make the shells work?" He already knew what he had to do to the shells, he had paid close attention to the scientist and her briefings back in Afghanistan, but it never hurt to get another opinion. And to be honest, he really hadn't worked out how to modify the nose plug to work from a Man Pad.

"Yes."

"Then I suggest you stay where you are and let me come to you."

"No. I am already on my way to you, and I have the building you are presently in surrounded. Anyone who tries to escape will be shot on sight." And he hung up. He dialed another number, one he had hoped never to have to use.

"Maribelle, good afternoon. We have had some difficulty these past weeks pulling the plan together, and we need your expert help. Can you get professional assistance for Adana?" In faraway France, Maribelle Françoise walked across her six-hundred-year-old carpet in her bare feet and stood at the gracious and tall gold-framed windows. Outside, the wind whistled, snow fell flying sideways, and the magnificent trees bent and swayed in the storm. Inside was the epitome of calm, splendor, and true antique elegance. The dress she wore was off the shoulder, a sparkling royal blue, and had once been worn by a mistress of Henry the Sixth. It had taken her months to get rid of the mothball smell.

"How professional?"

"The same level or better than Siobhan."

"Why?"

"She was inadvertently killed in a firefight we became engaged in."

"She was not supposed to travel outside of Ireland."

"Maribelle, you know what a strong-minded person she was. There was nothing I could do to prevent her. In the end, I gave her some of my best guards, who also fell during the encounter."

"I see. *Bonté gracieuse. Quelle insouciance de ta part. Elle était l'un de nos enfants les plus précieux.*" Badawi kept his opinion of Siobhan being anyone's treasured child, she had drunk like a fish, fucked like a spider, partied like a wild animal, spent his money recklessly, and yes, she had been very smart, and overall, he had enjoyed her. Right up to the time, she showed her cowardice by hiding in the toilet and screaming incomprehensible things at him in Gaelic when the Jews attacked his plane in Aleppo. So he had hacked at her with his knife, shot her several times, and silenced her annoying voice once and for all. At least he had in his mind, the truth being she had run out on him after the aircraft crash at Aleppo.

"I will provide someone, but you had better take care of her, or you will become an enemy and not a friend. Clear?"

"*Absolument. Merci, au revoir.*" Now all he had to do was get to Turkey, and he pondered his choices. A fast boat would take nine to ten hours, a helicopter a little over two. Time was of the essence. He had to regain both the shells and the nuclear material, but given he was in the process of collecting billions in gold bullion, he was not so much worried about the money he knew Abbas had stolen off the plane. He risked a short call to his banker, arranged for the exchange, and wrote down the contact he would give anyone who he needed to bribe or pay.

Life was good.

So long as he was in control!

# Chapter Thirty-Three

Sandra had a rare thought as her little jet — if you could call a sixteen-seat executive jet little-flashed over the Mediterranean Sea. This was what had started it all, in a way, an attack on the Vatican that had destroyed ninety-seven percent of the hierarchy of the Catholic Church and also destroyed thousands of years' worth of artifacts, icons, and documented religious history, by an aircraft that had been shot down probably close to where she was now. And just a day later, the boss, Jessica, and Pete had flown the exact route and made the discovery that turned the investigation on its ear.

Now, she thought, it was her turn. In control of an Israeli commando unit, Tom and his team, and with the help of the ex-FBI agent sitting opposite her, and as she was now a newly minted member of Section Five, she would be smart, so she thought through the way she thought Jessica would play it, snapped open her mini, dialed Tom, Fay, and Josephine into the conversation.

"Tom, hi! Are you in position?"

"Yes, Sandra, we have the premise locked down, but I need to warn you it is a very large, well-protected compound. We estimate fifteen to twenty guards, all roving patrols, as well as electronic surveillance. We over-flew a micro drone, and there seems to be no air defense, and the immediate area around the house, which is huge, seems to be kept free of patrols. It is a layered pattern, reminiscent of the way the West Germans set up their defenses during the cold war."

"Okay, we have five commandos from the 104 with us, plus your five?"

"No, we have nine. I borrowed four from Indigo to make up my squad."

"How are you dressed?"

"Smart casual, weapons concealed, light body armor, we have passed a number of people on our way here, as well as a police stop, and no one was particularly interested in us. We showed Interpol ID, not Section Five, and simply put, we were in transit. It's snowing and cold, so our outerwear is providing good camouflage. Bring a thick coat." Sandra did a quick mental calculation if Tom had eight, Josephine had five, she had thirteen excellent shooters who she would put up before a small army knowing she had the tactical and skills advantage.

"Tom, Fay, and I are coming in as suits, Inspectors from Interpol, with Red Notices and all the legal papers we need should we have to get heavy. Do we have the destination for the bullion yet?"

"Bob hit the first repository twenty minutes ago, they had been warned by the Ministry, who had made it clear that Interpol was in charge, so they were very helpful, even letting him inspect the proposed shipment, which had made it as far as pelleting. Bob has left one of his team in place, and the local federal police have sent a squad that will remain at the repository for as long as we need. He will be at location two in an hour, so we will have confirmation, perhaps. How long before you land?" Sandra looked at the flight tracker on the cabin bulkhead, did a quick calculation, and unmuted her mini.

"About ninety minutes."

"Good, we'll be ready, and I'll pick you up from the airport, as befits two such important people such as yourselves." The laughter in his voice relaxed Sandra, and Fay, who was watching her closely, saw some of the tension lift from her shoulders. This was the first time either of them had been in the field as the principals, and while the task might seem simple, getting it done would require tripping over a lot of potential landmines!

"Tom, this time, we are civilians, so no military behavior, just subservience, please." His laughter now was quite plain, and as she cancelled the call, she thought that being bloodied under combat conditions with people like Tom and Bob wasn't all that bad. Her mini buzzed. She opened the lid and saw a message from Bob via Tom, giving the physical location for the destination of the bullion, as well as the latitude and longitude. She thought that was backwards, she had been taught longitude then latitude, but it didn't really matter. There were also photos of the initiating paperwork, signed by the 'name', and documents from the federal Treasury approving the transfer, all witnessed by an unknown signatory. Fay swung her mini towards Sandra, the map on it showing a pulsing POI (Point of interest).

A very large building owned by the Buttenden Foundation, on the waterfront in Niece. Three minutes on, her mini told her the building was owned by a German Engineering company, held on behalf of a trust. It smelt like a corporate shell game, so she forwarded the information to Lyon, requesting a full check ASAP.

The location needed to be confirmed by Bob, and that would or would not happen in the next hour, so she settled back to think through her approach. Her German was spotty, but she thought that American English would give her an advantage. Maybe she could get on her 'deep south'.

"Fay, do you speak German?"

"*Nein, mein Kapitän, kein Wort!*" They all laughed. Her accent was perfect, if you were back in grade school!

"I'll take that as a no. Anyone in your team" she asked, looking over her shoulder at the Israeli contingent.

"*Nein,* what she said!" and they all laughed again.

This was the area where she would have to tread carefully with the 'name'. With his assumed wealth, he would have political connections at every level of government, potentially the military and the police forces. Ostensibly, there was no reason for him not to ship his bullion around as often as he wanted to. It was his registered and tax-paid asset. The link to Malik Badawi was not so much tenuous as subject to interpretation. But in her bones, she knew he was playing the game, for what benefit she had no idea, but if he thought he would get away with it, he was sadly mistaken.

"Fay, in your experience with the FBI, when you built a case, did you ever have doubts about the success you would have when you went to trial?" Fay smiled, relaxed back into her seat, closed her mini, and looked out the window at the clouds as they streamed past. Maybe she should issue them with a speeding ticket!

"All the time. And the more wealthy or well-positioned the perpetrator was, the greater the chance some high-priced fancy suit posing as a lawyer would get them off on some technicality. Never happened to me, but I saw it happen to others many a time." Sandra reviewed her notes mentally and recognized a potential weakness.

"Do you think he will have been tipped off by anyone in the Ministry?"

"If not, by someone in that food chain. He will know we are coming, and he will know most of the circumstances. Bob flashed the Red Notice and the World Court order and left copies for the director. Don't be surprised to find a really high-priced suit holding copies when we get there."

Sandra nodded to herself and thought through a seminar she had sat in back at the FBI Academy during her training for Interpol. It had dealt with making an arrest under difficult circumstances, where professional and legal resistance was being applied, and political influence trying to control the outcome. She made her decision on her tactics, called Tom, dialed in Josephine, even though she was sitting just a seat or two behind, then brought in Fay. Ownership and belief in what they were doing were key, and as the seminar had pointed out, the attitude of the arresting officers was everything.

"Tom, Josephine, I've changed my mind. Fay has mentioned that our target will have been warned by someone in the government that we are on the way and about the Red Notice, so I need you to be Section Five, paramilitary, and armed to the teeth. Tom, once you pick us up, you run this like a live fire exercise, front to back. Josephine, coordinate with Tom and work out your organizational structure, and tactics, Fay and I will still go in as suits but with our weapons and credentials visible. The Terrorist Laws give us the absolute right to incarcerate without trial, forcing the defendant to prove their innocence. If we have to, we take in the lawyer as well, and anyone else they throw in our way. In the case of armed resistance, I expect you to suppress it, but your safety and the safety of our team are paramount. I don't mind bodies, so long as they're not ours."

Sandra hung up, leaving Tom and the head of Commando 104 to sort out their order of battle and agree on their tactics. She leaned over until her head was almost touching Fay's.

"I know you're a hard arse, but I have to ask you a personal question. Can you pull the trigger?" Fay looked into Sandra's eyes, now a dark green with just a hint of black around the edges, but so intense they could light up a room.

"The FBI trained us-me-never to rely on our weapons but to use the law and the system and what it gave us. But since seeing how Jessica handled the Point Roberts situation, then Helena, and how she wrapped up the top echelon of the terrorists, I have no fear about using my weapon. I also think, in this case, the bad guys are the worst of the worst, and after watching you bitch and moan about getting shot, I'd rather do the shooting and not the bullet catching!" Sandra smiled, enjoying the joke.

"Hey, I didn't bitch and moan, and that ruined one of my best wardrobes!"

"All the more reason not to get shot again." Sandra nodded, agreeing with what Fay had said and grateful for the way she had said it. Jessica had hinted that Fay would learn from her, but in this case, she had learned from Fay, and it felt good to have such expertise at her disposal.

# Chapter Thirty-Four

The boss looked natty, the tailored suit stretching his well-built frame. His background was a very large arena-style room, all wood, and brass, with a huge skylight overhead. His white starched cuffs made his hands look framed, and I wondered how well he was adapting to his new environment.

"You called?"

"Yes. Jessica, I leave you alone for a week, and you get yourself all wrapped up in a political shit storm, and in Germany of all places." I shrugged, everything he said was true, and I was waiting for the punchline.

"Where are you?"

"Indigo and I are waiting for Abbas to land somewhere, and we are actively tracking Badawi."

"I'm told you have been rude to an admiral, pissed a ship's captain off, and basically created a storm up and down the Mediterranean."

"You didn't mention the helicopter we were in was attacked by a drone, and you missed half of Tom's team being taken out by an RPG."

"And you and Sandra being shot to bits as you rappelled down to the deck of a fifty-footer."

"Yes, well, these things happen, as you well know. Why did you call?"

"I have information for you and maybe a suggestion or two on how to find Badawi and Abbas."

"I'm all ears." He just smiled his alligator smile, making his scarred face look like a bad caricature from a comic book. Doctor Evil, I presume.

"First, your enquiry to Lyon regarding the ownership of the warehouse in Niece. Multiple shells, but they all come back to a trust owned and controlled by Herr von Speer. And interestingly, just last week, he rented it for three years to one Thana Praxidike, a.k.a. Malik Badawi. I've sent the data to Susan, Fay, Tom, and Bob. So you have your link, as well as the shipment documentation." I thought that through, under the Terrorist Laws, that was more than enough to restrain and incarcerate. Sandra would be jumping for joy in her scuffed boots.

"And your suggestion for finding our elusive terrorists?"

"I'd go with Abbas, having landed somewhere in Southern Turkey. The transponder going offline could be no more than the pilot shutting down, as you well know."

"We got a lat/long from the navy on the point of shutdown. It coincides with an airport recently completed near Adana. Fay has a drone on its way there, but I had them positioned at the other end of the Med, so it's taking them time to get there. Arie is considering an overfly that might happen in an hour or two."

"And Badawi?"

"We've tracked him through the desert. He was physically sighted in Khan Unis less than an hour ago. Arie has a spotter following him and has been for the last four hours. We're missing four shells. We know Abbas has two, as well as the nuclear material and apparently a lot of Badawi's money, which he stole from under his nose at Aleppo. "How do I know all this?" you ask, and I humbly reply, our geeks are bloody good, and they have an intercept on Badawi's satellite phone, and we just listened into a fascinating conversation."

"Give me the guts, and you've never been humble."

"Badawi is on his way to the warehouse in Turkey; they had an argument about that. Abbas wanted to travel to Gaza, but Badawi nixed it and is on the way. Abbas confirmed the two shells and is working out how to load them into a propulsion system. And then we had a second call from Badawi to someone he called 'Maribelle', whom he asked for a replacement for the Irish nuclear scientist we were previously tracking. 'Maribelle' seemed very pissed that Siobhan is no longer on the scene and made a threat or two."

"So we have a puzzle. Where are the missing shells, how will they load them if they can, and then how will they fire them, again, if they can."

"In her early research, Sandra identified a range of Man Pads that could successfully be used to fire a sabot with the shell inside. But that's not the optimum solution. I vote for crushing them both the moment Badawi lands. We take out at least the two shells Abbas has in his possession now, plus the nuclear material. Then we worry about the other missing two." The boss nodded slowly. He had always been a fan of shock and awe and personally loved to overload an enemy at every opportunity.

"You know we can't do that. The material will implode and you'll have a four-and-a-half thousand-ton nuclear explosion on your hands, with all the attendant fallout, in a friendly country. You have a plan. What is it?" I looked at him critically, he had been my boss, mentor, teacher, and confidant for the last six years, and we had both survived some very interesting and dangerous situations together. Not always in one piece. And I still had a crush on him, a constant embarrassment whenever I brought it to mind. I wondered if my plan would be similar to what he would come up with.

"My plan is to let them hook up, let the new scientist arrive, then take them by surprise, probably midday tomorrow. Arie will lend me sufficient resources. The navy won't play. Their rules of engagement are too strict. Plus, I've got Indigo, and he is already moving support into the area, under the cover of a food supply for the thousands of displaced people in that area. The word is Abbas has twenty shooters, we can only guess at Badawi's support, but it won't be more than twenty or thirty. So fifty on the ground shouldn't be a problem."

I could see him trying to look into my mind to hear what wasn't said. "Confined area, refuges everywhere, the opportunity for collateral damage is extremely high, but you will have thought of that. Why the middle of the day?"

"Who would expect it? Early morning is the usual time for a dark operation, and Indigo thinks he can organize a distraction that will pull a large number of their troops away or at least divert them long enough for us to take the shells. Looking at the plans for the building, it looks like the work area for the chemistry laboratory is downstairs, below ground slightly, with offices upstairs. If that is how it is, we'll get inside and then work back out to the street."

"Wait another day."

"Why?"

"Lull them into a false sense of security, let whatever plays out between Badawi and Abbas play out, even if it means they split up. You can let Badawi run, Arie's people will not let him disappear, and he may take you to the missing shells. Abbas will try to load the shells he has on-site, and I'd like to see how he attempts it."

"You would?" I smiled. So would I, but not at the risk of losing either one of the terrorists or any of the shells. "Can't do that. The risk of them doing something stupid is too great. Our only play is to take them out of action at the earliest time. Once we confirm the shells via an overflight, we move." He nodded, comfortable with my tactics, and the relief that gave me was palpable.

"Just make sure the Turkish Government knows who and what is going down. I don't want any local interference." Again, he nodded. Not unexpectedly, the political side of things had gone exceptionally smoothly since he had moved into the upper echelons of Interpol.

"Got you covered there. Stay safe." And he disconnected just as another call came in.

"Commander, Badawi has landed. He has taken some of the metal tubes we think to contain the nuclear material, his men have attacked Abbas's troops, the firefight killed many on both sides, and Badawi is again airborne, heading back to Gaza."

"How could this happen so quickly without you knowing about it?" The little Israeli agent looked crestfallen as if he had committed a huge sin. I changed my tone immediately. "Apologies, you caught me off guard. What happened in your pursuit?"

"Our helicopter was delayed, only twenty minutes, but by the time we were close enough to regain visual contact, the damage had been done."

"Could we successfully attack the compound now?"

"It would be the best time, in my humble opinion. There is still local fighting going on, and part of the building is burning, but the confusion will be to your advantage."

"Stand by, don't disconnect. Indigo, can you get your troops in now?" Next to me, Indigo was staring at his little screen, conversing in Italian, a magical language under normal circumstances, but just now, its musical, lyrical sounds grated on my ears.

"We can attack in five minutes. The Israelis will be onsite in three, your instructions?"

"Get the shells, the material. No prisoners required, but I would like a word or two with Abbas."

"Done." And he went back to his mini, and I opened the channel to the agent. "We will attack within five minutes, stay safe, and let me know the outcome as soon as you can."

"Yes, Commander." And he clicked off. It was too fast, we would not go in coordinated, the chances of the Israelis shooting the Italians and vice versa were great, and they were both moving into an already fluid situation, and I had to trust the instincts of the agent, and Indigo's skill at commanding a multi lingual-multinational force from several hundred kilometers away from the action, then I looked over his shoulder and saw he had live bodycam footage, very jerky, but very explicit. Bodies were falling all around the operator, and the UV patches on the arms of our troops stood out like beacons.

A wedge shape of troops poured in and down a dark stairwell. Sporadic firing lit up the confined area, then the wedge burst out into a lit but burning area, obviously, the laboratory where Abbas had been planning to work. I grimaced as a flashbang went off, flooding the camera with blue/white light. Then when the image returned, I saw the two boxes that should contain the shells. It took another minute of fierce fighting, but the camera slowly panned down. One box was opened, and inside lay the sleek brass/copper substrate torpedo. I mentally cheered. The camera panned around the area. All I could see now were shattered bodies, all in that gruesome pose of 'just shot, thanks for asking', then the agent's screen lit up on my mini.

"Commander, shells secured, and two metallic containers matching the description you gave us have been secured. Of necessity, I will have to leave this area now."

"Thank you, appreciated." But the screen had already gone black. "Indigo, status report?"

"No sign of Abbas. A vehicle was reported fleeing the compound just as we arrived. If it only had five people in it, perhaps he was one of them.

"The Israelis are taking the captured material back to Israel, with my permission." I nodded. Arie was collecting quite a stack of evidence should we ever have to use it.

"What do you want us to do with the building?"

"Check it out thoroughly, sweep the area for tangoes, eliminate all resistance, go back to supplying food for the refugees, put out any fires, and let them have the building." And I wasn't being sarcastic. The refugee problem in southern Turkey was critical, with hundreds of thousands of displaced people living hand to mouth, most without any sort of protection from the elements. If our little incursion could help ease some of their discomfort, it was a benefit that we could be proud of, off-setting the pain and agony over the casualties we would have taken. And I needed to know that. Indigo beat me to it.

"Five Israelis, three our ours, several walking wounded, but we are now in control." I nodded, knowing that nothing I could say would make any difference, but this chapter of the terror attacks had taken a greater toll than any of the previous actions.

As the boss had said on several past occasions, 'sometimes you get the donut, sometimes you get the hole'.

# Chapter Thirty-Five

S andra and Fay stood at the open doorway of the jet, looking down
on the long Mercedes Benz waiting for them at the bottom of the
stairs. The back door was open, and a uniformed policewoman
held a large umbrella over her capped head in expectation. Two black
4-WD's formed up behind, the rear one with its big door open and
another uniformed policeman holding an umbrella. Tom had brought
reinforcements as well as his team, but they were federal police, so she
would have to keep them out of any shooting that might eventuate if
she could. Tom walked to the bottom of the stairs.

"Inspector, if you will come this way?" He indicated the open
door of the limousine and stood to one side. The women entered the
vehicle and moved over so Tom could sit in front of them but facing
them on the bench seat. The four Italian special forces followed them
down the stairs and walked to the rear 4-WD.

"Tom, are you up to date on the situation?"

"Yes, Inspector, the site is still secured. Nothing has changed
since we spoke last. We have a squad of federal police backing us up,
permission from the Chancellor to proceed as we see fit, I have my
hybrid team in the 4-WDs, and we are waiting on your brief." He
handed Sandra a small headset.

"Tom, before we start, Indigo and the 104 have taken casualties
in Turkey, I would really like to make this a zero-sum game, but without knowing how Herr von Speer will react, all I can say is keep the
Germans out of any firefight."

"Copy that." She put the little headset on and relaxed back into her seat, letting the information in her head arrange itself.

"Listen up. Anyone who doesn't speak English, make yourself known." She paused, waited for any reaction, then continued. "Good. This is a sanctioned Interpol operation authorized by the World Court and the German government. We have a warrant for the arrest and detention of Herr von Speer and any associate who may interfere, in the matter of aiding and abetting acts of terror, financing acts of terror, and financing the procurement of weapons of mass destruction.

"The German Federal police members will provide perimeter defense, no one in or out, you are authorized to use deadly force if necessary. Keep your weapons in a safe position, and only shoot as a last resort. Questions?" Again, there were no comments.

"The members of Section Five will be clearly identified as Interpol, we have a Red Notice as well as the warrants, and you are to take your instructions from the Master Chief. Questions?" Silence again.

"The troops that arrived with us will stay with Agent Remer and myself as personal protection. Questions?" As no one spoke, Sandra took the headset off and handed it back to Tom.

"Your turn. Why don't you stop the convoy, reform as needed?" He nodded.

"Good idea." So they stopped, and the four Italians moved from the rear 4-WD to the limousine. Tom got out and, with a smart salute, left the women, and organized the federal police and his mixed team into the two vehicles. The convoy moved on until it was at the gates of the chalet in Buchenbuhl, where the first 4-WD stopped. The limo and remaining 4-WD climbed the hill, passing roaming guards who looked on with suspicion but took no other action. The vehicles stopped at the impressive portico entrance, a magnificent marble patio with towering Greek-like columns. Sandra and Fay exited and were immediately surrounded by the Italians. Tom kept his contingent inside their vehicle, watching the action through a button-hole camera stitched into Sandra's long leather coat, on the back of which was stenciled 'Interpol'.

Before they reached the door, a massive double three-meter wooden affair, carved with cherubs and winged creatures, a butler dressed in stiff black formal wear, his starched wing collars sticking out of his neck like petals on a flower appeared, bowed and gestured them in. Tom made a hand signal, and his entire troop exited and formed up into two rows, and started to walk around the perimeter of the villa in opposite directions, one stopping every twenty meters, facing outwards. By coincidence, Tom and his 2IC reached the extensive sheltered patio at the same time Sandra and Fay, and their guards were ushered through the massive glass doors to where Herr von Speer sat, dressed in a royal blue and burgundy smoking Jacket. He raised a cut crystal glass to them in welcome but remained sitting, putting Sandra and Fay at a disadvantage. Sandra solved part of that with a small hand signal, which caused her four-person team to surround them all, facing out. Fay moved slightly back, swept her jacket aside, and rested her hand near her weapon.

It was a provocative move, one that had von Speer putting his glass down on the back of a black glass swan-shaped table with some force.

*"Meine Damen, bitte, Sie sind in meinem Haus willkommen, warum all diese Aggression?"*

*"Herr von Speer, wir sind hier, um Sie gemäß den Terrorgesetzen in der Fassung von 2022 zu verhaften. Dies ist kein sozialer Besuch*, and we will speak in English from this point."

"Arrest me? No. I'll make one call, and you will then leave the way you have come." And he reached for a small transmitter on the back of the swan's head, and in response, gunfire broke out over the entire campus. The butler reappeared with a double-barreled shotgun and was immediately gunned down by the guard facing the doorway. Tom raced up the stairway just as von Speer pulled a Lugar pistol out of his jacket, only to be pistol-whipped across the temple by Fay, who then shoved the barrel of her weapon into his neck with such force his head tilted to one side.

"Enough. Call your men off, or they will be killed." Sandra's voice was steady, firm, and had an edge to it, so much that von Speer raised his hands in surrender. Fay didn't move her weapon. The gunfire continued, although now it was sporadic. "Cuff him." Sandra stood back while Tom jerked von Speer's hands behind his back, with Fay's weapon sticking to his neck as if it were glued there. She kicked him behind the knees, forcing him to the ground. She wiped the blood off the barrel of her gun on the tail of his jacket, then stood back.

"Herr von Speer, as previously stated, you are detained under the Terrorist Laws as modified in 2022 for aiding and abetting acts of terror and financing same, as well as the procurement of weapons of mass destruction. Let's go." And dragging the heft of von Speer, they moved back through the villa to their limo and the 4-WD.

"Where do you want him?" Tom's troop started to appear from both sides of the villa and, after a short conversation with Tom, filed back into the 4-WD. Pointing to the 4-WD, Sandra jerked her thumb.

"In there. And don't be gentle." He just smiled, thinking he had a Jessica clone on his hands and wasn't that just what they needed in this asymmetric fight? They had lost no one, and as he climbed back into the limo, he saw the question in Sandra's eyes.

"Sixteen tangos accounted for. Five escaped in a vehicle of some sort, but there is smoke and fire down at the gates. The Federales probably accounted for them." And sure enough, as they crested the small rise over the rainwater gutter at the bottom of the road, an upturned vehicle was burning, thick black smoke eking its way up into the grey overcast, with at least one body hanging half in and half out of one door. The police were just standing by, arms folded over their weapons slung across their chests, letting the vehicle burn, so Sandra asked to stop, dismounted, and found the captain in charge. He saluted with a crispness Sandra appreciated.

"Inspector, they tried to ram us. They were firing their weapons, so we returned fire, with the result you see here. Unfortunately, there are no survivors."

"Anyone hurt on your side?"

"No, Inspector, all is well."

"Thank you, Captain, excellent work, you may care to investigate the villa and its grounds. Someone in your government will have to determine what will happen to it next. There are also several bodies that will need to be dealt with."

"No problems, Inspector, we'll get on it right away". And following another crisp salute, he turned on his heels, gestured to his sergeant, and started to walk back up the driveway.

"You know, it always amazes me how arrogant the super-rich are. Von Speer fully expected to just sit there and have us walk away with our tails between our legs because he was so filthy rich, so well connected at the government level, he had his guards wandering all over the villa, and probably, the most insulting aspect of all, we were mere females." Fay looked pissed, and her voice had taken on a hard edge, which had some of the team moving slightly away from her. Sandra rubbed her arm in support.

"Arrogant, yes, but free? Never again. And best of all, no one shot on our side for once." Tom nodded; he had been thinking the same thing. What had made the difference in this engagement was the fact that his team had gone in ready and prepared to shoot at the first sign of any provocation, so when the alarm had been triggered, the body language of the guards on the property had been enough to start the deadly exchange, which in spite of some return fire, had been almost over before it had started. He had seen the exact same attitude when he had fought with PJ, with Jessica, and now with Sandra, although he had a feeling that her partner, the bewitching ex-FBI agent Fay Remer, who was obviously seriously pissed at Herr von Speer, would not be far behind in the 'shoot first and don't worry about the questions' department, a philosophy he totally agreed with when it came to facing down terrorists.

The trip back to the aircraft was uneventful. He half listened in on the conversation Sandra had with Jessica, then let himself drift off into a relaxing semi-sleep as he considered his options. His present tour ended in just over a month, and as he had his twenty years in, his pension wouldn't get any better if he signed up for another tour. Besides, people in his profession rarely got to retire, other than in a pine box if they were lucky. He wondered if he should give his old friend PJ a call and see if there might be a role for him in Interpol.

He liked working with these young, tough, plucky women who performed so well under pressure, and besides, they were not hard on the eyes by any stretch of the imagination!

# Chapter Thirty-Six

Malik Badawi's helicopter landed in the desert, right behind the tattered fence of the Rafah Refugee Camp, on the corner of the Gaza strip. He had nuclear material, and he knew where Abbas had hidden two shells, very cleverly, right in the middle of the tent and cardboard city that housed thousands of refugees. To describe the camp was to imagine the worst possible conditions that human beings lived under, and the daily death toll was in the hundreds. Most from starvation, some from wounds from bullets or knives, and some just from lack of hope. And the smell was atrocious, with funeral pyres streaming dense gray and black smoke up into the leaden sky as if the pillars of smoke were all that was holding the sky up and stopping it from crushing the camp.

Since the latest attack by the terrorists, the camp had swollen by thousands, so any attempt to organize relief had been abandoned. As Badawi moved through the fringes, his guards simply pushing refugees out of the way, he fleetingly thought of the long conversations he and the Irish scientist, Siobhan O'Cleary, had enjoyed over cocktails on his balcony that overlooked Dublin. She had been engaged emotionally as she described the objectives of the first terrorist attacks and the plans the women had for relocating millions of child refugees around the world. And had succeeded, and were still succeeding, as different countries brought online the ecological plants that produced the panels and power packs, allowing huge population centers to be constructed and filled with refugee children.

She had explained the help they had received from the old man of the desert, the incredible help 'Helen' had been, and the daring raids made on the oil well heads, gas terminals, and coal mines by Shetani and his mercenaries. She had glossed over the millions killed, either directly or indirectly, and enthused about their current campaign, designed to add pressure on the surviving world to accelerate the removal of children from the refugee camps.

He had listened patiently, assisted her in every way, from setting up the factory in Afghanistan to working with Abbas on the shipping of the shells, and engaged her tremendous mind in the rebuilding of the ship with its purpose-built electromagnetic rail gun.

Not once had he bothered to really 'see' her vision, having recognized early that here was the perfect vehicle from which he could launch attacks on his enemy with both impunity and massive force. Billions of euros were ready for the taking and the most powerful weapons any terrorist had ever had control of.

It had only taken him a few months to seduce the beautiful red-headed scientist and convince her that her agenda was his. And he had enjoyed every minute of the façade, reveling in the heady projection of a young, rich, and smart couple in love as he paraded her both in Ireland and on the French Rivera. And she had freed up the funds for him, providing a war chest so large he had yet to imagine how to spend it all. And it had given the poor humble boy from the desert a taste of the rich and powerful high life, a drug too powerful to resist, one he fully intended to consume for the rest of his life.

He had billions in gold bullion on its way to his leased shed in Niece. He had enough nuclear material for the two shells he was about to collect; he had a replacement scientist being flown in from somewhere. It didn't matter from where, only that she arrived on time and did his bidding.

His men physically forced a group of huddling women out of the way, allowing him access to a small tent. He pushed open the flap, peered into the dark, and saw a crying baby in one corner and a weeping woman, obviously sick, in the other. But no green boxes. In a fury, he shot the woman and was about to shoot the baby when three men rushed in and pinned his arms against his sides.

They forced marched him outside, where his guards had formed a ring. He was thrown into the center, lost his balance, and posed on one knee for a second, then slowly straightened. He recognized the man who stood before him and listened intently to what he whispered in Farsi. He looked around, saw that he and his men were heavily outnumbered, pointed back the way they had come, received a nod. The people parted to let him and his men through, closing ranks behind him.

Inside, he was at the boiling point, wanting to kill everyone around him, men, women, and children, then burn the camp to the ground. He visualized the roaring flames in his mind's eye, a snarky, evil grin splitting his face, making it look like he was suffering a stroke, the rictus so pronounced his men hurried away in front of him, not daring to look in case they became handy targets for his wrath.

Once again, Abbas had outsmarted him. He would die a horrible death, and it was only this thought that kept Badawi calm enough to climb into the helicopter and instruct the pilot to take him to Khan Unis, where he would regroup and plot his revenge against the leader of Hamas. He would secure his gold, and then he would have all the power he needed to wipe the co-leader out.

The irony of a master terrorist wiping out one of the most troublesome terror groups in the Middle East was lost on him.

He had the nuclear material. He would make more shells. He would get more shells. He would not be stopped by anyone or anything.

# Chapter Thirty-Seven

I sat in the large boardroom we had been allocated in the hotel, secured by some of Arie's and Indigo's best commandos. No coffee machine, for that matter, no Indigo, as he was out hunting for one as a matter of urgency. Bob, Tom, Sandra, and Fay, and their respective teams were on their way back. I had decided to get everyone under one roof for a day or two until we could get a clear indication of where Abbas and Badawi were. Arie's people were a class above the best I had ever worked with, and he had one deeply embedded agent following each terrorist, reporting as and when they could.

Yes, we could have just eliminated both terrorists, and I don't think I wasn't sorely tempted, but we still had the small matter of missing nuclear material and at least two shells. And the information Amira was feeding back to us from her laboratory in Israel was, on one hand encouraging, on the other, as scary as your worst nightmare.

The shells could only be opened by the application of a nanomaterial and closed the same way. That meant that an expert in nanomaterials was required. Samples of the nanomaterial had been captured with the shells taken from Badawi's ship, and Amira had been able to replicate them. Stands to reason, as she had been the one who had invented the first iteration of the nano bugs some five years previously.

The issue of how to get the shells to explode was just as complicated. The bulb nose was designed to break off under tremendous force and then penetrate the two chambers allowing the nuclear material to mix and the fission process to commence.

In her opinion, any attempt to drill through the bulb and insert a movable plug that would require much less force to operate would possibly create an unstable reaction within the shell, possibly leading to a premature explosion. I put the report down, it was depressing me, and like the angel he was, Indigo came back in, followed by two troopers carting a massive brass and silver espresso machine.

Within minutes it was plugged in, filled with water, and had beans grinding away in a separate brass tube. The noise filled every corner of the room and had everyone in it laughing in anticipation as they stood rooted to the floor. A large silver jug was filled with milk and attached to a steam tube, which immediately started to send out long lines of condensed super-heated steam, adding a screeching sound to the grinding noise. I couldn't remember a more enticing combination of sounds, and I mentally relaxed.

"Commander, your espresso will be just a minute, but you have a call from General Saunders." I took the mini off Indigo and walked back out into the corridor, where the sounds of happy anticipation were muted.

"General, you called?" She looked calm and relaxed. I hoped that was a portent for what was happening more broadly across the United States.

"Jessica, I need an update for the president on the nuclear threat." I looked at her, obviously in her office, the folded flags behind her adding a level of gravitas to her words. She was in uniform, but with her jacket and all its medals sitting snugly over the back of her chair.

Her flat green bow tie held her pristine khaki shirt together, and I thought she looked every bit the general she was.

"General, we still have to find two of the original shells; and some of the nuclear material is missing. We have tabs on Badawi and Abbas. They had a disagreement in Turkey where we took advantage of the situation and attacked, took two shells and material into custody, but missed Badawi and Abbas." She looked at me with a very hard and concerned stare, and I felt my hackles rise up. I hated Monday morning quarterbacking, and as I prepared to let her know that, she soft-ened her face, almost smiled, then relaxed in her chair.

"Jessica, my apologies. That means you have recovered what — twenty-two of the shells?"

"Yes." She nodded and tilted her head to one side as if thinking of something.

"Do you still need my navy assets?" Now it was my turn to think, I had put the admiral and his ships on the back burner, but to my mind, they still had a role to play.

"Yes, general, we still have to find the missing shells, and they have the detection gear that could help locate them. Also, a physical presence might force the terrorists to make a mistake." Again, she nodded, accepting my words at face value. "I'll let the admiral know. Keep in touch." And she clicked off, as was her usual habit. I accepted a huge steaming mug of coffee from Indigo, who was grinning from ear to ear.

"Commander, an army marches on its stomach, but I swear Interpol marches on caffeine!" I laughed with him, savoring the incredible smell of the newly brewed beans, and noticed that practically everyone else in the room had stopped what they were doing to mimic me sniffing my coffee. My mini jolted me out of my caffeine haze.

"Commander, what do you want us to do with the 'name'?" Sandra's face was distorted as she was peering over Fay's shoulder, looking down at the screen.

"Do we need any data from him?" She shook her head.

"We have all the proof we require to either retire him or lock him away. The proof is irrefutable. No way out." I thought for a minute, did we need more? A question formed in my mind.

"Do we know the details of the deal he did with Badawi?" She nodded.

"He had dictated a memo to his assistant, listing the seven targets, the agreed timeline, and the payment terms. There was a separate deed giving Badawi, under the name of Thana Praxidike, which we know is the alias he was using in Ireland, use of the warehouse. It's always easier when they write it down."

"What were the targets?"

"A series of towns and cities in Germany, France, and Bavaria. As well as the warehouse, he agreed to pay fifteen billion in gold shipped in three deliveries over the course of eight months. His only stipulation was that the attacks had to be mounted before the end of the year. The lease on the warehouse expired twelve months after that. No one said anything, we got all this off the incredible records these bastards kept, but then, that's the German way."

"I wonder what Badawi will do when he realizes he isn't getting the money and if we can take advantage of that?"

"The German federal police have the warehouses under observation. All three depositories have been shut down until released by you, again federal police enforcing, and when we left, they were swarming over the villa with a real gleam in their eye. It seems they have been after him for decades, but he always managed to slither through thanks to his position and wealth and government contacts."

"Where is he now?" Sandra turned her head, looked over her shoulder, then back at the camera.

"Hogtied in the rear of the cabin. He is very unhappy, swearing in languages no one here understands, but his intent is clear. He wants us all hanged, shot, or just killed and thrown out of the aircraft. He even tried to bribe one of the Israelis, who just laughed in his face."

"He really doesn't like you." She smiled and stood up so all I could see was her vest, now stained by perspiration.

"No. So, where do we send him?"

"Leave two of the commando 104 with him. Send him on to Arie with our compliments. When will you get here?"

"About an hour."

"Indigo will arrange ground transport for you. See you soon, and tell everyone a good job." My turn to click off, and I handed the mini to Indigo. "I need ten minutes of thinking time; can you stall everyone until then?"

"*Certamente, comandante, mi farà piacere.*"

Of course, it was a pleasure. Just about everything was to our sturdy Italian head of Interpol. He was a treasure, and not just for his ability to provide espresso at the drop of a hat!

# Plan 'B'

Amir Abbas was pissed! He had Badawi's money, about six hundred million euros he estimated, but he had lost the shells and the nuclear material he had laboriously got to the factory where he had intended to make his nuclear bombs. But he had an ace up his sleeve. The two shells he had hidden in the refugee camp in Rafah he had moved just yesterday, and he had two tubes of the nuclear material hidden in with the cash he had taken back in Aleppo.

And he had only got away with his life because one of his men had seen Badawi land, and heavily armed men flooded out of the helicopter. He had kept the money under guard in his massive armored four-wheel drive, mainly to keep his men focused on their tasks. Without thinking, he had immediately run out the back, into the garage, and instructed his troops to go back in and fight.

As they ran one way, he drove like a maniac in the other and now looked back on the burning warehouse from the safety of a small hill six kilometers from the action. A constant press of civilian refugees flowed past him, carrying everything they owned in tied bundles or on small wheeled carts. Hungry eyes stared out at him, and his men and the women pulled small, dirty, ragged children into the folds of their robes to keep a distance between the vehicle and the column.

He didn't see the small, shabbily dressed man on the dirt bike stopped a hundred meters behind him, and even if he had, he would not have recognized one of Arie Rosenberg's superb agents. Old bikes, even a few rusted cars, still managed to move along this road, and the sight of a broken-down truck being pulled by a pair of aging donkeys looked totally normal. People used what they could to live as well as they could, even if that was limited to maybe one meal a week and dirty, filthy water that made everyone sick. The one thing all the refugees had in common was a total lack of hope. Every face, from the oldest to the just born, was vacant, creased, dirty, eyes huge far beyond their normal limits, skin shallow and drawn, and clothing more like discarded rags than something that could be worn with pride.

None of this is registered with Abbas. To him, it was just a sea of annoying people heading for who knew where and for what? A trip across the Mediterranean Sea in a leaky boat or a thousand-kilometer hike around the Turkish border to Syria or Iraq, where conditions were even worse? They should just lay down and die and save themselves all that trouble. As the leader of Hamas, he was fighting the Jews and the evil influence of the West, the great Satan. He most definitely was not in the business of saving refugees for any reason.

He turned his vehicle around and headed to Mersin, where he had a boat waiting. In a few days, he would be in a safe location, have reclaimed his two remaining shells, found his weapons expert, and be loading the nuclear material into them, creating two perfect tactical nuclear weapons with which he could hold the world to ransom. He smiled at the thought, his only wish at this time was that Badawi's helicopter would blow up and crash into the sea, ridding him of this nuisance once and for all.

# Chapter Thirty-Eight

The gang was all together again, busily eating hot meals and drinking coffee as if they had been deprived for weeks. Fay, Sandra, Indigo, Tom, and Bob were in one corner, comparing notes and readying a report to Indigo and me. Tom and Bob's team of mixed nationality commandos was in another corner, no doubt sharing war stories and telling lies. One of the things I got used to very quickly since joining Interpol from the NCIS was the amazing way everyone got along, no matter their nationality or their languages. I put it down to a shared and deeply held personal belief that terrorism, people smuggling, crimes against children, and drug trafficking simply could not be accepted or excused on any level, political or otherwise. And that the worst of the worst should be caught and punished to the fullest extent of the law, if not removed from the planet permanently. The United Nations and the World Court had finally realized there could be no compromise when dealing with terrorism, and the Terrorist Laws, as modified in 2022, made that clear to everyone worldwide.

Now we could, on the basis of hard evidence, remove anyone who supported, encouraged, or participated in any act of terror-the key difference here being 'supported or encouraged.' Arms-length third-party support of terrorism had been a weakness exploited by nearly every country that overtly claimed to not support terrorists but sanctioned such acts under the table for decades.

No more.

Nation states were called to account and severely punished with sanctions, naming and shaming, political castration, and sometimes direct attacks on lawmakers and high-profile supporters of the grow-ing band of international bad guys that saw an opportunity in the grief of others less strong and able than them. Slowly, ever so slowly, terrorism was being confronted in a way that made the bad guys afraid for the first time in centuries.

Then the women refugees launched their world-crippling attacks, killing all sources of oil, gas, and coal, the Internet, nine-ty-nine percent of all computers on the planet, and the social unrest, as a result, killed another fifty to sixty million people around the globe, while the economy of most countries simply stopped in its tracks. The accepted economic terms of 'boom' and 'bust' had been replaced with 'crashed' and 'frozen'.

Fertile soil for terrorists, gangs, militias, and your average stupid bad guy. But this third wave of terrorism had a different feel to it. Led by the joint commanders of the worst terror organizations in the Middle East, Hamas, and Al Bar al Shirak, the threat was nuclear weapons, tailor-made to escape detection and made from a substrate composite of copper and brass using nanotechnology, a signature of the early attacks by the refugee women.

Their original objective had been, at least, to their way of think-ing, simple.

Make the world experience the same conditions that existed in most refugee camps, and force a change in both the beliefs, then atti-tudes and approaches to managing the refugee issue.

Towards this end, once the attacks had stopped, and the world was thrown back to the nineteen eighties in terms of technology and the stone age in terms of the use of petrochemicals, they had offered help with generationally advanced nanomachine-produced technolo-gies that offered incredible power panels and power packs to restart industry and commerce, as well as provide housing, schooling, and life for thousands of refugee children.

This new wave of threat appeared to be solely terrorism based, with no apparent benefit for the refugee situation. Yes, we had seen the message board from a year ago in Ireland, promising a new upris-ing. But an uprising of what? And whom? With Brexit and then the EU cooking along, Northern Ireland enjoyed as much separatism as they could ever want, without a single shot having to be fired. We had seen this as a blind-a way to get us looking west when we should be looking east. This had been borne out so far, with attacks ranging up and down the Mediterranean and into Syria, Iraq, and now Turkey. That is, attacks by us and our allies on the assets of the terrorists in order to confiscate the shells and nuclear material, and in that, we had been reasonably successful.

By our count, two shells to go.

But the problem for us was, as President Bush had said before the launch of the attack on Iraq back in 2003, "The United States cannot wait for final proof 'in the form of a mushroom cloud'"; likewise, Interpol could little afford the luxury of seeing one of the shells exploded when we could take them out of circulation if we were smart and good enough.

So we would have to be smart and good enough. I called the team together.

"Who wants to go first?" I looked around the room as everyone settled, most sitting on the floor, a few ranging themselves around the far wall on metal chairs. Uncomfortable chairs seemed to be our penance for working in so many different places, as they always seem to be in abundance, like mosquitos near a swamp! Perhaps they reproduced during the night, and that's why they seemed to dominate our backsides.

"Commander, you have our summary, so I'll just add to that with an update from Agent Akili, our specialist linguist. She, with two of Indigo's German speakers, has been combing through all the documents we retrieved at the villa. In short summary, von Speer has been dealing with Badawi for over a year. According to Speer's diary, at their first meeting, they discussed the possibility of undetectable small-scale nuclear weapons, and he put his hand up for some when they were produced. No timing was mentioned at that point, but he gave Badawi half a billion euros to help finance the factory and development costs." We all looked at where Sandra was using a huge screen as a visual aid, the documents she was referring to flickering across like an animated cartoon. Interestingly, the crest of the Finance

Ministry appeared on several papers, and I wondered what that was all about. We soon found out.

"These ministry documents you see here were signed by the former director, so the ministry was possibly complicit in this enterprise from day one. Our federal friends are backtracking that. Let me say, at this point, we have always found supporting countries helpful, but never with the fervor of the Germans. Apparently, they have wanted von Speer in their box for a number of years but have never been able to get anything to stick."

"Your read is that he was truly one of the bad guys?"

"Yes, Commander, going back a lot of years, and the Captain of the federal police told us on the ground that he was suspected of financing the attack on the Olympic games over fifty years ago, but they couldn't prove anything."

"Could they now?"

"We haven't gone back that far yet with his records, but the really good news is that they are so meticulous he lists his nefarious activities just like you would a transaction for buying and selling a building. He's been in the terrorist business for decades, there is no apparent reference to the refugee women at this point, but it's early days."

I had noted Sandra's use of formal address and wondered why something I would ask her when we had a moment together. She nodded to Bob, who moved to the screen.

"Commander, my team interviewed the current director of the ministry, as well as the three depositories at Würzburg, Munich, and Stuttgart. As you know, we were able to get the data we needed to shut down the movement of the bullion, as well as the proof of von Speer's involvement with Badawi, which came from you. In my opinion, the current director is probably not involved, but we have suggested to the federals that they take a closer look at Fräulein Seidensticker. She felt off from the get-go. I'll hand it over to Tom."

"Commander, not much to tell, really. Our two inspectors managed the capture of von Speer without loss, we took a ton of records, which Sandra has already referred to, and the federals literally cheered us on the way out. They were so happy that we had taken von Speer out of circulation. Not much else to say." He started to move to his chair, and I stopped him with a hand wave.

"Master Chief, there's a little bit more to it. I'm told you had some twenty tangos to contend with spread out around the villa. How did that go?" He looked at me, trying to dive into my motives for getting him to enunciate the details of the physical attack on the villa. I had my reasons, and they were simple. In this business, you rarely got thanked or had what you had done well reinforced. It was taken for granted that you shot to kill, you shot first, you were the hardest of the hard arses in the valley, and you feared no evil. But Pete had taught me the value of acknowledging the skills our people developed and perfected by rigorous training and mental preparation, and I wanted everyone to understand that what we did might be sanctioned at the highest levels of government but would never be taken for granted under my command.

"Commander, we were briefed well, we acted in concert with Inspector Thomas and Agent Remer's penetration of the villa, we were ready for any attack, and when von Speer activated his alarm, we acted on sight as each tango responded. I should say we acted before they could accurately respond. A few got away but were stopped at the gate by the federals and dispatched accordingly."

"You were a mixed team of Americans, Italians, and Israelis?"

"Yes, ma'am."

"So while jetting to the target, you integrated three nationalities and combat styles brilliantly, took out twenty-plus tangos which were familiar with the grounds, which you were not, and protected your principals?" A wan smile crossed his face, and he unconsciously looked over to Bob for support.

"Ah, yes, ma'am, that would be correct." He looked embarrassed, something I had not seen from him in all the months we had been fighting together.

"Well done, Master Chief, to you and your team, and you too, Major. You both led your teams in an exceptional manner, and personally, I thank you for it. What we do is not easy. How we do it can be complex and fraught with danger, but you both have shown what intelligence, preparation, and leadership can do when applied the right way. Thank you." The sound of finger snapping broke out around the room, and Tom moved to his seat as fast as he could, his face flushed with embarrassment. "Colonel Kashasini, could you please update us on our favorite terrorists and their movements?"

"*Certamente, comandante, piacere mio.*" Indigo was taking the piss out of me by answering me in Italian, but I had a sneaky feeling he knew what I was doing and why. He was, after all, one of the most experienced and long-served members of Interpol and Section Five. But he suddenly turned somber, stood straight, and called the room to attention.

"Commander, at your instruction, I organized a joint attack using our Italian troops, supported by Israeli commando 104, to attack a warehouse/laboratory in Turkey, where Abbas and Badawi were engaged in a firefight, some fifty tangos engaged. The attack by our people was successful in that we captured two shells and two sets of nuclear material. Abbas fled the location in an armored vehicle; Badawi had departed by helicopter some minutes before our attack. Sadly, we lost eight soldiers in the fray, five Israeli and three Italian. I would honor their bravery and their sacrifice with silence." And every head in the room bent, eyes closed, and many of the commandos sitting on the floor closed their left fists, pumping them up and down, a time-honored tradition amongst the elite forces of the world in recognition of comrades lost. I waited until I felt the calm descend on the room like a warm blanket of sunshine.

"At ease. It's never easy losing good people, but I would remind us all that we have recovered all but two of the shells. Yes, we've lost people, and it's now up to us to see that their sacrifice wasn't in vain. Tom, Bob, Sandra, Fay, Indigo, on me, the rest, please take thirty, be ready for briefings within the hour. Well done, everyone, and I mean that. Dismissed." My senior team moved over to where I had set up camp. Not exactly suitable for what I had in mind, but we would make do.

"Sit, take the weight off, relax. We need to review what we've done and our next steps. Quick summary, Abbas has got onto a small fishing vessel and is headed towards Syria. His jet has been impounded, and it is being stripped as we speak. Our agent has not been able to follow Abbas, but we have a drone in the air that should be able to intercept his boat in around twenty minutes. Badawi took off by helicopter, but we've lost him for the time being. With all the coming and going of the shells and the nuclear material, we have to guess what the current situation is, and it's getting harder and harder to keep count. So, our best estimate is Badawi has nuclear material, as does Abbas. There are still two shells unaccounted for; we know Badawi called for a new scientist from the terrorist woman known as 'Maribelle'; what else do we know?" I looked around at the faces of some of the smartest and hard-hitting anti-terror specialists and saw fatigue, tiredness, and a little despondency.

Having people killed in operation affected everyone's morale, especially those in command. And I couldn't let that despondency take root.

"Fay, where are our drones?" Her head came up sharply, a little startled by the look on her face and my tone of voice.

"The command aircraft, the C-17, is in Israel, fully manned, fueled, and ready to go. The two drones will be overhead in fifty minutes. I need a destination for them. They both need fuel. The US Navy has helicopters scanning the northern Mediterranean shore from Palermo to Hatay, and Interpol has received overfly permission from both Syria and Iraq, conditional on not landing without expressed permission; my plan is to refuel the drones in Israel, put the C-17 in a holding pattern over Damascus, and then start a methodical scan of that entire area. I am worried about their technology. We never did pick up Abbas's aircraft, other than by its transponder transmissions. And it had the shells aboard we collected in Turkey, so if they use the same technology again, I'm not sure what our options are."

"My feeling from day one is that this is about the Middle East." I looked at Sandra, not expecting that from her. She was a critical thinker. It was one of the reasons I had brought her into Section Five.

"If we look at the movements of both terrorists, they have always been pointed in this direction. I think we need a deep dive on the equipment needed to build the shells; the source material; where nuclear material can be modified, not necessarily supplied; and the technical expertise required to make it all work." I thought for a minute and looked at Indigo, who had his own thinking expression on, his face seemed to smooth out to make him look younger, and his eyes closed to thin slits.

"Sandra, the equipment for the building of the shells came from Japan. That company we have frozen the assets of. I think Innomatchi was its name." She looked at him and nodded.

"Yes. At the time, I remember we only asked our agents to confirm that Innomatchi had shipped the hardware to Afghanistan. So a question now might be, did they ship any other hardware of a similar nature anywhere else?" Sandra looked up at me. I was still leaning against the wall, trying to stretch out a kink I had in my back. Tunnel vision again! I had been so focused on Afghanistan I had not thought to ask if there we other factories in play; it was a habit I was determined to break. I dialed up Nokomoto Senji, one of our two specialist agents in Japan. Asked him what we needed, and he passed me to his offsider, Aikido Namoki, who today had dyed her long hair purple and blue. Neat look for an Interpol agent!

*"Kon'nichiwa, shirei-kan, ogenkidesuka?"*

*"Kon'nichiwa aikidō, wa i, arigatōgozaimasu."*

And with the formalities over, she handed the mini back to Nokomoto. "Commander, over a year ago, back in November to be exact, a ship set of identical machines to those sent to Afghanistan were sent to Al Millihil, Iraq, via Bagdad. The funds came from Ireland. The delivery was addressed to Al bar Binti Corporation. Six months before that, a similar shipment was sent to an address in Shoci." I looked back down at the team.

"What's in Al Millihil?" I was met with silence. Noticed Fay was busy with her mini, then she surprised us all by jumping up and flicking the data to the big screen. A map formed, with a POI and the name of the town, then a data box started to scroll alongside, and photos of men in protective gear moving out of UN-badged 4WDs.

"A milk factory?" Indigo asked in surprise.

"Not just a milk factory, but a famous milk factory. In a way, you could say it was the reason why President Bush Junior invaded Iraq." I started to recall the details. We had been briefed on this back at the NCIS Academy as a case study in failed intelligence and how it had all come about. It was supposed to be a factory producing weapons of mass destruction, but after three frustrating days, the inspectors only found machinery relevant to the sterilization and production of milk. Yes, they had detected radiation signatures, and yes, again, they matched all the radioactive elements to those used in fabricating a nuclear weapon, but no real physical proof had been able to be produced for the world to see on the six o'clock news.

But Bush had invaded anyway, some said to finish what his father had started years before.

"And who is Al bar Binti Corporation?"

"No idea, no records available."

"Indigo, plans, drawings, photos, ASAP, please."

"It's not there."

"It's not where?" My voice nearly squeaked, but luckily, I managed a cough to cover it up.

"It's not in Al Millihil." The map on the screen changed to an aerial view of a small town, the biggest building being what looked like a two-story apartment block. Where the POI had been located, a large dam surrounded by short stubby trees providing dense ground cover stood swaying in the real-time images. It was a delayed live feed from a satellite, the resolution was better than half a meter, and we could see goat herders moving a small flock of black and white goats around the dam. I checked the code and noticed it was twenty days old.

"According to the UN data, the milk factory was completely demolished back in 2001, at the request of the central government, who saw it as an unnecessary reminder of three decades of persecution by the west." I shook my head. If there was no milk factory, then where did the shipment from Japan end up? And how could we track it now that nearly eighteen months had passed?

"Indigo, run a full data analysis, get our geeks to look back in time, find evidence of the factory, data about its destruction, find images of the year before and the immediate months after. Someone must have all that data, find them, and get it for us, please." He nodded and moved across the room, speaking rapidly to Luigi, our Italian geek. I had another problem.

"Sandra, back to Nokomoto Senji, have him do an audit of Innomatchi, what they sent where, and when, and who paid, go back five years. Discount the environmental plant ship sets we know about. Fay, get onto Arie and see what his people know about the factory. I need to think this through. Okay, let's break for half an hour, let all this new data settle."

The issue I was wrestling with was a question-who was the scientific expert running their nanomachine program now?

Amira had told me that while she had assistants and undergraduates working on her nano programs at Harvey Mudd during the time she invented the process of cleaning up oil spills, and we knew the Chinese scientist, Michele, was also involved, she never mentioned anyone standing out as her successor.

Now we had the third iteration of her original work, a nano process that allowed the fusion of copper and brass, creating a new substrate with remarkable properties. The factory we discovered in the airport hangar in Afghanistan was sophisticated in the midst of thirty-year-old infrastructure but had been assembled from a ship set sent from Japan. That started me thinking about the whole process, and a face and a name floated into my mind.

"Fay, front and center!" She was just in the process of walking out the door with 'call me Sally', and her abrupt halt nearly caused a collision with some of the commandos.

"You called?" she asked, a half-cheeky grin on her face.

"Yes. Sit down, or stand up, but run me through every step of what you saw in Point Roberts." She hung her head for a moment, her long hair falling over her face.

"Well, if I could access the diagram we took off their computers, that would help," I called to Indigo, still deep in conversation with Luigi.

"Indigo, sorry to interrupt. Can you get the data from Point Roberts up on this screen, please?"

"*Un momento, comandante.*" And that was all it took, and a schematic floated up on the screen. Fay turned to it and pointed.

"This is where the sea water enters the facility, through these massive pipes. As far as we could ascertain, there are no holding tanks.

If there is an overflow it simply returns back to the ocean through this second pipe." I nodded. That made sense. She pointed to three squares lined up in a vertical row labeled 'B-1, B-2, B-3.'

"These are processing buildings, the plant was some sixty feet below our viewing platform, so all we could see was massive pipes and big chunks of things that puffed and spat out steam." I nodded again. It was a very detailed diagram, but it obviously protected the company's IP by offering very little real information that wasn't immediately visible. She pointed to 'B-4, B-5, B-6', also vertical squares on the diagram.

"Building six was the one where we actually saw things coming out of machines, and we could also see the nanomachines flowing along a transparent chute, a silvery sparkly paste sort of thing. We saw the panels heading out a door to a collection area. This was also where they allowed us to photograph the schematics, which were on a large screen attached to the wall." So if I had to guess, the nano-machines were manufactured, assembled, and created; I didn't really know the technical term for their creation in the first three buildings somewhere. I needed a conversation with Amira, who not only understood all the correct terminology but had created the first generation of superbugs. She had also been down off the floor of the Point Roberts plant.

"Thanks, Fay. Carry on with what you were doing before I interrupted you."

"Going to catch a meal with the gang. You should come." I smiled at the invitation. Nothing more I would like to do than relax and decompress with the team, but I had stuff to do and places to be, so I just let her know gently I was going to be busy. She left with a shrug, and soon I was the only person in the room except for Indigo, who was still in deep conversation with Luigi. He flicked his mini shut, and his shoulders gave a huge shrug as he rotated them, obviously getting rid of some stress.

"What's up, Indigo?"

"We have a real problem tracking our terrorists. They are obviously using the technology Abbas had on his plane, which of course, had been stripped out before we could take it over. We know we have a problem, as we scanned his plane while he had the shells on board based on the location of the transponder and got no reading on the shells."

"US Navy or Fay's drones?"

"US Navy, twice. Long contact, over three minutes, we should have been able to read the shells during that period."

"Have you geeks got any idea on how to counter this?"

"Not at the moment. Malcolm and Shami are also on it. We have three teams working very hard, but as yet, no idea how to counter it." That didn't make me happy at all, and he saw that in my face. I was a little tired and not as in control of my emotions as I usually was. And his use of perfect English tipped me off. He was being not only polite but very precise with his report. He was as concerned as I was.

"What's your assessment of Abbas and Badawi?" He looked at me critically, dropped his head in thought, walked to the huffing espresso machine, and made two large mugs, which he brought over to me. We clicked mugs and sat on opposite sides of the small table I had purloined from the lounge of the hotel. I loosened the neck of my shirt, rolled my shoulders, and drew in a big breath, which brought a smile to his rugged face.

"Jessica, you need to take some time off. Remember how the boss would disappear for hours at a time, sometimes for days?"

"But never during an operation." He nodded.

"No, never during an op. You have been trained in psyops (psychological operations), so you know how to identify the personality and behavior aspects of a target and use that information against them. What I read from this whole situation since our very first notification from Israel is a blunt attempt to misdirect us, confuse us, and waste our time and resources."

"Agreed."

"However, you being who you are moved too fast for the terrorists and practically neutralized them before they could get started, even though they had years of planning and set up time. Look at the timing. They only invoked cloaking mechanisms after we had successfully attacked their ships, boats, and planes. And it was Abbas who first managed to disguise what he was doing. However, we never did get a reading on the shells in Turkey, so whatever technology they are using is transportable."

"I get that. How does that help you read the terrorists?"

"What if the plan all along was to let us know about the shells, encourage us to chase them all over the Mediterranean, only to have a backup plan where they get some shells loaded, and then use us as their credentials for whatever their threat is?"

"As in 'Interpol has seized some of these weapons, ask them what damage they could do if you don't give us what we want?'"

"To use one of your American expressions in a nutshell. Pardon the pun."

"Let's get back to the terrorists." He smiled, sipped at his mug, and looked up at me.

"Abbas is a thug. He has been playing terrorist with Hamas for two decades or more, but his reputation is not strong even though he controls some of Gaza. But Arie told us some time ago that not even ISIL or other groups would let them into the controlling clique in that region, so to a certain extent, he is not really connected to the main players on the Strip. Look how quickly everyone believed that a competitive terror group attacked his shed to reclaim the shells. You were there, and what you saw didn't impress you. So I'd give him a 'B-minus' for strategy and tactics, and the ease with which Badawi attacked him in Turkey, took what he wanted, then left, all in just minutes, suggests that of the two, Badawi is perhaps the smartest."

"That doesn't exactly fill me with joy, Indigo. You'll have to do better than that!" He looked at me with a shrewd look, his eyes sparkling in the light.

"Look at Badawi's behavior. Beds down in Ireland, rebuilds a huge ship, jets off to Afghanistan, builds a nano factory, produces thirty-odd shells that we know about, gives Abbas ten to transport to the west, and keeps ten for himself, all lying quietly on his ship waiting to be loaded. Serious work, well planned and executed. Then as we round up Abbas and his shells, suddenly Badawi ups and leaves his ship, taking with him seven shells and heading east. We now know his change in plans was due to getting a better offer from the German industrialist. But what was his original plan?" I must admit, this had baffled me for some time. Badawi had a purpose-built launching system for the shells, a production facility on his ship, and at the time, at least one scientist who could do the work necessary to turn the shells into nuclear weapons.

Why would he abandon his original plan and walk away from the ship, the laboratory, and the launching system? It didn't make sense.

Unless.

"Could it be that Badawi's role was also as a dupe and that he had no planned targets when he moved to the ship from Ireland?"

"More likely, he had not yet been given his targets." I furrowed my brow in thought. This had never occurred to me, but then I had been consumed with the chase, not the motives. Another blindness! I really did have to up my game.

"You're saying, in essence, there is another party in all of this, controlling the traffic, as it were, creating chaos, scaring the hell out of us, and getting us to look in all the wrong places while they do what?" He smiled and nodded, took my empty mug, stood, refilled it from the huffing expresso machine, then returned.

"Commander, Jessica, the Arab and the women first time around had a thirty-to-forty-year plan, underscored by the skills of 'Helen'-Natasha Trotsky, the East German spymaster. The tactics were worked out by two brilliant children building computer games who combined weapons stolen two decades ago with state-of-the-art nanotechnology. Why not look at the possibility that we are again being played by experts, another long game, as part of the original strategy, but with new players and new elements?" I looked at him with my mouth open. I was lost for words. We had just spent days and days, massive resources, and the lives of good people tracking down and removing these shells from circulation, as well as the nuclear material. We had physically involved the Israelis, the Americans, and the Italians; we had badgered the governments of Turkey, Syria, Iraq, Iran, Jordan, Lebanon, Ireland, France, Germany, and the Gaza Strip through their proxy and who knows else, and made a nuisance of ourselves all over the Mediterranean.

Had we been duped? It slowly dawned on me this was a very likely scenario. I didn't feel as stupid as I should have because we had been reacting to a genuine threat. Old security system adage and alarm is an alarm, prosecute it as if it were real; right up there with the famous intelligence community motto, if there is doubt, there is no doubt.

So we had been correct in cleaning up the threat as fast as we could. But if this were a bigger game, we would have been very late to it, we didn't know the rules or the players, and we needed to catch up. And I needed more data on the factories that used the nanomachines.

"Indigo, you have given me cause to think, and I thank you for that. You never did actually answer my question. You have profiled Abbas. How about Badawi?"

"Highly educated playboy playing at the terrorist, using Abbas and Al Bar al Shirak as a cover. My instinct is he wants money, lots of it, and doesn't really care who or how many he has to kill to get it. But there is one important difference between Abbas and Badawi; he has direct contact with the women refugees somewhere. I know we tracked his end of the call; did we get the other?"

"Yes, it was made to and from the United States. Specifically, a little suburb of Roanoke called Cloverdale. The interception was made at a distance. The satellite was off-axis, so the plus-minus distance was around three miles. But now we have it, we will monitor that location for the next call."

"Jessica, my instinct is this goes back to the refugee women. Is there any way we can find out if more of them are behind all this trouble?" I looked at Indigo, my mind winding around all that we had learned in the last three months.

"Okay, I've suddenly had another thought. Have you got the list of the people Amira worked with at Harvey Mudd?" He reflected for a minute, referred to his mini, then looked back up at me.

"Yes."

"Send them to our favorite FBI agent, get her to dig deep on their families, their backgrounds. If they haven't got either, then we have another refugee terrorist." He got busy with his mini, and within a second my mini buzzed.

"Anna, hello, we were just sending you a message." The lovely and very relaxed face of FBI Senior Supervisory Special Agent Anna Bernstein filled my screen.

"Yes, that's why I called. Fill me in."

"Well, we need to trace a number of people who worked with Amira at Harvey Mudd, specifically on the nano bugs. I was hoping you could do a deep dive on that for us as a priority."

"My information here is that you are playing with potential nukes?" I smiled. Such a simple explanation for such a complicated action.

"Yes. But we've just started to unravel what we think is really going on, so we need your help."

"How's Fay doing?" My turn to smile and nod.

"Really excellent. She took to our operational methods like a duck to water. You just can't discount intelligence and willpower. Can't thank you enough for her. She is a real asset."

"Good. Glad she's fitting in. Now, what do you need?"

"Indigo has sent you a list of people who worked with Amira. We need to find the refugees among them. I'm looking for a nano expert. What we are unravelling looks very complex, but it all revolves around the nano bugs we have dealt with before."

"Got the list. I'll start working on it right away."

"Thanks, appreciated. Give Roger our regards."

Indigo had been following my side of the conversation. He gave me a quizzical look, nodded, and smiled.

"I like Agent Bernstein. She's one of your clever girls as well."

"That she is. Okay, what haven't we considered?" Before Indigo could answer, Sandra came back in, looking refreshed and as pretty as ever. I envied her ability to regenerate with such vigor!

"Indigo, you're sacked. Jessica is mine again. Tom and Bob want to see you outside." He bobbed his head in acknowledgement but still managed a huge smile.

"*Comandante, ispettore, vi saluto!*"

"He took the piss!" Sandra bounced up and down, waving her arms around as if chasing flies.

"Well, you both did just impersonate Inspector when you brought in von Speer," I said with a smile. I had a feeling that both she and Fay would be the subject of a lot of jokes over Fay's rapid self-awarded promotion! "Now, what do you want as well as coffee?"

She looked at me critically to see if I was taking the piss and decided I wasn't, so she stopped her windmilling and bouncing, retreated to the espresso machine, poured a mug, then sat down opposite me.

"I've debriefed with Tom and Bob, written it all up, they need Indigo for the same reasons, and it's my turn to babysit you." My smile didn't reach my face. This was something I would have to put an end to. We simply did not have enough people to waste one looking after me. It was as if she had read my mind.

"And before you sack me, the boss called me direct just five minutes ago, looking all gooey and bright in his uniform, specifically reminding me that his instruction was not to be violated for any reason. He had intel that the bounty on you is now up to fifteen million euros. For an old guy, he sure does look good!" I let it sit. Nothing to be gained by fighting it now. I would do it in my own good time. And as for the 'old guy', the boss was just forty or so by my count.

"I've got Anna running down the people who worked with Amira back at Harvey Mudd."

"Looking for nano experts."

"Yes."

"And I'm unpicking the manufacturing process used in Point Roberts, and I'm going to compare it with what Agents Yang, Yarmuth, and Drishya Singh describe at the hangar in Afghanistan. You've given me Point Roberts. I'm about to call the team in Pakistan." She nodded.

"Call Drishya. She went back in with the team and did a very thorough post-inspection, and interviewed a number of the ground and airport staff. She also sent a diagram of their setup, which we can compare to the factory-supplied instructions." I shook my head. I had missed the post-inspection and never considered the factory instructions. My operational blindness was staggering. If I didn't lift my game, I would have to call the boss and get him to appoint someone else to run Section Five. The very thought burned a hole in my gut, and it must have shown because Sandra leaned in and ran her hand up and down my arm.

"Jessica, I only know this because, in the last fifteen minutes, I have been thinking about what you asked me for before the break about Point Roberts, so I followed up with everyone and joined the dots. The reports were as good as filed, no one had seen them, and there had been no communication about them." I took a deep breath. She was absolutely correct, there were millions of details I would never see, so I had to learn to think more critically and faster. I had been sucked into the vortex of finding the shells before they could be turned into nuclear weapons and lost sight of the external picture. A good lesson and I hoped it would be my last big one for the time being. Later, I would ask the boss how he had managed all the data and see what he said, but for now, it was time to get back on the hunt.

"Thanks. Your support counts more than you can know. Okay, back to the task at hand, we find the nano expert; we find out how the nanomachines work; we find Abbas; we find Badawi; what have I missed?"

"We find the missing shells?"

"My money is on them being with either Abbas or Badawi, but I have Fay running searches on this side of the Med and the navy on the other. Have we made any progress on the technology they are using to mask their activities?"

"Not yet. Luigi and Shami tell us they are close but can't tell us how long before we have a solution. I have a suggestion if you want it." I looked at her, nodded, and wondered why she would even ask.

"Remember way back when I was in Chicago, and we had lost the Internet and most of the computational power around the world? The director of the FBI took a suggestion we made to heart, and it produced great results."

"Think old school?"

"Yes, think old school. Boots on the ground. But this time, we need eyeballs on the ocean and on the ground. HUMINT (Human Intelligence). We still rely on the geeks too much. I guess that is partly due to our training and the way we've worked in the past. But I bet someone has seen Badawi's helicopter and Abbas's boat."

"I agree. I've got every station head looking, and Aire had physical assets on both before they split from Turkey. He is now getting deep into the physical, looking up and down the coastline, but so far, no joy." My mini buzzed, so I swiped the image up on the big screen.

"Agent Singh, good morning or good afternoon. How are you?"

"I'm fine, Commander. Thank you for asking. I'm informed you want a report on the manufacturing facility in Afghanistan?"

"Yes, Drishya, if you could please." And a very good hand-drawn image emerged from her covered face and head, a strange transition that caused us to blink in surprise.

"Drishya, just one minute, please. Sandra, can you bring up the factory instructions?" She pulled her mini out, fiddled on the small keyboard, then flicked her screen so that the hand-drawn image sat next to a professional engineering drawing.

"There's not much difference that I can see. There are no inlet or outlet pipes for the seawater in your drawing, Drishya. How did they manage that?" A red line with an arrow appeared over her drawing and circled a box at the very start of the production flow.

"They installed two five-thousand-liter tanks, which they continually filled from tanker trucks. We interviewed one of the drivers, who said they were paid five thousand euros cash for each load, so as you can imagine, they tried to make as many trips as they could, with three drivers to the truck. They commented that the return seawater was left to run out onto the desert floor, which created some headaches for the airport crew. The round trip took them in and out of Pakistan, but they had no issues at the border. It seems that they had been taken care of separately."

"How far do you estimate their round trip was?"

"We plotted it at just over two thousand kilometers. And they had a tanker there every day for six months."

"Thanks, Drishya, excellent work. We'll send you any updates as they come in." Before I could disconnect, Sandra pushed in front of me.

"Drishya, before you go, Sandra here. Rude of me to butt in, but have you secured that plant?" Her smiling face replaced the diagrams, and her eyes lit up.

"Sandra, hi. Hard to do from here, but my boys installed micro cameras before they left, which give us excellent pictures of everything that happens. Plus, we counter-bribed the airport manager, and he will keep us informed."

"Excellent."

"We have one other thing up our sleeve. We let it leak to the local Taliban commander that they were building nukes in his territory, and they were not very happy about that, so we may have an added layer of protection."

"Clever. Thank you, Drishya. Well done." And I shut the connection, and Sandra shut her eyes, and we sat in silence for a moment.

"Badawi may or may not have nuclear material. He may or may not have shells. He may or may not know his ship has been taken and his gold embargoed. But he is expecting a new nanoscientist to arrive somewhere. And we have a ship set identical to the one delivered to Afghanistan sitting in the desert unaccounted for near Al Millihill in Iraq.

"Abbas may or may not have nuclear material; he may or may not have the shells. But he doesn't have a scientist who knows their way around the technology, and his natural habitat is the Gaza Strip. Both of them seem to have cloaking technology. Have I summed it up sufficiently?"

"You've managed to scare the shit out of me if that's what you mean. The thought of Abbas trying to make a nuke in the Gaza sets me vibrating, and not in a nice way!" I smiled; it was something that worried me as well. But Arie had a strong relationship with the Iman, who counselled a number of the terrorist organizations in the Gaza, and he might be able to help us. I'm fairly sure he would not want a nuke in the Gaza. It was already a hotpot of fanatic terrorist activity, with Hamas shelling Israel at every chance and other groups charging border stations at will. It had been going on for sixty years and would probably still be going on in another sixty.

"You know, if we're correct in our assumptions about a broader attack, and the activity we are seeing right now is to distract us, is a beard, I start to wonder if those shells can actually be exploded."

"Where in the hell did that come from?" She erupted, vibrating from head to toe. She was, after all, a battery bunny in human form! I just smiled at her with a sheepdog look on my face, largely to see how she would react. To my surprise, she suddenly stopped dead still, her arms right across her stomach. Slowly they started to wave back and forwards as if she was compressing something with her hands. She looked at me with a beatific smile, her whole body slightly vibrating again.

"You're not just a pretty face wrapped in a dangerous body. Strategically, if I were the women terrorists, playing with the likes of Abbas and Badawi, given how badly the infamous 'Shetani' got out of hand, that's exactly what I'd do. Design a simple technological marvel that wouldn't actually detonate as a nuclear bomb. Brilliant! All threats but no bang for your buck. I wonder if that's what they did?" I stood, stretched, rolled my shoulders, and dialed up Amira.

"Hi. I was just thinking about you. I hear you're looking for a nano expert?" I smiled into the camera lens. Amira had her long hair up in some sort of twisted tornado bun, which increased her already impressive height by six or seven inches.

"Yes. Do you want to freelance?"

"Depends on the Terms and Conditions. And thank you, by the way, for arranging for the stipend I lost when we froze all the terrorist bank accounts to be paid out of the confiscated funds. My family and I appreciate it." I had forgotten all about that. Part of the conditions she negotiated when she was, what, sixteen or seventeen? Was a payment the equivalent of $2,000 USD made in favor of her parents. It had been paid by the terrorist banker, Mohammad bin Azaria, right up until we froze the Sovereign Wealth Fund, but Arie, at the boss's request, had arranged for the Israeli government to take it over. They, in turn, had collected and kept billions of euros from what we took off Shetani's terrorist groups.

"No sweat and I mean that. You have more than made up for the things you did before you joined us, and everything you did was stunning and for the right reasons. Now, nano expert of mine, I have a question for you. Will those shells actually detonate?" She looked confused, shook her head, and looked at me with wide-open eyes. "Of course, they will. As I said previously, smash the bulb nose into something solid at eighteen hundred meters a second, and boom!"

"Have you tested one?" She looked shocked as if I had challenged her credentials.

"I ran tests on the material, calculated the density, the porosity, and the velocity required to break the bulb off and smash it into the membrane and through the two chambers. My calculations are not wrong!" She was as fired up as I had ever seen her, but I held my line.

"Amira, no one is doubting your calculations, but do us a favor and go physically smash one into something and tell me if it works as advertised, please." She looked flustered and ran her hands through her hair several times, disturbing the big bun, which exploded into a hair fall that partially hid her face.

"I will do as you ask immediately." Her clipped voice fading as she clicked off, still angry at me for doubting her. She was a pure genius, her work was several generations ahead of anything created anywhere in the world, and all done five years ago before she turned twenty-five. But the women terrorists had taken her work and bastardized it for their own purposes, albeit in the first instance to create massively powerful solar panels and power packs, which the world was slowly inculcating into its infrastructure fabric as we climbed out of the economic and emotional hole the terrorists had deliberately thrown us into.

The second iteration was a little more aggressive, as it attacked oil, gas, and coal, turning them into silver slag and removing them from use forever.

The third iteration of her brilliant work on nanomachines had been used to fabricate capable nuclear shells out of a new substrate of copper and brass. And nanomachines were used in opening and closing the shells, which then created an undetectable nuclear weapon with the explosive equivalence of one thousand five hundred tons of TNT.

Then an odd thought popped into my head like a rice bubble exploding in warm milk. Snap, crackle, pop!

I suddenly remembered what had happened to the ship sets in Japan, those that had been sent to specific destinations in Canada, Greenland, Chile, Portugal, Ireland, Denmark, Norway, Finland, Estonia, Sri Lanka, Solomon Islands, New Zealand, Japan, and Iceland. The US had taken three or four to install on the east coast. The others still on the dock had been frozen where they were when we took over Innomatchi. The women terrorists were super smart, all genius level at the very least, so it wasn't fanciful to imagine that they had a behavioral specialist on their team who might have anticipated America's reaction to the Japanese company and its amazing manufactured ship sets.

And the pain caused by the terrorist attacks, Internet and computer denials, and loss of carbon-based fuels had created for the American population. Yes, it had happened all over the world, but America was still the big dog on the block, and as altruistic as the government may or may not be, it was always going to be 'get our house in order first' and then worry about the rest of the world.

Maybe this was the real motive behind all the devilment we were currently experiencing. America had, after all, derailed a significant part of their plan.

But how to find out? How to contact them and establish a dialogue? I called Nokomoto, floated my idea with him, then let him get on with it.

We had so much outstanding information to collect I started to wonder why I was here, in the hotel, that was, and I remembered it had been to wait for Abbas to appear in Gaza somewhere. Was that now valid? I looked at Sandra-just call me 'Sally', comfortably sitting across her chair with her booted feet hanging over one edge, playing with her mini.

Fay walked back in, headed straight for the expresso machine, filled her mug, came to us, and sat next to Sandra, who raised her eyebrows in welcome.

"Crapped out with the drones, and the Navy has the same null result. The shells are not in our immediate area, or they are, and we can't see them. I've put the drones in long holding patterns, covering Gaza and all the way up to the Syria/Turkey border, with one drone in the air at all times. The Navy is still focusing on the northern coastline and blockading the entrance to the Med." I looked at Fay, who was showing signs of being stressed. Hunting something as potentially dangerous and serious as nukes and not being able to find them tended to wear you out.

I made a snap decision.

"Sandra, get Indigo to move us to Venice, Tom and Bob's teams to link up with the C-17, and Indigo's to come with us. Ask Arie if I can drop in on him on the way back and ask him if we could arrange a teleconference with General Saunders and the directors of the FBI, NSA, and CIA. Ask that they include the admiral we're working with within the Med." I got a quizzical look from her, but she bounced up as if she had been sitting on a spring, opening her mini.

"Yes sir, ma'am, commander, Jessica, at once!" I just smiled, happy to have her back at her sarcastic best.

# Milk Factory

From the air, it looked totally harmless, the big lake surrounded by the dense stubby and gnarled trees a sudden contrast to the surrounding bland and monotonous colors of the desert. Apart from a small ramshackle shepherd's hut off one end, the nearest building was over one hundred kilometers away to the west. The sheep and goat herders were genuine and had been using the lake for the past two decades without issue. But if you got one alone, away from his family, in a trustworthy environment, they would confess to you that the entire area gave them the 'spooks' as they described it.

Strange sounds from under the desert floor, stinky bursts of bubbles in the lake, rotten piles of vegetation floating around the shores, moved randomly by the wind until they washed up and discolored the sand to the point where the herders couldn't risk letting their flocks drink at those points.

But it was the only water source for hundreds of kilometers, so they put up with it, and dealt with things as they came.

One hundred meters under the surface of the lake lay a massive tri-level factory, clean and abandoned twenty-four years previously. On the bottom level, six massive Level Four bio-secured laboratories sat back-to-back, each filled with limp space suits that were both radiation-proofed and impervious to any bacteria or germ known to mankind. The room was kept at a chilled 14 degrees centigrade, and fans pushed air around the rooms in a deliberate pattern that forced-fed the HEPA particle filters installed in every corner. The submarine-like door, five centimeters thick, separated the corridor from the entranceway, where the double door of a massive lift waited. It went down one level to a small nuclear power plant and up to the other two floors, then stopped against a thick concrete roof that covered an area of ten football fields.

The middle floor was full of machines, benches, negative pressure, laminar flow rooms and laboratories, and high-tech equipment from centrifuges to particle separators. In one corner, a massive electron microscope waited patiently for someone to use it again, silently reporting its condition to a massive supercomputer tucked away against one wall every five minutes. The only light came from the constant flickering of the colored liquid diodes that covered almost every square centimeter of the computer.

The top floor was designed to house the staff, with a massive cafeteria with a centralized kitchen that would make any five-star restaurant proud, huge cold rooms and storage areas, and two massive lounge rooms that could comfortably hold sixty people each, and small, but comfortable motel-like private rooms each with their own bathroom facilities.

At its peak, the facility had been home to over one hundred scientists and support staff and had been the best-kept secret for over five decades of conflict with the western world. Once the topside infrastructure of the milk factory had been destroyed, access to the underground facility had been restricted to just a few technicians each year who came in to do the maintenance and keep the nuclear reactors running. The lake was no accident. It was the cooling pond.

The entrance was well-disguised and some five kilometers away and led to a long-running tunnel that had a rail-sled fitted inside. Massive fans pushed air along the corridor with a sound that was reminiscent of a fighter jet.

The colonel who managed the rotating teams ensured the ongoing security by having the technicians posted to the furthest locations imaginable in Iraq, where if they were lucky, they served out their time in the military, but sadly, most we killed in unfortunate accidents that seemed to follow the technicians like an ominous dark cloud from the time they left the facility. All in all, only three of the two hundred technicians who had ministered to the facility and its unique machinery were still alive, and in a quirk of fate that was harder to believe than a comic book, the colonel and his entire staff were assassinated on the same day earlier in the previous year, supposedly by Israeli commandos.

Israel vehemently denied any such action, and the Central Iraq Government postured and protested to their fullest extent, but no proof was ever found to enable blame to be laid at anyone's door. As if by coincidence, all the drawings, schematics, plans, photos, and reports gathered over fifty years while the facility had been built in secret, floor by laborious floor, also disappeared one day after the colonel and his staff met their gruesome end. The bomb that had taken out all twenty of his staff had been so powerful that it had levelled the three-story barracks attached to his office and a motor garage off to one side. Ninety-seven other soldiers had been killed at the same time, and the inspectors from the directorate of military affairs concluded that that attack had been targeted, successful, and annoying.

Annoying because central command had made it its business for the last twenty years to know and record nothing about the facility, adding credence to their public denials that Iraq had any sort of nuclear program. After thirty years of on-again, off-again sanctions, two massive invasions by the US-led coalition, and the constant threat to their peace and tranquility, the Iraqis, apart from desperately wanting to bomb Israel back to the stone age, had concluded that any nuclear program was too risky and fraught with difficulty, especially with the Chinese and Pakistanis sniffing around offering any type of nuclear weapons they wanted, from long-range missiles to airborne cruise missiles and bombs, just for the cost of a little 'accommodation'.

Of course, the terrorist attacks just months ago had put a stop to that, and Iraq, like so many countries in the region, was overrun with refugees, and civil unrest, the lack of fuel, gas, and oil brought most of the infrastructure to its knees. The economy crashed, and the political and military power base was seriously threatened from the inside for the first time in years.

The milk factory had been destroyed for all the world to see. It was dead, as were all and any who had ever set foot in its airconditioned white-walled corridors.

Except for two men and one woman. The woman was a refugee from Sudan, trained in France as a nuclear physicist, where she was moved to as a girl. Her name was Maribelle Assiano. She was now just thirty-three years old, was now also an expert in nanotechnology, ran marathons, lifted her own weight with ease, stood one-meter ninety-eight centimeters (six feet five inches) in her bare feet, spoke six languages, and at the moment was in love with a rock star who she had seen on the cover of a record cover six months ago.

She had one purpose in life, and that was to see her sisters' plan carried out to fruition and the refugee children cleared out of the camps around the world once and for all.

She lived with another refugee woman, tiny in comparison. She had moved to the United States at the age of nine, studied human behavior and psychology at both Medical Doctor and Ph.D. levels, and at just nineteen years of age, published a paper on how to change the beliefs and attitudes of large groups of people which stood to this day as the epitome of smart thinking on this subject. Rena Niele and Maribelle had lived together for six years, had their own independent source of funds thanks to the Sovereign Wealth Fund and Mohammad bin Azaria, had the benefit of working with and learning from 'Helen' for three years, and then had been on the fringes of everything that had been planned and executed by the female terrorists and the mercenaries from day one.

But not involved. Their mission was to see that the original plan of using the environmental ship sets manufactured by Innomatchi was distributed to the nineteen countries identified as perfect locations for the migration of large numbers of children and also ensure that additional ship sets were manufactured and shipped as required until every child had a new home, and new hope!

And hope was what they would give them, come hell or high water.

# Chapter Thirty-Nine

"On this call are general Saunders, White House, general Rosenberg, Sin Bet (Retired), directors Julius Bronstein CIA, Frank Reynolds NSA, Roger Winslow FBI, Colonel Kashasini, Interpol, Colonel Borowitz Israeli Intelligence, Anna Bernstein SSSA, FBI, Malcolm Tannery NSA, Interpol Inspector Sandra Thomas, Agents Fay Remer, Nokomoto Senji, Drishya Singh, and observing from Lyon Inspector General P J Anthony, Interpol. Thank you all for your time." I looked at the big screen, where everyone had their own little box, their name, and their rank listed below. "Those of you using minis will only have the current speaker on your screens, but you have a list of participants in a sidebar you can access when you need to. Questions?"

The president's general, Bridget Saunders, looked slightly amused, but otherwise, most were just playing calm, looking intently at their cameras, trying to give nothing away. There were no questions. Yet.

"I'll start with a very short summary; we have sent you each a data package with full details, or as full as we are prepared to share at this point, for your consideration following this meeting.

"In the past fourteen days, with the help of Israeli Intelligence, the US Navy, commando units from Italy and Israel, and computer experts from both sides of the Atlantic, we have been able to take twenty-two nuclear-possible shells out of circulation.

"A pair of gentlemen by the names of Malik Badawi and Amir Abbas, who head terrorist organizations identified as Hamas and Al

Bar al Shirak, are our prime suspects in this activity. During the first series of terror bombings three months ago, you may remember two automated attacks on Israeli supermarkets. We believe that one or both of these persons, using technology developed by the women terrorists, were responsible for both.

"They have now gone to ground, somewhere in the Middle East, using technology far beyond their capabilities, one in a boat, one in a helicopter, and we believe they may be chasing down the two shells we have not yet recovered. They both may have nuclear material, but we can't confirm that.

"However, thanks to the geek squad, we intercepted a call from Badawi talking to a new player, one 'Maribelle Assiano', who we believe to be another of the refugee women. He called to request a new scientist. It appears he lost the one he had previously, one Siobhan O'Cleary, who was also a refugee woman, brought up in Ireland with dense credentials in nuclear physics and nanotechnology. We have established this Assiano is most likely one of the woman terrorists due to her background having been entirely scrubbed." The director of the CIA signaled he had a question.

"Yes, Julius?"

"Jessica, how do you explain we apparently have full details on the Irish-woman, Siobhan O'Cleary, but not on the latest scientist?" I nodded; I had been anticipating this question.

"Julius, I will explain our current theory in just a minute. The answer to that question speaks to the hypothesis I hope to present to you all." He waved me on, not rudely, but firmly, which for no reason I could fathom, gave me confidence in what I was about to say.

"The FBI is tracking one end of that call, and we followed up on this end, but Badawi had gone by the time we got boots on the ground. Anna, do you have anything on that end, please?"

"No, Jessica, we have scanned the entire area around Roanoke, not just where the signal was tracked to in Cloverdale, and we found nothing. However, we have parked sensor-equipped vehicles in a two-hundred-mile area, so if he or she calls again, we will locate her." I nodded, it was what we had expected from our analysis, and we had more, but it was part of what we were holding back to keep everyone focused on the big picture.

"Thank you, we expected that. So, to summarize, we have two known terrorists with nuclear bomb-making matériel, 2 shells in an unknown location, and a nuclear physicist about to join one of the terrorists-we presume, to assist him in completing a nuclear shell." I let the silence speak for itself, this was still an untenable situation by any standards, and no one on this call had any doubt about the potential danger of two nuclear bombs that could not be detected.

"Okay, I feel that I have your attention." Several people smiled, grinned, or just grimaced, but the tension I had let build up diminished as I intended. I needed every one of these experts on their game if we were to win this asymmetric battle. "You will remember the Japanese company, Innomatchi, who manufactured the environmental ship sets for the terrorists. What you don't know is that they also manufactured the equipment and nanomachinery that was established in Afghanistan to build the thirty-odd shells that we know about. We tracked the second shipment of similar machinery some eighteen months ago to a location in Iraq." Now some of the faces hardened. That was the only way I could describe it, eyes narrowed to slits, mouths compressed, and an almost feral look on their faces.

"Where in Iraq?" General Saunders asked the question on everyone's lips so quietly I almost missed her question.

"Al Millihil."

"What in God's name is in Al Millihil?" Roger asked, a seriously confused look on his face.

"Nothing we can find at the moment, just a lake, lots of stubby trees, goats and sheep, and a few locals who seem to live in a little hut at one end of the lake." I waited to see if anyone would remember, then general Saunders leaned forward.

"Not your best work, Julius, or yours, Frank, although both of you were probably still in nappies. It was the location for the most famous milk factory on the planet." Both directors looked horrified. The intelligence failure was one of the biggest at the time, only to later be surpassed by 9/11.

"No sign of the factory now?" general Saunders asked.

"No. It was destroyed back in 2001, the central government grew tired of the innuendos and constant sniping by the US, EU, the UN, and they use it as a means of getting concessions on the embargoes we had all placed on them."

"So where did this machinery end up?"

"The addressee is nonexistent. It happened eighteen months ago we have had no overfly or satellite footage of the area for several years, no one in the system has any relevant data, and it's disappeared like so many of the terrorists' toys so often do."

"You believe this machinery has been or will be, set up somewhere in the Al Millihil area?"

"Yes, general, I do. And that brings me to point two of this briefing and an answer to your earlier question, Julius. But first, I'd like you all to look at these pictures and graphics and tell me what you see in them." And all the heads disappeared, to be replaced by screenshots of the original message from the Irish bulletin board, photos of the ship Badawi had modified, photos of the shells, and shots were taken of each capture, both on land and on the ocean. Each shot was time/date coded, with the location, details, and outcome, including fatalities and wounded. The presentation took just under eleven minutes, and each user could speed it up or slow it down at will. A little counter on my screen told me who was doing what, and it took no time at all to see lots of slowing and backwards and forwarding of certain images. The eleven minutes turned into twenty.

"Jessica, what I see is a brilliantly coordinated rolling series of strikes over a thousand miles or so and an integration of different skills and tactics that will make for a great lecture sometime. What I don't see is the point." I let the screen revert back to the headshots and noticed several people were now holding conversations off to the side with their support staff. I had to get their attention back to me, so I hardened the tonality of my voice.

"General, one question. Are you bothered by the threat of these shells?" Several heads shot around, all looking at their cameras with worried expressions on their faces. She held my gaze for a full minute before answering. Next to me, Indigo, Sandra, and Fay had tensed, staring into their minis as if ready to defend me. It had been their idea and brilliance to put the slide show together, thinking correctly that showing the photos would be a much more poignant statement and a faster method of making our point than just telling them about it.

"Yes, it does worry me. The threat appears to be real, you have fought and lost soldiers in these fights, and the behavior of Badawi and Abbas is that of dedicated terrorists following an agenda of some importance. At least to them."

"Thank you for that, and that is the whole point of this attack; we believe it is a feint, a beard, a tactic to get us looking in one direction while the terrorists work in another. The question in my mind has always been, why? Why would the women, having been so utterly successful the first and second time around, suddenly create a threat that would kill any sympathy for their cause that may have started to develop in the community?" I let that sit, gave them all breathing space to absorb what I had just said, then answered Julius's question.

"And the reason you have O'Cleary's detailed background and credentials, and nothing on the other is as simple as establishing their credentials for the level of threat they are posturing."

"Well, it worked. Now tell us what you think is really happening." She looked glum, unhappy, almost distressed, and I shared her fear, for what I was going to lay out for them was a huge step above simple untraceable nuclear weapons, a whole lot more complex and complicated.

"I have agents Fay Remer, Sandra Thomas, Nokomoto Senji, Drishya Singh, and Amira Abramowitz on this call to answer any specific questions you may have of them going forward, as each has played a significant part in putting all this together. Let me lay out a hypothesis.

"Firstly, the shells we have intercepted and still hunt for were never meant to explode." Every face except Arie's, the boss's, and my people goggled as their minds recoiled from first fearing an atomic attack, then suddenly hearing someone tell them it was just a huge bad joke. General Saunders practically jumped down my throat.

"Explain!" the edge to her voice was pure command, and I imagined many a soldier under her watch had their balls shrivel up at the sound of her bark.

"The shells cannot be exploded once loaded." The silence was profound. You could have cut it with a blunt knife. Beside me, Sandra started to vibrate, her face almost splitting with a smile, which she quickly hid with a polite cough. I elbowed her in the ribs. The last thing I needed now was my side looking anything but deadly serious. And this was as serious as it got under the conditions we were now all living under.

"Amira, would you please explain."

"General, it is my fault we only learned of this earlier today. When we reclaimed the shells, we studied them like we would any new discovery and pursued the nano implications to their fullest. The nano bugs are a derivation of my original work, much further advanced, but certainly, in the general area, we were experimenting in. The nanomachines were not only used to construct the substrate, but they have to be used to open and close the shells for loading. That gives them their impermeability and makes it impossible to track them using Giger counters or other radiation detection devices." Once again, silence reigned supreme, and I let it flow for a minute to once again let everyone comprehend what Amira was saying.

"It was only when Commander Riley insisted we test the shells physically as they were designed to be fired, that is, at a velocity of eighteen hundred meters per second, into something solid, that we observed the physical characteristics under test conditions did not match our theoretical work."

"And?" Amira had the good grace to look a little embarrassed, but how could I reprimand her for being tunnel blind over the science when I had been just as blind several times during this case? We would all learn from this lesson, and thankfully, it was a critical one in building my case.

"The nose bulb did not sheer as expected. It simply snapped off at the neck. Nothing penetrated the chambers of the membrane, and we proved this with four other tests. Once sealed, the shells cannot be exploded by any means we are aware of."

"Thanks, Amira, your thoroughness is appreciated." Arie put his hand up, and I noticed again how frail he had become over the last few weeks. I mentally shook my head. I needed his experience and wisdom for the next steps in my plan, even though he didn't know that yet.

"General, we independently tested two shells here in Israel, also at the request of commander Riley, and can confirm Agent Abramowitz's findings." She nodded, went into deep thinking mode, turned her head to one side, and fired a question at me like a rocket-propelled grenade.

"Does this mean you will stop looking for the other two shells?"

"No, general, it does not. They, Badawi and Abbas, are on the top of our 'to-do' list." She gave me a frosty stare, still thinking at a million miles an hour. I could see the action going on behind her gray eyes.

"So, your hypothesis?" I smiled to indicate I was not taking her blunt manner personally, she was just a general. I understood that, and to a certain extent, she needed to maintain her position relative to the directors of the NSA, CIA, and FBI, being a woman in a man's world and responsible for representing the military view of the world to her president.

"Proof of life."

"Explain!" Sharp and to the point, and I noticed that every head was paying close attention to their screens.

"I prove to you that I can make a nuclear capable undetectable bomb, let two known terrorists spread them around the Mediterranean almost in the open, but leave enough breadcrumbs around so we can find them, engage with them, have some success in reclaiming the shells, and all the time we are proving to ourselves that a genuine threat exists, and the elements are particulate nano machined shells, nuclear material, and a launching system that fits the assumed specifications. What is the outcome?"

"We believe there is a credible threat."

"Yes, and we all do, don't we?" This time the silence was underscored by a lot of worried looks.

"Alright, yes, we do. So what's next?" Now I needed to sell the other elements of my hypothesis, none of which I could yet prove.

"I suggest there is a second shell manufacturing plant, probably in Iraq, under the control of the women, running or not as yet to be proven, but certainly able to manufacture dirty bombs that will work this time and can be used in a massive worldwide blackmail attempt. And the motive is simple, and I suggest we do something like this; restart manufacturing in Japan by freeing up Innomatchi; cancel the Red Notices on the terrorist funds secured in the USA, Canada, Greenland, Chile, Portugal, Ireland, Denmark, Norway, Finland, Estonia, Sri Lanka, Solomon Islands, New Zealand, Japan, and Iceland, and allow them to be used for building the environmental sites as originally planned, then build the towns using the panels and power packs, all of which is within the number of funds that have been provided.

"And?" Not so sharp now, she was getting the picture I was painting, possibly all too clearly.

"And allow the migration of the refugee children as managed by Red Crescent, Red Cross, or Médecins Sans Frontières also as originally planned, to their time-table, without further interference."

"Is that all?" I looked at the general's face on the screen, it had hard edges to it, but her eyes were still bright and signaled she was fully engaged and working furiously on the consequences of what I was outlining.

"For now. I fully expect a new set of demands to double or even triple the number of environmental ship sets, we have over twelve million refugee children around the world, and I can see how they might want to migrate all of them at some point.

"Well then, you'll just have to find them and stop them, won't you?" And she disconnected, closely followed by her three directors, albeit with sheepish looks on their faces. Anna stayed on, as did everyone else.

"Thank you all. Please read the data we have sent to you, and for the next few hours, we will be available to answer any questions you may have. Anna, you have a question?" She smiled, and I felt the warmth all the way over the Atlantic.

"No, not particularly, but in view of your hypotheses, I think you may need updates on Helena, Roanoke, and Dargaville."

"Go for it, lovely idea. It's not as if we have forgotten, but we have been a little busy this side of the Atlantic." She smiled, nodding in agreement.

"Helena is the most advanced due to all the underground infrastructure that had been established five years before the attacks. If you remember, the benefactor's plan was to build a housing estate of some thousands of homes and infrastructure. Essentially all we have to do now is ship the panels and power supplies from Point Roberts, build the houses, schools, shopping centers, etc., then let the people who have migrated to that area agree to the terms of the contract and settle in. Around one thousand refugees arrive every twenty days. It's like a train of boats, all converted cruise liners, mostly put out of business by the Covid pandemic three years ago.

"They are shipping teachers, health care workers, managers and administration staff all from the camps, and of course linguists, although everyone who steps off the boats has a working knowledge of English and American history. In one sense, it is a magnificent plan, and the detail behind it is astonishing."

"Are you seeing any difficulties with the children settling in?" Anna's face took on a frown, quickly cleared, then went back to a full-on smile.

"Initially, we thought there would be issues, the first one being only around eighty thousand families had migrated into the area up to one month ago; however, there is now a constant stream of around one to two thousand families a week pouring in, all looking for a new home, and stability. Our psychologists believe the shock of the past three months, the chaos and uncertainty, huge death tolls, and civil unrest, has forced people to think small, Maslow's hierarchy, food, water, shelter, society, and family. And when you look at the terrorist offer, it's not a bad one by any means."

"What's the story in Roanoke?"

"A little different. No infrastructure originally, but the plans had been approved, they are just waiting on the Federal Government to provide the funding, which they now have, and work is progressing at warp speed. The president has made it a cornerstone of our recovery program and invited cities and towns from all over the country to apply for the same benefits. As fast as a house goes up, it is occupied, and the first ship of refugees arrived two weeks ago, the same story as for Helena. In many ways, the families are almost too willing to adopt. It's as if they are paying penance for past sins. And we have been informed that a second ship will dock next week, so the terrorists are matching the build rate."

"Which means they have on-the-ground intelligence."

"Yes. We are noticing a lot of highly trained social and medical staff turning up at both locations, almost out of thin air, and yes, we have backgrounded them, and they all have families and histories, and when we question them, all they say is that is what they have waited for all their lives."

"All young women between the ages of twenty and thirty?"

"Close, but no cigar. Twenty-one to thirty-five, so they were in all tranches of the refugees taken by Mohammad bin Azaria and 'Helen'-Natasha Trotsky."

"We know there are refugee women up and down the west coast, and I'd bet that a large number, if not all, of the people coming in as support staff for the refugees now, were also refugees themselves. So, as we thought, they took many more than we originally estimated."

"But we can't, and won't, prosecute them for their backgrounds."

"No, we can't. But we have a new terrorist cell now, one that is playing with nuclear fire, and we can and will prosecute them." She smiled, nodded, then sat back a little, causing the camera to zoom in and out to hold focus. It was an eerie look and reminded me we were thousands of miles away from each other, looking at two-dimensional screens.

"Jessica, I'd expect nothing less from you and your team. Now, are you interested at all in New Zealand?" My turn to smile, and I felt Sandra stiffen up alongside me. She had been the senior agent in charge of the New Zealand 'visit', and had taken a number of the refugee women terrorists into custody-as well as one of the young girls who had programmed the game that delivered the attack strategy for the terrorists.

"Go."

"No obvious initial infrastructure in Dargaville to start, but they had a trust fund set up like all the other potential sites, and there had already been a distribution of funds to companies in the area for sewerage, power, waste management that had been in operation for some five months before the first attack on the Vatican. It was believed to be government-sponsored, so no one outside of the area took any notice. Panels and power packs had been shipped sixteen weeks prior to your arrival at the plant on Great Barrier Island, and some eight hundred houses were completed. After your visit, it all went into high gear, and they now have some three thousand houses, five school and hospitals, shopping centers, reactional parks, and transport hubs. What they were lacking were families to fill the houses." I frowned. It made no sense to build a town with no one to occupy it. What would be the point? I was about to ask Anna when she put some photos up, and I saw the answer.

"They are recruiting families from other towns and cities."

"Yes. Similar offer in Helena. You left the New Zealand SAS in control of the plant. Once the government worked out what was happening, they fully endorsed the plan, let the plant resume but under their management, and made a big deal about it up and down the country. The civil unrest there was quite minor, and the government has always been on the green side of life and very empathetic to migration and immigration." I nodded. Somewhere in the back of my mind, I had been aware of that, but it was lost to me now as I suddenly felt the pressure to get the hunt for our new crop of terrorists underway with a vengeance.

"Thanks, Anna, hope to see you soon." And she disconnected, so I looked around at my Team, the geeks, and spoke to Arie and the boss.

"Arie, boss, if you could please stay on the line, everyone else, thank you, excellent work. We'll catch up again in a couple of hours." I waited patiently as, one by one, my expanded team left the meeting, I elbowed Sandra in the ribs, giving her a hint to make herself scarce, then looked at the image of Arie, looking older than his years, and worn, and the boss, resplendent in a pristine suit, starched white shirt, and blue regimental tie, his hair actually combed. The contrast between mister clean and his usual beach bum look was amazing!

"Gentleman, thank you for your time, and I appreciate you waiting for me just now. There is a potential political issue looming if, in fact, the machinery is in Iraq; without setting the bushes on fire, we will need to have a handle on that fairly soon, I suspect. Boss, I'm counting on you to make that happen. I will want full physical access, total control, legally and practically, and no bitching and moaning to the UN if something should go down. Arie, I will need your intelligence and muscle, and I might need your cruise missiles again. Do either of you have anything for me at this time?" The boss looked serious, said nothing, and shook his head. Arie looked slightly bemused, even entertained, which caught me off guard.

"Jessica, we will, of course, provide anything you need if we can, but when you ask for intelligence, are you asking what I think you are asking?" Now he looked as serious as the boss, and I briefly wondered if I could prevaricate.

One word-no. Not if I wanted Arie behind me all the way to the bitter end.

And I most certainly did. His people had died alongside ours in this mess, and they had more than just their country at stake. Besides, I wanted him to remain as the surrogate grandfather I had never enjoyed.

"Have you now, or have you in the past, any HUMINT in Al Millihill?" His frosty stare confirmed my suspicions, and he just gave a slight nod to the camera, his features giving nothing away, as you would expect after leading the Israeli intelligence world for nearly fifty years.

"We cannot confirm or deny that the Milk Factory episode was decades ago. Most everyone lost interest in it when the Iraqis' blew it up back in 2001."

"Maybe so, but my money is on you. I want a simple chat, it can be anywhere convenient, but I want it now. Please." He looked at me with anything but a grandfatherly smile, nodded sharply, then cut the connection. The boss sat back and looked directly at me.

"Jessica, I can feel where you are going with this, and I agree with your tactics, but remember we need evidence, evidence the world court can act on, not supposition or rumor. If you're thinking of doing what I think you are, you need to be very buttoned up." I gave him my best and most confident smile, feeling anything but disconnected. I slumped in my chair. He was correct. We would have to get hard evidence before we could do anything about the plant, if it existed, and if it were a threat. But I had started to understand the warped, if not brilliant, logic these female terrorists were applying to their 'change the world' project. I was getting a feel for their arrogance, their daring, their cunning, and in truth every genius I had ever met had that creepy 'I know something you don't know' feel about them and the look in their eyes when they stooped to explain something to a lesser mind; what really pissed me off was they were always correct!

But in my gut, I knew the old Milk Factory was in play somehow, the hypotheses I had offered solid, and now it was up to the team and me to prove it and act on it before the world had another problem that was too big for most people to comprehend and fix as in a nuclear attack on an unprecedented scale.

And if that made me arrogant, so be it!

# Homeboy

A mir Abbas had landed on the beach at An Nuseirat in the Gaza Strip. It was where he had started his career in terrorism, graduating with honors. No sooner than his boat had slipped up the shallow shore, hundreds of well wishes and admirers, mostly under the age of fifteen, all carrying AK-47s or cheap Chinese copies, swarmed him. On tough tattooed youth, a scar running from cheek to jowl, a red bandana circling his unruly jet-black dreads, a tattered black sleeveless shirt with a Grateful Dead illustration on the front, moved through the pack and controlled the mob by his very presence. To demonstrate his superiority, he addressed his commander in English, he could have just as easily used Spanish or Russian, but he knew no one in this mob understood English, so he used it to his advantage.

"Imam, welcome back. I have everything ready for you, my *shakhs mutafawiq*, and we have found teachers who can do the work you requested."

"Excellent. You have kept the power pack running as I requested?"

"Yes, Iman and the container you instructed to keep with the boxes has been plugged in at all times." Abbas just nodded, pushing rudely through the shouting throng. A cart followed with a huge battery connected to a long cylinder, and a pair of containers lay alongside the battery, each marked with the ubiquitous black and yellow radiation symbol. A jeep waited, the battery and cylinders were loaded into the rear seat, Abbas into the front, and the youth stood on the footstep, hanging on for dear life as the vehicle spun its wheels and raced off.

High overhead, one of Fay's drones religiously photographed the area, sending its laser detector in a wide arc covering the equivalent of three kilometers. The shell detector didn't ring, but the camera alarm did, causing Fay to interrupt her sandwich when she flicked open her mini. She watched for a full three minutes, then called me into the screen.

"Jessica, no word on the shells, but we have found Abbas's boat. It appears that he has taken the cloaking device with him. All we have is a moving blob of a blur, but it is heading inland somewhere, wait, another blur, larger this time, and the moving blur has merged into it." I signaled to Sandra and Indigo, flicked the image up on the big screen, used the zoom control until I could see the individual faces of people in the crowd that had welcomed the terrorist home, then tracked where the blob had gone, then stopped my scan when the bigger blob emerged from a row of buildings.

"Indigo, best guess address, please," I snapped out, and Indigo pulled up a military aerial view of the area, and very quickly located the area where the blob was, then zoomed in his own shot until we could see the building that was not there in the drone shot. It was squat, two stories high, looked to be in good condition, and in less than a minute, Indigo had the history of the building scrolling alongside the image.

"Ah, this was used as a testing laboratory during the pandemic. It's been vacant for the last year, owned by some Middle Eastern conglomerate, supposed to be a school. I can get the details if you need them."

"Thanks, Indigo, do that but hold the data. I have to think this through."

"What can you do in a bio lab?" Sandra had stood and was now scanning the big screen with an intensity that made me feel warm. She was back, no doubt about it, the emotional turmoil of her getting shot was behind her.

"From what Amira has told us about the loading procedure, you apply the nanomachines to the shells, they open, you load them, you apply the nanomachines again, the shells close up, and you're ready to go."

"So the tricky bit is decanting the nuclear material and loading it."

"Theoretically, yes."

"But wouldn't you need a clean room, radiation protection, and all the equipment that requires to decant and load the shells?" Sandra turned away from the screen, where Indigo had superimposed his hard image over the blob. It was amazing what you could do with computers, it never felt old, and for a minute, I forgot that the wider world had been deprived of all their technology just months ago, with only very small pockets around the world recovered, predominantly government controlled or military.

"Amira believes someone skilled wearing a Level Four bio-suit, with a pair of inert tongs, could make the swap in complete safety. Her observation from the canisters we recovered from the plane in Aleppo is that the terrorists paid for the material to be pre-shaped, as in a long cylinder for the plutonium and a round ball for the Uranium 235. She actually demonstrated a load/unload the day she received the shells and canisters. The two words she used all day were 'brilliant', and 'simple'." I smiled at that. In a way, having a genius accord those two words to your work would be high praise indeed.

"I guess she was impressed."

"She was, right up until you requested a physical test, then she just got pissed."

"Yes, I heard it in her voice. Now, if we theorize that Abbas has the shells and the nuclear material, and is about to load one into the other, knowing what we know, what should we do next?" She looked at me, bouncing up and down on her toes, clenching and unclenching her fists, so maybe her getting shot wasn't all done with, but I'd cope with that if it became necessary.

"My first instinct is to gear up and go kill the bastards. But I can see by the look on your face that's not an option."

"Yet. Remember where that building is."

"The Gaza Strip. So what?"

"Their government, if you can call a bunch of terrorists that are not supporters of Interpol, not members of the UN, and are the sworn enemy of Israel, and on its very best day the Gaza is a powder keg, is just waiting for a reason to go ballistic." She held her hands out in the 'so what' gesture, her fists still clenching and unclenching.

"And your point is?" I gave her a very hard look, but it went unnoticed. She just kept bouncing up and down. I reached out and stopped her bouncing, pushed her into a chair, and crouched down to be at her eye level.

"I know you're still pissed about being shot, and it was Abbas's men who shot us, but we need to remember who we work for and what is required of us. Absolute proof, proof we can take to the world court with confidence, then we can go in and shoot the shit out of anyone and anything we like." She smiled at the thought, nodded, then gave me one of her trademark battery bunnies looks.

"Sorry, Commander, I let it get to me. You're handling this a lot better than I am."

"I've had more practice getting shot!" And I stood, glad to have avoided what I sensed might have developed into a nasty meltdown. I needed all my team on the same page and at their best. This was the single biggest threat we had faced since the original terrorist attacks, and for some reason, I couldn't put my finger on it. We had more momentum back then. Just as I had that thought, my mini buzzed.

"Hi Aire, how are you? Before you go, I have some news for you." I said quickly, scanning his craggy face for signs.

"Jessica, I'm good, capture this data, keep it very tight, and let me know how you go." He paused; I could feel his finger poised over the cancel button.

"I'm sending you a data pack. Forewarned is forearmed." And he went to black, leaving me looking at a screen of type, which I promptly saved, then snapped the lid shut. I considered my options. Sandra was still buzzing slightly, but I knew she would be an asset. Indigo had more experience, but I needed him to anchor the Homeplate, Fay was coming along very nicely and was developing a lovely hard edge, and Tom and Bob were professionals with long experience in the field. I made a quick decision and called Indigo in, holding my hand on Sandra's shoulder to keep her in place.

"Indigo, I need a helicopter ready to leave in twenty minutes with two of your very best. Back of the church, please; relieve Fay from her overwatch on the drones, and send her back. Briefing in five."

"*Certo, comandante, subito!*" Now I had something tangible to do and somewhere to do it. I made a quick call to the boss, got his busy signal, and left a brief voice mail, which I knew he would act on immediately.

# Chapter Forty

Arie Rosenberg had a problem. Technically, he was retired from the leadership of Sin Bet (Shabak), one of Israel's prime intelligence agencies. Technically, he had been reinstated without a title but with unilateral power to prosecute the terrorists that had blown up the Dome of the Rock and the Western Wailing Wall nearly three months ago. During the attacks that followed, there had been two incursions by robotized vehicles on supermarkets close to the Gaza border, which had indiscriminately killed over a thousand people, both Arab and Jew, and mostly women and children.

He had negotiated an immediate Peace with an Iman he knew and respected, who had influence with the terror groups that made the Gaza strip home. By choosing not to retaliate with bombs and rockets, a modicum of peace had been maintained, and since that time, he had made it a habit to have a coffee with the Iman on either side of the border at least once a fortnight to keep him abreast of the latest developments. Indeed, before Israeli troops dressed as Arab terrorists under the command of Jessica Riley had reclaimed the two shells Abbas had hidden in small electric trucks in northern Gaza, Arie had met with the Iman and explained what would be done and why.

He just hadn't mentioned the who or the when.

The fact that the attack had been concluded just before they met did not take any shine off the conversation, as the Iman understood only too well the dire consequences for him and his people of having nuclear weapons found in the Gaza. They would be annihilated, totally and completely, and the world would silently cheer.

Now, with this new threat, as yet not proven but with a very high probability factor, Arie had to find a way to let the Iman know about the possibility of extreme danger without triggering any pre-emptive action. He gave it some thought as he walked into the secret and heavily secured laboratory that Amira had made her own. After passing three inspection points, using both his thumb and facial recognition, and lastly, a voice command, he ducked his head under the hard edge of the submarine-style bulkhead door, which closed behind him with a long 'hisssssssssss'.

"Mr. Rosenberg, good to see you again, sir."

"Relax, Amira, I'm not here to give you grief. I need your input on something." She looked up from the electron microscope she was using, moved what she was working on to a small box-like chilled storage facility, turned the microscope off, spun around on her stool, took off her protective gloves, and put her long-fingered delicate hands into the pockets of her white smock. Her shoulders slumped; she was obviously still irritated by her mistake of not testing the physical attributes of the shells earlier. He smiled, put one hand on her shoulder, and rubbed some of the tension away.

"Amira, what you're doing here is a miracle. What you have done is miraculous and a great achievement. The fact that your brilliant work has been taken by the terrorists and used against us is not your fault. Besides, if you think about it, the use of the nanomachines in making the panels and power supplies is a fantastic use of the technology and is helping to make a real difference in our recovery from the attacks." She looked very young, tired, and deflated. She looked up at him from under her long lashes, her face a mirror of confusion.

"How can I help?" Her voice was shallow as if she had only used a small part of her lungs to push the words out.

"Look at this photo." He held out a large glossy color photo of a power plant, obviously underground and very small, using the size of the pallet loader in the shot as a reference. She pulled the photo over to a projector and threw the image up onto a huge electronic screen that ran across the wall behind the microscope.

"It's a small nuclear power plant, probably around one-megawatt output.

Where is it?"

"In a facility we are interested in. How long could this run for, and how much maintenance would it require?"

"Over a hundred years, and as you can see here, the rods have been pulled, so according to this gauge," and she pointed to a meter on the control panel in the photo, "it's only dribbling out about five hundred watts, enough to maintain any electronic equipment, lights, air-conditioning, small appliances. As for maintenance, very little, probably a visit every five years to check for the integrity of the facility. It's more than likely that the aircon would break down before this plant would."

"Could this plant produce the material needed to make a nuclear bomb?"

"Absolutely. All you need is plutonium, which is a natural byproduct of this type of facility, and uranium 235, which has been used as a source for generations. If you're asking me if the material we took off the terrorists was made here, unless this plant is in France, then no, it didn't."

"The containers we took at Aleppo came from France?"

"Yes, every manufactured nuclear material has a signature, and that signature is registered with the Atomic Energy Commission, and Interpol." He nodded his head as if she had said something he agreed with.

"Thanks, Amira, that's very helpful. I'll let you get back to your work." Just as he spoke, three white-coated technicians came in, flushed with success, but as soon as they registered the old spymaster, they froze in place, their hands behind their backs. Arie turned to them, smiled, bobbed a short bow, then left the laboratory. They waited until he had cleared the pressure lock, then exploded into action again, flocking around Amira.

"You were correct. We ran test after test, and your idea was absolutely correct!" She looked at her interns, all as young and as bright as she had been at their age, smiling faces radiant with discovery, vibrating bodies alive with the promise of world-shattering work, and to a man and a woman, madly in love with this princess of the nanoworld.

"Have you documented this yet?" The leader, a tall, thin African woman with a head full of tiny woven dreads, shook he head.

"No, ma'am, we'll do that now." Amira smiled, happy for their discovery but unhappy with the professional blindness that had prevented her from testing the shells physically until she had been asked to by Jessica.

She'd get over it, but it would take some time.

Arie, having his worst fears confirmed, climbed into the waiting helicopter, looking like he had aged twenty years in the last twenty minutes. He mulled over what Amira had said, opened his case and, pulled out more photos, scanned them, then shrugged his shoulders. He looked out the windows at the ground speeding quickly below them, noticing that the built-up area had succumbed to the inevitability of the desert and that rolling sand dunes bereft of any sign of human contamination looked peaceful and serene, and he wished his mood could mirror the vista.

The camouflaged helicopter, which had been shadowed by a pair of long-range drones, both loaded with air-to-air and ground-pounding Hellfire missiles, landed softly in the sand, unremarkable in that it looked like every other bit of sand as far as the eye could see. As if in a coordinated ballet, two other helicopters landed alongside, their blunt noses pointing in different directions. The rotors wound down to ground idle, the whap-whap sound synchronizing in the strange way that all physical objects did, and as he stepped out, bending and holding his hat on his head, two women exited one of the helicopters, a solitary man from the other.

Arie moved out of the turbulent rotor wash, then waited for the others to join him.

"Jessica, Sandra, this is my agent 'Hamish.' He will answer any questions you have, and in this briefcase are the photos we have on file of the facility. I must emphasize that this meeting never took place, and nothing discussed here or in this briefcase can ever appear anywhere electronically.

"Physical records only?"

"Physical records only."

"Hamish, I'm Commander Riley, and this is Inspector Thomas. We're both from Section Five, Interpol. Thank you for risking your safety in meeting us."

"General Rosenberg said it was critical to our survival, and I would have come anyway if I had seen photos of your both." His cheeky smile only added to the humor, and not for the first time, I wondered at the incredible courage and dedication a deep cover agent would have to have.

"Thank you, in any case, can you tell us about the current condition of this plant and where exactly it is?" A huge smile lit his face, which was the color of tempered chocolate, his red and white checkered shemagh held in place with a beautiful embroidered blue headband framing it, which moved slightly back and forwards from the rotor wash.

"I though you would ask that, and I have a hand-drawn map for you, apologies for the running ink. We tend to use whatever comes to hand where I'm presently located. If you use a military survey map of the area, circa 1999, USA Cartographer Series 554, and overlay this, you will get your location. As for its current condition, as of my last visit, which was some two years ago now, the power plant was in low idle, but everything in the factory and accommodation levels was in working order."

"Why were you there?" He looked puzzled, probably anticipating that Arie has given us some detail about his activities.

"I was part of the regular, as in every three to five years-maintenance crew that is taken in to ensure everything still works." I nodded, having read a top-secret report that made this assumption about a number of plants and factories hidden around Iraq, but typical for the period of the information, it was heavy on supposition and low on facts.

"How is it guarded?"

"There is a small nomad camp three kilometers from the entrance, and the guards rotate out every twelve months as they get really bored with nothing to do. They walk foot and camel patrols that cross the line I have indicated on the map, effectively blocking any approach, at least in daylight."

"No NVG? (Night vision gear)."

"No. Low-rent guards, probably doing it for the food and pocket money, more than likely conscripts. And they don't know what they are guarding, only that they can kill anyone who approaches who isn't wearing an army uniform."

"How would you recommend we go in?" He thought for a minute, looked at Sandra critically, then at me, and tilted his head to one side.

"I know your reputations, but I think you would need more than the two of you, and I would suggest you approach at night from the dead side of the entrance. The doorway looks like a sandhill, the doors are blast-proof, the locks are electronic, but if you use this," and he reached into the folds of his thawb and pulled out a small device, "you won't have any trouble getting in. However, once you are inside, the tunnel is five kilometers long and slopes down at a ten-degree angle has motion sensors. I don't know what alarm they trigger. It might just be internal for the facility, but you will need a disruptor to be safe. And if they catch you inside, the advantage is all theirs, which is why I suggest more than just the two of you." I nodded, all good advice, and I mentally calculated how long it would take to jog five k's, carrying a full combat load, and realized we would need an hour for the incursion, plus whatever time we needed to eradicate any tangos inside or outside the facility. I looked deep into his jet-black eyes, noticing there was a faint ring of gold around his irises. Seeking any sign of prevarication or deceit, saw only compassion and excitement, and I could feel Sandra start to vibrate beside me.

Birds of a feather.

"Thank you, we respect your information, and we will keep it to ourselves. Arie." And with a nod to them both, I led Sandra back to our waiting helicopter, where our Italian guards were nervously peering out of the massive sliding doors, the relief on their faces when we reappeared almost comical.

With a small tornado of sand ripping up the desert floor, we climbed away, leaving the other two helicopters looking like abandoned insects amongst the rolling dunes.

"What are you thinking?" Sandra looked intense and excited and was almost bubbling over with enthusiasm.

"If you don't calm down, I'll leave you behind." She went into an immediate physical sulk, and if I hadn't come to know her as well as I had, I would have been fooled. "Stop it. This is serious shit!"

"So, how do you intend to handle this serious shit?" I gave her a withering look to absolutely no effect. She still vibrated in her seat, her face alive and her eyes glowing. I considered pulling my weapon out and shooting her, but then I would have to clean up the mess I made, so I just sat back and started thinking.

Exactly how did you attack a hidden facility deep inside Iraq's borders and make a safe getaway? I wasn't sure I had all the answers, let alone the questions, but I bet I knew who did. I sent a message to the C-17 pilot we had on standby in Israel and gave her specific instructions. I looked at my tactical watch, calculated the shifting time zones, and called general Saunders.

It was a fast conversation. She was with the president on some matter or other. She listened intently, grimaced, then nodded and gave me one last instruction.

Come back in one piece.

Easier said than done in this business, but I would do my very best to obey her. She was, after all, a general, and I was just a lowly commander!

# Back To School

At long last, Abbas was a happy man. The chemistry lab in the school laboratory on the first floor of the brick building seemed to have everything they needed to turn the empty shells, which now sat gleaming and radiating promise in their cradles, into nuclear bombs. The two science teachers that had been recruited moved pompously around with their stained and patched smocks flapping around their legs as they moved from bench to cradle. They muttered to each other, first in Arabic, then Farsi, then in what sounded like Russian. Each grunt earned a nod from one or the other, and Abbas felt completely left out of the conversation and the process.

He motioned to his subordinate and gave the young tough instructions on how to guard the two teachers while he went downstairs to review his rat-tag army of disenfranchised teenagers hungry for anything that shed blood. Mostly, they just sat around untidily in groups, smoking or pretending to sleep, their red arm-bands declaring their allegiance to Abbas and everything he stood for fluttering when someone moved.

He stood at the base of the stairs, wondering where all this might lead him. In a few hours he would have two armed and undetectable nuclear bombs, but he still had to solve the problem of delivery.

He had understood that Badawi's exotic plan had involved a huge ship, which he had purposely designed and made, and some sort of electronic sling, which he believed would deliver his bombs fifty kilometers into the heart of the enemy.

Abbas had shorter dreams.

He would be happy to just leave one of his bombs in a very public place in Israel and watch from a distance as the mushroom cloud earned him a special place in heaven as the most successful terrorist ever to have graduated from the Gaza strip University of Hard Knocks. He almost split his sides laughing at that thought, then noticed that his young and eager recruits were looking at him.

He stood straight, raised one hand in salute, his red armband fluttering as he did so, causing all his toughs to do the same.

Except they screamed out and yelled, and some of them even fired their rifles and machine guns into the roof.

Abbas looked up, glad that the roof was made of concrete and that the enthusiasm of his followers hadn't blown them all to kingdom come!

He walked back up the stairs to check on the progress of the teachers. He clearly saw their futures. He only had to decide if he would kill them personally or let the boys below have all the fun.

Decision, decisions!

# Chapter Forty-One

I t was the classic time for an attack, just half an hour past midnight, and the C-17 cruised easily at forty thousand feet above the desert floor, partially lit by a fleeting moon, which was playing hide and seek with a raft of high-flying puffy grey cumulonimbus clouds. Apart from the rippling exhausts and vortices from the huge cargo plane crashing through the frigid air, all was still, the ground far below passing with a majesty and monotony only long-distance pilots understood.

"Two minutes, stand up, the last check, face the ramp!" The loadmaster shouted through his oxygen mask, turning to check that his charges on both sides of the aircraft had heard his instruction. The aircraft was already unpressurised, the massive rear cargo door open to the dark night sky, the air so thin that the noise of the engines was a muted roar. For once, I was not in the lead, Tom was on my side, and Bob was on the other. This had been decided by a coin toss, which I was sure was rigged. So I stood bowed, weighed down by a sixty-pound pack, a steerable parachute, a smaller emergency one strapped to my chest, a small green metal bottle of oxygen hung off my webbing on one side, my weapon hung off the other side, and to top it all off an uncomfortable hard helmet with a face shield, oxygen mask, and NVG goggles made me feel, and probably look like, something out of a science fantasy magazine.

"One minute, look for the green. Good luck, ladies and gentlemen. Enjoy the ride. Better you than me!" And to a man and a woman, we laughed at the gallows humor, a HALO (High altitude, low opening) jump at any time was a taxing effort, but at night, over a featureless desert, with very little illumination from the moon, we would be relying on our night vision goggles for all physical clues, like when we were about to smack into the desert floor, or each other for that matter. The loadmaster held up his fist and started moving his arm up and down. We all hobbled forward slightly, one hand on the shoulder of the person in front of us, then the jump lights went from red to amber, then seconds later green, and we literally ran along the cargo ramp into the night, initially tumbling uncontrollably until we could extend our arms, and our legs as far as they would go, then 'fly' away. The blinking infrared lights on everyone's helmets told me where I was relative to my stick, and if we weren't going to war, the sight of a descending line of fairy lights against the black hole we were diving into would have been a stirring sight.

"Thirty thousand." The call had come from either Tom or Bob, and I checked my own altimeter for confirmation. I was falling at terminal velocity, which at this altitude was around one hundred and twenty miles an hour, so I had just over two minutes to enjoy the view before considering pulling my chute open. We would open at five thousand feet, or the jump master, in this case, Tom, could call for a later opening, depending on how he saw his stick laid out and the actual weather conditions at the critical altitude. The whole purpose of a HALO jump was to be as invisible as long as possible to any enemy below, so opening as close to the ground as possible was the optimum tactic.

And to have the noise of the aircraft far away from the jump point.

Ten thousand feet, a small led on my arm signaled, and I slowly reached for my guide chute, packed loosely into the folds of my suit. I moved slowly so as not to disturb my falling posture, which was as perfect as it would ever get on this jump. "Pull at three, repeat, pull at three!" The command came in loud and clear, and I made the necessary mental adjustment to accommodate the change in the plan. Either Tom or Bob had seen something or sensed something that had them change our release altitude. Less time to be seen and less time to find a good spot to land on, but the desert floor was starting to perceptibly rise in my visor, which meant there was some light from the moon, and that could easily silhouette us as we rocketed down.

I watched my altimeter wind down, it seemed to have accelerated the closer to the ground we got, but that was just nerves and anticipation.

Four thousand, three thousand, "Pull at one, repeat pull at one!"

Which came up so fast I almost missed it, but I threw out my guide chute, felt it streaming out into the slipstream, then felt the tug as my main chute pulled out, then a jerk as it partially filled, then seconds later a sharp pull up and jerk in my crutch as it deployed fully, and my altimeter read just two hundred feet. I stabilized my chute, focusing on the helmet lights of my stick, and saw them starting to turn into a circle. I followed, then braced my legs for impact, pulled the risers up as hard as I could, and tiptoed onto the sand. Settled. Let my chute collapse. Turned and pulled the risers in until I had an untidy bundle in my arms. Shrugged my chute pack off, forced the black silk into it, then kneeled on the top to help compress it, listening for any sign of trouble.

"On me." Whispered in my headset, and an infrared flare waved off to my right. Holding my pack in one hand and my weapon in the other, I walked through the sand until I came to a cluster of discarded oxygen bottles, packed chutes, dropped my own in a mess, then knelt next to Tom, who was watching an electronic instrument swing around like a compass. Everything was green, with an overall snow-like effect, the illuminated bits and pieces flaring bright white at times, but like everything else, once you got used to NVGs, you took them and the magic they performed for granted.

"We're clear of tangos, Commander, and less than half a click to the entrance."

"Disperse as planned, get Bob and his team into position; I'll follow you to the entrance, then you set up our backstop. Good jump." I patted him on the shoulder and noticed that Sandra, Fay, Indigo, and the minute form of 'Ira", our Israeli nuclear expert, had formed up around me, with Indigo's team formed up behind them. Wearing their NVGs made them all look like strange bug-like insects out on the town, and with no fuss at all, we all moved out to our agreed positions.

In an earlier conversation with Tom, Bob, and Indigo, who between them had over sixty years' experience plotting and executing battle plans, we had agreed that the tunnel left us vulnerable to an attack from the rear, so we would set up two teams both with long guns and squad automatic weapons in two arcs, one to act as a trip-wire, the other a purely defensive position. Indigo and his team would move with me down the tunnel, and we would post 'talking sticks', those little electronic repeaters we all loved so much, every half a kilometer. This would ensure we wouldn't be cut off no matter how deep we went into the complex.

In a hot zone, communication was everything, almost as good as having a long-gun shooter able to hit a fly at two thousand meters in the dead of night. And we had a couple of those on this trip, and I silently prayed they would bring cold barrels back to the rendezvous point when we were finished. It would be so much better if we could get in and out and no one was the wiser. We arrived at the massive sand-covered blast doors and noticed that they were built at an angle, allowing the buildup of sand along the top, creating a natural camouflage from drones or aerial observation. It also allowed us to huddle under the shelter of the cap-like brow as the three teams knocked fisted gloves before setting off to their positions.

Two of the team dropped the bundle they had been dragging from where we had landed, and it was tucked into the side out of the way. It didn't do to leave equipment lying around as proof of your presence. The teams faded away, their helmet lights extinguished, and the only proof of their existence the collapsing boot marks on the desert floor. The light wind would cover their tracks in no time at all. Indigo applied the electronic lock breaker, and with a hum-click-whirr, the massive blast doors opened. A team of four shooters set up in each corner, two to a side, one squad weapon, one long gun, belly down and dressed in Ghillie suits. They would be literally invisible to anyone approaching, and the long guns had massive night vision scopes attached, which would reach out far beyond any tangos' ability to see in, no matter what electronic equipment they had. And our information was that the guards were poorly equipped, so it was probably overkilled, but it was my backside and those of my team on the line, so I stopped worrying about it.

We moved in, dragged the blast doors until they were nearly shut, fed the first talking stick through the small gap we left, checked

448

the comms, then with two of Indigo's team-leading with disruptors to shut down any motion sensors, we started jogging down the tunnel. Going down was easy. Getting back up would take some doing, so I started to plan that in my mind.

"Indigo, leave a pack every five hundred meters, odds and evens, water and food, and spare ammunition repack if necessary. Plan for a sprint back up."

"*Certamente, comandante.*" I smiled at his use of Italian; he was letting me know in that super smart way of his that he had my back. We made good time, averaging eight minutes a kilometer, two of those shedding packs and reloading the explosives we had brought with us. We got to the first building wall. It looked like a garage, our advance team slipped in, and a short time later, huge halogen lights came on, creating a flash so bright I had to flip up my NVGs.

"Apologies, Commander, they were on a motion sensor. Do you want them to remain on?" The green and white flashes still blinded me, so I shut my eyes, squinted, rubbed a gloved hand over my eyeballs, and slowly reopened them. The world came into focus, and I turned and looked back up the tunnel, glad that the glare only reached about two hundred meters.

"How come your disruptors didn't cancel them out?"

"They're localized, not part of the security system." I nodded, not really understanding the difference but appreciating that our way was now well-lit.

"Clear the area, Ira, Sandra, Fay, Indigo, on me, straight down to the power plant." We headed to the metal stairs that wove their way down in a series of curves and noticed that as we got deeper, it got colder until we reached the floor to the reactor room, which was, as expected, a series of air-tight doors in a tunnel, so you had to shut one to open the other. We filed in, Fay leading with a Geiger counter, which clicked and buzzed in a very non-threatening manner. We reached the control room, and 'Ira' took out a small camera and started filming everything. Then she moved to the massive window and saw what had captured my interest. The entire pit, rods, and all were solidified in a silver crud that ran up the walls and across all the pipes and vents.

Nano bugs again.

We had seen photos from the nuclear facilities that had been attacked by the terrorists way back in the second month of the attacks, so no surprise there, except it was unexpected here in a supposedly nonexistent nuclear power plant. Sandra and Fay were sucking the two computers dry of their data, and I started to work out the best way to put this plant to bed permanently. I signaled to the troops and moved them all back up to the top floor, where Indigo and his men waited patiently. "Blow this floor down to the next, and the second likewise, we will bury this once and for all. Mine the tunnel to collapse behind us. I don't want anyone to be able to get in here ever again." He nodded, and my group started the long climb back up to the surface.

"What can you tell me?" I asked Sandra and Fay on either side, and 'Ira' tagged along as fast as her shorter legs would let her. I slowed my pace. I wanted information, not heart attacks. I was getting pissed again, the women terrorists were several steps ahead of us, and I was running out of options to stop them in their tracks. "Ah, Commander, from the quick read I managed, the power plant was last at full power just over a year ago. It ran for five months, then shut down. I will be able to tell you what was produced once I get back to my lab."

"Jessica, the machinery on the second floor was used recently. There were radioactive filings in waste bins. One of Indigo's troops gave me this." Sandra held out a small sealed box with the nuclear sign stenciled on the top. Fay ran her meter across it, the needle didn't move appreciably, which caused a mass release of breath, so much, so we all started to laugh. We picked up the first of the packs and didn't stop, but I handed out water bottles to everyone I could reach, then passed the pack back.

"We need a deep dive on everything we just got, and we need it fast." And just like that, our peaceful incursion into enemy territory came to a sudden halt with the unmistakable sound of sniper fire. The fifty caliber long-guns made a distinctive 'crack' even with a muzzle suppressor fitted, and the even pace with which the sound reached us suggested a sustained attack from somewhere. I lengthened my stride, I trusted my teams, and as yet, there had been no verbal report, so my job now was to get the inside boys and girls safely back to the surface. Half of Indigo's team ran past us, stopping only to fit an explosive pack to the wall every now and then. They were green-speckled blurs in my NVGs, but I knew everyone was a person and, as usual, was running to the fight, not away from it.

Warriors all.

The sniper fire was joined sporadically by the running cracks of a squad weapon, and you could actually count the three-second bursts as they burped. There was something comforting in the radio silence. What it meant, I didn't know, but we all had open hot mikes, and I couldn't even hear deep breathing, but I knew the troops would be using 'clickers' rather than voice.

The firing stopped just as the remaining half of Indigo's team raced past us. Indigo jogged to my side, and handed me a large pouch, which I slipped over my chest. "Data from the office computers. If you want my best guess, what was left for us was left for us to find." I took that in, rolled it around, added it to all the other signs and signals we had been collecting these past weeks, and wondered just how scared the terrorists wanted us and why.

I was just starting to get somewhere with my thoughts when a massive explosion ricocheted through my headphone, so loud I could even hear it with my naked ear.

"What the fu…"

"Commander, enemy helicopter down. We are taking prisoners. We need you all back here ASAP!"

"Casualties?"

"None on our side, several in the helicopter, and we have taken two long tubes similar to the ones you showed us photos of."

"They may be radioactive!"

"Negative, no blip on the detector. They are marked with the nuclear symbol, but sealed. Instructions on the prisoners?" Now I had two more unknowns to deal with, the prisoners we had taken off the helicopter and the tangos who must have heard the explosion and would soon arrive to investigate. I decided on deceit. Asymmetric warfare relied heavily on it for the success of many of the terrorist raids we suffered all year long.

"Hood and cuff the prisoners, blow the chopper and evacuate to the landing zone. The closest team to the door covers our exit. The building will blow in four minutes. Move!" A series of 'moving', 'roger', on the way' echoed through the net, as we squirted out the doors pulling the 'talking stick' behind us. Started running across the desert floor, looking for the little infrared tell tales we had left behind like breadcrumbs. I felt rather than saw our teams form up, we keep discipline and a lookout at the same time. I wondered what we would look like on a drone camera, little sparkling blobs racing in a pyramid formation leaving behind a burning chopper, and with a mighty heave of the desert floor, which had some of us stumbling and having to grab onto the person nearest us to keep our footing, the collapsed underground facility.

Just as we came in a range of our markers, three huge helicopters landed in the trail, doors open and guns manned. We literally fell into them, and in less than a minute, all forty of us recovered, with the helicopters lifting off into the night sky. No one shot at us and the last thing I saw thrown into the hold was the massive carry bag that had all our oxygen bottles and chutes. No mess, no fuss. I switched to the command frequency, waited to see who was on the channel, then asked what had to be asked.

"Who were we firing at just before the helicopter?"

"Commander, we had tangos come at us from two sides, we had them between our two positions, so I instructed the gatekeepers to take them out while we kept our heads down. The boys and girls did their usual fine job, then buggar me if the chopper didn't land almost on our head. We had no option but to take it out." Fog of war, no plan survived the first shot, always expect the unexpected, all the usual ditties about warfare flashed through my mind.

"Number of prisoners?"

"Three. One of whom you will want to meet personally. He came out of the chopper firing, so we took him down, then found he was still breathing."

"Who is he?"

"Well, according to the ID photos we carry, he is either the infamous Malik Badawi or his father. You can work that one out." I smiled. Sometimes coincidence was a bitch. What were the odds of us at the facility at the same time as Badawi made his end run? And we had his nuclear material. One down, one to go. But we knew where Abbas was holding out. We had the building under twenty-four-hour surveillance, with troops ready to go in on a moment's notice. How much time would he need to load his bombs? Because we now knew something he didn't, and it had changed the entire complexity of the chase. I mulled that over the whole trip back to Israel, then dialed Arie as a matter of courtesy.

"Jessica, good to see you. It looked to us as if you had a bit of fun on the way out?" I smiled at the little camera. He was looking a little relaxed for once, no doubt happy we had lost no one and had a relatively easy operation.

"Got a present for you, one Malik Badawi from all accounts, which would make it a very good day. Movement in Gaza?" He frowned and gave me an intense look.

"It's never a pretty picture there, he has around one thousand youths, all wearing tracksuits and high tops, head scarfs, throwing rocks at the soldiers on the other side of the border. They, of course, and using tear gas and rubber bullets, but the young men keep coming in waves."

"And this is near the building we have tagged?"

"Yes, right at the back of it." I thought for a moment, trying to understand why Abbas would knowingly draw attention to himself. Then I got it.

"He thinks we haven't located him." Arie nodded, sitting back in his seat. "We agree. This type of behavior happens every day, up and down the wire, it never stops, and many times it is worse than today. But we are keeping our heads, and I have a strike force sitting ready ten minutes away. Just say the word." I looked at Arie. It had never occurred to me that he would abdicate the decision to attack Abbas in favor of Interpol. Yes, we had issued the Red Notice, yes, we had got a judgement in absentia on Abbas, and yes, Arie had contracted his friend the Iman across the wire to warn him of the possible outcomes, so legally, we were covered. I mulled that over, then pointed to Arie.

"Hey, you're setting me up! You take the bastard out." And he grinned, enjoying the joke. I knew at the slightest sign that Abbas had the bombs, Arie would authorize the strike. He was playing games with me.

"Come home, and we'll talk about it."

# Chapter Forty-Two

The youths Arie had referred to had swollen in number, their red and blue tracksuits considered normal day apparel, their red arm-bands worn with pride, some not yet past their tenth birthday. The real tragedy of the Gaza was that there were now four generations of refugee children fighting for recognition and a place to live. In the way of the jungle, the strong survived by picking on the weak, and the various terrorist organizations used the swelling ranks of angry, dispossessed, and hungry children to their advantage.

Give one child money for food, or even just a few loaves of bread, and you could ask anything in return. Run drugs, act as a secret messenger, and even do sexual favors if that was your predisposition. While the worldwide average was one child under the age of ten dying every few minutes in refugee camps, in the Gaza it was one every two minutes, a tally that was only exceeded by the death count in Syria. The world knew of this problem, but the terrorist groups made it almost impossible for any of the Aid agencies to make a difference. And Abbas had made his bones utilizing tough, young recruits who viewed an AK-47 as the perfect recognition of their loyalty. And put fifty of the armed and invigorated youths together, and you had an army that could be crushed but would rise up again the next day with an even worse attitude. And now Abbas had called in his reserves, and there were now almost one thousand armed youths jittering around the back of the building, some drugged to the eyeballs, some just high on euphoria, taking potshots at the Israelis anchored in their weapons carriers and light tanks.

Understandably, the Israelis were getting nervous, thinking that this could escalate into a run on the border. The command channels were alive with reports and thoughts as the high command considered their options.

The real tragedy was that there were lots of younger children running between the armed youths, some just seeing the fun in it all, some trying to look tough and part of the action. Some just watched a brother in awe, hoping at some time to be able to emulate him.

Abbas watched this melee with glee, drinking Irish whisky straight from the bottle. He was just an hour away from having his bombs, and then he would turn the Middle East on its collective head. As he glugged the scotch, the two school teachers finally agreed on how to unload the canisters, then load the bombs. They had set a workbench up and were now outfitted in goggles, dirty white laboratory coats, gas masks, huge flameproof gloves, and wielding massive tongs. Their considered opinion was that the only threat of radiation would be the short time it took to lift the plutonium from the containers into the shells. Handling the uranium would require the same process-open the container, garb the machined ball, load it into the shell, then seal the shell with the nanomachines.

They stood side by side, tongs at the ready, looked at each other, nodded, and opened the first container.

The mushroom-shaped fireball rose fifteen kilometers into the morning sky, the dense fuming black and red plume initially obliterated by the sun-like flash of light, which could be seen three countries away, and blinded thousands unlucky enough to turn to look towards the noise. It was a sound many would never forget, a dark rumbling roar that erupted into a shouting match between the Gods. The blast force was so great the five armored vehicles on the other side of the fence six hundred meters away were picked up and thrown like tissue paper over a kilometer back into the desert. The mass of children waving their guns was simply vaporized, the shadows of some burnt into the sides of the few buildings that survived within the blast zone, creating a stark montage of death.

A fire so hot it burnt or vaporized buildings, concrete, tar, glass, flesh and blood, bones, and steel, and from above, where the drone had been flying before it had been shattered into a thousand pieces, it looked like someone had just cleaned the ground of all people and buildings with a giant weed wacker, leaving a massive blast hole in the ground that was lined with molten lava.

It was all over in less than five minutes, the blast wave moving faster than any cyclone or hurricane ever recorded and with a million times more force, sweeping all before it until it finally ran out of puff twenty kilometers away. No one knew how many people died from the blast, it was in the thousands, and thousands more died at a later time, often in agony from radiation poisoning.

Many of those blinded died in agony, unable to look after themselves or find anyone who would do it for them.

The Gaza strip had a hole in it that could be seen from space. Abbas had achieved the infamy he had striven for. He would be remembered as the man who let an atomic bomb off and killed thousands of his fellow men, women, and children and achieved exactly nothing in return except the condemnation of everyone with a voice.

I became aware of the tragedy when Fay burst into my space yelling 'that the shells had become visible in the Gaza!'. I calmed her down, sat her down, and used all my skill and empathy to get her to explain what had happened. She was wound up by whatever she had learned and was in danger of hyperventilating and losing consciousness.

"They bombed the Gaza with an atomic weapon, thousands were killed, but the shells have suddenly popped up on the detectors!"

"Who bombed Gaza?" I asked incredulously. She looked shell-shocked. I could understand her angst but not her almost frantic behavior. My mini buzzed, and I almost ignored it, but I opened it to find Arie looking a hundred years older than just hours ago.

"Jessica, the building where Abbas had roosted, has been destroyed in a nuclear explosion." I stared at him with disbelief all over my face.

"How on earth did he manage that?"

"We don't know, but the radiation is moving slowly out to sea, all our monitors are going wild, and the US navy is reporting they have a ship in the area, and it is reading radiation levels not seen since Hiroshima."

"How many did you lose?" Here was the reason for his gray pallor, his hunched shoulders, his deathly look.

"The incursion team, all thirty of them, another hundred and fifty in the armored regiment we had at the wire, and a lot of civilians who were close to the border, but the majority of the blast and radiation went out to sea, thank God. But we will have radiation poisoning to deal with long term, and blindness from the flash, potentially thousands damaged long-term."

"Khan Yunis is the widest part of Gaza. You might have got lucky there. Just how bad is it on the ground?" He looked at me and grimaced.

"The Knesset wants immediate retaliation. I've pointed out this was an individual, and he is now well and truly accounted for, but we are on a full-out war footing. I may need your help in calming all this down."

"I can be with you in ninety minutes." He nodded, looked off-camera for a moment, then back at me.

"We know the radiation signature is French, and the blast level was that of a kilo-ton bomb. Amira figures that three of the canisters would equate to that were they exposed to each other. Interpol can calm this down, but you have better come prepared." I looked at the blank screen and thought about how best to handle a hysterical government, one that had been on edge for longer than I had been alive, one who was constantly squeezing bits of the Gaza and would, in all probability, welcome what they would see as a cleansing war to end the Gaza drama once and for all.

"Sandra, Fay, get dressed, best street clothes, no weapons, Indigo, dress 1A's, we needed to be in Tel Aviv yesterday!"

Sandra looked at me, smiled a thin smile, and nodded, but I could see in her eyes she would disobey me.

I would deal with it when we landed.

We arrived in Tel Aviv to be greeted by a swarm of fully armed troops and armor vehicles. Many of the guns were pointing in, which was to be expected at this point.

A rabbi in a black three-piece suit, white shirt shut tight at the neck, wide-brimmed hat, long dregs, harsh, thick black glasses, and a grimace that would make little children run, bowed to us, and silently led us to a blacked-out vehicle.

We sped away, the trip only took ten minutes, but I promise you that in that short time, we hit every pothole and curb in Israel. Indigo just looked stoic, Fay was starting to get the color back in her cheeks, her stylish suit over a mild blue shirt looking very professional, whereas Jessica looked like she had just stepped out of a fashion magazine, her long blond hair sweeping the sides of her face every time she moved her head. She had not only gunned up, but I could see the telltale shape of a weapon under Fay's arm, and Indigo had a presentation holster, all shiny patent leather on his colorful belt, and I just bet he had his favorite nine mill fully loaded hidden away in it.

At the last minute, Sandra had pushed my Beretta and a pair of magazines at me, so I had also gunned up against my better instincts. We stopped. The doors were pulled open. We were in a tunnel. The light was dim, but soldiers were everywhere, and some formed a human tunnel along which we marched.

Bright warm light met us as we emerged into a huge high-roofed space, where a large circular table had been set up in the middle. The ubiquitous electronic equipment made its presence felt, with snake-like cables lying around and little yellow and black striped safety tunnels announcing where you could safely walk. Screens had been dumped on boxes, and a massive electronic whiteboard played a drone view of the blast site.

Around the table, three women and four men sat uncomfortably, all focused on the white-haired woman who currently led the country after numerous political fits and starts that had seen her in and out of office three times just this year so far!

"Madam Prime Minister, thank you for inviting us here." We stood to attention, then moved to our seats when she just waved her hand, somewhat regally, towards where she wanted us.

"General Rosenberg tells us we should listen to you before we make our decision. I should tell you we have already made it, and all it requires is for me to give the 'go'. Why should we listen to you?

As far as I can tell, you allowed this situation to develop in the first place." I felt Sandra bristle next to me, and I kicked her under the table. The Prime Minister had attacked, and rightly so, but from long experience with politicians who acted first and never bothered to ask the right questions, I appreciated the opportunity to make our case. And I sensed something else. They might have made the decision to attack, but I felt it had been far from unanimous.

"Madam Prime Minister, we stood back and let the terrorist known as Amir Abbas have the time to load the nuclear material into the shells because, in our opinion, it was the safest place for it to be." The room erupted, with three of the men standing and shouting at me in Yiddish. It was a little comical in a way, fists waving, faces spewing, and all in the most prestigious chamber in Israel. The PM waved them back down into their seats. She turned her full attention on me, turned her body in her chair to face me, and made it clear it was now one-on-one.

"Explain." Her steely grey eyes burned into me, but we had come prepared. I pulled my mini out and looked directly at her.

"With your permission?" She just nodded, her face set in a very hard way, reminding me that the fate of two million lives depended on what I said next. I pushed the image of a shell onto the whiteboard, waited a few seconds, then stood.

"Madam Prime Minister, we have been chasing these shells all over the Mediterranean for nearly three weeks. We believe there were some thirty odd manufactured originally, with one destroyed during that process. You will have been briefed on how we tracked down and recovered all but two." I looked at her waiting for acknowledgement. Her eyes narrowed, then she nodded slowly, so I continued.

"During the testing of the shells we recovered, we discovered that they could not be fired via the nose bulb as we originally thought; once sealed with the nano-machines they could not be opened again by any means we are aware of, and they cannot be exploded by external forces." I clicked on the next image, showing the abandoned shells at the bottom of the crater recently made by Abbas's stupidity and arrogance, both intact, but layered beneath the debris that no doubt would be very radioactive.

"Our thinking was if Abbas loaded the shells, we would have effectively removed his nuclear material and he would be left with two useless bombs we could take off of him anytime we chose to." You could hear a pin drop in the room, it became so quiet, and even Sandra held her breath, a sure sign she was reading the room the same as I was.

"Have you recovered these shells?"

"General Rosenberg is organizing a radiation hazard team to scour the area as we speak. There is already a huge effort being provided by both yourselves, the Palestinians, and international aid agencies, to locate and help survivors, but so far, little has been able to be done because of the high levels of radiation." Her chin was now resting on one fist, and unconsciously she started scratching the bottom of her chin with her forefinger.

"Why did this tragedy happen?"

"Abbas or whomever he recruited to load the shells made a simple mistake. They opened the canisters the wrong way, they mishandled the material, we may never know. But they did not manage to load the shells."

"What would you have us do?" I looked at Sandra. She was staring at the men and women seated opposite us, all of whom looked confused. I looked around the room, trying to get a gauge on where the strongest reaction may come from, and fixated on a little grumpy wizened man who was crouched so low in his seat only his head could be seen over the table.

"Make a statement that you will not retaliate if the Palestinians hand over every member of Hamas and Al Bar al Shirak within twenty-four hours. If not, you reserve the right to sweep the Gaza for them yourselves. This will give us time to recover the shells and try to learn what happened, but to be frank, the chances of anyone being left alive who know the story are very slim."

"Are there any more of these shells lying around?" And with one simple question, she had my hypothetical balls in a vice.

"Have you been briefed on our recent operation in Iraq?" She sat back in her seat, so suddenly it moved under her slightly.

"Yes."

"Then, Madam Prime Minister, all I can tell you is we found evidence that nuclear material had been manufactured in the last year, machined into an unknown configuration, and an unknown substrate in unknown quantities may have also been manufactured at the same time. However, we believe this was a much higher level of operation, possibly run by a group of female terrorists aligned with those who attacked us originally."

"Huh!" And she thumped the table with both fists, and everyone but the gnome jumped in their seats, except for Sandra, Fay, and Indigo.

I was proud of them.

But this was what was wrong with politicians in any investigation. They always wanted answers before we even had the questions, which was why so many of them made so many bad decisions.

There was an old adage in the technology world, the people that paid the money didn't use the equipment, and in the case of politicians, the people who declared war didn't line up to get shot or butchered. I sat down, sensing that they had all they needed and that more information may well confuse them. Sandra squeezed my hand under the table, and I inwardly smiled. It was nice to have a backup. A furious dialogue broke out in Hebrew on the other side of the table. The PM let it run, and it fizzled as quickly as it had started.

In essence, what had been said I totally agreed with. The women terrorists had upset the world and should be hunted down and prosecuted to the ends of the earth. They may be refugees, geniuses, and women, but they were killers.

"We will make a statement, give you time to recover the shells, and you report back to me personally. I have one of your precious computers. I will send you my address; twenty-four hours, not a minute more." Before I could answer, she stood and stalked out of the room, soon followed by the other members of the Knesset. The gnome waddled, obviously restrained by age, and I momentarily felt sorry for him. In today's high-tech world, even one thrown back fifty years into the past by the terror attacks, it was hard to live a normal life if you were less than perfect, as others saw you. A failing of humanity for thousands of years. We stood, and a flood of armed soldiers poured in, formed up around us, and marched us out.

The trip back to our helicopter was uneventful, right up until we lifted off, when the missile detector in the cockpit started screaming, and the aircraft started to fishtail and spin around in a crazy circle, jerking from side to side, throwing us against our seatbelts. The sounds of explosions and gunfire rippled through our headsets, our helicopter regained some semblance of control, and we temporarily raced across the buildings with about three meters of clearance until we smacked into the side of one and literally fell ten meters to the ground. The rotors made a frantic attempt to keep turning but simply managed to shatter when they hit the brick wall, sending bits of red-hot aluminum through the cockpit and into the cabin.

Overhead a tremendous roar followed by bomb bursts shocked our senses, which, when added to our compressed and bruised bodies, made for an interesting look on Sandra's face. She had her weapon out and was heading for the door on her knees, blood running from her head and staining one arm.

"Stay here, don't move, Indigo, cover me!" And she leaped out. Fay shook her head groggily and looked around as if she didn't know where she was. Then the sound of incoming fire registered as pings and thuds worked their way through the fuselage. A hole suddenly appeared in the sidewall, and all three of us fell to the floor in a pile. Then I heard the measured single shots of a pistol, Indigo and Fay rolled out the door, and I did my best to follow, just in time to see Sandra kill three figures dressed in black as they surged towards the helicopter.

We formed a ragged line, hiding as best as we could behind bricks and debris, flat on our bellies, scanning for targets. I shot at one who popped up almost at our side, Fay shot his companion, and Indigo stood and blasted their position while we both ducked back down.

"Fuckers think they can take us by surprise. Well, I've got a surprise for them!" Sandra shot again, this time to her right, where a similar pair had made their presence felt, and her angry frame rotated around like a searchlight, all taught and tight, her hair flowing in the wind, her eyes feral in the mottled light. A flood of Israeli soldiers suddenly appeared, so we stopped firing but didn't lose our focus. I could feel the anger in Sandra. She was seriously pissed. Fay wasn't a whole lot better, her lip pealing back and her teeth showing in a look that would have any mother hiding her children.

*"Comandante, Sandra, Fay, tutto bene?"*

*"Sì, Indigo, tutto bene, grazie."* It was comforting to have our personal paratrooper stand in front of us as if shielding us from bullets, and I admit he did cut an imposing figure in his blue and red formal uniform, his jauntily perched cap, and the almost casual way he stood facing the approaching troopers. One came up to him, saluted, and babbled for a minute before he realized Indigo wasn't taking any notice of him. He stood and just looked perplexed.

"He wants to know if we are alright and why we are standing in the wreckage of a helicopter," Indigo said out of the corner of his mouth. He slipped his pistol back into its polished holster, then reached down and pulled me up, Sandra did the same for Fay, and we looked at each other, wondering who in the name of Hell had shot at us this time. I pulled my mini out, saw that it was fatally smashed, and slipped it back into my pocket. Sandra handed me hers, so I dialed Arie and asked him if he could arrange for us to be collected by someone smarter than the current crop of soldiers who were now milling around the wreckage as if they had never seen one before. Thankfully, the pilot and co-pilot stood near the nose, apparently uninjured. I walked over to them, shadowed by Sandra and Fay, with Indigo covering our rear.

*"State entrambi bene e chi ci ha abbattuto?"*

*"Grazie comandante, stiamo bene, ed era un drone armato. Nessuna identificazione."* So the ubiquitous armed drone, no identification, and our pilots were okay. Thank God, I was getting a reputation in the ranks for being dangerous to fly with! I sat down with my back against the brick wall we had crashed into.

"Jessica, I hate to say this, but someone had a real hard-on for you. By my count, this is the fourth time someone has tried to kill you. Who did you upset so much?" We all laughed. We knew the root of the problem. There was a twenty million euros bounty on my head. Who wouldn't kill for that much money? The bounty had been going up by five million euros every three days or so for nearly a fortnight.

"And you wanted to leave our guns behind!" I grimaced, she was correct, and without our weapons, we would have been killed or taken, without a doubt.

I sensed we were getting deeper and deeper into the mire with precious little to go on. We had a partial location on one of the women. We had eliminated the two terrorists and their shells; the fact that one had eliminated himself didn't really count. We had shut down the dreaded Milk Factory once and for all, but the evidence, which I had not yet had the time to examine, pointed to more shells and nuclear material out there somewhere.

And this time, possibly in the hands of someone who knew how to really use them. But why? Was our hypothesis about their motive correct?

# Chapter Forty-Three

**M**aribelle Assiano and Rena Niele huddled over their screens. The implosion hole that had been a part of the Gaza strip was centered in it, with a running commentary from one of the local radio studios, presently limited by their lack of technology, but the crater was visible to anyone who had the ability to look beyond all that had been denied by the terrorist attacks when they so efficiently killed most of all technology.

"That fool Abbas has blown himself up!" Rena shook her head in disbelief. The reason why they had used the terrorists in the first place was that they lacked the ability to load the shells, and they were counting on them being captured to create the fear they needed for their plan to work. And if by some miracle, the terrorists did manage to load the shells, the shells couldn't be reopened or exploded. Unless you handled the nuclear material the wrong way and, even then, they had color-coded the canisters to help prevent that from happening.

"We need to move the other shells now before Interpol puts two and two together. I've got the five delivered from Afghanistan, plus all that we made at the milk factory, and I figure we have a solid forty-eight hours before they do, and in that time, I can be out in the Atlantic a long way from everyone. If I leave now, I can be on the ship and on our way in less than thirty minutes." Her voice was sad, but Maribelle had a toughness that came through the disappointment, and she packed her go-bag and walked out, carrying her satellite phone with her.

"You know, I was starting to think that one of them would get our message across for us, but I'm not unhappy it comes down to us." At the other end of the call, in a little house just outside Roanoke, Rena hunched down on the couch she was laid out on, locking the phone with its small screen between her cheek and her shoulder as she reached for the rug to pull up over her legs. It was a cold day, and even with the fire burning, she couldn't get warm enough. She was just getting settled again when her front door blew open, and five masked, and heavily armed shadows stormed in, pulled her roughly off the couch, laced her hands behind her back, bagged her head, then kneeled vigorously on her prostrate form. One figure picked up the satellite phone, looked at the screen, made the 'cut across the throat' sign for silence, then put his ear to the handset.

At the other end, just before she terminated the call, Maribelle whispered 'goodbye and bless you', then hung her head in sorrow. Now she was the only one left to deliver their message and see that the threat behind it was honored. What she didn't know was that both ends of the call had been located and that she was just minutes away from incarceration herself, which she escaped simply by being on her way out of the accommodation complex as the Federals drove up on the far side. She mounted an electric motorcycle and sped off down a small lane, turning into the highway and heading for the coast. In another twenty minutes, she was mounting the skids of her helicopter, the rotors already spinning as she had used her remote control to start the chopper while she was still five minutes away.

She lifted off, let the aircraft move through the bumps and burbles of transitional lift, then hauled the collective up as hard as she could, dropped the nose, and pushed the little machine to its top speed, holding just meters off the tops of the waves. Her ship was not as grand as Badawi's was, but at eighty feet in length, with a fine narrow hull and two powerful engines, it could push through the ocean at a good eighteen knots all day long. That would get her across the Atlantic in an easy six or seven days, weather permitting.

As she was sliding onto the helideck of her ship, the accommodation where she had been hiding was raided by armed members of the Irish Federal Security Forces, who literally tore the place apart, only to be frustrated by both the lack of a physical target, or any evidence that she had even been in the room other than a warm seat.

I was reading their after-action report when I received a transcript of the call that had originated the attacks in both the United States and Ireland, one by the FBI, the other by the IFSF. I looked at the words on the screen, tried to imagine the state of the minds of the two women, and found that I didn't really have enough information on either of them to do so. I knew they were passionate about the refugee situation, specifically the fate of so many young girls in the camps spread around the world. I knew they were geniuses at the top of their games, but as yet, I didn't know their individual specialties. Although it was a fair guess, one of them had deep technical knowledge about nano bugs. I wondered if the other was the psychologist we had hypothesized the women's terror network might have.

We had guessed their agenda, and the short conversation we had recorded seemed to support our intuition. And if getting the nineteen countries to accept and use the environmental plants and then handle the migration of thousands of refugee children, we knew where the blockages were, but not necessarily the level we would need to reach for us to work around them. I felt the pressure to do something, and I ignored it and followed my instincts. Called the head monk, someone I owed a huge debt to, moved away from Sandra and Fay, saw Indigo look over at me, then carefully placed himself between everyone and myself.

Another I owed a huge debt of gratitude to, and not just for his magic hands and his coffee-making abilities or his accuracy as a shooter!

"Stefarino, thanks for taking my call. I need to ask you for a favor again, you may or may not be able to accommodate me, but I have to ask."

"Jessica, hello, how are you all? We've been following your adventures back here in Venice with some interest." I smiled at that. The thought of Stefarino watching us tramp all over the Mediterranean made me smile.

"In the main, we're all fine. Stefarino, I need your genius with technology again. This time it may prevent World War Three breaking out." He gave me a somber look, nodded, then looked up, his grey-green eyes sparking with interest. "You want me to track that woman on the end of the phone in Ireland?" Did his question surprise me? Not really. He and his geeks had kept us in the game for over three months, so anticipating my needs would be logical. But I needed more from him this time.

"Thank you, do that, but I also need you to go back in time, maybe eighteen months, and track all movement to and from the Milk Factory. I need to know where they took what they made there. I expect it will be protected by their black hole technology, but you have cracked that, so you should be able to tell us something." He nodded and looked up as if thinking.

"Eighteen months, you say?" I nodded and waited silently for his next question.

"Can I use your geeks and Malcolm and his team?"

"I'm counting on it, and Indigo will have everyone on standby for you within the next five minutes."

"How important is it?"

"Top of the list. I need proof of what these women are doing, and I need it quickly. I probably only have a day or two before I need to take action, and I can't afford any mistakes." He nodded, waved his hand in the sign of the cross, and disconnected. Indigo, who had been pretending not to hear my call to his brother, looked at me, saluted sloppily with a huge smile, pulled his mini out, and went to work. I dialed another of my friends to whom I also now owed favors. At this rate, I would be on my knees for weeks!

"Anna, how goes it?" She looked fresh and satisfied with herself, always a good sign for the most senior member of the FBI next to the director.

"We have your terrorist, although we can't announce it due to the fact we rid ourselves of the female terrorists two months ago if you remember?" I smiled. The US president had decided to keep the women out of the recent terror stories, preferring to blame Shetani and his men, visible and known mercenaries who carried the blame well, now that they were dead to a man and a cat.

"I need her held somewhere very remote and safe. I'm on my way to you in a matter of hours. I'll do the interrogation with you when

I get there. Is that okay with you?" She looked down at her hands, beautifully manicured long fingers stretched out over the small keyboard. Having Interpol in the house would send up flags politically, and the president didn't need any more grief than she already had. The country was in the best shape it had been in three months, but it was a delicate balance between social unrest and hope for some sort of brighter future.

"Can you make the Gerald Ford?" I looked up, mildly amused, not sure of her agenda.

"Where is it?"

"Mid-Atlantic."

I thought for a minute, two birds with one stone. Logistics, logistics, always bloody logistics! Then I had a genuine brainwave.

"We need to get Admiral Rogers back to that carrier and your newest friend. Can you make the necessary travel arrangements for her on your end? Let's set the meet-up for tomorrow at ten hundred hours local time, but you must keep our guest isolated, hooded, and secured."

"Not my first rodeo." She smiled and cut me off, so I dialed the general. "Sorry to interrupt again, I've just asked Anna to get a prisoner you hold to the Gerald Ford. My intention is to fly out to where Admiral Rogers is now in the Med, board with my own prisoner, then travel with him to the Ford. Do I have your permission?" She looked at me with wide-open eyes as if I had shocked her. She saw how serious I was, and no doubt she was up to date on what we were doing and why.

"You want me to order Admiral Rogers back to the Ford; is there an imminent threat to us?"

"Yes. And I might need Admiral Rogers to remove it for us. Can you warn him before we meet?"

"Will you take over the ship?" I thought hard and deeply about that. It came down to culpability and political expediency.

"I would prefer for Rogers to give the order at the instructions of Interpol, suitably accredited, and with all the necessary paperwork. If it turns out the way I think it will, the US Navy taking this action will be seen to be righteous and timely." It was her turn to think, and she did this by tapping one bright red fingernail on her teeth.

"I just heard about your latest little nuclear episode in Gaza. Should I be scared?" She smiled at me; she wasn't scared yet. Generals didn't get scared. They got pissed. But if we fucked up, it would be more than fear and a pissed look that would ride her pretty face. She nodded. "A world court order and a Red Notice will be sufficient proof. I will instruct him to act on your orders and your orders alone. Clear?" Crystal, it would all come back on me, and that was the way I preferred it.

"Clear." She didn't need to know about the prisoners. That was very much Interpol's business. Even though the FBI had bagged the terrorist, we would interrogate them and then take whatever action was necessary. I dialed Arie and got the top of his head, which turned into his face, where he perched a pair of reading glasses precariously on the tip of his nose. He smiled, and I laughed. It relaxed us both.

"Arie, I need our latest guest and myself, plus one ferried out to Admiral Roger's latest command in the Med. Can you arrange that, please? And I need to be aboard in the next hour if possible." He just smiled, waved his hand as if to say 'go away', and closed the call. I thought for a moment, then called the admiral directly. After all, he had a mini and could join in any call we made on them at his heart's content. And probably had done so because I would have been in his position.

"Admiral, good to see you."

"I've just been briefed by the president's military chief-of-staff, not that she told me very much. How fast can you get here?" He was dressed in day blues, a faded pattern that didn't do his big frame any favors. He had a sleep crease on one side of his face, which only added to his rugged looks.

"Two hours, tops, and if you could, can you get that destroyer you plugged the Med with, out into the Atlantic, fastest speed possible, around the top end of Ireland? You're looking for a boat. No details yet, but it will be moving fast and toward the east coast of the US. I'm guessing it will be under one hundred feet, and it will be electronically invisible, so mark one eyeballs are the order of the day."

"Does that mean you are finished with us here? We rolled a destroyer in your latest little episode, had to wash the ship down to get rid of the radiation, and a few heads banged, but no real damage, thanks for the warning." His sarcasm cut through my tiredness, I kept forgetting all the chess pieces we had in play at any one time, and while we had constantly relayed everything we knew or suspected to his fleet, maybe I should have thought of the possibility of the terrorists blowing themselves up.

Could-a, should-a, would-a, yeah, if only I had known! Where was that million-dollar lottery ticket I kept meaning to buy and that crystal ball?

"It took us all by surprise. Arie lost a lot of troops and civilians. It's only that your magnificent fleet of brut ships is so awesome it drew off the radioactivity before it could cause more damage on land that saved the day." He had the good grace to smile, but I understood his pain. An invisible enemy with invisible nuclear weapons. Well, I thought to myself, I wonder how he will handle a direct attack on a nuclear-armed vessel at close quarters? With no physical proof.

A question for later.

Indigo gave me the thumbs up. I rolled the stress out of my shoulders and looked for Sandra. This next conversation would be telling.

"Sandra, light combat gear, wear your rank and Interpol chevrons on your chest patch, jackets for cold and wet weather, personal weapons only, ready for sea duty, pack for five days. Got it?" She looked at me with an intensity that I was getting used to as she tried to figure out where we were going.

"What rank?" I laughed.

"You liked being an Inspector, so that should work!" This time she laughed as well.

"Fay, I need you back in the C-17. Arrange for midair refueling with Indigo. Plan on two or three days. I'll give you your grids to search for sometime tomorrow. Take three shifts with you. It will be long and intense." She just nodded, no doubt thinking about how to survive in an aircraft for three or four days with twenty or so people. Just the food and water requirements would be hard to manage, not to mention waste disposal, but apart from the little island we had force landed on after being shot down by an armed drone some time ago, Serra de Santa Barbara, with its International Aeroporto das Lajes, there simply wasn't much in the way of stopping off points in the lower sections of the Atlantic.

"Indigo, I need the geeks' data soonest, and I will need Red Notices and world court orders for our two terrorists. I know the name of one but not the other. Take care of that, please." I looked around at everyone, their faces infused with anticipation as we were on the hunt again, at full throttle.

Was there any other way to be?

# Chapter Forty-Four

T he pert little gunboat was just a little under one hundred feet long, but with a very fine bow and two colossal Rolls Royce turbines driving the very latest in variable blade technology, giving the ship a clean speed in rough weather of eighteen knots and a sprint speed of twenty-four. Originally built for the Iran Navy, but decommissioned a few years ago due to the sanctions being applied by Western nations made maintaining it impossible, it was now painted a royal blue color, with red and white key lines around the superstructure, making it look like a pleasure craft or some rich person's toy. But it still had its hidden torpedo tubes, three very large guns built in behind added superstructure, a complete set of antiair missiles and sea skimmers, and a set of armed drones, and all the weapons were fully automated and could be engaged from the armor-plated bridge.

In fact, this was where the terrorists had spent their money, with a state-of-the-art electronic control center that would allow one person to fight any enemy to death from the comfort of their command chair. Big screens surrounded the console, and when they had the drones up, they would be able to see out to one hundred and fifty nautical miles in every direction. Sophisticated sonar gave them a measure of protection against submarines, although there were precious few of them left serviceable after the initial attacks. And smart undersea bombs and torpedoes would give them another layer of protection should they be hunted.

And then there were the nuclear weapons. All they had to do was load them, then use any of the three means they had designed to ignite them, and that would be that.

But crossing that Rubicon came at a price, and in truth, their objective of freeing up the funds and the plants and the flow of refugees had to take precedence over their survival and the use of the nukes.

Still, they had them, and by now, they believed the major players in their world, the Americans, Israelis, Italians, Europeans, and of course Interpol, and many of the Middle Eastern states would know of their existence and possibilities. They were counting on it to get those countries to change their collective minds. Fear was a strong motivator, and the possibility of a whole society rising up and killing their politicians was an even more frighting motivator, and all their studies showed that if one of their bombs were to be targeted appropriately, and the surviving population came to understand that it was an avoidable threat, and all it had required was loosening the control over things that made little difference to the ordinary person, then revolution and purge would follow.

As the ship rounded the headland of Ballycastle and cut a swath for Lough Swilly, the terrorist known as Maribelle Assiano managed its helm with an expert touch. At just thirty years of age, as well as an expert in nanotechnology, she was a fitness fanatic and, at six feet five inches, could bench press her own weight, which she did at every chance.

She was also an expert coxswain, having trained with the US Coast Guard Reserve. She only had a crew of four, one to look after the gas turbines and all the mechanical guts that went with them, one to cook and clean, one to relieve her at the helm, weapon controls, and help with the navigation, and one to guard her treasure, deep in the bowels of the speeding vessel. In specially made cradles, twenty-five elongated tubes shining in the red lights of the storeroom lay inert, and a second cylinder with the well-known yellow and black-propellor shaped radioactive sign stenciled on its side lay beside them. These cylinders were also nano-manufactured substrates of copper and brass, but twice the size of the original torpedoes, except for the five smaller ones made in Afghanistan, and when loaded and activated, would explode with a force of more than one megaton.

They also were also undetectable, but then so was her ship. How Interpol had found the original shells, the women had put down to dogged detective work and sloppy processes by Badawi and Abbas. They had watched with amusement as Interpol, Israel, and the US Navy had chased all over the Mediterranean Sea looking for the shells, only to have that cretinous idiot Abbas blow himself up trying to load his shells. But it had been an excellent outcome for the women because it proved they had the technical ability to manufacture undetectable nuclear weapons, and they were counting on the sheer fear that would strike into the heart of the American politicians specifically to achieve their agenda. And fear into the hearts of Interpol, who would be seen to have been the reason for the attacks in the first place with their accursed Red Notices.

All she and her fellow sisters wanted was all nineteen of the trust funds, in the USA, Canada, Greenland, Chile, Portugal, Ireland, Denmark, Norway, Finland, Estonia, Sri Lanka, Solomon Islands, New Zealand, Japan, and Iceland-freed up by Interpol; all nineteen countries had already accepted their environmental plants from Japan, and all nineteen counties once they built their eco-friendly homes fill them with child refugees from all around the world.

Was that so much to ask?

She stood with her feet apart, braced against the sway of the ship as it crashed through two-meter waves chopped up by a local storm, and she thrilled at the firm feel of the wheel as the ship bucked and bulleted like an angry broncho. Spray flew across the bridge with a swoosh, and the rotating wiper pane did its best to shed the load and provide a clear view forward.

She enjoyed the sheer pleasure of fighting the weather, the Irish Sea, and the whole dammed world if it came to that, but she mourned for her lost sister, just twenty-six and a bit, as she would want to say, someone she had lived with and cherished for a very long time. They had both been refugee children from the same camp in Syria, both parentless, and both plucked out before their tenth and sixth birthdays, respectively, simply because they had both shown a talent for reading and writing. In a sense, Maribelle felt responsible for the fate of Rena because she had left her alone in America, but the truth was Rena was a slight woman and wasn't really cut out for combat. She had a massive intellect, had sailed through school and college, and was possibly the most intelligent and brilliant psychologist to graduate from Harvard before her seventeenth birthday.

The papers she had authored on mass change processes, political warfare, and social injustice had set the whole tone for the refugee women's terrorist campaign. She had been the one to determine, using massive computer models, that you could tear down the modern world and change people's beliefs in days, using shock to overwhelm disbelief. Specifically, shock that encompassed and destroyed belief in social balance, personal safety, and collective security. Change a belief, and you could change an attitude; change an attitude, and you could change a value, and then change behavior.

Change behavior, and you could change the world.

And she had been proven correct, for once the enormity of the attacks around the world had registered on ordinary people, the Internet and most electronics killed, and oil, gas, and coal eliminated from use once and for all, the social unrest and civil disturbance that unfolded was like a tsunami of emotional proportions not previously experienced since the extinction of the dinosaurs. This emotional cathartic shock forced ordinary people to reexamine what they really believed in. And the proof of this was how fast the populations of the major cities were taking to the roads and moving into the country, seeking rural shelter and a chance to provide for their families. And how quickly refugee children were being taken in by ordinary families in Helena, the site of the first environmentally focused resettlement, and in faraway New Zealand, with a tiny population by comparison but a far bigger social heart.

Roanoke was coming along, but as a government-sponsored settlement, the usual stop-start of politics was delaying the flow of refugees, although the US had allowed the forged credentials of the refugee children and their support staff to pass immigration. And the Americans had already taken five of the environmental plants from Japan and were building them on the east coast, which meant that to get all nineteen countries up to speed, more plants would have to be manufactured by Innomatchi, yet another Red Notice, the women, needed to be rescinded by Interpol.

And now bright young Rena had been taken into custody and was now where? Who knew? She fervently wished she could do something to help, but she was on her course to facilitate major change in the world once and for all. She would make her pitch and see where it led her.

The ex-patrol boat cut through the water like a knife, and Maribelle noticed a small blip on the radar. She tuned in the image, amplified the signal, then applied a proprietary computer program to it and resolved the image as an eighty-foot fishing vessel.

Perfect! Something to practice on, to get the rust out of the weapons systems. She selected one of the smaller ship-killers, pushed the red dot onto the image, and fired. Forty seconds later, the screen bloomed, whited out, then regained its full-color image, the blast still resonating in the turbulent water spout and fireball.

Flotsam and jetsam rained down from the sky, thumping silently into the waves like confetti at a wedding.

She smiled; it was good to know that what you might have to rely on under pressure would work as advertised. They were Russian missiles, like everything else on the ship, probably provided during one of the many intense periods of fighting with Iran's neighbors. They were old but well-serviced and proven in too many battles to count. She rounded the last of Northern Ireland and changed her course to the great circle route that would take her to New York.

She called up her shipmate, handed the helm over to her, and went below to catch some sleep.

# Chapter Forty-Five

Malcolm, Luigi, Shami, Indigo, and three of the monk's best geeks shared the screen, the center of which was a moving map with a time/date running off to one side. Shami was in the lead, moving his mouse like a gun barrel, pointing at everything in quick double time. The map was scrolling at sixty times normal speed, creating the illusion that anything that moved did so at a fantastic rate, so much so that the constant blurs on the screen started to annoy. Before anyone could complain, the screen suddenly froze, holding the same image.

"Here, you can see the helicopters landing and people moving into the bunker. We don't have a great angle for face recognition, but a fast scan suggested that one of the women likely matches Amira's list of colleges from Harvey Mudd-89% probability. I've checked with her, and she agreed. This is most likely because Maribelle Assiano, a former refugee from Syria, moved to the United States and then Ireland. She majored in nanotechnology and mathematics and was working on the subproject Amira had running on metals conversion."

"When was this?" Indigo looked at the big screen, trying to read the detail which had shrunk when the screen had been frozen.

"Twelve months ago. There were a series of people coming and going for the next few months, then the mass exodus just five months ago, two months before the first attacks on the Vatican and the Dome of the Rock." I looked hard at the image and tried to imagine what the woman felt leaving her hidey-hole for the last time, given that she must have known what was coming.

"Was the guard camp occupied during this time?"

"No."

"Can you see what they are carrying out of that bunker?" In response to my question, Luigi changed the image to a close-up of the line of people moving out in the dead of night, wheeling what looked like boxes. An awful lot of boxes.

"No chance of scanning them to see what's inside?"

"Yes. These are, for all intentional purposes, live images, and I can scan them back as they were and look at what is in the boxes." Amira's lovely young face popped into the screen next to her huge electron microscope. "Here's what we found."

Now the image was dark, with seriously black holes in the middle, running up and down like a ladder. Inside each black hole was an irradiated shape that looked like a cylinder, and against each one was a smaller version of the same thing. They moved like ghosts up the screen until; they disappeared.

"Where did they go?" My voice squeaked; I couldn't help it. I was tense, and only a small part of that was due to the fact I was convinced I was looking at more nuclear possible shells, albeit of a different design to the original torpedoes.

"Into the aircraft. Which, if you look closely, disappears until we uncloak it. They were still using the old 'black hole' technology at that time. Watch what happens next." We all followed the image over a dark background, typical of tracking a helicopter at night. The frame rate speeded up, then went too fast; it was a blur, then steadied again.

"That was two and a half hours' worth of time. Here it lands, nothing happens that we can track, but our military geeks tell us it refueled, it then takes off again, three hours plus, then here it is at its last stop."

"Where is that?"

"Tartus, Syria. Watch closely."

The image of the shiny outlines punched up again on the screen and, this time moved away from the helicopter and onto what I guessed was a flatbed truck. It was still nighttime, and just as my eyes got used to the dark images, they sped up again, blurred across the screen, then stopped.

"Here, they are transferred onto a ship. We hunted up a daylight version, and this is what was here." A beautiful blue-hulled ship with a snazzy red and white trim sat at the docks, a crew dressed in whites standing on the decks. "Remember, this was eight months ago, and because we love you, Jessica, we tracked it to where it stayed until last night. Guess where?" I was incredibly impressed with the geeks' work. They had gone the extra mile and a half. It must have taken them hours to dig all this up from months and months ago.

"Northern Island, probably Belfast."

"Give the girl a teddy bear! Yes, Belfast, where a certain terrorist was chased away from just hours ago. The boat became a blur three months ago, a day after the attacks started in Italy and Israel. It was still a blur yesterday, but now it has disappeared. We can't find it anywhere." I screwed my face up in concentration. Even if they were using the electronic cloaking device, we should see where they weren't, but Luigi said quite clearly, 'can't find it anywhere'.

"Do they have a new way of hiding things from us?"

"It appears so. But we have eyes. We know what they look like. We need to get eyes in the sky ASAP." I nodded. It made sense, pity. I had pulled Fay and her drones out of Ireland a week ago to chase Abbas and Badawi all over the Med.

"Do we have air-sea rescue in that area?" Silence, then Indigo chipped in. "Yes, A Garda Síochana or the Irish Coast Guard. There's an air unit at Shannon, rotary wing." I considered my options; how far could that ship go in twelve hours?

"Indigo, how fast is that ship?"

"Cruise at eighteen knots all day, sprint at twenty-four. If you're asking how far they could have got so far, then my estimate would be just over two hundred nautical miles."

"How fast are their helicopters?"

"Plan on one hundred and ten knots."

"Endurance at that speed?" He waved his hands in the air, dived into his mini, then looked back up at the camera over the big screen.

"Six to eight hours, maybe more, with an extra fuel bladder or two." I nodded as I had expected.

"Indigo, get one airborne ASAP, maximum fuel, have them fly out for two and a half hours due west, then due north, until they are abeam the northern tip. Tell them not to stop, just look like a rescue helicopter, and tell us what they see." He nodded and bent to his mini. Because we had based Fay and the C-17 and drones in Ireland initially, we had excellent contacts in government circles, so I believed Indigo would have no issue there. I checked my watch. Only twenty minutes before we had to leave to fly to the admiral. Sandra was already dressed, her form-fitting combat outfit looking like something out of a fashion magazine.

She had tied her long blond hair up into a ponytail, which shot out of the back of her black baseball cap like a fountain. She pointed at me mimed, looking at her watch. I nodded. I would have to break off the meeting and get dressed.

"Excellent work, everyone, and I mean really excellent. Continue briefing Sandra. I'll be off the air for twenty minutes." And I left the room to get into my own slightly worn, definitely not fashionable combat duds, which comprised of a many-pocketed pair of baggy trousers, my usual well-worn boots, a sleeved shirt with a few additional extras, and my own version of a baseball cap. I strapped my weapon onto my hip, a pair of magazines on the other, and an SOG combat knife behind them. Then I bent and strapped on a four-inch Beretta in an ankle holster. After all, a girl couldn't have too many weapons, could she? As I walked back to find Sandra, I ran into Indigo.

"Coast Guard will be airborne just after you, on station in three hours. *Comandante, abbi cura di te stesso e non lasciare che Sandra ti metta in troppi guai!*" I certainly would not let Sandra get me into trouble, and I would try to look after myself, but who knew? There was a bounty on my head, bound to draw someone's attention.

"*Grazie, Indigo, prenditi cura di tutti per me. Stai attento.*" I gave my favorite Italian a hug, then headed to the door. The helicopter was the same one we had flown in the day before, same crew, so I just relaxed back into my seat and let them do all the work. Next to me, Sandra mimicked me, restful for the first time in days. Our most recent prisoner sat locked to his seat, head bagged.

The admiral met us on the helideck. We stooped until it had taken off. He led us to a huge brute of a helicopter the size of a double-decker bus, its massive floppy rotors hanging down as if exhausted from their previous efforts.

"Flight time will be a little over six hours, so make your selves comfortable. Stretch out if you like. There's only the five of us." And as we climbed in, I saw the master chief who had originally met us when we had first landed onboard the US Navy ship. He was in day camos, well-armed, but also well-rested, and very, very calm as he transferred our prisoner. I took this as a good sign. The admiral looked at the prisoner, his man, then over to me.

"The chief will act as your interpreter once we're on board. Anything you need or want goes through him. I take it you intend to keep your weapons?"

"Yes, sir, we do." He gave me one of his very hard looks, the type that would freeze junior officers to the deck, then just grinned and sat back.

"I expected nothing less. Do you have the paperwork for me?"

"No, sir, not yet. It is being prepared in Lyon for you. It will be transmitted directly to your ship and copied to us." I held his eyes with mine, motioned to Jessica to put headphones on the prisoner, waited patiently, then turned so I faced the admiral head-on. "Admiral, I hope you understand that our rules of engagement are very different from yours?" The look he gave me could have melted rocks, and I swear I saw fire in his eyes. Then he blinked, and he smiled.

"Commander, I have been well briefed. I expect to go to the wall for you, I don't know exactly what that may entail at this point, but we will not let you down." I nodded, not knowing what to say next. I was saved by the intercom, suddenly blaring out my name.

"Commander Riley, call for you, channel four." I switched to four, then hunkered down to create the illusion of privacy.

"Commander, Jessica, sorry to bother you, but I have some very interesting news for you." If Amira could be any more excited, I would be surprised.

"Go."

"The hazmat team that visited the blast site in Gaza brought the shells back with them. Jessica, they have no radiation signature at all, they are pristine, and frankly, I am in awe of what these women had done with their nanomachines!" I wondered how to include Sandra in this call, then gave up, not having the faintest idea of how to achieve that in this flying truck. The five of us sat in webbed seats up one end in the monstrous hold, which was empty from stem to stern.

"Explain what that means, please." I moved away as far as the headset cord would allow me, then the chief moved to a panel, pulled out my plug, motioned to me to follow him, plugged me back in the middle of the cargo hold, then hobbled back to his seat. I waved my thanks to him and looked at Sandra. She took the hint, then mirrored the chief's movements, and sat down beside me with her thumb up. "Amira, I've got Sandra here with me now. Can you repeat what you said and then explain, remembering I am not a geek. And we're on an open line." Laughter rang in our ears, then she quickly sobered up.

"Sandra, hello from the geeks who rule. By the way, we recovered the shells from the Gaza bomb site, and they show no signs of radioactivity, and they are not damaged in any way." Sandra looked at me, surprise in her eyes.

"And that means, what, exactly?" I tried not to let exasperation get into my voice, but it was really hard dealing with all this technical stuff day after day.

"When they are sealed, they are a binary neutral electromagnetic neutral substance. Nothing can get in or out of the substrate. This is a fantastic discovery; you have to believe me."

"I do, but what does that mean to us?" I could hear her young face collapse at my ignorance, and I wondered why she had not used her mini. Then I remembered we believed the military net we were using had been penetrated by the terrorists, and I wondered who was behind the decision to let them know we had worked out a secret of theirs. I smelled the work of an intelligence agency, and I would have to follow that up sometime in the future.

"Well, in simple terms, they can't be destroyed, at least not by any means we currently have." I sat back, thinking about the cylinders we had seen loaded onto the converted gunboat.

"What does the lack of radioactivity tell us?" Sandra beat me to the question by a hair's breadth.

"Good question. It means that the substrate is atomically stable and neutral."

"I'm none the wiser, but thanks anyway. If the shells can't be destroyed, how do they blow them up?" I heard her face smile again, her voice several tones lighter.

"They can't blow up. That's the whole reason for the design. The shell creates a barrier against any explosive force or mechanical for that matter."

"No more bang for the buck?" Sandra's sarcasm was back in full swing, and I just laughed.

"So, in summary," I said, just a little tired of it all, "we can't destroy them, and they can't blow up. They are just a clever piece of engineering designed to scare the shit out of us." I heard Amira suck air into her lungs. I think she had finally realized we were not happy with her findings or enchanted with the technical marvel that was the dual-metallic substrate.

"Sorry, I should have thought more about the consequences."

"It's okay, not your fault. Keep up the good work. We appreciate it." I pulled the headphones off, leaned in close to Sandra's ear, and whispered.

"Our options are now very limited. Stay with me while I work it all out." I sat back in the webbed seat, closed my eyes, and tried to remember all that I could about the Atlantic Ocean. I had been in the navy, and we were well versed in the oceans and seas of the world, but it felt like a thousand years ago when I sat in that particular class back at the NCIS academy.

But the deepest trench was near Porto Rico, far too close to civilization to risk it, and today we had submersibles that could dive to thirty-six thousand feet, so I needed a better strategy when the time came.

I must have dozed off because Sandra was shaking me by the arm, and the helicopter was making huffing and puffing noises, with very loud electronic whirring sounds coming from the sides. We thumped down, and I realized we were on the carrier, wherever it was.

I waited until the rear door opened, looked back to make sure the chief had our prisoner, then stepped aside so the admiral could lead us out. Much fanfare, whistles, tannoy announcements, flight deck crew racing around like demented dogs, the massive rotors swinging down close and closer to our heads as they wound down, all very exciting but completely lost on me as I followed him to the door in the superstructure that led to the bridge.

"Chief, you may already have another prisoner onboard, the one from the States. I need them separated and ready for interrogation in ten minutes, please. Their comfort is not a priority." He gave me that hard look of his again, and I could see the busy work happening behind his bushy eyebrows. He just nodded, then pulled the prisoner away as if he weighed nothing. I followed the admiral to the bridge. Sandra had obviously followed the chief, and when we arrived, the same pomp and ceremony occurred as had at our arrival on deck. A cockswain blew his whistle, and someone shouted, "Pacific Fleet aboard!" while I just stood by and watched. The Captain and the Admiral shook hands and had a brief conversation, which earned me a hard look from both of them, so I just pulled my flight helmet and goggles off, looped my hair back behind my ears, and put my baseball cap back on.

It was a man's world, but the three women on the bridge were all looking at me out of the corner of their eyes, faces neutral. One was a lieutenant; I couldn't see the ranks of the other two. The Captain turned to me and held out his hand.

"Commander, nice to have you aboard. Can I get you anything?" I shook his hand and decided to be polite, at least for the time being.

"Sir, I have two prisoners to interrogate. They are known terrorists, and I need to attend to them first.

"Then I need nautical charts from Ireland to the US please, annotated with the current position, speed, and heading of every ship we have, as well as the destroyer that left the Mediterranean yesterday. If a paper is not possible, I'll need a tablet that I can draw on. And, sir, you will need to change course soon. I will advise you of our heading as soon as I can work it out. Do you have long-range observation aircraft onboard?" He looked curious, more than annoyed at having his fleet taken over by a woman of uncertain origin, but having arrived with the admiral probably gave me some temporary credibility.

"Yes, we do, four of them, sub hunters, twelve-hour endurance. Why do you ask?"

"Sir, I'd appreciate it if we could leave the Q&A for now. Can you have them ready to launch in an hour, and can they be air-refueled?" He nodded, I wasn't sure which question he was ageing to, but I chose to think it was both. "Sir, I need permission to leave the bridge."

"Granted." I followed a sailor out of the bridge and made the long trip through corridors, down ladders, and around corners until we were in the maintenance hangar, where the chief sat on a metal desk smoking a small cigar.

"They'll kill you, you know," I said conversationally. He just smiled.

"If they don't, you and your pretty companion will probably get me killed in any case. How do you want to play this?"

"Hard arse, worse arse, giant pain in the arse. Let's start with the woman." He crushed his cigar out, and I followed him to a steel cell built out of a container. I entered, and he stood at the door in the at-ease position, hands behind his back and his face fixed with a scowl. Sandra sat opposite our prisoner, drinking a coffee and flicking through some paperwork.

"Red Notice, world court judgement, in absentia, summary execution recommended, all good." She looked at the young woman who sat opposite us, her face streaked with tears, her hair messed up from the bag that had been over her head for hours, her hands shackled to the top of the desk, with a chain leading down to her ankles. The faded green boiler suit disguised her body shape, and she looked as miserable as it was possible.

Good.

Advantage us. I flicked a look at Sandra, giving her the lead.

"What is your name?" Her dry, bored tone was as discouraging as the scraped walls of the container.

"I want a lawyer, I want a phone call, I want my rights!" she sobbed, bending her head to her shackled hands to wipe the snot and tears from her face. I looked up from the paperwork and smiled at her.

"You have no rights. You are not entitled to a lawyer, a phone call, or a piss in the corner. Nothing. Not even a cup of this terrible coffee.

"You are being held under the Terrorist Laws as modified in 2022, which are quite clear. If you plan, plot, organize, or perform an act of terror, assist in any way and enable such an act, support persons or entities in any such act, or even breathe the same air as anyone who does such things, you are guilty under the law, and the penalty is death." She looked shocked at her nonexistent boots, her face now a complete mess of terror, fear, confusion, and more fear.

"You were asked your name. What is it?" She looked like a deer in the headlights, her skin color washed out by the harsh lights, and her eyes were darting back and forth between Sandra and myself at a million miles an hour.

"My name is Rena Niele, and I am a citizen of the United States of America, and I demand my rights!" She screamed out the last, slumping forward in her seat to bury her head in her arms. I let her cry, her sobs not reaching even a millimeter into my heart. Here was a woman who had planned with other women to use nuclear weapons on an unsuspecting population without fear or favor and obviously without any thought of the consequences.

"Inspector Thomas, add the name Rena Niele to the warrants, master chief prepare the firing squad."

"At once, ma'am." And he opened the door, then slammed it shut behind himself. Our prisoner looked up in horror, her fear was palpable, and she started to vibrate.

"If you tell us what we need to know, I will suspend your execution, but I want answers now, and they had better be correct. Who was your partner you were talking to on the phone?" She wiped her face on her sleeve just as the chief crashed back in.

"Firing party ready, sir, at your command." I nodded and held my hand up in the 'stop' position.

"Hold, for now, chief, but stand by." He crashed out again, the bang of the door shaking the whole container and reverberating around the small space.

"Name?"

"Maribelle Assiano, my partner for the last five years." I nodded and made a show of looking through the papers as if confirming what she had said. The chief crashed back into the container and stood with his arms folded behind his back.

"And where is she now?"

"Somewhere in the Atlantic."

"Headed for?" She paused, probably trying to think how much we knew versus how much she should tell us. I smashed my fist down on the table, making a noise that would wake the dead and caused the papers we had collected to jump into the air, some falling onto the metal floor where we let them lay.

"We know she is on a converted gunboat; we know when she left and where she left from. You have one last chance to live. Where is she headed?"

She looked so pathetic I almost felt sorry for her, but the memory of Sandra and I getting shot as we boarded the terrorist boat holding some of the shells flashed through my mind, then the image of a rocket blowing up half our squad and all such thoughts disappeared.

"America. I think New York, but that was to be determined after you responded to our demands." I looked at her, put a forced smile on my face, and decided to play a little rough and dirty.

"Tell me, how does holding the world to ransom using nuclear bombs help your cause with the refugee children? Do you really think we will forgive you for the terror this will create?" I laughed, looked at Sandra, and punched her on the arm. "Do you believe these people?" She laughed back at me, enjoying the moment, probably wondering where I was going with the interrogation. The prisoner had a totally different reaction to the one I expected. She drew herself up, sat straight, squared her shoulders, and looked me in the eye.

"All our computer modelling showed that if you believed strongly enough that we had the capability of making and using nuclear weapons, the fear of that alone would be enough for us to get what we want." And I heard the pride in her voice, the last thing I expected, then I threw out a hook to see what else I could catch.

"You're the genius psychologist who worked all this out?" I laughed, this time for real. I couldn't help myself. Didn't they realize the thin wedge of social stability that existed because of their previous attacks couldn't survive yet another type of threat? Particularly one that used weapons of mass destruction.

"Yes. I am Harvard-trained, and I studied and modelled this for nearly three years. I helped plan all phases of the attacks, it was designed to work, and we anticipated that America, with its normal capriciousness and self-interest, would steal some of the environmental plants to gain an economic advantage over the rest of the world. This threat was designed to reverse that action and make everyone realize once and for all that creating political situations where defenseless children are left parentless and homeless rotting in their wake is unacceptable." This last was shouted with a passion I understood, I had an internal conflict over this very issue since day one, and I knew the boss had seen it in me and been concerned it might weaken my resolve.

Wars and skirmishes raged all over the planet in a never-ending series of political moves designed for gain, either economic, or worse, conquest or ethnic cleansing, and had for thousands of years. Maybe it was a part of the human condition to want everything your neighbor had, but in what had been the modern world, surely, we could have found a peaceful way to live side by side?

Wishful thinking. Time to get back to business.

"Your plan was destined to fail from the first bomb."

"All you have managed to do is enrage the world, create social chaos, destroy economies, kill millions, and empower every creep on the planet with a gun or a knife. Oh, and by the way, your actions have directly led to the creation of millions more refugees. How do you reconcile your actions with that?" I stood suddenly, causing the rest of the papers on the desk to slide onto the floor.

"You will remain here why I decide your fate. No last meal, no calls to mum or dad begging forgiveness, you helped create this chaos, now suffer the consequences." Sandra bent behind me as I stomped out, collecting the paperwork. The chief slammed the steel door shut with such force I feared it might bend, but it locked tight, and the three of us stood uncomfortably thinking about our prisoner and her future if she had one. Sandra ran her hand down my arm, and I turned to look at her. "We have the names now. At least the paperwork will be accurate. I need a coffee and not that mud you passed off on Sandra." The chief laughed, reached for a wall phone, mumbled into it, hung up, then sat down on the desk again. "You ladies play hardball; I admire your style. Would you really have her shot?" I held his gaze and felt Sandra's eyes on me, so I just smiled.

"Chief, a lady never gives up all her secrets." A steward arrived with a covered tray, and as fast as we could manage it, three mugs of coffee had been poured, and the three of us then eyed off the cookies that had been placed on a paper plate. I ignored the calories, inhaled the smell of the brew, then just slurped it down and refilled my mug.

"This is where I miss Indigo," I said, letting my eyes close as I wallowed in the caffeine high.

"Who's Indigo?" I looked at the chief. He was a curious person, and as I remembered it, Indigo had not been with us when we had first boarded the navy vessel some weeks ago.

"Indigo is Colonel Indigo Kashasini, head of Interpol Italy and the best coffee maker on the planet." He nodded. No doubt, with all his experience, there was an Indigo somewhere in his life, so he could relate. And a question that had been floating at the back of my mind suddenly rose and demanded attention, so I moved away and dialed my mini. It only took a minute, and I had my answer. I turned to the master chief.

"Okay, next, same roles, but this one might be in three or four languages." He looked bemused, then led us to another container just a few feet away. He banged on the door. It opened, and a marine gunnery sergeant loaded for bear stepped out.

"Chief."

"Gunny. Stand very by, have a coffee while you wait." We entered the same setup, except that this time Badawi still had the hood on his head. I reached over and pulled it off. I started with English to see his reaction.

"Mister Malik Badawi, aka Thana Praxidike, previously commander of Al Bar al Shirak, is friends with one Amir Abbas. I regret to inform you Mister Abbas won't be joining us today, as he destroyed himself, his men, and a good chunk of the Gaza strip recently. Made quite a mess. Now, to you. You are charged with several capital crimes, all involving terrorism, and you have already been issued with a Red Notice, tried in absentia by the world court, and sentenced to death. Is there anything you would like to say before we execute you?" And I sat back from the table and just looked at him. Sandra pulled her weapon out and laid it on the table. His eyes flicked from hers to mine, then over to the chief, who, this time, was leaning insolently against the door. They were just a relaxed, happy bunch of people delivering a shitty message to someone who didn't really deserve more than a minute of our time.

He remained silent. I couldn't read his eyes or his face. Perhaps he had given up all hope, having been shot and captured, then hooded and transported in total silence. I had read accounts of the strongest types of personalities breaking down under such conditions, which was why we used them.

Saved a lot of time.

"Chief, please unshackle the prisoner, and bag him. Then you and the gunny need to take a walk up to the NCO's mess, where we will join you."

"Ma'am," he stood rigid, saluted, moved to the shackles, bagged the terrorist, then pulled him up by his wounded arm. Sandra grabbed the other, and we filed out into the massive space of the maintenance hangar, littered with aircraft with their wings folded, some in pieces. Sandra and I took one arm each. I held his chains, and we walked in one direction towards the huge aircraft lift that ran down from the flight deck, the chief and the gunny in the other.

We reached the huge open side of the aircraft lift and stood Badawi facing us with his back to the ocean, streaming past with the occasional slap of a wave. I looked at Sandra, and she looked at me, pulled her weapon out, and shot him in the head. I shot him in the heart. He started to topple forwards. We caught him and simply pushed him backwards until he fell into the ocean. We policed our brass, I punched Sandra on the shoulder, and we walked off to the NCO's mess.

"What are you going to do about the woman?" I shook my head.

"I don't know. We kept many of the other women alive. They are living in cells with no daylight and no privileges. They may as well be dead. Executing these terrorists in this manner makes me sick to the stomach, but it's what we signed on for, so there is no value in complaining. These bastards kill men, women, children, and babies indiscriminately. They are the worst of humanity. They have no conscience, no morals, no standards, just greed, and fervor. And this bastard had what he thought were nuclear weapons he could use anytime he liked on anyone who took his fancy. And in the end, he was doing it for money. If we don't take care of them, then who will?"

"You'll get no argument from me. What do we tell the chief?" I looked at her and smiled, feeling lighter than I had an hour ago.

"Is it too late to shout 'man overboard?" She laughed from her belly, a raucous sound that was music to my ears. We still had some hard yards to cover, but at least we now knew the who and the what, and the why of the current attacks.

"Chief, gunny, any chance of some food?" We sat down opposite them, the gunny poured coffee and passed a plate of sandwiches across, and we all sat silently for a moment.

"Chief, I need you to get the woman prisoner back to Israel. If you contact Interpol Italy, they will give you the details. The admiral has the contacts on his mini. And I need those charts please, soonest, and a meeting arranged with the Admiral and Captain in an hour." He passed a massive laptop over the table, then an electronic pad the size of half the table.

"This belongs to the navigator, he considers it a precious possession, so if you break it, you own it. Charts on the computer, slide them to the pad and scribble with the pencil. Is there anything we need to clean up in the hangar?"

"No chief, no mess, no fuss." His look said it all, but as in all things military, if you didn't put it into a report in triplicate, it didn't exist, so he let it go. I knew he knew, and he knew I knew he knew, so we both left it at that.

"Then, if you're happy here, we'll let you carry on and arrange for your meeting." I nodded, and he and the gunny left, closing the door behind them, but not before I saw the gunny take up a position outside. So we wouldn't be bothered, but we couldn't go anywhere without an escort, either, thank you, Admiral!

I pushed the laptop to Sandra.

"Ireland to the east coast of the US, plot me the thumb line, then add in all our ships in the vicinity." I pulled the pad to me, fired it up, and marveled at its clear, crisp resolution, then I bent to look at the data Sandra was flicking over to me. It was clear we had a good position to intercept our speeding terrorist and probably two days to do it. I had decided we needed deep water to sink her in, and no record of the location, and I had no idea how to manage that. It was something I needed to work on in my spare time!

"I picked up the fact that Amira said the shells can't be exploded. Do you believe that to be true in this case?" I thought about her question. It was one of the variables I was worried about.

"My thinking is that if we sink her in deep enough water, it won't matter. We know from the Abbas experience the tubes of nuclear material will explode if fractured, which gets a nice mushroom cloud, and if the shells do or don't explode, so long as they sink to the bottom, it doesn't matter. The problem I am wrestling with is how to disguise the location of where we sink her."

She looked at me with a question in her eyes, thought about it, started to speak, then swallowed her tongue. She finally scratched her head. She studied the laptop, nodded to herself, then looked back up at me.

"Well, what do we need to find her, then sink her?"

"We have Fay in the C-17 starting a grid search. The Irish coast guard should have finished their grid, and we have four sub-killers aboard we can put up to get eyeballs on the ocean. So let's assume we find her in the next day or two. You asked what we need to sink her?"

"Yes. We need to take out the boat completely, definitively, and quickly. We need it broken up into little bits that sink like stones, never to be found again. And if the shells won't explode, then they need to disappear and never be found again."

"Should we plan on boarding her rather than sinking her?" That got my attention. I thought about this for a moment, then shrugged my shoulders.

"Good plan, so long as the bombs are inert and don't play into her defense strategy." I thought about my chat with a certain spymaster earlier and decided to share.

"Arie put the 'can't explode' message out over the military net to give us an advantage. We know they are listening to Milnet, so they know we know."

"I figured that when I heard Amira. But consider this. These bombshells are three times the size of the torpedoes and have different shapes. Maybe these ones will go off." She had a good point, one I had wrestled with, and the answer I kept coming back to was to destroy the female terrorist and her ship as completely as possible, in the deepest water possible, then hide the engagement from the rest of the world. I moved the positions of the fleet around with my pen, then had an epiphany.

"We've got some subs with us?" She stared at me with a bemused look on her face.

"Yes, four of them, I think, the standard for a fleet of this size." I nodded. Now I had a picture of how we could run her down, box her in, and destroy her utterly and completely. I was just congratulating myself when my mini buzzed. I opened it to find Fay's face filling the screen with tears in her eyes.

"Fay, what's up?" She absently wiped her eyes with the back of one green Nomex gloved hand. She was obviously in the C-17 somewhere.

"The Irish helicopter was shot down, and all the crew was lost. We have the position. We're over it now, but no sign of the target. It happened at least three hours ago, but it gives us a datum to work from. The real problem is the weather is seriously bad, with cloud down to three hundred feet, up to forty-five thousand feet, heavy rain, squalls, and near cyclonic winds. We can't see a bloody thing on the radar, and our eyeballs are useless!" I felt for her. She was initially trained by the FBI, had become a superior agent who had caught our eye, and was a refugee child herself; so, like me, she had strong feelings about the women and no doubt about the crew of the search and rescue helicopter.

She was compassionate caring and had pistol-whipped a terrorist without a second thought, so she had the stones we needed in Section Five.

495

"Fay, not your fault, I underestimated this woman, and we won't do that again. Stay in the air, for now. Fly the grids we gave you. If the weather doesn't clear in four hours, return and wait on the ground."

"Yes, Commander. Do you have any new information from the prisoners?" I thought about how to answer her, then just sighed.

"Unfortunately, Malik Badawi turned out to not be able to swim, and we're sending the woman back to Israel. We're on the hunt. Call you later."

"I heard that. Pity about the Coast Guard, they're all volunteers, civilians, in Ireland?"

"All but the aircrew, yes. But she's given us a datum, so move your great circle route accordingly. We need to talk to the admiral." I stood and opened the door. The gunny was relaxed, but his index finger was right alongside the trigger guard, so he was primed, for what I had no idea.

"Gunny, we need to speak with the admiral, please." I turned just as he pulled the door closed and risked a small smile.

"They are afraid of us." Sandra made a 'pump up the muscles' move with one arm and cheered me up to no end. I thought about the many ways the boss had broken the tension and realized that while we now had a different mix of personalities, we had the same emotional needs. Shooting someone who was handcuffed, in chains, with a bag over his head had stained me emotionally, given me an acid stomach sucked all the joy out. But the alternative wasn't any better, just longer and more drawn out. The only difference was this way. We carried the baggage and not someone else. Although Sandra seemed just fine, so maybe her natural battery bunny sunny disposition made all the difference.

The door opened, and the Admiral and the Captain walked in, moved straight over to the coffee urn, helped themselves, then sat opposite us. The admiral gave me the stinky eye and looked at me over the rim of his mug.

"I'm told the ship's complement is now one short?" I looked back at him with as bland a face as I could manage, given I was on the verge of insane cackling at the ridiculous way he had asked the question.

Here was a man who commanded thousands of sailors on a war footing, with enough weapons to blow up half the planet, and he was quizzing me about a missing terrorist who had used nuclear weapons to threaten innocent civilians in the Middle East? Seriously, how could anyone with a brain get upset over that?

"He couldn't swim. Now, if I may, I need to ask you some technical questions." His stare was long and hard, but he spoiled the effect with a thin smile as he nodded for me to proceed. I held the tablet up so they could both see it. The Captain swung around pressed a little control panel on the wall, which then slid soundlessly down into the floor, revealing a huge flat screen. I flicked the images to it, and they both reversed themselves in their seats.

"I'm not going to insult either of you by asking for technical or performance details on the fleet, I'm simply going to paint a picture, and I need you to resolve a viable solution. In terms of the outcome, there is only one, I want a specific vessel completely destroyed and sent to the deepest part of the ocean, between fifteen hundred and eighteen hundred nautical miles from the coast of Ireland, and I want no record of the sinking in the operational plans." I watched their faces glaze over as I mentioned deliberately attacking a vessel on the high seas without a declaration of war. And got the predictable questions.

"This is a civilian vessel?"

"Ex-Iranian gunboat, but yes."

"Country of registration?"

"Don't know, don't care, this boat goes to the bottom of the ocean and somewhere in this area." I pointed to the box we had created based on the small amount of data we had and what I remembered from my NCIS days. They both peered at the screen, the Captain raising to run his finger around the dotted lines of the box I had drawn electronically.

Did I mention I failed finger painting in kindergarten?

The box was a little wiggly on some sides and encompassed an area of some two hundred and forty thousand square nautical miles-the box was six hundred by four hundred nautical miles, with the long side between Ireland and the United States. I had added little dotted lines out to the sides another two hundred nautical miles on either side, just in case.

"And so you don't think this will be easy, think about this, the terrorist who is in control of this boat is a genius-level technical wizard, who has built thirty to forty nuclear bombs, each capable of at least a ten megaton blast, and she wants to get to New York as desperately as I want to sink her. So, gentlemen, what about it?"

The Captain sat down and looked at his admiral. They held a silent look-deep-intomy-eyes-conversation, then rotated their chairs around, so the big screen was now at their backs.

The Captain was the first to speak, perfectly calm, in that wonderful Boston accent that was both slow and concise. It could turn a woman to jelly under different circumstances.

"Commander, unless I received orders to the contrary, I cannot sink any civilian ship on the high seas unless there is a perceivable threat to my country or a declaration of war. What proof do you have that this vessel is carrying nuclear weapons?" I smiled and nodded, but my patience was wearing thin, I needed these naval experts to put their minds to how we found this needle in a fifteen million square nautical mile haystack, and I needed them started on it now. But before I could fire back, the admiral held his hand up to stop my retort.

"Captain, I will give you those orders, and will allow you to confirm them with Admiral Ocher, currently C-in-C Surface Fleets if you need to." He looked straight at me and held his hand out. I passed him the Red Notice and the world court order, and the first thing he noticed, of course, was the blank space where the name of the vessel usually went. He put the papers on the desk and folded his large hands-on top.

"Can you walk us through your reasoning in reaching your conclusion that this specific vessel is your target?" I nearly boiled over, then remembered the navy played by much cleaner, nicer rules than we did, so I sat back and gestured to Sandra.

"We can, but I need you to work on your solution starting now, and on the basis that you will not be required to sink anyone for an hour or two, can you accept that?" The admiral looked at his captain, and the captain looked at me, probably wondering how come a badly dressed woman openly armed, who he really didn't know anything about, could negotiate face-to-face with a fleet admiral.

"We can do that. Meet us in the tactical space in thirty minutes, ready with your story." They both got up and left. The door remained open, and the gunny remained outside, but this time he looked at a loss in terms of what to do. Then the chief came in, sat down, looked at me, and smiled.

"You sure can get people worked up. Never seen the Admiral, or the Captain for that matter, so pissed off." I just rolled my shoulders; the stress was starting to get to me again. Sandra had her head deep in her mini, using a pair of remote earphones for privacy. I stood, walked out back into the corridor, looking at the chief who had followed me, pointed up to the flight deck, and set off. I waited until we were standing in the open air, between the back of the Island and a brace of Hornets fully loaded with missiles but wings folded and chained to the deck. Little red flags fluttered from where they had been attached to the missiles, signifying they were inert.

"Chief, we are in a world of hurt. Since I first met you, we have recovered twenty-four capable nuclear bombs from terrorists all over the Mediterranean, and one of the bastards behind that is your missing man. Now we chase a boat that has potentially thirty or forty more nukes, all many times more powerful than the ones we captured. I know you think we are cowboys, but the rules we play by are designed to eliminate the very people who do these things for no better reason than they want to attack someone or something because they're pissed off." He looked away out to sea, where the horizon indicated we were in for some of the storm Fay had mentioned. The Gods were angry, no doubt about that. I just hoped they weren't too angry with me.

"Commander, Jessica, if I may call you that," I nodded. He continued, "When you look at it from our perspective, we are a highly trained and disciplined force designed to work under the toughest of conditions and protect our country from all threats, both foreign and domestic, although, frankly, the domestic issue is beyond my comprehension." I waved that comment away, I couldn't blame the navy for anything that had happened on land during the terrorist attacks, and they had been as helpful as they could be, supporting us every time we needed them.

"But by your very nature, you represent a clear and present danger. You exude tension and threat. Even our marines are scared of you, and that says a lot. Our life is simple — we get up in the morning, eat, train, muck around some, then sleep, and repeat. We respond to orders, we have an established hierarchy, and we always know what to do and how to do it. We look to our officers for direction and good judgement." He looked at me with a kindness in his eyes I had rarely seen in a military man.

"On the other hand, you and your people seem to make everything up as you go along, you constantly flout tradition and rank, and you bust balls at the drop of a hat." I smiled at that. I'd have to remember what he had just said so eloquently and take it back to the team in Italy.

"And then I remember you are experts at asymmetric warfare, you chase fucking terrorists for a living, there are no rules in your game other than get there first, survive and kick terrorist arse. I get that, but for the love of me, I couldn't do what you do day in and day out. I would shatter under the pressure of the constant need to be so flexible, open, and ready to change direction in a heartbeat. We like structure, we like predictability, we like rules, we like form and shape, and know what comes next, who to look up to, and who to follow, what it is we have to do, and how to do it. That's all I'm saying." I looked at him, a big hefty man, probably in his early forties, greying a little around the edges, but with a tough well-worn face and eyes that held both intelligence and passion.

And he had just described us and our mission to a tee.

"Chief, thank you for that. We really don't mean to scare anyone. I guess it's just an attitude thing, in that we have to be prepared to meet any threat from wherever it comes and whenever it comes.

"And that threat doesn't usually announce itself or walk in the front door. And we rely on you and others like you to apply your disciplined military skills to help us succeed. We are a very small team, believe it or not, if you don't count all the geeks and technical staff we steal from our member countries, I have less than six direct reports, and two of those come from your own military command. We function by force multiplying through stealing the best of the best from the armies and navies of our members. That's why we are here, on this boat, at this time. I asked your president's military advisor for the admirals help, and here we are." He looked a little lost at this statement, his eyebrows scrunching up in thought.

"The president's military advisor?"

"Yes, General Saunders."

"No wonder you walk with heavy boots. I had no idea you were connected so high up the food chain." I smiled, the tenseness had gone out of his stance, and he seemed genuinely relaxed as if I had settled something inside him. A sailor popped his head around the corner of the Island and snapped to attention.

"Chief, the Admiral wants you and the commander in the tac room." We followed the sailor, and I felt that the animosity that had always circled the chief was no longer present. I would think on that. Maybe I needed to have a better approach to the rank and file in the future. We met Sandra escorted by the gunny outside the impressive double steel doors pained dark blue, with the words "Pacific Fleet Tactical-all you who enter here be smart!" wrapped up in white painted rope with a sailor's bowline knot at the end. Someone had a sense of humor!

The Captain and the Admiral were sitting with three senior offices, all dressed in day-camo, sea, that mishmash of light and dark blue splotches that looked like a three-year-old had painted them, all with laptops, all looking very serious. I immediately filtered what I had been going to say, held Sandra back by her arm.

"No details, just the bones." She gave me a silent nod. No way we would share our operational data with so many people, no matter who they were. The admiral saw our little connection, scowled, then tilted his head sharply to one side. Once again, he reminded me why he was an admiral and I was just a tolerated visitor.

"Gentlemen, please wait on the bridge. Commander, the Captain and I are ready for your briefing." The three offices stood, collected their laptops, and left, not looking at either Jessica or myself directly. I had to give the admiral points for that. He had read as well. I decided to use my newly modified approach, all three minutes old and looked the captain straight in the eye.

"Captain, I am Commander Jessica Riley, and I head Section Five of Interpol. Inspector Sandra Thomas and I are here at the invitation of the president's military advisor, general Saunders. Is there anything else you would like to know about us before we start the briefing?" He had the good grace to smile and just bobbed his head in acknowledgement.

"Get on with it." The admiral had obviously lost patience with us, so I sat back and let Sandra take them through our investigation over the last three weeks — just the high points, with images and pictures time/date stamped. When the image of the step-ladder-like photo of the new shells went up, and the data box beside enunciated the ten-megaton blast prediction, potentially times thirty or forty, both sailors froze. "And you say these bombs are undetectable?" I noted the Admiral's use of the word 'say' and not some lesser words like 'belief' or 'think'. Points to Sandra for her excellent assembly and presentation of the facts as we knew them. And points for the admiral finally understanding we were not here with the direct support of his president because we were sloppy with our data and analysis.

"Yes. From the very beginning, from the first attacks on Rome, Israel, and the United States three months ago, the terrorists have been using a clever mix of technology to create black holes in satellite and visual data; we have crashed through two iterations of their technology, but the most recent one still has us working on it. This is the blob or blur you see in these aerial shots." They both looked at the screen and nodded, the looks on their faces no longer neutral or suspicious but engaged and thinking. Being military men, they would instinctively know the damage a ten-megaton nuclear weapon could do in an urban environment, and it was anything but a pleasant thought.

"The other issue is that these bio-metallic shells are not detectable by their radiation signature, but we have worked out a method to make them visible with the right conditions — conditions you exploited, admiral, in the Mediterranean." He sat silently for a moment, considering his options.

"What, specifically, do you want us to do?" The admiral's hard look was enough for me to realize our dog and pony show had done its job. Now it was up to me to give them a solution they found palatable, one that fit their tight rules of engagement, one that gave them enough flexibility to be able to take credit for what they achieved. This was critical-we needed them to take ownership of the solution because Interpol by itself couldn't do anything as simple as sink a terrorist ship in international waters without the overt support of one of our members.

The admiral didn't know I had Arie in reserve and would never know if this worked out.

"You have a photo of the ship. You need to visually identify it, then sink it as fast as you can, in as deep water as you can, then disguise the location of both the attack and the wreck. This is critical. The information we have suggests that the shells cannot be destroyed by an external blast, so we don't ever want them to surface again. On this point, I am not negotiable." The admiral scratched his chin, looking at the images on the screen.

"You have a few conflicting options here; I wonder if you have considered them all?" He suddenly looked at me as he finished speaking. I was back in the limelight. He still needed proof that we were in the game for real.

"I conferred with nuclear specialists and weapons experts, ones we consider to be at the top of their game, and they offered different alternatives, all of which, except for the last one, had the same result." He waved me on, obviously wondering what mere civilians could come up with that was better than the military. He forgot that we worked with everyone's military when it suited us, not just the Americans.

"The first option mooted was a physical confrontation on the high seas, board the vessel, take prisoners. Reclaim the shells and the nuclear material." He continued to look at me, but this time with a sly grin.

"And how many people were killed in that scenario?"

"All aboard any ships in the area within sixty miles and the target vessel, plus the possibility of them launching a nuclear missile before the boarding was executed, was not out of scope."

"Next?"

"Use a kinetic missile to sink the vessel from long range, may or may not implode the nuclear material, hard to model without knowing exactly how and where the material is stored. But we judged that to be a very high risk." He just nodded, not agreeing or disagreeing.

"Then the third option, the one I like, is to set up a fallback position between the point of planned impact and the east coast of the United States, close the attacking vessel to a hundred miles, clearly identify the ship, then sink is as fast as you can, with the biggest and fastest weapons you can muster."

"You drew a box on the board where you wanted all this to happen."

"Yes, optimal location by our reckoning. You would have noticed the dotted lines on each end of the box. That should give you some flexibility."

"And all this is based on your guess as to where this ship is headed?"

"It's not a guess. The woman who is running this attack's girl-friend confessed to us on this boat just an hour ago that New York or the east coast of America was their prime target. I have a record of the interview if you need it, but in the interests of time, I'd prefer you just take our word." The Admiral sat back, the Captain looked as uncomfortable as a senior officer in charge of an aircraft carrier being asked to sink a civilian ship in international waters could, but neither said anything.

Our word it was then, one more hurdle crossed. I held the admiral's eyes. His look gave nothing away, then the captain spoke in that slow, rolling Boston brogue that could, under normal circumstances, set a lady afire.

"Commander, as you requested, we have a strategy to find and track the vessel, then sink it expeditiously. Do you expect a nuclear explosion when we do?"

"Yes. Fifty to one hundred megatons, at the very least."

"Do you have any idea what such a blast in the open ocean is likely to create?" This time the admiral sounded pissed, seriously pissed, but not I judged us, but at the untenable situation we had brought to his door.

"Yes, a tsunami of five hundred to a thousand feet wave height, blast radius of fifty to eighty nautical miles, radiation blast probably twenty or thirty miles beyond that due to acceleration by water, and the wind direction, and a bloody great big mushroom cloud possibly as high as one hundred thousand feet. Then a fireball which will be a righteous bastard we will need to protect against it as well as the fallout. The tsunami will probably make itself felt right across the Atlantic, but if you hit the ship in the box we have indicated, the wavefront should have mostly dissipated by the time it hits land. Did I miss anything?"

The admiral's stare told the story. My numbers had been the same or close to those they had generated, so we had passed another critical hurdle. He still looked cranky.

"I have a choice, I can trust you with the operational details of how we intend to strike or just keep you in the dark. As tempting as that is, when the order to fire is given, I want you standing with me on the bridge, with your finger on the same button as mine, understand?" I was surprised that he would want to share, but suddenly I thought that a lot of his anger was aimed at the position Interpol had been placed in as well as the navy.

"One more thing-the target is a terrorist boat crewed by terrorists. There is to be no mention of women in any subsequent conversation." I looked at him, realizing he had been briefed by general Saunders, and reminded that as far as the US was concerned, there had only ever been the one woman terrorist. Everything else had been done by mercenaries led by 'the Devil'.

"We can easily lay the entire episode at the feet of Al Bar al Shirak." I paused, to let him take that in and saw confusion in his eyes.

"The second terrorist we had on board here was the leader of that terrorist group, he was one of the two we chased all over the Med, they are well documented, and we have already let it be known we have accounted for Amir Abbas, his partner, the other one we chased."

"How did you do that?"

"We let him blow himself up in Gaza, and let it be known that it was all his own fault that he killed all his people and blew a hole in Gaza that can be seen from space." He suddenly smiled, and I felt the tension in the room dissipate.

"You're sneaky as well as devious. Maybe that's why I like you. Okay, Captain, spread the word. We are hunting a ship containing a wanted terrorist with possible nuclear devices. Prepare the fleet for action. I'll brief these two devious Interpol agents on how we are going to do it."

And he did, and any worry I had about the US navy and their rules of engagement disappeared like a cloud of early morning mist. I asked Sandra to amend the paperwork. Accordingly, she went off into a corner to do that. I made my leave and went to the quarters that had been assigned to us.

We had a little over forty hours before the ship would be in our hypothetical box, so I willed myself to sleep right after a long hot shower and a huge mug of coffee from a jug, like a percolator that had been set up in our room.

Not up to Indigo's standards, but under the circumstances, acceptable.

# Chapter Forty-Six

The storm was a pure bastard, something the Atlantic whipped up at a moment's notice, a sure sign the Gods were angry. The clouds thundered their way up to fifteen thousand meters, some higher, and the rain squalls moved across the cresting waves at close to one hundred kilometers an hour, sideways, and mostly in the wrong direction if you were trying to go somewhere.

While Maribelle loved the fact that she and her cargo were invisible to any satellites that may be working, now she was invisible to anything trying to fly through the massive storm or find her on the surface of the boiling ocean. Her own visibility was less than ten meters by her reckoning, probably more like five, and she peered through the rapidly rotating clear-screen, watching the massive waves as they crashed across her bows, sending cascades of angry, furious white spray as far as the bridge. The sheer energy of it excited her. This was nature at her best, both incredibly threatening yet also fascinating in her fury and temper.

All her crew was with her on the bridge deck, all clinging on for dear life as the gunboat buckled and heaved with every wave. She had reduced their speed to just six knots, yet they were still thrown from crest to crest as if they were a cork from a discarded bottle. Her weapons expert, a pert little redhead with a figure straight out of a sex magazine, was intently watching a radar scope.

"Belle, we have a large target six hundred meters on our starboard bow. It is either a freighter or a cruise boat. It will pass us in fifteen minutes." Maribelle looked at Carol, another rescue from the refugee camps and one who had lived and trained in faraway Argentina. She had entered the Argentina navy at sixteen, with a double degree in physics and mathematics, and by her twenty-fourth birthday, had risen to the rank of Capitán de Corbeta, the equivalent of a lieutenant commander in most other navies.

"Carol, work out a targeting solution. Let me know when you are ready and what weapons you want to program." She watched the younger woman work furiously on her keyboard, accepting and then discarding graphics and data boxes in equal measure. Her blue booted feet tapped to some unheard rhythm, then she looked up with a huge grin.

"Belle, in this weather, I want to use a pair of ASR-65s and four wire-guided torpedoes. Strike time is seven minutes and twenty seconds mark! You'll have to turn twenty-six degrees off the current heading for one full minute." Maribelle nodded, catching the excitement in the eyes of her companion, checked her position, and judged the sea state, which was simply horrible, but the gunboat had the chops to weather a slightly broadside roll or two. It would be uncomfortable but survivable.

"Button down everyone. Strap in and get ready to rock and roll!" And she fired up her personal electronic playlist, switched to the speaker system throughout the ship, and suddenly, over the already screaming and shouting of the storm, the most famous war chant of the last forty years flooded the decks.

'We will, we will, rock you!' thundered out, with the crew joining in at the top of their voices. Their clapping and foot stomping matched the rocking bass and drum lines, and as the master attack controller marched down the seconds to firing time, Maribelle swung the bow across the waves until she had the desired heading.

Just as she reached the crest of a massive wave, the ship rolled, shuddered from the sheer volume of water that had poured over it, then popped back up like a cork. Twin exhaust plumes flooded the windscreen with dirty black smoke, the fire from the rockets almost invisible in the drenching rain. Then the port side thudded, followed by the starboard side.

"Weapons away, one minute to impact!" Maribelle pushed the little hand controller over, sending the bouncing ship back on its prior course, heading straight into the melee. Mentally, she counted the seconds, then at sixty-one, she heard a loud explosion, closely followed by a second, then Carol's shout broke her concentration.

"Two hits, center of mass, topsides down, counting for first torpedo impact, ten, nine, eight, seven, six, five, four, three, two, bang! Dead on target, second hit — NOW!" she shouted, then clapped her hands in joy. She had just killed her first major ship, having only a lonely coast guard helicopter and a fishing trawler to her credit so far. She was amazed and bursting with pride at the immaculate performance of her weapons, even in such atrocious weather. She fitted a pair of headphones, still nodding to the music, held a thumbs up, and pulled the headphones off, so happy she was almost bursting.

"Captain, breakup sounds on its way to the bottom."

Everyone on the deck cheered. She let them for a minute or two, then shut down the music.

"Back to business, team. We ride out this storm, then we get down to what we came all the way here for."

Five thousand yards away, in trail with the gunboat, the USS Campbell, a one-year-old hunter-killer nuclear submarine, heard the attack, heard the impact and breakup of the ship, creating a problem for its captain. She would not break cover, but she could get an undersea message to the destroyer one hundred and twenty nautical miles off her stern, speeding through the storm as if it didn't exist. At five hundred and fifty feet below the turbulent surface, the Campbell moved through the freezing water silently and smoothly, her speed matching exactly that of the gunboat.

Her orders were simple-locate and track, don't let the target know you are doing so, and stand by for orders to dress the boat for a nuclear attack. The Captain had to go to her safe in her tiny cabin to get the orders for that, and once confirmed by her number one, had six of her ship-to-ship missiles reconfigured and four of her torpedoes. As explained to her, the target was an ex-Iranian gunboat, one hundred feet long, possibly carrying nuclear weapons intended for the shores of the United States.

This was information very much held close to her chest and would be so until she had orders to fire.

But there was a bit to go before that could happen.

Another eight hundred nautical miles until they were in the 'box' as sent to her, and at their current speed, that might take some four days unless they sped up. And the storm was getting a little more fierce, so maybe they were in for a slog.

Then she had to get close enough to make a visual identification, get digital photos as absolute proof, then retire to shooting distance again before taking any direct action.

She composed a message and went to her radio officer.

"Sparks, send a tight beam to USS Indiana, the ship sunk by missiles and torpedoes, give this latitude and longitude, and request they investigate."

"Aye, ma'am."

"Then send this to the fleet, telling them what we have asked to be done." He nodded, concentrating on turning his laser tight-beam sender to the proper frequency, then fired off the first message. He changed the frequency, then fired off the second message. He was about to confirm both when he received an incoming message from their sister submarine, the USS Echo. He pulled the little digital pen out of his console, handed it to his captain, then bent back to his console.

The Captain looked to her number one, who looked to the chief of the boat, then left to go to her quarters.

"Chief has the conn!"

The two women, both dressed in amorphous at-sea overalls, a rank-blue color and a shape that could have hidden the finest female form without effort, moved effortlessly down the tight corridor and through the waterproof hatches with their sharp shin killers. The Captain plugged the pen into her laptop, watched the message scrawled across the screen, then tapped the 'freeze' key. She leant forward to study it, wishing she had her reading glasses. She turned to her number one, some ten years her junior.

"Have a look at this, Roslin. Tell me what it says." The number one bent to the laptop screen and looked back up at her captain.

"Basically, the same message as ours, but she is five thousand yards off our target's beam, so she would be much closer to the ship they sunk.

"Do you think there are any survivors?" The Captain rolled her head to one side. "In this weather, and given the severity of the attack, not likely, but you never know, and I want that ship identified if possible. I need to know exactly why our target risked giving away their position to sink a ship in the middle of the Atlantic."

When the messages reached the admiral, he called me into his cabin, having woken me from a dreamless sleep. I was unwashed, unpolished, my overalls were unpressed, my hair straggly, and I had no makeup, but that was normal for me, and I hadn't had any coffee, but I made it to his stateroom under escort in three minutes from bunk to door.

"Sir, you called?" And mentally froze because he had his senior cadre in with him, all bright and polished, shiny, creased to knife point, hair smoothed or cut military style, all with nice smiles on their faces, no doubt having been shocked out of their minds by my shoddy and inappropriate appearance. The only good thing about dressing so fast is by sheer habit, my weapon was on my hip, so I could shoot the bastards if they gave me too much trouble. Before I could develop this thought, the chief moved forward with a monogrammed mug of coffee, handed it to me, smiled warmly, then retired back to his seat. The admiral's face gave nothing away. He just waved me down.

I pretended I couldn't see him, lost myself in both the aroma and the taste of the coffee, and slowly felt my body come alive. After a suitable pause, I looked up at him.

"Commander, thank you for joining us so quickly. Here are two messages you need to read." The electronic pad passed from hand to hand until it got to me. I looked at the screen, ignored the 'Top Secret', 'Eyes Only' stamped top and bottom, and looked back up at the group of polished, shiny sailors.

"How far is this from our picket line?"

"We're still sailing to our final position, but the datum you nominated for the center of the box is a thousand nautical miles from where we will locate. The Campbell is five thousand yards in the trail, at five hundred and fifty feet. The Echo is five thousand yards on the starboard side of the target, matching its pace. The destroyer, Indiana, is five thousand yards further out again but will now close in on the impact point and look for survivors. They'll be there in twenty to thirty minutes, subject to the storm they are sailing through."

"Do we know what ship they sunk?"

"No. No satellite data, no shipping information." He looked up.

"When Lloyds was shut down during the first attacks, the shipping register they maintained ceased. Our own satellite systems are still not giving us good coverage, and until now, there was no reason to have this area covered." I nodded at his words, accepting the logic, but I had an ace up my sleeve. Pulled out my mini and dialed my favorite geek. Marked the conversation 'private' so no one could dial into the call.

"Stefarino, apologies for bothering you again. Can you do a search of the Atlantic around the target vessel? You're looking for a large ship, probably a tanker, cargo vessel, or maybe even a cruise liner, though I have no idea who would be on that now. It's just been sunk, and I need to identify it."

"Jessica, you are never an interruption. Give me a minute." And his head turned to one side, and the musical sounds of rapid Italian flowed like water rushing over rocks. He face-turned back to the camera, and I saw the warm grin on his face turn into a massive frown. He sent me a data package. I opened it and saw the infrared heat signature of a massive burning vessel.

"Hold another minute. We'll run this backwards until we get a clear image."

"Take your time. Send it to me when you get it. And thank you, once again. Your help has been invaluable." I looked at the admiral, and pointed to the large screen off to one side of his stateroom, one of his officers clicked it on, so I swiped the data package onto it for all to see.

"Real-time satellite infrared, you'll have to tell me how Interpol does that sometimes, given we lost all our satellites. Big ship by the images, best guess around one hundred and eighty thousand tons, might be more, could easily carry five to six thousand passengers, fifteen hundred to two thousand crew. Why the hell did they risk giving their location away to sink it?" I thought for a minute, rolled everything I had come to know about these genius women terrorists and the people they chose to play with.

"Arrogance. They don't know we have them located; they probably don't even realize we are looking for them. And they strike me as the sort of people who love to play with things, high technology, super gadgets. I wouldn't be too surprised to find out they were just testing their weapons systems for something to do." Just as I finished, my mini buzzed, and another data package arrived. I gave it a quick look before I swiped it onto the screen.

A huge multilevel cruise ship came into focus, looking a little the worse for wear but still seaworthy by the proud wake streaming out behind its stern. The view was from five hundred or more kilometers above the earth, so we could not see any name on the stern or the bows. The annotation said that it would be tracked back to the port of origin, but that would take another twelve hours.

"Indiana might give us something more. Do you object to us sending these images to them?" I thought about that, the fact that we had better electronic resources than any country wasn't exactly a well-kept secret, but I could moderate how much was shared.

"Certainly, but no attribution beyond this room, please. A girl has to keep her secrets." Mild laughter acknowledged my attempt at humor, but I suspect the thought of thousands of people blasted violently into the freezing Atlantic limited their normal enthusiasm. The Admiral got busy, and his sailors started to chat amongst themselves, so I stood.

"Sir, if I may take my leave?" He nodded and went back to whatever he had been doing. I left them to their own devices and found no one waiting for me, so I walked back to the cabin that I was sharing with Sandra. My mini buzzed again. I stopped in the corridor, looked at the screen, then lowered my head. I had no way of knowing why the terrorists had killed that ship, but I now knew it was possibly the biggest single mistake they had made in three months.

# Chapter Forty-Seven

Aboard the USS Campbell, three digital clocks were counting down. The first, right above the main steering station, counted down the hours and minutes until the sub was in the 'zone'-that area of the ocean the higher powers had designated as the perfect place to sink the target vessel in.

The second, a much smaller one, counted the elapsed time the sub had been on its latest course, now making fourteen knots. Above, the waves had dropped to a mere six feet in height, and the rain squalls had shrunk to a constant dribble of freezing rain. The cloud base had risen to around five hundred feet, and the visibility was now thought to be around two to three nautical miles. The destroyer had reached the wreckage of the ship, found no survivors but plenty of debris which had confused the ship's crew, and was now pacing the gunboat ten thousand yards away, ready to stop or slow down at a moment's notice should the visibility improve.

The third clock was counting down the minutes and seconds before the little 'bug' reached the target vessel, having been released some ten minutes previously. The 'bug' was a tiny robot, almost invisible to the naked eye but electronically neutral, and was capable of sending back video images without detection. The captain, first officer, and weapons officer were hunched over the consul, watching little pictures of waves wash over the 'bug'. Then out of the rain and mist, the blue hull of the gunboat came into focus. The bug slowed down automatically, then crept forward until the whole side of the boat was clear. The red and white stripes confirmed in the captain's mind that they had found the target, and she sent the images by laser tight-beam to her sister sub, the destroyer, and to the fleet.

Seconds later, she received confirmation of the target from the fleet.

"Chief of the boat, make ready for nuclear attack, designate vessel as target one, lock in all engine and wash sounds, change heading forty degrees to port, and have Echo mimic our positioning. Time to the box?" She looked around at her control room crew, all very young by her standards but all fresh-faced and steady as far as she could judge. Obviously, the thought of a nuclear encounter didn't faze anyone, and she wished she could be as calm about it. They were not going to fire any of their nuclear weapons, but it had to be assumed that the target vessel may well retaliate using theirs, or the nuclear material she had been briefed on would detonate as a result of the attack by the submarines.

"Eleven minutes, forty seconds, sir!"

"Call 'mark' at ten to run, count down from thirty seconds, ready vertical launch tubes one through four, torpedoes tubes one through three, I want a firing solution in five!"

"Aye, aye, Captain, running angles now." The chief of the boat, a diminutive sailor as black as the ace of spades, made his presence felt with a voice so rich and low it automatically made you think of barbershop quartets.

"I want the missiles on target one second before the torpedoes hit, fore, middle, and aft, and I want Echo to follow our shoot by five seconds. Make it so!" The tactical plan was simple, at the appropriate time, swing the bow to line up with the gunboats course, fire the missiles, crib the heading over just a touch and fire the torpedoes, then have Echo duplicate all that five seconds later. Of course, they would possibly be shooting into an atomic storm, time would tell, but the explosive force of the missiles and torpedoes would be enough to sink an aircraft carrier, let alone a one-hundred-foot gunboat.

The admiral had been very clear. Sink it as fast as possible, and leave nothing bigger than a matchbox to sink to the bottom of the ocean.

Artificial intelligence automatics on both submarines would synchronize the firing of the weapons, and the two subs were now linked with a semipermanent laser tight-beam, guaranteeing the accuracy of the firing solution to the millisecond. Both boats would be at five hundred feet depth, heading deeper and away from the blast zone the second their last torpedo left its tube. If nuclear material was involved, there would be a severe disruption of the surface initially, then as the tsunami wave built-in height, it would suck water up from thousands of feet below, but that process had been timed during tests at around two to five minutes, so she expected to get thumped in the arse, possibly rolled, maybe a bit of elevator-like rise and sink, all of which could last from minutes to hours, depending on the quantity of nuclear material that exploded.

The Campbell and the Echo were only one year old and had the latest technology available at the time of their commissioning, and both boats could safely dive to two thousand feet if needed. The computer told her they would be at nine hundred feet, heading to a thousand at the time of impact, so, fingers crossed, the experience should be no more than a fast, rough ride at the county fair.

Watching the clock and monitoring her crew's challengers and responses as they worked the solution, as the big clock reached zero, she straightened her shoulders.

"Rig for damage, rig for an attack, fire on my command!"

"Aye, sir, fire on your command." She tapped the little digital screen linked to the fleet and sent three words.

'Ready to shoot'.

On the flight deck control room of the carrier, the Admiral and I stood shoulder to shoulder, radiation suits touching in lieu of skin.

Sandra and the other sailors stood a respectful distance behind us, as silent as church mice, but I could feel Sandra watching my back like a hawk.

"All ships change heading, rig for nuclear attack!" The Boston accent was nice to hear, but the words belied the warmth in the captain's voice.

The Admiral looked at me, rolled his shoulders, held the small digital transmitter in his palm, grinned, and nodded his head. The big boxy antiradiation helmet made him look like the marshmallow man in a scene from Ghostbusters.

"Your call, commander." I nodded, looked out to sea in the direction of the target, then pressed the send button, and the words 'permission to fire granted' ran across the screen. We all fitted flash suppressor shields over our face masks as seawater started to vomit all over the superstructure and deck of the carrier.

Nothing happened. We held our breath.

Then something happened, and a huge bright red and yellow fireball rose into the sky, fighting its way through the storm. Flared briefly, washing out all the color and detail, then faded as a dense black cloud hid the horizon again, leaving us all temporarily blinded.

"Rig for collision!"

"Aye, Captain, rigged for collision." We waited again. No one said a word. Everyone was intently looking out to sea in the direction of the black cloud. No one started to fidget, but you could feel the tension start to build.

It took fifty-six minutes to arrive, but when it did, I feared for the lives of the crews in the subs and the destroyer.

It was monstrous, a fury of piled high ocean spewing white caps and spray as venomous as a snake, as it rose up and up until it obliterated the sun, and thankfully, we rose up with it as if we were on an elevator until we could look down into the trough a thousand feet below, then we were plunging down the backside at a fantastic speed, the bow digging in at the bottom, only to be thrown back out and up as the next wave hit us. And the next, and the next, until we were just being assaulted by fifty to one hundred footers every five minutes. The amount of water we took over the deck was amazing, so much so that the captain had ordered the superstructure wash to be stopped.

"Radiation count!"

"Five percent above normal background, it peaked at twenty-seven percent, but we are now well within limits." Good, the radiation suit I was wearing was cooking me from the inside out, like being in a microwave oven. I turned to look at the captain, comfortably seated in his command chair, his big boxy white suit making him look like an alien. No one moved to take off their helmets, so I suffered a little longer. When in Rome. The waves had dropped to little twenty-footers, and we almost had stopped bouncing up and down when the captain called for a damage report.

Aboard the USS Campbell, it was a totally different story. Weighing in at eighteen thousand tons and diving for twelve hundred feet at her maximum speed, which was classified, the massive eruption she and her sister's submarine had caused sucked her up as if she was a feather, then slammed her back down as the tsunami formed, and to describe the sea as boiling was to make the understatement of the year. Against the full force of her massive shrouded propellor, driven by a state-of-the-art nuclear reactor, she was sucked backwards and upwards at a rate of knots that defied the cockpit instrumentation to calculate it.

Then she simply went dead in the water, her crew held their collective breaths, and someone muttered "breath in, breath out, poor buggar us when it does!" then the Campbell started down again, but this time with a vengeance that had her knot meter bending against its stops. The captain feared for a moment that she would lose control and her ship would simply bash its way to its ultimate crush depth, and that would be that.

Her worst fears were not realized, as after four repetitions of the same incredible up and down motion juddering movement, the Campbell, at last, started to respond to its turbine and headed for its intended depth at her maximum diving speed, under a semblance of control.

"Damage report!"

"No leaks, but internal damage to sections three and five, two of our missiles have been damaged, and their tubes are out of action. And if this instrument is to be believed, our hull has been bent three degrees off plum." Running down the exact center of the massive hull was a tiny tube that linked the bow and the stern, through which a laser light measured any swelling or shrinkage of the hull. Unlike earlier submarines, the Campbell and her sister submarine, the USS Echo, were constructed out of exotic materials developed for the space industry and, as such, were designed to allow a little flexibility.

Was three degrees too much? She looked at the crew, some of whom had been thrown around the control room by the sheer violence of the aftershock of the nuclear explosion, many with blood running from various head and body wounds. She had maintained her position by hanging on for life to the bottom of the periscope barrel, linking her arms over the handles, and now felt as if her shoulders had been pulled out of their sockets.

But the three helmspersons were still strapped in their seats, and the monotonous call out of their diving depth resumed, albeit with a bit of a tremble in the navigator's voice.

"See to injuries, report section by section!" And as they did, the captain wondered how to describe to command what had happened.

The USS Indiana had a totally different experience. The massive wave reared up over her like a dragon seeking a meal, then crashed down on her so hard she was forced several hundred feet under the water. And while she had every hatch and opening well battened down, the sheer weight of the water crushed through her smaller entry points, like her missile tubes, gun ports, and lower deck portholes, so when she bobbed back up to the surface, before being pummeled several more times in just minutes, water poured out of her as if she had sprung several leaks, and someone had turned on the fire hoses.

When she finally stopped flopping up and down, she started to lean over to one side, then rapidly and viciously snapped back to the other, a motion that emulated what a backhand across your face from God might feel like.

There was no one left alive on the bridge to call for a damage report, and the shattered bodies of the crew, at least those that didn't drown, flopped and spewed blood in every section of the ship.

Deep in the bowels, in a small waterproof room, an engineer who had been strapped into a sturdy seat shook himself awake, feeling like he had been crushed by a ten-ton elephant.

Nothing worked.

No power, no engine noises, no people noises, just the huge snap and rumble of the water smashing into the superstructure of the ship. He reached for a relic-a sound powered repeater that linked him to the engine room, command spaces, and pilot house.

Nothing.

Then he noticed the smallest trickle of water seeping through the bottom of the waterproof door, which, as he looked at it, seemed to lean towards the left. He shook his head to clear his vision, and before he could properly focus on the hatchway, it burst open, the huge flood of water drowning him in minutes.

To the credit of the shipbuilders in faraway Norfolk Naval Shipyard, Indiana remained afloat, bobbing and swaying in the aftershock of the explosion, where she was recovered almost a week later.

Out of respect for the hundreds of men and women of the crew who had been literally physically battered to death or drowned trapped inside the buckled hull, the decision was made to sink her in place. She was the only official casualty of the event that was simply recorded as an 'at sea' volcanic eruption, the magnitude off the scale, possibly five times bigger than that at Tonga, way back in 2022.

Strangely, the epicenter of the eruption was reported several hundred nautical miles to the northwest of the actual location, something that remained a mystery for years.

# Chapter Forty-Eight

I t had been a week since we sunk the gunboat, and as I read the report on the Campbell, Echo, and Indiana, I thought about the waves that had crashed onto the shores of Ireland, Wales, Spain, Northern Africa, and the USA. No real damage, no fatalities, just another sign that climate change was going to punish us for as long as we chose to ignore it. I was sitting in the anteroom just off the Oval Office with Sandra and Indigo, waiting for the president's pleasure. Sandra was checking in with the geeks, who had uncovered a series of transmissions from the gunboat prior to its sinking to a location somewhere in North Africa.

A new name had become our focus, a cleric by the name of Mohammed bin Usha Rashad, who had previously only been identified as one of the terrorists who had made contact with Amira during her college career in Israel and Harvey Mudd. The conversations between the gunboat's captain, Maribelle Assiano, and the cleric were marginally frightening.

Firstly, it was he who had put the bounty on my head, now up to thirty million euros. He had also warned Maribelle not to head for the USA with her bombs, preferring to use them as had been planned for the original shells that Abbas had managed to destroy. He had shouted at her about this so much that some of his words were unintelligible. That started me thinking, and a picture of the woman master psychologist came to mind, and I wondered what she thought of him.

And he wanted her to link up with another woman, 'Justine', who was presently sitting on another batch of shells but had no nuclear material. Apparently, Maribelle was supposed to deliver her part of what she had taken from the milk factory but had not done so yet. The geeks said he sounded very pissed and shouted at her to stick with the plan. She had defied him, told him to go back to the desert, and cut all connection with him.

All this happened during the first two days she had been at sea, and as our focus had been on the gunboat and its cargo, the geeks had put these conversations on the backburner. I started to mull over the timing, then the boss walked in, as pristine as you like, light grey suit and starched white shirt, old boys club tie, and even had his hair cut. He squashed down in the leather chair next to me, punched me lightly in the arm, then looked around for coffee.

"What are you doing here?" I asked, wondering if I had missed something. "Direct request from the president, via the general, they even laid on an aircraft." I looked at his smart suit, the creases so sharp you could cut yourself on them, and wondered if he had flown himself. He looked at me, his deep blue eyes sparkling with interest, a crocked but evil grin on his craggy face.

"And to answer your question, no, flown over in a small jet. Very nice."

"And yes, I dress like this now."

Before we could continue, a marine captain in immaculate dress blacks, the red stripes on his trousers making him look ten feet tall, came to attention, saluted, and waited until the boss, Sandra, and I stood, and the boss returned the salute.

"General, Commander and Inspector. Please, come this way."

And turned on his heel with military precision and led us into the Oval Office, where the usual suspects were already sitting and helping themselves to coffee and tea. We all sat in the spare seats, and found ourselves facing the president at her desk, but surrounded by the directors of the FBI, NSA, CIA, and Homeland Security, the general and her aide, and three people I did not recognize, one a beautiful black woman whose face reminded me of someone, but it didn't come to me. Anna sat next to Sandra, who sat next to me, obviously no accident, and Malcolm sat next to the boss, also not an accident.

We sat across the bottom of the 'U' shape seating arrangement, and it was clear that the seats and table had been brought in specially for this meeting.

"General, thank you for coming so quickly. Commander, good to see you in one piece. Let's get down to it. The three people you probably haven't met our are Director Stephenson, Federal Circuit Judge Advocates Office, Justice Maison Oakley, Supreme Court, and Jennifer Middleton, my new media advisor." Then her face clicked. I had seen it on several broadcasts earlier in the year somewhere.

Long before the attacks, then I remembered a piece she had written on child exploitation and had alluded to an anonymous attack on child traffickers that had been very successful. An anonymous attack that I had led just a year before. A shiver went up my spine, and I gave the boss a gentle nudge in the ribs with my elbow. He just replaced his permanent smirk with a faint sneer, telling me he had remembered her as well.

And he hated all media shrews, talking heads, network anchors, in fact, anyone who had anything to do with the media, social or otherwise.

Interesting.

"I have requested this meeting to enable us to close off several elements of your investigation and get from you firsthand exactly where you are up to and what you intend to do next." The president sat back in her chair, seemingly relaxed, but I could see the stress lines radiating out from her mouth, and no amount of makeup could hide the bags under her eyes.

I felt sorry for her. She was in an almost untenable position.

"Admiral Rogers tells me he had a successful intervention in the Atlantic and that the undersea eruption did minimal damage if you discount the destroyer and its crew. Was that your observation?" I looked at the president, mildly confused by her description of what we had just survived, but she had claimed credit for her admiral, so that was well and good. The USA owned the solution, whatever that turned out to be officially.

Local ownership was something we worked very hard at achieving in every operation. Interpol could only work through its member countries, not on its own initiative, except for the master database of criminals and terrorists we held and collected on behalf of every country. But now I was unsure whether or not in this eclectic company to mention I had been on the bridge at the time of the attack and had been initiated on the gunboat. Had, in fact, sent the 'fire' message, thanks to the admiral wanting Interpol to put its balls where its mouth was.

"Madam President, it is a tragedy that you lost Indiana. Those underwater volcanic eruptions are unpredictable and can be a very disturbing threat. Sadly, this one was and we are sorry for your loss." She nodded, and just the faintest smile crossed her eyes but never made it to her mouth.

"So, Commander, can we now regard this whole sorry mess of incidents and attacks by the mercenary terrorists to have been concluded?" She looked at me with such a forceful glare that I found myself trying to read her mind. What was the message here? Anna, Malcolm, her general, and her directors knew exactly what the current position was, but the clear signal I was getting was a long way from reality. Again, in this company, some of whom I did not know, walking the line would be easy for me. I'd say nothing that wasn't public knowledge.

"Madam President, we believe the terror cell Al Bar al Shirak and Hamas responsible for the attacks have been neutralized. We have accounted for their leadership and a very large number of their members. Whether or not another cell might or might not pop up somewhere is not yet known to us, but we will keep a watchful eye on the situation."

"Excellent. Once again, thank you for your dedication and excellent work." And just like that, we were dismissed. Malcolm, Anna, Sandra, the boss, and I stood, nodded to the group, and walked out, following the marine who had ushered us in. Sandra started to speak, but the boss just put his arm around her, and we eventually emerged into the wintery day, sleet falling in little flutters making the White House gardens and trees look spectacular. We entered a large vehicle and were soon on the beltway, heading for an unknown destination.

"Are we being kidnapped?" Sandra asked, swiveling on her seat and resting her hand on the top of her weapon. The boss pattered her hand, pulled it back to her lap, smiled that alligator smile of his, and looked outside at the empty beltway speeding by the darkened window.

"Easy, easy, good work Jessica, told them nothing, gave them everything."

"But where are we going?"

"Another meeting, some of the same players, maybe a new one or two." I let that sit for a moment, wondering what that dog and pony show had really been all about. I was about to ask the boss when the whole world turned upside down. We were bashed from side to side, then top to bottom, a massive explosion shattered the relative silence, and we found ourselves rolling over and over, crashing into each other, arms and feet flinging all over the place, hitting faces and bodies indiscriminately. A smaller explosion seemed to go off out front near the engine, then the unmistakable sound of a large caliber chain gun cut through the chaos, and with a final jarring crash and thump, we came to rest, rocking from side to side, the roof of the vehicle where the floor usually was. We unbundled slowly, Malcolm reaching to pull Sandra from between the seats where she had lodged, the boss reaching down, or was that up? To pull me towards a door.

The shoulder that I had just invested weeks in rehabbing hurt like a bitch, and my pants suit was shredded, but when I saw the blood running down Sandra's face, and Anna rolled up in the fetal position, blood soaking her suit, I forgot my own worries and looked for a first aid kit. I didn't find it, everything went very grey, out of focus, and the last thing I remember was a helmeted soldier peering into the vehicle upside down.

A gunship had landed on the beltway, rotors turning determinedly, whipping up the predictable snowstorm, and another military vehicle stood on the verge, silhouetted against the darkening sky. The sleet was still falling, and I felt its cold embrace as I lay on the hard wet ground, trying to remember where I was and what I had been doing. Then I saw Sandra, weapon in her hand, lying across my legs, pointing up at the roadside, leaking blood from her head and face. Anna was lying on her stomach, blood seeping out of her hair, down her face, and from her hip. The boss was crouched in front of her, and his weapon was also drawn. No Malcolm I could see. No shooting I could hear. I looked around, and then we were swamped by soldiers, and in a matter of minutes, we were all in another vehicle, this one an army armored troop carrier. Sandra was being stitched up, Anna was prone on a stretcher with fluids being pumped into her, Malcolm was alongside her, no idea of his condition, and I had been immobilized once again, my arm strapped to my body, but this time right over my suit jacket. My ears still rang from the missile attack, but the boss seemed in the best shape of us all and held his finger across his lips to keep us quiet.

So I sat, shut up, and glared at him.

What the fuck had just happened? How had we been attacked in broad daylight, on the beltway, in Washington, under a military guard and the auspices of the president of the United States? The helicopter gunship and armored personal carrier made sense; we had used the same tactics when we had been in Montana chasing the terrorists. But we had been hit by at least two missiles, big ones, so who had the intelligence assets to track us from the president's office on an unknown route and hide successfully from a helicopter gunship until they fired?

I looked at the boss again. He was too calm, too placid, too relaxed. He knew something, I was sure of that, but something else was going by the way he wanted us to keep quiet.

And I really started to worry, because in a calm state the boss did his worst damage. I looked over at Sandra, her head bandaged, her face cut and bruised, but she still had a smile lurking around because I could sense her bubbling impatience.

"You know, if the boss had told me I would get shot at, shot down, blown up, and attacked by rockets as often as we have to work with you, I would have stayed in Chicago!" I laughed with her, the boss breaking out into a smile, and apart from the injuries to Anna, all seemed right in our little cloistered world if you had a seriously warped sense of humor as we apparently did.

We had been headed for a meeting with someone, and I wondered how we would now manage that. And who the someone was.

And I still didn't understand what had happened at the meeting we just had with the president and her chosen few.

We arrived at our destination, still unknown, and after much twisting and turning, stopped and let the troops move us into a huge building, where medical assistance was in abundance. Anna was spirited away on a stretcher, I was manhandled until I almost shouted, then Sandra was looked at, with Malcolm and the boss looking down on us as if we were slacking on the job. Malcolm had not a single scratch on him, his surfer blond hair still waving all over the place, but his suit did look a little stressed, as in perspiration rings under his armpits and a few small rips here and there.

The boss looked immaculate as if he had enjoyed a ride in a limousine and not been bounced all over the insides of a people carrier after a rocket attack. But his eyes never stopped moving, and when I finished my private pity party, I noticed that Sandra and the boss had bookended us, effectively providing interference for anyone still wanting to kill us.

Or me.

Was this an attack on Interpol or just another attempt by someone to collect the bounty they had placed on my head? Then a tattered and bleeding man was brought in under guard and stood up in front of me, held by two very large marines, both of whom had blood and matter splattered all over their creased uniforms.

"Ma'am, this gentleman asked specifically to talk to you." I stood as straight as I could and looked the terrorist in the eyes. He didn't flinch, his head held high, but tension spoiled his posture because his shoulders and hands were shaking, hopefully from some pain or broken bones. Sandra edged between one of the guards and my good shoulder, and I felt the boss at my back, and even Malcolm had arranged himself on one side, so now I was flanked. I stared at the prisoner, trying to think why he would ask for me. Who was he? Where did he come from? He looked around thirty, his skin a mild coffee color, but his features were not Middle Eastern, more Slavic. Thick black hair dotted his head in patches, in between bandages which were wrapped around his chin in an untidy parody of 'the wounded man'.

And right now, I couldn't ask anyone where we were. That might give the prisoner an indication of just how unprepared I was to interrogate him. I had to trust my instincts and, going with my gut, spat out an order.

"Take him to the nearest small room, and hold him there until I am ready." The guards dragged their prisoner away, and the sheer look of anger on his face gave me a thrill. I turned to the boss. "Coffee and Anna's condition before I do anything." He nodded and looked at one of the troops standing around watching the spectacle, but before they could react, a marine in full dress blues snapped to attention and saluted.

"Commander, if you and your team could come this way, please."

"I want the condition of FBI Agent Bernstein before I go anywhere." He didn't flinch, just stared to his front.

"Ma'am, she is being treated at this time. I do not know her condition except she regained consciousness and is coherent." I looked right through him, thinking about what I should do next. Anna was a part of our team. She had taken hostile fire beside us, never complained about the atrocious conditions we sometimes experienced on this mission and had been a huge moral support to me both emotionally and mentally.

"Where do you want to take us, and who is it we are meeting?" He continued to stare to his front, his face devoid of any expression.

"Ma'am, I am to escort you into a conference facility we have here, but I cannot tell you with whom you will meet." Then before I could react, General Bridges marched in, gave the marine a sharp look, then pulled to a full stop in front of us. "General. Commander, follow me, please. Anna is okay, just a little shaken up.

"She will join us when they have finished tidying her up." The marine marched off after rigidly saluting the general. We followed her down a long dark corridor, then into a brightly lit conference room with enough technology in it to launch a moon shot. Huge wall screens wrapped themselves around three sides, and the long conference table had a row of embedded small screens and keyboards all lined up like little soldiers. An aide moved over and pointed out four seats for us, and Malcolm, the boss, Sandra, and I sat down as comfortably as we could. Then Sandra suddenly stood up and moved to the seat on my right, and the boss moved into the seat she had just vacated.

Surrounded again!

And before I could snarl at either of them, Malcolm moved into the boss's old seat, and that was that. My scowl said it all, but the general just smiled and sat next to Sandra. The directors of the NSA, CIA, and FBI walked in from the other end, arranged themselves along the table, and the seal of the president of the United States filled the wall screens. Her face swam into focus, she was alone, and the camera panned right around the space, showing us the empty walls and relatively feature-less furnishings. She was obviously in a bunker somewhere, and again I wondered what was up all of a sudden in Washington.

"Thank you all for your patience. General Saunders will brief you fully in a minute. Firstly, I need to know what is really happening and where you are really up to." She stared at the camera, her look of determination quite fierce, then she suddenly leaned forward and pointed. "Jessica, Sandra, why are you bandaged? You've both got blood on your jackets. And where is Anna?"

I started to answer, then the boss put his hands on my thigh under the table and squeezed.

"Madam President, we had a little trouble on the way here. All taken care of. I'll let the commander bring you up to date."

I held my breath to see what happened next, but the president remained quiet. "Madam President, it would help with my report if I could understand what our last meeting achieved."

She sat back in her seat, rested her chin on one hand, and fur-rowed her brow. I would have described that look as 'sulky-pissed-off-president'. Then she leaned forward in her seat again and smiled.

"Jessica, thankfully, you rarely have to deal with politics in what you do, and I apologize for not having you briefed. That was simple, so I don't get impeached. The other side is making snide accusations, and I had no choice but to cut them off at the head." I nodded. Thick as I was, it had taken me nearly half a day to work that out.

"Madam President, we have removed the initial threat, or more correctly, your navy has, but we are now working on a third possi-bility, a terrorist that goes all the way back to the original banker,

Mohammad bin Azaria. All we have at present at a series of satellite calls intercepted by our geeks, which we are working on as we speak. And a new name, one Mohammed bin Usha Rashad, a cleric who we believe once met with Amira. We are chasing this down with some urgency, as the conversations indicated he was managing the attacks they had planned with the nukes, the inference being he also had some shells and possibly nuclear material." She shook her head, sat back, her face went to neutral, and tilted her head to one side. "Thank you, I'll let you get on with it." And the big screen went blank. So I turned to the general and speared her with my dirtiest look.

"So, what gives?" She didn't flinch. You didn't get to be a general, and a female one at that, by letting sharp words cut you.

"Jessica, the president is under a tremendous amount of pressure. As you know, there have been a number of casualties amongst the congressmen and women and representatives she sent back to their electorates. The opposition is using this against her, claiming she sent them off to be killed to reduce the chances of their candidate getting re-elected. You know why she did it, and so do they, but the opportunists among them, mostly the same ones that still maintain the election was stolen five years ago, will do anything they can to tarnish her with this whole dreadful terrorist situation and make it her fault."

"Glad I'm not a politician."

"Me too." And she smiled, relieving the tension that had built up in the room. Then Anna walked in, looking very much the worst for wear, and we all stood up and crowded around her. She held her hands up in defense.

"Hey, back off. I'm okay. What did I miss?"

Sandra just hugged her, and unashamedly I followed, then we all settled down again but with a much lighter spirit. We were a very small core group, and having one of us down and out left a very big hole to fill. Her boss, Roger Winslow, stood and watched all the fuss, smiled a little, then just rubbed his hand down her arm.

"Nice to have you back in one piece," he said, leading her to her seat.

"Yes, Anna, good to have you back. And sadly, you've only missed a political dog and pony show, so now we can get down to tin tacks with the general and the directors." General Saunders threw me a dirty look but remained quiet. I looked at the boss, and he just waved me on.

"Okay, now that we are all here, who would like to answer the first question. How did someone know our movements well enough to ambush us and try to kill us on the beltway?"

I watched the three directors as closely as I could, given that they were arranged to run away way from where I was seated. I saw the CIA director, Julius Bronstein, look away first, telling me all I needed to know.

"You were penetrated again?"

"Yes, well, not exactly. We might still have some bad guys hidden away in our networks somewhere. Frank's geeks picked up local chatter while you were in transit, but the ambush site was settled sometime yesterday after we swept the highway."

I shook my head in wonder. Just how far had these refugee women penetrated our systems? And how many of them were still hidden away, waiting for their time in the sun?

"No profit in bitching about it now. What happens next?" The general turned to look at me, this time without any malice in her eyes.

"The original purpose in calling you here was to get a debrief on what you did and how you did it in eliminating both cadres of Abbas and Badawi's networks. But frankly, in view of current circumstances, maybe we should just disperse and let you get on with it."

"General, with the greatest respect, we are not finished here by a very long way. I need to know the status of Helena, Roanoke, New Zealand, and the other seventeen countries that have the plants waiting to be set up, and we haven't even spoken about the elephant in the room." Every head swiveled towards me, and for a fleeting second, I wondered if I should raise the subject here now or continue to keep it to myself and not share the burden and see what happened.

"America will provide technical assistant to any country that requests it, and we assume Israel will do the same when the time comes to start them up." The general all but barked out her statement, straightening her shoulders and sitting up straight in her seat at the same time. I decided to spoil her pitch and probably the appetite of everyone in the room except Sandra and the boss. I also had a prisoner to interrogate and, in what I considered to be a brilliant strategic move, stood, looked around the room, and placed one hand on Sandra's shoulder.

"I'm calling a ten-minute break. Sandra and I have something to do. In the meantime, can I suggest you read the after-action report prepared by Admiral Rogers? I know you have it, I know it exists, I cosigned it." And I walked out with Sandra, just as the boss gave me an evil grin with half his face but a warm look in his eyes. He knew what I was doing and had probably sussed out why. Then I had a sudden insight, maybe the geeks tracking data from Israel hadn't been shared in the report. Maybe the identity of the ship that had been sunk by the terrorists had not been listed.

Why? And by whom?

Interesting, because that would infer a change to the report after I had signed it off as factually correct. More trouble than it was worth, but why do it in the first place?

We reached the guard outside the door to the little room where I assumed our prisoner was being held. The guard saluted us, stood aside, opened the door, and chained to the desk our terrorist sat hunched over his elbows, his head covered with the orange telltale of antiseptic over blood stains.

"You wanted to speak with me." He looked up, looked at Sandra, and shook his head.

"Not her, just you." My turn to shake my head. He looked down at his cuffed and chained wrists and seemed to be thinking.

He had no discernable accent, suggesting he was comfortable with English. But I used the silence trick and just stood there, looking at him with what I hoped he perceived was total disdain.

The silence dragged on, then he shook his head again. "No. Only you." I shrugged my shoulders, turned on my hee,l and walked out.

"Get rid of this cretin. He is of no interest to us, and please bury him in a very deep hole somewhere."

Sandra rubbed my good arm in what I took to be simpatico. She soon dispelled that illusion. "You're a bad arse and a hard arse, no doubt about it. Maybe he had intelligence that might have been useful?"

"Then someone else can play his game. We've got bigger fish to fry."

"Such as how did the enemy know our moves?"

"No, got that one figured. The States have been penetrated by 'Helen's' homegrown terrorists. She didn't give us all of them. Pity, she can't help us now."

Sandra gave me a funny look, then she smiled and relaxed. "Yes, a real pity.

"I must admit I enjoyed every second of putting her in the ground."

I let it go. It was the nastiest and hardest part of working for Section Five, and even though we had a world court determination and judgement in hand, the act was a huge emotional catharsis. Thankfully, in my time with this specialist section of Interpol, only three people had the responsibility to act on the court's behalf.

We entered the conference room, where the directors and the general were having a vocal altercation, voices raised, tempers barely held in check. In complete contrast, Malcolm and Anna were drinking their coffee and eating sticky buns. I smiled as Sandra joined them, filling a plate that she placed between our seats. I helped myself to more coffee, sat, then looked pointedly at the general.

"Can we continue?"

The four of them suddenly looked as if I had fired a gun and returned to their seats.

"Well, general, do you or your directors have a question for me?"

She attempted to frost me with an icy look but failed, as I was now stuffing a cream bun in, suddenly realizing I was hungry.

"Commander, we skimmed through the report, and it seemed to be quite clear and precise. Why did you insist we review it?"

So the identification of the ship was not in the report that they had received. Now I would have to tread very carefully in case... a thought was better left unformed until later.

"Are you all happy with the report?"

They all looked at each other as if seeking permission from each other to answer my simple question.

"Yes. Is it accurate?"

I shrugged my shoulders, casually dismissing its providence as I wiped my sticky fingers on a hand towel.

"Must be. The Admiral signed it. Now, to other things. If you have no objections, Sandra, Anna, and I have to get moving. We've got a new terrorist to catch. Malcolm, great job. Get in contact with our geeks and get up to speed. They have a way of penetrating the latest black hole the terrorists are using. General, thank you for your hospitality. Such as it was, we needed to get out of here. How do you suggest we do that?" I held her stare. I would brief her personally at a later time, she had a mini, and I would make it a condition she shared with no one.

She stood, looked at her directors, then back at me. "I apologize for the attack, we don't yet know how they tracked you, but we'll get you back to your aircraft and provide a military escort to wherever you are going next. As for Helena and the other places taking refugees, we can touch on that later at your convenience."

"Thank you, happy to have been of some help." And I let that little piece of sarcasm slip out with a smile.

We left, reentered the armored personnel carrier, took off like a speeding bullet, and shook and shimmied all the way back to the airport, where a shiny midsized jet awaited, all resplendent in military colors and markings.

We settled in, the boss up the pointy end with the pilots and us women down the back, the seats were all the same gigantic size, so it really didn't matter where we sat. I whispered in Sandra's ear, then leaned my seat back until it fully reclined and closed my eyes. I heard Sandra call the cockpit and was asleep before the wheels retracted on takeoff.

# Chapter Forty-Nine

Brother Francis pulled his well-worn and often patched brown robe over his bearded head, rolled his shoulders to settle it on his lean but fit frame, bent to tie his equally worn hiking boots, then slid his mini in one large pocket and a sandwich and prayer book in the other, judged himself ready for his mission. He strapped on his thin and scuffed portfolio holder, this time loaded with a sturdy notebook and a clutch of sharpened pencils, and one half-used biro just in case. A very large black floppy hat completed his ensemble, and he smiled to himself knowing all who saw him would only see a man of the cloth, well-worn and humble, and not a secret emissary from the brotherhood who had their headquarters in an underground cathedral in faraway Venice.

His passionate interest, besides his calling, was studying the oral history and then documenting stone dances throughout Ireland, and he had, over the years, managed to record over two hundred conversations that hinted at both the light and the dark in times past. This time had was headed towards the west coast, to a little structure outside Pollatomish, in Country Mayo, some three hundred kilometers away. His guidebook on the area described the fallen ruins as an old church, perhaps even a castle, but ruins they were and claimed to be over a thousand years old and with a magnificent, if not small, stone dance just a kilometer away.

Ireland was full of legends and stories, and many a time, he had arrived at a location only to find that the locals had created the legend and embellished the stories in an attempt to draw tourists' dollars into their meager coffers, something he could not blame them for. By his very habit, he represented the poor and down-trodden, and his oath to his Order, eschewing possessions and wealth in his mind at least, made him one of them. It was also a great cover for an intelligence operative, something I had come to realize when I first met the head Monk, Brother Stefarino, Indigo's brother, deep in the bowels of their hidden sanctuary under a two-thousand-year-old church in Venice.

This order had taken it upon themselves to record everything they could discover about all religions and their genesis and had done so for fifteen hundred years, and by a quirk of fate, now found themselves to be the most sort after the library in the world, following the bombing of the Vatican and the destruction of the catacombs and three thousand years of Roman church history and icons. Members of the same terrorist cell we now chased all over the globe with their super-hi-tech bimetallic bomb shells had devastated the world with a series of attacks that had effectively thrown us back to the nineteen seventies in terms of technology and almost back to the stone age in terms of fossil fuels.

Brother Francis was on the move again due a specific request I had made.

It had been two days since we had been attacked in the US, and Serafino, the head monk, had not hesitated to call his brother on the minicomputer I had left him within an earlier encounter, and he had passed on my simple request, and the coordinates our geeks had calculated from the conversation they had pulled of a French satellite the terrorists were using; a conversation between the now deceased Maribelle Assiano and a cleric, only known as Mohammed bin Usha Rashad, but someone we had heard of previously. Our super geek, the genius that had invented the nanotechnology the terrorists had used so successfully in shutting down all oil, gas, and coal production and then producing undetectable bimetallic shells designed for nuclear material, had met this cleric back in her early years. He had tried to recruit her over to the dark side, working with the terrorists to kill modern society and boldly throw the world into the same living conditions found in many refugee camps.

Initially, the terrorists had succeeded, and a large number of refugee children had migrated to the United States and New Zealand, and it was possible that many other countries would soon join in if only to get hold of environmental plants designed and built by the terrorists, that gave hope to the ordinary person that their lives could be lived again in modern comfort.

These plants used technology derived from Amira's work, and they were, if I said so myself, amazing! But suddenly, this new series of threats using nuclear weapons that could not be detected by conventional means, in my humble opinion, threatened to change any positive attitudes that may have formed around the refugee issue into a hardline negative.

It didn't make sense. Why would people so smart make such a fundamental mistake when the challenging nature of human behavior was on show twenty-four-seven for all to see?

Which was why I was back in Israel, in a small uncomfortable room facing the partner of the now dead gunboat captain, a young woman who looked about fifteen but was probably in her mid-twenties and had already told me in an earlier interrogation that she was the brains of the terrorist organization, in that she was a forensic psychologist, a human behavior specialist, who had used a supercomputer to predict what every government would do at every level of their planned carnage, attack by attack.

I remembered a meme my own computer instructor had drilled into me — GABO — garbage in, garbage out. Somewhere along the line, this young genius had programmed in some really wrong assumptions about human behavior, or I was missing something altogether, something so important I was getting quite worried about it. So I sat in front of Rena Niele, now dressed in pale blue overalls, chained to a desk by her hands and feet. She had lost some of her youthful luster and shine in the past few days and had a distinctive hang-dog look to her.

"So, Rena, we meet again. I hope your accommodations are acceptable?"

"Maybe if you were a dog or a pig, but you didn't mean that. You are just trying to get under my skin," she snapped at me. I looked at her, she had a backbone, and I could work with that. In a sense, I was conflicted. Half of me was constantly appalled at what these genius ex-refugee women had done, the other half was amazed at the sheer talent and smarts they had exhibited. But right now, I was well and truly pissed, having had to give the signal for submarines to blow the gunboat out of the water and, in doing so, set off an atomic explosion that had sent a crashing tsunami onto both sides of the Atlantic, doing untold damage, not to mention the radioactive cloud that floated around the Atlantic.

"Tell me, Rena, how did you predict the behavior of the Middle East to the presence of multiple atomic weapons? How did you factor in the crazies and the dedicated jihadists who would love nothing more than to blow themselves up and everyone else with them?" She looked at me with a mean smile. Obviously, I was so below her level of intelligence it was insulting. She shrugged her shoulders leaned back as far as the chains would allow her, and flicked her hair at me. Casual to a tee, but her eyes showed genuine fear.

"Our choice of using Hamas and Al Bar al Shirak was computed to have a ninety-six percent chance of success and would have if you hadn't got lucky." I looked at her, amazement on my face.

"How did we get lucky? And who is the 'we'?" She shrugged her shoulders again and gave me a disdainful look, but I could see that the effort of maintaining her rigid control was taking its toll on her, probably due to her jail diet.

"Interpol. We factored you in based on what you did during our preliminary attacks but underestimated the speed with which you raised nation-state forces against us. And you got lucky because one of our sisters betrayed her heritage and her history." I thought about that, shouted "at the door", stood, and left her statement hanging.

"Where's Arie?" The guard looked at me with a small smile on his face, reached into his pocket, and pulled out a little communicator, which he handed to me.

"Arie."

"Jessica."

"Amira is a target."

"We know."

"They weren't after us. They were after Amira."

"Yes, we worked that out after the second attack on the hospital and its surrounds."

"Have you got her secured?"

"Yes. Stop worrying. Go back and get what you need from our prisoner."

I could hear him smiling at me and mentally patting me on the head, and I almost lost it, then remembered I had always wanted him as the grandfather I had never had. I took a seriously deep breath, then Sandra walked up, sipping on a huge coffee mug. I snatched it out of her hands and drank heavily. We had agree on the strategy for this second interrogation. She would not come in until I signaled her or she thought the time was right.

"Thanks." Went back in. Sat down. Breathed through my toes. Calm, calm, calm. But internally I was righteously pissed. How did I miss that Amira would be a target? It never entered my mind. Talk about tunnel vision, which I was ashamed to admit, I had exhibited right from day one. I would have to ask the boss, who was now back in Lyon, how he avoided it sometime.

"Well, Rena, talking about luck, it seems you miscalculated there, Abbas blew himself and a thousand of his followers up in Gaza, and we have Badawi in a cell not too far from yours. Oh! Wait, sorry, he was sentenced by the world court to death, so he has been executed. My bad." And I grinned, just to let her know I thought that was the perfect epitaph for a terrorist who had tried to use nuclear weapons on ordinary, everyday people. I had one more bullet to use, and I sensed my timing might be right on the money because her face had gone a pasty gray color at the news about Abbas and Badawi. I waited, watched, wished for coffee, and as if by magic, Sandra opened the door and handed me a gigantic mug out of which real steam was rising in little wisps. Soundlessly, she placed it in front of me and sat next to me, nursing her own mug.

I nudged her under the table with my knee, giving her point.

"Miss Niele, there is one other thing you need to know, and my apologies. We haven't been introduced. My name is Sandra Thomas, and I'm an inspector with Interpol."

"We know who you are. We know every one of you, so enjoy what time you have left." This was said with such finality my skin started to crawl, but miss battery bunny next to me just laughed, literally rolling around in her chair.

"Oh! That's so funny! You in chains, your partner now nothing but a distant memory in atomic mist, your cohorts dead, and you try to threaten us?" She continued to laugh, rolling her mug between her hands, looking at me as if I should be joining in, but I was watching Rena's face, and I saw what I wanted.

"What my associate is saying is your partner, Mirabelle Assiano, was killed in an unfortunate nuclear explosion a day or two ago. We're very sorry for your loss."

"Speak for yourself, Commander. If she had a grave, I'd be dancing on it!" Sandra laughed as she spoke, obviously infuriating our prisoner. The look on the young girl's face told it all. They had been more than just partners. I needed to do two things, calm Sandra and probe Rena while she was emotionally weak.

So I led with the biggest news of all, that only Sandra and our geeks knew.

Maybe, Arie, I wouldn't be surprised at all if he was in on the secret.

"Rena, if you're such a genius at understanding human behavior, a forensic psychologist to boot, with a huge computer to do your dirty work, where, exactly, did you get the idea to sink your own refugee ship with the loss of all five thousand souls onboard?" Her face went white, her bottom lip started to tremble, and tears started to leak across her face.

"You're lying. We would never do that. Never! Those little girls are our future!" I looked at Sandra, now leaning back with her arms across her chest, a seriously evil grin on her face.

"Well, future or not, your erstwhile partner sent a brace of torpedoes and rockets and destroyed the ship in open waters, sunk it in seconds, not a single survivor. Wasn't that part of your grand strategy?" The prisoner shook her head, trying to shake the image of the massive ship sinking to the bottom of the ocean with five thousand frightened refugee girls on board, and couldn't quite bring the image into focus.

"No. You are lying. I refuse to believe you."

"Refuse all you want; it is a fact. Your precious partner, Mirabelle Assiano, deliberately sunk your refugee ship and then sailed on for two days as if nothing had happened." Sandra picked her mug up, sipped, then, posing as if she had suddenly thought of something, put the mug down with a loud 'clack'.

"Perhaps that was your master stroke, to engender sympathy in the hearts and minds of the world, a not-so-subtle call-out on the atrocities suffered in the refugee camps?" She turned to look at me as if seeking agreement. I shook my head.

"No, inspector, this was no simple act to get world attention. This was simple, unadulterated murder on the high seas, pure and simple. We have the attack on audio and live footage of the wreckage after the attack. It doesn't make for comfortable viewing. Why did your partner sink that ship?" I snapped out the last question, hoping to unnerve her to the point she told me the truth.

All I got for my effort was a mournful wail as the girl broke down, sobbing as her head lay in her manacled hands. Sandra and I exchanged a look, nodded to each other, and relaxed back in our chairs to wait her out. We had all day, and in all probability, we also had our answer. Sinking the refugee ship was not on their planned agenda, or at least was not known by the miserable woman sobbing across from us.

They really didn't make terrorists like they used to, all gritty, tough, bearded, swarthy, sulky, and I felt myself losing it as my mind wandered. I stood, walked out, pulled the door behind Sandra,and parked my back against the wall.

"You take her from here. Get what you can. I need to get to Arie."

In faraway Ireland, in one of the prettiest areas in Country Mao, Brother Francis stood in the sleeting rain, his cassock saturated, his boots sodden, smiling as if he was the happiest person in the world. The reason for his happiness was he had just been invited into the lonely cottage he was walking past by a tiny woman who looked to have reached her century some many years before. Hunched over from the waist, dressed in a long worn gray flannel dress, well-worn slippers on her feet over yellow socks, a bright green jumper, and a red beanie over long fading hair, her smile was infectious.

"Get ya sodden self in here, lad, and don't ya being trapsing any mud on my floors, or I'll paddle yer arse!"

"Yes, ma'am, and what might I call such a fine lady as yerself, then?" he asked with a huge smile plastered all over his face, his green eyes twinkling in the twilight, where the yellow sun had finally lost its battle to poke through some low flying clouds. She stood as erect as she could, still bent slightly from the waist, put her hands on her hips, and turned fully to look him up and down, then just stared up at his bearded face.

"Well, a cheeky one you are, and that's for sure. You are calling me Miss Mauve, and get out of your wet things before you catch your death of cold." She wandered off and soon returned with a massive green checked dressing gown, spotted with red and black patches, cuffs well frayed, and elbows patched with leather squares. "This was my dear departed Ryan's, and for sure, he won't be minding you putting this on. Now get out of your wet things and put them before the fire. Get with you now!" And she threw the dressing gown and two well-worn towels of an indiscriminate color at him and shuffled off somewhere.

He smiled to himself, completely at home in this warm and inviting cottage, shed his cassock and underthings, took his boots off, then his socks, dried himself as best as he could with the tiny, thread-bare towels, then hung everything on the post that had been set before the fireplace.

"Here now, get this into ya, warm yerself from the inside as well." She handed him a battered mug with the strong smell of whisky, holding down the strong tea beneath. He sipped at it, instantly feeling at home, then bowed slightly to the tiny woman.

"Miss Mauve, I'd be thanking ya with all my heart, for sure as can be outside is a little miserable at the moment."

"Who would you be then, trudging through that terrible weather so close to nightfall?"

"I'm Brother Francis, of an order of monks who try to grab a little bit of history here and there. I'm heading for the stone dance outside Pollatomish. I understand there might be some ruins of an old church there as well, and if so, I'd like to get its story."

"Would ya be doing all that, then? Well, come in and sit, I'll put dinner on, and maybe we can talk about your grand adventure." And she shuffled off again. He realized he was embarrassed to be taking food out of her mouth, for it was painfully obvious that she had very little in her cottage, so he walked up behind her.

"Please, don't you be taking any trouble over me, I'm perfectly fine with the tea, and I thank you for it."

She gave him a hard look, shook her head, then marched out to her kitchen jut. "There isn't a soup in the world that can't do with an extra cup of milk. Now sit yerself down, boy, and mind yer manners."

He looked at her shrunken frame, trundled back into the small sitting room, and found a tattered armchair that had seen many a bottom in its long, long life. He fired off a quick, silent prayer that he could give her something in return for her hospitality and was immediately worried he might insult her by offering some of his travelling expenses. But apart from his notebook and pencils, he had nothing else to gift her. Then the question became moot as she placed a steaming bowl of soup in his hands, topped with fresh crusty soda bread she had obviously made herself.

"Blessed be, Miss Mauve, and I thank yer for this fine bounty from the bottom of me heart."

She just waved one arthritic hand as if it was nothing, but he was very much aware that he was probably eating her next meal, and possibly the one after that as well, and he vowed to go back to the small village he had passed on the way, and replenish her meager supplies before he continued on his quest. He spooned the soup, all the while smiling, marveling at the warm, common courtesy of the ordinary person in extraordinary circumstances, something he believed in his experience was innate in most Irishmen and women.

"Miss Mauve, would you have heard any stories about the dance I'm interested in?" Her well-worn face squinted as if she was dragging up memories from far away.

"I remember when me da was still around, himself telling me there was a fairy sídh just near the dance, and at the end of harvest, you could see and hear them playing in the grass. Of course, I was very young then and inclined to believe me da no matter what he said. I went there once, right on Samhain, but even as my youngest self, I couldn't see any fairies or elves. Still, I believed me da, just didn't think I had the magic in me to see them." He nodded. This was a story he had heard many times, all over Ireland, particularly where stone dances were involved. Fairies and elves frolicking in green grass, singing, and dancing. The only real difference in these stories was who did the telling.

"Did you ever hear anything about the ruins of a church, or perhaps it was a castle?" he asked, putting his empty bowl on a small rattan table. She turned her head to one side and looked at him with wide-open eyes.

"Not from stories from me da, mind you, but I hear just recently, maybe a year or so ago, that strange things happened in that place, things that are better left unsaid." He smiled. This also was a common theme around the many ruins in Ireland, most accused of harboring the dark spirits of the dead or the angry ghosts of those passed on unhappy with their fate.

"Can ya recall any examples?" he asked, smiling to lessen the intensity of the question, for this was his real mission. Interpol had tracked one side of the conversation with the gunboat's captain to the location of the ruins, and he knew that the fabulous Jessica, with her smart mind, stern looks, and marshmallow heart, had dispatched air assets at the same time as his brother had sent him on his quest. He didn't know what, but he guessed it might be the Israeli C-17 and the drones that they had sent the first time. Miss Mauve sunk in on herself, looking smaller and frailer than she had just moments before.

"Some in the village said that foreign strangers had moved into the ruins, some said that convoys of trucks and helicopters had buzzed all over the village for months and that men with guns now shooed anyone away that came close."

"Did anyone comment on how they were dressed?" She gave him a canny look as if sussing out his real intentions.

"Well now, I seem to recall they were dressed in farm clothes, but with big guns, but those that had a mind to tell of them all said they were foreigners, and not from just England, mind. Real foreigners, like the ones you see in Europe." He shook his head, understanding exactly what this treasure of an old woman was alluding to. And his skin tingled, excited as he was to get on his way, but that couldn't be before tomorrow and only after he went back to the village to replace her generosity.

So he nodded and changed the subject.

"Tell me then, Miss Mauve, all about your Ryan. He was a good man to you, I expect?" Her face lit up, and he swore he saw the light come on in her eyes.

"For sure, he was the finest of men, a handsome one, let me tell you, and didn't he look after me like a princess for over sixty-nine years?" He felt the warmth pulsing out of her and relaxed back to hear of the wonderful Ryan, whose presence suddenly seemed to be in the room with them.

# Chapter Fifty

Fay had been airborne for some twenty-six hours, minus a short stop to refuel and was feeling the effects of the pressurization, cabin altitude, noise, and cramped seats. She had her drones out, some one hundred nautical miles to the west of their current position, just over Omagh, where they flew a racetrack pattern at reduced power in a holding pattern that would be visible to any aircraft controller who looked. But they had arranged for a cover story, part of a national geodetic survey, and their transponder was broadcasting a code that was recognized as belonging to the government department responsible for such things.

Both her drones had overflown the ruins, both at a height as to make them invisible to the naked eye, and both stealthily cloaked electronically to protect them from detection by ground radar. And both had sent back encrypted images of bi-metallic shells stacked in boxes well below the surface of the ruins.

She called her drones back and instructed her pilots to return to the old and closed strip at Galway, which was only four thousand feet long, but plenty long enough for their C-17, and mostly unoccupied, and therefore perfect for a clandestine mission.

Galway airport had been officially closed back in 2013, but in spite of losing its license, it was still used by the Garda, Life Guards, and the military when it suited them. Arie had somehow arranged for fuel for them to be shipped there, as well as four long self-contained airconditioned mobile living quarters, and even had provided a chef who cooked like a Michelin Five Star restaurateur. Sometimes,

Fay thought to herself, living in the boonies wasn't all that bad! And she had been warned that a contingent from Israel and Venice was inbound, due sometime later today.

"Drones in formation, breaking off for Galway." Her pilots were thorough, as you would expect from the Israeli Special Forces, and not for the first time, she marveled at the sheer professionalism and skill exhibited by anyone Jessica involved in her operations, which was in part what had attracted her to transfer from the FBI to Section Five. The FBI was good, great in fact, but Interpol was better, more exciting, and even a little more unstructured, giving its operatives wide leeway in working a case. Her musings were interrupted by her mini buzzing in her pocket.

"Fay, good to see you. We have you moving towards base."

"Yes, we just turned. Drones recovered on the ground in less than thirty minutes."

"Good, we just landed, and we're dressed like the film crews here. We still need to keep a low profile, but that should be easy with all the crew here now."

"Yes, we saw them all when we refueled, don't use all the hot water!" I laughed. It was good that in the middle of the most severe operation we had ever faced, we could argue over who had the longest shower.

"Did you get any images?"

"Yes, sent them to you all just now. Have you heard from the monk?" In the caravan which Jessica had claimed as female quarters, she turned and looked at a map of Pollatomish stuck on the wall, and her eyes glazed over.

"No, not for some time. I hope he's okay." She disconnected, then thought about her options with brother Francis. His last text said he was at the dance half a day later than planned due to having to backtrack, no reason given, but he was now moving towards the ruins, then nothing for some six hours. Sandra sprawled opposite her, eyes shuttered to the ugly neon lights. The Israeli Colonel, Josephine Aria, who now headed commando 104, was fast asleep in a corner, her rucksack used as a pillow. Two other female Israeli commandos slept in other parts of the long mobile accommodation, all happy to have their own space, if only for a few hours. Amira was also sleeping, but she had taken a small room and had locked herself in, which had pleased Jessica as it was one less thing to worry about. She had still posted Tom and one of his troops outside in the corridor, but they were far enough away to maintain the illusion of female space. Where was the brother, and what was he up to? According to the map, the stone dance was approximately two kilometers from the ruins, which were fifteen kilometers from the village of Pollatomish. The aerial shots from the satellite clearly showed the ruins, well burnt out and broken chunks of stone lying haphazardly in a pile that reached forty meters and was probably one hundred meters wide. Clearly, heavy vehicles had been to the site, as their tracks were unmistakable in the long grass and small screed that covered the area. There had been a major disaster in the area back in 2013 when peat slid off the surface and caused a massive landslide that rolled all the topsoil into the ocean, and much of the area had not recovered any ground cover since that time.

But there was a modern gas line running through the area, and it could easily be construed that all the tracks belonged to vehicles and trucks working on that project.

But to Jessica and Sandra, with whom she had discussed the data, it was clear. The terrorist had built an underground facility using the ruins as a cover, and as the drone footage clearly showed, they now had a massive stack of bimetallic shells stored there. In her mind, the giveaway was the twin pipes that led from the ocean to the ruins. The geniuses used sea water and sand in their nanotechnology, and while the twin pipes had been covered in places, if you knew what to look for, it was as clear as day.

But the question remained, what else had the terrorist built? Did they have nuclear material with which to load the shells? What timetable were they working to? And how many of them were there, and how well could they defend the ruins? Bombing them back to the stone age was out of the question, if they had nuclear material and it imploded, the blast alone could wreck a third of Ireland. It all depended on something Amira had told us when she first tested the shells we had taken off Malik Badawi and then Amir Abbas. If she was correct, and I had no reason to think she wasn't, then we might have to force the issue. I mulled that over, then my mini buzzed, Sandra's eyes shot open, and in seconds we were looking at the tired and muddy face of brother Francis.

"Jessica, hello Sandra, forgive my informality, but I am all out of pomp and circumstance!" He laughed a long belly laugh that had him leaking tears. "Apologies, but with what I have just had to put up with, you can forgive me."

"Forgive you for what?"

"Being so casual. Anyhow, look at these pictures, and I'll talk you through what I have found." A row of images filled the screen, building a series of windows, one sliding under the other like a series of steps. I quickly pushed them into a viewer, then brought up the first image.

"Ruins, burnt out, very old, hard to know if it was a church or a castle."

"Yes, for you, maybe, but our records back in Venice tell us this was a church ransacked by heathens back in the fifteen hundreds."

"Good to know. These are tire tracks, heavy vehicles."

"Yes, recent, in the last month or so, but the locals tell me the gas pipeline before it was shuttered by the attacks last month would have accounted for most of the heavy equipment moving through the area."

"But these tracks are recent?"

"Yes." I flicked to the next three images, which showed the sides and one end of the ruins, and just off to one side, a thin sliver of shiny material could be seen.

"That looks like the lining for some sort of entry."

"No, it's an aluminum door frame that was trashed here. There are multiple examples of rubbish left lying around. It's a crying shame to see a site as old as this desecrated by hoodlums and vandals." I felt for him, but my patience was stretched, and I needed to get to the meat as soon as I could wrangle him.

"Did you find an entrance?"

"At the ruins, no, but two kilometers away, yes. There is a tunnel running alongside the gas pipeline, which seems to be boarded up, but I actually saw it open and close. It's quite ingenious."

"The tunnel didn't show up on the drone footage." He shook his head as if the drone footage was of no consequence.

"Jessica, I saw it just before I was bundled away in a truck by heavily armed guards purporting to be Garda; a massive door opened, a long truck carrying timber drove in, and the doors closed again. I managed to talk my way out of the Garda station, which looked real but was fake, protesting an attack on the holy church and my mission to visit the ruins and the dance. What worries me is that all but two of the people I saw were Irish, of varying ages, but dressed like townspeople and not farmers, except for the fake Garda who was in uniforms."

"How do you know they are fake?"

"I asked at the village, and the real Garda told me about the setup that no one in authority knew about, except for a few locals, all of whom have dubious backgrounds. The fake Garda claims to have been commissioned by the gas pipeline people, out of Belfast, to provide security."

"And the timber truck? What is that all about?"

"I asked at the village, and they tell me timber arrives by truck every few days or so, disappears along the pipeline, then comes back empty six hours later. No one in the village knew any of the people driving the trucks or their companions other than they were Irish, but probably from the south, according to their accents. The drivers did stop at the local pub on occasions but were close-lipped about who they were and where they were from." I studied the one photo he had managed of the truck and saw the dressed timber at least sixty feet long in a huge stack on a long flatbed truck with a faded sign on the door. I made a note to get that examined by our geeks.

"What are your intentions now?"

"I'm going back to the dance. I'll write it up as I normally would, then I might just go for a walk after it's dark to stretch my legs, as you see." I thought about that, the inherent danger of him being swept up, imprisoned, tortured even; simply not an option. If his brother, the head monk, Stefarino, didn't skin me, his brother, our own very Indigo, surely would!

"Brother Francis, please wait. I'm sending you a couple of scholars to help with your work. They'll arrive tonight, near the dance, so if you could please wait for them, I would be eternally grateful." He bowed his head; I had no doubt he had worked out what I was doing. He looked up and smiled.

"I guess I'll see you later, then?" And his laughter echoed through the mini as he disconnected. I thought hard. Who were the most studious-looking operatives we had? Who spoke English, Arabic, maybe even old Irish, and would look bookish enough for suspicious people to only see 'scholars' and 'religious students'?

Sandra started bouncing up and down on the balls of her feet, her hands making some sort of wavy motion. I could feel her intent, smiled at her and called for Fay and Tom. They both arrived, so I led them all outside into the fresh air. The rain had given up for a spell.

It was still chilly but in a refreshing sort of way.

"Tom, I want to put a team together to go with Fay, Sandra, and I; you and your team initially dressed in civies as scholars and students. You can have two or three dressed as monks in that lot. Those of you in civies will carry only weapons that your jackets will conceal. Your monks can carry what they like, so long as they pass the smell test. I want everyone to have miniature NVG (night vision gear) and secure encrypted comms, and we need civilian tents for the entire team plus one, and rations for five days. There should be fresh food in the rations, and the water carriers should be local. Organize that from Pollatomish, truck it into the dance where brother Francis is located." I paused, letting my brain catch up with my mouth.

"You need to either drive there now or get there somehow and find a vehicle you can hire-scrub that, not going to be possible. Find a beat-up vehicle you can put your team in, and get going. Take two if you need to, but on the ground, we need to look like a university dig team. Tom, you and your team, are to be there by the last light tonight. Get to Pollatomish as a team of scholars joining brother Francis at the dance, do your shopping, make a little noise, maybe drop into the pub, but sell it, and sell it well. Set up camp between the ruins and the dance, which can be as public as you like. Got it?" He smiled and nodded and strode away with a purpose in his body language.

"Fay, I want overhead drone coverage, live, for the next five days, I don't want anyone on the ground to be able to see them, and I want the feed to our minis on demand. Set it up, but then give it to one of your team. You're coming with Sandra and I. Oh, and I want us to HALO in tonight, on the ground by twenty hundred hours local time; I want to hit the area between the ruins and the tunnel. Make it happen. See you at the aircraft by eighteen hundred hours. Sandra, on me." We headed over to the military base on the airfield, where we could get a thorough weather briefing and a briefing on the local area around Pollatomish from the real Garda. And data on the gas pipe line. And the condition of the ground, which in all the satellite photos, looked like someone had scraped off the topsoil in vast swatches of areas, leaving behind a boggy, muddy mess.

"Sandra, while I get the met briefing, go over to the Air Sea Rescue (ASR) people and see if they are interested in getting justice for their helicopter that was shot down. Light on the details, but suggest it might involve airlifting some of our boys and girls into and out of the target area, maybe tomorrow, maybe the day after.

"Warn them that our people will be heavily armed and that they may be flying into a hot zone." She nodded and rushed off. Shadowed by two of Indigo's best, I got my briefing, then asked a casual question of the forecaster.

"Do you know any of the Garda here?" The mop of red hair bopped up and down as the young woman's smile cut her face in two.

"To be sure I do, missus, me very own brother commands the squad they keep here for no good reason we know of would you be keen to meet with him?" I smiled back, and nodded. She picked up an ancient faded brown handset, dialed a short number, then, in Gallic, asked him to come over to the weather shack. Her voice was musical, surrounded by happiness, two qualities I genuinely envied the Irish for. They had a way with them, and I wish I could sit still long enough in one place to get myself fully immersed in it. A middle-aged man with an equally unruly head of red hair stepped in, straight to his sister, whom he hugged unashamedly before turning to me.

"You'd be the lass wanting a chat, then?" again, that beautiful smile must run in the family.

"Sergeant, thank you, could we have a private word, please? I'm Jessica Riley, Interpol, and I had some questions for you." He looked

552

a little startled, then recovered quickly, straightened, and looked at his sister. She nodded, then he pointed to a small back room behind the briefing counter. I followed him in and waited until he settled behind the desk, his back straight, shoulders back as if expecting to be dressed down. I sat, held my hands out placatingly, let my shoulders relax, and smiled.

"Sergeant, we have no trouble here. I want to talk to you about something else." He visibly relaxed, put his elbows on the small table, and leaned forward. "We knew you were not with the film crew, and our office in Dublin simply said to stay away from your encampment and let you be. That, of course, caused us to be a little suspicious. But we did notice the Israeli cargo jet and that a lot of your people carry weapons, all of which are illegal here in Ireland. So we have been watching and noting, so it is with some pleasure that I look forward to you telling me all that is going on." I sensed a highly educated mind here, his eyes held mine, and I sensed a level of professionalism that belied his posting to what was now considered a backwater now the airport had lost its license for the second time. I wondered about that, then decided to simply ask.

"Why are you and your Garda unit here at Galway airport? It's been officially closed for years." He leaned back, smiled, then got serious.

"Aye, that it has, but it doesn't stop the odd duine dána from dropping in to do a little business now, does it?"

"People smugglers, drugs, contraband?"

"Aye, cigarettes being the least offensive. Then the hard stuff."

"Where from?"

"The Americas, groups in expensive jets, posing as celebrities out for a little jaunt. Mostly that's stopped now, what with all the fuel being contaminated, but my bosses want to wait and see what comes down the road at us." I thought for a minute, filtering what I could tell him and what I couldn't. Always a thin line to tread when speaking to the LEOs (Local Enforcement Officers).

"Sergeant, we have a team just outside Pollatomish, working with one of your well-known Irish scholars at a stone dance, who tells us he was arrested just today by a group of people dressed in Garda uniforms, which the locals believe to be false." And I stopped there and watched him closely as he processed what I had just said. His face turned to stone, and his eyes hardened noticeably.

"We've heard rumours of that, aye, we have, but my bosses decided to let it go for the moment as there doesn't seem to be any real harm in it. And we only have the one officer in Pollatomish, and a young one at that."

"Well, tell your bosses that the situation has changed and that we will put an Interpol-authorized squad in that area, and if they choose to give us grief, we will accommodate them. After all, this was a monk on a sanctioned quest to record the details of the dance and to assess the condition of the church ruins nearby. And no way should have been interfered with by anyone." His stare turned frosty. He stood up and irritably rolled his shoulders, which were well-muscled.

"I hear your anger, madam, and as I don't really know or under-stand the circumstances, I can't be commenting. But I will say that I will pass your message on to my bosses, and I will let you know the outcome. As for any sort of interaction with this Garda unit, I'd advise you to tread carefully, for I know that our head office did approve pri-vate security for the gas pipeline people."

"So you're okay with private security dressing up in Garda uni-forms?" I gave him a very thin smile. There was something he wasn't telling me, something he knew. "And by the way, I'm a commander with Interpol, that's the equivalent of a one-star general where you come from, so if you know something I should know now's the time." I stared him down. He seemed to be thinking, his eyes flicked from side to side, considering. He reached for the handset on the desk, punched in a long stream of numbers, and pressed the speaker function.

"Sir, I apologise for interrupting you. I have a commander…"

"Riley," I filled in for him.

"…Riley, Interpol, and I think we should listen to what she has to say."

"Go ahead, Commander."

"Firstly, who are you?" And my tonality clearly indicated I was pissed at being thrown from person to person.

There was a prolonged silence at the other end of the phone. "Okay, I have a better idea. My boss will call you." And I hung up, dialed the boss on my mini, and his svelte but well-worn face swam into view.

"Jessica, what's up?"

"I need you to call your counterpart in the An Garda Síochána, find out what they have going down in Pollatomish, and clear them out of the way, please. And I need it now."

"Done." And he hung up. The Sergeant looked at me as if I had grown horns, but I was too far gone to have my feelings hurt by a sulky policeman. Sandra saved me from further depression as she bounced in, bringing happiness and light back into my life, instantly saw I was out of sorts, and cleverly inserted herself between the sergeant and myself.

"SAR guys are happy to help, they are pissed about their crew, and now they only have two helicopters available. I told them that if we used them, maybe we could find it in our budget to replace the one they lost." I smiled. In the broader scheme of things, given that billions of Euros had been salted away by terrorists all over the world and tens of undetectable nuclear weapons were being readied in an underground cavern less than a hundred nautical miles from us, what was a few million Euros for a new chopper? The Sergeant looked shocked, but before I could comment, my mini buzzed. I set it up on the desk and opened it so all three of us could see the screen.

"Jessica, you are cleared into Pollatomish and its surrounds. Any resistance of any sort may be dealt with as you see fit; the real Garda will stay well out of your way." And before I could thank him, the boss hung up.

"I guess that clears it all up. Thank you, Sergeant. We'll stay out of your way." I moved out back into the now freezing drizzle, wondering what the fuck the Irish were really doing in our target area, but quickly put it behind me. I now had clearance to do whatever I had to do to secure the nukes or the shells, and then the noise from three heavy vehicles roared through the rain as our convoy headed off. Now all I had to do was make sure we were properly prepared and equipped. We reached our long shinny accommodation, and I dialed the boss again.

"I'm thinking I need you to work me through the choice of a weapon." His craggy face smiled. He was obviously rested. There were not the usual batch of stress lines on his scarred face, and I envied him.

"Shoot."

"Do you know of a ground penetrator powerful enough to collapse two to three hundred feet of rock and earth without exploding anything in the process?" He looked at me, his eyes glazing over as he thought it through.

"You're worried about a chain reaction like you achieved in the Atlantic."

"And what Abbas managed to do to himself."

"Got that. But we know something they don't know. Have you thought about that?" I gave him my best stare, but in truth it was definitely an option, just not a good one.

"I trust Amira explicitly. That's not the issue."

"You're worried they may not load all the shells."

"Yes." He nodded, turned his head sideways on his shoulders, and for a minute stared at me sideways.

"Your only real option is to check for bolt holes, seal them all up, weld the door shut, and let them stew in their own brilliant ideas." My turn to smile.

"I did have that idea, but the end game is too unpredictable." He nodded again, looked a little serious,

"You're dealing with an unknown jihadist. He may take it upon himself to shut it all down, take everyone up with himself, once and for all."

"We have to take that risk." He nodded again, looked right into the camera, and leaned forward.

"Be careful." I nodded and cut the connection.

"What do you know about nerve gas?" I asked Sandra. She looked at me with a serious frown, looked at her fingernails, then back at me.

"The FBI in Chicago trained with fast-acting nerve agents that incapacitated, but they were flaky in my humble opinion, the dispersion was never equal, and they took too long to work."

"Exactly. So we'll do it old school, it will be bloody, but it's the only way I see we can get in with a chance of taking them out once and for all. What do you know about timber?" She laughed and held her fingers an inch apart.

"About this much, but I suspect I'm about to get an education."

"Yes, you are. Get onto the geeks, find out the name of the yard that is supplying the timber, locate it, then get back to me. I'm going to take a long run to get the kinks out."

"Not without me, you're not." I had forgotten the boss's mandate about Sandra sticking to me like the proverbial sandfly.

"I'll take Fay. She needs the exercise." Sandra didn't look happy, but she moved off to work with the geeks. I had an idea, one as old as history, but first, I needed to decompress. I stood stock still in front of my room and dialed my mini.

"Brother Francis, describe to me how the timber truck got through the doors." He was used to my lack of politeness, so he just smiled.

"Ah, Jessica, you look lovely in the gloom. I was just standing in the tree line, the truck drove up, the driver flashed his lights four times, the doors opened, then closed behind the truck."

"How many in the cab?"

"Two, both males, mid-thirties, nothing remarkable about them, dressed as farmers."

"Thanks. You'll have company in a few hours, help them settle, then if you feel like taking a walk later, head towards the tunnel entrance around ten tonight. Bring Tom with you, don't be concerned if he looks a little military." He just smiled, and I headed off for my run. It was a gloomy day. Drizzle fell in waves, and it was a little cold, but the magic that was Ireland fought through every time the sun won its battle with the low-flying clouds, and the ocean, always angry around this side of the Atlantic, postured and spewed as wave after wave crashed on the broken rocks of the foreshore. It was rough, elemental music that spoke of long-lasting elements that timed life in the millions of years, a reminder of just how fragile human beings really were.

Fay ran smoothly beside me, holding her peace, a tight little smile filtering across her eyes every so often. She ran well, balanced, and belied hidden power. But her head never stopped rotating, looking for the unimaginable, which kind of spoilt the overall effect. I huffed out a breath and had a thought.

I needed Bob and his team, and I made a mental note to call him when we finished.

# Chapter Fifty-One

The HALO jump went as planned, and Fay, Sandra, and I shed our parachutes with the assistance of brother Francis and Tom, and I noticed Tom had brought a canvas sled case to stuff everything in.

Good thinking. No mess, no fuss, and nothing to indicate we had ever been here.

We were all dressed in black, including hooded face masks. Only the brother brought any color into our little world, and then only the grubby brown of his often patched and repaired cassock. Low light intensifiers masked our faces, including the brother, so we all had an insect-like appearance whether we liked it or not.

"The entry." He nodded and moved off, surprisingly quiet for such a large man. But I had learned that those that worked for Stefarino and his order were a cut above the rest, similar perhaps to those we recruited into Section Five. Their geeks were world-class, as they had demonstrated on many an occasion over the past few months.

We moved silently, with Tom taking up the rear and doing a sweep every thirty seconds or so. He leaned forward to whisper in my ear.

"Contact left, ninety meters, three targets, on foot, making their way to the same point we are." I held up my fist, tapped the brother on the shoulder, and he crouched, his cassock forming a tent over his substantial frame.

"We wait."

We did, and when they, whoever they were, were fifty meters in front of us, we followed until their red heat signatures seemed to merge with the ground. We followed, tranquilizer weapons pushed out in front of our bodies, the rubber strap that linked over each shoulder taught with tension. The brother was now in the middle of Fay, Sandra, and me, with Tom still covering our rear. Just ten meters from where they had disappeared, the earth suddenly caught fire. We all snapped our NVGs off, and with our naked eyes could clearly see the massive blast doors opening, the light from inside shooting up into the night sky like a beacon. They closed silently, and we continued our creeping until we could just see over the ledge that protruded out in front of where the doors were located in a massive pile of dirt.

This was very clever work. You could not see the doors unless you were very low to the ground, and then only if you were looking straight up the axis at them, and there was another huge mound of dirt, now growing weeds and wildflowers just twenty meters away, which would effectively prevent that from happening. All of this would have been dug and built as part of the gas pipeline, and no one would have given it a single thought at the time. As it was, the pipeline was the most visible thing on the horizon, where huge stacks of unused pipe lay piled on top of each other, waiting to be joined and linked to the system. Interestingly, the two seawater pipelines we had picked up in the aerial photos disappeared straight into the ground just past the pile of dirt that hid the doors.

At some time, we needed to have a chat with the people running the pipeline installation, but that could wait. What fascinated me was that the people who had entered the tunnel didn't have a man-sized hatch or doorway somewhere, and I wondered about that. I leaned over, snapped a series of pictures, panned the immediate area, placed a tiny satellite camera in the mound covering the door, then signaled my team to backtrack.

We got back to where we had landed, Tom hitched the sled to his shoulder rig, and the brother led us back towards the tent camp. As we passed the ruins of the old church, my hackles started to rise, and trusting my instincts, I called the team to the ground.

"Someone there, in ruins, Tom, Sandra, with me, Fay, move the brother back to the tent line." We crept forward, air guns at the ready, the last thirty meters on our bellies.

"Three targets, reference large jutting rock, to the right fifteen degrees." Tom's whispers were just that, but our comms system amplified his voice in my head, so I turned to look down the line he had indicated, and there they were. Three heavily armed people, all lining up on the camp, either on a recon mission or just a group of civilians out for a sport. Their red body signatures had a yellow haze, indicating some type of body armor, cutting down on their infrared signatures. That spelt tangos to me, so I sent Tom off on his own to cover them, and Sandra and I crawled back away far enough to be out of sight and legged it to the camp.

"Shit!" I couldn't help it. Out of the gloom came the image of four of our people being held at the end of the barrels of guns by four tangos; first question, where were the rest of our people? Second question, where were the brother and Fay? Third question, who were these tangos? Fourth question, was our mission blown before we had started it? I held in place, listening for all I was worth, trying to glean what was actually going on. Then I saw pulses in the infrared and realized Tom's team had us surrounded and had gone to the ground.

Working with the best of the best never gets old.

I looked for Fay's telltale blink and saw it twenty meters to our immediate left, now with three others. Good. Out of harm's way. I signaled to Tom to hold, then Sandra and I split off to have the four tangos in a pincer movement. I counted to ten, then stood up, and advanced as fast as I could, firing my tranquilizer darts at the four shapes, Sandra appeared out of the gloom, and in seconds they were down. Making the sign for 'silence', then 'advance on me', had the entire troop milling around, guns pointed at the ground, bug eyes from the NVGs glowing in the dark. Tom had returned and secured all four tangos, checked them for comms gear, and found miniature sets that were showing green flicking LEDs, indicating they were live.

I motioned to Tom, and he pointed to the ruins that were invisible in the gloom. I motioned again, splitting the team into two, one half to stay and secure our base. The other formed on me as I walked very slowly toward the ruins. Sandra put her hand on my shoulder, and this was repeated down the line, and I felt rather than saw Tom moving ahead of me slightly to my right. He had a pair of NVG

Extenders on, making his head look like he was wearing a Lego set. He suddenly knelt and held up a clenched fist, so we all followed his lead and knelt in place. He signaled three tangos to the right, the ones we had detected previously, and four to the left, sixty meters ahead. I turned and faced my line, waved my hand up and down and across in a manner that any special forces trooper would understand, split them in half, and sent them on their separate ways. Within a few heartbeats, they had all disappeared into flanking positions, leaving Sandra, Tom, and I to move up the center line.

Then at around fifteen meters, the tangos became visible, and could you believe it, two of them were smoking, creating little bright orange and white spots on our NVGs. I paused and looked at Tom. He bent his head to listen to the clicks of our team as they reached their positions, looked at me with his extended bug eyes, nodded, and counted down with his fingers.

We rose and stalked, then shot and followed our darts in to secure the tangos. The cigarettes were stomped out by someone, immediately returning the view to the flickering green, a welcome relief. I signaled half the team to take the prisoners back to our base, then kneeled on the stone wreckage, and thought for a minute. We had taken out eleven tangos. They were all dressed in Garda uniforms, appropriately badged but not appropriately armed. They carried a mix of AK 47s and M-16s, with flash bangs and grenades hanging off their vests. No Irish policeman I knew ever went after a suspect loaded like that unless they were on attachment to special forces.

I needed a conversation with the brother.

I signaled again, and our half-team spread themselves across the ruins. Tom patted me on the shoulder, then Sandra and I moved swiftly back to our camp. We found our troops looking outwards, with the tents and the brother safely secured in the middle. The eerie glow of the NVG's lenses gave an ethereal and unnatural feel to the camp as if it were being guarded by insects. My back was wet with nervous sweat, and I felt the chill under my armpits as well as in my crutch. Tension, adrenalin, and heightened situational awareness could do that to you, even on the coldest of nights, and I hoped the team had made provision for us to be able to deep clean at some point because the smell could get worse when the sun came up!

I leaned over the brother, held my pad under his nose, and wrote my question.

"How many at the fake Garda headquarters?" He took the pen from me and scribbled.

"Fifteen." I thought about that, three in the tunnel, maybe one left behind to manage the store?

"Where is the HQ?" he took the pen again, marked the camp, the ruins, and the entrance, then made an 'X' off to the left of the entrance. I patted him on the back and looked over at Sandra. Thought for a moment, then signaled her to go find the Israeli Colonel from commando 104 and held up two fingers. She nodded, scrambled off, and was back in a minute or two with three black-faced commandos behind her. I drew on my board again, held it up for all to see, got four nods, rolled onto my stomach again, and started to crawl away. When. I judged we were out of sight from the ruins. I stood, pulled them around me, and told them what I intended to do.

We made good time, with, as expected, the Israeli Sgan Aluf taking the lead with her own version of Tom's extended NVGs. Because she was so broad-shouldered and somewhat squat, the image was that of a thick monster leading with a high-tech head that reached out beyond her feet! I smiled at my poetic license. After all, we were in Ireland, and we were camped under the influence of a fabled stone dance that was supposed to be full of magic!

The headquarters of the fake Garda Unit was well-lit. They were not making a secret about it, so I left three outside to cover our backsides, and with Sandra just knocking on the door and striding in, our NVGs cranked up over our helmets. The lone occupant, dressed like a rural farmer, sprang up and reached for an automatic weapon, which Sandra disabused him of with a slap to his wrist with the barrel of her air gun.

"Sit, be still. What is your name?" He looked at me, grinned like an idiot, then broke out into laughter.

"Oh, aye, the gods have worked their magic again, for all I see is thirty million euros when I kill you!" Sandra moved behind him, applied the cuffs, tied a second set around his elbows, then squatted on the floor. She grinned like an idiot.

"Do you think I could collect if I killed her for you?" she asked the prisoner, poking him in the chest with her weapon. Then she shook her head.

"Jessica, it's amateur hour, no doubt about it. In less than an hour, we have cleaned up the fake Garda and took their HQ. I really thought we would face some serious opposition this time around."

I grinned back at her, and so had I. But there had to be a reason for the lax security, and maybe the daylight would reveal more secrets at the ruins. We moved out, taking their portable comms gear with us. I waved to the Israeli commander, told her to mine the small building, then waited until she and her team had finished. She placed a microsatellite camera twenty feet away in some dirt, then signaled she was ready to move back to our camp.

We got back to find everyone still on their bellies, but I noticed that most of Tom's team was missing, so I assumed they were at the ruins waiting for the dawn. The silence was absolute, so after looking around, posting a four-point guard, mimicked everyone else into a sleeping bag and gave them three hours of downtime.

Sandra had taped the prisoners' mouths and hog-tied them. The only thing I was worried about was a listening device or camera set up in the ruins that might give us away, which is why I was waiting for the dawn.

It came soon enough, and Sandra and I joined Tom and his team and crawled through every nook and cranny, and to our surprise, we only found a massive satellite dish hidden in a pile of rocks, with a thick cable running off into the ground. We scanned every inch and found no surveillance devices, another sloppy move by the terrorists, so we placed our own, set up a detector next to the dish, and returned to the camp and a hot meal.

"What do you want to do with the prisoners?" I looked at Tom, currently with his head half buried in a tin cup, the unmistakable smell of coffee disguising any body odor, and clicked my mug to his.

"We need to get them away somewhere. If the three that went into the tunnel come out, we'll know. If they go back to the HQ, they'll be surprised, then dead, and if they come back here, different surprise, maybe not dead, but they might as well be. Bob should have the truck here in an hour or two. I think we just have to walk them as far away as we can and wait until it is all over before we arrange transport for them. Agreed?" The Israeli Sgan Aluf was standing just off to the side of us, listening in, and I saw her head nod. Good, all are on the same page.

"What about the brother?" I looked at the diminutive Israeli, sans headgear and body armor but still armed with a weapon slung across her chest. She was eating with a fork on a metal plate, and from the twisting and shaking going on, I guessed spaghetti or pasta of some sort. Gone were the days of RATPACKS and K rations! "If he goes, we can send him with the prisoners, or he can stay here in the camp. I'll ask him." And I wandered off to where the brother was enjoying a chat with some of the team, arguing about something by the way hands and arms moved all over the place.

"Ah, just the person we need to settle this with, Jessica. these heathens are trying to tell me there's no such thing as magic!"

I looked at the mix of men and women, ranging in skin color from black as the deepest dark night of night to warm coffee color to bleached white, all experts in the art of killing their fellow man, and could not imagine a more literal bunch of people if I tried. I raised my mug in a mock salute.

"Of course, there's magic. How else do you explain how the sun comes up every day?" And I laughed and patted the brother on the shoulder.

"We need to brief in two. Toss a coin if you need to resolve this argument." And I wandered back to where my commanders were chatting. Considering what we had planned for the day, they were all very relaxed, and the camp had a smooth sense of purpose as tents were struck, rubbish bagged, weapons checked, and we got ready for war.

"Okay, listen up. Tom and Josephine will select two team members each to go with Sandra, Fay, and I. That will make seven for the penetration plus Bob's team; Tom, you take the North side, Josephine the South, post overwatch, and I want the doors jammed one centimeter from closing, make it look like a rock or something, then when we call you pry them open enough to provide ingress and jam them; place the satellite repeater in clear view of both the tunnel and the sky; make sure to protect our backsides as well. When possible, use air guns. We don't know how many, how they are organized, or how they are armed, but we will act as if they have video surveillance on the doors in the tunnel. Our objective is to capture any nuclear material and any shells, loaded or unloaded, then secure the facility. Questions?" I looked around at the blackened faces, not a flicker in any of them, and we all knew that attacking a hidden location with unknown numbers of the enemy was sure to cost us lives, so their stoic looks reinforced just how powerful the 'special' was in special forces.

"Timing. When the doors open, kill the satellite dish, kill all detectors, cameras, and everything electronic, flood the area with noise, and remember our comms are immune to the jamming we will use but be ready for the loss of comms at any point. Questions?" One hand went up, an Italian from Indigo's team I recognized.

"*Scusi, comandante, ma perché non interroghiamo uno dei prigionieri sul tunnel e sulla disposizione?*" That was a good question, but I answered in English for the benefit of our Israeli friends.

"We suspect the prisoners will only tell us lies, and to be brutally honest, we will all fight better if we are alert and on our game. We will have the benefit of surprise, at least initially, and by the behavior of the prisoners so far, we are not expecting expert troops by any means." He nodded, and no one else indicated a question, but before I could continue, my mini buzzed against my leg. I held my hand up, "Wait, one."

Bob's craggy face swam into focus, his background whipping past at a furious rate. "Jessica, I'm sending you a drawing of the tunnel, the clearing area for the truck, and a lower open working area that has been set up as a lab. You will see accommodation facilities off to one side and work spaces off to the other. It has been described to us as like a giant spoon. Sean O'Malley is riding with me. He's the big boss of the timber company. Without counting the outside guards, he estimates no more than fifteen people, half of whom are women. We're thirty minutes away. Where will you join us?"

"We'll meet you on the track half a click from the ruins. There will be seven of us. If you stop, we'll find you, and you and Sean can brief us then."

"Roger that. See you soon." I brought up the drawing on my mini, scrolled it, zoomed it, pinched it, turned it around, and poked it under Sandra's nose.

"Notice anything familiar?" She took the mini off me, did her own scrolling, then handed it back.

"It's a clone of the one we took down last week. The only addition I see is the roundabout where the trucks unload. The rise is only about three degrees, so that should be easy to traverse. No upper and lower levels, but those were built when the Milk Factory constructed thirty-five years ago. This looks relatively new and a much simpler design."

"The pipeline construction has been going on for two years, so that's when they dug this out. I wonder if they have a pile in there somewhere?" She gave me a very hard look.

"They better not have, or I'm claiming danger money!" Everyone laughed, the tension that had been building up from the start of my briefing dissolving with the laughter. I made one last quick call, briefed Amira and Indigo, then looked around at my team, all keen and eager to get on with it.

"Let's get into position everyone, ruins team, listen out for our call; one last chance. Any questions?" Every head shook in the negative, so I pumped my fist up and down twice, and we broke up.

My seven jogged to the rendezvous with the truck, Tom and Josephine jogged off to the tunnel, the ruins team moved away with a purpose, and the low-hanging haze turned into a full-on mist, with sheeting, freezing rain hidden in it, just to make us feel at home. It was eerie, I had to watch my GPS to maintain course, but twenty minutes in and with a soaking that ran down my back and right through everything I had on, we reached where the truck would eventually drive by.

The unmistakable sound of a laboring diesel engine filtered through the mist, and I wondered where the driver got his fuel from. I saw Tom before he saw me, I waved, and the truck with its piled high sixty-feet timber lengths bounced to a stop. Tom and the driver, whom I assumed was Sean O'Malley, jumped out.

Before I could move, Sean embraced me in a massive bear hug, then stood back, his face split with a huge grin.

"Aye, you're the one the brother told us about, pretty as a picture, and glad to be able to help yer I am." If I looked astonished, it wasn't an accident. How on earth did an Irish truck driver I had never met know of me?" He broke into laughter, pointed, then dropped his head.

"I am confusing you, I see, well now, wasn't it my very own brother that drove your holy man all the way back home from Dublin just weeks ago? And didn't he regal you with stories of the most beautiful princess he had ever met being sent here by the Gods to save us from heathen foreigners bent on destroying us?" The twinkle in his eyes sparked from bright green irises flecked with gold, and that itself was disturbing enough, and I wondered who else the brother had a conversation with.

But this was Ireland, and when in Rome, etc, etc..

"Sean, lovely to meet you. What do you know about the tunnel?" I held my mini out, with the drawing on it of the spoon. He tapped the screen with one finger, the nail of which had seen better days, then looked me straight in the eye.

"You won't be harming the women folk, now would ya?"

"Not if we can help it. How many are there, and where do they come from?"

"Well now, four not from here-a-bouts, and pretty and regal are they, all with a very strange language, if you ask me. But the other four were hired months ago to provide cooking and cleaning for the men, who are a little rough by my standards and also speak a strange tongue. But I've not seen any guns to speak about, except for the Garda, but you would expect that."

"When was the tunnel built? And where does your timber fit in?"

"They dug it when the pipeline reached the creek, the work team was all foreigners, and they all left months ago when it was finished. They used my timber initially to line parts of the tunnel, but now they build boxes and crates of all sizes and shapes, but the three woodworkers, all of whom are locals, use the old method of joining and gluing, so it's almost works of art they are making, for sure."

"Do they allow the civilians, the locals, out of the tunnel?"

"No, not for some months now, but they allow us to pass mail and small packages back and forth from their families, and I don't see any real duress on the faces of any of them. After all, they are being paid like I am, in gold bars, worth many times more than any paper money, I suspect. We all had to sign a document forbidding us to talk about our experiences, and the Garda checked on us from time to time." I nodded. Civilians in the mix made our job all that much harder, so I pulled a photo of Mohammed bin Usha Rashad onto the screen and asked if he had seen him.

"For sure, he was there at the start, then left some months ago, but came back just this last week, very unhappy he was, snapped at me in that strange language of his, yelled at me to hurry up, and leave. As I was back just the day before yesterday, I didn't see him, but I've no doubt he is in there somewhere, as everyone was on their toes and had unhappy faces. And I noticed a tent of some sort had been erected down at the end of the chamber, with hoses and pipes running to it from a control room of some sort. I didn't think to ask what was going on. Everyone had their heads down."

"You won't be suspected of coming back so soon?"

"No, I was told by the carpenter I normally see to come today or tomorrow. It seems they are now in a hurry to get done, whatever it is they be doing." That gave me pause for thought. Now I had a tactical situation to consider as well as civilians. "Stay here, please. Sandra will look after you, Bob, on me." We moved away, I pulled out my mini and dialed my two flank troops.

"Tom, Josephine, we may be dealing with loaded weapons as well as shells and nuclear material. Come prepared." I looked at Bob. He understood what I had just said, nodded.

"We have twenty containers in the truck. I can call for more. We can use the Coast Guard to deliver them." I nodded, my thought exactly. But not yet.

"Put them on standby. Let's get back." Sandra was in deep discussion with Sean, who had loaded a huge pipe but not lit it. Thank the gods!

"Sean, thank you for all your help. When you get to the turn-a-round point, I want you to stay in your truck, no matter what. Can you promise me to do that?" He looked at me, thinking, holding his pipe proud of his lips, and nodded.

"Aye, missus, I can make that promise." I tapped him on the shoulder, and looked at Bob in his farmer's outfit, covered by an old battered leather coat, that not only looked the part but smelt it as well. I knew it covered a variety of weapons and comms gear that would be essential for our success. We crunched fists and knuckles.

"Luck!"

"Back at you, see you on the other side."

# Chapter Fifty-Two

"**S**he wants you to do what?" The president sunk back into her chair, a beautiful Italian leather lounger she had been brought for Christmas by her family. Enjoying her first few hours off in months, she had been slowly drinking a chilled glass of California chardonnay when the admiral had burst onto her screen like a bomb. The admiral out on the high seas in the Atlantic thought himself clever to be out of immediate physical reach. The president had reacted so quickly to his news that she had inadvertently slopped some of the sparkling greenish wine over her sleeve.

"She has asked for three MKR-56 guided missiles, one second apart, to fly inbound from one of our ships, which is steaming into position as we speak, just in case you approve this, and then over the Irish coast, she will give us an electronic signal to follow from a drone, then she wants us to fly down into a tunnel, alongside an abandoned gas pipeline, of all things." The president brushed at the stain on her sleeve, put her wine down with her reading glasses, turned the book she had been reading, and collected her thoughts.

"I know we can drop guided munitions through truck windows, but can a missile hit that target with such accuracy?" The admiral paused, looked at his screen where the technical data was scrolling, tapped a section, then shrugged.

"According to our data, yes, this one can, plus or minus half a meter. If we do fire three 56's for her, we'll have them in the trail, one meter below each other, with the lowest targeted on the floor height plus two meters. According to the specifications, and God forbid, a hand-drawn diagram, the tunnel is fourteen meters across by twelve meters high and has a three-degree downslope to the end. These missiles have excellent visual tracking ability, LIDAR (light detection and ranging), and topical mapping capability. They are very, very accurate."

"I see. What is the situation on the ground?"

"She is currently launching a physical attack on the tunnel and assures us that they will have all personal and any radioactive material secured before they call for the launch."

"How big a hole will these missiles make?"

"Madam President, a standard cruise missile carries one thousand pounds of explosives. The 56 carries three times that amount, and three of them going off in enclosed space seconds apart will have a synergistic effect that will multiply that blast effect by a factor of five, maybe six." She nodded, accepting the admiral at his word.

"What are the chances of collateral damage to villages or towns in the area?"

"The Commander tells me the area is clear apart from some ancient ruins, which sit on top of the tunnel's endpoint. She believes that the damage will be minimal due to the depth of the tunnel and the solid construction of the ruins."

"Do you have any images?" He flicked his screen, then sent the images had been sent to the president. She leaned forward in her chair, putting her reading glasses on.

"So this is the tunnel-the doors closed in this picture?"

"Yes, Madam President, but the commander tells us they will very much be open when she gives the command to fire."

"How will the Irish feel about us attacking their country?" He smiled; this was the only bright light he could see in this entire mission.

"General Anthony has cleared the way there. The Irish government is thankful Interpol is dealing with the problem and has offered any support the commander might need. Towards that end, she has requested three squads of the Irish Special Forces to be on standby and had requisitioned three of their transport helicopters to be at a site between the ruins and a stone dance of some sort where an Irish priest will be waiting with some prisoners, I didn't get the gist of all that, but in simple terms, no issue with the Irish government."

"You're not up with your Irish fables, admiral." He looked uncomfortable, not sure if the president was having a joke with him or suggesting he should know something he didn't. He chose to let it go.

"So, Madam President, do I have your approval to support the commander as she has requested." The silence was absolute, the digital signal linking the two totally inert, as it should be. She liked Jessica, thought she had done a remarkable job under the worst conditions imaginable, and, more importantly, she trusted her and her team. "Yes, admiral, give her all the support she asks for." The admiral bent to his mini and sent a short text message.

I got the message just as the truck stopped at the blast doors of the tunnel. Just two words.

"Mission approved." I smiled to myself. Good to know you had the US Navy on tap to do a little damage to your local terrorists! The truck lurched forward, and I started a mental countdown and watched the big hand on my wristwatch. Old fashioned, it was an analogue, given to me by my mother when I graduated from the NCIS Academy. To pay for it, she must have saved for years, something I would never forget.

Right on nine minutes, we lurched to a stop, and then all hell broke out. "Go, go, go!" Bob shouted, leading a team who fell out of the back of the truck from the temporary space we had constructed under the timber, like ants from a hill doused with hot water. I was one of the ants, and my team headed in the opposite direction to Tom's, shooting anything and anyone that moved with our air guns, and then I heard the unmistakable sound of automatic gunfire, returned by the short stucco of controlled three-round bursts from a tactical weapon, then the inevitable silence that filled any void after a firefight.

"Report!" I shouted into my mic.

"Three tangos down, two of ours wounded." I crossed my fingers that the wounded were not fatal but kept running down towards the tent and the big hoses that ran to it from a smaller control room of some sort. Every time a head appeared, the body attached to it got shot, the little air pistols huffing away comfortably in a steady rhythm.

"Gun, down!" Sandra's shout had the desired effect. We hit the dirt, literally, and both she and I fired a short burst from our tactical weapons at the same time, shredding the flimsy side of the control room and the terrorist who was now half in and half out, having collapsed over the wall, and before I could move, the team behind us were up and running to the large tent.

"Hold, hold, hold!" I shouted as we could now see that the one who had fired at us was a man wearing the unmistakable suit of a man from the desert, and as I turned his head, the lifeless eyes of Mohammed bin Usha Rashad stared at us. Our team was ranged around the tent, weapons poised, then Tom's team joined them from the other side, and the frozen tableau looked like something out of a Kabuki theatre play. As we watched, four people in white hazard suits walked out of a split in the side of the tent, hands held high, pulling airlines behind them.

I checked my radiation counter. Sandra checked hers. We were all wearing masks and goggles as a precaution. I could see Tom checking his meter, we all looked at each other, and I made the decision for us all.

"Josephine, take the suits away and out of the tunnel. Move everybody out except the clearance team. Get them and their containers now. Maximum exposure time for us from now, mark! Ten minutes. Move it!" As it was, the radiation level was high enough that we would need antiradiation pills as soon as we could swallow them and maybe a trip or two to a decontamination site. But if we kept to the timeline, we would only have been exposed to about as much radiation as we would normally get in a year.

The four white-suited people were collected, stripped of their suits, and four really beautiful women appeared, all dressed in a grey overall, all very young, and with obvious Asian or middle European heritage. Their masks were left on, and they were cuffed and marched away. The clearance team, wearing masks and lightweight hazard suits, moved through the slit, pulled it apart so we could see what was happening from where we were standing, and ever so slowly, the entire team moved backwards, seeing the open containers we recognized from our last encounters with the shells. They had been loading the shells, which was good in one way, because, secret, we knew something the terrorists didn't; but the bad news was several of the long tube containers that had held the nuclear material were open and carelessly thrown around the floor.

"Tom, more hands are needed. Call in the Coast Guard, and I'll get the Army Ranger Wing to use the doors as a locus. Shells and nuke material on the Coast Guard helicopters, prisoners except for the four women with the Rangers. I'll brief them accordingly."

"Sir!" And people started to move with more purpose. The timber was rolled off the truck, the temporary hide we had hidden under the timber pulled off, and the massive flatbed was backfilled firstly with people, then empty shells in wooden cases, filled shells in wooden cases, then lastly tubes of nuclear material bundled together in piles of three. I did a quick mental count and got to thirty-six before I got distracted.

"Tom, leave two of the women here with me." Sandra and Fay were watching the clean-up of the laboratory when a head suddenly poked itself around a hidden corner. A gun followed, and before I could react, both Sandra and Fay had fired and reduced the threat to a bloody mess. Tom saw the firefight hand waving four of his troop off to check for any others. Two of Tom's team approached, each with a woman in restraints, their hands behind their backs.

"Do either of you speak English?" They both nodded, so that was a start. "How many people down here?" One looked to the other, and who I judged to be the youngest took point.

"If you count the bloody Garda, fourteen. Four of those are Rashad's bodyguards, four are locals who clean and cook for us, and the other three were here when we arrived."

"Was Rashad in command?" They looked at each other, and I got the sense whatever they said next would be a lie.

"Tom, bring the other two, please." One of them would turn out to be the boss, I was sure. They arrived, one limping rather badly, with a rip in her overalls and blood coagulating on her leg.

"I'll ask again. If Rashad wasn't in command, then which one of you was?" All four looked at each other. I saw what I needed to see, just a little hardening around the eyes, pointed to three of them, motioned them away, and was left with the woman with the torn leg.

"What is your name?" She looked at me out of deep black eyes, her hair short and equally black, but her face was chiseled and shaped so much so that I was reminded of an ad for a beauty product.

The one that promised all the good-looking men I could ever want!

"You'd be the woman from Interpol, the one that hunted down our sisters," she said with a hard edge, her eyes never left mine, her whole body tense.

"Hunted down terrorists that killed the spirit and the hope of the world, and millions of innocent people to boot, not to mention the economic and social chaos they created. I asked one of your so-called sisters just last week what you hoped to achieve with nuclear weapons," I paused and looked at Sandra, "....was that before or after one of the other sisters sunk a ship carrying five thousand refugee children?" I asked her, hoping she had clued in on my interrogation approach.

The involuntary gasp from the prisoner told me she hadn't known about the sinking but had known about the ship.

"I ask again. What could you possibly hope to achieve with nukes? Didn't you realize you would scare the crap out of everyone, and any social capital you may have gained, sympathy for your cause, would disappear as fast as a puff of smoke?" I shook my head, motioned towards the exit, and she was taken away. Inside the tent, the clearance team was running over the floor with a Giger counter, and one turned to us and held up a thumb, then they moved towards the truck.

"Sandra, Fay, one last sweep, electronics, documents. Tom will have most of them, but let's make sure."

We found little. Tom and his team had done a thorough job, so we moved to the truck and climbed on. The driver, who had obeyed me to the end, tipped his cap to me as I walked past the cab. We rumbled back up the ramp twice as fast as we had come down, and I had time to marvel at the skill of the tunnel builders. They had really done beautiful work. The timber that lined the roof and walls was joined seamlessly, and the bright lights highlighted the grain. The sound of helicopter blades cutting through the dense air flooded down the tunnel, and I was snapped back to the present.

Outside, two muddy brown and grey helicopters sat, their fat bodies shedding the rain that was being sprayed far and wide by the turning blades of their rotors. A team of Army Rangers stood under the canopy of rotating metal, seemingly unbothered by getting wet. While Tom sorted out the prisoners, two Coast Guard helicopters, red and yellow, floated down face to face with the Army ones. They looked at each other like dogs in a park, then people started to move toward them, and I moved to the ranger captain.

"Captain, I will give you a fuller brief at a later time, but for now, please take these prisoners. Four of them are locals drafted for cleaning and cooking, and three are carpenters, also local. When you prove their credentials, get them back to their homes. They have been paid in gold bullion, and they are entitled to keep that. You will find some more who posed as Garda to be collected to the south of the ruins. The brother's coming with us. These are first-class terrorists, and if they give you any grief, terminate them, clear?"

"Yes, commander."

Sandra, Fay, and I were left with the leader of the women, who were still guarded by one of Tom's men. Once the three women, the shells, and the tubes had been loaded on the coast guard helicopters, I pointed to Fay, then Tom.

"Keep them alive, but separate them when you get back to base. Send a chopper back for us. We'll be at the stone dance. Fay, load everything in the C-17 and get it to Israel. Keep however many of the boys and girls you think you need to be safe; we'll get air-to-air refueling for you if you need it, and you will have an aerial escort, thanks to the admiral. Happy?"

"Good to go. Should I take the Israelis back with me?"

"Yes, good idea, thank Josephine for me. I'll see her when I get back." Fay walked off. I turned to the prisoner and pointed to the truck.

"Let's go."

We did, entirely uneventful, and we found the brother sitting under a Colman light reading a book, the rain held off with an army poncho older than I was. The fake Garda we had captured sat in the rain, looking miserable, guarded by a mix of Italians, Israelis, and Americans, all of whom were deep into an argument about something or other. In contrast to the prisoners, our troops looked positively happy. The sound of a helicopter broke the silence. It landed, the prisoners and the troops departed, and the brother put his book away and stood up.

"Well, that was entertaining. What happens next?" his smile would light up a room, and it was simply impossible to feel anything but joy in his presence. I reached for my mini, and Sandra moved surreptitiously to stand between the computer and the brother. He didn't take offense, just shook his head. I dialed up the view from the drone, sent the location signal, then gave the drone a command to hold its position. I sent a text. The admiral acknowledged. I motioned for us all to sit facing the ruins, which we could just make out in the rain and mist. I rested my back against one of the stones in the dance, feeling its heat warm me. A warm stone in freezing rain? I laughed.

"Now, we wait and see if the earth can truly move as if by magic," I said, and sometime later it did, when the ruins seemed to lift themselves up off the ground, then gently slide down to it again, as the mist was sucked down through the old stones as if being vacuumed by someone in the nether world deep under the ground. We felt three firm thuds through our feet and backsides, so close together that it felt like one continuous kick. Then we heard the thunder of the explosion, which reverberated around the stone dance like the percussion section of an orchestra. The stones vibrated, and I felt it all the way up my back. Magic indeed, thank you, Admiral.

"Brother Francis, you are free to pursue your passion, or we can get you home." He looked at me, looked at the sky, which was clearing, a faint grey drifting through the haze, and he stood up, looked around at the dance, then back at the ruins.

"Commander, thank you, I'll stay awhile. Bright blessings on you all." And he wandered off towards the ruins, now bathed in weak sunlight, but sparkling from the rain. They looked magnificent.

I pointed at the truck, and the driver nodded and doffed his cap at me again.

"And where would I be taking you, pretty ladies, then?" My turn to smile, I was wet from head to foot, probably slightly radioactive, and dirty, so in the eye of the beholder it surely was, and I felt a chuckle rise in my throat at my use of the Irish phrase!

"To Galway airport, if you please, kind sir, and don't spare the horses!"

He didn't, and when we arrived, Fay had the C-17 loading, with the Israeli team providing the guard, so I walked over to their Sgan Aluf, pulled her aside, and briefed her.

"How are you wounded?"

"Flesh wounds, both are back in action. The woman on Tom's team is in the base hospital. She's stable but took three rounds to her legs." I nodded at this news, having already established the condition of the injured on the way back to Galway.

"Okay, Arie will know what to do with the shells and nuclear material, but I want Amira involved at every step. She has point until such time as she is ready to send everything off to deep storage. Keep the prisoners isolated and separated. I will want to interrogate them when I get back. How are you faring?" She looked at me with a squint as if trying to see behind my question. Then she smiled, and the tension flowed out of her body in a rush of relaxation.

"I admit, we were all a little spooked when we saw those canisters open, but all good there. The medics cleared us when we landed. It has been a privilege and a pleasure to work with you, Commander, and I hope to be able to do so again." I smiled and patted her on the shoulder.

"Don't take this the wrong way, but I hope not. I'm tired of chasing bloody terrorists all over the planet and back." She nodded. Held out her hand. Shook mine.

"Understood. Stay safe." And she walked up the open ramp, which closed behind her, leaving me to sort out the unholy mess we had inherited.

I still did not understand why the women thought they could be successful in using nuclear weapons as a bargaining chip. It just didn't make sense, given their supposedly humanitarian cause. And why had the gunboat captain sunk the refugee's vessel? Up until this latest series of attacks, the women had been focused on their strategy of creating the same conditions in the general population existed in many refugee camps, and force a change in the belief system of the ordinary person.

It was a deep psychological experiment on a worldwide scale, and initially, it had worked, but the sheer randomness of the social disorder that followed their attacks on the major religions, the crashing of the Internet and computers everywhere, and the denial of oil, gas, and coal had led to widespread chaos and a massive loss of life. Over thirty-three million that we knew of, and maybe another ten we didn't.

They had managed to get three sites up and running with their inventive power panels and machines, two in the United States, and one in New Zealand, and the first three tranches of refugee children had been or were being settled. Then at the point where hope had been given back to the world, with the discovery of superior power supplies invented and manufactured by the terrorists, we suddenly became aware of the potential for small, undetectable nuclear bombs being distributed around the globe.

It just didn't make sense.

But now I had to report to the admiral, his president, the Prime Minister of Ireland, whose country we had just subjected to a massive missile attack, my boss, the head of the Israeli Intelligence Service, and then interrogate several terrorists and try to understand the 'why' and the 'what' they were trying to achieve with their latest attacks. And find another twenty or so women terrorists who had yet to show themselves and their skills.

Dealing with geniuses in any form was a pain in the neck! But what I needed most now was a good cup of coffee!

Read about how it all started

**THE TEARS OF HOPE - BOOK 1 OF THE TRILOGY**

Somewhere in a refugee camp one child under
10 years of age dies every eight minutes

# The Mentor

"We had a plan, a good plan, but like all plans, once we war-gamed it, we discovered it would not have survived the first few minutes of battle. So now we have created several plans and strategies; you might call them one for each force element. You will be self-tasked on your timetable under your command and control. You will have just one primary target, with a secondary only if the primary becomes compromised. You will be expected to work from our data and fit into our overall timing schedule. Still, the logistics, personnel, weapons, delivery systems, and exit strategy are for you to create. And only for you to know. It's your backside, and we trust you to keep it in one piece out of self-preservation if nothing else." The two people, one at the penultimate stage of a brilliant career, the other still radiating the bloom of the fast-tracked youth, sat opposite each other, the late afternoon sun creating exciting shadows across their faces.

"Imagine you committed an atrocity—an act of terrorism so vile that literally, half the world would be trying to either kill you on sight or incarcerate you forever in a deep hole, you would never see natural light again. Imagine that others, like you, committed this heinous act in parallel to you another five or even six times in the same seventy-two-hour period. Thousands, possibly tens of thousands, dead or worse, broken, maimed, or damaged and mentally scarred for the rest of their lives. Predominantly collateral damage, civilians, real innocents of the finest type, with a small mix of real targets, but sadly in the minority. Where would you hide, for the rest of your days, assuming that you were still alive at the end of it all. Where?" The general's piercing green eyes bored into the young woman, looking for the faintest sign of discomfort. The woman smiled back, completely at ease, confident and comfortable with the concepts being discussed. After all, war was just politics and the projection of power by other means, however and wherever politicians might apply it.

Their cause was possibly the justest cause ever underpinning a warlike action.

And the woman was a warrior.

Trained from an early age to instinctively follow the Code of the Warrior to the point of death.

"Sir, the only place that would be safe."

"And where would that be?" the general asked, somewhat amused by the sense of calm that seemed to exist between the two of them, given the nature of the discussion and the difference in their experience, rank, and age. The woman smiled again, twisting a small gold band over and over between one thumb and forefinger.

"Sir, the only place where people like us could survive. In plain sight."

Read the next exciting book in
The Tears of Blood Trilogy – Book 2

## THE TEARS WONDER
## BY PETER A. HUBBARD

# Flashback

T he Boss stood; everyone else in the conference room ringed outside by Israeli soldiers in full combat gear sat, mostly uncomfortable on the small metal chairs. They formed a circle, so everyone could see everyone else without turning their heads, and for once, there wasn't a single presence of electronic equipment in evidence. On the contrary, a massive sign on one wall said, "אזהרה! איןמכשירימאלקטרונייםמורשים, זהומתקןאטומומאובטח. עוש." I wondered how many years of jail time I would serve if I breached the no electronics rule, then forgot about it as the Boss started to talk.

"Firstly, thank you, Colonel, for your excellent performance in bringing down Shetani and his mercenaries and for your support in getting Mohammad bin Azaria and his henchmen." The Israeli Sgen Aluf, head of the Shayete 104 commando troop, looked anything else but happy, the stoic look on his face giving nothing away. "Colonel, Tom, I'm asking you both to leave at this point and pass our thanks to your men and women for excellent work." Tom, who Pete had forewarned that this would happen, stood, smiled, looked directly at the Boss, and saluted. He walked out behind the Israeli commando, whose body language was anything but compliant.

"We now enter a difficult phase of our investigation, and I'm going to hand over to Captain Riley to summarize where we are and what we will do next." And he sat down in the seat vacated by Tom and looked expectantly at me. I looked around the faces I was now so familiar with, Indigo with his little smile, as if all was right with the world; Anna, a little grim-faced, probably still lagged from her flight back across the Atlantic; Pete, relaxed, although anyone who knew him would easily spot his eyes casually scanning every inch of the room. Arie, looking all his years, the past weeks had taken a heavy toll on him, yet the sparkle in his grey eyes was encouragement in itself. General Bridget Saunders, now dressed in mufti, looks like someone's mother but is not able to disguise her military bearing. She had flown over with Anna, an afterthought by the president, who was feeling distinctly not in control of her country or the events that were unraveling at such a frantic rate.

The room we were in had been organized by the local Interpol office in Tel Aviv, and in recognition of this, Senior Agent Beth Arezzo was also sitting in. As I had had the pleasure of briefing her just an hour ago, I was again impressed by the caliber of agents Interpol attracted.

At just thirty-two, she ran one of the busiest offices in the area and worked under the same duress as every other Israeli citizen from the constant rocket attacks on the city.

She was married, had a child, and dressed like a fashion model, currently wearing a tight red sheath with a purple-and-gold scarf dropping between her arms. A lightweight cotton jacket in peach completed the ensemble, no doubt concealing her weapon and credentials. She also spoke five languages like a native. I stood up, breathed in deeply, held my hands loosely in front, and relaxed as far as I possible. "We have Mohammad bin Azaria and his lawyer secured and under guard; we have left the Jesuit priest to his own devices, but we have asked him to remain to be debriefed sometime tomorrow. The electronics and intelligence we recovered from both successful attacks are now being examined, and we expect the first summary within the next hour. This meeting aims to determine exactly what we will do from here on and who will be responsible for each activity. "While we have used paramilitary tactics against the terrorists and the mercenaries, this is, still, essentially a police action. Interpol has been commissioned by several countries as well as those represented here to discover and bring to justice the persons responsible for the attacks that were initiated last month in Italy, Jerusalem, Abu Dhabi, the United States, and, more recently, the international consortia that controlled the International Space Station.

"Our investigations uncovered the mercenaries led by Shetani, who was responsible for at least two mass bombings, the destruction of the Arabia oil field, and the destruction of some three hundred and fifty oil and gas pipelines and fracking sites. Needless to say, every country impacted by these attacks has requested us to add their support to our mandate, which we have accepted on the condition that all political interference be withheld until a satisfactory outcome has been achieved."

"And what, exactly, do you think a 'satisfactory outcome' looks like?" asked the general in a tone more suited to the parade ground than a meeting of the minds. I turned slightly to look at her and sensed the Boss flexing his shoulders, a sure sign he was going to jump in, so I paused in my reply to let him do so.

He didn't.

I continued.

"For some days, we have been working closely with one of the refugees who was groomed to participate in developing the technology weapons used in the attacks. She quit and ran, years before the attacks were launched.

"Apart from helping us to uncover the internet destruction, she had records of her time with some of the other participants, who we are now identifying and tracking.

"When you look at the possibility of combining what the Jesuit priest can tell us, what your secretary of state can tell us, the intelligence we are now unraveling, we may well get a better understanding of how to find the refugees who did participate in the attacks."

"You'll have to go through the president to get to the Secretary," the General barked, "and you'll have to go through me to get to the president."

"We understand the circumstances. We have been briefed by both Roger and Julius." The general seemed to be thinking about something; she nodded to herself and tilted her head to one side. She looked directly at me with an intensity I felt in my bones. She held up one manicured hand, her perfect nails showing just a hint of clear polish, and ticked off her fingers, one by one.

"So, firstly, you have identified and taken out of play a mercenary terrorist crew in Canada responsible for shutting off the oil and gas pipelines as well as destroying the fracking sites across northern America and Canada. Secondly," as another finger flicked up, "you seemed to have solved the UAV attacks on the sports arenas, at least in the US." I held her eyes, determined to hear everything she had to say before I acknowledged anything.

"Then you have masterminded an attack on Arabia, forcing the third regime change in two weeks, destroying the mercenary terrorist leader Shetani in the process."She watched me for any reaction and saw none; I played poker with people so hard to read you had to actually rely on the cards you were dealt! A wan smile crossed her eyes, her thin lips struggling to follow.

"Fourthly, you have identified, located, and captured the banker and prime suspect in the organization of all the attacks and currently have him here somewhere under guard." I held her eyes as hard as I could, not giving any sign of acknowledgment. The silence in the room was deafening; I could almost hear everyone breathing. She wasn't exactly attacking us, but her tonality suggested she was after something, but I wasn't sure what it might be. I nodded, just once, to see what she would say next. Her hand opened up so all fingers could be seen as she ticked off the last on her list.

"The problem I'm having is seeing exactly where a military action starts and stops, and a police one takes over." The tension in the room ratcheted up a notch, and I saw Pete stiffen out of the corner of my eye and Indigo visibly lean forward as if to pounce on the general. Before I could answer, the Boss stood up again, rolled his shoulders as if preparing for a physical fight, and motioned for me to take my seat.

"General, as you would know, my unit within Interpol is authorized to engage and utilize military forces as and when we see fit. As you know, our standing guard is made up of US Special Forces on loan to us from the Pentagon.

"The two attacks in the desert were led by an Israeli Colonel supported by Israeli commandos, whom you have been introduced to, and Interpol simply provided an observer in each of those two attacks. And before you point it out, yes, we had more boots on the ground when we took down bin Azaria; the situation was judged to warrant it. And don't forget the Canadians and all the other countries who have used lethal force in attacking the various arms of Shetani's network of mercenaries, including your very own, on several occasions, all without any Interpol presence." The look he gave the general was anything but contrite; the edges of his face would have cut glass. If there was one thing the Boss hated, it was Monday morning quarterbacking. The general, to her credit, immediately sat back as far as her little metal chair would allow and shook her head.

"Colonel, I apologize if it seemed I was attacking your tactics. I fully realize we would not be as far down the comeback road as we are without the excellent efforts of Interpol and your team. I was just trying to see where the line in the sand was; please put it down to bad manners and bloody-mindedness." The Boss visibly relaxed, and with one simple gesture, the tension drifted out of the room. Pete sat back, Indigo relaxed, and even I felt some existential crisis had been avoided.

But I still did not know what was behind her verbal attack.

"General, we're all a little wound up, and I suspect if you have had as little sleep as my people, more than just a little tired. The fact remains, and I freely admit it, we have used national troops for various parts of our investigation, with the overt approval and under the direct control of each country involved. In the case of the mercenaries, we provided intelligence to some sixteen countries, and each country then dealt with them as they saw fit—the US is one of those countries. All within our mandate. And I took the measure of checking in with the director of your FBI, NSA, and CIA, and even yourself and the president, as warranted before we initiated any direct action." He flexed his shoulders again, looked down at his scuffed boots, raised his eyes in surprise, then looked up back at the group. Maybe he had meant to clean them?

"So as for a satisfactory outcome, while we have involved the politicians at every step so far, what we do next will be determined by what evidence and data we can analyze and which direction it suggests we move in. And to answer your unasked question, no, we may not collaborate with anyone nation-state at that point. The next moves will be an Interpol police action, full stop."

"You suspect a nation-state of masterminding the attacks, or at least covert support of the banker?" she asked.

"We have from the very start. The fact that the earliest attack on the computer systems in the US and Europe took place on the back of the Y2K debacle, now over twenty-five years ago, which would make the women we are chasing just out of nappies at that time, means that someone was setting all this up well before the use of the refugees was even thought of. Or, at the very least, concurrently. We have a statement from the Jesuit priest that the discussion regarding taking the children occurred around twenty years ago; we can't be definite, but we might get closer to the actual date once we chat with him tomorrow.

"Whatever that outcome, someone paid a lot of talented people for decades setting all this up. Look at the chronology—backdoors were set up in secure systems; tactical munitions were stolen from secured storage and transshipped around the world; aircraft and UAVs are either stolen or purchased outright and secreted in—we think, but can't prove yet—Turkey; a decommissioned nuclear missile base is taken over, refurbished, extended, all under the noses of both state and fed initially at least two world-class universities we know of, then moved underground and perfected. In fact, we have evidence that an early version of the nanomachines that took out the world's oil pipelines were trialed off the coast of Nova Scotia in full public view! The resources needed to support all this were more than just a handful of talented women. No doubt they played a part, but someone else played a much bigger one for nearly thirty years."

"How many women from the refugee camps do you think were involved?"

"Good question. In fact, a great question. Indigo?" The Boss turned, then yielded the floor to our Italian head-of-station in Italy. His thickset body was in direct contrast to the Boss's, but you couldn't miss his natural swagger or, for a change, his perfect English. Must be wanting to impress the general!

"General, Colonel, good people, our computer experts, with the help of Anna and the FBI, have run simulations working backward from the ground zeros of the attacks, based on the real-time mirror-attacks, both the Colonel and the Captain ran. Allowing for the Hercules and the UAV to have been housed in Turkey, adjacent to the terrorist base we discovered there, we estimate one woman pilot, one engineer, and or one technology specialist. There would have to have been a support crew at some point to keep the aircraft in flyable condition, and the bombs and missiles maintained, but they could have been locally hired from the airport. That is being ascertained as we speak by local authorities."

"Two to three women for the attack on the Vatican and the Dome of the Rock!" the general exclaimed, her tonality dripping with disbelief and sarcasm.

"Yes, at a minimum, but easily doable with the right equipment and training."

"The Grand Mosque? Lloyds of London? The nuclear attack on the Arabian oil field? The bombings in Avion? The UAV attacks in England and Germany?" Deftly, the general had held up her fingers again, counting off the attacks. She stopped at five, looking very hard at Indigo. He wasn't ruffled one bit by the intensity or harsh tone, choosing to smile and bow ever so slightly towards her.

"General, I know this is on the very edge of believable, but then, I would suggest if we had come to you a month ago with an outline that these attacks were even possible, I believe you would have laughed us out of the room as conspiracy theorists." The general latched her fingers together, shut her eyes for a minute, obviously getting herself under control. There was something behind her continued aggression; I wished I could divine it.

"Colonel,I apologize; I am letting all this get to me when I should be listening to your reports and helping you move forward. Please forgive me." Indigo bowed slightly again, a huge smile causing his whole face to light up.

"*Generale, per favore, capisco il tuo dolore, questo ha causato a tutti noi un po 'di dolore, e noicomprendiamo il tuo.*"

"*Colonnello, lei è troppo gentile. Per favore, continuate. Dovreicongratularmi con lei per isuoieccellentisforzi, non appendendo il mio dolore per-*"

*sonale al collo*." We all smiled, Italian being a second language for all of us except Indigo, and were warmed by the general's words.

"So, General, to answer your questions, we believe that the order of battle was-the Grand Mosque, mercenaries; Lloyd's was the women, the nuclear attack on the Arabian oil fields was the mercenaries using a weapon developed by the women; Avion was the mercenaries, and lastly, the UAV attacks were mercenaries using weapons designed by the women." She nodded, the list obviously lining up with one she had in her head.

"Just humor me for a minute. What makes you so sure Avion was the mercenaries?"

"The investigators found no bodies in the burnt-out trucks. Mercenaries are not known for self-sacrifice or becoming suicide bombers." She nodded again, then seemed to relax a little. She played the finger game again.

"How about the attack on West Point, the Alaskan pipeline, the Australian gas terminal, and the Russian/Chinese pipeline attacks?"

"West Point was the women, as was the space station. The pipelines, gas terminals, and fracking sites were mercenaries using weapons provided by the women."

"You see a distinct difference in the roles and responsibilities here?"

"Yes, we do. The women provided the weapons, the hardware, and possibly the tactical plan, although, to be frank, we can't prove that, and our best strategists have summarized that our nation-state player might eventually get the credit for that. We do not believe the women played any physical role in any bombings, truck-based UAV attacks, or oil and gas system attacks other than, and not yet proven, the design, manufacture, and fitting of the UAV bombs in the trucks and possibly communication—as in giving the 'go' order. In a sense, you have them as the planners, designers, inventors, creators, and possibly the manufacturers, although we have yet to track that down. The mercenaries were the hired hands that did all the on-the-ground dirty work.

"And at a stretch, if the women were using artificial intelligence or remote control for the aircraft attacks and never physically present, it could be tough to convict them." I started to see what might be lingering behind her animosity towards how we had developed our case so far. I looked at the Boss; he saw me out of the corner of his eye, nodded minutely, then gestured to Indigo. Indigo nodded and sat down. I stood up. My next words would be critical if we were to keep the Americans behind us and onside.

"General, let's take the case of the Hog pilot. We have her on video doing an engineering pre-flight in the hangar, gearing up, entering the cockpit, starting the Hog, and taxiing out to the holding area. From that point on, it could be argued that she left the aircraft—maybe or maybe not under her own auspices—on the ground idle and had no notion of the intended attack. She could claim that she was paid to get the Hog to the holding point and nothing more—or that she was coerced out of the cockpit and taken prisoner. When she left the aircraft, as far as we are able to prove at this time, the armaments were not live; the safety pins had not been pulled; the inflatable was not in use; all she had done to that point was get the aircraft into position as per her filed flight plan." The general looked gob-smacked, this alternative narrative on the actions of the Hog pilot who had caused so much death and destruction at West Point obviously never having occurred to her or anyone in her orbit. But we were Interpol—and we worked to policing mandates that required absolute proof to support a conviction in the world court, or the court of any civilized country on whose behalf we were operating, not a military organization that could shoot first and ask questions later. I wasn't going to let her off the hook.

"Take the case of the refugee child who was established in a home in Israel twenty-three years ago. Yes, she later developed the nanotechnology that would be used by the terrorists to take out our oil and gas reserves. At the time she left the program, she had successfully demonstrated a genuine ecological solution to oil spills. She developed a system that was supposedly for environmental reasons. She left years before the final development of the nano weapons, played no part in it, and freely admits that she was a refugee who was taken out of the camps and placed in a normal home when she was but a child. It is the intel that she acquired during her time at various universities that we are now plumbing for information on some of the other players. But what, exactly, would you hold her guilty of?" The general looked like she had swallowed an apple whole; her whole body showed extreme stress, and I was afraid she would start to hyperventilate. Then the crisis passed, and she shook her head violently from side to side. Military training had its advantages.

"You cannot tell me that the woman that set up the Hog to attack West Point, killing thousands, not to mention the joint chief of staff, can get off scot-free?" She rose to her full height, an impressive one-meter eighty-eight, the look on her face enough to make a lesser person cringe.

"No, General, I'm not. I'm just putting it out there that we have a lot to do to prove beyond a shadow of a doubt the complicity and guilt of anyone involved in the attacks. And I'd like to add to what Colonel Kashasini said to us earlier. If you look at the attacks in the US critically, you really don't see a role for more than three women." I remained standing, held her icy stare, and braced myself for whatever might come. She seemed to be considering her options, but what was going on behind those icy eyes was hard to fathom.

"Captain, you graduated from our NCIS academy?" she asked, her voice frosty and hard-edged.

"Yes, General."

"And at that academy, were you exposed to the nightmare of what is now regarded as the 'Terrorist Laws'?"

"Yes, General. In fact, I helped write some of them after the attacks in Egypt on our Air Force base. If you remember, we had a medical facility there that specialized in burns and reconstruction. It was destroyed, killing all sixty of the doctors, nurses, and scientists there. The fact that it was someone else's sovereign soil, the base was not listed as a US military establishment, and the terrorists escaped initially over the border into Libya made it all the more difficult to prosecute a case."

"But you did get them and prosecute them?" she asked, knowing fully that I could not answer the question. Two reasons: I had signed a non-disclosure agreement issued by the Justice Department, the downside of that being thirty years in the stockade, no parole. The second reason was that NCIS had tracked them down using Special Forces on an illegal, unsanctioned mission that had resulted in a one hundred percent kill rate, with the small sample of proof recovered after the attack enough to justify prosecution but not lethal force. The whole sorry episode had thrown the military lawyers into turmoil, and to prevent anyone from ever uncovering anything about the retribution, it had been buried deep in the Pentagon files.

"General,as you well know, that prosecution caused a lot of debate in legal circles, and that was why we wrote the 'Terrorist Laws.' Cross border jurisdiction, arrest, and detention versus weapons-free, nation-state permissions, you know the content. And you also know I cannot answer your question." The general smiled for the first time, not much of one, but enough to crease her face somewhat.

"Well, as you know, under the 'Terrorist Laws,' it is perfectly legal to arrest someone on suspicion of aiding and abetting a terrorist act, providing comfort to identified terrorists, being suspected of arranging or planning a terrorist act, and the kicker, as far as I am concerned, physically or substantially providing materials or substances that were or could be used in a terrorist act. Now, if I am not wrong, Interpol operates under these laws, is that correct?" I looked at the Boss to see if he wanted to take this; he just stared blankly at the general, leaving me to my own devices.

"General, the laws under which we operate are those struck by the world court. And we are allowed to also act under those laws mandated by the countries who support us, providing such laws do not contravene any law of the world court. What's your point?" I asked, this time letting my voice have just a little edge. I was getting a little tired of all the legal mumbo jumbo. The Boss, Indigo, Anna, and I had discussed all the rules of engagement we would operate underway back at the start of this horror show; it should be no surprise to the Americans, or anyone else for that matter. At least she had the good graces to sit back in her chair and hold her hands out as a sign of acquiescence.

"Captain, again, my apologies. The idea of the Hog pilot getting off on a technicality riled me somewhat. Let's get back to the main conversation. If I have heard you correctly, you are saying the total number of women used in these attacks is five or six?" she couldn't disguise her lack of belief, but there was no longer a bite in her tonality.

"Yes, we are. At least in minimum terms. Your own special forces reported on their clean-up of the silo and the discovery of the helicopter in the underground hangar. The documents of the local municipality show that the restoration was done in plain view; only one woman was identified on the applications; she no longer exists, of course, but the local workers whom your FBI questioned said they only ever saw the one woman, and that the work was completed over a year and a half ago. The physical records exist, but the electronic ones are gone."

"And we have no satellite footage of the data cable channel being dug or the underground hangar." I nodded; this was the real sticking point. The terrorists had used their black hole technology on the entire site and one hundred miles from the site to hide everything that had happened for over two-plus years from any intelligence agency. Maybe.

"No, General, not at this time." And I left it at that, happy to have an ace up my sleeve. In this case, Amira believes that she could reverse engineer the code she had been sent from Michele and reveal the actions of the terrorists.

"This 'satisfactory outcome'—what exactly is it?" she asked, folding her arms."

"We view the capturing and disbandment of the mercenary terrorists and the banker as a significant phase in this case. Our next objective is to interrogate those captured and ascertain their roles in the attacks. At the same time, we will analyze all the captured data and mine all the intelligence opportunities we have now within our grasp. Then we will sit down and determine what to do and how to do it. It's that simple."

"And that would be your 'satisfactory outcome.'"

"For this phase, yes. We may have to rejig our approach to what we do next, depending on the intelligence we might have. We might require different resources and engage with different technologies. We are not forgetting anything, just thinking through what we might need to finish the job." The general remained still, her head bowed slightly, a neutral expression on her face.

"How long before you decide on this future action?" she asked. I looked at the Boss, and he nodded.

"We will take an official break of twenty-four hours to rest our people and let things settle, then we expect to have the intelligence sorted within three days and a comprehensive plan in another two." The general nodded twice, stood up, looked around the room, and probably saw the same tiredness in everyone's face that I saw—at least, I hoped so. Arie stood up, nodded to the Boss, smiled at me, making me feel warm inside.

"General," he said, "why don't you and I have a chat and let these good people do what they have to do?" he gently took the general's arm and walked her out of the room. The bright shaft of sunlight that suddenly flooded through the open door caused me to shield my eyes with one hand. I had forgotten the time, the day, and, for that matter, the month.

Time to calm things down a little.

Look for Book Four of the Interpol Section Five stories

## THE ISLAND OF TEARS

**Due Out End Of 2023**


**If just 1% of families around the world adopted a refugee child, the problem would be solved. Forever. Families create Hope – and Hope gives Life.**

www.ingramcontent.com/pod-product-compliance
Lightning Source LLC
Chambersburg PA
CBHW020427130626
46549CB00001B/11